The Dryden Press

Texts in Education

GENERAL EDITOR

M. J. NELSON
*Dean of the Iowa State
Teachers College*

METHODS OF TEACHING IN

Town and Rural Schools

REVISED EDITION

E. L. Ritter and L. A. Shepherd

The Iowa State Teachers College

THE DRYDEN PRESS · NEW YORK

Copyright, 1942, 1950, by
The Dryden Press, Inc., 31 West 54 Street, New York 19, N.Y.

Manufactured in the United States of America
by The Haddon Craftsmen, Inc., Scranton, Pa.

PREFACE

THIS REVISED EDITION of *Methods of Teaching in Town and Rural Schools* differs from the original, 1942 edition in several respects. The authors believe that the following five changes have materially increased the usefulness of the volume:

1. Several entirely new chapters have been added, as well as wholly new sections to certain chapters included in the original volume;

2. The work as a whole has been subjected to extensive rewriting, largely in order to take cognizance of significant developments within the last eight years;

3. The chapters have been grouped into larger units, in order to achieve a more manageable organization of elements;

4. A large number of sketches and drawings have been included as a functional aid to the discussion.

5. The text has been made considerably easier to read.

The authors have stated in the opening chapter the educational philosophy which pervades the principles and suggested techniques set forth in this book. This statement may assist present teachers in crystallizing the basic principles which have largely determined their attitudes, purposes, and procedures in teaching but which have remained more or less undefined in the shadows of their thinking. Perhaps this statement will help also to direct the thinking and action of prospective teachers into channels educationally productive and socially secure.

The main objectives of the book, as related to teachers both experienced and prospective, may be summarized as follows:

1. To help teachers become more aware of those stages in child development which are proper for the utilization of subject matter and the acquisition of learning skills;

2. To present for the consideration of teachers certain tested practices and effective techniques which may be used in their classrooms;

3. To stimulate teachers to experiment with different and possibly new procedures and to guide them in perfecting and using fruitfully the results of such experimentation;

4. To help teachers themselves to develop efficient study skills, with the suggestion that they in turn teach their pupils how to grow in the ability to study;

5. To disclose, on occasion, a glimpse of what really artistic teaching

can do, of the tremendous importance to our nation of this kind of teaching, and of the high place such teachers occupy in the total picture of human development. These and other equally important possibilities are brought to light in order to help every teacher realize the almost infinite power he can wield, and to help him catch a vision of what an inspired teacher can accomplish.

Grateful acknowledgments are made to the thousands of teachers in Iowa whose teaching the authors have been privileged to observe, and whose influence undoubtedly appears on every page.

The late Professor C. A. Fullerton, of the Iowa State Teachers College, wrote the chapter entitled "Growth Through Musical Experience" for the 1942 edition. His daughter, Miss Margaret G. Fullerton, of the Iowa State Teachers College, has revised this chapter for the present volume.

Professor John W. Horns, formerly of the art staff of the Iowa State Teachers College, now supervisor of art in Contra Costa County, California, originally wrote the chapter "Acquiring Art as a Language." Both the principles and the techniques of teaching seemed to fit present-day ideas in this field; hence very little change has been made.

Miss Ethel O. Gergely, formerly instructor of art at the Iowa State Teachers College, made the drawings for the revised edition. The authors believe that these illustrations, because of their functional nature and artistic effect, enhance the value of this volume as a book for teachers.

The authors herewith express deep gratitude for these helpful contributions, and for the privilege of including numerous references. Without doubt the authors have been influenced by many readings and suggestions not mentioned in the footnotes. Sincere acknowledgment is also made of these.

Finally, the authors owe much to their colleagues in the Extension Service of the Iowa State Teachers College; especially to its former director, Professor I. H. Hart, for his interest, encouragement, and advice, and to members of the various departments of this college who have contributed directly many of the illustrative materials, and indirectly valuable suggestions in their respective fields.

Cedar Falls, Iowa
April 1950

E. L. R.
L. A. S.

TO THE STUDENT

There are at least three ways in which *study helps* may be of value.

1. They may point out the essential elements of subject matter.
2. They may help the student organize and direct his study attack. This may be done in these three steps:
   (1) The student meets and masters the fundamentals of the subject matter,
   (2) he uses these fundamentals to deal with problem situations,
   (3) he summarizes both the fundamentals and problem solutions by giving his own individual reactions to them.
3. They may organize the study attack to fit individual student differences in as large a degree as possible.

The study help materials for each chapter of this book have been constructed with these purposes in mind. The Facts are the essential elements without which no thorough study can be made. The Problems encourage or even impel the student to use the fundamental facts in their solutions. The Personal Reactions invite the student to give his individual ideas after the facts have been assimilated and used.

This organization of study helps fits approximately the various levels of student ability usually found in an unselected group. (1) All students should be able to discover the answers to the fact questions. (2) It takes a higher order of ability both to master the facts and to use them in solving problems or meeting problem situations. (3) Undoubtedly, even better ability is required to react individually and intelligently to the practical application of specific material.

Study helps over a single text are used in an almost endless variety of ways. However, a good student uses them somewhat as follows:

1. He reads the section of subject matter to be covered, first in perspective, then in detail.
2. Then he answers the fact questions, either mentally or in writing, depending on the use to be made of them later. He refers to the text if necessary. Close reading should necessitate very little reference to the text in answering the fact questions.
3. He works out and notes (mentally or in writing) the problem situations. Reference readings may be necessary in doing this. He puts facts together and makes reasonable answers or solutions.
4. With the facts and problem answers in mind or on paper, he puts himself into the conditions set up in the Personal Reactions and thinks out his response.
5. Finally, he has a period of discussion with a classmate on his "reactions." This is not necessary but is desirable, especially if a student is required to defend his reactions.

EDITOR'S INTRODUCTION

THE FIRST EDITION of this volume proved to be highly successful: not only has it enjoyed a wide sale and distribution, but users in considerable number have commented on its excellent organization, its useful and practical materials, and on the fact that it is an exceptionally "teachable" text. This revision, with completely new sections devoted to health and safety education, speech development, literature, audio-visual instruction, and several other areas, gives the reader a text of even greater usefulness.

The authors of this text are no "arm-chair" educators concerned only with the highly theoretical considerations involved in the education of the elementary school child. Both of them have spent many years in the Extension Service of the Iowa State Teachers College, during which time they have devoted themselves to the improvement of instruction in hundreds of small elementary and rural schools. Each of them has discussed problems of method with groups of teachers, with county superintendents, and with elementary school principals, as a part of his weekly routine. As a result of these experiences, as well as their summer work in teaching college classes of teachers-in-service, they have come to know the exact problems that confront both the beginning teacher and the teacher of considerable experience.

College teachers of education, elementary school supervisors, and elementary school teachers will find in this text a wealth of illustrative material. The prospective teacher or the teacher of limited experience will want to refer to it often, for it is a veritable storehouse of practical and usable ideas for both town and country teachers.

M. J. NELSON

CONTENTS

Part III: Elementary Mathematics

Part IV: Social Studies

Part V: Science

Part VI: Development Through the Arts

PART ONE

Introduction

CHAPTER 1

THE FUNCTION OF THE SCHOOL

CHILDREN are the reason for the existence of schools. Whatever contributes, therefore, to happy school experiences for children and opens the way to real life and growth individually, in their school groups, in their communities, in their nation, and in their world should be of prime concern to the school. It is the school's obligation to direct the wide range of attitudes, interests, urges, and needs into the most promising channels.

Society has evolved two ways to meet this obligation. One is by transmitting to the present generation carefully selected parts of the accumulated culture and knowledge of the ages up to the present, with directions for using this heritage beneficially and adding to it if possible. The other is by developing the present generation of children individually and collectively to function efficiently in the activities of the democracy and the world in which they live. The table on page 3 presents these ideas graphically. The following paragraphs explain this table in some detail.

The child. No two children are alike in all respects. Even those who come from the same home and have had practically the same environment, possess divergent personalities. All normal children, however, even though they differ, have many urges in common—to play, to use materials, to communicate, to inquire, and to learn. These urges give rise to needs: children feel a need to make objects to play with, a need to ask questions, to receive attention, and many more.

The Function of the School

THE CHILD Society's Obligation	THE SCHOOL Society's Agent			A GOOD CITIZEN Society's Goal
Undeveloped capacities, attitudes, interests, urges, needs, such as	Factors in the School			Characteristics essential for living together well, such as
	The *Teacher* with desirable characteristics, such as	A *Plan*, such as	*Equipment*, such as	
Play Work with materials Communication Curiosity Admiration of beauty Collecting Investigation Interest in pets Interest in plant life Interest in other children Appreciation of praise Interest in stories Enjoyment of social recognition	Good health Sympathy Resourcefulness Knowledge of subject matter Knowledge and use of good techniques Naturalness of manner Ability to stimulate interest Ability to inspire pupils with confidence and to work Fairness Tact Humor Refinement Pleasing voice	General techniques of method, such as Group instruction Individual instruction Units of work Study guides and helps Skill development Measurement of teaching Course of study, including provision for Communication skills, such as language, reading, spelling, writing Social studies and elementary science The arts Elementary mathematics	Clean and pleasant room Proper lighting Proper seating arrangements Instructional materials Textbooks Reference books A library with recreational reading material Play materials Artistic objects Bulletin board Reading table	Fairness Honesty Kindness—thoughtfulness of others Humor Loyalty Industry Progressiveness Open-mindedness Leadership Ability to follow good leaders Ability to select good leaders Interest in government Co-operation Good health Respect for property, law, ideals

Children develop naturally as they give expression to these inherent urges and are able to satisfy these needs. The simplest and most sensible procedure in developing children, therefore, seems to consist in supplementing and guiding those elemental factors with which nature has already fitted them.

The school. The outstanding question for the school is this: How can it shape the activities of children as they naturally express themselves and their needs, so as to develop worthy individuals equipped with attributes essential for living well together? It is the hope of the authors that the following pages will assist teachers in making their schoolroom practices function in this direction. The three basic factors essential for conducting a good school are the *teacher,* the *plan of work,* and the *equipment.*

There seems to be no question that the *teacher* is the most important factor in the situation as it is seen in the adjacent table. She should know the attitudes, interests, wants, and urges common to children; appreciate the big goal toward which the school is working; possess the necessary equipment as the tools for her job; follow a plan or program of procedure; realize the benefits children receive from the give and take among members of the groups; and arrange the school activities so that this interchange of ideas and opportunities for mutual helpfulness is possible. The teacher should realize that through the plan and the equipment she creates an environment about the children which is stimulating to their developing capacities and which tends to develop abilities for satisfying their needs. Under such guidance, children should develop individual personalities of the type deemed desirable for good citizenship. To illustrate, the teacher should teach pupils to read and to compute in order that they may use these tools and others in their business of living.

Little is accomplished in any undertaking without *a plan* and conducting a school is no exception. This plan should be flexible enough to be changed easily. It should include good techniques of method, such as adequate provision for varying individual abilities, guidance in building good study habits, and organization of material on the unit basis or otherwise. The plan should also contain a course of study that provides for the acquisition of tool-subject skills and for information in the field of content subjects. It should make sure that important parts of the material accumulated through the past are made known to children, and it should indicate how this material may be used in meeting life situations. The whole plan is shaped and set up with the child as the center and his development as the main objective.

No workman can succeed without tools and other necessary *equipment*. This is also true of the teacher. A hygienic, attractive place in which to work is desirable. Artistic touches add to the general atmosphere. No longer are textbooks considered the only indispensable instructional material. Reference books and recreational reading material are also essential. There should be maps, globes, bulletin boards, reading table, play materials, aquarium, terrarium, and equipment and supplies for construction work.

A good citizen. If the main purpose of the school is to develop individuals who will be able to live together happily in a democratic manner, what characteristics should the individuals have? Consider a few listed in the table. A good citizen shows *fairness* in dealing with others, not only people in his home community, but those in other parts of the world. Children readily sense the presence or lack of this trait in their associates. How can the school make this fairness an intrinsic part of each child? *Kindness* and *courtesy* add to the happiness of all. Real courtesy is the use of kindness in a polite manner. In social relations, children soon learn the effectiveness of asking with a smile and a "please," instead of a frown and a "give me!" attitude. *Humor* smooths out many unpleasantnesses. A good laugh saves many a trying situation. Children's ideas of what is funny often appear crude to the adult but through guidance and direction this tendency may become a very desirable asset. *Loyalty* means not only faith in, and support of, one's country, but also loyalty to friends, to school, to community, to oneself, and to ideals. The most loyal child is the one who, among other things, stands for good principles of citizenship in the school. *Leadership* is much easier for some than for others. Many, on the other hand, can acquire abilities necessary to become leaders. They learn to conduct meetings successfully, to be chairmen of committees, or to lead in playground activities if they are given the chance, and to understand some of the requisite techniques. If there is leadership, there must be those who can *follow a leader,* who can be good contributing committee members, who can ask useful questions in a meeting, or who can take their places and do their parts in a game. Our form of society makes two basic requirements of an individual: that he be a good leader and a good follower. Are the schools providing the necessary experiences through which children can acquire these abilities? *Co-operation* is necessary if democratic government is to function. All public schools, especially the one-room rural school, offer good situations for teaching children to work with others, to help each other overcome individual difficulties, and to promote the feeling of working for the good of all through mutual helpfulness. *Good health* is a social obligation as well as a comfort to the individual. A person can seldom be ill without inconveniencing someone else. To what extent can the schools develop the attitude of consideration of others as one goal of keeping well?

QUESTIONS—PROBLEMS—REACTIONS
(see page vii)

SECTION ONE: *Facts*

1. What opportunities should the school offer children?
2. What is the prime reason for conducting schools?
3. What are two prominent obligations of the school?
4. What are the three main headings in the table "The Function of the School"?
5. What are given as "Factors in the School"?
6. Which of these factors is the most important?
7. Under what form of government will these characteristics of good citizenship function best?

SECTION TWO: *Problems*

8. Observe some children and list any manifestations that correspond to the items given in the first column of the table.
9. Check yourself +, —, U(ncertain), for the characteristics given in column two.
10. Show what capacities in column one would be utilized when teaching the communication skills, as they are given in column three.
11. For which items in column four will the teacher be responsible? Be able to defend your choice.

SECTION THREE: *Personal Reactions*

12. In column five of the table, star the items you deem most important at the stage of elementary school development.
13. What other institutions in your judgment have a very strong influence on child development?
14. Add more items to those given which you think would belong in each of the five columns of the table.

SUGGESTIONS FOR FURTHER READING

Anderson, J. E. "Child Development and the Growth Process." *Thirty-eighth Yearbook of the National Society for the Study of Education*, Part I, pp. 15-25. Public School Publishing Co., 1939. This material aids teachers in understanding child development and the conditions and factors involved in the learning process.

Breed, Frederick S. *Education and the New Realism.* Macmillan, 1939. This book compares the pragmatic philosophy with the realistic as applied to education, with leanings toward the realistic. It is in a sense a reply to certain pragmatic principles as expounded by educators of that philosophical preference.

Cole, Luella. *Teaching in the Elementary School.* Farrar and Rinehart, 1939. Part II, "The Teacher and Her Class," has helpful suggestions on motivation, control, and general guidance of group instruction. Other sections discuss the teacher's relations to various factors of her work.

Forty-sixth Yearbook for the Study of Education. Part II. "Early Childhood Education." The University of Chicago Press, Chicago 37, Illinois. 1947. From this book one can obtain ideas basic in planning the most suitable school program adapted to the best development of young children.

Jersild, A. T. and associates. *Child Development and the Curriculum.* Bureau of Publications, Teachers College, Columbia University. 1946. A fine help in understanding children, this book describes child development from infancy through adolescence.

Leonard, E. M., Miles, L. E., and Vander Kar, C. S. *The Child at Home and School*. American Book Co., 1942. This is a comprehensive treatment of child development and the meeting of child needs in school.

Stratemeyer, F. B., Forkner, H. L., McKim, M. G., and committee members. *Developing a Curriculum for Modern Living*. Bureau of Publications, Teachers College, Columbia University, 1947. This book shows the relationship of society to the curriculum of the present-day school.

CHAPTER 2

GENERAL TECHNIQUES

THERE are various effective techniques which the school can employ at different levels to educate boys and girls in good citizenship. "Study your lesson" is not sufficient. In addition each pupil should be taught *how* to study and work independently. A well-equipped pupil has plans for attacking problems. He has methods for studying topics. He utilizes guides for using books and objective materials. He possesses the means for acquiring facts, developing skills, and measuring his own growth. To assist teachers in guiding pupils to greater independence in their work, we discuss in this chapter some details of the following techniques: audio-visual instruction, unit procedure, group and individual instruction, study guides and helps, skill development, and measurement of teaching.

In the succeeding chapters these techniques are referred to frequently as they are applied to various fields of learning.

AUDIO-VISUAL INSTRUCTION

Much teaching is being done and has been done with words, our most convenient tools for conveying ideas. Even though convenient, words are useless unless they are meaningful to the user. Word meanings vary with individuals, depending upon the individual's background of experiences. The ideas or concepts which words represent in any person's mind are the results of the fusion of experience elements, whether actual, vicarious, or imaginary.

9

Therefore, the principal aim of audio-visual teaching is to develop broad, clear, rich, usable concepts as foundation stones for children's learnings, understandings, and attitudes—these to be acquired through the senses by means of first-hand contacts, models, pictures, the radio, and recordings. To illustrate, a child who has never seen a garden could scarcely react intelligently when he hears the word "garden." How might he obtain this understanding? The most real experience would be for him to make a garden of his own. If he could not do that, he might visit one; or, he might plant a miniature garden in a box at school. If he could not experience the real thing, he might see gardens in a movie, or in other pictures. By such means he would acquire ideas and form concepts of "garden" which would have a meaning depending on the experiences he has had and the manner in which they have been organized.

There has been a tendency to think of audio-visual instruction merely as the use of the movie film, filmstrip, radio, and recordings. This is a very narrow interpretation. Audio-visual instruction includes actual first-hand experiences, as those obtained through excursions, visits to museums, and acquaintance with models; it includes experiences with objects also through the less direct mediums of photographs and other pictures; and it includes experiences in abstract forms, such as charts and graphs. In general, we may say that it implies educational materials which are mainly independent of printed words.

The following *principles* should help teachers in the use of this teaching technique:

1. Audio-visual techniques should be an integral part of the whole plan of teaching. A museum, for example, should function in both social studies and language arts.
2. Teachers should select the types of material which most nearly meet the requirements of the situation. Thus a movie may be desirable for a jungle study, still pictures for a study of the Capitol at Washington.
3. Direct-experience teaching materials should be selected on the basis of practicality. Thus, growing popcorn may be feasible in Iowa but not in Detroit, although Detroit pupils can pop the corn and eat it.
4. Selection of materials should be based on pupil background of experience. A diagram would suffice to give the idea of a tunnel if children knew about culverts.

5. The value of visual aids is proportional to the degree of reality they bring to children. A pupil operating a toy model of a steam shovel may get a clearer concept than one who sees the actual shovel in operation.
6. Visual aids should stimulate further activity. Thus a good movie may motivate reading or other types of investigation.
7. Teachers should utilize all materials provided by both the immediate environment and other sources, such as objects from the home and films from the outside.

The field of audio-visual instruction is very broad, as has been indicated; therefore, only some of the more important aspects of present-day *methods* and *materials* will be discussed.

FIELD TRIPS
REAL

First-hand experiences are fundamental to learning. Youth learns by seeing, hearing, feeling, smelling, and tasting. One spring a group of kindergarten children in a midwestern community illustrated this by participating in the making of sirup. The trees were tapped; the sap was caught in pails and carried to the school kitchen, where it was boiled. Some of the sirup was made into maple sugar. Thus the students learned the principles of sugar making more thoroughly by actually going through the steps of a pioneer process. In a similar manner children may learn about butter making by churning, about cloth making by spinning and weaving, about furniture making by building school cupboards or a play corner.

The *museum* is a means of making accessible to children objects which they otherwise would not see; it thus provides enriching and broadening experiences. As pupils collect and arrange the articles of

MODELS

a museum, they gain in ability to organize ideas and to work out general principles. Articles in these collections may be those brought by the children; those obtained in the community, such as hobby collections; articles from foreign countries; those offered by business concerns; and those in private and public museums. The items displayed may be real objects; samples, such as of building materials in a house; miniatures, such as toy tractors; or parts of a thing, such as a twig from a coffee tree showing the pod and seeds.

A real purpose should precede the establishment of a school museum. It should be a growing project and should not be regarded as complete in any specified time. The objects should be identified by labels which are fairly uniform, neat, and well written. Duplication should be avoided as much as possible, and special care should be taken to avoid making it a collection of curios. Dale[1] suggests these questions to evaluate exhibits:

1. Does this specific exhibit attract attention?
2. Does it sustain interest?

[1] Dale, E. *Audio-Visual Methods in Teaching*, p. 437. The Dryden Press, 1946.

3. Can it be easily understood?

4. Does the audience get the message?

Excursions are a means of helping children learn by going to the scene and observing at first hand such things as construction in bridge building, processes in a cotton mill, civil-service work in a post office, bird life in the woods or park. The steps necessary for a successful excursion are given in the chapters on techniques and on science and are applicable for all field trips.

Demonstrations bring understanding to children in much less time and often more clearly than is possible by reading. It is much easier to show how to tie a knot than to tell someone how to do it, and children often benefit even more when they participate in a demonstration. (See p. 507 for further discussion.)

Dramatic plays, pageants, pantomime, tableaux, and *puppet shows* all may contribute to the building of concepts. Those who profit most are those who take part. Therefore, it is a good idea to have many of the pupils as actors. Such plays may be the incentive for reading, observation, and interviews in order to assemble information and materials for an accurate, interesting presentation.

There are two main kinds of *motion picture*—silent and sound. These may be in black and white or in color. Instructional and school

MOVIES

entertainment films are commonly 16-mm. (millimeter) and are mostly of the sound type, although a few of the older ones are silent. The following suggestions may be helpful in the selection and use of motion pictures.

1. Films which are selected and shown should clearly relate to materials being studied. Pupils should not be compelled to view a film which does not directly enrich their subject-matter programs.
2. Every film should be previewed before it is shown to the children.
3. Manuals and guides accompanying the films should be studied and their suggestions used.
4. The teacher should prepare children for viewing a film by:
   a. setting the background, as one would motivate any other type of lesson,
   b. presenting and explaining any new words, if it is a silent film,
   c. making other necessary explanations,
   d. assuring a good showing (no waste of time in setting up and adjusting the machine),
   e. following the first showing with discussion and questions,
   f. supplementing with other materials such as objects, pictures, charts,
   g. reshowing the film, perhaps even a third time, if there are enough unanswered questions or parts not clear,
   h. relating the film to the unit or subject being studied,
   i. checking with lists of questions to see what pupils have gained. (This also helps them realize that the movie is an integral part of teaching.)

The still picture—and this term includes the stereograph, the different kinds of slides, the filmstrip, photographs and prints, and the projections of the opaque projector—is more versatile and more practical than motion pictures.

The *stereograph* gives pupils the feeling of reality as they look through the stereoscope at the three-dimensional views. The stereoscope is not expensive and the views are plentiful. Often only one picture is needed to make clear the size of the redwood trees or the height of the Rockies. The "blinders" on the frame make it easy to imagine that one is on the location looking directly at the objects in the picture.

Slides can be purchased or made by the teacher or children.[1] They

[1] Directions for making slides: (1) *Ordinary glass slides:* Children draw pictures or print words on paper in an area $2\frac{1}{4} \times 3$ inches. Lay a slide or piece of good window glass $3\frac{1}{4} \times 4$ inches over the drawing or printed matter. Trace the picture or words on the glass with India ink. Let the ink dry. Slides used frequently should have the tracing covered with a cover glass and both pieces bound around the edges with binding tape. If permanency is not desired the ink may be washed off and the glass used again. Pictures cut freehand from lightweight paper, black or a color which will not allow the projector light to pass through, may be pasted on the slide. (Use a cover glass if obtainable.) The result will be a silhouette on the screen. (2) *Etched glass slides:* Follow the above directions except that colored pencils may be used for trans-

may be used (1) to stimulate interest in a subject, (2) to make clear or emphasize points during periods of discussion or study, (3) to review a unit of work, (4) to aid pupils in presenting a topic, (5) to give pupils standards with which to compare their work, (6) to project a picture or map on a large sheet of manila paper or blackboard so that it and additional features may be drawn over the projection.

Dent offers good advice for teaching the child how to look at the slides:[2]

1. The child should recognize such technical points as finding a known element with which to compare height, size, or distance of new elements.
2. He should acquire the ability to determine the perspective of the view; whether it is close up, as of a flower; at a distance, as of a mountain peak; or from above, below, or on the same level.
3. He should see the picture as a whole and never lose the meaning by taking it apart.
4. He should only be *guided* by his teacher—not *told* what to see.

Filmstrips are a series of still pictures in film form. They are small rolls, easily filed, stored, or shipped. They may be black and white or in color. They may be purchased or school-made. Photographs or illustrations, such as charts, maps, cartoons, and drawings, may be made into filmstrips. If the filmstrip is composed entirely of pictures, oral explanations may accompany the showing, or explanations may alternate with pictures on the filmstrip. Sound filmstrips are also available.

Filmstrips can be shown through a regular filmstrip projector or, with an attachment, through a slide projector. The room does not need to be completely darkened, and discussions proceed in a livelier

---

ferring pictures or printed matter to the glass. Colored pencils come in sets of six and cost about $.50 per set. These slides may be cleaned with a kitchen cleaning powder. The dry glass may be cleaned with an ordinary eraser. (3) *Lumarith slides:* This material withstands heat. It comes in sheets about 20×50 inches (priced approximately $.55 to $1.50, depending on the weight) and can be cut into pieces with scissors or paper cutter. It is furnished by the Celluloid Corporation, 290 Ferry Street, Newark, New Jersey.

Directions for making slides are given in Dent, E. C., *The Audio–Visual Handbook,* pp. 56-68, Society for Visual Education, Inc., 100 East Ohio Street, Chicago, 1942.

[2] *Ibid.,* p. 70. Adapted.

manner for that reason. Filmstrips for use in many fields of teaching, such as nature study, social studies, and literature, are available.

The *opaque projector* enlarges on a screen any flat nontransparent object or printed material. The room needs to be quite dark and the projector is rather cumbersome, but it has many advantages. It is excellent for group teaching on any level. On the lower level, for example, it can show experience reading charts or the pictures pertaining to a unit (*e.g.* different kinds of leaves gathered); and on the higher levels, pupils may be shown maps of areas for comparison, graphs in arithmetic, pictures of life in different regions, pupils' English work for discussion, creative work for enjoyment, and tests.

The *microprojector* is a way of projecting small images in enlarged forms on a screen by means of an attachment applied to a microscope.

From early times *pictures* or *drawings* have been used to convey ideas. Those most commonly used for teaching purposes now are photographs and the different kinds of prints.

Photographs and prints are easily obtained from many sources and are usually not expensive. Some teachers delight in using their cameras to obtain shots for school use. Magazines and newspapers often contain suitable photographs. Sets of views pertaining to units and topics may be procured from commercial organizations, and some industrial concerns, especially transportation companies, send out splendid material. The illustrations in textbooks are usually an integral part of the content, and the children should realize this and "read" the pictures in connection with the text matter. Every teacher needs a file (if nothing more than a cardboard carton) in which to keep pictures ready for use. Numbering each picture also helps, for the number can be filed under several field categories and topics in connection with which the picture may be used. Teachers would do well to keep these standards in mind when they select pictures for specific purposes:

1. Are they good pictures from the standpoint of focus, arrangement, artistry?
2. Will they increase knowledge or affect attitude?
3. Are they true to conditions with which pupils should become familiar?
4. Do they depict a typical aspect of an area or topic and not an an exceptional case?

There are gradations in the manner in which children "read pictures. They may (1) simply *name* the objects seen, (2) *describe* what is happening (in an action picture), or (3) *explain* what it means.

Much could be said concerning the use of pictures under different conditions. The entire class as a group may view a picture, or it may be passed from child to child if it is not projected. It may be posted on the bulletin board or placed on the reading table.

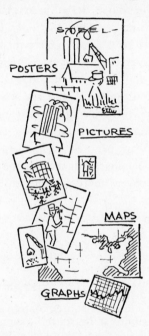

Young children may use pictures (1) to organize information in a scrapbook, such as classifying and mounting pictures of farm buildings, livestock, machinery, and crops; (2) to illustrate experience reading lessons, (3) to illustrate number concepts. Older pupils may use them to illustrate notebooks, to show customs and clothing of other periods and people, and show scenery of different regions.

Graphic materials, such as cartoons, posters, maps, charts, graphs, and diagrams, are not as objective as other materials discussed but are often sufficient for clarification.

The *cartoon* aims to influence the reader by an appeal to his emotions. Consequently it may be desirable or undesirable depending on the school's standpoint. The explanation is usually meager, and the depth of understanding generally required is over the heads of most elementary-school children. Nevertheless elementary-school pupils should begin to acquire a certain familiarity with such commonly used representations as Uncle Sam symbolizing the United States and John Bull representing England.

The *poster* can be teacher-made or pupil-made, or obtained from some agency outside the school. Its purpose is to emphasize some one idea forcefully, and it is not necessary that every pupil in a room make a poster. It is better to have a few posters made for the purpose intended and displayed in a conspicuous place. (For further suggestions see p. 624.)

Maps vary in kind. Children should begin with very simple maps of their environment, which they may make on the floor. A road map is easily obtained and has interest because of the children's travel over the familiar highways pictured on it. Children in grades above the primary should be familiar with the "air-age" maps and their use. Of course, the globe conveys more accurate impressions of the world than flat maps.

Charts are classified by Dale[1] as follows:

1. Time charts show time sequence, such as railroad timetables.
2. Stream or tree charts, such as a family tree or a river system, depict development or growth.
3. Organization charts represent by rectangles (sometimes circles), lines, and arrows the functional relationships within an organization, such as the United States Government.
4. Comparison and Contrast charts tell a summarized story by the simple device of showing two or more sets of data in column form.
5. Pupil Achievement or Progress charts record and may show the work of each child in column or line form. Most teachers use these as incentives for stimulating pupil effort.
6. Direction or Guidance charts present, in simple statement or outline, certain directions for the pupils to understand and follow. The reader will find this type of chart in subsequent sections of this book. (See "Charts" in Index.)

Graphs can vitalize statistics and give them a direct appeal. In presenting information in this manner to children, the simplest form should be used first, such as different-sized baskets of corn to show

[1] *Op. cit.,* pp. 287-288. Adapted.

the amounts raised in different years. The baskets may be changed to bars later. It is essential that the data be accurate always. If they are taught how to make graphs properly, children will read graphs more readily and give them more attention when they appear in books. (See pp. 388-389.)

Diagrams are frequently used both in teaching and in the explanations given by pupils who may, for example, thus demonstrate relationships in the solution of arithmetic problems or in a scientific experiment. Colored chalk often increases the value of diagrams on the blackboard. This is one of the ways in which the blackboard functions as a visual aid.

FIGURE
PROPORTIONS

Blackboards are accepted equipment in elementary-school classrooms. Perhaps because they are so common, their value as a vivid means by which to present certain types of audio-visual teaching has not been sufficiently realized. They are a vital part of group instruction. They may be used by teachers and pupils alike. The bodily action connected with their use tends to focus group attention. Finally, the materials employed may be quickly and easily changed.

Many teachers hesitate to make sketches and illustrations on the blackboard because they lack drawing ability. Almost anyone, however, if he looks at objects carefully and perceives the general outline, can portray ideas with simple lines or stick figures sufficiently well to convey impressions graphically. This skill may require a little practice, but it certainly should be acquired.

To make effectual use of the blackboard: (1) Keep it clean. (2) Be sure all the children can see the material. (3) Avoid glare (looking at it from the children's position). (4) Make material legible. (5) Do not hesitate to use the ruler, compass, or other guide when necessary. (6) Stand so that children can see what you are writing, or work quickly and step aside. (7) Do not have too much on the board at one time. (8) Save space, if necessary, by using mimeographed or dittoed sheets for certain exercises.

Picture the children in the primary room of a two-room school in a small community. They are seated on the floor in front of a *radio*. At 1:30 the teacher sets the dial and a voice, familiar to them by this time, introduces the storyteller and the story "The Five Chinese Boys." They settle themselves for a period of real enjoyment. As the plot unfolds, their attention and facial expressions show their interest. At the close, they voice their opinions in a lively discussion; some draw pictures of the story's scenes; a dramatization is planned. Some have objects from China which they offer to bring. This type of experience is repeated over and over in all types of school and in many fields of subject matter.

"Educators have come to realize that radio marks an advance in education comparable only to that brought about by the invention of printing."[1]

These suggestions should assist in utilizing the radio:

1. Arrange the day's program so that the broadcast ties in with the regular work.

2. Use the guides sent by stations in planning the radio teaching.

3. Prepare the pupils for listening to broadcasts by means of pictures, discussion, reading, and otherwise.

4. Enrich the broadcast by the use of other visual aids, such as maps or pictures. Point to pertinent places on a map or show related pictures as the broadcast is heard.

5. Follow the broadcast with discussion, drawing, investigation, construction, or other activities that may fit the broadcast and the day's program.

[1] Miller, R. W. "Through Radio," *Using Audio–Visual Materials with Children,* p. 25. Association for Childhood Education, Washington, D. C., 1947.

6. Assign reports on programs broadcast in out-of-school hours. Follow these with reports and discussions in school.

7. Organize school broadcasts both actual and imaginary. This requires careful preparation. Such broadcasts may be of the following types: a straight talk; an interview, panel, or round table discussion; an on-the-spot report, a quiz bee, a classroom pickup forum, or debate, a dramatization, a program of music, or a demonstration lesson.[1]

Among sources of information on programs are local radio station weekly schedules and the *Journal of the AER* (Association for Education by Radio).[2] Several of the large school systems, state departments of education, and university-owned radio stations issue program logs, station schedules, and utilization handbooks which are of value to those schools within the areas of "coverage."[3]

Recordings have advantages over the radio as an audio aid. They can be (1) previewed, (2) repeated, (3) stopped at any place and discussed, (4) used at any time, (5) made in the school room and kept.

Recordings were used first in schools to teach music, and they continue to be thoroughly effective for this purpose (see p. 571). They contribute much to rhythmic expression and to games. Recordings are used to improve speech; others are available which test knowledge of the basic facts of addition and subtraction;[4] still others bring to the children bird calls and the sounds of jungle life.

Unbreakable records are now made which add to the possibility of children's using the phonograph independently. Wire and tape recordings are very satisfactory if the equipment is available. There is no breakage and the wire or tape can be cleared and used again and again.

Audio-visual aids may be used in *testing* and *evaluating* the results of teaching in several of its aspects.

1. Audio-visual aids may be used for testing in content and tool subjects. Mention has been made of the use of phonograph records for testing arithmetic knowledge. Other uses are: using test questions in

[1]Levenson, W. B. *Teaching Through Radio*, p. 48. Farrar and Rinehart. 1945. Adapted. Levenson also (p. 141) lists sources of information about programs.

[2] Published monthly (except June, July, August). 228 N. LaSalle St., Chicago, Illinois.

[3] One is the *News Letter* published monthly, except June, July, August, and September, by the Bureau of Educational Research, Ohio State University, Columbus, Ohio.

[4] Developed by E. L. Ritter. Obtained from J. S. Latta and Son, Cedar Falls, Iowa.

connection with maps, pictures, graphs, and tables to check information and/or skills acquired; matching labels in a museum with the correct article; identifying trees by means of leaves and bark. Many more will occur to the imaginative teacher.

2. Audio-visual aids may be used in checking growth in audio-visual skills. For example, the three levels in "reading" pictures—naming items, description, interpretation—may be used to indicate growth in this skill. Another example involves the abilities to read and make graphs of increasing complexity—the more complex the graph, the higher the ability.

3. Audio-visual aids may be used to evaluate general development. This evaluation, though largely subjective, may be very valuable. A chart such as the one shown below, to be filled in at regular intervals, should help in this kind of evaluation.

Name	1. Powers of observation	2. Interest in the community	3. Use of environmental resources	4. Use of audio-visual aids out of school	5. Interest in other than book materials	6. Self-confidence	7. Tendency to carry on independent activities	8. Contribution of home materials	9. Acquisition of word meanings	10. Interpretation of reading materials
Anderson, Jane										
Andrew, Tom										
Beavo, Harry										
Burr, Mary										

To *summarize*, let us think of a day in a school with four or more grades. How might audio-visual techniques function?

The *flag* is raised and saluted (citizenship). Children sing accompanied by the *phonograph* (music). Teacher and children make plans for the day, which are written on the *blackboard*. *Samples* of materials—such as wood, glass, cement—pertaining to the house unit carried on in the primary grades are shown, discussed, and labeled (language). The upper-grade pupils see a *movie* on the technique of studying. (This had been borrowed because some were having trouble in locating and understanding reference material.) The middle grades write explanations of a *field trip* the school has taken to the creamery. These are to be placed in notebooks and illustrated with simple sketches or cut-out *pictures* (health and language). The second grade interprets a story read by *dramatization* (reading and oral language). The teacher asks one child to *demonstrate* to the others at recess a broom-handle stunt (physical education). All the children are prepared for listening to a weekly *radio broadcast* on conservation (science). Different *objects*, such as games and puzzles, are available for use during the noon hour (number, science, literature).

Audio-visual aids have become vital factors in the daily teaching of most schools. Development in these aids and their uses will undoubtedly advance and will continue to challenge resourceful teachers.

UNITS OF WORK

In many modern schools much of the procedure is organized around a theme or center of interest instead of being limited to the order of materials in textbooks, or to strict adherence to a course of study which presents materials in definite subject divisions, such as history, geography, reading, and language. Terms used for this type of procedure include: projects, problems, activities, centers of interest, units of work, and areas of experience. The term *unit of work* is commonly used when referring to the type of procedure in which teacher and children plan, obtain materials from various sources, integrate their findings around a central theme, and form their own generalizations. Hockett[1] gives this definition: "The term *unit of work* is used to designate the various experiences and activities that grow out of, center in, and contribute to a chosen theme." The plan of unit teaching is applicable to any type of school. Conditions in a small one-room rural

[1] Hockett, J. A. and Jacobsen, E. W. *Modern Practices in the Elementary School,* p. 64. Ginn. 1938.

school are especially favorable for this procedure; pupils of different age-levels work together there and the opportunities for individual instruction are greater because of smaller enrollment.

Psychological bases for organizing and conducting work on the unit plan are these: (1) It stimulates and directs thinking in a way not possible by such older methods as the use of questions and answers based on textbook material. When learning by units, children set up problems for which they are eager to find solutions. Thus thinking is stimulated and guided toward definite ends. (2) Learning takes place and facts are mastered because they are encountered in their natural functional relationship to one another. For example, when pupils learn how sugar is produced, facts in agriculture, climate, transportation, and processing are all normally correlated as the problem is solved. (3) Also new connections are made, new relationships developed, and broader concepts formed in solving problems involved in units. For example, children are interested in transportation. They already know about travel by automobile as they begin to study airplanes and they know that the routes automobiles travel are called roads and highways. They learn of the airways, of why and where they are planned. Thus their conception of the term "route" is broadened and enriched.

Some *advantages* of the unit plan of teaching are: (1) It helps prepare children for democratic living. The able teacher finds many real-life situations in the activities of a unit which can be utilized to develop children's initiative, responsibility, co-operation, and other desirable traits of a good citizen of a democracy. (2) It provides good opportunities for personality development. Teachers can observe natural traits and tendencies more clearly if they get the children's views freely expressed and observe children's activities self-directed and self-controlled. These observations may present openings for commendation or redirection by the other children as well as by the teacher. (3) Units of work offer opportunities for developing good leadership as well as the ability to follow and assist through committee procedure effectively employed. (4) Such a plan increases ability to make adjustments essential to happy community living. A good unit presents many unpredictable situations which necessitate developing the ability to shift procedures and find new solutions. (5) Facts take on real meanings and skills may be acquired with less effort under this plan than under some others, because there are definite motives back of the efforts and the learning takes place in natural settings. (6) Units furnish splendid opportunities to organize for future use knowledge which children acquire when working on the theme. For example, they may know of houses as places to live in, but in the home unit these may be classified as bungalows, apartment houses, two-story houses, etc.

There are also *dangers* in conducting work organized on the unit basis. (1) Some teachers are unprepared for this type of teaching through lack of suitable training or insight. (2) Unless the choice of units is based upon carefully determined criteria, time may be wasted on nonessential topics or those unsuitable for certain groups of pupils. (3) There may be a lack of necessary control of pupils or an absence of effective organization of efforts toward definite goals, resulting in pupils' acquisition of poor habits of work or even antagonistic attitudes toward co-operative enterprises. (4) Essential facts and skills may be neglected because too much responsibility is placed upon the children without proper teacher guidance. In such cases, objectives and checks are often overlooked in the program. (5) Sometimes, too much time is devoted to manual activities at the expense of important concepts, subject-matter facts, and basic skills. A train may be constructed as part of a unit on transportation and the building be made the all-important factor, while the understandings of our dependence upon transportation receives little, if any, consideration. It may be that such concepts could be more effectively presented by means of an excursion —seeing a train or riding on one.

There are different *ways of organizing* units. Only three will be discussed in this chapter. *First,* the teacher who has plenty of training and experience and the right attitude may be able to organize all or the major part of the curriculum around units of work in such a manner as to enable the children to acquire important facts, master essential skills, and develop desired appreciations. *Second,* for the majority of teachers it seems wiser to use the following plan of organization: (1) to set aside a part of the day's program for the unit work, (2) to have other periods during the day to work on the regular content and skill subjects, and (3) to tie up these two parts of the program as much as possible. For example, the unit under consideration may

be "Foods." Reference reading and reporting may be done during
the regular reading period, letter writing to manufacturers during the
language period, and chart-making in the arithmetic period. Necessary drills on the four fundamental operations of arithmetic, work-
type reading skills, language usage, spelling, and writing should find
places in these regular class periods. It is often desirable that the
period devoted specifically to the discussion and evaluation of the work
of the unit be the first one of the day and thus facilitate the planning
and launching of the day's work. *Third,* in the upper grades, some
instructors prefer to organize units around specific subject-matter fields,
centering the interest in geography, history, health, or science. For
example, the unit might be based upon a logical division of subject
matter, such as the Civil War period in history. Children would
then consult several books, hunt up specimens for a museum, find
pictures of that period, consult descendants of war veterans, use songs
of that period, and perhaps organize all their material in outline form,
giving their information and conclusions concerning this period of
United States history.

Regardless of the type of organization selected, the following
factors have been found *useful* as bases for the *teacher's planning:* (1)
making the approach, (2) setting up the unit, (3) planning the procedure, (4) determining the activities to be incorporated, (5) arranging
the subject matter to be included, (6) summarizing the findings, (7)
forecasting the outcomes in terms of anticipated appreciations, knowledges, and skills, and (8) providing the materials and equipment.

The chart on page 28 illustrates the possibility of planning a unit of
work which covers a broad field so that children of different levels of
ability can work simultaneously on different phases. This is especially
adaptable to a schoolroom of several grades, such as a one-room rural
school.

At least *four requirements* are *essential* for *successful unit teaching:* (1) insight and effort on the part of the teacher, (2) equipment,
(3) understanding on the part of the community, and (4) knowledge
and use of community resources.

The *teacher's role* is of utmost importance in carrying on units of
work. The following qualities are essential: (1) The skill to adapt
herself to the various abilities, individualities, and experiences of her

group. (2) The ability to see what subject matter is related to the theme to be studied, where materals pertaining to it may be got, and how these can be organized into an effective working procedure for children to follow. For example, when organizing material in a unit, such as trying to determine Europe's place in the agricultural world, the teacher guides the children to use not only history and geography

UNITS OF WORK—

TRANSPORTATION

RAILROAD ROUTES

Various levels of ability can work on the same unit.

texts but also bulletins, reports, exhibits, and sources of information found in their immediate environment. (3) The ability to see the potentialities of and the necessity for tool subjects (such as arithmetic, reading, writing, and spelling) and to help children to feel the need for practice and development of these necessary skills. (4) The ability to organize children for work. A good teacher allows freedom, but retains control, so that confusion is avoided and respect for each other's privileges is maintained. (5) The ability to recognize the character-

TRANSPORTATION

	First Grade (Age six)	Second Grade	Third Grade	Fourth Grade	Fifth Grade	Sixth Grade	Seventh and Eighth Grades
GENERAL DISCUSSION OF MANNER OF GOING PLACES							
Special Interests for Each Grade							
	Automobiles	Trains	Airplanes	Boats and ships	Transportation in other lands	Manufacturing industry. How one form of transportation is built, as automobile	Organization of a transportation company, as bus line
SUBJECT MATTER AND PROCEDURES INVOLVED IN THE UNIT							
Reading							
	Experience charts Labels Captions Books	Books Folders Pamphlets Advertisements Information on bulletin boards	Same as second	Same as second Reference material Landing or docking notices	Reference and story books Geography texts Poster captions Descriptions	Folders from industrial companies Books Advertisements	Charters Advertisements Folders
Language							
	Discussion Group compositions Vocabulary development	Discussion Group compositions Dictating letters Making captions for pictures Vocabulary development	Same as second Riddles Dramatization	Discussion Riddles Dramatization Writing letters Vocabulary development	Same as fourth Outlining Vocabulary development Grammar, common and proper nouns (names of and parts of boats)	Same as fifth Writing ads	Same as sixth
Arithmetic							
	Counting Reading numbers Gaining concepts of size, distance, measuring	Telling time Reading recorded time Learning of distance, money (price of tickets)	Same as second Reading time schedules Using multiplication	Same as second Learning of size, weight, money (shipping rates) Using fundamental operations	Same as second Comparing rates Using charts and graphs	Using percentage Appreciating values of materials, wages paid, fair number of working hours	Having experiences involving capital, interest, stocks, banking
Social Studies							
	Places visited Kinds of automobiles for different types of business	New trains compared with others Extent of railroad travel Railroad map	Around-the-world trips as they are being made Other trips of public interest Safety for those traveling Qualifications for pilots	Routes for ships Distribution of commodities Development in ship building	Reasons for certain forms of transportation in different countries Changes in transportation in other countries	Places where automobiles are sold Constant improvements in automobile construction	Economic situation requiring organization or large business enterprises Capital and labor

istics essential for good citizenship and for happy individual living. This should always be part of the teacher's planning and work, so that she can offer guidance in good living habits. For example, a child is having trouble finding reference material. How much should he be directed and encouraged? Other similar situations offering opportunities for experiences in good living will arise when children work and play together. These may all be used by the teacher in developing good citizens.

Equipment is the second requirement for carrying on unit study successfully. More can be accomplished if there is enough space to allow painting at easels, meeting in committee groups, and construction with materials. Desks and seats of the older type may be fastened to runners, thus permitting rearrangements of such space. Bulletin boards and screens for mounting purposes; shelves or tops of low cupboards for display of a museum or of illustrative material; tables for work; some provision for a workbench for construction with carpenter tools —these are also necessary items of equipment. One textbook is not sufficient in any grade where unit study is used. Not only are books for reference work by the children desirable but also those for teachers, particularly in the lower grades. In addition, there may be actual objects, pictures, and materials for construction, drawing, and modeling.

A *sympathetic community* plays a direct part in making this type of teaching successful. Sometimes patrons need to be convinced of its value. Most parents are glad to co-operate in school arrangements if they understand the reasons why children go on excursions or make soap in school. Often success in introducing newer methods of teaching can be traced to preliminary effort spent by teachers in preparing the community for them.

Much help in connection with unit teaching is to be secured by *utilizing community resources*. The teacher who sets out to make a survey of the available materials in her community will probably be surprised to find how much assistance she can get from various occupational groups, institutions, and recreation centers, and from nature itself. She may find occasions for children themselves to contribute directly to the life of the community through their own efforts—working toward beautifying the community, assisting in clean-up campaigns, and providing clothing and play materials for less fortunate groups. She may find parents, older residents, and others capable of making special contributions. These may be invited to share with the children knowledge and skills, showing them, for example, how to dye cloth, keep bees, and arrange flowers. The versatile teacher not only collects materials herself but encourages her children to find items to add to the school's equipment: museum collections, pictures, movies, radio, reading material, and natural specimens. She also locates points of interest which she may have the children visit, either individually or on a school excursion. The excursion can be a very important feature of a unit of work. Tippett[1] gives these purposes for "school journeys": "(1) to gain information needed to answer questions, (2) to verify conclusions reached in the classroom, (3) to enrich classroom learning by direct experience, (4) to create a closer understanding between teacher and pupil, (5) to develop a spirit of co-operation, and (6) to establish an appreciation and understanding of how people work and live together." Children should feel that there are reasons for making a trip, that it is more than simply "going some place." The teacher planning an excursion should make a preliminary visit to learn what is to be seen, to decide on the manner of going, and to make any necessary preliminary arrangements. The children should state the purposes of the trip; discuss and list items that they will look for and questions they wish to have answered; look at pictures that will provide the background for the trip; and formulate rules of conduct. After the excursion the group should discuss the experience as a whole, list answers to the questions, make records, and thus tie up the excursion with the unit. The excursion may be a means of initiating, enriching, or culminating a unit of work.

As a unit is launched and carried on, many specific problems present themselves for solution. For example, in the transportation unit suggested previously, the children may learn what safety devices are used on the railroad, how automobiles are retailed, or what preparations are made for a trip around the world. There are *definite steps* which *children may follow* in solving each of these problems. *Sensing* and *stating* the problem is the first step. The children should clearly understand the problem to be solved. Perhaps this can be stated by

[1] Tippett, J. S. *Schools for a Growing Democracy*, p. 66. Ginn. 1936.

the children or by the teacher and children together. Writing it in a definite form often helps. *Planning the solution* is second. The children should plan (usually with guidance) the methods of attack and the materials to be used. Often a list of questions or items or an outline will serve as a guide for the work to be done. Perhaps one effective procedure is to arrange for committees to work on different phases; for example, one committee to read about sugar, another to consult the grocer, and another to bring different kinds of sugar for study. *Collecting data and materials,* the third step, requires ingenuity and time. The fourth step, *predicting the solution,* usually comes in the form of a tentative solution. This may not always be possible, but it is one of the best ways to help children to think and to draw upon their own resources. It tends to show them their inadequacies and to stimulate them into remedying these. It offers an incentive for judging the data collected. This prognosis, however, should be based upon real thinking. It should not develop a tendency to guess or jump at conclusions without substantiating reasons. *Solving the problem* is the fifth step. The data collected should be assembled by individuals or by committees and should be organized for use. Let us assume that the questions are answered, the items checked, or the outline filled in. *Judging and checking results* is the sixth and last step. Some solutions are more easily checked than others. If the problem is to furnish living quarters for a pet rabbit, its success is easily determined by use. If it is planting a flower garden, the success is made evident by the appearance of the flowers and the pleasure which they give. If it is a unit on finding out how food is transported, there are less objective means of checking.

In comparison with other definite techniques of instruction, the measurement of results of teaching by units is more difficult. The facts and skills acquired can be measured. But the more or less intangible changes in personality, in attitudes, understanding, interests, and ideals cannot be as accurately determined. Probably the best way to judge growth in these respects is through observation of children's conduct. For example: Pat, a rural school lad, had an unfortunate home background and was a little old for his group. The teacher was especially eager to have him feel that he "belonged" and she made particular efforts to understand him and to bring out desirable traits, even taking him on a special trip in order to establish rapport. His election as class president by the children gave the teacher the chance to help him meet the new responsibilities and to carry them out. He assumed this leadership in a splendid manner and by the end of the semester showed real personality growth along desirable lines.

GROUP AND INDIVIDUAL INSTRUCTION

Any statement which attempted to cover adequately the wide spread of meanings connected with the term *group instruction* would reach from the most barren question-and-fact-answer recitation to the most interesting and helpful developmental group activity. For the purposes of this book, however, it may be sufficient to say that group instruction is a group activity which stimulates growth in desirable individual and group traits. Such a definition includes the class instruction or recitation period as well as the seat or individual activities in which all pupils strive toward a given end. It embraces all aspects of an activity unit or an area of experience or any other group undertaking in which all members work toward recognized objectives and assume responsibility for reaching them. The meaning should become clearer as we now proceed to discuss some phases of group instruction.

Planning by the teacher and pupils is one aspect of group work. Both pupils and teacher should participate in working out the plans by which known objectives are to be reached. Though perhaps not all would agree that pupils need to realize fully what the ultimate objectives are, everyone admits that pupils should have clear ideas of the purposes and the ways and means of reaching the more immediate goals. For example, first- or second-grade pupils may not fully understand just how learning to read will help them to be better citizens but they should see that learning to read will enable them to get along better in school, take more pleasure in books, read newspapers, and obtain information. Even though no exact lines of demarcation can be drawn to separate the *types of planning,* it is possible to make some useful distinctions by considering the purpose of the planning. Certain rather definite forms appear.

Preliminary or survey planning is used when leading the pupils into a wide area of exploration, when attacking a large unit of work, when beginning the solution of a problem, or even when starting the study of a given section of subject matter. In short, such planning is employed when there is need for long-range thinking ahead by both teacher and pupils. This planning might include: (1) the objectives, (2) ways and means of reaching these more or less specific objectives, (3) ways and means of checking progress and final results, (4) the evaluation of the procedure and of its effect on the pupils. All of this planning is in the nature of an overview of the whole undertaking before it is actually begun. It is taking a look at the woods before entering and making more or less definite plans as to what shall be done after the actual entrance is made.

Another type of planning pertains to the *daily work* or the *smaller activities* that go to make up the larger parts of the whole and eventually the whole itself. To illustrate: What shall be done first today? What shall be required to make the corners square? Some factors to consider are these: (1) Organization on the part of both the pupils and teacher is necessary to make this short-range planning most successful. The teacher's job is to look ahead and estimate as nearly as possible everything necessary for the day, taking into consideration each pupil's ability. The pupils' job is to look ahead and find as nearly as possible what they will need in the immediate future, and make arrangements to obtain such materials or data. Some individual activities may be so arranged that materials, books, floor space, and so forth will not be needed by several pupils at the same time. (2) Co-operation among the various members of the class is perhaps more important in the short-range planning than in planning for a longer period. For example, Jack may find in the course of his reading on commerce certain information that Clara could use in her search for data on the history of water transportation. (3) Courtesy in the busiest workroom or recitation is an absolute essential for most effective and pleasant relations. This factor usually needs no special planning, but in the press of excitement or individual desire in the daily group activities it often necessitates attention. (4) Additional factors enter into the planning for the short-time activities. Among these are individual differences of pupils, likes and dislikes of pupils, and time available for activity.

Planning for a special occasion often occupies the attention of teacher and pupils. Getting ready for an auditorium period, arranging an exhibit, preparing to report on a finished unit of work are some examples. This is different from the other types of planning in that it implies an audience that is uninformed about the activity or the results of it and wishes to become informed. This situation has the following implications: (1) The uninformed audience should be of first consideration. Plans should include all angles of information, as well as the capacities and inclinations of the audience, and the program should be made to fit all conditions as nearly as possible. (2) The individual abilities of those reporting should also be considered in plans of this nature. That is, if dramatic ability is needed and John is the best qualified, John should be assigned to take the lead in acting, other factors being equal. Sam is good at writing stories. In order to produce the best that the class can give, Sam is assigned an important role in story writing. Such planning does not suggest that May, who is capable in neither dramatics nor story writing, should get no chance to participate in either or both. Probably she would have minor roles in these activities and be given an opportunity to use her talents in other ways. (3) All plans for such periods or activities must provide for some means of evaluating results. This may be done by a committee of pupils or faculty or by judging the audience response. If the evaluation actually reveals the strong and weak points it is obviously of marked help to all engaged in the activity.

By way of *summary* it may be said that while planning is an important part of instruction of any kind, it is especially important in group instruction. This is true not only for the teacher but for each member of the group. Planning clarifies the objectives, the means by which the objectives are to be reached, the type and amount of checking to be done as the work progresses, and the kind of final evaluation which is to indicate how well objectives have been reached.

A second element of group instruction is the *assignment*. The meaning of this term as used in the following pages is broad enough to cover all activities which prepare pupils to work as individuals or as a group on the task at hand. It may be merely, "Take the next five pages," or it may be an elaborate and well organized plan for a semester's work on which teacher and pupils have spent days or even weeks.

Whatever the level of excellence of the assignment there are certain basic factors to be kept in mind by all concerned, especially the teacher. *Establishing motives for work* is among the most important of these. Generally speaking, the loftier the motives the greater the chances for desirable development. For example, a pupil knowing that his own success and that of his class or school are dependent on his efforts in a particular piece of work, has greater possibilities of desirable development than a pupil motivated by fear of punishment or of failure.

Some aids in establishing healthy motives for work follow: (1) The immediate goals and even those that are remote should be made clear to the pupils. Emma should know that the original story she is copying goes directly to a group of fifth-grade pupils in London, England. Henry should realize, if possible, that the habits of reading he builds in his grade-school work may be the ones he will retain as long as he lives. (2) The goals should not only be clear: they should be attainable through reasonable effort, difficult enough to challenge, yet easy enough to encourage. (3) The goals should seem valuable to the pupils. That is, they should be worth while and interesting to them. (4) Undoubtedly there should be clearly stated directions to follow in reaching the desired goals. These may differ with the various levels of pupil ability. The lower levels of ability will, in all probability, need more specific and simpler instructions. (5) Appeals to the pride of the pupils are powerful motives in getting work done. This is true in most cases both as to quantity and quality of work. Children simply do not like to see their friends or their classroom or their school excelled in any way and they usually will spare no effort to prevent this. (6) A fair check on the work accomplished by pupils serves to activate them. This is certainly true when they are progressing to a marked degree. But it is no less true when the degree of progress is not unusual, provided that the checking is done under proper guidance.

A second factor of the assignment for group work is the *material to be used*. Materials are usually provided in a more formal way by the course of study, the textbooks, the references, and a wide range of related printed materials, possibly from several fields. The teacher usually has a good deal of leeway in this area and is encouraged to use it. The less formal materials come from pupil and teacher experiences, data collected by the pupils themselves, contributions of persons indirectly connected with the school, and other similar sources. Whatever the materials used, the general tendency at present seems to be to use them as tools to develop the powers of the pupils, not as ends in themselves.

A third factor in making assignments involves the *procedures used*. Such procedures vary widely in effectiveness. On the lower levels we find assignments given in the form of page numbers without any illuminating remarks, or possibly in the form of topics without any interrelationships suggested. A little higher on the scale of assignments we find page numbers or topics with more or less definite directions for study. Higher still on the scale appears the problem or project attack, especially if the problems grow out of pupil thinking and are self-assigned. Perhaps near the top of effective assignments would be the class-developed ones, arranged on difficulty levels and suitable to the various abilities of the pupils of the group.

The types of procedure in assignments are affected by *other factors*: (1) the general kind of subject matter (such as content or skill subjects); (2) grade or ability levels, (such as first-, fifth-, or eighth-grade); (3) the rate of progress, (such as normal, subnormal, or supernormal); and (4) remedial materials designed for special purposes.

A third important element of group instruction is perhaps best indicated by the term *sharing*. This element may be divided into two types: (1) sharing the materials which have been assigned for definite study (examples: reports by individuals, presentation of a piece of work for criticism by teacher and pupils, reading for group pleasure, regular class recitations); (2) sharing information acquired independently of regular assignments (examples: news items, magazine stories, personal experiences, such as travel, interviews, or observations; books for recreational reading). All pupils should benefit from this sharing with others; those who give, no more nor less than those who receive.

A fourth element may be termed the *clarifying* factor. Difficult procedures, operations, or skills often can be taught to a group as well and as easily as to an individual. When this is possible, group instruction saves the teacher much time and effort. Some difficulties, however, are largely individual and little can be saved by clarifying these through group instruction, whereas much may be lost in decreasing interest for those who already understand.

The fifth element is the *checking* of the results of teaching. The types and means of checking vary widely according to the purposes for which they are used. Generally speaking, the teacher checks on the work of the assignment and expects the checking to indicate to some degree the kind and amount of effort expended by the pupil on the assignment. Teachers should also try to check the undirected work by securing brief statements or reports from the students. This undirected work reveals the extent of pupil interest.

The usual definition of *individual instruction* stresses the idea that pupils be given the opportunity to develop at their various individual rates over a prepared course of study. This course of study is sometimes worked out in great detail and exactness. Schools organized on the individual basis, however, usually include some group work. For example, pupils have a chance to work as groups in such subjects as the manual or domestic arts, physical education, music, reading of various types, and other skill subjects. Thus pupils are given training in the co-operation necessary to engage successfully in group activities. This of course is needed in actual life experiences both in and out of school.

Among the *advantages* claimed for individual instruction are these: (1) Each child may develop in his own way and advance at the rate normal for him. Hence, time is saved for the fast-moving pupil because he does not wait for the slower ones, and the slow pupil has as much time as he needs to do his task well without being pressed by those who lead. At the same time both fast and slow pupils face the continuous challenge of meeting and mastering definite life situations which confront them each day. (2) It eliminates unequal competition among pupils doing the same work. Such competition is often detrimental to all concerned. (3) It offers a better opportunity to adapt the subject matter to the abilities of the pupils because the learning situations may be arranged in the order of difficulty. (4) It can be used with slight adaptation in schools of any size. Small one-room rural schools often use this type of instruction out of necessity.

Perhaps some of the *disadvantages* should also be mentioned. (1)

Some pupils seem to lose incentive when working alone. To keep working at their best they apparently need the stimulation of direct contact with others of their group. (2) Frequently administrative difficulties appear, such as (a) pupils' spending comparatively too much time on one subject, and (b) uneven growth in the various subject-matter fields (a pupil's grade level might be 3.5 in history and 7.5 in arithmetic). (3) Some individual-instruction procedures allow little time for exchange of ideas among the pupils concerning the situations studied. (4) To be used most successfully individual instruction should be carried on by well trained, experienced teachers. These are not always available to all schools.

In individual instruction, as suggested previously, it is comparatively easy to *adapt the materials of study* to the *abilities* of the *pupils*. In fact this is almost a necessity if the plan is to work most successfully. Some types of methods used in this adaptation follow. *First,* the same materials are used in different ways on the various levels of difficulty. The fundamental facts of a history lesson may be all of the assignment that is required of the lowest level of pupil ability. The solution of problems based on these facts is met on the next level by pupils of higher ability. Pupils at the highest level should supplement the actual history materials with their personal reactions based upon wide reading. All of these, however, would take place over the same subject-matter base. A *second* type of adaptation provides that the materials used be on one level of difficulty only and be varied in amount. For instance, a bright pupil might read five readers on the fourth-grade level while slower pupils read only two. A *third* type of adaptation suggests that different materials on several levels of difficulty be provided for a single grade. To illustrate, an easy text in arithmetic is used for the minimum assignment, to cover the simplest fundamentals of the topic studied—say, addition of fractions; a different text, possibly with a different and more difficult treatment of the addition of fractions, is selected for a higher level of ability; and still another text of even more difficult subject matter, for the highest level of ability.

Individual instruction by the nature of its procedure requires relatively closer *checking* than do some other types. Frequently the checking is done by daily or other small units either by teacher or pupil or both. Other tests are carried on over blocks of subject matter covering larger areas, or over whole sections. Provision is also made for checking progress in the acquisition of skills necessary to use the instructional materials effectively.

In *summarizing,* it should be noted that much individual instruction occurs even when the main part of instruction is carried on in groups, and that much group instruction occurs when the main emphasis is on the individual child. The main difference between the two forms is one of emphasis. When the stress is put on group work in a class or grade, we call the procedure group instruction; when on individuals working separately and progressing at different rates with the same materials, we call it individual instruction. Both have their advantages and disadvantages and both are valuable as techniques of teaching.

STUDY GUIDES AND HELPS

If we accept the educational theory stated in Chapter I, we believe that the function of the schools of our nation is to fit individuals to live happily according to democratic ideals. This means that children must be given an opportunity to learn to meet life's situations. Children come to school to learn and they ought to increase their competence by developing techniques of learning. Study guides and helps contribute much in this regard. The time was when teachers guided their pupils simply by telling them, "Study your lesson." Such teachers usually expect pupils to read, remember facts, and repeat them. Facts are an essential element in meeting life's situations successfully. Furthermore, the habits formed in the process of learning facts often live as long as the pupils who form them. Because of this, much more stress is now placed upon teaching children how to study and upon developing techniques for individual, independent growth in all phases of the child's being—physical, emotional, mental, esthetic, and social. Thus the school accepts the challenge of helping pupils to develop effective behavior patterns.

There are many *ways to learn.* The following is a general list:[1] listening, enjoying, observing, writing, reading, looking at pictures, thinking, organizing, playing games, memorizing, discussing, asking

[1] Jones, A. J., Grizzell, E. D., and Grinstead, W. J. *Principles of Unit Construction,* pp. 62, 63. McGraw-Hill. 1939. Adapted.

questions, looking up references, drawing maps, making outlines, dramatizing, interviewing, experimenting, going on excursions. A great
deal of undirected learning occurs in children before they enter school
and this should be continued and encouraged. If the learning has been
started in undesirable channels the school may redirect it into desirable
ones, as well as help establish in the child new ways of learning independently. At this point we encounter various devices to guide pupils
in their study.

There are *different types* of *guides* and *helps* for study which aid
pupils in relying more and more upon their own initiative. Some of
them are: (1) broad plans of procedure covering a large area of material, such as an outline form for the problem method of studying a
unit in history, or contract forms, with sheets of specific problems
over a section of geography; (2) specific outlines of study effective in
acquiring skills, such as the weekly unit plan for studying spelling;
(3) definite procedures for specific learnings, such as the look-and-
recall method for learning to spell a word or to master an arithmetic
combination fact; (4) self-help guides or directions to show pupils
preferred methods or steps in certain learning activities, such as a list
of items stating what to do in order to read well orally or silently; (5)
techniques which aid in learning facts, evaluating, organizing, and
remembering, such as the manner of using the different parts of a book
—the index or maps—taking notes, and using a library.

There are marked *advantages* to teachers and pupils in using such
guides for learning purposes. (1) Teachers are helped to see the scope
and organization of a block of work—for example, a unit in history and
geography—and can better unify the learning processes and outcomes.
(2) Such guides are objective and lessen the personal element. That
is, children do the task according to a plan so as to attain the results
set forth, and not merely to please the instructor. (3) Pupils are encouraged to think, reason, evaluate, and draw their own conclusions
and to feel responsible for results. (4) Pupils often increase their
efforts to follow plans and work up to goals, because they may have
taken part in setting up the guides and standards. (5) A pupil can
advance in accordance with his natural rate of progress and his individual capacity. (6) Such guides and helps, if properly administered, may
augment the desire to learn.

Suggestions for developing *specific abilities which may be used by the pupils* in independent learning will be found frequently throughout this book. A few general techniques are elaborated in this chapter: steps for problem solving, taking notes, outlining, making paragraph headings, and using books and libraries.

The basic *steps* to use in *thinking through a problem* is one prominent study pattern which pupils should acquire. The steps usually followed are those given in the section, "Units of Work," pages 30 and 31. If pupils acquire this pattern, it should help them meet a great number of situations both in and out of school.

Pupils often have occasion to *take notes*. Do the majority know how or why? In the first place, there should be a definite *purpose* for the note-taking. The notes should be of value to the pupil for remembering or for immediate or future reference.

Second, there are certain *occasions* where note-taking is expedient; for example: (1) recording information one has collected from various sources; (2) recording information given by some such person as an outside speaker or the teacher; (3) making minutes of the proceedings of a meeting; (4) recording incidents pertaining to an excursion; and (5) making notations when thinking through and evaluating material on a topic.

Third, the notes should be made in neat, legible *form*. If the gist of the thought is recorded, the items will be brief yet full enough to convey the meaning when read at a later date. If the material is copied, pupils should be impressed with the importance of copying accurately and indicating quotations with quotation marks. The name of the author and title of the book are probably best given at the head of the notes made from books. The page references may be written in the margins. Although many notes will be in sentence form, children should realize that other forms are acceptable, such as incomplete sentences, phrases, and the outline.

Fourth, certain *methods* may help develop *note-taking* ability. In the primary grades, the following are suggested: (1) A short paragraph may be read orally and a child asked to state briefly what it tells. The teacher writes this on the board and the pupils copy. The process may be repeated for other paragraphs. (2) While investigating a problem, different pupils bring information obtained by asking, observing, listening to the radio, and other means. This information may be stated briefly by each pupil, put on the blackboard, copied in notebooks, and later used for discussion and evaluation of the problem. (3) Pupils may be encouraged as they are working on a problem to make notations of the ideas and conclusions occurring to them as they work. These may be used later in class discussion.

After pupils develop ability through these co-operative activities, they should be encouraged to continue independently and to enlarge upon the same procedures. With such a basis, note-taking should be an intelligent, independent learning device for intermediate grade work.

The ability to *outline* is a study help that aids pupils to organize and to keep material for reference. By this means relationships are noted, less important details omitted and facts arranged in appropriate order. Simple beginnings may be made in the primary grades as a part of language or reading instruction, thus initiating pupils into the idea of classification. The pupils may dictate the items and the teacher write them on the blackboard. Later such a list may be numbered and copied by the pupils—for example, listing like items under one heading:

Fruits	*Vegetables*
Apples	Lettuce
Pears	Bean
Grapes	Carrots

Gradually subheadings may be included and the regular outline sequence begun:

Transportation

I. On land	II. On water	III. In the air
A. Train	A. Canoes	A. Airplanes
B. Automobile	B. Steamers	B. Dirigibles

More advanced work will include additional subheadings:

Transportation

I. On land	II. On water
A. Trains	A. Canoes
1. Passenger	1. Birch bark
2. Freight	2. Aluminum
B. Automobiles	B. Steamers
1. Car	1. Passenger
2. Truck	2. Freight

The following is a more inclusive outline form:

Transportation

I. On land
  A. Trains
    1. Passenger
      a. Local
      b. Limited
    2. Freight
      a. Local
      b. Fast
  B. Automobiles
    1. Cars
      a. Sedan
      b. Coupe
    2. Trucks
      a. Delivery
      b. Cattle

II. On water
  A. Canoes
    1. Birch bark
      a. Construction
      b. Use
    2. Aluminum
      a. Advantages
      b. Cost
  B. Steamers
    1. Passenger
      a. Luxury liner
      b. Transport
    2. Freight
      a. Lake
      b. Ocean

For a yet more detailed outline the Arabic numbers and small letters with parentheses are used, such as

I.
  A.
    1.
      a.
        (1)
          (a)

Although it may seem desirable to have one standard outline form and to use generally the same sequence of figures and letters, this is not always followed in practice. Nevertheless the order ought not to be varied within the same outline. There should be more than one subheading, for otherwise the idea is incorporated in the previous heading; for example, there should be an A only if there is a B, a 1 only if there is a 2. Sometimes only sections of the outline form are used:

A.   B.   1.   2.
  1.   1.   or   a.   a.
  2.   2.   b.   b.

It is unnecessary always to begin with the Roman numeral, but whatever part of the outline is used, the usual sequence is followed, as shown above. The same form of wording is usually used as far as possible in the same section: the paragraph, sentence, participle, prepositional phrase, noun, modifier, and similar structures. For example, in the outline above, the main headings are prepositional phrases; the first sub-headings, nouns; and the additional co-ordinate subheadings, nouns or adjectives.

The ability to make *paragraph headings* indicates skill in organization, evaluation, and summarizing. It is often expressed in the outline form. In order to develop this ability gradually through the first few years of school, the following *graded exercises* are suggested for use at the different levels of children's maturation:

1. Show mounted pictures that have been cut from magazines. Discuss them with the pupils. Show how pictures tell something. Ask for names for the pictures. Write these names on the blackboard or suggest them as captions for the pictures.

2. Ask pupils to suggest names for recorded compositions or experience reading charts. Use the names as titles for them. Usually such a chart consists of several sentences and presents a unit of thought concerning one topic; it may be considered a paragraph, although often it is not in paragraph form. Thus the title is really a paragraph heading.

3. As soon as pupils meet the paragraph form in their books, speak of the sections as paragraphs. Stress the main thoughts expressed by questions or statements, such as, "What did the boys do with the money they earned? The next paragraph tells," or "The first paragraph tells what happened when they drove through the puddle. Read to see if it was fun."

4. Ask each pupil, as he reads a selection which lends itself to this type of procedure, to draw a picture of the thought expressed in the first paragraph, then to do the same with subsequent paragraphs. Ask each to name his pictures. Have the class discuss the different sets of pictures and titles and revise the titles, if desirable. Have each pupil copy the names of the pictures in outline form. Show them that they really have provided names for the paragraphs. The following outline might be the result of such a procedure as applied to a dog story:

a. The dog   c. The accident
b. The boy and dog playing   d. The rescue

5. Construct paragraph headings for a selection. As the pupils read each paragraph, refer to the corresponding heading and discuss why

it is good. The heading is suitable if most of the paragraph discusses it. For example, in the following, all but the first sentence discuss what Jane saw at the airport.

Paragraph	Paragraph Heading
Jane lived near the airport. Every day she watched the planes glide down the field. She could see the people get on and off the big liners. She liked to watch the lights go on at night.	What Jane saw at the airport

6. Help pupils to match paragraphs and headings. This exercise can be used on the advanced primary level.

7. Help pupils to select the best headings from a group which has been made for each paragraph. It appears to be harder for pupils to select a heading than to match paragraphs and headings.

8. Give them a list of the paragraph headings arranged in incorrect sequence covering all the paragraphs of a selection. After they have read it, have the pupils number these headings in the correct order.

9. Give pupils paragraph headings for a selection they have read, in the form of completion exercises. This is an easy step toward formulating headings for themselves. For example, after reading several paragraphs about Indians, they might fill in the following:

a. Of what _____ the Indians made houses
b. How they got their _____
c. What they used for _____
d. What _____ they kept

Key: a. materials b. food c. clothing d. animals

10. Ask pupils to make alternate headings, every other one being supplied. For example, after reading about a sudden call to the city, they are to supply the missing headings:

a. The trip to the station   d. _____
b. _____   e. The arrival in time for
c. Missing the train   the appointment

Pupils might supply some headings similar to the following: b. The flat tire; d. The fast drive to the city.

11. If pupils can comprehend the material they read, they probably should be able to formulate paragraph headings independently. This

certainly would be possible if they have had plenty of practice with graded exercises (similar to those given above) spread over the period of the early elementary grades.

Since the correct use of *books and libraries* aids learning, pupils often need special instruction on these facilities. *Information about books* should be presented to children according to their ability to assimilate it at the different learning levels. They should learn the names of parts common to most books and the purposes of each part. For example, the title page contains the name of the book, the authors, the illustrators, the publishers with the city or cities in which they have offices, and sometimes the date of publication. The date when the book was copyrighted usually appears on the back of the title page. It is important for pupils to learn to look for the publication date, since changes in all fields occur rapidly, and material in a book with an old copyright date might be questionable and even incorrect. Similar presentations may be made for the introduction, preface, or foreword; the table of contents; the index; the glossary or word list; illustrations, maps, and charts; the appendix; footnotes; bibliographies; reference material; and cross references.

A unit on the schoolroom library is a good means of introducing pupils to the *use* of a *school* or *public* library. Some of the information and skills which will help them in using such library facilities independently are as follows: (1) The knowledge of the most common resources of a library—encyclopedias, atlases, magazines, pamphlets, daily papers, collections of pictures and clippings, yearbooks, reference books in different fields, and government documents. Guidance is essential if pupils are to understand the importance, contents, and manner of using such resources. (2) Skill in locating material in the library is developed through instruction in the purpose and use of the card catalog—(a) the alphabetical guides on the outside of the drawers, (b) the alphabetical guides inside of the drawers, (c) the title, author, subject, and other cards. Some understanding of the order of arrangement of books on the shelves may be expected of pupils on the higher grade levels. (3) The making of a bibliography, or a list of books on one topic, should have definite attention. It should include the author's name, title of book, publisher, date of publication, and library call number if feasible. These should be listed under the proper heading:

Animals

Friskey, Margaret. *Seven Diving Ducks*. David McKay
  Co. 1940.
Stearns, David. *Wisk, the Story of a Chipmunk*. Farrar
  & Rinehart. 1941.

Use of the *dictionary* is extremely important in pronunciation, word meanings, and similar language aspects. Therefore, special lessons should be conducted to influence pupils to rely upon the dictionary for frequent aid. There are several current editions especially suitable for the elementary grades. Available pamphlets and books offer suggestions for instruction in their use.

These limited suggestions as to study guides and helps may point the way and stimulate the resourceful teacher to find other avenues for providing guides for learning and helping pupils to use them. The teacher's purpose should be to help pupils direct their own activities along lines of desirable independent learning.

SKILL DEVELOPMENT

It may be well, at the beginning, to make a brief statement of what is meant by skill development. Various terms—drill, practice, skill training—indicate the activities involved in building into habits certain often used facts or processes. The processes may be predominantly mental or physical, as in learning to solve arithmetic problems or to do handwriting. The exercise required to make the use of these facts or processes to some degree automatic—this is the meaning of skill development.

Current theories about skill development vary all the way from the extremely progressive to the extremely conservative points of view. (1) The radically progressive would have no so-called drill because it would tend to detract the pupil's attention from the centers of his creative interest. According to this theory of education, the pupils would acquire such skills as are needed in the processes of working out their larger units of activity. Furthermore, this theory asks: Of what use is drill if it is done apart from the situation in which it is used? (2) At the other extreme, the conservative asks: How can a pupil reason without facts, how can he create profitably without the command of certain fundamental skills, or develop reasoning power without having basic information? These skills, the extremely conservative attitude maintains, must be fixed in habit by practice whether the pupil likes it or not. (3) The more liberal attitude takes a midway position, maintaining that practice is undoubtedly necessary if pupils are to secure an efficient use of the essential facts and processes of learning, but that this practice should be as meaningful and effective as possible. For example, in practice on the simple addition facts each pupil should work on the ones he does not know, not indiscriminately on all. He should not even be introduced to them until he has acquired sufficient maturity and then only after a preparatory background has been built up. Finally, the pupil should be aware of the purpose of the work he is doing and have definite ends in view. The liberal says: Yes, there should be skill development, but by selected, purposeful exercises.

Four factors which directly affect skill development should be discussed at this point. These are not all of the factors which pertain to the technique under consideration, but they seem to be of the most immediate interest to teachers.

First of all, teachers should clearly realize that it is *impossible to teach any skill wholly apart from every other*. This is true because a child is a unit organization and each part of him is directly connected with every other part. He learns as a whole. Learning a comparatively simple skill like writing the letter "m" involves holding the pen or pencil, hand and arm positions, holding the paper, body position, and perhaps many other more or less complicated skills. Improvement in writing "m" involves improvement in some or all of the conditions connected with the making of this letter. What teachers usually mean when they say certain skills are "practiced" is that those particular skills are emphasized more than others; not that no other skills are developed at the same time.

The second factor in the most effective type of skill development can best be indicated by the term *stimulation*. By this is meant the motivation necessary to make pupils function in practice somewhere near the upper limit of their ability in the skill being developed. Teachers know that in general pupils progress most rapidly in skills when doing their very best; not when loafing at half their ability.

Teachers also know that most pupils do not naturally tend to work near their top limits of performance; they usually need a certain amount of stimulation to spur them on. Ordinarily, high levels of performance for each pupil can be maintained only for a comparatively short time.

A third factor in developing skills is *checking*. The type of check, of course, varies with the purpose but, in general, skill checking should be both immediate and rather rigid. Checking serves in a sense to direct the pupils' efforts. It keeps them from straying mentally and from acquiring detrimental work habits. If stimulation is the accelerator, checking is the steering wheel. These go hand in hand and should be properly balanced. Too much stimulation often produces guessing, nervousness, false or even slovenly reactions. Too much checking may result in slowness, over-cautiousness, and time-wasting repetitions.

The fourth factor is that of *teacher guidance of pupil effort*. This is perhaps the most important of all, but the least effective suggestions can be made concerning it. Such efforts must of necessity be personal and depend upon the pupil's varying needs as he develops; his attitude; his home and school environment; the teacher's personality; and numerous other factors, many of which change from day to day. For example, Helen has had trouble with outlining. This particular day her reactions are unusually poor. It is difficult to know whether she tried and failed or did not even try. The guidance given by the teacher, it would seem, must be formulated to meet the needs of such a situation after the situation appears. Certain broad principles of guidance may be learned beforehand, such as the use of patience, the ability to sense the true pupil attitude, the giving of sympathetic consideration, and the use of easy materials at first. Even more specific facts or conditions pertaining to various difficulties may be kept in mind:—Can Helen select the main and subordinate ideas of a paragraph or section? Does she have a method of outlining? Does she seem to perceive relationships of any kind? The teacher must, if necessary, be able to react according to her own diagnosis and formulate on the spot the suggestions to meet each individual situation.

Types of *skills* used in school are sometimes classified as follows: (1) Skills predominantly mental, such as memorizing a poem, finding the central thought of a paragraph, summarizing a chapter; (2) skills predominantly physical, such as manual or athletic dexterity, skill in playing an instrument, typing; and (3) skills about equally mental and physical, such as oral and written spelling, oral reading, vocal music. It is obvious that the types of skills suggested are not separate categories but shade gradually into one another. The main difference seems to be that a certain phase is more prominent in one type than in another. Perhaps another difference is the ease or difficulty of observing or measuring growth in the three types. Generally speaking the predominantly physical skills may be observed and possibly measured most easily.

Some *results* of effective skill development are: (1) It increases the efficiency of pupil work, both in the original learning of subject matter and in the maintenance exercises later. For instance, a pupil who has well developed reading skills will be able to attack his history or science assignments more efficiently than a pupil who is defective in these skills. Moreover, these same reading skills would give a pupil a distinct advantage in making a periodic review or summary of his history or science materials. (2) It is possible and probable that a command of skills in any field would aid in creating and maintaining healthy pupil attitudes. The fact that a pupil can do a thing well tends to give him a spirit of mastery and helps to foster self-respect and self-confidence. These may in turn reflect favorably on all the work he does. In short, we like to do the things we can do well and we may dislike those we cannot do well. Effective skills assist in learning, and hence in achieving a favorable attitude toward learning. (3) When the result of effective skill development is carried to its logical conclusions it appears to contribute to personality growth. Teachers working in the remedial fields testify again and again to the radical personality changes resulting from more nearly normal pupil functioning brought about largely by the acquisition of a basic skill, such as reading. Undoubtedly a command of the basic skills required in normal living plays a large part in determining the strength and quality of personality.

Practical suggestions for skill development are of direct interest to teachers. The following include some of the more important ones in effective practice: (1) Keep all pupils profitably busy all of the time. Many teachers use this as a measuring stick to test their practice devices. Teachers know that they have reached an ideal situation when this suggestion applies one hundred percent. Any device that keeps only a part of the group profitably busy is not the best device and one that keeps only a few or none profitably busy should be discarded. (2) Vary practice exercises to avoid monotony. That is, shift the emphasis, or change the procedure of an exercise before pupils tire of it. This assumes that the difficulty of an exercise suits the pupil or grade level and is arranged in the most attractive form. (3) Keep pupils happy. This may be done by keeping the exercises animated with the game of play element prominent. Usually the pupils share the zest of the teacher and react to her stimulation. Pupils also enjoy the sheer activity of interesting, lively exercises. They may be predominantly mental or physical or a mixture of both depending on the grade level and materials practiced. Consciousness of success colors pupils' attitudes. They like to feel that they are getting somewhere as they practice skills. (4) Check exercises carefully. Perhaps the most effective checking is done with small units and immediately following the exercise. Such checks should usually be as exact as possible and quite rigid. Exceptional situations may arise when exactness and rigidity of checking are undesirable but they should not occur too often. Furthermore, the checks should be objective when possible. (5) Show progress (change) by charts. This device may be used profitably in charting results of both informal and standard tests. Textbooks suggest it in a wide variety of ways. A chart that shows change over the longer period of time is the more valuable. Charts may be made for a class or an individual. The class chart shows the central tendency of the group as a whole, while the individual one is usually kept by each pupil for his own information. Practices in using charts of both kinds vary greatly.

MEASUREMENT IN TEACHING

The human mind probably has always asked the question, "How much?" We know it has been asked from the beginning of written history, and to answer this question the human mind has invented countless measuring instruments. We ask the same question today in teaching: How much learned? How much development? How much taught? How much improvement?

Perhaps the mention of some *fundamental factors* in the measurement of teaching would help toward a better understanding of this important field of instruction. In the first place there must be some sort of *measuring instrument*. (This will be discussed more fully later in this section.) Secondly, in trying to measure the results of teaching, one must measure *mental elements* or *activity* which are not easily observed. If trouble is encountered in measuring with exactness things we can see, much more difficulty may be expected with things we cannot see. A third factor is the *unstable force* that must be measured. A pupil's mind is constantly changing not only because of school experiences but also because of all the influences which play upon it from every source. This makes measuring the results of teaching similar to measuring the distance between two points which move constantly, and often irregularly. A fourth factor is the *widely varying pupil capacities* with which teaching must deal. The original endowment of pupils extends from the moron or below to the genius, and successful instruments to measure the results of teaching must function reasonably well with all levels. A fifth factor involves the *making of standards of performance or of growth, or of both*. Even if the results of teaching could be measured accurately the question of what pupils of given age, ability, or capacity levels are able to do would not be answered. To illustrate, a pupil can be weighed quite accurately, but the figure obtained does not indicate what weight he should have. His weight may be far above or below the desirable weight of a healthy boy of his age. Some standards are comparatively easy to make, while others are difficult, if not altogether impossible.

This mere enumeration of factors indicates some of the *difficulties* involved in measuring the results of teaching. Among these are: (1) Many variable and practically uncontrollable factors, such as environment, inherited tendencies, pupil attitudes, tend to invalidate the measurements. (2) Constructing the measuring instruments is a difficult matter. (3) The more or less technical nature of some of the tests make them hard to use. Teachers may be inexperienced; pupil factors may vary; the test results may be erroneous through faulty administration or scoring, or they may be misinterpreted. (4) A host of other causes may stand in the way of proper measurement of teaching, such as lack of funds to secure the best testing instruments, inability of school officials to appreciate the value of good testing, teacher resistance because of fear of having their pupils tested, and previous unwise use of test results. But in spite of these difficulties, considerable progress has been made, as the following paragraphs will show.

The *types* of *measuring instruments* which have been evolved to date may be roughly classified under three heads: achievement tests, mental tests, and diagnostic tests. *Achievement* tests are used to measure the results of teaching in the subject-matter fields. They include both actual subject-matter materials and the skills involved in learning. There are two types to be considered. The first is the *standard* test which has standards or norms of performance set up by previous experiment. These norms may be in the form of scores on the test, or of age or grade levels. For example, a teacher using a standard test in reading in her fourth grade can at once compare her pupils' performance with the standard, both as a group and as individuals. This may be done in terms of score, reading age, or reading grade, provided those standards are given for that particular test. A second type of achievement tests is that *improvised* by the teacher. If each test item of this type admits of only one correct scoring the test is called objective. If some items allow the leeway of several scorings, the tests are only partially or semi-objective. When test items call for a rather extended written answer or opinion the test belongs to the essay type. Each of these types of tests has its advantages and defects. The standard tests have the obvious advantage of direct comparison of results both with the standards and with different tests throughout the year—those obtained at the beginning, middle, and end of the school year. But such a test is rigid and often does not fit the subject matter taught in a particular room or school, although it may do well in testing basic skills. Improvised classroom tests have the advantage of flexibility, but do not offer the standards of comparison. The essay tests allow full expression of pupil opinion but have little or no objectivity.

Mental tests are designed to measure the *innate* or *inherited capacities* of the pupil. Since the *environment* affects the child, however, it is impossible to get an accurate result. For this and other reasons some teachers question their validity. Mental tests are generally of two types: the *individual*, which must be administered individually and which requires considerable technical ability on the part of the administrator, and the *group*, which may be given to two or more pupils at a time. The scores of both types are usually translated into years of *mental* age, which in turn is divided by the *chronological* age to obtain the intelligence quotient (I.Q.).

Diagnostic tests may be either of the achievement or mental type and, as the name suggests, are designed to find defects which may be inhibiting proper development. They are used most frequently to locate deficiencies in study skills or in basic facts in a given field. For example, a pupil is having trouble with the mechanics of long division. A diagnostic test might show that he is deficient in several of the simple subtraction facts and does not know the basic multiplication facts well enough. Such tests can also be purchased, but teachers usually make them to fit their own particular class and pupil situations.

In order properly to interpret and use the results of the various types of tests, especially those of achievement, it is necessary to have command of certain commonly used *statistical techniques.*

First, some *measures* of *central tendency* will be discussed. Suppose the following per cent scores were obtained by a class in spelling: 86, 87, 95, 93, 88, 99, 94, 85, 91, 96, 93, 82, 96, 94, 83, 85, 92, 91, 84, 90, 91, 89, 91, 90, 92, 91, 90, 89. If the teacher wished to find a single figure to represent the class (measure of central tendency) she could add the scores and divide by 28 (the number of scores) to find the *average.* This is 90.3, and is usually called the *"mean"* in statistics. Should the teacher want to know more about the relationships of the scores she might arrange them in order of size as: 99, 96, 96, 95, 94, 94, 93, 93, 92, 92, 91, 91, 91, 91, 91, 90, 90, 90, 89, 89, 88, 87, 86, 85, 85, 84, 83, 82. By counting half way down (14 scores) from the top or half way up from the lowest one the teacher could find the *midscore* to be 91. This is another measure of central tendency.

Finally, the teacher may wish to make a *frequency distribution* in which all the steps appear. Notice in the list above, in which scores are ranked according to position, there are no 97, 98, or 100%. A frequency distribution of the same per cent spelling scores, using a two-step scale, is given below.

Distribution of Spelling Scores   Grade X   School *B*

% score	No. of scores	
99–100	1	1
97–98		
95–96	111	3
93–94	1111	4
91–92	~~1111~~ 11	7
89–90	~~1111~~	5 (13)
87–88	11	2
85–86	111	3
83–84	11	2
81–82	1	1

Total scores   28

The teacher may find the *median* (mid-point) of the scores from this distribution. It is calculated as follows: (1) ½ of 28 (the no. of scores) is 14. (2) Begin at the bottom of the "No. of scores" column and count (add) up to the number which if added would make 14 or more, as $1+2+3+2+5=13$. If the 7 in the next step were added the partial sum would be greater than 14, hence past the mid-point of the distribution. Therefore, the median (mid-point) is in the scale step 91-92. (3) Since 13 scores were counted to get up to this step, only 1 in it will need to be counted to reach the mid-point (14), or in this case it will be ⅐ of the scores (1 of the 7 in the step) in the scale step (91-92) and ⅐ of the distance through the step would be ⅐ of 2 (units in the step), or 2/7, or .3 (approximately). This correction is added to the beginning of the scale step $(91.0 + .3 = 91.3)$ which is the median by actual calculation. Many of the test norms are expressed in terms of medians.

The *measure of relationship* ordinarily used is known as the coefficient of correlation. This is usually represented by the symbol "*r*" and may extend from −1.00 through 0.00 to +1.00. The −1.00 represents a perfect negative correlation. This means that there is a large amount of relationship between the two factors, but a negative relationship. For example, this kind of relationship might exist between the number of days of drouth and the size of a crop. The greater the amount of drouth, the smaller the size of the crop. That is, as one factor grows the other lessens in a relatively equal degree. A perfect positive correlation is represented by +1.00. This might be illustrated by the relationship between the diameter of a circle and its circumference. The longer the diameter is, the longer the circumference will be. That is, as one factor grows, the other grows relatively. The complete lack of correlation (relationship) is represented by 0.00; that is, the trend in one factor has no relationship to the trend of the other. This might be illustrated by the amount of direct sunlight to the earth as related to the amount from Polaris (North Star) to the earth. The sun might cease to shine and Polaris send the same amount of light; or Polaris be blotted out and our sun send the same amount as before. There seems to be no relationship between these two sources of light. Hence there are no trends or relative changes, and the coefficient of correlation would be neither negative nor positive, but zero. Such a situation is seldom found in schoolroom activities. Usually some degree of correlation, either positive or negative, is present.

If the reader is interested in further knowledge of these statistical devices he should consult books in theory and uses of elementary statistics.

QUESTIONS—PROBLEMS—REACTIONS
(See Preface, "To the Student")

SECTION ONE: *Facts*

1. What gives meanings to words?
2. Describe the elements which are included in audio-visual instruction.
3. What types of still picture are suggested?
4. What are the different phases of general techniques of teaching discussed in this chapter?
5. For which do you have the best background of knowledge and experience?
6. What is meant by group instruction?
7. What five phases of group instruction are discussed in this chapter?
8. What kinds of planning aid group instruction?
9. What factors make assignments effective?
10. How may teachers check the results of undirected work?
11. What is meant by individual instruction?
12. What advantages and disadvantages result from this type of teaching?
13. What phases of teaching need special emphasis in individual instruction?
14. What is the main difference between group and individual instruction?
15. What is meant by "organization of instruction on a unit basis"?
16. What are some arguments in favor of such organization? Against?
17. What are some different types of unit?

18. What requirements are essential for sucecss in such organization of work?
19. What factors should help in planning any unit?
20. Of what importance is development of the ability to study effectively?
21. What are some of the usual ways by which we learn?
22. What are the helps and guides which may assist students to study independently? Describe each briefly.
23. To what extent are study helps furnished in textbooks or accompanying pamphlets?
24. What are some of the advantages of the modern dictionaries planned for elementary schools?
25. Note how many books you use in one day which have the elements listed in this chapter.
26. What other terms are used for skill development?
27. Give four factors that affect skill development.
28. Make a heading for each type of skill suggested. List examples under each.
29. What are some effective practices that promote growth along this line?
30. What fundamental factors deserve consideration in planning for the measurement of teaching?
31. What are the different classifications of tests commonly used in teaching?
32. List the explanatory terms given under these two headings: measures of central tendency and measures of relationship.
33. Select from the methods and materials for audio-visual instruction those best suited for a unit on clothing. Why do you select these?
34. Compare the values of the motion picture and still pictures in education.
35. Which aspect of evaluation in the audio-visual field would contribute most to habits of independent study? Why?

SECTION TWO: *Problems*

36. Explain which form or forms of planning in group instruction would contribute most in a unit pertaining to Indian life.
37. In what fields of subject matter would pupils profit by periods for clarification? Why?
38. Show how to check individual progress for assignments made.
39. Compare the values and dangers, as set forth for unit teaching. Evaluate the differences.
40. Make clear the relationship of, and help from, the community in unit teaching.
41. Why should the pupils participate in the selection and planning of a unit of work?
42. List three units and show for which level each would be appropriate.
43. Suggest several excursions suitable to your locality and indicate their educational value. With what units might they be correlated?
44. Illustrate how checking can be done in units of work.
45. Bring notes you have made for some occasion. Analyze them on the basis of the discussion in this chapter.

46. Outline the section on Group Instruction, using the outline form suggested in this chapter. Be able to defend your arrangement of items.
47. Indicate which of the three current theories concerning skill development would assure the acquisition of necessary information and skills and yet permit attention to individual development. Reasons.
48. Select some desired skill and show how the four factors suggested will function in teaching it.
49. Give illustrations for drill that include at least three of the principal suggestions discussed.
50. Can the maker of an automobile judge the results of his labor better than a teacher can judge the results of her teaching? Why?
51. Which types of tests would be more valuable in helping to determine the grade in which a pupil should work?
52. What type of test would you recommend for checking weekly progress in geography? For weakness in multiplication or division? Why?
53. Do you deem the essay or objective type test the better for showing a pupil's real achievement? Why?
54. Would the class "average" show the distribution of grades more easily to a teacher than the class "mid-score"? Why?

SECTION THREE: *Personal Reactions*

55. Which of the seven principles given to help teachers in using audio-visual techniques do you consider most important to a beginning teacher? Which next in importance? Why?
56. Which do you think should be given more attention—the concrete experiences, the use of all kinds of pictures, or graphic materials? Why?
57. What do you consider to be difficulties in or objections to the use of the radio in school?
58. Do you believe it well to use more audio-visual techniques and fewer textbook assignments? Why?
59. Select a topic for group study. List what you consider some good teacher objectives; some good pupil objectives.
60. Which of the aids in establishing healthy motives do you consider the most helpful to pupils?
61. Select an assignment for study and show how you would arrange the assignments so as to meet three levels of pupil ability.
62. List five desirable and five undesirable study motives that you have experienced or observed.
63. Judging from your experience, does group or individual instruction receive greater emphasis in schools at present? Which do you think is the more effective? Which do you think the more difficult to administer?
64. Why, in your judgment, is unit teaching not used more extensively?
65. Do you think unit teaching would adjust itself better to a conservative or to a progressive philosophy of education? Explain how.
66. How much help and at what level in your education did you receive instruction in how to study?

67. Analyze the solution of some situation you have experienced, using the steps referred to for thinking through a problem.
68. Which have you retained better from the teaching you have received, information acquired or habits of work?
69. Select one exercise for developing ability to make paragraph headings. Select some material and show how you would present it to children according to the exercise selected.
70. What is your opinion of the value of keeping notebooks?
71. Would you recommend a course in high school or college on the organization and use of the library? Why?
72. To what extent do you believe people generally work to the limit of their capacity?
73. Which of the five practical suggestions for developing skill do you consider would require the greater teacher effort to make it effective? Why?
74. Some people question the value of judging pupils' abilities by testing. Do you think they have justification for this stand? Why?
75. In your judgment, are these "General Techniques" of equal value in rural and town schools?

SUGGESTIONS FOR FURTHER READING

Bowen, G. *Living and Learning in a Rural School*. The MacMillan Co., 1944. This is a splendid book for a (beginning) rural teacher who wants to conduct a school according to present-day theory. Question section with paged answers is good.

Caswell, Hallis L. *Education in the Elementary School*. American Book Co., 1942. The present-day philosophy of education is set forth in its various aspects of planning, organization, and techniques of teaching.

Dale, Edgar, *Audio-Visual Methods in Teaching*. The Dryden Press, 1946. This book gives a very complete picture of audio-visual materials and procedures. It also furnishes good material on general teaching methods and is written in an enjoyable style with an abundance of good illustrations. A good book for all teachers.

Dent, E. C., *The Audio-Visual Handbook*. Society for Visual Education, Inc., 100 East Ohio Street, Chicago, 1942. This handbook is concise and specific in explaining how to make slides, use projectors, and utilize other visual and audio materials effectively.

Forty-eight Yearbook of the National Society for the Study of Education. Part I. "Audio-Visual Materials of Instruction." The University of Chicago Press, Chicago 37, Illinois. 1949. This gives an inclusive presentation, dealing with many aspects of this area of teaching.

Forty-ninth Yearbook of the National Society for the Study of Education. Part I. "Learning and Instruction." The University of Chicago Press, Chicago 37, Illinois. 1949. This yearbook should help teachers to accept the declaration that "classrooms should cease to be lesson-learning rooms and become laboratories for learning."

Foster, J. C. and Headley, N. E. *Education in the Kindergarten,* Second Edition. American Book Co., 1948. This is a very valuable book to one who is fitting herself to do effective work with children of the kindergarten level.

Garrett, Henry E. *Statistics in Psychology and Education.* Longmans, Green, 1937. This is a readable discussion of the elements of statistics. It is amply illustrated with drawings and problems. It also contains more advanced statistics.

Griffith, Coleman R. *Psychology Applied to Teaching and Learning.* Farrar and Rinehart, 1939. Chapters 6 and 7 contain interesting discussions on habits and skills. Many tables and charts of experimental data illustrate and verify the statements.

Hockett, J. A. and Jacobsen, E. W. *Modern Practices in the Elementary School,* pp. 7-63. Ginn, 1938. This book offers suggestions for practical ways of guiding learning procedures in a school conducted according to modern ideas. Teachers will find help here in organizing work on the unit basis.

Levenson, W. B. *Teaching Through Radio.* Farrar and Rinehart, 1945. This book deals with the radio as an instrument for bringing radio programs into the schoolroom and with children's broadcasting. It discusses, among other topics, sources of information for teachers, the home use of the radio, and the teacher's part in guiding children's listening. It also has a chapter on recordings.

Macomber, F. G. *Guiding Child Development in the Elementary School.* American Book Co., 1948. One can find much help on unit procedure in this book. It also offers assistance in teaching the various subjects on a day's program with the idea of developing abilities effective in daily living.

Mott, C. and Baisden, L. B. *The Children's Book on How to Use Books and Libraries.* Scribner, 1937. A workbook entitled *Children's Library Lesson Book* accompanies this book. This is for the upper elementary grades. The style is appealing to children, and the material gives excellent guidance for techniques required in carrying on study and solving problems by means of independent reading.

Nelson, M. J. and Denny, E. C. *A Practical Guide and Workbook in Statistics for Teachers.* The Dryden Press, 1939. This is a summary of the theory and practical application of statistics in one volume. It has both explanation and problems.

Smith, D. V. and Frederick, R. W. *Live and Learn.* Scribner, 1938. This book shows how children learn in the modern school. Pictures add to its interest.

Wofford, K. V. *Teaching in Small Schools.* The MacMillan Co., 1946. This is a book for teachers to use in planning and as an aid in techniques.

PART TWO

Communication Skills

CHAPTER 3

READING

INTRODUCTORY

THE person who can read rapidly and with a reasonable degree of comprehension has access to unlimited resources of information and enjoyment. Reading is an acquired ability, not a natural tendency like hunger and gregariousness. Besides, it is a very complex process involving movements of the eye, mental processes of recognition and interpretation of symbols, thinking, and in the broader interpretation, the use of acquired information. The old idea that saying words in consecutive order constitutes reading has long since been discarded. Needless to say, when one reads, words must be recognized, but that is far from being enough, for actual reading means comprehending ideas expressed by words in the various forms of printed and written language. The words used and the ideas expressed, however, are not interpreted in the same way by any two persons, because each interprets them in the light of his own experiences.

Reading is essential in all walks of life, for the least informed person and for the one who is profoundly educated; for the poorest manual laborer and the corporation president. Growth made by reading is absolutely necessary to all who wish to keep abreast of the times. Without the ability to read, a person cannot enjoy his share of the world's cultural heritage.

That *modern conditions affect reading* is self-evident. Some of these may have a tendency to decrease, some to increase the amount of reading done. Some contemporary agencies that tend to *decrease reading* are the radio and television, which bring news directly to the listeners almost as soon as the events happen; motion pictures, which tell of current happenings pictorially as well as verbally; public forums, which help to shape public opinion; various means of travel, which broaden individuals by firsthand contacts with conditions. Agencies that tend to *increase reading* are better library facilities, making books accessible to rural as well as urban families; more leisure time, which challenges people to make good use of it; keener competition in most industrial and professional fields, which make necessary the use of related reading materials; unsettled social and economic conditions, requiring enlightenment on national and world affairs. People read more because there is so much more to read—papers, periodicals, and books made accessible promptly through rapid transportation and improved library facilities.

Although conditions have changed, the *purposes* for which people read have remained much the same. "The broad objectives of reading; namely to enrich experience, to broaden interests, to develop appreciations, and to cultivate ideal and appropriate attitudes have changed but little during recent years."[1] In general, there are two types of reading: (1) study reading—to gain knowledge or to solve problems and (2) recreational reading—for enjoyment or fun. The first usually involves reading content subject materials which are almost entirely factual. The second uses literature for the sake of stories and poems. Study reading may also involve the development of certain skills necessary for the improvement of reading, such as increasing vocabulary, improving comprehension, and establishing good study habits. It is the purpose, not the material, that largely determines the classification of reading. The same material might be used for either recreational or study reading. Further discussion of these matters may be found in the section, "Reading in the Grades Above the Primary."

From the standpoint of *form*, reading is classified as *oral* and *silent*. Oral reading predominated during the early days of our nation. Storm

[1] Gray, Wm. S. *36th Yearbook of the National Society for the Study of Education.* Part I, p. 18. Public School Publishing Co. 1937.

and Smith [1] tell us that in the colonial period people learned to read in order to read the Bible. The member of a family who could read read the Bible to the others, and oral reading served a definite purpose. As time went on and the colonies were settled by "various peoples" oral reading served as one means of bringing about greater uniformity of speech. Noah Webster gave this as one purpose of his Blue-backed Speller, "the first textbook prepared by an American author." During the Revolutionary period "It is estimated that 75 per cent of the population was illiterate." Information had to be broadcast. To meet this need, orators presented information and news directly to the people. Thus the aim of teaching reading became "that of developing eloquent and expressive oral readers." Much stress was placed upon correct habits of pronunciation and clear articulation. Emphasis upon oral reading continued for over a century and was so strong that the expression "to read" usually meant to read orally. One still hears the expression, "to hear the reading class."

Today conditions of life demand much less oral and much more silent reading. Some specific reasons for this situation are: (1) A very large percentage of our population can read for themselves; therefore much oral reading is unnecessary. (2) People have access to more reading material and use silent reading because it is faster. (3) Educational studies have proved the advantages of silent over oral reading.

Some skills required in oral and silent reading differ. Silent reading is usually thought of as involving the recognition of symbols and the interpretation of meanings. Oral reading involves not only the skills of silent reading but also those of speech. Ordinarily we read silently to get the thought only, and orally both to get the thought and to transmit it to others. Both forms should be taught from the time reading instruction begins. In recreational reading, we usually read silently for pleasure but opportunities often occur for sharing a good story, a poem, a joke, or a beautifully worded selection. Study reading is predominantly silent, although sometimes a sentence or paragraph is read to others to prove a point. The minutes of a meeting, announcements, and reports are read orally.

In order fully to understand the *present methods* of teaching read-

[1] Storm, G. E. and Smith, N. B. *Reading Activities in the Primary Grades,* pp. 26-31. Ginn. 1930.

ing, one must know something of former practices. The most important of these were the alphabetic method, the phonetic method, the word method, the phrase-and-sentence method. The *alphabetic method* was used as far back as the time of the Greeks and Romans. Children taught by this method learned the words by spelling them. It may have been an advantage to learn the spelling and pronunciation simultaneously, but needless to say, this was a laborious, meaningless, and uninteresting approach. The *phonetic method* was a step in advance, since there is a relation between the combined sounds of letters and the pronunciation of a word. This method consisted first of sounding out simple words and later using them in sentences. While it has the advantage of helping children to work out new words independently, it has the disadvantages of lack of interest in learning the sound of a symbol, the disregard of word meanings, and the non-phonetic character of many of the words in the English language. The *word method* is more rational. Children learn words as units, not as combinations of symbols. There are two outstanding advantages of this method. First, it is a natural step to learn the forms which stand for "mother," "car," "dog"—words already familiar as auditory impressions. Children have a large store of these when they start school. Second, meanings as well as pronunciations of words become an important part of initial reading instruction. In the *phrase-and-sentence method*, children learn phrases and sentences first. These larger units are later broken down into words. The best methods today are combinations of the last three mentioned.

Several *changes* have recently been made in the *teaching of reading*. (1) Initial reading is now postponed until children have greater maturity. (2) Since reading comprehension is dependent upon an accumulation of experiences, activity work is more common, especially in the primary grades. (3) More attention is now given from the start to teaching children "to read to learn" as well as "to learn to read." (4) Degree of ability rather than chronological age has received greater consideration in selection of books and in grade placement of pupils. (5) More emphasis is placed on teaching reading or on practicing skills wherever it is needed. Materials in the content subject fields are used as well as reading texts. (6) The type of material and the reading purpose affect the emphasis placed on the rate of reading.

(7) Better teaching techniques from the beginning are urged, thus lessening the amount of remedial instruction needed.

There are a number of *basic factors* underlying reading instruction in the elementary school. Six are discussed below in a general way: periods of growth, ability grouping, relation of reading to subject-matter courses, vocabulary development, eye movements, and remedial work.

The *periods of growth* in children's development require careful consideration. Studies in this field have led to the realization that the physical, mental, emotional, and social growth of children are of paramount importance in planning for reading instruction at each level. Materials and methods should be selected with this in mind. Success in reading at any period depends to a great extent upon children's readiness to accomplish the work presented to them. Consideration of this fact and selection of procedures adapted to each period are perhaps the best preparation for success.

The following *four broad periods* in reading instruction are given in the *Iowa Elementary Teachers Handbook on Reading.*[1]

1. *The period of reading readiness.* This involves the years before the child comes to school and a part or all of his first year in school, and with certain children even more than this.
2. *The period of beginning reading.* This involves the first experiences the child has with formal reading from a preprimer, experience charts, from primers, and sometimes first readers. Ideally the child will be six and one-half years old mentally before entering this period.
3. *The period of expanding power.* This takes the child through reading levels covering his earlier books, first and second readers, perhaps an easy third reader.
4. *The period of growth in the use of the reading tool.* This period begins in about the third or fourth grade, when children are reading second, third, and possibly fourth readers. It continues throughout the elementary years.

Since each child develops at his own rate, much attention should be given to *grouping* children as they pass through these periods in reading instruction. For example, observations of pupils' general reactions, interests in independent reading, intelligence tests, reading-achievement tests, and other checks may indicate to teachers the

---

[1] "Reading." *Iowa Elementary Teachers Handbook.* Volume II, p. 17. Department of Public Instruction, Des Moines, Iowa. 1943. Adapted.

pupils who would profit by reading easier material on one or more levels and those who would need the challenge of more extensive reading matter of about basic-reader level. This means dividing the class into two or more groups and planning suitable instruction for each. In a room of twenty or more pupils, it is usually advisable to arrange for two or three divisions. Most careful consideration should be given to planning for more than three groups because of the teaching load it involves.

Often in rural schools where there are several grades in a room, two or more of the middle and upper grades may be combined for reading instruction if the pupils show similar abilities. In other instances it may be advantageous to disregard grade lines and group according to ability.

Reading is vitally related to the teaching of all subjects. In any of the elementary grades, reading should be taught not only in the reading periods but also in all the periods where reading is required; when using history, geography, arithmetic, health, or other textbooks. In other words, all lessons that involve reading should have as their aims teaching the tool subject, reading, as well as the subject-matter material.

The possession of an extensive *reading vocabulary* is essential for effective reading. Often pupils read sentences orally in a fluent manner and yet do not comprehend what they read because of insufficient knowledge of word meanings. Successful reading instruction includes continual stress upon building rich, meaningful reading vocabularies. Furthermore, knowing one meaning is not enough. In our language many words have more than one meaning or shade of meaning. This fact causes an added burden. For example, a child knows the word "face" as a part of his body. Later it may mean the "face" of a cliff, or the "face" of a note. The various subject-matter fields have vocabularies with meanings peculiar to each field. These meanings should be made clear so that pupils will understand them in their new relationships—"coast" and "divide" in geography, and "note" in arithmetic.

Word meanings are based upon experiences, and no two people have identical experiences; consequently the concept of a word may differ with each individual. This implies that our understanding of any reading material is determined by our previous experiences; and, therefore, we can never translate the exact thoughts which the writer sought to express by the words he has used. The more extensive the pupils' experiences have been the broader and richer their vocabulary knowledge will be.

As pupils advance they should learn to recognize words by using different techniques. Some techniques used are: (1) obtain the word from the context or meaning of the sentence, also from illustrations of the story; (2) look for known parts in a word, such as "be" in "begin"; (3) remember a word as used in a previous setting; (4) sound the word; (5) use the dictionary; (6) ask someone who knows; (7) use more than one of these techniques. As soon as the child has a sufficient background, it is well to help him realize that such methods exist and to urge their use frequently. The child is fortunate who acquires a curiosity about words early in his reading experience, develops several methods of interpreting new words, and thus finds pleasure in mastering them independently.

Certain *movements of the eye* are involved in reading. The eyes move along a printed line in a series of sweeps and pauses. Seeing the words occurs during the pauses or *fixations*. The material interpreted during a fixation is called the *perceptual span*. The person who reads slowly will probably have a shorter average perception span and longer fixations than one who reads rapidly. It is estimated in normal, mature reading that the eye makes from 4 to 14 fixations per line. The eyes sometimes move backward along the line because the reader loses the place, meets an unfamiliar word, does not grasp the thought quickly, or misses the first word of the next line. These movements are called *regressions*. When the end of a line is reached, the eyes swing back to the beginning of the next line in a return sweep. When reading aloud, the eyes move ahead of the voice. This difference of distance is called the *eye-voice span*. Usually the faster the rate of oral reading the longer the eye-voice span is. Regularity and speed of eye movement differ with the material read and the pupils' powers of comprehension.

The fundamental habits of eye movement are established in the primary grades. Cole [1] says, "In the first half-year of school a pupil's

---

[1] Cole, Luella. *The Improvement of Reading,* p. 62. Farrer & Rinehart. 1938.

fixations are so numerous and the focusing of his eyes so inaccurate that his silent reading is no more rapid than his oral." "By the second grade, however, the eyes can move about twice as fast as the voice. If the children continue to receive intensive drill in oral reading they develop the eye-movements and the pronouncing habits necessary for reading aloud." Thus it is evident that silent reading should be taught from the start, so that the comparatively slow reading habits produced by pronouncing words will not be stressed unduly.

With increasing maturity and comprehension in reading, the fixations normally become fewer and of shorter duration, the span of perception increases, regressive movements decrease, the eye swings to the next line in a rhythmic motion, the eye-voice span increases, and the normal rate of silent reading far exceeds the oral.

Remedial teaching is the term used for techniques designed to help a child who is reading definitely below his capacity. This instruction is usually more difficult than the initial teaching of reading, because it requires a two-fold task: undesirable habits need to be broken up and new skills acquired. A good time to check a pupil's reading ability is when he begins a new stage of work. Such a check may indicate some of the following *deficiencies:* (1) lack of vocabulary; (2) weakness in the mechanics of reading, such as poor eye movements, pointing to words; (3) poor attitude; (4) insufficient skill in interpretation; or (5) lack of good work habits. It is desirable to learn not only how he reads, but to get all pertinent information available from parents, former teachers, the school records, and other sources. There should be a minimum need for such instruction if a well-organized developmental program (initial teaching) predominates in the classroom.

Some conditions, often uncontrollable, which may cause deficiencies are: physical handicaps, including those of sight, hearing, speech; non-readiness for beginning reading; unsuitable materials—too difficult, or not adapted to pupil capacities; or emotional disturbances, such as fear of punishment, failure, and a feeling of insecurity. Specific suggestions for remedial instruction on the primary levels are given on page 87, and for the higher grade levels on pages 130-131.

Teachers sometimes find it difficult to distinguish between the mentally *retarded* child and the one who is normal mentally but needs remedial reading instruction. Teachers who have not been specially trained in mental testing may find the following suggestions helpful.

Mental tests are the best scientific means available for determining the child's status. It is well to supplement such tests with data obtained by observation and other means. Among such data might be facts on the child's physical condition, muscular control, play habits, adjustment to social situations, and reactions to numerical problems requiring little or no reading.

Some techniques of teaching may be used in both remedial and retarded cases: progressing at a slower pace, using easier materials, expecting less in achievement, and giving sympathetic and careful guidance.

The retarded child, undoubtedly, needs more drill and should have it perhaps in more varied forms than one who learns faster. Assignments should be such that successes, even though small, are possible. The feeling of achievement is a vital incentive for continued effort. The slow learner needs more individual attention. Sometimes subjects may be profitably combined, as reading, writing, and spelling. Reading may be made more meaningful by connecting words with pictures and activities. Of course, retarded children cannot reach as high levels of attainment as the normal child and should not be expected to do more than is possible for them to do.

READING IN THE PRIMARY GRADES

THE PERIOD OF READING READINESS

Since the *reading readiness* period is the first of the three periods in the primary grades, it should be discussed in detail. Teachers who have attempted to instruct children in formal reading at the beginning of the first grade, irrespective of individual abilities, welcome the emphasis that is being placed upon reading readiness.

Each normal child has his own pattern of growth. At certain periods he should begin to walk, to talk, or to show his readiness for different activities. If a child is forced to engage in these activities before reaching a proper level of development, failure and its accompanying emotional disturbances may occur. If we affirm that each child has a right to a successful start in school life and at the same time fail about 25 per cent of first-grade children each year mainly because of reading, something should be done to make our performance more nearly fit our objectives. One of the chief contributing factors to this paradoxical situation is lack of readiness to read.

Children must make many social adjustments before starting to read. Coming to school is a decided break in their lives. They sud-

play corner

denly find themselves part of a large group; they are cut away from the protection and care of the home; they are in a strange environment; they are expected to play with others; they need to develop more self-reliance; they must get acquainted with the teacher; and they need to make many other adjustments. Time should be allowed for these adjustments before the teacher begins the regular reading instruction.

Reading readiness depends mainly upon background and maturation. For example, a certain eye maturity is necessary for close reading. Teachers often ask what to do with the children during the early part of the first school year if they postpone the teaching of reading. The following *suggestions* answer this question and at the same time indicate ways and means to prepare for reading.

Varied and rich experiences help develop concepts which aid children in interpreting what they read later. (1) Units of work, such as studying pets, planning and giving a party, and making a play corner, not only give information and understanding, but furnish opportunities for acquiring new words and developing a better use of English. (2) Excursions may be arranged to give first-hand contacts. The trips may be made in the immediate vicinity—about the school building—or there may be trips to the store, court house, depot, library, or airport. Children should be guided in observing and exploring, for this will stimulate them into thinking for themselves. (3) Nature materials offer excellent possibilities. A goldfish, bird, rabbit, or other pet may be brought to class for a day, or longer, to study their care and habits. Plant forms may easily be observed, responsibility for their care assumed, and their beauty enjoyed.

Constructive activities, such as building a hutch for the rabbit, furnish many occasions for planning, executing, and for judging results. These stimulate real thinking.

Varied use of oral language tends to increase vocabularies and to improve the ability to use English effectively. Much of the work presented in the section on language may be carried on in the reading-readiness period. Carrying messages is a good method of developing memory and holding a series of ideas in mind.

A *library corner* is a means of acquainting children with books and developing in them a desire to read. As they sit around the table they learn how to turn pages and to handle books. They tell stories from the pictures and so learn to follow a sequence of thought. As the teacher reads to them, she may direct them in several ways: (1) by showing how she follows the line from left to right, then swings down to the next line, (2) by stopping and letting the children supply the next word, (3) by giving the first sound of a word in a sentence and letting them guess the word from this sound and from the context, and (4) by talking about the fun the children will have when they themselves can read.

Labels, signs, and charts help children realize that symbols stand for spoken words. Children are not expected to read labels but to know that they have a purpose; for example, color names on crayon boxes, names of objects contained in boxes, and children's names to designate their lockers and belongings. They may be told the meanings of different signs, such as "Wash hands before looking at books," on the library table; "Do you want to draw a picture?" on the easel; and "John will feed the goldfish today," on the bulletin board. Charts which record the events of an excursion, show the list of committee members, or tell of the events of a holiday may be read to children, much to their satisfaction, after they have helped in dictating the sentences.

Auditory and visual discrimination exercises help children develop ability to hear and see likenesses and differences in objects, symbols, and sounds. Counting taps, repeating nursery rhymes individually or as a group, giving words that begin with the same sound as the one given by the teacher, and repeating a short sentence are illustrations of exercises to develop auditory discrimination. These exercises may help in developing visual discrimination: matching like words, letters, objects, colors, numbers, etc.; drawing a simple picture or pattern after a short exposure to view; giving the number and description of a group of objects after a short exposure to view; recognizing their own names.

Exercises that train the eye to move from *left to right* across the line and then *swing back* to the beginning of the next line are given in published workbooks prepared for the reading readiness period. In addition to these exercises and the devices which help children follow a line from left to right when the teacher is reading to them, the teacher may do the following: (1) say as she writes on the blackboard, "I always begin at this side and write across, then come back and begin again"; (2) swing the pointer without stopping from left to right, carefully avoiding pointing to individual words as she reads experience charts to the children; (3) instruct the children when looking at a series of pictures on a page, to begin at the left side of the page and explain that people do this when they read.

Cooperation of the home can be especially helpful in making a reading readiness program successful. It is traditional that children learn to read when they come to school, and parents take this for granted. Usually, if parents are helped to realize the value of a delayed program, they will cooperate wholeheartedly. There is the possibility, however, of delaying reading too long. Some children may acquire other interests or be satisfied to have stories read to them. To determine when pupils should begin reading, teachers need to refer to all available information, study the children, and use their best judgment. Reading readiness activities should be continued for those not ready to start reading.

Certain *tests* may be used to determine children's readiness to read.[1]

Certain evidences of reading readiness have been determined by reading authorities. A *composite list* is given in the chart below. Teachers often use this type of chart to check children's attainments at the close of the reading-readiness period. Charts of a similar nature may be made to check children's reading abilities at the close of each successive period or stage.

	Children's Names						
Directions: Check the items which each child has attained to a reasonable degree. Use the following symbols, +(yes), −(no).							
A. Mental and physical development 1. Has he a mental age of six to six and a half?							
2. Does he have reasonably sound physical development?							
3. Does he have sufficient eye maturity?							
.....acuity of hearing?							
..........good speech?							
B. Abilities 4. Does he use a broad speaking vocabulary?							
5. Does he have a reasonable facility in using English effectively in expressing ideas?							

[1] The following intelligence tests are recommended: Probably none is better than the Stanford Revision of the Binet-Simon Scale, published by Houghton Mifflin Co. This is an individual test and requires practice in order to administer it satisfactorily. Teachers can give one of the group tests more easily, such as: Detroit First Grade Intelligence Test, published by World Book Co.; Pintner-Cunningham Intelligence Test, published by World Book Co.; Pressey Primary Classification Test, published by Public School Publishing Co. The following reading-readiness tests are available: The Betts Ready to Read Tests (individual), published by Keystone View Co.; Gates Reading Readiness Test (Group) published by Bureau of Publications, Teachers College, Columbia University; Lee-Clark Reading Readiness Tests (group), published by Southern California Book Depository; Metropolitan Readiness Tests (group), by Hildreth and Griffith, published by World Book Co.; Monroe Reading Aptitude Tests (group and individual) published by Houghton Mifflin Co.; New York Reading Readiness Inventory, Forms A and B (group), published by Bureau of Reference, Research and Statistics, Board of Education, City of New York; and Reading Readiness Test by Van Wagenen (individual) published by Educational Test Bureau. Publishers of sets of reading texts have charts and tests accompanying their books.

	Children's Names							

Directions: Check the items which each child has attained to a reasonable degree. Use the following symbols, +(yes), −(no).

6. Does he have some ability in using sentences?

7. Does he show average ability in anticipating words in common phrases?

8. Can he detect likenesses and differences in the sounds and appearances of words?

9. Does he show medium ability in using ideas in meeting problem situations?

10. Does he have normal ability to think abstractly?

11. Can he remember directions?

12. Can he quickly find likenesses and differences in pictures, geometric forms, colors, words?

13. Can he match correctly in seatwork exercises?

14. Can he copy from a sheet triangles, rectangles, squares, 4, 3, etc., without making reversals?

C. Habits
15. Has he good work habits, such as giving attention to one task for a period of time and usually finishing a task begun?

16. Can he follow a left-to-right sequence fairly well in telling about a row of pictures or making a series of drawings?

D. Social adjustments
17. Is he well adjusted to the teacher and children in school?

18. Has he fairly good social habits, such as ....sharing?

..........waiting turn?

........giving attention?

...........self control?

E. Attitude
19. Does he want to read?

THE PERIOD OF BEGINNING READING

PREPRIMER PHASE

The *period of beginning reading* may be divided into two phases. The first includes the introductory work of preparing for primer reading. The second consists of reading from the primers, and in some cases from first readers. The first phase is sometimes called the pre-book, or *preprimer phase*. The latter term will be used although materials in addition to those of the preprimers are advocated. The normal child, who often has had some reading-readiness experiences at home, in the kindergarten, or during the first few weeks of his first year, comes to this period with many concepts, understandings, and a desire to read for himself. In a class of normal size there will probably be wide variation, necessitating adjustment of procedure to meet individual requirements. The main task is to help each pupil make the transition from the spoken words, to which he is accustomed, to the written or printed symbols. The following are some ways of helping children make this transition: (1) using materials from the blackboard, charts, and incidental reading material; (2) using definitely organized material, such as the introductory material of a basic series of readers—charts introducing preprimers and other supplementary material; or (3) using both (1) and (2). The materials of a basic reading series have the advantage of systematic preparation with careful selection and gradation of vocabulary and subject matter of interest to children in general. On the other hand, materials based upon children's own immediate experiences have a decided interest value. For these reasons it may be advantageous to use both. Groups may profit by using school-made materials containing the first part of the vocabulary to be met soon in the basic preprimer. After beginning the basic preprimer, both types of materials may be used.

Since manuals accompany basic texts and give directions for the effective use of the preprimer, nothing more concerning their use will be said. The materials that may be worked out by the teacher and children, as well as certain procedures, are briefly explained under the four headings below: (1) silent reading exercises, (2) incidental reading, (3) experience reading charts, and (4) handling books.

Silent reading exercises should be a part of the first reading material used. Children are always interested in their own names. Therefore, the possession of an individual name card helps each child to learn to recognize his name. When the teacher writes "John" on the board, saying "Will —— bring the books?" he matches his card with the name on the blackboard and decides whether it is his name or not. Combining names with action words, such as "John run," "Walk Mary," "Helen skip," furnishes directions for children to read silently from the blackboard or cards, and to carry out these directions with no oral reading involved. An action word is best presented following the activity—teacher asks the children to run, then the word "run" is written on the board to name the act. This activity helps children to understand from the beginning that reading involves meaning. It is more than simply oral repetition of words.

Incidental reading includes labels, captions on pictures, signs, and bulletin board notices to which the children were exposed in the reading-readiness period and are used, at least in part now, for reading purposes. (1) Labels should be used where found useful, as to name articles in a museum or to designate contents of boxes. (2) Children may dictate titles to be attached to mounted pictures taken from magazines or to their own drawings. Also the teacher may place below an especially good picture the following:

"This is Henry's picture.
It is the picture of an airplane."

(3) The sign "Quiet please," will help those at the library to remember. (4) Notices on the bulletin board or blackboard, if vital to the day's procedure, stimulate interest and effort in reading, and often aid in learning words, especially if those words met in books are repeated in the notice. (See bulletin board suggestions, pp. 91-94.)

Experience reading charts are used very commonly. These are often accounts of school experiences made co-operatively by teacher and children. The making of the charts should be carefully planned. The topic should be of real interest. The following are suggested: (1) school activities—what children like to do at school, what was seen on an excursion, or what was done in a unit of work; (2) holiday events—what happened at the Hallowe'en party; and (3) home experiences—caring for pets, going on a trip, or playing with friends. By asking "leading questions," the teacher paves the way for the most satisfactory responses. For example: the question "Who lost his pet yesterday?" will more surely bring the response, "Ted lost his pet yesterday," than would the question, "What happened yesterday?" Some editing may be necessary if incorrect forms or poor constructions are given, but it is better to use the children's own expressions as much as possible. If the experience stories are to be retained after they are read from the board, they should be copied on large sheets of paper with crayon, broad-pointed pen, or stamping outfit (observing such items as three-inch margins, uniform spacing between words and lines, and good lettering). Pictures, either magazine or children's drawings, often add to the interest. These may be mounted below or above the story if the sheet is posted as a chart, or the opposite page, if in booklet form. The teacher may duplicate smaller copies for the children to mount in booklet form (9 inches by 12 inches or larger), illustrate, and take home to "read."

Some *disadvantages* in the use of experience reading charts are: (1) It is hardly possible to have much repetition of vocabulary if the topics are of immediate interest and the sentences are dictated by the children. (2) Unless teachers know how to direct the work of the children, the sentences may be too long and the sequence faulty. (3)

Teaching reading by the use of such charts may cause children to become weary of them and uninterested in all reading.

Some *advantages* of their use are: (1) They interest pupils in reading because the children help make them. Thus such material helps create a good pupil attitude toward reading from the outset. (2) They can be made about current happenings in school, thus connecting reading with children's activities. (3) They furnish opportunities for line reading, thus aiding in developing good eye movements. (4) They give opportunities for identifying sentences. (5) They provide a chance to learn words which will be met later in preprimers. (6) They show how a story progresses line by line. Generally speaking, it would seem that experience charts have an important place, not only in the preprimer period, but throughout the primary grades. Using them for occasional or reference reading, however, appears preferable to using them for regular reading purposes.

In addition to experience charts, *other types of charts* are of value at this stage: (1) The color chart displays on movable strips the colors and the accompanying descriptive sentences, such as "This is red," "This is orange," etc. (2) The number chart illustrated in the chapter on arithmetic may be used when children are able to count. (3) Charts can show plans for the day's procedure:

Things to Do (For individuals)	Plans for Wednesday (For the class)
John will paint.	Work in the garden.
Mary wants to dress the doll.	Make shelf in the store.
Tom will mend the table.	Look at books.
	Learn a new song.
	Bring things for the store.

(4) Record charts help children realize their own accomplishments. They may have headings, such as "Poems We Know," or "Songs We Sing," or "Stories We Like." (5) A chart for room care is one means of helping children feel their part in sharing the responsibility for the appearance and routine of the room. Different name cards may be inserted to complete sentences, such as "——— will feed the fish. ——— will take care of the books. ——— will place the chairs." (6) Vocabulary charts help in acquiring words, stimulating interests in word meanings, and suggesting classification, for example:

Mothers	Babies	Vegetables We Like	
cow	calf	potatoes	peas
cat	kitten	tomatoes	beans
dog	puppy	carrots	

The more reading opportunities of this nature children have, the greater their interest will be and the broader their concept of reading. (7) Commercial charts introduce different systems of reading and are to be used before and in conjunction with the preprimers.

It is probably safe to assume that some familiarity with the *handling of books* will have been acquired before the preprimer phase. Before reading from books, however, it is important that some of the following mechanics become habitual. (1) Turning the pages by using the right hand on the upper corners needs to be taught. This can be done informally as pupils are looking at and discussing the pictures, while they leaf through new books at the reading table. (2) Holding the book at the proper distance from the eyes (between fifteen to eighteen inches) is important. Placing the book at an angle gives a better focus for the eyes than is possible when it lies flat. (3) Following the line and keeping one's place should be attempted before reading from books. Often children place a small cardboard ($1'' \times 5''$) below the line as a teacher reads to them, follow across, and move the marker down to the next line. This habit is at least partially formed before the pupils themselves attempt to interpret what the lines tell.

When these four types of activities are employed, namely, silent reading exercises, incidental reading, reading charts, and use of books, interspersed with preprimer reading, children have occasion to see the same words in different reading situations; they experience variety in their reading, and they are given a good foundation for reading from primers. The length of time necessary to reach the standards set for the preprimer phase varies with the ability of each child, his home training, and the school conditions. The *36th Yearbook* [1] gives from three to eight weeks, but if children enter before six it may take longer to prepare for primer reading.

[1] *36th Yearbook of the National Society for the Study of Education.* Part I, p. 93. Public School Publishing Co. 1937.

PRIMER AND FIRST READER PHASE

The amount of preprimer reading done before beginning the *primer phase* depends upon the plan followed. One plan is to read several preprimers before a primer is started. The reasons for this are: (1) the material is on approximately the same level of difficulty, and (2) most preprimers have many words in common. The other plan introduces the basic primer as soon as the basic preprimer is completed. The reason for using this second plan is vocabulary arrangement. The first part of the primer of the same series often is easier than a preprimer of another. If the latter procedure is followed, it is well to use, as supplementary to the first primer, several other preprimers. Reading from sources other than books should be continued.

The main emphasis in the primer phase should be upon helping children (1) to acquire a reading vocabulary, (2) to get the thought from what they read, (3) to enjoy reading. Variety in conducting the work is desirable for keeping the children's interest. The *steps* of *effective procedure* in presenting a selection from a book are these: (1) Arouse interest and desire to read by discussing the picture or experiences which the children have had and which are similar to those in the story. (2) Present new words by placing them on the board as you talk about the story, or by including them in blackboard sentences containing other familiar words. Then ask the children to find the new words in their books. (3) Ask the children to read a line or more silently, in order to find answers to questions; discuss what they have read, and continue in this way through a brief selection. If it is too long for one reading, it will be better to use different sections on different days. (4) Have them re-read orally the consecutive thought units with discussion and evaluation. (5) Ask for re-reading, later, of certain designated parts; for example: "Read the part that tells where they found the dog." (This may be the next day.) (6) Carry on supplementary activities which give an opportunity to re-read the same words in other settings. These activities may include (a) using seatwork pads, (b) reading different sentences on the blackboard, or (c) using supplementary booklets. Re-reading words in this way furnishes excellent vocabulary practice.

Some children may be ready for *first readers* during the first year in school, others will profit by delay until the second year. If the latter plan is followed children should read preprimers and primers at the beginning of the second year in order to review their reading vocabularies and re-establish good reading habits. The *procedures* used with the primer are usually effective with the first reader. Naturally pupils should be able to read silently longer units necessary for finding answers to questions. Repetition of vocabulary used in content should continually be emphasized and periodic checks made to determine pupil achievement. Incidental reading as suggested in the preprimer phase should continue, and new types of material should be introduced both for pleasure and for informational purposes. Children should read books on one level adapted to their reading abilities before attempting more difficult materials. Usually the rate of silent reading in the first reader period does not surpass that of oral reading. Therefore, a reasonable amount of oral reading, in all probability, would not retard proper skill development in silent reading.

THE PERIOD OF EXPANDING POWER

The period of expanding power follows that of beginning reading. The importance of work during this period is hard to overestimate. Unless pupils have the necessary foundation in skills, habits, and attitudes when they undertake the reading and study needed in the following periods, they will be handicapped. Usually at the opening of a school year, some time should be spent on reading materials of an easier level of difficulty than those read at the close of the preceding year. The connotation of the word "readiness" is thus broadened to apply to all periods. "By the end of the third period of development pupils should be able to read independently and intelligently, both silently and orally, the various types of reading materials used widely at the beginning of the fourth grade." [1]

Children's *interests* at this period extend beyond their immediate environment, and reading is a vehicle for further developing such interests. Pupils are able to read materials other than those in the reading texts and to do more independent reading. Therefore, the reading equipment may include children's newspapers; magazines;

[1] *Ibid.*, p. 99. Adapted.

arouse interest and desire to read
by discussion, pictures, etc.

presenting new words

read silently

reread orally

pamphlets on topics studied; simple books on science, health, and community life; as well as good stories. This should help guide them in personal development and in social, scientific, and civic understandings.

Oral and silent reading each has its place, but "The speed of silent reading gradually surpasses that of oral reading, and the habits involved in rapid silent reading and fluent oral reading become clearly differentiated in general pattern." [1] Occasions should be arranged for audience reading. This gives pupils a chance to read to others the selections which they have prepared and to realize both pleasure and profit in so doing; pleasure from the satisfaction of reading, and profit from the suggestions for improvement made by the audience. Much of the independent silent reading may be related to current units of work.

Some *purposes* which pupils may have for reading follow.

Silent reading
1. to enjoy a story
2. to get information on a topic
3. to find answers to questions stated by the teacher, or by the pupils and teacher
4. to learn how to make something
5. to decide if a story is true
6. to find out if a story in one reader is like that read in another
7. to make questions to ask others
8. to find out what is happening in a picture
9. to determine if a selection is suitable for dramatization, using these standards:

Re-reading silently
1. to prepare for dramatization: finding characters, places, things needed
2. to prepare for audience reading
3. to divide into parts
4. to select beautifully worded parts
5. to remember
6. to judge suitability of a title
7. to select paragraph headings

a. Are there several characters?
b. Are the characters doing things?

Oral reading
1. to give pleasure to others
2. to test one's ability
3. to prove a point
4. to practice for dramatization
5. to read the most humorous part
6. to answer questions
7. to prove ability to find part designated
8. to read a beautifully worded section
9. to enjoy a poem

c. Can we do, or play we are doing, what they are?
d. Is there talking?

[1] *38th Yearbook of the National Society for the Study of Education.* Part I, p. 200. Public School Publishing Co. 1939.

There are some *important general factors* that underlie reading instruction in all the primary periods. These are pupil grouping by levels of accomplishment, small group instruction, correlation of reading with units, use of books, remedial instruction, and development of vocabulary. These will be discussed in turn.

Any group contains pupils of varying abilities. Some teachers maintain that *grouping according to ability* is discouraging to the slow child, that he profits by his contacts with the brighter children. The answers to this are that the faster children are restrained from working up to their capacity, that the slower children become discouraged because they are surpassed by the others, and that it is difficult to provide suitable material for the wide variation of abilities in one class. As soon as variations in ability among individual pupils are apparent, the teacher may find it advantageous to group her pupils according to levels of ability. The classification should be flexible enough to allow shifting if relative abilities change. The children should not be embarrassed because of grouping.

Another problem is how to find time for this *smaller group instruction*. More can be accomplished in less time with greater uniformity of ability in the class. The teacher who plans carefully can arrange more independent silent reading with suitable checks for the faster group, and personally supervise more closely the slower groups, giving them their proportionate amount of time. If a class is large it may be divided into small ability groups with a few leaders. Exercises can be arranged for the specific needs of each group: (1) sheets containing stories, with questions to check comprehension on the back of these sheets, (2) oral reading of a story previously read silently, (3) vocabulary games, (4) matching exercises consisting of questions and answers and, (5) pupil discussion and further investigation (by brighter groups) stimulated by and growing out of class work. In conducting these groups, the teacher may spend her time chiefly with one group or may move among them all, giving her attention where most needed. This should not be taken to mean that the slower groups are to have the majority of the teacher's time at the expense of the faster moving pupils.

Correlation of reading with units stresses reading for definite purposes. Since primary readers contain materials on science, family life, pets, play, Indian life, community activities, and other fields of interest, it is possible for pupils to acquire information independently, which they can use in discussions or in other class activities. By reading a wide variety of materials, children acquire new words and new meanings, which they will need later in studying content subjects. In addition to reading from books, reading from experience charts may be utilized. These may show the pupils' plans, lists of materials needed, directions for work, as well as records of what they have learned or accomplished. For example:

The Airplane	*What We Know About Bananas*
We saw an airplane.	We buy them at the grocery store.
It carried people.	Bananas grow in other countries.
It flew from city to city.	They come to us in big boats.
This airplane traveled high in air.	They grow in bunches.
It looked like a bird.	We eat them when they are yellow.

Charts of questions which pupils dictate about a unit and the answers when they have found them, may also be read. For example:

What We Want to Know	*What We Learned*
Why are there stamps on letters?	Stamps help pay for carrying letters.
How much do stamps cost?	Some stamps cost one, two, and three cents.
Where are stamps made?	Stamps are made in Washington, D. C.
Why are there marks on stamps?	Cancelled stamps cannot be used again.

It is important that children learn *how to use books properly*. It is a pleasure to present a new book to children. When doing so, discuss the general format by calling attention to the title on the cover and title page, the author, the table of contents, and the titles of the stories. Pupils in their early reading, if so directed, soon learn that the title tells what the story is about. Later, they learn that headings for parts of chapters serve the same purpose. Children easily form the habit of using pictures to enhance the meaning of what they read. (See section Study Guides and Helps for additional suggestions, pp. 46 ff.)

The teacher's *evaluation* of basic reading achievements at the end of this period may be made by the use of an adaptation of the chart on pages 74-75, or by the use of appropriate standard reading tests.

Remedial instruction should be carefully planned if it is to be administered at all. Some general suggestions for remedial work are: (1) Find materials the pupil can read easily. Increase the difficulty of the material gradually as he shows improvement. It is very difficult to do corrective work when using reading material beyond the child's ability. (2) Increase the pupil's knowledge of words. One of the best ways of doing this is to furnish many opportunities for the re-reading of the same words in different contexts. This implies the use of several books on one level of reading difficulty. (3) Test the pupils for physical handicaps. Parents and teachers are often unaware of the most severe disabilities.

Perhaps *hearing* and *seeing* are the two senses most closely related to reading. If a child is inattentive or does not carry out directions it may be that he does not hear. Testing with a watch to determine at what distance it can be heard readily may indicate whether or not a more extensive examination is needed. Reading involves eye-strain. Children's eyes must become accustomed to seeing small words accurately. Cole [1] concludes as a result of observations and studies that between a third and a half of the children who enter the first grade are unready to read on account of defective or immature eyesight. Children are often unaware that their vision is different from others, since their own eyes are the only ones they know about. One very near-sighted eight-year-old was unconscious of his disability until one day his mother made a remark about the lines between the bricks in a building across the street. He was unable to distinguish the mortar and did not know that others could. Children seldom complain even when aware of faulty vision; but struggle along, failing in achievement, and building up defense mechanisms of various kinds. Teachers should be on the alert for symptoms of visual deficiencies. These may be noted by the appearance of the eyes, the manner of holding the head, squinting, shading the eyes, distance between book and eyes, carelessness in reading, nervousness, becoming fatigued easily, headaches, and dizziness. Room conditions favorable for good vision should be arranged: (1) by providing sufficient light; (2) by avoiding glare in

[1] *Op. cit.*, p. 34.

children's eyes, such as often occurs when facing windows, and from reflections from desk; (3) by preventing shadows on books or work; and (4) by writing on the blackboard so that the material is easily read.

Faulty *eye movements* are indicative of poor reading habits. Improvement in vocabulary knowledge, extension of comprehension, and the use of easy material often improve eye movements. Specific remedial exercises may be desirable in certain cases. Eye movements may be roughly checked by observing the pauses, regressions, and return sweeps in a small mirror placed on the page opposite to the one being read. Use large print at first.

The following are some of the more *specific reading defects* with suggestions as to how they may be avoided or remedied: (1) Reversals sometimes occur. Do not leave to chance the acquisition of the left-to-right movement across the line or word. From the beginning, use devices which will cause children's eyes to move from left to right, such as (a) moving a pointer without pause or stop on the lines of a chart or blackboard story, (b) putting phrases or word cards in a wall pocket in that order, (c) showing pupils how to look at a word from left to right or, if restudying it, to go back to the beginning of it each time, (d) using manuscript writing. For remedial exercises Gates [1] gives this suggestion: Have the children name the letters in the order they appear in the words, or sound the letters if the word is phonetic, or use a rubber stamping outfit. (2) Jerky, halting word reading is usually avoided by (a) readiness before beginning to read, (b) materials suited to the ability of the readers at each period, (c) non-stop movement of the pointer or hand along the line on charts or the blackboard. If remedial work is necessary, discontinue oral reading by the pupils for a time. Arrange to have the children hear good oral reading and to learn to differentiate between smooth and halting performance. Later, come back to oral reading. Have the children read the selection silently, check on their comprehension of the material, and then read it aloud. (3) If help is needed in keeping the place in initial book reading, give children markers as described in the preprimer phase or suggest using their thumbs as marginal guides. In remedial instruction, use the

[1] Gates, A. I. and Bennett, C. C. *Reversal Tendencies in Reading*, p. 31. Bureau of Publications, Teachers College, Columbia University.

markers when needed. (4) Vocalization with lip movements should be discouraged from the beginning. Early silent reading of short sentences, such as directions with emphasis on "lips closed," inhibits this tendency in children. If it persists, use a blackboard chart headed, "I Can Read With My Lips Closed." Ask children to read a page or to read for a minute, and list on the chart the names of those who succeed in keeping their lips closed. Compel them to read so fast that they cannot use lips. Use flash exercises, gradually increasing the number of words exposed. (5) Difficulties in comprehension should receive specific attention. Finding the answers to questions develops the habit of reading for thought. This should begin in the preprimer phase. A good sequence to follow in reading a sentence in the preprimer phase is: Question—Silent Reading—Answer—Oral Reading. For remedial work in comprehension, use easy materials and simple questions. All exercises, such as matching, true and false, and multiple response, although used as checks, may also serve as incentives for giving more attention to thought. (6) Lack of interest is unnatural. This is not common with children who have good beginning reading instruction. It may be the result of (a) failures in reading, (b) excessive phonic teaching done too early and with too much stress on word recognition at the expense of thought getting, or (c) some procedure connected with reading which gave the children an aversion to it. In remedial work, first discover the cause of the lack of interest. Easy materials are the key to success in many cases. Once a child masters easy material he will be interested in trying the more difficult. In short, interest may be developed by using easy reading materials on subjects of special interest to the children and from that leading out to other fields of less initial interest.

Through a variety of experiences, a child early acquires a speaking vocabulary which is the basis for the *development* of his *reading vocabulary*. In this stage of the reading program the teacher has three requirements to meet: (1) providing many opportunities for children to build concepts; (2) developing a speaking vocabulary related to the expression of these concepts; (3) developing skill to recognize the printed words as the symbols of the words in the speaking vocabulary. The first five suggestions given for developing reading readiness (pages 71-73) are also desirable for developing meaningful speaking vocabularies. In addition to these, children acquire words by discussing pictures, by labeling museum items, and by acquiring an interest in words as words.

A word may appear as a very complicated hieroglyphic to a young child who is just beginning to read. He may not even realize that it consists of separate letters, or that it should be scanned from left to right. The wise teacher advances slowly at first, and bases her procedure and rate of progress on the age, mental ability, and former experiences of her group, keeping in mind the three requirements listed above. Words at the start are usually presented in sentences and children learn them as *sight words*. After children have a sight vocabulary of 100 to 200 words, *phonics* may be especially helpful to independent word recognition in silent reading. "Teachers must understand that 'getting' a word involves recognizing it by sight, acquiring the ability to pronounce it, and understanding its meaning. Phonetic ability can do only one thing directly,—give assistance in pronouncing words." [1]

Before teaching children the sound elements of words, they should have experiences with *ear-training exercises*, hearing words with like initial and final sounds; thus they will realize that words can be divided into component parts. Later they may be taught to see the different parts, note similarities, and recombine these into new words, such as (1) using "pen," "hen," "ten," to call attention to "en"; (2) then meeting "en" in new words, as "men" and "den"; and (3) recombining and pronouncing these words. This diagram illustrates the cycle idea in presenting phonics.

(Begin here)

Read in stories new words containing the element ← 5 . 1 → Read stories

Recognize and use the element to interpret new words, as men, den 4 — 2 Select familiar words with like elements, as pen, ten

3 Note the sound of this element *en*

Since the fifth step is the real purpose of phonics, the teacher should be careful to see that children understand the relation between phonics and reading. Other suggestions to keep in mind in helping children

[1] Hahn, J. L. *Child Development Readers,* First Grade Manual, p. XXVIII. Houghton, Mifflin Co. 1935.

acquire and use phonetic skill are: (1) Teach children to apply phonics when doing silent reading. (2) Instruct children to scan the words from left to right. (3) Help children to look at words carefully and to notice likenesses and differences. (4) Help children to look at the parts of one word, think their sounds, and then the word as a whole. (5) Teach children to combine the use of phonics and of context in attacking new words. This will help them to make an intelligent guess, as "It is a c—— winter morning." Naturally the word is "cold." (6) Postpone the use of diacritical marks until children need them in glossary or dictionary work. (7) Stress the adding of elements—of "s" to make plurals, and of prefixes and suffixes—in making new words. (8) Guide the children in using syllabication to attack unknown words as soon as they can. (9) Refer to letters by names occasionally when they are used in words. (10) When pupils are ready, give graded exercises to teach the use of dictionaries. Follow the procedure for presenting phonics given in your manual, if you are using a modern textbook, whether or not it agrees with the above suggestions, and remember that the non-phonetic words must be presented as sight words. Guard against making children excessively word-conscious by too much intensive and formal practice.

The *bulletin board* affords opportunities for reading in addition to those derived from books. Two children came into a first grade room one morning and, after greeting the teacher, went immediately to a bulletin board (made in the form of an easel) which stood in a conspicuous place. There they became engrossed in the material posted. One child sought help with an unfamiliar word from another child. Finally, with an expression of satisfaction, they left and went to a bulletin board on the wall where they inspected the children's drawings which the previous day had been selected by the class and teacher as worthy of being displayed. This incident illustrates two purposes of bulletin boards: one, to furnish information, some in the form of notices, directions, and descriptions; the other, to exhibit good work done by the children. Another purpose is to clarify topics discussed. To do this, materials, such as pictures and objects, may be shown on bulletin boards in order to arouse interest in and enrich the topics studied.

Bulletin boards may be *constructed* satisfactorily from several kinds of materials—wood, cork, beaverboard, and composition board fibers, such as celotex. Inexpensive, yet satisfactory ones, are made by covering heavy cardboard with manila wrapping paper. Bulletin boards should be placed where children can see them easily, as near an entrance where they often pass. Those placed above the blackboard are usually too high for reading material. They may be used, however, for display purposes. Hinged commercial frames make it possible to have enough surface for mounting in a condensed space. Teachers will find many uses for movable boards that can be placed on a ledge or on an easel. The height from the floor of bulletin boards containing reading materials varies with the ages of the children who use them. The following distances are recommended: for lower primary rooms, 18 inches; for third and fourth grades, 30 inches; and for grades above, 36 inches.

Some factors of *arrangement* which pertain to mounting materials on bulletin boards are: (1) balance the arrangement, (2) make the general effect attractive, and (3) avoid a cluttered appearance. A cluttered effect is often the result of having too much on the board without systematic arrangement. If there is only one unit, the objects in it should balance. If there are sub-units, they should balance each other. There should be margins. The bottom margin should be the widest, the side margins equal, and the top may be the same as those of the sides. There should be spaces between parts and these should be less than the margins.

Careful *preparation* must be expended on the materials to be posted. Pictures are much more attractive if mounted on some color that blends with the picture, not lighter or darker than the hues in it. Children's work that goes on display should have real merit. Sometimes less rigid standards are used for the sake of encouragement, if the work is the best a child can do. Children as well as the teacher may be responsible for the material to be displayed. Children should be encouraged to bring information and objects and post them. The material should be changed often.

The two children described above had the *habit* of *reading* and *observing* the materials posted on their bulletin board each morning. This is very desirable if bulletin boards are to have real reading value.

In order to check this type of reading, it is well to have the bulletin boards read at some time during the day, especially after the posting of new materials, or to ask questions about the materials to find whether they have been read or not.

The list on page 94 is suggestive of some of the *types of material* that may be posted on bulletin boards.

The *library* is an essential part of a complete reading program. (1) It gives children in the reading-readiness period a chance to handle and to enjoy looking at picture books. (2) It gives older ones opportunities to select their own reading materials. (3) It is a means of enriching the regular school program. (4) It gives the teacher a chance to check and direct the children's reading tastes. (5) It is a means of developing good library habits. (6) It offers opportunities to develop consideration for others. (7) It may add to the attractiveness of the room.

There are various ways of *equipping* and *arranging* the library. The tables and chairs should be of the proper height for the children. Make the library furniture refreshingly different from the rest of the room's equipment. Sometimes a small rocking chair and rug give a home-like touch. If the table is in front of a window, see that the children do not face the light. Open bookcases or shelves encourage the use of books. Labels may indicate where the different kinds of books are shelved, such as Story Books, Picture Books, Funny Stories, Animal Books, Stories of Pets. A magazine rack may hold the newspapers, magazines, and large school-made booklets. Book ends, a runner for the table, and other accessories create a pleasant library atmosphere. Reading-table books should be changed from time to time. Lack of school funds need not prevent having a library. Resourceful teachers have found many ways of providing the equipment. At the close of this section are suggestions for such furniture as children can make.

It is desirable to provide a *variety of reading material*, such as picture books, single copies of readers, short story books, and sets of pictures. There should be some material to be read for information and some for fun. The varied abilities of a group must be considered when selecting material. Most of it should be easier than the textbook

1. *Greetings*
"Good morning, girls!"
"Good morning, boys!"
"Good morning, children!"

2. *Days of the week*
"This is Tuesday."

3. *Order of the days*
"This is the first day of the week."

4. *Months*
"The new month is December. Christmas comes this month."

5. *Weather conditions*
"This is a rainy morning. Some children wore raincoats."

6. *Children's experiences*
"Tom went to town Saturday. He went to the court house."

7. *Seasons*
"Spring is here. Find signs of spring."

8. *School activities*
"Yesterday we took a trip. We found many seeds."

9. *Items about our school*
Post some descriptive sentences. Each day use a new sentence. "How many windows are there in our room? Count to find out."

10. *Achievements of a class*
"The First Grade have read their fifth primer."

11. *Items from daily papers in children's vocabulary*
"The circus is here today."

12. *Announcements of school activities*
"Indoor recess today. What shall we play?"

13. *Safety rules*
"Look before crossing the street."

14. *Special day salutations*
"Merry Christmas!"
"Happy Birthday!"

15. *Notices of articles lost and found*
"Has anyone found Mary's glove?"

16. *Achievements of individuals*
"George can read without a marker."

17. *Notices of new school material*
"There are new books on the reading table."

18. *Requests for materials from home for class use*
"Bring cloth tomorrow for aprons."

19. *Assignments of schoolroom duties*
"Plants....... John
Cupboards... Marie"

20. *Direction of attention to a new picture*
"This is a trick pony. How can we tell it is?"

21. *Names of visitors*

22. *Number neither absent nor tardy*

23. *Results in health inspection*

24. *A good joke*

25. *An original poem*

used in class work, some books should be on about the same level, and a few books more difficult, to serve as a challenge to the advanced pupils.

If funds are meager for book purchasing, the following libraries are suggested as *sources* of material; state, county, town (often rural schools have access to these), and the libraries in county superintendents' offices. Other materials that may be used are: advertising material; scrapbooks and story books made by teachers; good stories, salvaged from discarded readers and made attractive in bright covers; children's-experience stories made into typed or written booklet form; books children bring and share with others.

It is desirable to have some *time* on the daily program assigned especially *for library use*. Otherwise, some children may never get the opportunity to do free reading. The time between classes, when regularly assigned tasks are completed, also can often be very profitably spent in the library. Younger children may find pictures they wish to show to others, or stories and poems that they wish the teacher to read to them. Older children may find material on a unit being studied, select a story to read to the class, or select a part of a story to tell in order to interest the others in reading it.

At first very little *checking* of children's free reading is done. In upper second or third grade, where children are able to read simple story books and to select stories from books, the teacher may find different ways of checking and recording their reading. There are definite values in knowing the types of reading interests which children have, their reading comprehension, and the amount of reading they have done. On the other hand, since one main purpose for this phase of reading is to develop a desire for leisure reading, certainly no chances should be taken to create an aversion to it by too much reporting and checking. The following suggestions may be of use: (1) Large charts containing the children's names with spaces for recording the books or stories read may stimulate some other children to read more because of competition. (2) A card for each child filed in alphabetical order, with spaces for the record, eliminates undesirable comparisons which may be possible in the chart form of number (1) above. (3) Individual cards for reporting may serve as a check on individual reading, for example:

Child's name	Grade
Name of book	
Writer of book	
How did you like it? Very much ☐ Not very much ☐ Not at all ☐	
What is the book about?	

(4) A set of such question cards for different books or stories may become permanent equipment. (5) The other children and the teacher ask a pupil questions about his story or book, after they learn its title. This is preferable to telling the stories that have been read. It is difficult for children to tell stories in their own words interestingly and for this reason, the enthusiasm of others for reading the same selection may be lessened.

If the teacher wishes to introduce her class to simple library *procedures*, a visit to a town library is a good means of so doing. This may be a good way of initiating a library unit, or of continuing the unit in the school if the library is already equipped. The latter will involve planning, appointing children as librarians, learning how to draw out books, and when to return them. A file will be needed which contains a card for each child recording the name of each book and the date taken out. Children accept this responsibility surprisingly well and enjoy the procedures.

The following are *suggestions for furniture* that children may make for a school library.

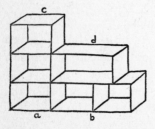

BOOK CASE

Materials:
   3 orange crates (use only 2½), a, b, c.
   1 grocery box slightly smaller than
      orange crates, d.
Steps in making:
   Nail boxes together.
   Sandpaper and paint.

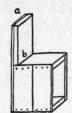

CHAIR

Materials:
  1 orange crate
Steps in making:
  Remove one end.
  Remove two opposite, upper sides.
  Use the end that was removed to rein-
    force the back a–b.
  Sandpaper and paint.

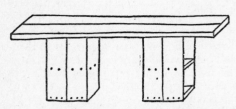

READING TABLE

Materials:
  2 orange crates
  Pine board $1' \times 8'$
Steps in making:
  Saw off four inches
    from one end of
    each box.

Replace ends to make the top more firm.
Saw pine board in half and nail side by side on top of the crates,
  which are about eighteen inches apart or far enough for the
  chairs. The open side of each crate should face toward its
  respective end to serve as a place for books
Sandpaper and paint.

DESK

Materials:
  2 orange crates
  1 board 12″ by $38\frac{1}{2}''$
  1 board 5″ by $38\frac{1}{2}''$
Steps in making:
  Take the ends from the crates
    and saw the sides to the de-
    sired height.
  Nail boards across the tops.
  Sandpaper and paint.

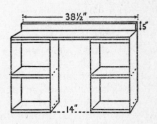

The term *seatwork* as used in this section includes the activities
of the time between the class instruction periods, whether at the desks,
the library table, or in other parts of the room or building. Such
activities may include those for:

1. Building reading vocabulary
  a. Make dictionaries by arranging pictures alphabetically.
    The teacher may make labels which the children paste
    below the pictures. These serve as dictionaries for find-
    ing new words which are given in sentences on the black-
    board, for example:

Draw a big *airplane* ———— (new word to be found in dictionary)

Draw a boy.

He wants to ride in the big *airplane*.

The children not knowing the word "airplane" find it in their dictionaries by matching. The picture gives the meaning.

b. Work with puzzles. Simple ones may be made of pictures cut from magazines and mounted. At first, cut the picture only into three or four parts. Later furnish word cards to accompany the puzzle, some of which are labels for objects in the picture, some are not. Direct children to separate the labels of objects in the picture from the unrelated labels. Increase difficulty by using phrases and sentences. These and other vocabulary exercises may introduce words to be used in future reading as well as in reviewing those already introduced.

2. Developing habits of independent work
   a. Use the library. (See p. 95.)
   b. Place on the easel a sentence written on a strip of paper and have pupils draw at the easel to illustrate it.

3. Directing thinking and checking comprehension in reading
   a. Work on different kinds of checks covering the material read, such as thought questions, true-false, matching, multiple choice, and completion exercises.
   b. Guess riddles. Several groups of riddles kept in envelopes may be used repeatedly if the cards are numbered and the children answer by drawing or writing on another sheet and numbering the answers correspondingly.
   c. Match (a) like forms, (b) like pictures, (c) pictures with labels or with short reading sections, (d) sentence strips with experience chart story, (e) colors and color names, (f) Arabic numbers and number words.
   d. Place phrases in the four sections made by folding a large sheet of drawing paper twice at right angles through the middle. Pupils illustrate the phrases with drawings. This suggestion may be adapted to either easel or desk work.

4. Correlating reading and manual activities
   a. Carry out directions involving drawing, cutting, tearing, pasting, and sand and clay modeling. The words "cut," "draw," "make," "color," "mold," and "paste" should be learned in the preprimer period. This is also a means of reviewing vocabulary by combining the appropriate words from the selections read with the words listed above.
   b. Make scrapbooks and label the pictures. Organize these as books of pets, of a boy, or of a dog, showing the activities of each with the pictures.

5. Applying ideas gained from reading. Draw illustrations for a movie telling a story which the pupils have read. Place a descriptive sentence under each picture. The children read these sentences as the movie is shown.
6. Continuing activities of the class period. See purpose for rereading silently on page 84.

In a schoolroom where there is more than one class, it is necessary to arrange for considerable time to be spent in the seatwork periods. *Suggestions* for effective work in these periods are: (1) Plan exercises that will be easy enough to be done independently. (2) Plan for all members of the class to be employed the full time. Plan extra activities for the faster pupils. (3) Make the assignments clear, being certain that children understand all procedures to be followed. (4) Help children to understand the purposes of the seatwork exercises. (5) Arrange to have variety in the work assigned. (6) Grade the difficulty of the exercises. (7) Give plenty of opportunity for showing initiative and doing creative work. (8) Give children some choice of activities. (9) Furnish keys where it might be advantageous for the children to check their own results. (10) Check the results, offering help as needed. Give recognition for achievement in some way, such as showing to class, posting, or discussing.

CHAPTER 4

READING: GRADES ABOVE THE PRIMARY

OBJECTIVES

TEACHERS wish to know first of all what a reasonable expectation of *accomplishment* for *intermediate* and *upper grades* in the field of readings is (the fourth stage of reading development is indicated on page 66). Below are the well-considered and clearly stated "Major Aims and Objectives,"[1] for grades 4, 5, and 6: "(1) To extend and enrich the experiences of pupils through wide reading in the various fields in which pupils are and should be interested at this stage of their development. (2) To broaden and elevate reading interests and tastes and to establish the habit of reading regularly for recreation and pleasure. (3) To promote the development of increased power and efficiency in various important phases of reading. This includes rapid growth in recognition and meaning vocabularies, in accurate comprehension of increasingly difficult materials, in breadth and depth of interpretation, in speed of silent reading, and in quality of oral reading. (4) To stimulate, in conjunction with work in the various subjects, the development of attitudes and habits that enable pupils to engage effectively in different study activities that require reading. (5) To make continuous studies of the attainments and needs of pupils in reading and to provide necessary corrective and remedial instruction." Added to these is the following objective for the junior and senior high school not specifically mentioned for the intermediate

---

[1] *36th Yearbook of the National Society for the Study of Education.* Part I, pp. 110 and 123. Public School Publishing Co. 1937.

grades: (6) "To improve and refine habits involved in good oral interpretation, particularly of informational, literary, and dramatic selections, and in connection with public and class activities that require reading to others."

Extending and *enriching pupil experience* might mean: (1) That each pupil would touch, through reading, constantly wider and different fields of experience; not only read more stories and books of the same general nature but also those of different kinds, such as biography, travel, nature, science, history, and fiction. (2) If pupils read more widely in varied fields they become, as a result, broader in their concepts of human life and its relations. For example, persons who travel are usually broader in sympathy and tolerance than those who do not; this breadth of attitude may be gained by vicarious travel through story. (3) If pupils are broader-minded, more tolerant, and sympathetic, they are likely to be better balanced, and their reactions to be more sane in any given situation. Better balanced citizens are exactly what any democratic nation needs in as large numbers as possible.

Widening and raising the level of tastes and *interests* in pupils' leisure reading invites the teacher to find: (1) each pupil's present level and variety of interests, (2) the level of difficulty of the materials he can read with pleasure, (3) his attitudes toward reading, and (4) some promising indications for future guidance. For example, he now reads detective stories or possibly "big little" books almost exclusively. The teacher asks herself by what means or over what route he can be directed into more fruitful channels.

To develop greater effectiveness in the *basic skills* of *reading* is one top-ranking aim. It seems that success in attaining all other aims is conditioned by this one. Pupils who can read well almost always like to read. If pupils like to read, they usually read widely all available materials. If they read widely, they are less likely to be prejudiced for or against certain types of reading matter. In this event the basic aims are more or less fully realized. This aim will be discussed fully later, under methods of improving reading abilities.

Building more efficient study habits is a justifiable aim about which comparatively little has been done. This aim should be stressed because: (1) Better study habits help the pupil in his school work now. (2) Habits of work are enduring; long after subject matter has been forgotten the habits acquired in learning it are still functioning. (3)

Efficient mental work habits often transfer directly to life activities. To illustrate, a reading rate built up to 400 words per minute would function every time certain types of reading were done.

Often we think of *diagnostic* and *remedial measures* as applying only to the slow or dull pupils. The best teaching applies diagnostic and remedial treatment to the best pupils as well as to the poor or average ones, for the following reasons: (1) The brilliant student, more often than the slow student, does far poorer work than he is normally capable of doing. (2) The teacher wishes to know the exact deficiencies of her most able pupils as well as the deficiencies of the average and poor ones, in order to be able to deal more intelligently with all groups. (3) Much energy and time can be saved and desirable pupil attitude developed if a teacher realizes reading defects in time.

Higher levels of speech activities should be given special emphasis in the upper grades or junior high school for the following reasons: (1) Such activities as reading dramatically or actually performing in a play make the literature more real. (2) As a selection becomes more real, it has a greater chance of becoming part of the actual experiences of the children. (3) Helping children re-live the experiences of the literary selections seems to be a fundamental aim of literature teaching. (4) Such activities tend to develop poise in public speaking and platform presence and other qualities highly valuable in life.

TYPES OF READING

The *two general types of reading* (as indicated at the beginning of the chapter) with which teachers are concerned are oral and silent. Every teacher should be intimately acquainted with the uses, values, and dangers of teaching each type. These are illustrated in the following diagram:

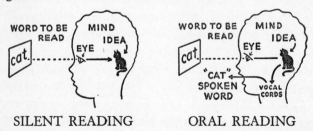

SILENT READING   ORAL READING

In *oral reading* the reader transmits the thoughts of the printed page directly to others by means of the spoken word. Some of its *values* are: (1) an aid in the early stages of reading in associating word meanings with the printed forms (if a pupil says "dog" as he sees the printed symbols which mean "dog" he seems to have a greater chance to connect the symbols with the concept already in his mind and to remember it), (2) a means of teaching voice control for pitch, loudness, quality, enunciation, and pronunciation, (3) a factor in developing a taste for good literature, (4) an opportunity to develop into a good reader in public. This accomplishment is rarely used, but its attainment wins great respect for the performer, as in dramatic reading and broadcasting.

Perhaps a word of *warning* should be uttered concerning the use of oral reading. (1) Oral reading is less important than silent reading to the pupil both during school and later. (2) Oral reading habits which might interfere seriously with silent reading should not be formed. (3) Undoubtedly oral reading is much slower than silent reading and hence less efficient in getting thought from the printed page. (4) Although oral reading is of some value in early instruction, it seems to help very little after the second year. (5) Oral reading is more difficult to teach well, because more learning activities are involved. (See the diagram above.)

Silent reading is classified on the basis of use into two types: recreational—when one reads for pleasure, and study reading—when one reads for a more or less definite purpose. Of course, there is no exact line of division between these types. What is reading for fun at one time, may be work under different conditions. Generally the purpose indicates what type of reading it is.

Perhaps the larger portion of silent reading is done for *recreation*. *Values* that may be expected from it are: (1) a profitable use of leisure time, provided the guidance has been effective; (2) a permanent interest in reading good periodicals, newspapers, and good books; (3) interests in special fields, such as the stock market page, sports, editorials, advertisements; (4) a desire to keep informed in as many fields as possible, such as politics, science, education, international relations; (5) a broader conception of human relations with a better understanding of their implications.

It seems that *caution* should be unnecessary in recreational reading.

There are some chances to go wrong, however. (1) Improper guidance, or none at all, may result in unbalanced development or thinking. To illustrate, too many mystery or detective stories or too many wild west stories might give the avid young readers an out-of-focus impression of life. (2) Too much reading of even the highest level at the expense of play out of doors is not desirable. (3) Great care should be exercised by both teachers and parents to avoid disabilities of sight or posture. (4) Finally, an excessive amount of careless reading may

Reading
for
fun

considerably reduce the levels of comprehension or retention. A brief oral or written check over the main points of the story, a short discussion of the story's outcome or its purpose, will help the children to retain the story.

Study reading almost invariably is of direct and immediate as well as lasting value to pupils. Some *values* of this type of reading activity are: (1) the ability to appraise quickly and to attack effectively any task which involves reading: to solve a problem, work out a lesson assignment, find the answer to a question; (2) skill in summarizing a larger unit of reading, and putting the summarization into a few pithy words fully expressive of the larger unit; (3) the ability to use books, libraries, reference guides, and source materials (such as newspaper files) efficiently; (4) the development of the ability to organize the main and subordinate ideas of the printed page into some orderly form mentally while reading, and in written outline, later; (5) last, but by no means least, the ability, basic in any study-reading training, to acquire new vocabulary by using the old. New words are being encountered daily in the different subject-matter fields and the skill that aids in assimilating them contributes directly to successful learning. The habit of assimilating a new word comes from good training in study reading.

Suggestions as to possible *wrong conceptions* in teaching study reading may be helpful: (1) Teachers often stop short of establishing fixed habits in the training of pupils in the various study-reading skills. For example, pupils learn how to outline or select the central thought of a paragraph from their work in study-type readers, but they may not use this knowledge in their daily study of content subjects, thus converting it into habits of study. (2) Some teachers think that special exercises should be used only in the development of study-reading habits. They do not use the regular content subject matter materials to teach both the materials and the good study-reading habits at the same time. (3) Often teachers forget that each content subject-matter field is more or less specialized and the pupils need reading instruction in each field. For example, training in the ordinary reading period may not be sufficient for good reading of problems in arithmetic. (4) Sometimes we get the conception that study-reading skills are separate activities and that we can develop pupils in one and not in the other. This is not true. For example, an exercise in finding the central thought depends on the child's vocabulary, ability to summarize, ability in finding sentence meaning, and other reading skills.

METHODS OF TEACHING

Methods of *teaching reading* may be divided for convenience into the classifications of oral reading and silent reading with the subheadings: recreational reading and study reading.

ORAL READING

The best development in *oral reading* requires more skill in teaching than is now commonly used. Many teachers believe that all they need to do to develop their pupils properly in oral reading is to have them read orally a selection previously prepared by silent reading and vocabulary study. The teachers, of course, listen closely for mispronounced words, faulty voice control, wrong pauses, and other shortcomings. Given equivalent equipment and schoolroom conditions, almost any normal person could do what these so-called teachers do, and with the same results. If teachers really wish to develop their pupils efficiently by using oral reading, different methods from the one just mentioned should be used. The following statement by Gray[1] hints in a general as well as specific way at what is meant by "Effective Oral Reading."

"Effective oral reading presupposes a thorough mastery of the fundamental habits of recognition, accuracy of pronunciation and enunciation and efficiency in comprehension and interpretation. It also includes a variety of important attitudes, habits, and skills, of which the following are typical: (1) A definite motive for reading to others. (2) A sense of the importance of the message. (3) Sympathetic regard for the listener. (4) A clear understanding of the meaning and purpose of the selection. (5) Clear oral presentation of thought relationships. (6) Adjustment to, and the expression of, changes in character and mood presented in the subject matter. (7) Vocal adjustment to the rhythm of poetry. (8) Appropriate facial expression, subordinated to the thought of the selection and indicative of the reader's understanding and appreciation. (9) Controlled bodily movement and breathing. (10) Confidence in one's own ability, freedom from tension; naturalness and sincerity; and convincing speech and manner.

"The foregoing attributes of effective oral reading suggest interesting instructional problems. Each problem must be attacked systematically in stimulating reading situations if desirable results are to be attained. Appropriate attitudes on the part of the listening group should always be cultivated; for example, thoughtful attention to the materials presented and responsiveness."

This quotation sets up standards toward which every teacher should strive. This brings us to the next part of this discussion, namely: What are some ways and means of attaining these standards? Perhaps we should first suggest some *basic factors* of *oral interpretation*.

[1] Gray, W. S. *36th Yearbook of the National Society for the Study of Education.* Part I, pp. 69-70. Public School Publishing Co. 1937.

Most students agree that oral language activities are affected mainly by two agents, the voice and the body as a whole. (1) The voice can vary oral language meanings by certain changes. (a) Inflection or pitch in ordinary terms is the highness or lowness of the tones. (b) The loudness of tone is determined by the force put behind its utterance. One reads or speaks differently to a group of ten people than to one of five hundred. One exerts more vocal force in the latter situation. (c) Speed of oral communication has to do with both the rate of speaking the words and the amount of time used between each word. These are varied to express different situations. One would say, "Look at that beautiful sunset!" differently from "Look! A tornado is coming!" The words in the latter sentence would be spoken faster and the length of time between them shortened. (d) Quality of the voice consists of numerous attributes, hard to describe but very evident. These are the characteristics which enable us to know the voices of relatives and friends as well as or better than we know their faces. Even when the words are matter-of-fact, traces of anxiety or annoyance may be detected in the voice quality. We do this so easily and naturally that we think little of it, but quality of voice is an extremely important factor in conveying meaning orally. (2) The body as a whole is generally used in oral communication. Perhaps only the face or the hands are employed, possibly the tenseness of the whole body or its posture may be brought into play, or it may be a physical alertness which seems to heighten the quality of oral interpretation. Thus the good oral interpreter uses eyes, head, hands, face, posture, stance, and a myriad other bodily actions to enforce his interpretations. Another way to show the importance of the body in oral speech is to point out that one can be understood fairly accurately through pantomime when making his wishes known to a person who does not understand his language.

Modern methods used in *teaching oral reading* may be summed up under two headings: (1) the laboratory type of teaching in which both teacher and pupils work to improve the reading of each and every pupil and (2) the audience reading type in which the purpose is to give a fine performance after thorough preparation. In the judgment of most teachers these two types of reading work should be kept separate, just as practice periods in music are different from recital, and are thought of in different terms. The learning is done in the practice or laboratory periods. The results of the learning are shown in the audience periods.

Following are some *basic factors* of *laboratory period* procedure. (1) The pupils should know what constitutes good oral reading. This may come from examples by the teacher or pupils or both. The essentials should be before the pupils in chart form during their practice periods. Any form of clear statement of these requisites will do. For example:

Were the words and phrases enunciated (spoken) clearly and at a proper rate?
Were all words pronounced correctly?
Was the reading done in a pleasing quality of voice?
Were there any distracting mannerisms?
Did the reader have good posture and did he seem to have the proper attitude toward the audience?
Did the reader seem to know or understand what he was reading?
Had the reader made a suitable selection for his reading purpose?

Other essentials may be added. Teachers find that the best procedure is to start with only one or two characteristics of good oral reading on the chart and then add to them. (2) There should always be an individual pupil purpose for the reading in a laboratory period. This may be different for each pupil in the group. Tom may be trying to avoid monotony in the pitch of his voice. Harry may have trouble with mannerisms and posture. Tom and Harry each had practiced at their seats, at home, or elsewhere the different phases of the selection to be read in the laboratory period. That is, each did everything possible himself to eradicate his particular difficulty. The class is informed about the problem upon which each pupil is working. By this procedure pupils do not need to have the same books. In fact, it would be better to have different ones. Thus the reading materials in these laboratory periods are used as tools to improve the pupils' reading abilities—not as so many pages to be read. (3) The suggestions made by the teacher or pupils should be helpful and encouraging, and focused solely on the immediate purpose for which the pupil is reading. Making constructive criticisms may be as beneficial to the person who makes them as to the one who receives them. (4) Extreme care should be taken by the teacher in the organization of class and individual practice work. Each pupil should work on his own problems in both the class and individual practice periods and should have definite instructions as to the next step in his practice work. Teachers of smaller groups of pupils have an advantage in such a plan of teaching. Those in the one-room rural schools perhaps have the best opportunity of all. Their work is, or may be made, practically individual.

More specific *suggestions* for work in *laboratory reading teaching* are: (1) Sight reading (with no previous preparation) is an excellent exercise for pupils who are sufficiently advanced. The selections should be comparatively easy. This should help to keep the pupil's confidence in himself and encourage a healthy attitude toward reading. (2) The teacher often participates as a reader in order to stimulate interest or to illustrate a particular factor in the reading. At the beginning of the term she may do this frequently, using different devices, such as: (a) reading a selection and stopping for pupil comments now and then; (b) reading a poem or group of poems without mentioning the titles and asking pupils to give titles for them; (c) reading jokes or funny short stories solely for enjoyment. (3) A reading club may be formed whose membership is based upon certain oral reading achievements as well as accomplishment in other types of reading. Some clubs have objective standards set by standardized tests, some have standards based upon the books read and reported, and some have standards based on other checks. The standards should not be so high as to discourage slower pupils or so low as to be uninteresting to the better pupils. (4) Teachers frequently use some kind of semi-objective standards to score oral reading of the laboratory or audience periods (usually in the form of a score card). The essentials of oral reading (p. 106) may be put in this form and each pupil's reading be scored, Good, Fair, or Poor by both teacher and pupils. This gives the teacher and pupils data in objective form which may be used by them for remedial purposes. (5) Teachers find plenty of opportunity for class oral reading in the incidental readings from text and reference books. This type is assured of a critical audience and therefore must be read carefully.

Sometimes teachers do not understand that the use of the laboratory plan of teaching oral reading is radically different from the old plan which arranges for each pupil to take his turn in reading a selection, with little or no attention to individual needs. The following arrangement shows some of the differences:

Laboratory plan	*Old plan*
1. Each pupil works on his own deficiencies both in class and in his study.	1. Little attention is given to individual defects insofar as assignment or class work is concerned.
2. Each pupil may select his own practice materials in any book.	2. All pupils read the same subject matter from the same book.
3. Subject matter is regarded in the light of its relationship to pupil needs and performance.	3. Attention is given to subject matter, such as reading materials which pupils study. Some attention is given to pupil performance.
4. Objective of laboratory teaching is, first, to develop pupils, then to teach subject matter.	4. Objective is to teach subject matter, then develop pupils.
5. Stresses pupil co-operative activities and constructive suggestions in class work.	5. Stresses individual performance with teacher as judge.
6. Aims to aid pupil to find and remedy his own defects of oral reading.	6. Aims to provide opportunity for pupil to read same selection as other pupils and compare himself with them.

The laboratory plan of class work frankly emphasizes the oral reading skills and treats the subject matter as a tool for strengthening them. For this reason, probably, laboratory or practice periods should not be considered reading in the sense of studying literature, or as leisure-time reading. Perhaps an oral reading laboratory period should not take more than one-fifth of the total class reading time. A good arrangement might be literary reading two days, free reading two days, laboratory oral reading one day. If the pupils need practice in silent study reading, the laboratory activities may be extended to two days and include specific exercises in study reading.

Audience reading, as mentioned above, involves situations in which the reader is "put on the spot." It is, in a way, a test of performance or a check on the effectiveness of drill. Some qualifications of audience reading as adapted from Paul [1] are: (1) The audience reading period

[1] Paul, Vera Alice. *36th Yearbook of the National Society for the Study of Education.* Part I, pp. 314-315. Public School Publishing Co. 1937. Adapted.

should be unique among the periods of the school day. Children and teacher should approach it with pleasure and anticipation. The persons responsible for the period should stimulate interest and curiosity in the material to be used. (2) The material read must be something that the group actually wants to hear. (3) Audience implies listeners. Only the reader should have a book. The pupils should be seated as informally and comfortably as possible. (4) There should be no interruptions or distractions in the audience reading. Pupils should receive the same courtesy that adults receive. (5) It is important that no poor audience reading be done. Every child should succeed in as many ways as possible. The teacher should not allow a pupil to try to do something for which he is not ready. Pupils should be encouraged to think of audience reading as a high-level performance.

Situations in which *audience reading may be done* are found in the pupils' own schoolroom and elsewhere. Among these situations are: (1) reading a story or poem at an assembly, (2) reading a report of a committee to the school club, (3) reading current events to the class, (4) giving a report of a trip to a lower grade or another room, (5) a pupil reading as some of his classmates pantomime what he reads, (6) pupils reading dialogues or plays as they take the character parts, (7) pupil reading his favorite poem. It is not necessary to have a special time on the program for audience reading although this would undoubtedly add much to its significance. Assignments may be arranged so that this type of reading will occur in any regular reading period.

choral group

They sing together. Why not read together? Have you tried it?

Group or *choral reading* is, as the name suggests, oral reading by groups and may be used in either laboratory or audience situations. In the intermediate and upper grades the groups are usually divided into "low" and "high" voices for variation in reading. Sometimes a single voice carries the reading. Often antiphonal effects are achieved by group divisions. This type of reading can be used from primary grades through college. The readers and the audience both seem to get a unique emotional reaction from choral reading. Moreover, the teacher can often draw reactions not possible in any other way from reticent students. There are excellent opportunities for the teacher to get in some effective strokes in teaching the fundamentals of oral interpretation, such as phrasing, diction, and voice quality, as well as to emphasize the relationship of all oral expression to the emotions. Thus pupils as a group may be taught the basic elements of speech when time would not permit teaching them these as individuals. There are rather definite limitations, however, on what can be done with this type of training and if these are recognized there will be little danger of wasting time.[1]

Finally, while it is generally agreed that oral reading is not used as much as the silent forms, it is sometimes extremely important—for instance, reading a secretary's report at sight to a group of a hundred people. In view of this fact, oral reading will in all probability continue to be taught. If it is, the methods of teaching it certainly should continue to be improved.

SILENT READING

Silent reading, as suggested above, may be thought of as recreational or as study-type. The satisfaction which is derived from pleasant recreational reading associations encourages a child to read more and to develop further. Likewise, study reading will generally improve with normal and above-normal conditions of study. This improvement, in turn, enables the pupil to study more effectively. These conditions, however, are not always true; furthermore, the normal development is scarcely ever what it would be if it received special attention. It is true that many pupils have defects in their silent reading abilities and these should be discovered and eliminated, but it is also true that the abilities of the so-called normal pupils have not been developed to a point even approaching their limits of growth.[2]

[1] For information on materials and techniques write Expression Company, 16 Harcourt St., Boston, Mass.

[2] Data which verify this statement are given in a later section. (See table in study-reading section.)

The suggestions below are given in the light of these facts and possibilities.

Abilities in *recreational reading* may be developed in varied and numerous ways. Before making more practical suggestions, a few facts which show the need of developing pupils in this respect should be given.

A recent study of the reading of 466 girls and 641 boys now out of school was made by the Iowa Planning Board.[1] They had an average age of 19.8 years at the time of the study and an average grade of 10.5 when they left school. More than half had completed high school and many had attended college. Approximately 29% said they enjoyed reading more than any other leisure activity, but 43% had read no books since leaving school. Only 5% had read magazines of at least average literary quality. Leisure reading in colleges seems to be woefully deficient, and adult reading, in the words of one writer, savors far too much of the "garbage can."

If this be true, *what,* if anything, *can be done about it?* Perhaps some of the best practical answers to this question are given by Horn;[2] in adapted form, they are as follows: (1) Separate literature teaching from instruction in reading skills. He suggests the use of other subject-matter fields such as geography, history, and science to develop reading skills because they contain more logically arranged informational materials. (2) Stimulate a reading interest in all the content subjects by using the subject matter of those fields as a start for reading. (3) Change the method of teaching literature from that of critical analysis to one of direct appreciation, from that of prepared lessons to one of real "leisure reading" in an informal atmosphere, from intensive to extensive reading. Some time should be devoted, however, to teaching pupils how to read good literature. (4) Provide reading materials to fit individual abilities. Horn gives data in his discussion of this suggestion to show that a ninth-grade group of 30 pupils varied in reading ability from the fifth-grade level to the median for college freshmen. A larger group of students would undoubtedly have shown even wider variation. This means that the leisure reading for these 30

[1] Starrak, J. A. "Survey of Out of School Rural Youth in Iowa." (Unpublished study)

[2] Horn, E. "The Improvement of Leisure Reading," *17th Yearbook, Department of Elementary School Principles,* N.E.A., pp. 339-346. 1938.

pupils should contain materials ranging in difficulty from fourth-grade level up to and including the first year of college. (5) Provide materials that children like. Children do not dislike literature; only the literature we select for them. Research has shown again and again that children do like good literature in both prose and verse. Teachers can secure graded book lists containing names of books selected by the children themselves.[1] (6) Spend more money for suitable books. Horn reports in 26 eastern cities of from 50,000 to 425,000 population the median expenditure was 10 cents per pupil. In one midwestern state the expenditure was less than one-half of one per cent of the total disbursement for schools. (See literature section, p. 133.)

More specific suggestions and *devices* which have proved effective may be mentioned: (1) A library table attractively displaying special books for the week may be provided. (2) A bulletin board chart show-

"...AND WHAT DO YOU THINK HAPPENED NEXT?" *stimulate reading*

ing the number of books read and reported by each pupil may be made by using a very small colored folder for each book read. (3) A book club may be formed. Membership is earned by reading a certain number of books. Certain desired privileges should accompany club membership. (4) A book or story is read by the teacher up to a very interesting place with the suggestion that the pupils finish. (5) Some interesting happenings in a book or story are told by the teacher up to a certain point, with the question, "What do you suppose happened

[1] The American Library Association can give information on various book lists. Usually each state has a selected list for the various grades.

after that?" (6) A weekly free reading period of at least one hour, when everyone is required to read literary material other than that used in regular class work, often encourages a pupil in reading who otherwise might not desire to read at all. (7) Books borrowed from other rooms, other schools, libraries (local and state), should help to meet the range of interest and achievement among the pupils of the room. Perhaps the most valuable asset pupils acquire from the elementary school is a healthy attitude toward reading. In other words, teaching pupils to like to read is one of the most important of all the activities of teachers. Leisure reading plays an important role in creating this desirable pupil attitude.

The commonly used *study-reading skills* are quite widely recognized, but comparatively few teachers do anything definite about teaching even a knowledge of them, and a smaller number help pupils to transform knowledge of these skills into efficient study habits. To be frank, comparatively little development of effective study habits is going on in the intermediate and upper grades. This is indicated in at least three different ways.

The first is the objectives toward which teachers work. The course of study usually directs them to teach subjects, so many pages in a textbook, a given number of problems, or stated activities. In all such courses of study the emphasis is on subject matter—the things to be learned, or the things to be done. Seldom does one find a course of study or a teacher setting out primarily to develop pupils and considering subject matter as a necessary but secondary tool. If teaching subject matter is first in education's plans and the pupil's needs subordinated, it is doubtful that his individual study habits will be properly developed.

The second way is indicated by the methods of teaching. The assignment is ordinarily in terms of books. The seatwork relates largely to subject matter and the recitation is based on subject matter, often in a dozen ways. Rarely is an attempt made to find just what Tom needs, rarely is the subject matter shaped to meet those needs. This is shown even more strikingly in the tests teachers use. About the best they can do to date is to check on facts of subject matter learned. Sometimes they rise to the level of testing ability to use facts. They do not test to discover, for example, exactly to what degree and

Table I.   Data on Identical Pupils for Preliminary and Final Tests
(27 Counties)

Grades	4	5	6	7	8
1. Town and Consolidated Schools Number of Pupils	2678	3036	3176	2786	2878
Median Score in Tests 1–5—Final	60.0	84.1	109.5	126.9	146.3
(comprehension) —Preliminary	35.5	57.6	84.0	106.7	126.6
—Gain	+24.5	+26.5	+25.5	+20.2	+19.7
Standard gain in score from .2 of yr. to .8 of yr. (Tests 1–5)	9.0	13.5	12.0	10.0	13.0
Per cent of standard gain made in Tests 1–5 (comprehension)	272%	196%	213%	202%	152%
Per cent of standard gain made in Test 6 (rate of work)	320%	140%	31%	22%	73%
2. One-Room Rural Schools Number of Pupils	1171	2057	2000	1281	1329
Median Score in Tests 1–5—Final	51.5	75.1	94.2	116.6	136.4
(comprehension) —Preliminary	30.7	49.5	68.5	91.1	115.1
—Gain	+20.8	+25.6	+25.7	+25.5	+21.3
Standard gain in score from .2 of yr. to .8 of yr. (Tests 1–5)	9.0	13.5	12.0	10.0	13.0
Per cent of standard gain made in Tests 1–5 (comprehension)	231%	190%	214%	255%	164%
Per cent of standard gain made in Test 6 (rate of work)	380%	207%	123%	22%	−33%
3. All Schools Number of Pupils	3849	5093	5176	4067	4207
Median Score in Tests 1–5—Final	57.5	80.7	104.2	123.6	143.4
(comprehension) —Preliminary	34.1	54.5	78.1	102.5	123.2
—Gain	+23.4	+26.2	+26.1	+21.1	+20.2
Standard gain in score from .2 of yr. to .8 of yr. (Tests 1–5)	9.0	13.5	12.0	10.0	13.0
Per cent of standard gain made in Tests 1–5 (comprehension)	260%	194%	218%	211%	155%
Per cent of standard gain made in Test 6 (rate of work)	340%	173%	63%	22%	40%

in what respects Tom has changed during the year in his ability to think with history materials or to organize ideas as he reads. Teachers are even less able to measure accurately his changes in attitude. Rarely do they think about testing such factors, not because they consider them unimportant but because as yet they are unable to do so. If educators had devoted as much time and energy to measuring the various phases of pupil development as they have to measuring the results of teaching subject-matter facts, they would probably now be able to measure the skills and possibly the attitudes above mentioned at least as well as they now measure the results of teaching subject matter.

The third way is by the results obtained when definite effort is directed toward certain study-reading skills, and content subject matter is used to develop them. Table I shows the gains which were made in certain study-reading skills in a six-month period in the rural and urban public schools of 27 counties in Iowa. The Iowa Silent Reading Test for Elementary Grades [1] was used in both preliminary and final tests. This test purports to cover six skills: (1) paragraph meaning, (2) word meaning, (3) central thought, (4) sentence meaning, (5) location of information, and (6) rate of reading. The first five types mentioned are thought of as testing comprehension, the last, rate of reading. During the six-month interim between the preliminary and final tests very little was done by way of supervision to assist the teachers, especially those of the one-room rural schools. Identical pupils are those who took both tests in one school system and were in it the entire time of the experiment. When pupils double or triple the normal gain in any given time, as shown by the test standards, one can safely conclude that the abilities of these pupils were not previously developed up to the limit. In fact it would seem reasonable to think that in comparison with what might have been done, only a meager amount had been accomplished.

The per cents of standard gain show that approximately equal gains were made in graded and one-room rural schools. This would seem to indicate that in both situations comparatively little development in study-reading skills is normally being made. If we compare grade

[1] *Iowa Silent Reading Test*, Elementary. The Bureau of Educational Research and Service, The State University of Iowa.

medians, however, the town and consolidated pupils lead those of the one-room schools by an average of approximately .6 of a year.

An excellent *classification* of *study-reading teaching problems* for the junior high school has been made by Gray [1] which with slight adaptation can be used in teaching the intermediate grades:

"1. To expand the meaning vocabulary systematically and to develop greater independence in deriving or finding appropriate meanings of words.

2. To promote increased power of comprehension and interpretation. For example:
   a. Comprehending exact meanings.
   b. Recognizing the broader meaning or significance of what is read.
   c. Appreciating the quality or worth of the ideas presented.
   d. Making critical judgments concerning the relevance and validity of the facts presented.
   e. Sensing the author's aim or purpose, and the assumptions that underlie his arguments.

3. To develop an insight into the procedures involved in reading different kinds of material and for different purposes. For example:
   a. An interesting story versus a detailed description.
   b. Reading to identify a sequence of events versus reading to judge the quality or worth of an author's ideas.

4. To improve efficiency in study activities involving reading. For example:
   a. Selecting facts from different sources.
   b. Searching for relationships.
   c. Determining effects resulting from certain conditions or factors.
   d. Applying principles, facts, and ideas in interpreting new situations.
   e. Generalizing on the basis of evidence secured.

5. To train pupils to adjust the speed of reading to the purpose at hand, varying from very careful reading to skimming."

This outline of reading activities is by no means all-inclusive, but it does give an idea of what might be in a program of teaching reading to develop skills for purposive reading. Granted that problems similar to the ones quoted above must be met, *what assistance* can the teacher get to aid her in the task?

One very fruitful source is the newer *study-type readers*. These, of

[1] Gray, W. S. "The Nature and Organization of Basic Instruction in Reading." *36th Yearbook, National Society for Study of Education.* Chap. XV, pp. 124-125. Public School Publishing Co. 1937.

course, should be used in study-reading fashion, keeping clearly in mind the four factors of skill training explained previously; namely, development of the child as a whole, stimulation, check, and teacher guidance of pupil effort. Each skill should be well learned, so that probably several lessons will be necessary for each. This should be comparatively easy with the reader materials because they are especially adapted to the perfection of particular skills. The teacher should select skills according to the needs of her pupils—not as they happen to come in the book. She may add to or subtract from the exercises the book gives. In any case she should keep in mind that the text is a tool and that she is using it to develop her pupils. When the knowledge and skills acquired in the reading process are carried over into the study of the different content subjects, the teacher increases measurably the chances that they will be translated into study habits.

Special study-reading exercises are used to help in building effective habits of study. Often they supplement the reading text. Sometimes they are used as original teaching materials. In the latter case the teacher usually contributes something of her own by way of check or directions. Exercises of this type are not a substitute for the actual subject matter of the content subjects, such as history, geography, science, etc. They do, however, supplement and lead up to it. The following sample illustrations give concrete ideas of what these exercises may be:

VOCABULARY—Wrong Word in a List

Directions: One word in the list does not belong with the others. Cross it out.
1. cheese   apple   bread   stone   pie
2. paper   book   top   pencil   tablet
3. tree   batter   bat   runner   ball
4. church   schoolhouse   girl   store   home

CENTRAL THOUGHT—First Level

Directions: Read the first paragraph, then find the central thought which is connected with the first paragraph and put a number "1" on the line just before it. Put a "2" in front of the central thought that belongs to the second paragraph. Do this for all the paragraphs. There is one extra central thought which is not needed.

Paragraphs	*Central Thoughts*
1. You probably have seen a hen trying to frighten some animal or to keep a hawk away from her chicks. She fluffed her feathers until she seemed much larger than she really was and squawked at the top of her voice.	—— How a cat tries to frighten its enemies
	—— Some animals "play dead" to trick their enemies
2. Everyone has seen a cat arch its back, stand up tall, spread its claws, show its teeth, and spit to scare the dog away.	—— How one fowl tries to scare its enemies

CENTRAL THOUGHT—Second Level

Directions: Read each paragraph carefully. Then read the central thoughts and put an "X" in front of the one which best tells what the central thought of the paragraph is. Re-read the paragraph if you need to do so. As soon as you finish one paragraph, go to the next. You should make but one "X" for each paragraph. If you have time, look back over the central thoughts to see if you have made any mistake.

Paragraph	*Central Thoughts*
Our schoolhouse was made of wood. It stood on a hill about ten rods back from the road and had six tall pine trees near it.	—— What our schoolhouse was made of
	—— Where our schoolhouse stood
	—— Our schoolhouse
	—— Six tall pine trees

CENTRAL THOUGHT—Third Level

Directions: You are to find the main idea or central thought in each paragraph and write it in as few words as possible on the blank lines at the right of the paragraph or on your test paper. Remember you are to find the one big thought in each paragraph with which most or all of the parts of the paragraph are connected.

Paragraphs	*Central Thoughts*
Then the storm came. It was like a hundred trains running right over us. The ground shook. It was dark in the cellar and we stood close together.	_____ _____

Paragraphs	*Ceutral Thoughts*
In a little while Miss Jones sent us home to say that we were all safe. She told us to be very careful not to get hurt by things blown across the way. It was cold and the road was wet with the rain.	_____ _____

ORGANIZATION—Paragraph Headings

Directions: Number the paragraph headings in the order they should appear in the story. Let number '1' be first in the story. The sample has been done correctly.

Sample: __3__ On the way home from school
         __2__ A day at school
         __1__ Jane goes to school

1. —— Preparations for the visit
   —— The trip back from the country
   —— What Harry saw on Uncle Jim's farm

2. —— How we went to the factory
   —— Reasons for the trip
   —— Reports about the trip

SUMMARY—Selecting a Title for a Paragraph

Directions: Read each paragraph and write on the line above it the best short title you can find.

1. Title: ————————————————
     I lie on Mary Lou's desk most of the day. I'm easily bent but I spring back into shape again. I help Mary Lou change her errors in writing. I'm made of a kind of rubber.

2. Title: ————————————————
     If you hear or see me coming you run to your storm cellar. And you have good reason to do so for I might kill you if I caught you up in my whirl. I crush houses like you crush eggshells.

Another suggestion (previously mentioned) is the *use* of the *content subjects* to develop study-reading abilities. The later sections on history, geography, science, and others contain further materials for study improvement. The recommendations given here are applicable to any subject-matter field with proper adaptations. Furthermore, they may be used in various types of school organization, ranging from an eight-grade, one-room rural school to a room containing one grade only. The plan of work given below is made for a one-room rural school of eight grades, using a rigidly set program often found in such schools. If a procedure can be made to function under such conditions it is quite probable that it will work in simpler schoolroom situations and be adaptable to them.

The *plan of procedure* can best be shown by using a specific subject chosen from among those in which it could be used, say fifth-grade history. The rural school mentioned above allows 15 minutes twice a week for recitation time for this particular history class. While the assignment would not usually be made in pages, it shall be in this instance, because of increased ease in talking about it. Suppose the two 15-minute periods come on Monday and Wednesday. A skeleton outline of the procedure is given first. This is followed by a more detailed one.

SKELETON OUTLINE

A. Monday
1. Check on previous assignment ⎫ class time
2. Directed reading ⎭ time
3. Assignment of new work (seatwork)
   a. Fundamentals of assignment
   b. Problem situations growing out of materials used
   c. Additional work

B. Wednesday
1. Check on Monday's assignment
2. Directed reading
3. Assignment of new work
   a. ⎫
   b. ⎬ On these three levels same as Monday
   c. ⎭

DETAILED OUTLINE

A. *Monday* (15 min. for 5th grade history recitation)
1. *Check on previous assignment*—pp. 165–169 (10 min.)
   a. Teacher reads answer to fact questions or checks other forms if used (1 min.).
   b. Pupils give and discuss answers to problem situations —time and place for free pupil reaction with reasons pro and con (6 min.).
   c. Hear brief reports—if any were called for—on outside assignment.
      Teacher may need to check the reports herself.
2. *Directed reading* (5 min.)
   a. Base always on the new lesson materials (pp. 170–175).

    b. Stimulate pupils to utmost effort in the skill being taught and check each effort.

    c. Give each pupil, regardless of ability, a chance to do his best in the skill being emphasized.

    d. Keep in mind that the focus is on teaching pupils how to study, not on teaching history.

    e. Use procedures of these types: Pupils find page and close books on fingers. (1) Teacher asks question on new history materials, pupils race to get the answer. Close books on fingers when right one is given; (2) Pupils start together to read a selected paragraph or section. When half or two-thirds have finished all stop. Teacher asks questions to check reading, being careful to place questions according to amount pupils had read. The pressure on time or accuracy is for the purpose of stimulating pupils to exert the utmost effort.

    f. Suppose only pages 170–171 were covered in the directed reading period.

3. *The assignment of new work* for Monday

The study period (30 minutes) immediately follows the directed reading period. Assignment for pp. 170–175 is fully written out on the board or carbon copies provided for each pupil. It should be sufficiently long or difficult or both so that no pupil can finish with perfect preparation in the time allowed (30 min.). All should begin at the beginning of the assignment and work straight through. Each pupil should be scored on the basis of what he does correctly in the time allowed. All work is put in notebooks. The *first* part of the assignment is concerned with the fundamentals (in this case certain desired *facts* from pages 170–175). These facts may be in the form of questions, completion sentences, a partially filled in outline, or other forms. In any event it should include all of the main ideas the pupils are supposed to get from the history text or other sources. These facts should be included regardless of what happened in the directed reading period. The *second* part of the assignment is of a little higher level of difficulty and should include the use of problem situations. These should cover the same materials the facts cover (pp. 170–175) and if possible be made up from the facts themselves. Related materials previously learned may be used also. This part should be designed to help the pupils to use the facts to meet certain problem situations. The problem situations should be gauged in difficulty to fit the ability of the class. The *third* and last section is composed of additional work, either in the text or outside of it. This

work may not be a prerequisite for further work in 5th grade history.   It is, however, very helpful, and if a fast-going pupil brings it to the class, everyone will profit thereby.   For example, pupils do not need to know the story of the compass to learn about the discovery of America by Columbus, but it may add interest to the story if they do.   This is not just "more work," but includes additional tasks which add definite values to the group study.
  B. *Wednesday*—(15 min. recitation time)
    1. Check previous assignment, pp. 170–175 (10 min.). See Monday's discussion.
    2. Directed reading over the new assignment, pp. 176–180. See Monday's discussion.
    3. Assignment—pp. 176–180. See Monday's discussion. The next week's procedure would be the same as this week's only with new materials.

Some values of such a procedure are: (1) A definite time is provided for teaching pupils how to study. (2) Pupils are taught to study by using the subject-matter materials of the new assignment. (3) Definite assignments that stand on their own merit must be prepared. Apparently much of our poor teaching results from poor assignments. (4) Pupils given the benefit of such procedures for a semester in only one subject make marked improvement in study ability and attitude. (5) Pupils like it if it is well done.

Some difficulties which may be met are: (1) It requires time, energy, and initiative on the part of the teacher. (2) The teacher needs to know good study habits herself. Up to this time she may have had very little help from her teacher training or experiences as a pupil. A goodly amount of common sense, a willingness to experiment, and an ability to learn from books will help. (3) The trail has scarcely been blazed and the hardships and disappointments of the pioneer may be expected. (4) Pupils may not like the idea at first and parents and school officials may not understand. All of these should be won over before, or shortly after, the start is made. (5) Subject matter may not be suitable. Start with the easiest textbook and with the most capable group of children.

What happens when pupils are given this sort of encouragement and opportunity to grow? Table I on page 116 shows this in terms of "per cent of standard gain." Another way of saying it is in years and months of reading age. Table II shows changes in reading age for ten counties in one section of Iowa, made during the reading experiment mentioned in Table I. In this section, the experiment ran an average of about six and one-half months. Only pupils who were in the same schools the entire time between the preliminary and final tests are included in the data of Table II.

TABLE II. CHANGES IN MEDIAN READING AGE OF COMPREHENSION IN TEN COUNTIES OF ONE SECTION OF IOWA IN SIX AND ONE-HALF MONTHS

Grades	4	5	6	7	8
Town and Consolidated Schools					
Number of pupils	723	864	919	636	594
Final (Tests 1–5)	10–9	11–10	13–0	13–10	14–9
Preliminary (Tests 1–5)	9–2	10–7	11–7	12–8	13–10
Change in Reading Age	+(1–7)	+(1–3)	+(1–5)	+(1–2)	+(0–11)
One-Room Rural Schools					
Number of pupils	337	940	814	180	205
Final (Tests 1–5)	10–4	11–6	12–4	13–5	14–2
Preliminary (Tests 1–5)	8–8	10–2	11–1	12–2	13–5
Change in Reading Age	+(1–8)	+(1–4)	+(1–3)	+(1–3)	+(0–9)

The data from this section of Iowa are quoted because the procedure for utilizing content subjects suggested above was widely used there. Table II shows that the pupils of the fourth grade in the town and consolidated schools grew 19 months in reading age in six and one-half months (the time of the experiment). The same grade in the one-room rural schools grew 20 months in the same time. It would seem, therefore, that among other factors the methods used were reasonably effective.

Teachers *measure* the *results* of their teaching of reading by two means: teacher-improvised tests and standard tests. *Classroom tests* measure results well or poorly according to the care used in making and administering them. Often this type of testing is not fully objective. Some suggestions for testing follow: (1) Make and keep a record of the classroom attitude of the pupil when reading. This may be in class, at work on an assignment, or during the free reading period. (2) Observe reactions to materials when he reads orally. Does the reader interest the other pupils? Does he seem to comprehend what he reads? Are his enunciation, pronunciation, voice quality, and other performance excellent, average, or poor? (3) Use silent reading materials of approximately known grade difficulty in rate and comprehension. Each pupil finds the page of new subject matter to be used and closes the book on his finger to keep the place. At a given signal each pupil opens the book and reads the designated paragraph, section, or story. He closes the book on his finger instantly when the designated portion has been read once. The pupil notes the time as marked on the board by the teacher in 15-second units. The teacher checks with a 10-item (or longer) objective test on the board or paper. Each pupil calculates his rate in words per minute, and checks his comprehension by scoring the objective test. Sections for tests should not be too long, perhaps not over 500-1000 words. For a slow reading group they should be shorter. Some excellent inexpensive books containing interesting stories with the words numbered and objective tests on each story are available.[1] (4) Make tests to check specific skills in study or other types of reading, such as finding the central thought of a paragraph, knowledge of vocabulary, making an outline, etc. (See exercises for teaching study reading, pp. 119-121.) (5) Keep a class record (average) of the results of each test mentioned above in item 3 and make a chart to indicate change. This is usually made on cross-ruled paper with half-inch squares; the vertical lines showing the various weekly tests, the horizontal lines showing the rate of reading or per cent of accuracy in comprehension, as the case may be. The longer the period over which such a record extends, the more valuable it is. A semester or year record is much more valuable than one kept for six weeks. (6) Arrange for each pupil to keep his own record in the same form suggested for the class record above. (Drawing page 127.)

The second means of measuring results of the teaching of reading

[1] Educational Department, The Reader's Digest, 353 Fourth Ave., N. Y. 10.

The Reader's Digest Reading Workbook, Sixth Grade, Part One and Part Two, and Reading Skill Builder, Fifth Grade, Part One and Part Two (in preparation).

Four and Twenty Famous Tales—upper primary.
Forty Famous Stories—Lower intermediate.
From Washington to Lindbergh—Upper intermediate.
Wonder Stories From Nature—Upper grades.
Webster Publishing Company, St. Louis, Mo.
Practice Readers—Series.

is by the use of *standard tests*. This is particularly true of study reading. (1) Comparisons may be made for both class and individuals with the standard score, the standard reading age in years and months for the grade at any given time of the year, and the standard reading grade in terms of grades and tenths of a grade. (2) If tests are given at the beginning and end of the school year (a) a measure of the growth in the abilities tested may be secured for the class as a whole or for each individual, (b) individual differences may be shown at the beginning of the year when maximum use may be made of the information, (c) the test data may be used to motivate pupil effort in

the desired fields. (3) Use may be made of class and individual charts to illustrate and add meaning to the test data as suggested for the teacher-improvised tests outlined above.

The measurement program should be utilized to the fullest degree. The test records may profitably be studied, analyzed, charted, discussed, and used by the administration when studying the results from the school system as a whole and by the teacher when working with the group and individual pupils of her own room. Teachers should remember that measurement is a double-edged instrument. It reveals not only conditions pertaining to the pupils but also those pertaining to the teacher. It shows both how pupils have or have not developed and it also commends or indicts the teaching methods used. The fact that our measuring instruments are as yet very crude should be borne in mind. We are unable to measure accurately, if at all, the results of teaching many of the most important factors of healthy development. At best, the test results show only indications, not the whole and absolute truth of the pupil's situation. In short, common sense is to be used in interpreting and using the data from any type of test materials. If this is done, much good may accrue from the measuring materials now available.[1]

Almost every teacher has pupils who need *diagnostic* and *remedial treatment* in some part of the reading field. The brief suggestions below are only "first aid" and should direct the teacher to fuller and richer sources of assistance.

[1] The following reading tests are recommended. Diagnostic Examination of Silent Reading Abilities, published by Educational Test Bureau; Durrell-Sullivan Reading Capacity and Achievement Tests, published by World Book Co., Gates Silent Reading Tests, published by Bureau of Publications, Teachers College, Columbia University; Gray Standardized Oral Reading Paragraphs, published by Public School Publishing Co.; Iowa Silent Reading Tests (New Edition), published by World Book Co.; Metropolitan Achievement Primary Reading Test and Intermediate Reading Test (Revised), published by World Book Co.; The Nelson Silent Reading Test, published by Houghton Mifflin Co.; New Stanford Reading Test published by World Book Co.

CHAPTER 5

READING: DIAGNOSTIC AND REMEDIAL

SOME *characteristics* of *disability* in *reading* are: (1) In oral reading, a slow, halting manner, accompanied by inability to pronounce words is common. (2) Frequent errors in pronunciation, by substitution, omission, repetition, and change of order of words, are other traits. Weak readers appeal by word or gesture for signs of encouragement from the teacher. (3) There is often a lack of comprehension of the materials read orally, even if the words are pronounced correctly. (4) In silent reading, the rate may be slow or the comprehension low, or both. Usually these are accompanied by movements of the vocal organs, particularly of the lips. (5) Frequent eye pauses on a line of reading indicate small perceptual units. (6) There is often an attitude of fear which may turn into antagonism to reading. (7) Doubt and hesitation or frequently just the opposite— a bold attempt to pretend with a total disregard for meanings—may be manifested.

Some *possible causes* of reading disabilities follow. (1) Although low mental power is the cause of probably less than 2% of reading disability, it ranks high as an alibi for failure in the teaching of reading. The fact that the school assigns mental deficiency as a cause of disability, or allows it to be so designated without proper investigation, occasionally causes mentally normal pupils to be moved to the intermediate grades with a reading ability of the low primary level. (2) Poor teaching is the prevailing cause of abnormalities in reading abilities

This cannot be wholly charged against the teachers. Some of the responsibility must go to the system of organization under which they work and to the homes which do not co-operate to the full extent. (3) Physical defects are a frequent cause of trouble in reading. The eyes, ears, clogged throat or nasal passages, malnutrition, and a host of other physical conditions may be contributing factors to poor reading. (4) Bad habits of eye, voice, or mind, or combinations of them, may retard progress. For example, if pupils have been taught to read orally to the exclusion of other types and their minds have become accustomed to perceiving one word at a time (as in oral reading), they are quite sure to have trouble learning to do silent reading of any greater speed than oral reading rate, because of the one word-at-a-time rate of the oral reading perception. (5) Sometimes emotional instability, which may grow into unfortunate attitudes toward reading, may be a disturbing and retarding element. To illustrate, an extremely excitable child having trouble with her reading may develop all sorts of erroneous ideas about her classmates' ridiculing her.

DIAGNOSTIC METHODS

Among the *diagnostic methods* usable by the average teacher in a pupil reading situation are the following. (1) Observe the child without his knowledge in the various reading activities. This will catch

Do you know your pupils?

his general attitude and habits of work—the "outside" evidence of what the pupil does when he reads. Make notes in some detail for several periods of observation. (2) Arrange personal conferences with the pupil. The object of this is to help the pupil tell or show just how he studies a particular subject or lesson in that subject. Several brief conferences may be better than one long one. The teacher should make notes during these conferences or immediately afterward. The confidence of the pupil must be obtained for the best results. (3) Get his case history, from himself, his brothers or sisters, parents, previous school record, and other sources. It should contain the pupil's class standing, physical data, social adjustments, home environment, church and community relationships, and similar data bearing on the reading situation. (4) Use standard psychological and educational tests designed to clarify the problem at hand. These tests may be group or individual. The tests should be reliable, valid, as objective as possible, and accurately diagnostic in nature. (5) Use, when accessible, mechanical measuring instruments, such as the Betts Ophthalmic-Telebinocular,[1] with which the eyes singly or together can be tested for such factors as distance vision, vertical and lateral imbalance, eye co-ordination, and the like, or the Ophthalm-O-Graph,[2] which takes a picture of the eye movements in reading a selection on a moving film, which may be studied at leisure. Through such devices definite data may be secured.

REMEDIAL TREATMENT

The *materials* and *methods* used in *remedial reading* work may be designated roughly in the following categories. (1) The reading materials should fit the pupil's needs. If, for example, a sixth-grade pupil should be found to have the reading ability of a pupil half way through the first grade (1.5), he should be supplied with materials on the 1.5 level or below. Some teachers still think that remedial reading should be of the grade level in which the pupil happens to be classified. "If not," they ask, "how will he learn to read sixth-grade materials?" They forget that growth in most abilities starts on easy levels of performance and that higher levels of ability are built up from the lower ones. All phases of reading are remedial in these same general ways: (a) find the pupil's level, (b) begin there with remedial treatment, (c) as a pupil grows, raise the difficulty level of materials used. (2) The instruction should be fitted to the needs of the individ-

---

[1] Betts Ready-to-Read Battery, Keystone View Co., Meadville, Pa.   Revised 1936.
[2] American Optical Company, Southbridge, Mass.

ual pupil. Whatever it takes to interest, to stimulate, to encourage, and to assist him should be used by the teacher in her methods of remedial teaching. This is found by using the information about the pupil obtained from all sources and sometimes by trial-and-result procedure if every other method fails. (3) Records of change are generally effective to demonstrate to the child the results of his efforts. If intelligently used, these may be stimulating regardless of whether the change is favorable or unfavorable. These should be kept on charts by the pupil himself, in a form that will indicate change over a long period of time. (4) The teacher would do well, before attempting to do any difficult bit of remedial work, to consult and use books written especially as aids in this field.

CHAPTER 6

LITERATURE

L ITERATURE portrays all phases of life—the real and the fanciful,
the present and the past, the immediate and the remote—
by means of the story, poem, and play. All youth should have
the opportunity to profit from this rich abundance of cultural material.

Literature is the material commonly used for teaching recreational
reading. This phase of reading instruction should not be crowded out
by the zeal to introduce children to beginning techniques, to expand
their powers, and to develop abilities needed in study reading. The
Iowa Elementary Handbook, Volume II,[1] states, "At least a half of
the total reading time in grades three through eight should be given
to this [literary] type of reading."

Weeks[2] gives this as one interpretation: "The term literature has
been used in a broad and inclusive sense to cover good, wholesome
reading matter as well as reading matter of fine literary quality. At
the elementary school level, literature for children would be a very
small body of literature indeed, were it limited to the prose, verse and
drama which satisfied all criteria that characterizes fine literary writing."

SOURCES AND SELECTION

According to this criterion reading texts are one good *source* of
literature. It is preferable to use such selections in readers, in general,

[1] *Reading*, p. 22. Department of Public Instruction, Des Moines, Iowa. 1943.
[2] Weeks, B. E., *Literature and the Child*, p. 7. Silver, Burdett & Co. 1935. With
permission of the publishers.

for enjoyment and appreciation rather than for study reading as sometimes has been done. Other sources of literature for children are the home, school, and local libraries and bookshops. The home atmosphere and reading experiences have a marked influence in initiating children to this field of enjoyment and growth. A shelf designated as the child's own on which he keeps his books adds definitely to his interest. In the home he may hear or read his favorite stories more often as a member of the family group. It is profitable to have cooperation between the home and the school in the selection, the guidance, and the sharing of such reading matter.

The school-room library increases the number of books available and makes them easily accessible. The local library usually cooperates with the teacher in lending books to the school and to individual children. It is very advantageous for children to establish early the habit of using the local library. It is one way of initiating an inexpensive recreational activity that can be used throughout life. In some rural areas the bookmobile brings the library to the readers.

Although bookshops may be thought of as places usually visited by adults, they can be patronized by children also. Where better can a child invest his allowance? Even browsing through the displays and looking at the attractive covers stimulates the desire to own and to read books.

There are many *aims* for using literature in guiding children's development. Some of them are: (1) to furnish a means for wholesome enjoyment, (2) to learn of the interests of individual children, (3) to direct children to materials that meet their individual needs, (4) to help pupils understand themselves and others better, (5) to build desirable attitudes toward people and conditions, thus avoiding or overcoming prejudices, (6) to introduce new fields of interests— perhaps to provide a hobby, (7) to help children satisfy curiosities, (8) to provide good humor, (9) to furnish opportunities for relaxation, (10) to help make children's lives richer and broader.

To summarize, children should acquire through their recreational reading activities an appreciation of the values of literature for the purpose of meeting their various individual needs. This can be achieved most fully when the teachers, parents, and other adults understand children and appreciate literature themselves.

The question of *selecting books* for recreational reading is not one of finding, but of choosing from the abundance that is available. The first problem is to know the children who are to use the books, that is, their individual intellectual levels, emotional trends, and the types of experience to which they are accustomed. Weekes says,[1] "It is essential that the child have a wide variety of reading material in harmony with his interests and experiences, as fine in treatment and form as possible. If horizons are to widen, interests change and strengthen, the literature for childhood must afford opportunity for the reader to satisfy the play of his imagination, permit escape from the realities of life for a brief space; to explore the unfamiliar past and to venture into the unknown future, or into the remote spaces of the universe. Balanced reading for a child is preferably a mixture of fiction and fact; the imaginative and the real in prose, poetry and drama form."

Studies have been made concerning children's interests according to age levels and sex. It is worth a teacher's time to familiarize herself with the results of these in order to facilitate her selection. Weekes[2] has a good summary of several such studies. It is probably safe to conclude that the fanciful is more enjoyed in the early grades and the realistic later. However, the best indication, no doubt, as to preference is the material a child selects freely without direction. There are approved lists[3] to help teachers in selecting good books and to use in guiding pupils' choices.

Each year, awards[4] are made for outstanding contributions to juvenile literature. These prize-winning books should be included.

Attention also should be given to the reading difficulty of the

[1] *Ibid.* p. 39.

[2] *Ibid.* pp. 18-26.

[3] *A Basic Book Collection for Elementary Grades* by Joint Committee of American Library Association, National Educational Association, and National Council of Teachers of English. American Library Association, 503 Huron Street, Chicago, Illinois. 1943.

Best Books for Children, issued annually by Iowa Pupils' Reading Circle, 409 Shops Building, Des Moines 9, Iowa. Free.

Children's Books—For seventy-five cents or less—1947 revision. Association for Childhood Education, 1201 16th Street, N. W., Washington 6, D. C. A classified list of inexpensive approved books for children, 36 pages. Price 35 cents.

A supplement to *500 Best Books for Children* compiled by Nora E. Beust and Mrs. Eleanore F. Clift. U. S. Department of Interior, Office of Education, Washington, D. C. 1945. Price 5 cents.

[4] John Newberry Medal Awards—to writer of best American literature for children. Randolph Caldicott Awards—to artist for the best picture book.

literature selected. If children are to read for pleasure the difficulty level of most of the material provided should be a year or more below that of the basic text.

METHODS OF TEACHING

Customarily, teachers and pupils look with pleasure to the period devoted to literature. In addition to the regular periods for recreational reading and free reading, literature may be enjoyed together at the opening of the day's work, in spare minutes during the sessions, and at the close of the day. There should be at least two designated class periods a week for the primary grades. (See time allotments, p. 110, for grades above the primary.)

There are two main reasons for presenting literature orally to children. First, much literature can be understood and appreciated before pupils have acquired sufficient skill to read it independently. Second, the beauty and musical quality of the language used is obtained chiefly by hearing it.

STORY TELLING

Although *story telling* brings pleasure to pupils of any age, it is most commonly used on the lower levels. All primary teachers should have the thrill of successfully telling good stories in these grades. In order to do so, thought should be given to the selection, preparation, manner of telling, and discussion. The following directions may help in these four respects.

The *selection* should be given careful consideration. (1) Know in general the interests and experiences of the group in order to determine a suitable type of story. (2) Select carefully the story to be told. The lists previously referred to should help in choosing. Do not hesitate to select such old classics as "The Three Bears," for they are new in each generation. (3) Consider the qualities that make a story appealing to children, such as familiar family characters, animals that talk, surprising events, absurdities, magic, incongruity, imaginary action, repetition of phrase and conversation. (4) Select stories with characters of contrasting types who are portrayed true to type—the wicked should be punished and the good rewarded. Children are not shocked by a cruel ending if it is deserved. (5) Be sure there is a plot—that is, a series of events, one dependent upon another, culminating in a climax and followed by a justifiable ending. (6) Try your hand at writing a story if there is none available which meets these criteria.

Time should be taken to make adequate *preparation*. (1) Be sure that you like the story yourself. Read it two or three times before deciding. (2) If it appeals to you, proceed to know the story. In order to do so, think through the story, incident by incident. Do not memorize it, but remember what occurs first, what follows that event and so on. If there are certain repeated phrases, or quotations, they should be told each time in the same form, such as "Somebody has been sitting in my chair," or "I'll huff and I'll puff and I'll blow your house in." When telling the story, children often like to repeat these parts with you, thus sharing in the telling. (3) When you feel that you have the story well in mind, tell it to an imaginary hearer or to yourself in the mirror. You will find nothing gives you as much confidence when telling the story to children as such a previous rehearsal.

The *manner of telling* is most important in conveying the ideas of the story. (1) Set the stage by bringing the children close to you, either in chairs or on the floor. An arrangement of seats in rows is not conducive to the right attitude for enjoying a story together. (2) Be sure that the children are comfortable and that you can see the eyes of all. With confidence and poise, begin. Remember that you are conveying the author's thoughts to this young audience. (3) Be natural in manner, tone, and quality of voice. Tell it as you would talk. Use everyday manner of speaking and acting. (4) If the story is humorous, suggest that the funny parts are coming by facial expression and a twinkle of the eyes. (5) Put feeling into the presentation. Tell it earnestly. Make the children feel that you like what you are doing. (6) If you should forget what comes next, do not stop but carry the story along, and the thread of the story will, no doubt, come back to you. If you should omit an unimportant part it will not matter. However, if it is essential to the thread of the story and you realize the omission later, you can bring it in with some such remark, as "I should have told you—." On the other hand, you may be able to insert the event in another place, and detract nothing from the general plan.

Discussion stimulates pupils' reactions. (1) When the story is finished, take time for the children to "digest" it. (2) Encourage pupils' remarks and questions, such as, "I would not like to have been the First Little Pig," "I bet Raggylug stayed in his nest next time when his mother went away," or "Why did the Little Red Hen carry scissors in her pocket?" (3) Make pertinent comments yourself. Do not point out "the lesson" implied, or ask questions simply to test the listeners' remembering of the events. Rather guide the children's thinking in ways to enjoy the story and solicit their reactions.

If stories are told to pupils in grades above the primary, the same procedures, modified to fit the age, will apply. For suggestions on story telling by pupils, see pp. 169-170.

It is possible now also to bring literature to the children by means of the phonograph record,[1] radio broadcast,[2] motion picture, filmstrip, and theater.

ORAL READING

Reading literature to pupils is appropriate on any level. When doing so, teachers should again select and prepare the material with care. As in story telling the responsibility is that of conveying the ideas of the author to the audience. The tone, inflection, and pitch of voice as well as the facial expression are all vehicles by which the meanings are conveyed. If necessary, there should be practice until it is a pleasure for others to listen. When using picture-story books, stop the reading to show the pictures and be sure there is sufficient light on the page for all to see.

When pupils have sufficient reading ability, they themselves may prepare and read selections to the others. (See suggestions, pp. 110-112.)

Poetry, to be thoroughly enjoyed, should be heard. But it must be well presented. The reciting or reading of it should convey the musical and rhythmical quality while, at the same time, expressing

---

[1] For information write to American Library Association, 503 Huron Street, Chicago, Illinois.

[2] Miss Gloria Chandler, Association of Junior Leagues of America. The Waldorf-Astoria, New York 22, New York.

the meaning, unless it is a simple jingle. Even the jingle type of poem needs to be recited with a tone expressing feeling.

In the early grades, short or especially rhythmical poems make the stronger appeal. Young children like poetry about familiar situations and experiences, or just pure nonesense rhymes. It is interesting that all ages, even adults, enjoy some of the modern poetry written for younger children by Aldis, Milne, Fyleman, and others. On the higher levels, longer poems, both humorous and more serious, should be provided.

Forced memorization of poetry has, no doubt, caused many to dislike this kind of literature. Nevertheless, knowing poetry does have values, (1) in interpreting references in other literature, (2) in personal enjoyment resulting from the ability to associate lovely lines with beautiful scenes, with the fragrance of blossoms, with the experiences of friendships, and (3) in the personal satisfaction of achievement. The dominant idea should be to find ways of stimulating the pupils' desires to want to memorize poems or parts of them. The time for memorizing poems easily is in the intermediate grades.

Some *suggestions for literature periods* devoted to poetry and for memorization follow. (1) Use Mother Goose picture book. Show pictures and read the accompanying verses. If some are familiar to the children, encourage them to join in the telling. (2) Choose several short poems. Create a setting for each by a remark or question that recalls some familiar situation of similar nature as, "Did you ever see a turtle?" After a few responses, remark, "This poem is about a turtle. Listen to what it did." After the reading, the children may want to say, "It lived in a box," "It climbed on the rocks," and so on. Continue in similar manner with the others. (3) Introduce and read several poems; then ask which ones they would like to hear read again. Reread those chosen. (4) Introduce and read several poems. After reading each one, ask the children to suggest a good name for each. Write those on the board. Also write the author's titles that differ, opposite those given by the pupils. Help them to compare and to decide which they think are the better according to the ideas in the poems. (5) After reading a poem, write the title on the blackboard. Do his with several. Suggest voting for the class favorite. To do so, each thinks of the one he likes best, closes his eyes, listens for the title, and raises his hand as he hears it. Read the titles and record the number of votes for each. Ask children to look at the results and to determine the most popular, the least enjoyed, and how many more the leading choice is above the second choice. (6) After hearing two or more poems, suggest that each child draw first a picture that shows which one he liked best and, on the reverse side of the paper, a picture of his second choice. (7) Suggestions (2), (3), and (4) for the primary grades can be adapted to the older children by selecting poems suitable for their ages. Frequently, older pupils have been deprived earlier of this phase of literature instruction and have little liking for poetry. In such cases these methods would be especially applicable. Often humorous poems appeal most readily in this attempt. (8) Assign periods when pupils read only poems of their own choosing. Follow with informal, voluntary discussion—perhaps children will want to read certain lines or different stanzas. At other times have no discussion—some poetry stimulates feelings difficult to express. (9) In presenting a longer poem; (a) Read the entire poem, unless it is a very long one, in which case divide it into thought units and read one unit at a time. Pupils listen without copies. (b) Encourage discussion and questions following the reading. For this part of the procedure each pupil has a copy to refer to, either in books or in mimeographed form. They may wish to read orally certain parts vital to the discussion. Participate in the discussion only to the extent of guiding and stimulating the pupils' thinking. (c) Read the entire poem again. If there is a pupil who can, with preparation, read the poem or section well, he might do so at the beginning and the close. (10) Encourage pupils to preserve these mimeographed copies in booklet form, also to copy some poems that they have especially enjoyed. Occasionally, plan a period when children choose from "their anthology" poems or parts of poems and read them to the others. (11) Suggest that pupils find and prepare to read poems pertaining to a current unit, such as farming. Devote a period to the enjoyment of hearing these.

Arrange for children to hear much poetry and choose the poems they may want to *memorize*. (1) Encourage children to ask for repeated readings of the same poem. Often they can repeat it with little extra effort. (2) Plan for motives that stimulate memorizing, such as letting others know the poems liked by giving them in an assembly or at a parent-teacher meeting. (3) After reading a poem, ask if there is any part that continues to come back to them. If not, suggest that they might like to learn that part. (4) Read a poem and ask children to listen for words or parts that seem unusual or make a picture they like. Then ask if they would like to learn such parts. (5) Use choral speaking to stimulate the desire to know poems in order to share in group activities. (See pp. 111-112.) (6) For aid in a group memorizing; (a) Read the whole poem. (b) Read part of a line, expecting the pupils to finish it. Alternate the parts given by the teacher and pupil. (c) Follow the same plan using alternate lines. (d) Devote additional effort to especially difficult stanzas. Soon the children will know each stanza and the entire poem. (7) Encourage applause when a child shows achievement. It pleases his ego and stimulates further effort.

SILENT READING

When a child has sufficient reading ability, he should be influenced *to read for himself* this rich heritage of literature, both prose and poetry. This implies more individual choice and the opportunity to improve his tastes, and to utilize the abundance of material available for acquiring desirable understandings and attitudes. Some types of lessons suitable for doing this follow:[1] (1) Free reading, or library reading—just reading for fun and doing nothing with it. (2) Reading a story to tell back to the class or group. (3) Dramatizing a story after reading it. (4) Making a movie of a story. (5) Making simple puppets to use to tell the story. (6) Illustrating a story or fable, and having others guess what is illustrated. (7) Recommending a book to other children—that is, making a brief but convincing sales talk. (8) Writing the recommendation and posting it on the bulletin board together with the book jacket. (9) Making a brief report on a book or story read—telling about it, not retelling it. (10) Preparing stories in groups and reading them to the rest of the class. (11) Finding and reading stories of a certain type (*Aesop's Fables*), or of a certain period (*Log Cabin Family*), or of a certain country (*Si, Si, Rosita*). (12)

[1] "Reading," with additions. *Iowa Elementary Teachers Handbook*. Volume II, State Department of Public Instruction, Des Moines, Iowa. 1943. Adapted.

Getting stories ready for a program or assembly. (13) Having a reading club. (14) Making original stories and reading them to the group. (Children love to write their own stories. Encourage it. Do not stifle the attempts by too much emphasis on form and perfection.)

RESULTS OF TEACHING

Some of the many *results* to be expected from the teaching of literature are: (1) Interest in a wide field of reading. (2) Improved reading tastes. (3) An interest in vocabulary and its use. (4) An appreciation of picturesque expressions. (5) Ability to choose better reading material. (6) Broad interest in different fields. (7) A better understanding of self. (8) Sympathetic understandings through acquaintance with various peoples and events. (9) Character development through imitation of characters admired.

To *summarize*, literature contributes to children's emotional experience and to their thinking as is done in no other way. By careful selection and well-planned and varied procedures, a capable teacher who likes literature and reads much herself can contribute immeasurably to pupils' cultural advancement.

CHAPTER 7

LANGUAGE

INTRODUCTORY

L ANGUAGE is the common means by which we satisfy our inherent desires to express and communicate ideas. Language ability grows and improves chiefly because of our natural social tendencies. We express wants and desires, give and ask for information, ask advice and give directions, in our normal human associations. We have more sympathy and better understanding of each other if we "talk over" situations. We acquire new ideas, gain food for thought, reach new points of view, and often find satisfaction in unburdening our own minds through such social intercourse. There are two other main uses for language: as a medium for recording events, thoughts, and facts; and as a tool for creative expression.

A consideration of some of the *relationships* between normal *oral* and *written language* may be of value to the teacher in this field. In the first place, oral language is the older form. Moreover, everyone knows that one is able to talk long before he learns to write. In fact, the ability to write has become necessary only in comparatively recent times. The relative amount of usage is a second factor of relationship. No one knows just what this ratio is, either in general or specific situations. Some writers guess that at least 95 per cent of language usage is in oral form. If one thinks of the days or even weeks during which he uses oral language in direct conversation or listens to it over the radio and does not write a single word, it would seem that 99.99 per cent would be more nearly correct. On the other hand, the morning

143

newspaper, weekly and monthly magazines, books, and personal correspondence remind us that written language is also widely and frequently used. In the third place, oral language seems to be not only the source of written language; even today it supplies some of the basic skills by which written language functions. Finally, lest the conclusion be reached that written language is of little value, it should be noted that most, if not all, of our progress in every field of human experience has resulted from our ability to write and record what we think, say, do, and feel. At present, however, much recording of oral language is being done by means of mechanical recording instruments.

Language occupies a very *important place* in the *school program.* It is the vehicle for conveying thought in all subject-matter fields. Practically every class period is to be considered a language period. The diagram expresses it graphically.

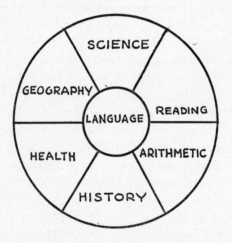

Every teacher, regardless of her subject-matter field, should feel responsible for teaching language. Nevertheless, there should be definite periods set aside for language classes, in order to present, to show reasons for, and to give practice in its specific phases.

There have been decided *changes* in the teaching of language in the elementary grades following changes in educational aims. One is the change of emphasis from its formal to its social aspects. The second change is the shift from grammar as an end in itself to that of a functional, mechanical aid in understanding and using grammatical construction in oral and written expression. In short, form has been subordinated to content of language.

One may assume that the *main objective* of language teaching is to make every child efficient in the following language situations. In oral language these are: taking part in conversation, using the telephone, participating in meetings, giving reports, naming things, making speeches, delivering messages, making announcements, giving explanations and directions, making introductions, using forms of courtesy, planning procedures, retelling stories, and creating stories and verse. In written language these are: writing letters, keeping records (including minutes of meetings and diaries), writing notices of future events, filling in forms, preparing invitations, writing advertisements, taking notes, making outlines, memoranda and lists, making a bibliography, and doing creative work.

Some rather *general suggestions* for achieving proficiency in these language situations in the elementary grades follow:

1. The schoolroom should be a place where children live naturally and happily if they are to develop the ability to use language effectively in real-life situations. This implies
   a. stimulating surroundings which furnish materials that appeal to the children's desire to manipulate, to investigate, and to ask questions;
   b. a warm, natural atmosphere in which children feel at home, have a personal interest in and respect for and responsibility toward the equipment provided;
   c. an understanding that teacher and children are working together for the growth of each pupil. This means a spirit of co-operation in helping individuals to overcome their weaknesses and in recognizing their successes.
2. Since language growth is a gradual development, the simple beginnings of the first year should be continued and broadened year by year. For example, children use, see, and read sentences in the first grade, and acquire, at least in a limited way, a "sentence sense." Later, a sentence becomes a unit of thought and in due time the pupils learn its parts and structure.
3. Oral communication implies at least two persons, the speaker and the listener. The speaker should always consider his audience and the audience give due courtesy to the speaker.
4. It is the teacher's duty to institute definite measures to improve the language usage of her pupils. This may be done by
   a. increasing and enriching her own vocabulary and giving special stress to her own speech forms, so that children hear correct forms constantly;

    b. arranging for children to hear good English in stories and poems;

    c. eliminating incorrect forms used by the pupils, such as "I seen," "you ain't," etc. Group practice may be inaugurated effectively when a large part of a group makes the same error. Class consciousness of language errors may thus be aroused and a definite class attitude toward them formed. The most effective and lasting work, however, is likely to be done when each pupil knows and corrects his own errors with the solicitous interest of his classmates. If some sort of record in chart form is made and kept to show growth or progress toward a definite goal, the situation is likely to be even more stimulating.

5. Oral language should be given more attention than written language, at least in the lower grades. The results of testing have shown the need for better oral ability.

6. Voice quality and tone should be given attention in language work. This point applies to both teacher and pupils. Phonograph records of good speaking voices may be used as models.

7. The language assignments should be definite and simple, so there can be no mistake in the child's mind about what he is to do and how he is to do it. All tasks, of course, should be well within the range of his ability. He has had, however, the stimulation of effort which comes from knowing exactly what is to be done and how he is to do it. Such assignments as: "Write a story," "Be able to tell a story in class tomorrow," would in all probability not be as stimulating or effective as: "Write a paragraph about the thing you liked best at the fair," or "We shall depend on James to have such a good joke and tell it so well tomorrow that no one can keep from laughing." Especially would this be true if these tasks were selected by the pupils themselves.

8. Children may be taught to work independently through the use of self-help charts. These may be set up by the teacher and children for different phases of work at different stages. If the items are stated in the form of direct questions, such as the ones below, children may feel a more personal appeal. Time should be taken to instruct children in the use of such charts, especially if it is one pertaining to written work. These charts show the standards expected and may develop a feeling of responsibility for individual growth.

For Oral Composition

1. Did I look at the people to whom I was talking?
2. Did I stand without leaning against something?
3. Did I have something interesting to tell?

For Written Composition

1. Did I begin the first word of each sentence with a capital letter?
2. Did I use the right mark at the end of each sentence?
3. Did I leave out any words?

For Oral Composition

4. Did I have an interesting opening sentence?
5. Did I have a good closing sentence?
6. Did I make my story clear to
the listeners?

For Written Composition

4. Did I spell each word correctly?
5. Did I leave a margin on each
side?
6. Did I tell something worth
while?

9. The results of teaching should be measured in some way. If this
can be done objectively, more definite outcomes may be expected. Many phases of language, however, as yet lack objective measuring instruments and the teacher is left to meet these
situations with her own ingenuity. Whether the measuring is
done with standardized tests, tests improvised by the teacher,
or estimate by the teacher, by the class, or by teacher and class,
it should be done on the highest level of accuracy and efficiency
possible. Some teachers think it is not possible to measure
certain qualities of language composition. Others are not
willing to admit that measurement of these qualities is impossible. Suggestions for measuring growth in oral and
written language on the lower grade levels are made on pages
212-214.

ORAL LANGUAGE

First and second grades are often combined for oral language
activities if both grades are in the same room. It is probably better,
however, that they be in separate classes for written work since the
second-year pupils usually do more writing than first-year pupils. If
units of work in content subjects are carried on, there are abundant opportunities for teaching language. It is wise to incorporate most of
the primary language material with units of work and other school
activities in planning the language program.

IN PRIMARY GRADES

The *different phases* of oral language to be emphasized in the
primary grades will be discussed under the following headings:
vocabulary development; conversation; oral composition. reports, and
speeches; names of people and objects; social courtesies; directions;
announcements and messages; telephoning; dramatic play; and recounting stories. Creative work, both oral and silent, will be discussed following the section dealing with written work.

Vocabulary development is a gradual process. It shows the greatest gain between the ages of one and six. "Between the eighth and the seventeenth months the first word appears."[1] Children's vocabularies grow rapidly during the pre-school and primary period—more than at any period of the same length throughout life. The following table shows vocabulary norms.[2]

Age	Number of Words	Increments
1 year	3	
1½ years	22	19
2 "	272	250
2½ "	446	174
3 "	896	450
3½ "	1222	326
4 "	1540	318
4½ "	1870	330
5 "	2072	202
5½ "	2289	217
6 "	2562	273

"Generalizing the increments, we may say that during the first year the child acquires three words, during the second year, 269 words; from then on to the fourth year, very close to 600 new words each year, after which the rate slows to 500 a year up to the age of six." Children use a large part of their vocabularies over and over again during a day. "Studies by Gale and Gale, Brandenburg, and Nice, record the total language responses of the child during a single day. For the two-year-olds studied by Gale, the total number of words used in a day varied from 4,275 to 10,507, with approximately 50 per cent of the child's total vocabulary being put to use. In the Brandenburg investigation, a three-year-old child used 11,623 words during the day, and the four-year-old child 14,930; the three-year-old child used 37 per cent, and the four-year-old child 23 per cent of his total vocabulary. The three-year-old asked 376 questions and the four-year-old 397 questions during the day. The total length of time a child was linguistically inactive was nineteen minutes, and the longest single period of linguistic inactivity was four minutes. These figures show the tremendous amount of practice the child gets in language during the day."[3] This refers only to chil-

[1] *38th Yearbook of the National Society for the Study of Education.* Part I, p. 212. Public School Publishing Co. 1939.

[2] *Ibid.*, p. 213.

[3] *38th Yearbook of the National Society for the Study of Education.* Part I, pp. 213-14. Public School Publishing Co. 1939.

dren's speaking vocabularies. Children understand many words they do not use, so their "hearing vocabularies" are even larger.

These facts would indicate the importance of paying special attention to the means of providing conditions which would *stimulate* the *acquisition* of *new words* when this tendency is strong. The following are suggested to teachers: (1) Make children "word conscious"—that is, stimulate an interest in words by talking about them, asking which of two words they prefer to use, asking for words to describe an object, listing all the words children can give to describe a picture, listing words on paper charts that pertain to a unit being studied, and commending children for using unusual words. (2) Use new words in the schoolroom. Children delight in hearing new words and often use them in conversation before the day closes. (3) Ask for meanings of words as they are met, in order to be sure that the children understand them. Encourage children to ask for meanings. (4) Plan for children to arrange a museum and to label the objects. Encourage children to use these names as they talk of the different specimens. (5) Play games of matching synonyms and opposites. (6) Call attention to words in children's reading which are appropriate for use in oral discussion. (7) Help children realize the importance of a varied vocabulary in keeping listeners interested. (8) Suggest that third-year children keep in booklet form new words which appeal to them. Many words will be learned indirectly; but teachers can, by definite planning in these and other ways, help children with little additional effort to gain a rich and broad vocabulary, and thus to express themselves more effectively, interestingly, and with greater ease.

It is a decided asset to be able to converse well. Situations in which *conversation* is used have been tentatively classified:[1]—at the table, at social gatherings, in discussion groups, at public gatherings, in public places, during introductions, during calls, in interviews, in greetings and partings, in asking directions, and in telephoning. All these different situations call for different types of conversation. That is, topics discussed at a family meal would be inappropriate following an introduction; taking one's part in formal group conversation is different from talking with an individual. In view of its importance in social situations, conversation receives less attention in the teaching

[1] Course of Study for Elementary Schools, p. 263. State of Iowa. 1928.

program than do some far less important phases of language. Because conversation is so common, teachers have not realized the need for instruction in the various problems of learning to converse.

Certain *conditions* to *develop* desirable *skills* in conversation should prevail in the schoolroom. (1) The relations should be informal. Children need to feel that their contributions are welcome. If children are always expected to ask permission to talk, natural responses will be limited. On the other hand, social courtesy requires development of the ability to await an opportunity to contribute. It may be that teachers sometimes expect too much self-control from first-year children. If the topic is of personal interest, the child's natural reaction is to express his ideas about it immediately. The ability to wait one's turn comes gradually. (2) The teacher needs a great deal of tact in order to draw out the reticent child, to curb the one who naturally contributes too often, and to try to arrange for contributions by all in the group. It means careful study and understanding of children. The teacher should try to feel herself one of the group and also play her part. Her contributions may be a means of guiding the trend of the discussion. (3) Conversation may be stimulated by nature specimens, materials for construction, toys, and pictures.

One of the first essentials to consider in *planning situations* for conversation lessons is that children talk spontaneously about the things in which they are interested and of which they know. This holds whether the conversation is carried on informally or with direction by the teacher.

Some such situations in the *intermission* or *free periods* may be these: a child bringing something to show others and telling them about it; a group of children playing with blocks, looking at books or other objects of interest, and talking with each other about their activities; children arriving at school and telling the teacher and playmates of happenings in the community.

Some situations in *class periods* other than the language period are: planning for the day's program, such as making a garden; discussing the information in a reading lesson or the activities that promote health and safety; or evaluating the results of an excursion or other activity.

Some situations for the *assigned language period* are: discussing the characteristics of good conversation and establishing standards in the different phases; pointing out the need for being good listeners; stressing the courtesies involved in conversation, such as how to include everyone in a conversation, and helping those who contribute infrequently; mentioning suitable topics about which to talk, where children can find interesting information, and their responsibility for having something interesting to offer; and practicing, often in dramatic form, different types of conversation, such as when entertaining a friend who is waiting to see one's mother.

The following *suggestions* in *method* may aid in developing abilities in conversation in the situations listed above. (1) Much of the teaching in connection with conversation is guided by providing occasions and materials which stimulate conversing. (2) The children should be directed to talk about something of interest to all. It is not enough for them simply to talk. (3) A teacher, by showing genuine interest in what a child says and giving attention to what he tells, as well as how he tells it, encourages him to further effort. (4) A teacher may arrange to have pupils discuss with one another personal experiences— for example, those about pets—or she may help the entire group to talk on one topic of common interest—for example, the airplane they saw pass over the school grounds. She may also arrange conversation situations for small groups of two or three (the most common group number in life outside the school). The teacher may help the child who finds it hard to contribute to group discussion by directing him to some new object of interest in the room. This may help him to gain material for conversation later in the day. (5) Pictures and objects may be used to suggest similar or related personal experiences.

Oral composition, *reports*, and *speeches* are closely associated with conversation, although they may differ somewhat in length and organization.

Modern school *situations* for developing skills in oral language arise naturally. (1) They may occur in recounting personal experiences, as when Mary returns from her uncle's house and tells of her pony ride. (2) They may be reports on investigations that had been based upon such a question as, "Which feet of the rabbit make the front tracks in the snow?" (3) Helen reports a plan for taking care of the new books in the school library. (4) There are speeches to be given in a program to which the parents are invited. These talks may be about some school activity, such as the making of maple sugar. (5) Taking part in the school assembly offers an opportunity to organize and tell of the activities involved in a completed unit of work.

In planning her *methods* for *conducting* such language activities, the teacher must remember that the material is to be the children's own and not something memorized from a book. They can be helped by using plans or simple outlines, for example, when telling about playing after school:

> "With whom did you play?"
> "Where did you play?"
> "What did you do to have a good time?"

The teacher may ask these orally or put them on the blackboard. When pupils talk of their gardens, it might be: "Who?" "What grew?" "What was liked?" to remind them to tell who took care of the garden, what grew, and what they liked best. Devices like these may be used even with first-year children. They aid by suggesting what to talk about and how to organize the discussion. Older children may help at first in setting up such guides, and later make their own simple outlines independently. Many oral compositions are spontaneous. Those to be given at the assemblies or programs should be thought through previously, practiced before a group, and improved as a result of the suggestions received. Teachers help children to be conscious of such standards by using a guide, such as the one on pages 146-147. Often children add interest to their compositions by illustrating them with objects or blackboard drawings. A first-grade boy was finding it difficult to make clear his description of a new electric train and track, so he stepped to the board and drew the track, then went on with his explanation. If children display articles, they should learn how to do it effectively. They should hold materials or pictures so that all can see and if these are too small, they should tell about them and then pass them around. Other items might be: "Did I keep on the subject?" "Did I tell all that was necessary?" "Did I begin without 'why-a' or other unnecessary words?" "Did I avoid using unnecessary 'ands'?"

Children show great interest in the *names* of *people* and *objects*. A visitor seated herself near a group of pupils working at a table. One child leaned over and quietly asked, "What is your name?" This was a natural reaction—an expression of a child's inherent curiosity. Often a child asks, "What is it?" when he sees an unfamiliar object. Names identify and give individuality to people and things. Names save time. The game is "tag," not, "the game in which you touch a hand and run." Names make it easier to think about people and things. Which book shall we read, "Little Black Sambo" or "Peter Rabbit"? Names help in remembering, even long after the dog is lost or the doll discarded. Names create interest. Neil has not merely a new coaster; he has a "Pony Express."

Participation by the children in selecting names utilizes their native initiative and originality. Sometimes they need help in selecting appropriate names. To start them on such a procedure, two or three names may be presented for their consideration to be used as a basis for selection. Below are some *situations* which occur in school and which involve the need for naming: (1) pictures which children make, bring from home, or which the teacher provides; (2) committees which involve room duties, or roles in some unit work; (3) classes—these names may be based on an activity or interest the class has at a particular time, such as the "Play House Class." A class may adopt the name of some member of the class (i.e., "John's Class") changing the name from time to time; (4) objects which children make with clay and wood— the figure is not just a boy, but "Jack Horner." The airplane is the "China Clipper"; (5) recorded compositions, original stories, poems, plays, and programs—the selection of the name usually follows rather than precedes the composition work; (6) booklets containing records, those connected with units of work, and those made of original stories and verse.

Using verbal *forms* of *social courtesy* is one way of expressing consideration of others. Although certain polite forms are desirable, it is the attitude of genuine kindness and thoughtfulness of others that teachers wish to develop. This attitude, expressed through the observance of common courtesies in social contacts, makes living pleasanter for everyone. Such expressions give pleasure to others and satisfaction to the person using them. An effective way to help children acquire these attitudes and habits is to provide an environment in which courtesy is practiced and children receive polite consideration.

Some obvious *situations* in which greetings are involved are these:

receiving guests, entertaining or being entertained, making requests and expressing gratitude, extending and replying to invitations, and being introduced.

Greetings given cordially to children when they enter the schoolroom usually bring forth a "Good morning" or "Good afternoon" in response. The "Hello John" from playmates is received and answered. This is a habit easily acquired. Often a short conversation follows.

Receiving guests in school involves asking them in, offering them a seat, asking if they can be helped, and answering their requests. The guest may often be a parent. The teacher may assign different pupils or a committee of pupils to receive guests. Planning and giving parties offer many situations for the exercise of courtesies—receiving, entertaining, and bidding goodbye to guests. Children should also have opportunities to learn how to be gracious guests and to express themselves courteously when leaving a party.

Making requests and *expressing gratitude* often require more than "Please" and "Thank you." The manner of asking may affect the granting of a request. The children should realize this and be taught some underlying principles, such as (1) the reason for the request, (2) the proper time for it, (3) the proper wording, and (4) the proper attitude.

Invitations are often extended verbally either over the telephone or in person; they are expressions of desires to show courtesies to others. Children need to learn not only how to give invitations pleasingly but also how to accept or refuse them politely. School situations involving invitations may include these: (1) giving a party for parents or other children, (2) one child asking the children of the room to come to see a new pet at his home, (3) inviting those from another school or room to see a piece of work that has been completed, such as a library corner, (4) asking parents or other people to an assembly or entertainment. Although it is undesirable to use any fixed form, since its use may prevent the person conveying the invitation from doing so naturally, children should be made to realize that a good invitation will tell: Who is giving the invitation. Who is invited. What it is to be. When it is to be. Where it is to be.

Introductions of new pupils to others, or of one of the parents visiting the school, make children familiar with the purpose and the manner of presenting strangers to each other. Knowing how to reply when introduced and being ready with a bit of appropriate conversation are additional attributes. The latter is not to be expected in the first part of the primary period. It is delightful to see a first- or second-grade child who, when presented to an adult, holds out his hand and says, "How do you do, Miss Carey." Usually a child stands when he is introduced. By the time he reaches third grade he can understand that standards

"mrs Smith, this is mary"

INTRODUCTIONS--

to remember are: (1) to introduce a child to an adult, (2) to introduce a man to a woman, (3) to say "How do you do?" and the person's name when being introduced.

When *practice* is needed in helping children develop abilities in social courtesies, dramatization may often be used. They may play at having a party, and receive or act as guests, extend or answer invitations, and make introductions. Situations can be arranged for practice of the polite forms, "Thank you," and the others; but usually enough occasions occur in the daily school procedure to allow for sufficient practice. Commendation for remembering to do and say the correct thing helps children develop good social habits.

Children need to develop abilities both *to take and give directions*. Hearing well-given directions should aid pupils in formulating clear ones themselves. A teacher has many occasions to give directions to children. Some examples are: how to use the paste, how to put away materials, and what streets to take on the way home from school.

Perhaps the best test of the effectiveness of directions is the manner in which they are carried out.

Some common *situations* in which children should be able to give and take directions are these: how to make something, how to perform some act, how to reach a place, how to play a game. Besides the usual opportunities for giving and taking directions in school, teachers can arrange for others if necessary—a child can tell how he made his auto. If practice is necessary, children should feel that it is for some specific purpose or reason and not an unrelated activity.

Children should realize that certain *essentials* should be kept in mind in *learning* to *give directions*, such as (1) they should know the material to be explained, (2) they should tell only what is necessary, (3) they should organize what they are telling, so that the steps are given in the correct order, (4) they should be brief and concise, and (5) they should speak distinctly. Sometimes words are insufficient and the directions are made clearer if the speaker shows the steps in the procedure; for example, in telling how to play a game. Goodrich [1] gives the following suggestion. "The teacher should point out to children that directions are often made more clear by use of such words as these: first; now; then; next; up, down; front, back; here, there; over, under." Guides similar to those below help children plan and give directions for certain purposes.

How to Find a Place	How to Play a Game
Tell in which direction to go	Tell how many can play.
Tell how far to go.	Tell where they are to be.
Use left and right; not north, south, east, and west.	Tell in the right order what they are to do.
Tell something about the place that will help one know it.	Tell how they know who wins.

Children *convey messages* and *give announcements* both in and out of school. Outside school, occasions often arise, such as sending in a message to a neighbor, calling someone to the telephone, or sending an announcement to several people. In school there are actual occasions for sending messages to the next room, to a neighboring school, to a teacher, to a principal, and to the superintendent. These messages may be information about attendance, supplies, and procedures of the day.

[1] Goodrich, Bessie Bacon. *The Language Program,* Grades One and Two, 1936, p. 29. By permission of Charles E. Merrill Co. 1936.

The announcement may be of a program, some object of general interest in a room which others may see, a holiday or early dismissal, lost articles, material to be brought from home, new play apparatus, a meeting for the parents, and similar occasions.

Teachers need to keep two *considerations* in mind when arranging for a child to carry a message or make an announcement. First, the task should be within the child's ability. The child should understand what it is and its purpose. Second, it should be easily understood by those to whom it is given. An announcement for the kindergarten children needs to be simpler than one for the third grade. In order to carry messages and make announcements effectively, children need to realize that they should understand the meaning, select the important facts to be told, give it briefly, talk with feeling, and speak in tones which all can hear. Guides may help, for example,

For Lost Articles	For a Program
Tell what is lost.	Tell what is to be given.
Tell how it looked.	Tell where it is to be given.
Omit unnecessary facts.	Tell when it is to be given.

If there is some special purpose for the program, it is well to include a statement as to why it is being given and its cost.

Since there are so many occasions for children to participate in these activities, it is easy to find a purpose for teaching them. In order that children may acquire skill in delivering messages and making announcements accurately and pleasingly, practice is necessary. There may be "try-outs" to teach children to select the best one to be presented. They may use guides similar to the ones above as the basis for their selection. Perhaps one of the best motivations is that a pupil understands the crucial importance, not only to himself but to the whole room, of the announcement or explanation he is making—that is, the candy sale, attendance at the program, the reputation of the room, all depend on the success of his effort.

The *telephone* is used so commonly that even primary children should learn certain accepted procedures in answering calls and in making calls, and some of the courtesies involved. How much and what phases depend upon the age of the children.

The *methods* of teaching this to children and of developing the necessary skills may vary. If children come from homes equipped with telephones, there may be relatively little to be taught them. Information, however, concerning the values and purposes of using the telephone is in order for all. Many skills suggested in the section dealing with conversation are applicable here. In addition, there are certain forms and procedures pertaining to telephoning that differ from face-to-face conversation. During a unit on communication, information and development of skills related to telephoning fits in naturally or this may come in the regular language period. Class discussions concerning telephoning usually include some of the following points: (1) Time and effort are saved by the use of the telephone. Children may give illustrations from their home experiences and observations, such as using the telephone for business or for convenience. (2) People experience pleasure because they can converse with relatives and friends in this way. Children may know of long-distance calls from friends whom they seldom see. (3) The service of the telephone in case of illness, fire, and other emergencies is familiar to some and the discussion may emphasize its value. (4) Children's appreciation of this means of communication may be developed by showing them how many different people are responsible for telephone service. (5) The names of at least two parts of a telephone (mouthpiece and receiver) and their use should be learned through observation and explanation.

More *specific suggestions* on method follow. A first-grade teacher acting as principal answered the telephone frequently, and capitalized on this fact by instructing the children to receive calls. In this way, she had actual situations in which children learned the accepted procedures. Where there are no telephones to use in this way, dramatization serves the same purpose. The use of toy telephones adds realism. Children may impersonate different people in the community—doctor, grocer, garage man, and others. These names and the telephone number each child selects may be placed on the blackboard. The teacher acting as the operator may receive the number and call the person indicated. Some terms for a child to remember and some procedures to follow are:

1. When answering the telephone
   a. to answer the call promptly
   b. to answer by giving his name, not simply saying, "Hello"
   c. if someone is asked for, to say that he will call him, or that he is not there and ask if there is a message

2. When calling someone
    a. before calling, to look in the directory and to remember the correct number
    b. to tell who is calling rather than wait for the one called to ask
    c. if the person answering does not give his name to say, "Is this John Smith?"
3. When answering or calling
    a. to talk distinctly
    b. to talk slowly enough to be easily understood
    c. to keep the lips near the front of the mouthpiece
    d. to speak directly into the mouthpiece
    e. to talk in a pleasing voice and not too loudly
    f. when the conversation is finished, to say, "Good-bye."

Dramatic play is natural for children. Before school age they prepare meals in the sand pile, stir imaginary cakes, and boil make-believe coffee. A box is their auto and leaves form the outline of the garage. A board across stumps is the store where they buy leaves for cookies and twigs for candy. Their make-believe includes many familiar situations taken from their own environment. One may be father or mother, big brother, grandmother, doctor, or machinist. Their impersonations include a wide range of acquaintances. Children grow through play of all kinds, but dramatic play is especially effective in increasing understandings, appreciations, and exact knowledge. This spontaneous activity of children is incorporated in the school because it has such marked educational value.

To keep this dramatic play free and natural, the schoolroom should be one that invites and encourages activity. It must have an adequate supply of *materials*, such as (1) a play corner with furniture for playing house, (2) blocks for making buildings, furniture, (3) a doll to represent the baby of the family, (4) toys—dishes, small broom and dustpan, wagon, trains, and animals—which add realism to housekeeping, transportation, farming, a circus, or other activities, (5) real tools and materials for constructing more buildings, furniture, means of transportation, and other play forms, (6) sewing materials for making doll clothing or an apron, cap, and other bits of costume, (7) miscellaneous materials—spools, boxes, string, rubber—for unpredictable uses. Materials such as these not only add to the pleasure in dramatic play, but often suggest new play situations. In fact one important function of the teacher is to provide such stimulating materials. By so doing she achieves one of the essentials to be remembered in effective dramatic play, that is, she keeps herself in the background. She guides indirectly by suggesting play through the medium of materials.

It is doubtful that in the more formal type of dramatic play, or *dramatization*, the activities dominated by a teacher are of enough value in children's personality development to warrant the time spent upon them. She can accomplish a good deal, however, by assisting in planning, by providing experiences as bases for dramatization, and by clarifying points when the children are in doubt, by participating in the evaluation, and by encouraging those who lack confidence. She should remember that it is what the children do, using their own initiative, that most affects their growth. The degree of perfection with which the production is given is of minor importance. Therefore, original conversation and children's interpretation of situations far outshadow any memorization of formal conversation and stilted imitation of action. Plays already made for children should either be excluded in these grades or used with discrimination.

What children use as bases for their dramatic play or dramatization depends upon their environments and interests. The following suggest possibilities: (1) Vital, worthwhile experiences should provide many occasions for dramatic play. These experiences may be got on an excursion to see bread made or butter churned, a ride on a train or bus, a trip to a circus, or a shopping trip to buy a doll. Such experiences or phases of these experiences are often relived later in the schoolroom. These wholesome activities may serve to crowd out the robber-and-killing scenes which are sometimes in evidence in children's play. (2) Units of work furnish changes for characterization of those—the mail carrier, the air pilot—and interpretation of activities in different fields—activities centered around the farm, the store, and primitive life. (3) In dramatization of literary productions, children undertake a more difficult task, namely, to assume the concrete activities of designated characters. They do not create their own as in the more spontaneous dramatic play. Mother Goose rhymes provide excellent opportunities for beginning dramatization of literary materials. These are often dramatized by pantomime and require little if any conversation. (4) Children should help select stories appropriate for dramatization. They may set up standards as a guide, somewhat along these lines: (a) Does the number of characters suit our school?   (In a large school it is advisable to have several characters. In a small one too many might eliminate the possibility of using the selection.)   (b) Is there action in this story? (c) Could we play or pretend what is happening? (d) Is the story too long? (If it is long, excerpts may be selected and played.)   (5) Children may compose more formal plays of their own. With the younger children, these may be group or individual productions dictated by the children to the teacher.

The following are some of the *factors* to consider *in planning* for and *conducting* dramatization: (1) The youngest children are unconcerned about having an audience. Older children often express a desire to have someone see their play, in which case the teacher may be the audience. (2) Advance planning for dramatization is often done by second- and third-grade children. This may be conducted as a group or individual activity. If done by one child, a fine chance is offered him to explain his plans, request co-operation, and direct the play—all furnishing splendid opportunities for oral language expression. (3) Children may plan the dramatization of a story by organizing the material under the headings: Parts, Characters, Settings or Places, and Materials. (4) If a play is to be given before an audience, there should be opportunities for children to practice their parts and receive criticism. Several may try out for one part, the other children selecting the players on the merit of performance. (5) Three aspects of dramatization may be considered: planning, playing, and evaluating. The last is of special significance. The standard for judging should be the naturalness with which the children portray the characters and interpret the situations, not the finish and perfection of the performance. (6) Elaborate costumes and settings are unessential. Frequently merely a touch, such as a crown, makes a child feel the part of a king. Children enjoy bringing the necessary materials from home. Often backgrounds can be made with wrapping paper, paint, or other inexpensive materials. (7) Appropriate music may be incorporated to add to the effectiveness of the play.

Puppets instead of children may be the characters. The children manipulate the figures and have the benefit of the language experiences without being seen themselves. Three kinds of puppets most commonly used in school are stick puppets, finger puppets, and the puppets controlled by strings. See art section for further suggestions.

Opportunities for growth and *ability* to *use language effectively* constitute a major value of dramatic play and dramatization. (1) Conversational skills are developed by carrying on conversations between imaginary characters. Phrases and expressions supposedly characteristic of the farmer, doctor, or witches are incorporated in children's speech. (2) Vocabularies are enlarged and enriched since different situations require words pertinent to the field reproduced. (3) Discussion is in order after a plan for a play has been presented. (4) Opportunities

PUPPET SHOWS

An oral language device especially good for shy children.

for giving and taking directions occur if a manager is in charge of the production. (5) Flexibility of tone and voice develops naturally through impersonation of different characters. (6) Clear tone and enunciation are necessary when there is an audience. (7) Ability to organize is needed in composing plays, since a play contains a sequence of events based upon a central theme, a climax, and a satisfactory conclusion. (8) Children become more familiar with literature by dramatizing worthwhile selections.

There are many occasions at home and in social groups outside the home when the ability to *reproduce a good story* adds to everyone's pleasure. It may be the retelling of a story, an anecdote, or a joke one has either heard or read. This is an activity which children enjoy also in school. It is successful when the person enjoys the story himself, the audience wants to hear it, and it is well told. On the other hand, one should avoid reproducing a story that all have heard or read, retelling a story too complicated or too long for the ability of the pupil, and retelling a story unsuited to the audience. When a suitable story is to be retold it is better for a child to practice in order to be sure of the sequence of events and unusual expressions that are essential. This is usually unnecessary when telling a joke or short story. The stories being retold may be illustrated by pictures, a movie, or a pantomime given by some of the other children. Friendly discussion by the audience of the reasons for liking or disliking the content of the selection and the manner in which it was told often helps the story-teller to improve.

IN GRADES ABOVE THE PRIMARY

Some of the phases of oral language already discussed were considered on the primary level, but it is necessary to continue work on them in the *middle and upper grades* in order to raise the level of pupil development. For example, the simple forms of conversation in the primary grades are elaborated into a business interview in the upper grades.

Some objective facts concerning *conversation* have been found, mostly of a mechanical nature, such as errors children make in conversational speaking, methods of correcting such errors, and the like. There seems to be little or no objective evidence to guide a teacher in a broad positive program of teaching this very important oral language skill. There are, however, helpful suggestions now being used by successful teachers and supervisors. Miss McBroom's [1] statement of *abilities* and *knowledge involved* in *conversation* is of this type. The following items are adapted from her list: (1) having something to talk about, (2) the ability to observe common courtesies in conversation, (3) the ability to use correct speech techniques, (4) a knowledge of and the ability to use a pleasing vocabulary, (5) the ability to be a good listener, (6) the ability to change tactfully the topic of conversation, (7) the ability to talk without the use of mannerisms, (8) a knowledge of topics appropriate to certain occasions, (9) the knowledge of where and how to get interesting conversational material, (10) a knowledge of when and where it is not appropriate to talk, (11) the ability to make an introduction and to follow up with appropriate conversation, (12) the ability to be enthusiastic during a conversation, (13) the ability to carry on a business interview, (14)

[1] McBroom, Maude and others. *The Course of Study in Oral Composition.* Unpublished report. University Elementary School, State University of Iowa.

a knowledge of conversation during calls. While these items do not constitute a complete list of abilities and skills which may be used in conversation, they indicate quite well the ones in common use.

In successful teaching of conversation the idea that one must *have something to talk about* in order to converse interestingly is planted when the pupil starts to school, if it has not already been done, and is cultivated throughout his whole school experience. The topic of conversation should be closely related to the child's experiences or interests and should be important, at least to the child. Some types of topics are: (1) hobbies, pets, games; (2) exciting experiences at home or in travel; (3) contests in school or outside; (4) movies or plays; (5) interesting books; (6) home or community incidents or news.

Teaching preparation is a prerequisite for successful conversation. John should know that he is to lead in the conversation period on next Friday and not only that he must be prepared but also what such preparation involves; namely, that he should have his subject ready and be able to answer questions of his classmates. If they ask none, he should be prompt to ask his own questions on his topic and request his classmates' opinion. The same or like preparations would be made if a committee were in charge.

Another element important in learning the art of conversation is the ability to *observe* the *common courtesies* of this type of intercourse. Perhaps most if not all of the habits and skills which add up to the sum total of courtesy spring from the pupil's attitude toward his fellow beings. If he is considerate he will generally show it in his conversation. If he is rude, selfish, domineering, or thoughtless, he will in all probability not be very courteous in his conversation. It is obvious that courtesy must be developed early if suitable attitudes are to be formed. Some specific "rules" are of the following types: (1) Always be agreeable. (2) Express likes or dislikes with moderation. (3) Differ with another's view tactfully. (4) Change an unpleasant topic to a pleasant one. (5) Avoid completing another's statement or monopolizing the conversation. (6) Never knowingly say something to injure another. (7) Know how and when to interrupt another in conversation. Many other more specific "rules" might be named but these are sufficient to illustrate the breadth of the subject.

Every pupil, if he is not already, should learn to *be* a *good listener*. This of course implies active and intelligent listening. Some specific qualities required for this are: (1) an interest in what is being said, (2) ability to understand what the other person is talking about, (3) frankness to ask if the speaker is not understood, (4) ability to ask an occasional pertinent question, (5) a sympathetic attitude toward the speaker, (6) a real enjoyment in listening. Perhaps a direct attack on this is best, that is, one in which pupils do listen. Occasionally to check effectiveness of listening, the pupils may be asked to take notes, mental or written, or to answer questions about the conversation, The second suggestion may be used in a surprise check.

The *ability* to *use correct speech techniques* is not absolutely essential to successful conversation but is very significant, especially in some classes of society. A personality may outweigh or offset the effect of incorrect speech forms but it often takes a powerful one to do it, whereas, correct speech seldom, if ever, detracts from personality. Some factors to be considered in this connection are: (1) incorrect grammar, (2) slang or swearing, (3) control and use of voice and speech organs, (4) sentence order in paragraphs, (5) word order in sentences.

The ability to *talk without mannerisms* is one most adults lack to some degree but which children, especially when they begin to talk, possess almost perfectly. This, of course, includes only ordinary conversation, not that of an angry or hurt child. Some of the common mannerisms are: (1) toying with parts of clothing with fingers, face, hair, or other parts of the body; (2) putting hands in and out of pockets; (3) assuming poor posture of body, slouching or leaning against something. The general method of attack is, first, prevention by teaching the correct skills before the child has had opportunity to form bad habits, and second, to replace all faulty habits with correct ones. The pupils may become aware of correct habits from textbook reading, from class discussions, by experiment, by dramatization, and the like. Each pupil should find what he needs to work on and try hard each time he talks to overcome those particular bad habits and to build good ones. The positive program should be kept in the forefront.

The ability to *change a topic* of conversation is often very important, not only in school but all through life. Children should have actual instruction and practice in this. Some things that may be done to change the topic tactfully are: (1) Concede a difference of opinion. (2) Call attention to some other member of the group by asking him a question slightly off the topic being discussed. (3) Postpone the discussion for the time being, by changing position of the group or by introducing an entirely new element in which all are interested, such as a call to supper. (4) Tell a good joke aptly applied to the situation to get a good laugh. (5) Compare the present situation with something else as different as possible yet which still applies. Methods of teaching this ability seem to require first, a thorough class discussion of how it may be done, second, examples actually dramatized in class—the latter after preparation has been made—and third, extempore class examples perhaps led by the teacher.

The ability to *carry* on a *business interview* includes conversation in any situation concerned with exchange of information between two persons or small groups in a formal or semi-formal way. This statement uses the term "business" in the broad sense. Exercises in this ability should include: (1) making arrangements and preparations for an interview; (2) a knowledge of the etiquette of an interview— how to open it, how to proceed, how much time should be used, knowing the time to leave, how to end it, how to express appreciation; (3) how to pick the best time; (4) agenda for an interview; (5) knowledge of the person to be interviewed. Some form of dramatization may be used. For example, one member of the class may be the employer, others the applicants for a position. The remainder of the group may judge the effectiveness of the applications. Or the activity may be a sales talk, a request for a contribution to a worthy cause, or a call for information such as a reporter would make. If a set of standards is set up, the results are likely to be better.

The group *may improve* the *effectiveness* of their *conversation* period by using the following suggestions. (1) Give everyone an opportunity to participate. (2) See that each pupil feels a responsibility for the success of the period. (3) See that only one pupil speaks at a time. (4) Insist that all pupils listen while one is talking. (5) Make clear that intelligent listening is as much a part of conversation as talking. (6) Encourage everyone to ask questions freely. (7) Make a summary of the period directing attention to the strong points as well as the weak ones for use in future periods. The last suggestion probably should be done by the teacher and should be constructive and encouraging.

The second general situation listed in which oral language is used is the *use of the telephone*. The task of teaching seems to divide itself into two parts, (1) knowledge and actual use of the telephone, and (2) the courtesies attendant thereto. Teaching the facts pertaining to actual use is usually started in the primary grades by class discussion, experience chart, dramatization, and other procedures. These are continued on appropriate levels through the intermediate grades. The same thing is true of common courtesies of telephoning.

The *factors* usually mentioned in connection with the use of the telephone are: (1) In answering, an individual should announce his name, or if answering for a business firm, he should give the name

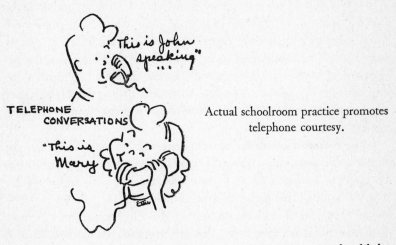

Actual schoolroom practice promotes telephone courtesy.

of the firm. (2) When completing a conversation one should be sure to replace the receiver carefully on its hook or cradle. (3) In making a call or closing a telephone conversation, certain steps are taken which ordinarily are taught in the primary grades. (See pp. 158-159.) (4) The telephone directory should be studied carefully to find what to do in case of emergency, such as fire, sickness, or accident. Pupils should know what to do to call a distant place, whom to call in case of telephone trouble, or lack of service. (3) It would be helpful to find out facts about the telephone, such as its history, number of 'phones, conversations (local and long distance), how the telephone works, and its importance in our everyday life. The telephone office of any city exchange would be glad to furnish some of the excellent available printed information.[1]

Another teaching device which may be used in any grade is a visit to the telephone exchange. If previous arrangements are made, the telephone management is usually pleased to co-operate in educating children to understand the telephone better. Preparation on the part of the pupils previous to the visit might consist of readings, class discussion, preparation of questions, organization of the trip. It probably is best for the pupils to work out the details of such a trip themselves. The teacher should see that important items are included, such as: What questions shall we ask? Who shall ask them? Who shall take notes? If all cannot see everything, who shall be selected? Should we talk little or much? If several grades make the trip (as in a rural school), how shall we arrange ourselves? Such precautions not only organize the expedition more effectively but tend to increase interest in it. It might be that the repair department would give an old telephone to the intermediate grades for experimental purposes. Possibly a student from the high school physics class would show just how the telephone works by using physics equipment.

The *common courtesies* of telephone conversation are much the same as for any other type. (1) Unless the call is urgent it should be made at a time likely to be most convenient to the person called. Early morning, late night, and meal-time calls are usually not welcome. (2) One should always respect the telephone rights of others and take no more time from the person called or the line than is necessary to complete the conversation. (3) Business telephones should not be used for social calls. When a call is made from a business office, it should be brief and appreciation should be expressed for the privilege. (4) Gossip, family affairs, or private business have no place in conversation over the telephone. Neither have long drawn-out visits of a half or three-fourths of an hour.

Another important form of oral language is *story-telling*. There

[1] The class might write for such materials to the American Telephone and Telegraph Company, New York City.

seems to be little doubt as to the value of this ability. In some form it can be used almost anywhere that oral language is used. Its interest extends through all ages. Some factors fundamental to successful teaching of this aspect of oral language in all grades are suggested below.

Both teaching and learning in story-telling should be *enjoyable*. If a large part of the class dislikes this activity, an investigation of the materials, methods, attitudes, and atmosphere of class work is most certainly due. If rightly done, story-telling is pleasing to both audience and story-teller in real life, and something is wrong if it is not so in the classroom.

The *character* of the story should fit the pupil. The teacher may restrict the pupil's work to certain areas but the choice within those limitations should be left to the pupil. The teacher may suggest that tomorrow is the day for jokes. This of course rules out adventure and all other kinds of stories for that particular period. But the pupil should be left free to select his own joke. The reason is obvious. If the pupil does his own selecting he is probably more likely to suit his own tastes and personality. If the pupil asks for assistance the teacher should be careful to help him to decide for himself—not to decide for him. To aid a slower pupil a teacher often suggests a list of topics or other information from which the pupil may select, or, better still, this may help him think of something himself.

There must be *standards* against which to measure performance. The success of teaching pupils how to tell stories depends largely upon the intelligent use of these standards. If they are too rigidly applied, or too prominently displayed they may ruin the informality and spontaneity of the learning and thus kill most if not all individual initiative. But if worked out and established one at a time by the children themselves, as their powers develop, all discreetly supervised by the teacher, they may become stepping stones to splendid levels of attainment. Such a set of standards undoubtedly would contain these:

1. Be sure to have a good story.
2. Be sure you know your story well.
3. Get so interested in your story that you show it to the audience.
4. Be yourself while telling the story; talk just as you always do.

5. Speak so that all can hear and understand.
6. Use words that fit the story well.
7. Do your best to use correct forms of speech.
8. Be as natural as you can in standing or sitting and look directly at your audience.
9. Vary the tone in which you speak.

Careful preparation should be made before attempting to tell a story. This preparation depends upon the type of story to be told, but it may include:

1. Deciding what story to use
2. Reading or thinking it through
3. Making an outline of it in mind or on paper
4. Thinking of a good way to open or introduce the story
5. Telling the story at least twice, preferably aloud, to one's self
6. Making any changes which should be needed
7. Telling it again to one's self with the changes

The wise teacher spends much time with the pupils in this preparation. Not only should this get better class results but it should aid in fixing the idea that such preparation should be made.

Class instruction periods may be divided into at least two types: The first is devoted to practice by pupils who wish suggestions and criticisms of their efforts. The practice class period is really one in which everyone works on his own deficiencies. The second is given over to the finished "products" of individual pupil effort. In this period each pupil does his best after adequate preparation. He is put "on the spot" as a performer. This recital type should be used with caution. If it is over-emphasized, enjoyment and individual initiative may suffer or be wholly lost.

The right use of *illustrative materials* makes a story more interesting and makes the telling easier. Teachers can assist bashful or timid pupils to lose their self-consciousness, by encouraging them to use materials as they tell stories. A good example of this use was in the story of shoes, in which the pupil showed the different parts as he told about the making of a shoe.

Each pupil should be *encouraged to be himself* and tell his story in his own way. Direct imitation of the teacher's vocabulary, qualities of voice, and mannerisms should be frowned upon. Without doubt some imitation is helpful, especially if the pupil takes merely the idea and applies it in his own way. This is asking a difficult thing of the teacher. Usually the stronger a teacher's personality, the more her pupils will be inclined to imitate her, and hence the greater the possibility that their own personality development will be retarded. Stimulating the pupil just enough to produce self-help and consequent self-development is certain proof of artistic teaching.

Formal public speaking is a type not used so often in ordinary pupil or adult life as other oral language abilities. At times, however, its need may be imperative. Furthermore, the person who can speak well in public has a distinct advantage over those who cannot. Since there are opportunities in the regular school life of intermediate and upper-grade pupils for public speaking there seems to be every reason why such training should be given. The teacher may utilize reports of meetings, experiments, hobbies, or visits and debates organized around historical, social, or economic subject matter fields. This type of work need not be done often but should be done occasionally and should be of a formal nature following thorough preparation. Different types of speeches may grow directly out of a wide variety of situations introduced in the classroom. A birthday anniversary, the return of a long-absent pupil, visitor's day, special successes of the class or some child, presentation of a gift, afford opportunities for practice in public speaking.

The *abilities required* in public speaking are similar to those outlined above for story-telling. Certainly among these would be the following abilities: (1) to choose a proper topic for the occasion; (2) to organize into an outline the main ideas of the speech; (3) to commit to memory the things to be said, or to write them into good composition form; and (4) to speak clearly to an audience without annoying mannerisms.

The *methods* of teaching may be on a more individual plane than in story-telling. Otherwise the same procedure may be used. One major objective is to keep the pupil in his natural frame of mind and retaining his desire to tell something of interest. Oratory may be left for high school or college.

Answering questions constitutes a considerable amount of oral composition both in and out of school. We answer questions for at least three reasons: (1) to give information—"What is today's date?"

(2) to meet an argument—"What reasons do you have for making such a statement?" (3) in response to an urgent request or demand—"Tell me, how did it happen?" This form of oral language is closely related to other forms and because of the direction given by the question in each instance, less attention to actual teaching is needed. Nevertheless, so many evasive answers are heard even among adults that one wonders if answering questions is so easy after all. Just one example will illustrate this. In reply to the question, "What is a difference between common and proper nouns?" this answer was given, "A common noun refers to all members of a class, while a proper noun refers to a particular person or thing." This response passed without challenge though it did not answer the question and gave only the definition for each kind of noun, leaving the listener to get the difference for himself.

Below is a list of *factors* involved in answering questions: (1) a clean-cut concept of what the question asks; (2) a straightforward reply without the injection of unnecessary words or ideas, whether the answer be positive or negative; (3) a true answer, not opinion or sheer guess; (4) an opinion labeled as such if the answer is unknown; (5) no hesitation in saying that the answer is unknown; (6) further explanation if a question is not fully understood; (7) plenty of time to analyze and think a question through; (8) a courteous and easily understood answer; (9) an evasive answer indicating the ideas or feelings of the person answering.

Children's answers should be stated clearly enough to be heard and should receive recognition. Some teachers have the deadening habit of repeating and correcting pupils' answers. This not only encourages slovenly replies but relieves the pupil of all responsibility for precise answers. In addition, it detracts materially from the artistry of teaching.

Questioning is done for a variety of purposes, such as motivating a pupil to pursue a topic further; determining whether the pupil has certain facts; and stimulating reasoning or the making of inferences.

The motivating question is often used to stimulate interest in a new situation, such as introducing a new unit, opening a class period, or starting a new topic. Such questions as "How would you like to find what makes this machine work?" open the door for an interesting preview of coming experiences. To stimulate further effort one might ask, "What do you suppose happened after that?"

It is comparatively easy to formulate questions that require factual answers—often only one word or a short phrase. This may be one reason why teachers use this type so much—perhaps too much. "Who invented the reaper?" "When did World War I end?" "What is the largest state of our country?" are questions of this type. The short-question fact-answer level of so-called teaching uses this kind of question almost entirely, usually with the textbook open before the teacher. This type of question, however, is used more effectively to bring out basic facts later used in problem solution, in checking vocabulary, in various types of directed reading exercises, and in other effective ways.

Questions that require reasoning through the use of facts, that encourage pupils to interpret printed or spoken matter, or that require the solution of problems are perhaps the most difficult to formulate and are undoubtedly of greatest value in teaching. Some questions of this type are: "Why can beef from Argentina be sold in New York (without duty) more cheaply than beef produced in Iowa?" "Why did Chicago grow where it is?" "How can the topsoil of Township X be most effectively conserved?" Not only are these questions difficult for the teacher to word; they are also hard for pupils to understand and to answer correctly. For example, to answer the questions about beef, a pupil must discover and deal with several factors, among which are: (1) beef cattle prices in Argentina; (2) beef cattle prices in Iowa; (3) cost of packing in Argentina; (4) cost of packing in Iowa; (5) cost of transportation from Argentina; and (6) cost of transportation from Iowa. The facts must be organized in much the same way as one arranges data in solving an arithmetic problem to insure a logical answer. In pupil development, one such question properly thought through and answered is worth all the time and effort it takes of all concerned. This kind of question is often also highly motivating.

Miscellaneous uses of questioning may include those which: (1) guide reading or thinking; (2) promote rapid reading, such as skimming; (3) point to word recognition and meaning; (4) direct organization of reading or discussion; (5) stimulate interest in a specific item or idea; (6) aid in the selection of the main idea of a paragraph; (7) guide in the use of glossary, charts, tables, maps, etc.; (8) help in the organization of information obtained from sources other than books.

It is obvious that one type of question may become another type, depending on the use made of it. For example, the fact question "What is the answer to this riddle?" may be highly motivating and could cause a lot of reasoning in the case of one pupil; whereas for another pupil, who has heard a similar question asked and answered correctly, it may arouse very little mental activity.

The ability to *conduct meetings* of a more *formal nature* has been receiving more school attention in recent years. One-room rural schools as well as the larger ones have clubs or groups which hold meetings and conduct programs at regular times throughout the school year. These are conducted by the pupils themselves with the teacher in the background. Pupils get excellent practice in simple parliamentary procedure, in proper decorum at meetings of this type, as well as in oral language forms. If the teacher makes sure each pupil knows why we have such formal procedures and knows their values, additional benefits will accrue. Textbooks have good outlines and suggestions to guide both pupils and teacher besides those of the regular books on parliamentary procedure.

Normal *speech development* in the elementary grades usually accompanies the oral language activities suggested above for the various grade levels. This development is conditioned by the pupil's experiences before starting to school and is modified later by his school and community contacts. In far too many instances,[1] however, speech does not develop normally, and elementary teachers find themselves confronted by a great range of speech problems. Teachers of the elementary grades, generally speaking, have had little specific training in speech and probably should not attempt to correct such difficulties as (1) a wide variety of voice problems involving quality, pitch, loudness, and melody, often accompanied by tenseness, lack of resonance, personality inhibitions, or faulty breathing; (2) defects of speaking rhythm, such as rapid speech with slurring of words or indistinct enunciation and stuttering, which most teachers recognize; and (3) major problems of articulation resulting from a partial loss of hearing, cleft palate, tongue-tie, or general nervous disorders. Cases of these

[1] In 1931, the White House Conference on Child Health and Protection reported that one million children in the United States needed remedial treatment and training.

types should be referred to specialists if such help is available. In the absence of such direct assistance, the teacher or school official should seek the aid of the state department of education, some state speech organization, or a college speech department to obtain competent advice if not actual personal direction. If thrown back on her own, the teacher may follow suggestions in manuals on speech correction.[1]

The three phases of speech education which the average elementary teacher can deal with will be discussed more fully. This is done with the understanding that speech practice work is made an integral part of all the regular school activities and is not put in a separate period for itself alone.

The speech education necessary for proper *social adjustment* is normally given in the oral language training of the elementary school. See pages 147ff. for suggestions on the primary level and pages 163ff. for intermediate and upper grades.

Development in *semantics* (use of words in their correct meanings) in its relation to speech is closely connected with the learning of oral vocabulary and other work in word meanings. For the primary level see pages 147-148.

Problems of *articulation in speech* are approached in much the same manner as those in any other communication skill. Poor spelling, poor handwriting, and poor phrasing in written composition are counterparts to improper letter sounds, poor speaking rhythm, and a monotone voice in speaking.

Since the consonants are a greater cause of difficulty in speech intelligibility than vowels, disabilities in them are usually considered first.

Fessenden[2] gives the following order of speech sound check and treatment:

---

[1] Manser, Ruth B. *Speech Correction on the Contract Plan.* Prentice-Hall, Inc., N. Y. 1937.

Birmingham, Anna I. and Knapp, P. K. *First Lessons in Speech Improvement.* Charles Scribners Sons, N. Y. 1922.

Avery, E., Dorsey, Jane, Sickels, V. A. *First Principles of Speech Training.* D. Appleton-Century, Inc. N. Y. 1928.

Fairbanks, Grant. *Voice and Articulation Drillbook.* Harper & Brothers, N. Y. 1940.

Gullan, Marjorie. *Speech Training in the School.* Evans Brothers, Ltd., London.

[2] Fessenden, Seth A. *Speech and the Teacher,* p. 178. Longmans, Green and Co., Inc., N. Y. 1946.

1. Lip sounds—*p*, *b*, *m*, *w*, *f*, *v*.
2. Tongue front sounds—*t*, *d*, *n*, *l*, *r*, *s*, *z*, *th*, *y*.
3. Tongue back sounds—*k*, *g*, *ng*.
4. Affricates and combinations—*sh*, *ch*, *zh*, *j*, *st*, *str*, etc.
5. Vowels—*a*, *e*, *i*, *o*, *u*.

The same writer[1] also suggests the order of corrective procedures:

1. Make a general selection of pupils with possible speech defects.
2. Analyze the speech difficulties of individual pupils who apparently need speech correction.
3. Ascertain if possible the cause or causes of the difficulty in each case. This step should indicate whether the teacher should attempt remedial work.
4. Help pupils to realize their handicaps and to want aid in overcoming their difficulties.
5. Be sure the pupil recognizes the differences between the desirable and the undesirable sound.
6. Help the pupil make the correct sounds and be sure that he knows that he is making them.
7. Help the pupil to use the correct sounds until they become automatic.

This should be done as much as possible under supervision. The latest research in speech training seems to show that much effective work can be done in group correction, especially with children who have similar types of disorder. Moreover, the added stimulus of group activities seems to give benefits not available through individual teaching. This later research assigns the regular classroom teacher a much larger part in speech correction than it had heretofore been thought wise for her to assume.

---

[1] *Op. cit.* p. 178. Adapted.

CHAPTER 8

WRITTEN AND CREATIVE LANGUAGE

WRITTEN LANGUAGE

IN PRIMARY GRADES

ALTHOUGH most of the language needs in the *primary grades* are satisfied by oral expression, there are situations requiring written language. If children are well developed, have good muscular control, and are learning manuscript writing, some simple beginnings are suitable even for the first grade. Before children attempt the mechanical techniques of writing, they can compose and dictate work to the teacher, such as notes, letters, stories, and compositions written by her on the blackboard. Thus they may become familiar with the physical forms of capital letters, punctuation marks, and sentences as well as of other types of written work. The two different phases of written work are the above introductory phases leading up to written language work, and the actual writing by the children which may be discussed under the following headings: writing letters (this includes greetings, invitations, and notes of thanks); making written accounts; filling in forms; making labels and signs; making memoranda and lists; and doing creative work. The order of discussion which follows is not intended to indicate either the importance or order of presenting the different phases.

When we consider the number of letters received every day in cities, towns, and rural districts, it is easy to believe that *letter writing* heads the list of written language forms used in daily living. Even a

177

young child delights in adding a scribble to his mother's letter to grandmother. Later he asks to enclose the letter which he has written with great effort, with many requests for help in spelling. One wonders why this pleasure is often lost in later years, and why the writing of letters and notes frequently becomes a burden. To some extent the schools have been at fault by neglecting to emphasize the needs, occasions, and content of letter composition, and by putting too much emphasis on form.

There are *needs* for writing notes and letters in every school, such as writing to a child who has moved away, writing for permission to visit some place of interest, or asking for materials to use in school.

The *methods* used depend upon the abilities of the group. Most children have some knowledge of letters when they enter school. (1) Begin by showing children actual letters. One might post a letter received by the school on the bulletin board. (2) Read letters of interest to acquaint pupils with the salutation, the signature, and the body, as well as other parts of a letter. (3) Explain the purpose of these parts to help them realize the reasons for letter forms. They should understand from the start that letters are written to carry information to someone and, therefore, that the content is important. (4) Help children to dictate letters co-operatively. This can be done early in the first year. (5) Give the children, when they have learned to write their names, an opportunity to sign the copy which the teacher makes. The first actual writing of a letter may come with the ability to write a sentence. Words they need to use may be written on the board for reference. Then pupils are ready for two essential parts of a letter, the body and the signature. The only new difficulties in completing the letter form are writing the sentence and the name in their proper positions. More complicated forms are taken up as pupils expand their capacities. Observation of addresses on envelopes helps in understanding their purpose. Third-grade children should be able to address their envelopes. Often the letter form which children copy on one level is used on the next higher level in independent letter writing.

The following are suggestions for *grading the difficulties* in presenting letter writing form beginning with the easiest and increasing in difficulty.

1.
    Please come and see us.
                  Jack

2.
   Dear Will,
     Please bring your dog
over.
                Joe

3.
          Sheldon, Iowa
   Dear Mother,
     Please come and visit our
school.
               Ted

4.
         Watertown, Ohio
         January 10, 1950

Dear Mary,
   May we come to see your
dog?
        Second Grade

5.
         Austin, Texas
         January 10, 1950

Dear Fred,
   I had a ride in an airplane
yesterday. We were up a
half hour. It was thrilling.
I'll tell you about it when I
see you.
        Your friend,
          Harry

Gradation of difficulties in teaching addressing of letters may be (1) Write names only, as the address for a note. (2) Copy full address. (3) Write full address by yourself.

Four other procedures that aid in obtaining good results in writing letters at the different levels of development are: (1) discussing its content with children before they begin to write, (2) reviewing, perhaps on the board, the form to be used, and (3) helping children to practice writing salutations, the name of town, state, and date before incorporating these into a letter. (4) Children may help themselves by questions in chart form, such as:

1. Did I tell things that the person would like to hear?
2. Did I make my letter interesting?
3. Did I spell the words correctly?
4. Did I put the parts of the letter in the correct position?

Sending *greetings* appropriate for the holidays and birthdays affords occasions for simple short expressions of good wishes. After different wordings have been discussed and the teacher has put the one selected on the board, the children may copy it. The greeting may be "A happy day" on their birthday cards to John, "I love you" in the folder for Mother's Day, or "Spring is here" for the Easter message. Making individual and original greetings should follow this co-operative work.

Developing the ability to extend a correct oral *invitation* is preparation for work in writing invitations. (See page 154 for suggestions.) Even first-year children can co-operatively dictate an invitation, which they feel is their own even though the teacher makes the copy that is sent out. Later, in the primary grades, they can copy one themselves; and still later they can compose invitations individually. Children should realize that an invitation calls for a reply—either an acceptance or a regret. Helping children to form these answers may be accomplished by using a plan similar to that suggested for making invitations. The following are examples of invitations:

1. Co-operative invitation to be written by the teacher

   Dear Third Grade,

   We are having a Hallowe'en party Friday at three o'clock. We hope that you can come.

   First Grade

2. Co-operative invitation for education week dictated and copied by the children

   Dear Mother and Father,

   We should like to have you visit our school next week.

   John

3. Individual invitation written by one child to a friend in another room

   Dear Mary,

   We have a pet turtle in our room. We hope you can come and see it.

   Helen

Frequently a *note expressing appreciation or gratitude* for some favor brings pleasure and satisfaction to both the sender and the receiver. An occasion for such a note may be in writing to thank people who have been connected with a school excursion, who have loaned some article, or who have talked to the school. There is even greater gain if this carries over into the home and the children receive encouragement from that source.

Some of the *desired outcomes* from practice in letter writing are: (1) understanding the reasons for writing letters, (2) understanding that different kinds of letters are appropriate for different occasions, (3) knowledge of the form of a letter, (4) consideration of information the receiver will enjoy, and (5) enjoyment in writing letters.

Through the ages men have kept *accounts in writing* of personal experiences and general events. Children of primary age enjoy this activity in various forms. Distinct values in language development result from the process of making, and later using, such accounts. (1) The first-grade pupils discover a booklet telling them of the farm trip the children of the previous year took and, after seeing it, they decide to enlarge on this experience by visiting the creamery and learning more about milk. (2) The second grade, at the close of the year, finds real enjoyment in reviewing the year's experiences by looking through their "Year Book." (3) The first grade dictates a composition to the teacher and uses it for a reading lesson. The reading of such accounts in whatever form they may be, helps children of any grade to realize that there is valuable reading material outside of books. (4) Children help to formulate rules and recipes which save time later on. (5) Greater respect and more appreciation of their own work is felt if a written account is made of it.

There are certain *factors* to keep in mind in helping children make accounts of their experiences. These accounts (1) should be childlike in composition form. If, in lower grades, these accounts are dictated by the children and written by the teacher, care should be taken to avoid using adult language. (2) Children should learn to select the important items and to realize that these accounts do not always need to be complete reports. (3) These accounts need to be clear and definite, whatever their form. A guide like the following one, used in chart form, helps children to make their accounts and to criticize them.

Is it interesting?
Does it tell the important facts?
Is it easily understood?
Is it true?

(4) Reports of experiences, to be of value must be accurate. Children should realize that unless accounts of happenings are true they are useless as records. In addition, an inaccurate record may be misleading and even detrimental.

Accounts of this nature may take a *variety of forms*—pictures, charts, dictated compositions, rules, recipes, newspapers, and diaries. The form will vary, depending upon the age of the children, the purpose, and the subject.

The use of *pictures*, drawn or cut out freehand by the children or obtained from magazines, is recommended. Individual drawings made after a trip and mounted with captions will tell the main features observed. These pictures may be combined in booklet form and placed on the reading table. One about "Our Trip to the Depot," might contain the pictures of the children riding in cars, at the depot, talking with the agent, in the train, near the baggage truck, and others. Catalog and magazine pictures cut out and mounted under the correct headings are means of depicting information gained. For example, in connection with the food unit, pictures of vegetables, fruits, meats, and beverages mounted on large charts under appropriate headings, or mounted on different pages for individual booklets, help in developing organization and in showing what information has been acquired.

Making charts is a graphic and simple way for young children to present information. Before they learn to write, drawings, cuttings, and other methods may be used to give the information. A large sheet of paper divided into sections headed with subtitles pertaining to the main topic gives the background for mounting the appropriate materials. Below is the suggestion for a chart to be used in connection with the transportation unit. This offers the chance for children to show the different means of travel they have observed. Such a chart may be large enough to enable the children, as the unit progresses, to indicate by drawings different ways in which people travel.

Ways We Have Seen
People Travel

On land
In the air
On water

Similar charts may have such headings as

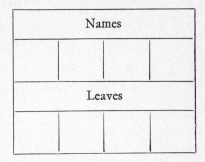

What We Raised in Our Garden

Vegetables

Flowers

Trees We Have Seen

Names

Leaves

Dictated compositions also have their place. With the youngest children the teacher's guidance by the means of questions and remarks determines to a large extent the wording of the composition. (See Reading, pp. 78-79.) Deciding on a title is important. Sometimes this is done before the composition is written, sometimes after its completion. When such a composition is finished and read, teacher and children can see the need of re-organization and editing. For example, if all the sentences begin with "We" or "It," other words may be substituted. The teacher will probably wish to copy the composition in permanent form, using good manuscript writing. It is then ready for use as a room chart or, if smaller, as part of a booklet for the reading table; or, if in a small edition, it may be put in individual composition booklets for children to take home. After children have contributed to the construction of composite compositions, they often dictate compositions individually to be used in these same ways. As they progress, they occasionally write their names as signatures to their individual work. If a booklet is made, a table of contents listing the compositions helps children to appreciate the book more, and understand better, that part of book "set-up." These booklets are more attractive if illustrated. When children have learned to write, they will write their own accounts of experiences and events. The compositions below were dictated to the teacher who copied them into booklets for the reading table.[1] The table of contents lists the compositions in one booklet.

---

[1] Campus Elementary School, Iowa State Teachers College.

FIRST GRADE—Booklet "Minnie's Birthday Party"
(made after returning from a party at Minnie's farm home)

JOHN GETS SCARED

When we went to visit the cows they were all lying down when we went in. They got up in such a hurry they scared me and made me jump. We went over to another place and there were some other cows that I didn't know about.

John

SECOND GRADE—Booklet "Our Trip"

THE RIDE TO THE GREENHOUSE

We went to the greenhouse on the streetcar. On the way we saw the water tower. We wondered what the white thing on the top of the tower was. We saw a big pile of leaves. We got off and went to the greenhouse.

Lavene

Rules may be long or short, but need for making them co-operatively often occurs in schools where children are "living." Perhaps there is too much talking at the reading table. This situation is discussed and the group decides to put up a notice. Effective wording is the next problem. Several suggestions may be offered: "Don't talk," "Please do not talk," "Please be quiet," and "Think of the others." There is discussion of these different forms of the rule and one is selected, written, and posted. As criteria for judging rules, questions in chart form are helpful:

> Is there a need?
> Does it tell what is wanted?
> Is it polite?
> Will it help?

Other situations involving a possible need for rules are conduct on school grounds, caring for materials, manner of going to and from school. These usually consist of several sentences and are put on the blackboard or chart.

Directions found in a school "Record Book" may include not only recipes for things to eat but also directions for accomplishing some piece of work as carried on in the past by a former class. Such guidance is of real help in a school using activities which involve different types of materials. The need may be directions for making maple sugar, firing clay, making furniture for the library corner, or for making jelly and cookies for a party. Some group may have experimented with more than one recipe and as a result composed one of its own or left directions of what it had done. To be of value, a recipe should be brief and accurate (as should all instructions), thus saving time, materials, and effort.

The school *newspaper* in the primary years consists mainly of items of outstanding interest which have occurred during the school day. These are usually dictated at the close of the day or early the next

An idea usable on all grade levels.

morning. Such items lack the organization around definite themes that is true of compositions. Children may become familiar with the days of the week and dates through writing successive issues of the paper. Large sheets of unprinted newspaper or wrapping paper serve admirably if newspapers are to be copied and kept. At the end of a week or two these sheets should be bound and added to the reading table material. Third-grade children may study the different sections of a real newspaper, plan, and carry out the make-up of a paper, which includes news, stories, sport items, science information, and cartoons.

Keeping diaries furnishes a fine motive for writing dates and sentences. When a school diary is kept co-operatively the children, by discussion, often decide upon the items to be used. These are placed on the blackboard and then copied into the school diary or into each pupil's book. Later, the children may want to keep individual diaries. One short, interesting, concise sentence is better than many sentences, poorly written. If keeping a daily diary is a burden, a short period set aside two or three times a week, over a period of a month or more, gives children an opportunity to improve greatly in sentence composition and form. Occasions will arise when it is desirable to refer to the diaries to find out or confirm when certain events took place. Children can make their own booklets to serve as diaries. Cover designs add to their attractiveness.

Filling in forms correctly is a necessary skill in daily life. It may be necessary, for example, to give information required to join an organization, or to fill in an order blank for a new bicycle. Two fundamentals are necessary for satisfactory work when filling in forms: (1) knowing where to write the information called for and (2) knowing how to write the information correctly. Children should understand that one reason for learning this is that they may be prepared when asked such questions, as, "What is your name?" "Where do you live?" "What is your father's name?" "What is your telephone number?" "How old are you?" As soon as the pupil is able to read, a simple form like the following may be put on the board, and each child asked to give his personal information orally. Later he will write it. Name ———— Home ———— How old ————. At first, explanations should be made concerning the use for all the common forms called for. After that, practice is justifiable in order to prepare the children for the various situations where the forms will be used.

In schools where children participate daily in the care of the room and equipment, the need for *making labels* and *signs* occurs frequently. Labels are used to show contents, to indicate ownership, and to specify location. The first occasions in school when children need to label are for indicating what belongs to them—a book, locker, rubbers, etc. Where there are materials and tools for school work, labels indicating where they are kept help save time and materials, as well as improve the appearance of the room. Labels show which boxes contain the scissors, the different colored crayons, etc. Certain spaces on the library shelves are assigned to the picture books, story books, and others. Nature study materials brought for display purposes; pictures for the room, and those that children make for booklets; folders for keeping pictures; containers for seeds to be kept until spring; jelly made and put away for the Thanksgiving party—all these should be labeled. Consideration of the children's age and ability should guide the procedures. Before children can read, some teachers give each child a picture to be pasted on his locker. This serves as a label of identification. Each child can learn to recognize a picture before he can recognize his name. He benefits by pasting these labels on the objects himself. Later the teacher may use the child's name for labeling his possessions and thus he becomes familiar with it before he can write. When he begins to write, using his name for labels will furnish a real motive for practice in writing it.

Signs are used as reminders or notices of procedures. In fact they may be briefly stated rules. Some illustrations of occasions and places where signs are needed and suggestions for such signs are given below:

In the library corner:
  "We have new books today."
  "Books in place."
  "Turn pages properly."
  "Come often."
Near the sand box:
  "Sweep up the sand."
In the museum corner:
  "Please do not handle."
On a piece of paper posted on the bulletin board, to be given to those making preparations for the noon lunch:
  "Hot lunch today.
  Write your name here."

When painting wooden objects:
  "Fresh paint."
Near the tool rack:
  "Keep tools in their places."
In the store:
  "Oranges—30 cents"
  "Fresh vegetables"
When making doll dresses or curtains in play corner:
  "We need some cloth.
  Who can bring some?"

The procedures for writing signs are similar to those for making labels. The making of signs often develops from a specific situation. This is discussed, and the children realize need for a notice. Teachers make the signs at first, and the children may post them in appropriate locations where they serve as guides. Later the children make copies and the best written copy is selected to be used. The fact that children see the need for signs and try to make them independently, shows real understanding of the value of rules.

The *appearance* of both *labels* and *signs* should be given attention. The following points to be emphasized are: (1) The size and shape of the paper should fit the wording and the posting location. (2)

There should be margins around the words. As with other mounted material, the rule of the bottom margin wider than the top and the side margins equal should be followed by older children. (3) A narrow edge of color adds attractiveness to the sign or label. This may be done by mounting the paper or oak tag on a slightly larger piece of colored construction paper. (4) Certain uniformity of size, writing, and paper should be observed in a group of labels or signs used together.

Memoranda, lists, and *outlines* are similar in form. All of these are good memory aids but there is an additional use for outlines, namely, promoting intelligent organization. Some of the occasions when children may use memoranda or lists are: remembering to bring articles from home, listing questions for which they wish to find answers on an excursion, showing the order of procedure in carrying on a piece of work. Some of the needs for classifying or listing items under proper headings are: listing "Food—Dishes—Games" when planning a picnic; classifying animals under "Pets—Those That Help—Wild" when conducting a unit on "Animal Life." Outlines considered as plans to aid in oral composition work are discussed on pages 146-147. The plan of procedure is this: (1) children dictate the items either co-operatively or individually and the teacher writes them, (2) later, the children copy the lists, and (3) finally, the children themselves, list the items in the outline under the proper headings.

IN GRADES ABOVE THE PRIMARY

A brief restatement of some *basic factors* underlying written language teaching as viewed from the *intermediate and upper-grade* levels might be helpful at this point.

First, both teacher and pupils should realize that each form of *written language has a purpose.* While we do not use some forms as much as others, each has its respective values which are important even though used infrequently. For example, most of us do not write reports as often as we write letters but when we do, we should strive for clarity of subject matter and arrangement.

A second factor concerns itself with the *ways* and *means* of *realizing* to the utmost the *values* of each form of written composition—for example, What is the most effective way of making an announcement? How should one make notes so that they be most usable? What are some helpful suggestions in writing a short story?

A third important element relates to the *type* of *pupil* being developed. How may a particular form of written composition be best fitted to the children? Undoubtedly the mental and social levels should be considered as well as the pupils' experiences, past and present, their immediate interests and attitudes, and even the possibilities of the future.

The fourth general factor is that written composition be *taught* in *natural situations*. Undoubtedly this and the third factor are closely related. It may be that not all language teaching can be done in the daily run of the pupil's experiences, yet advantage should be taken of every opportunity. Undoubtedly periods of practice on certain fundamentals will be necessary. To make sure of the final objective, pupils should have ample opportunity to make the different types of written composition function in actual situations.

The fifth factor suggests that some sort of *check* be made on the *results* of teaching and learning to determine progress and the success of methods used. Rather satisfactory measures of change may be made if objective tests of growth in ability in this field or even those which give a reliable cross-section of achievement are applied. If such tests are not available, the teacher and class may set up standards and occasionally judge a sample of each pupil's work by these standards. An individual pupil record of these ratings would give each pupil at least a subjective idea of his progress.

The work to be done in the grades above the primary usually is outlined definitely in the textbooks; and that sequence is followed by most teachers. Moreover, the foundations for most forms of written composition already have been laid in the primary grades. It seems, then, that the suggestions given here for grades above the primary would be most helpful if they (1) built upon the primary grade foundations and (2) rendered assistance in ways not ordinarily given in texts.

Perhaps the most important task in teaching written composition is effective instruction of *letter writing*. The extensions of this type of written language usually taught in the grades above the primary are: (1) re-emphasis on the purposes of letters and the variety of types of letters which corresponds to the various purposes; (2) greater emphasis upon meaningful and interesting content attractively arranged; (3) letters of more than one paragraph; (4) a closer check on language usage, greater insistence on correct forms, and less use of trite or meaningless phrases and statements; (5) some sort of measuring instrument to check both content and form. Elaboration of these extensions should be of value to the teacher.

The *purposes* of the various kinds of letters shold be stated so effectively that pupils will not only know what these purposes are but really desire to become more proficient in the use of them. The following may serve as good ways to make this emphatic: (1) Imagine (with the class) our own country with no means of sending messages of any kind, by letter, either printed or written. What effect would it have on each of us, our homes, our community, our country? Guide the pupils in making lists of the things we do by letter, lists of the kinds of letters we write, and lists of the ways letters help us.

It is hardly possible to over-emphasize good letter *content*. The purpose of the letter determines what its content should be. But whatever the purpose, the content should be suitable for the occasion, fit the personalities both of the writer and recipient, and fully convey the message intended. In searching for elements which make social letters interesting, one investigator [1] analyzed social letters of high quality. The factors which to him seemed to stand out are a spirit of courtesy, an air of informality, a delicate yet effective sense of humor, an attitude of cheerfulness, frank but careful expression of feelings and opinions, restricted scope of discussion, and clean-cut statements. The teacher, of course, should go further and make clear by example and suggestion that the "spirit of courtesy" usually is present in letters when it overflows from the life of the letter writer. One is likely to write courteous letters when he has a kindly and a sympathetic feeling toward the person to whom he writes. Form may make a letter attractive but only content can make it real. Form may please the eye, but content satisfies the spirit.

Children should be taught from the beginning that *each main thought* introduced in the letter should be put into a new paragraph. This is as difficult a task as any the language teacher faces. It sometimes helps to require pupils to put in brief outline form what they plan to write in the letter. Thus each main outline heading might be the mian idea of a paragraph. A most helpful device is one which

[1] Johnson, R. I. *English Expression*, p. 68. Public School Publishing Co. 1926.

compels pupils to think through what they plan to write and put it into some orderly written form before they begin the actual writing.

The intermediate and upper grades should be expected to *use written forms* on a higher intellectual and technical plane than the earlier grades. Correct and increasingly original expressions may be expected. Grammatical and spelling errors should disappear by the end of the upper grades or before. Moreover, pupil attitude toward them should become definite and strong. Perhaps this may grow from class discussions of why such improvement should be made, why letters without errors or trite phrases are better, and how this kind of improvement helps the pupils themselves.

Standards of some kind are necessary for the most effective teaching. This applies to both letter content and form. The standards for judging the excellence of the pupils' work can best be established by co-operative effort of pupils and teacher as suggested above for raising the level of language usage in letters. Pupils are more willing to be measured by the standards which they themselves have helped to set up than by checks obtained from a book or dictated by the teacher. Standards may be helpful even though they do not give objective measures. The following may be found helpful for *judging* the *content* of a social letter:

Directions: Check the phrase which best fits the letter.

A. The content of the letter is fitted to the type (social, business, etc.)
    1. Very well ____, 2. Moderately well ____, 3. Poorly ——

B. The amount of tact shown by the writer is
    1. Very large ____, 2. Moderate ____, 3. Very small ——

C. The quality of humor shown in the letter is
    1. Very subtle ____, 2. Average ____, 3. Rather crude ____

D. Courtesy as indicated by the letter content is
    1. Very effective ____, 2. Merely noticeable ____, 3. Non-existent ____

E. The manner in which the writer expresses his thought is
    1. Easy, natural, familiar ____, 2. Rather formal, unnatural ____, 3. Stilted, insincere ____

F. The topics of the letter are
    1. Limited to a few, well selected ____, 2. Rather numerous, fairly well selected ____, 3. Very numerous and irrelevant ——

G. The organization of the letter content is
    1. Excellent ____, 2. Fair ____, 3. Poor ——

H. The general effects produced by the letter are
 1. Very uplifting, cheering ____, 2. Little noticeable effect ____, 3. Definitely disquieting, depressing ____
I. The letter conveys the personality of the writer by its originality and genuineness
 1. To a large degree ____, 2. To an average degree ____, 3. Very little or none ____
J. The attitude toward the writer produced by the letter is
 1. Very friendly, favorable ____, 2. Neutral ____, 3. Antagonistic ____

A *rough summary* may be found by counting the number of checks at each of the three steps of excellence. If a more objective score is desired, the steps may be weighted. For example "1" might be given a score of 5, "2" a score of 3, and "3" a score of 1. With this weighting, a letter content might receive a low score of 10 or a high score of 50 or any figure in between. Perhaps the warning previously given should be repeated. Too rigid application of any kind of measuring stick means almost sure death to individuality. Common sense combined with a co-operative spirit and sympathetic attitude should be exercised by the teacher and pupils in applying standards of performance to all pupil effort.

A *score card* for *letter form* is easier to make and use. Such an instrument is based upon a standardized letter form. Once this form has been determined a score card [1] such as the following can easily be arranged. The same type of scoring device can be made to fit any type of written composition. The scores given the various items are arbitrarily set.

SCORE CARD FOR SOCIAL LETTERS

Score on these points:	Points	Pupil's Score
I. *Spacing and margin*		
A. Space at top of paper......................	1	____
B. At least a half-inch margin on left.........	1	____
C. At least a half-inch margin on right.......	1	____
D. Space at bottom of page...................	1	____
E. Space between heading and salutation......	1	____
F. Space between salutation and body.........	1	____
G. Space between paragraphs..................	1	____
H. Space between body and closing...........	1	____
I. Space between closing and signature.......	1	____
Total score for spacing and margins.....	9	____

[1] *Iowa Course of Study for Elementary Schools*, pp. 304-305. State of Iowa. 1928. Adapted.

II. *Heading of letter*

A. Heading at right-hand side of paper........ 1 _____
B. Punctuation at the end of lines: 1st, 2d, or 3d 3 _____
C. Heading on three lines.................... 1 _____
D. Heading in right order................... 3 _____
E. Comma after name of city................ 1 _____
F. Comma after day of month............... 1 _____
G. No unnecessary punctuation within heading 1 _____
H. No capitals omitted in first line of heading... 1 _____
I. No capitals omitted in second line of heading 1 _____
J. No capitals omitted in third line of heading.. 1 _____
K. No abbreviations in heading.............. 1 _____
    Total score for heading.............. 15 ═══════

III. *Salutation*

A. Salutation even with left margin........... 1 _____
B. Salutation appropriate.................... 1 _____
C. First word only of salutation capitalized,
    unless person's name is used............. 1 _____
D. Comma after salutation................... 1 _____
E. Ending at right of middle of page.......... 1 _____
    Total score for salutation.............. 5 ═══════

IV. *Ending of letter*

A. Word "from" not used in ending........... 1 _____
B. Appropriate ending....................... 1 _____
C. First word only of "ending" capitalized..... 1 _____
D. Comma after ending...................... 1 _____
E. Signature at right of paper................ 1 _____
F. Signature not crowded.................... 1 _____
G. First and last name given in signature....... 1 _____
    Total score for ending................ 7 ═══════

V. *Body of letter*

A. *Spelling*
    1. No misspelled words. (Take away 1 for
        each word misspelled up to and includ-
        ing 5. No points earned if more than 5
        words are misspelled)................ 5 _____
    2. No hyphen mistakes................... 1 _____
    3. No omissions or repetitions............ 2 _____
    4. No abbreviations in body (except certain
        titles and initials in connection with
        names)............................ 1 _____
        Total score for spelling............... 9 ═══════

B. *Punctuation*
   1. Punctuation in body of letter (1 point subtracted for each error in punctuation up to and including 5. No points earned if more than 5 errors in punctuation).... 5 _____
   2. Capitals in the body (1 point subtracted for each error to 5).................... 5 _____
   3. Paragraphs indented (1 point for each paragraph indented correctly, limit 3). 3 _____
     Total score for punctuation........... 13

C. *Grammar*
   1. No errors in grammar (1 off for each grammatical error up to 5)................ 5 _____
   2. No "run on" sentences.................. 3 _____
   3. Clear and complete sentences (1 point off for each unclear or incomplete sentence) 3 _____
     Total score for grammar.............. 11

D. *Composition*
   1. Material given in at least three paragraphs 3 _____
   2. Avoidance of slang expressions.......... 2 _____
   3. Carrying out assignment in regard to subject matter used and understanding of situation........................... 3 _____
   4. Subject matter clear to reader without reference to questions in the test......... 3 _____
   5. No use of trite phrases (I take my pen in hand, write soon, etc. One point off for each)........................... 3 _____
     Total score for grammar.............. 14
     Total score for body of letter.......... 47

VI. *Neatness of letter*
  A. No erasures, blots, or soiled places......... 1 _____
  B. Penmanship legible; letters made well; on line.................................... 3 _____
     Total score for neatness.............. 4

VII. *Miscellaneous*
  A. Additional points for the few outstanding letters in point of content (upper 5 or 6 per cent of class).......................... 5 _____
VIII. Total for whole letter...........................92

Additional types of *written composition* met by the pupils in their school life and later in life involve: (1) writing invitations, announcements; (2) completing blank forms of various kinds; (3) keeping records of events or experiments; (4) making notes, or outlines; (5) preparing a report, or summary. Little need be said of numbers (1), (2), and (3) because they are usually thoroughly discussed in middle- or upper-grade language books. Experience in writing these forms in actual situations should be provided and the children taught to master the techniques necessary in writing them. Moreover, greater skill should be expected of the pupils as they progress through the grades. Parties, programs, athletic events, displays, are the sort of activity which offers opportunity for invitations and announcement. Composition or test paper headings, library slips, questionnaires, enrollment cards, and various kinds of commercial blanks or coupons are examples of filling-in forms. Writing the school newspaper, the weather record, the rules for playing a game, the directions for making an article of furniture, are illustrations of record making.

Perhaps *making notes* or *outlines* should receive more detailed attention. Notes should usually be in outline form, even though rough, to be most valuable. Hence making notes and outlining may be and often are closely related. The secret of making an outline of subject matter (read or heard) is found in the ability to select the main ideas and the lesser ones which belong to each main idea. If pupils have not learned to do this in their reading and study, it should be taught in the language work, because nothing of consequence can be done in outlining until such abilities are acquired. Teachers may stimulate pupils to pick out the main points for their outline by suggesting that: (1) the title of the story be the main heading; (2) the main idea of each paragraph be a topic; (3) in picking out the main idea from each paragraph each pupil should ask himself if all or most of the paragraph is about that idea; (4) in selecting the lesser ideas each pupil should ask himself if that idea is connected with the main idea of the paragraph, or if not directly connected with it, of what idea it is a part; (5) the outline has definite uses and values after it has been made. The teacher should make very clear what some of these uses are, such as helps in organization, memory, saving of time, and others.

Preparing *reports* for class or other purposes is an activity frequently engaged in by middle- and upper-grade pupils. These reports may be on an article, reference, or experience. Certain basic factors in making reports should be easily recognized and utilized. (1) What is the purpose of making the report? (2) What materials will help best to realize this purpose? (3) How much time is allowed for the report—hence, at what length should it be? (4) What are the interests of the audience before which the report is to be given—therefore, what should be included in the report? (5) In what order should the material of the report be organized? The following order is suggested: (a) State the purpose briefly. (b) Give the sources of the data, facts, information. (c) Report the various items selected. (d) Summarize the report briefly, showing how it has fulfilled the purpose. (6) How can the reporter best be prepared to answer the questions asked by the group on his report?

Written *summaries* are usually brief yet comprehensive. They may cover a variety of activities ranging from the reaction to a three-minute report to the summing up of a semester's unit of work. Teachers often begin the instruction of this skill by teaching pupils to state the substance of a paragraph in writing, in one-half or less the number of words used in the original, to write a good title for a story, or to give the answer to a well stated conundrum. The length of the unit to be summarized usually determines the degree of difficulty in summarizing it.

In *summing up* the suggestions for teaching written language in the middle and upper grades, one should emphasize its all-embracing social importance. The purpose of this discussion has been to suggest that written language is not primarily a matter of form but of ideas; that while form of expression is important and easy to check, it should not be emphasized beyond its teammate, content.

CREATIVE EXPRESSION

Should the term *creative expression* be used? Does anyone really create? Probably not in the strict interpretation of the term. One recombines, rearranges, reconstructs, and calls the result a creative production. It may be new at least to the person doing it and so have the element of creativity for him. Stating it differently, mental activity produces something different from the commonplace by utilizing imagination and originality. It is not dominated by direction and imitation. Advancement of civilization has resulted largely from these characteristics of man's imagination and originality. The opportunities in the school for creative activities are exceedingly important because they may be used to develop children through self-expression. This expression may occur in the field of planning, or in the use of concrete materials, music, dance and rhythm, verse, stories, and drama.

IN THE PRIMARY GRADES

Some of the *purposes* for encouraging children in their creative efforts in verse, stories, and dramatic play *in the primary grades* are: (1) to develop individual personality by furnishing opportunities for the expression of feelings and ideas, (2) to use leisure time profitably by making children more independent and self-reliant in the field of language expression, which in turn would enrich their lives, (3) to draw out and promote any natural ability that children may have in language expression, (4) to help children appreciate good literature through their own attempts at literary production, which usually leads to better understanding of the writings of others.

Certain *conditions* are essential for stimulating satisfactory creative expression. There seems to be no definite method for developing it within the conventional type of teaching. The pupil himself must feel a desire or urge to create. A story is told, a verse composed, because the individual wants to express his feelings about, or give his interpretation of, an experience. This being true, the child's environment affects his expressions very strongly. Therefore, his immediate surroundings should be stimulating. Materials to handle, tools to work with, pictures to look at, toys to play with, all suggest activities in which children may be happy. Children usually do not feel like making a verse or story unless they have experienced strong feeling, usually one of joy or satisfaction. Beauty of various types is frequently a strong stimulus. Take children to see a beautiful tree, a bed of bright flowers, water rippling over the stones, the rhythm of machinery, the smoke of the engine; to hear the songs of the birds, the hum of the machine, the rustle of the leaves; to smell the air after a rain, the basswood blossoms, the newly cut grass; and to feel the softness of fur, the smoothness of satin, the roughness of a boulder. Why? The senses bring feelings of delight to the children—sensations which they often try to express by means of words. Have beauty about the schoolroom. It may be nature material attractively arranged or a bit of inexpensive pottery on a colored background which enhances its tone. One place in the room where there is always something beautiful, varied from time to time, furnishes a touch which appeals to the children's love for beauty and may elicit interesting expressions. The teacher should realize that children cannot be forced into this type of expression. It should come naturally because of an environment stimulating to their thinking and feeling. In addition, children need a sympathetic attitude toward their efforts, encouragement in their attempts, serious consideration of their contributions—not ridicule, which is one of the most deadly enemies of children's creative efforts. They should feel secure and normal in attempting to express themselves as their moods prompt them.

While children often produce stories and verse for the pleasure involved, there are times in school when their creative efforts are directed to *meet* a *special need*. To illustrate, a grade was conducting a program in which the children were to tell incidents of Lincoln's life. There were not enough stories to go around, so one boy volunteered, "I'll write and recite a poem about Lincoln." In addition to such a use in assemblies, there are the greetings for special days, such as Thanksgiving, Christmas, Saint Valentine's Day, and Easter. A girl or boy is pleased on his birthday to receive verses made by his playmates. A sick child appreciates being remembered with stories, verses, and riddles. The school paper calls for all these types of creative work.

The following *suggestions* may aid the inexperienced teacher in encouraging and directing attempts at creative production.

1. The teacher herself needs to cultivate the ability to see beauty in her surroundings, to use picturesque language on occasions, to try some original writing, and to realize the value of creative expression in children's individual development.

2. Children should be made familiar with all kinds of stories— humorous, realistic, and fanciful. Discussing the characters, the series and culmination of events, and story ending help children to feel the essentials of good stories. Children need to hear poetry that expresses feelings and tells of experiences within their comprehension. Thus they acquire the feeling of rhythm, they hear familiar experiences expressed in unusual wording, and they learn the meaning of rhyming.

They find, however, that poetry does not necessarily rhyme. A teacher who is familiar with the delightful poetry suitable for children, especially some by recent authors, will take advantage of many appropriate occasions for communicating it to children. For example, a button has been lost from a little child's coat and the teacher as she pins the coat for him repeats the poem "About Buttons," by Dorothy Aldis.

3. Hearing or reading a verse, or even an unusual expression made by other children, will often encourage pupils to try to express their own feelings. A little girl, as she walked through the dry leaves on an autumn day, said, "The leaves sound like my breakfast food a-popping." Expressions like these, commended by the teacher and placed on the blackboard or bulletin board, serve as an incentive to others.

4. Although definite directions seem out of place, attempts may be encouraged by questions, such as: What do our hammers say? What is the picture in the clouds? How does it feel as you wade in the water? A composite story or verse made by the teacher and the class may be a good means of helping pupils to make individual efforts.

5. The results of children's first endeavors should be encouraged even though they may not be good. If they are truly the children's own, they show a beginning and the results that occur later may be better. This requires patience, tact, and insight on the part of the teacher but often she is more than compensated by the results obtained.

6. Many children can express themselves originally and interestingly before they learn to write. It is desirable that teachers preserve in some form the children's unusual expressions.

7. Praise should be given when it is justified. Even the fact that a child has tried is worth praising. The second attempt may be an improvement over the first. There may be some especially good sentences to commend. Sincerity and originality deserve high praise. Thus the child is encouraged to persevere.

8. We cannot expect everyone to produce original material and if some seem unable to contribute after various approaches, they should not be made to feel unhappy or inferior. They may be talented in other ways.

9. Riddles give children patterns for their original work. Also others enjoy guessing the answers. Usually children guess many riddles before they construct them. Although originality and content are the

most important factors, standards of composition should be considered.

Children should feel the need for improvement. When they do, they may set up *criteria* for their own use, with the help of the teacher. Learning what constitutes a good story, poem, or play may be gained from the discussion of those heard and read. The following illustrate what may be worked out and used by the children in judging their work.

A Story

Is there a good beginning?

Does the story tell about one thing? (Centered about one idea)

Is there one most important part? (Climax)

Is there something different from other stories? (Originality)

Is there a good ending?

A Play

Is there a good beginning?

Do interesting things happen?

Do the characters talk as you would expect them to?

Does something very important happen near the end?

A Poem

Can we keep time as we say it? (Rhythm)

Does it give pictures we enjoy?

Does it tell in a beautiful way about something we know?

Riddles

Did I tell two or more things about the answer?

Did I tell important things?

Was I careful not to make it too easy or too hard?

Children may also improve in original expression by extended observation of the fields in which they are writing. For example, a third-grade class was making riddles about its experiences on an excursion to a farm. One boy thought that the corn was dry when put into the silo. Others thought it was green. In such a case, further investigation would be preferable to information furnished directly by the teacher. Also, time should be given to discuss and think over such experiences as nature trips, so that children may have opportunities to review events. Often teachers rush pupils too rapidly from one task to another. For example—the teacher might say, "The poem you wrote last week about the maple trees reminded me of the tree we saw today. Your poem called them golden; would you say the same of this one?"

The following are *illustrations* [1] of young children's creative expressions.

[1] Made by children in Campus Elementary School, Iowa State Teachers College.

A composite story by a second grade group:

THE NANNY GOAT

Once upon a time there was a nanny goat. She lived in the woods near a lake. She had two little babies. One was black and one was white. One was a boy and one was a girl. Every day they went upon a hill and ate sweet grass.

Now there lived a wolf near by. One day while they were eating the sweet grass the wolf saw them on the hill. When he saw them he smacked his lips and laughed. They heard him laughing and began to run. They reached their home safely. The wolf was very, very angry and said to himself, "I'll jump in the window and get those little goats yet."

Then the wolf tried to jump in the window but it was too high. The wolf was very, very, very angry but the little goats only laughed. The old wolf went home hungry and the three goats lived happily ever after.

A fanciful tale dictated by a third grade child:

THE MAGIC BALLOON

Once upon a time there was a magic balloon. It took people up in the air. One day a princess took a ride in a magic balloon. She went up, up, up, until she came to the moon. Then she tied the end of the balloon to the moon. Then she went to see the man in the moon and while she was talking to him the wind blew the balloon against the point of the moon and it went, bang! Then she went and asked the man in the moon if he had a parachute and he said he did. Then she went right down to her throne.

—Howard

These verses were composed by children in the second grade. The first shows how familiar poems or songs may become patterns for children in their creative endeavors.

My Valentine

I love you,
I love you,
Really, really,
Really, true.

—Jean

A Fairy Frog

When I was in my garden
I saw a fairy frog,
I looked at him—
He looked at me,
I wondered what he thought.

—Jean

The Rain

Little raindrops fell around
Sprinkling all the ground,
It watered the grain,
This lovely sprinkling rain.

—Frances

A play dictated by a first-grade group. All members of the group co-operated with Mary B., who was outstanding as a leader (but not so strong in English) to create this delightful bit of drama:

AN EASTER PLAY

People in the play: Easter Rabbit . . . . .Mary B.
Mother . . . . .Marilyn
Father . . . . .Richard
Marian . . . . .Sarah Lee
Storekeeper . . . . .Fred

Scene One—Place: In the yard

Marian: Hello, Little Rabbit. What are you thinking about?
Easter Rabbit: I am thinking about how many Easter eggs you want.
Marian: I am wondering if you would like to stay here with me. (Mother comes out.) May I keep this bunny?
Mother: Do you think he would stay with you? I'll go in and think about it. (Aside—I wonder if that would mean work for me. Maybe Marian could take care of it herself.) Do you think you would take care of the bunny yourself, Marian?
Marian: Yes, I think I could.
Mother: Then you may keep it here.

Scene Two—Place: In the yard

Marian: Here, Bunny, I want to put you on this leash.
Bunny: I don't know as I will like that so well.
Marian: I could take you to the store for more eggs if you will wear this.
Bunny: That will be fine.
Father: Well, whose bunny is that?
Marian: I found it this morning. Will you help me get a cage for him?
Father: I will see. I have a few boxes

Scene Three—Place: The Store

Marian: Come on, we are going to the store.
Storekeeper: What is it for you today?
Marian: I would like some eggs. I would like some Easter Egg dye.
Easter Bunny: Are those eggs for me?
Marian: Yes, in a way. No, in a way. I have to dye them, and then put them in a basket.
Easter Bunny: Should we go around with them?
Marian: Yes, we will go around with them.

IN GRADES ABOVE THE PRIMARY

The term "creative expression" which for the most part means "creative writing" on the *middle- and upper-grade* levels has already been defined. This type of writing is intimately related to the pupils' experiences, which is its principal asset as an instrument for developing language ability.

The question then arises: just how does written language of the creative type function? (1) Since creative language activities come or should come directly from the reservoir of pupil experience and since the pupil's experiences are of intense interest to him, creative language activities connect directly with his greatest interests, and hence have the greatest possible opportunity of affecting his thinking and acting. If the creative activities in writing can be kept on this high level, they may become definite factors in the growth of pupil personality. (2) Success in creative written language stimulates as effectively as success in any other field, if it is properly rewarded. To illustrate, who does not remember with a degree of pride when his first written article received recognition? (3) When free play of ability in any field is given to youth, the teacher and all concerned are usually pleasantly surprised at the special talents that unfold. This is true of creative writing. It gives a chance to the talented child and at the same time affords opportunity and encouragement to the ordinary one. (4) Without doubt the learning rooted in the centers of pupil interest and activity has the greatest chance of permanence. Creative writing is unfettered and, therefore, most adaptable to the individual pupil's most intimate thoughts and associations.

Conditions which aid in realizing the values of creative writing are comparatively easy to suggest but often difficult to carry out. For example, most teachers would agree that the atmosphere of the classroom is an important factor in successful creative writing adventures, but just how to get the proper atmosphere or to determine what atmosphere is best for any particular group is quite a different matter.

Previously it was hinted that a *background* is necessary for creative writing. The things which people "create" are in mind already,—put there by experience of some kind. The "creating" comes about when certain factors of experience line up in a new way, through the introduction of a new factor. For example, Jack is writing a scene for the health play. He saw a cot on the stage that morning. He had just been warned by the school patrol that riding double on his bicycle was against the school regulations. These, together with the fact that he must write this scene, prompted him to think of portraying a crossing accident caused by disobeying a school regulation. Thus preparatory backgrounds not only bring up old experiences but inject new ones, which under proper conditions, make new combinations with the old. The background may be one of reading, picture study, oral composition, or a combination of any or all types of experience.

It seems well for pupils to know that not all of creative work is stimulated by outside influences. Often the use of *memory, reasoning, emotion*, or other forces help produce what one wishes to create. In fact pupils should not get the notion that if they "just wait" the inspiration will come. Often a little work while the waiting is going on aids materially. To illustrate: The heroine of Janet's story is in the dumps— almost down and out. Should Janet wait for an inspiration to get her out or put herself in a like condition, size up the elements involved, and imagine how she would use them? In short, pupils should realize that loafing even if glorified by the idea of getting an inspiration usually does not end in the making of something new.

Undoubtedly the *teacher's attitude* and reactions, as well as those of the group, have a great influence on original production. If the pupil finds his teacher and classmates discerning, sympathetic, stimulating, and interested, he has a much better chance of developing in this difficult field than if the opposite conditions exist. The environment insofar as it encourages, judiciously guides, and adequately rewards efforts in a creative direction is certainly one of the most important factors in assuring the full measure of development. Teachers who have tried to direct pupils in creative work of any kind need not be told that plenty of patience is needed. But to those who may not have succeeded as well as they had hoped, or to those who are new in the profession, a word of advice may be of benefit. Most sources of information indicate that the Creator of the world took or is taking plenty of time to make the worthwhile things of life and nature. It is not probable that teachers can do them much faster. What is a week, a month, a year, if a pupil catches a vision or discovers in himself a possibility that gives new purpose to his life? Is this treading on air; just suggesting glowing generalities which never occur in actual experience; just asking teachers to chase a myth which never was and never will be; or is it a glimpse of the promised land which patience and artistic teaching disclose once in a great while?

If intelligent progress is made in creative effort, *evaluations* of this effort must be made either by the teacher, the pupil, or both. If evaluations are to be made, some sort of standard must exist by the use of which the evaluations may be made. These may be in the mind, possibly in the imagination or emotions, but they must exist somewhere or no intelligent judging can be done. It is essential, moreover, that these standards be clear and in a form both pupils and teacher can use. As yet no objective standards for creative writing acceptable to a majority of teachers seem to have been worked out. Perhaps the next best thing is tentative standards set up by teacher and pupils together, possibly in the form of the good qualities of any given type of creative writing. For example, Mary has just finished the rough draft of an editorial and has the following standards in chart form to consult:

> Is it clear?
> Is it concise?
> Does it discuss one idea only?
> Does it present the situation fairly?
> Does it present the facts?
> Is it in good form?

Other factors may appear in such standards by which Mary evaluates her editorial, or there may be fewer or different ones, but she must have some idea of what a good editorial is if she is to improve in ability to write one. It is a comparatively simple matter to evolve such standards, but effective use of them requires all the skill a teacher can muster. If standards are stressed too much, creativeness may be stifled or even killed. On the other hand, if no means of evaluation are used the pupil has little or no helpful suggestion in what he is doing. He has small chance of developing in the right direction or even of knowing what that direction is. The procedure some teachers find safe is, first, to encourage the children to write what they wish to, disregarding form but emphasizing ideas and, second, to suggest, when this is done, that the pupils evaluate their ideas by the standards evolved by the group. This method of teaching interferes perhaps less with the creation and expression of ideas than other procedures.

In the so-called creative writing the teacher has the supreme opportunity to use written language in developing her pupils. Even though it is most difficult to teach and is fraught with danger, it holds promise of being one of the most potent instruments of instruction as well as one of the chief satisfactions of her teaching experience. For example, creations like these certainly are a source of pleasure and satisfaction to a teacher who is able to secure them.

Mirth [1]

I saw some puppets performing
Upon a tiny stage.
I laughed at the awkwardness
Of the funny, feeble things,
Made to work by strings.

Perhaps
God laughs,
Gently,
At the awkward antics
Of us, puny puppets,
Performing on our tiny stage
The earth.

—Ray Cline, 8A

So Why? [1]

I cannot grow quite fast enough,
And my mind won't speed me
  there,
But I wish I were a little older,
Just enough to wave my hair.
I wish for a fancy "formal,"
And a saucy, furry wrap,
A pair of silver slippers,
Without a childish, stupid strap!
Yet I wonder after growing old,
My youth, like Auntie, will I
  try to hold?

Marigail Stewart, 8A

[1] *Young Voices.* Original verse produced by the pupils of the Sarah Scott Junior High School, Terre Haute, Indiana. Georgia A. Brewster, Instructor of English. 1932.

CHAPTER 9

FORMAL ASPECTS OF LANGUAGE

IN THE PRIMARY GRADES

THE formal aspects of language in the *primary grades* are taught in order to intensify the effectiveness of expression. Often the value of what is said is weakened because of poor form, incorrect usage, or undesirable speech practices.

In *oral language* teachers usually meet a twofold problem: first, to help children substitute correct for incorrect speech habits and, second, to introduce new techniques. A teacher, through observation, can determine the poor practices most common in her group. Listing these will help her to decide which to select first for elimination. The bases for selection may be, (1) those which are the most offending; to illustrate, "John and me" is so common that it is acceptable to some authorities, while "me and Jane" is to be discarded without question; (2) those suitable for the different age levels; for example, we do not expect children to distinguish between the use of "well" and "good" in the first grade, but we do try to substitute "I saw" for "I seen."

Some *suggestions* that may help both in acquiring new techniques and in substituting the good for the undesirable ones are: (1) Be alert concerning your own manner of speech, such as quality and pitch of voice, correct pronunciation, clear enunciation, correct form, and variety in expressions. (2) Develop the idea that our speech is for the purpose of conveying ideas to others and that speech forms do make a difference in the hearer's understanding of what is said and in his opinion of the speaker. (3) Help children develop a consciousness of good English. Pupils who have been exposed to poor English often do not know when they make errors. The development of "a good English" consciousness increases the chances not only for individual self-improvement, but for the development of the whole group. The use of mutual corrective practice in a co-operative spirit establishes a receptive attitude toward better English. (4) Concentrate the efforts on one or two forms at a time. (5) Insert tactfully the correct form as a child is talking. This usually causes him to repeat it correctly and often to continue without being otherwise disturbed. This procedure is sound because he substitutes the better form immediately. Repeating the correct form after the child's complete statement has been made is sometimes better, especially if he is a beginner or is sensitive. (6) Teach few rules since they seem to be of little value in the primary grades. It is the actual doing that forms the correct habits. (7) Use regular language periods to make explanations about better language usages and to give direct practice. However, the use of good language should be taught in all periods. (8) Put practice on deficiencies. It should be motivated; that is, children should understand why they need to say "singing" not "singin'," "get" not "git." Exercises should be so arranged that the repetition is brought in as naturally as possible. Ready-made language games, as formerly given in books, were often of very little value. Games may be of some help if properly planned and conducted. To be effective they should incorporate a form on which the group needs practice and which is repeated in situations similar to those in which the expression is commonly used. (9) Eliminate the tendencies to begin sentences with "Wella," "Uh," and other such expressions. Place the same sentences on the blackboard, omitting these introductory words. Ask children to read them, and ask which they think sounds the better. Helping children to see their errors usually is a step toward improvement. (10) Be careful in eliminating the unnecessary "ands" and do not expect children to omit them too early. It may help to ask a child to repeat his story, suggesting that he tell one thing, then stop. Write this sentence on the blackboard. Do the same with the next sentence and the next. This will show objectively that all the "ands" are not necessary.

To prepare for *written language work* the teacher may take advantage of many activities in the early primary period for developing sentence sense and correct usage, as well as for directing attention to capitalization, punctuation, and arrangement.

The idea of *sentence sense* may be initiated and developed in the following ways:

1. The dictated or recorded composition is one means. The teacher as she writes the children's contributions might say, "That is a good sentence," or "That does not tell anything. Can you give the whole sentence?" or "Who has another sentence?" When the composition is completed, the children may count the sentences.

2. Explanations of pictures in booklets (as explained on page 182) is another device. The children dictate such sentences and the teacher writes them in the booklet.

3. Captions for pictures may be used. These may be posted with the pictures on the bulletin board or in other places in the room.

4. Question and answer exercises are an easily used device. Sides are chosen. Those on one side ask questions of those on the other side who answer in sentences. The questions may concern some topic of interest in a unit, such as how certain farm animals help, how some wild animals prepare for winter, what materials different freight cars carry. They may also ask for additional information following reports given. This is not a suggestion to be followed in ordinary discussion; that is, it is not desirable to expect children habitually to reply in sentences. Such procedure is stilted and unnatural both in school and outside.

5. Commendation for good sentences also helps. Justified praise given to children when they happen to use unusually good sentences in appropriate situations helps to establish the feeling of sentence sense.

6. Sentence and nonsentence exercises are frequently used. These may be given as children advance through the grades. The teacher says, "I am going to say some sentences and also parts of sentences. Close your eyes. When you hear a sentence, raise your hand. When you hear words that do not make a sentence, keep your hand down." The standard for judging should be that the sentences tell or ask something. The closed eyes prevent imitation of classmates.

7. Sentence and nonsentence card exercises are helpful. Each child has an envelope containing cards. On some are written sentences, on others only groups of words. The sentences are to be placed on the left-hand side of the desk and the nonsentences on the right.

8. Reading material of all kinds may aid in the task. Early in children's reading from books, the teacher speaks of what a sentence tells and often asks children to read one or more sentences.

Punctuation, capitalization, arrangement, and *correct usage* may also be called to children's attention before they themselves write, through their recorded compositions and other dictated work discussed previously. Their attention may be directed to the differences between the large or capital letters and small letters, to the periods and question marks, and to the spacing on the paper,—that is, the margins all the way around with a wider space at the top. If children dictate sentences which contain incorrect forms, the teacher should help them to re-word the sentences and to use the correct forms. Later, as the teacher places their sentences on the board, they may put in the periods themselves and sign their individual productions.

When children actually begin to do *written work* they have plenty of opportunities for writing and developing the necessary skills in the formal aspects of good written form.

Some ways of developing these skills are:

1. They may write sentences in the situations discussed under the heading "sentence sense." In addition, they may write line-a-day diaries or simple notes of one or two sentences. It is better, at the beginning, to limit the writing to one, then to two, and to three sentences. Perhaps they can write part of a recorded composition.

2. In the latter part of the primary period the compositions should take the paragraph form with the first word indented and sentences not on separate lines. The idea of all the sentences telling about one topic, of a good beginning, and of a closing sentence will have been emphasized in oral compositions and in the compositions dictated to the teacher. These recorded compositions really make a good basis for understanding the meaning of the paragraph, since all of the sentences tell about one topic, the title.

3. Punctuation, capitalization, and arrangement which have been

discussed previously in their recorded work should be reviewed and connected with their various writing experiences.

4. Children's first written work will probably be copying. It is desirable for children to have a motive for this and to understand the material they are to copy. Occasions for copying have already been suggested, as memoranda, signs, invitations, stories and sentences in books, items for diaries, and others. It is better if, as soon as possible, they use the word as the smallest unit to copy, and gradually develop the power to write two or three words without looking again at the original. Unless children are encouraged in this they may continue to look up for each letter they write. They should also be directed to check their work with the original.

5. In the latter part of the primary period, children may benefit by writing material from dictation. There may be few needs for such writing but the main idea is to give practice in the formal mechanical aspects of written language without being responsible for the thought expressed.

In all probability, more *practice* than that furnished by the actual needs will be necessary to make these common techniques habitual with all. If such is the situation, it is desirable to learn what is needed by the different individuals in a group and to help each improve his own skill. Teacher and pupils should not lose sight of the fact that the purpose of practice is to make one able to express himself correctly in independent, original work. On the other hand there is danger of losing interesting content by making a child unduly conscious of form.

Self-help guides like the following may help by keeping before the pupils what is expected and giving them standards by which to check their own work.

Sentences	*Title*
Did I begin each with a capital letter?	Did I write the title in the middle of the first line?
Did I use the right mark after each one?	Did I begin each important word with a capital letter?
Did I leave out any words?	Did I leave out the period after the title?
Did I spell all of the words correctly?	Did I leave a space between title and the first sentence?
Did I leave a margin on each side of the paper?	

A Paragraph

Does the first sentence tell what the paragraph is to be about?

Do all of the sentences tell about the main idea?

Are the sentences in good sequence?

Is the first word indented?

The following *score sheet* is suggested for the purpose of helping the teacher find some of those abilities in which children of the first two grades may need practice and also to help her note individual progress. The teacher may wish to add other items. Nothing is given for the third grade since textbooks are usually used at that level.

Provide activities which will help determine children's abilities as set up here. The three columns in each division furnish the opportunity for comparisons. Record the children's standings at the beginning of the year, in the middle, and at the close. Those that are starred are expected only of the second grade. The following is recommended as the manner of indicating children's reactions: *U*sually, *O*ften, *N*ot at all.	Children's Names								
Oral:									
1. Does he show interest in new words?									
*2. Does he show interest in meanings of words?									
3. Does he voluntarily contribute to a conversation?									
*4. Does he feel responsible for having something of interest to tell?									
5. Does he listen when others are talking?									
*6. Does he consider the feelings of others when talking?									
*7. Does he correct the person speaking in a polite manner?									
8. Can he follow a plan when giving an oral composition?									
9. Does he use a good speaking voice?									
*10. Does he stand quietly and with good posture when talking?									
11. Does he speak plainly?									
12. Does he speak loudly enough for all to hear?									

Provide activities which will help determine children's abilities as set up here. The three columns in each division furnish the opportunity for comparisons. Record the children's standings at the beginning of the year, in the middle, and at the close. Those that are starred are expected only of the second grade. The following is recommended as the manner of indicating children's reactions: *U* sually, *O* ften, *N* ot at all.	Children's Names									
13. Does he begin without unnecessary words?										
*14. Does he show a tendency to omit unnecessary "ands"?										
15. Does he stick to a topic?										
16. Does he use polite forms appropriately?										
17. Does he greet people in an acceptable manner?										
*18. Can he give an invitation remembering the essential items?										
*19. Can he introduce people and acknowledge introductions in an acceptable manner?										
20. Can he give a direction that others can follow?										
21. Can he follow a direction that he hears?										
*22. Can he deliver a message correctly?										
23. Can he answer the telephone properly?										
*24. Can he call someone over the telephone properly?										
25. Does he enter dramatic play with enthusiasm and enjoyment?										
26. Can he reproduce a story of a few sentences that he has heard so that others will enjoy listening?										
27. Does he show improvement in correct usage?										
28. Does he detect some incorrect forms?										
*29. Does he commence a story with a good sentence?										

Provide activities which will help determine children's abilities as set up here. The three columns in each division furnish the opportunity for comparisons. Record the children's standings at the beginning of the year, in the middle, and at the close. Those that are starred are expected only of the second grade. The following is recommended as the manner of indicating children's reactions: *U* sually, *O* ften, *N* ot at all.	Children's Names								
30. Can he give a report if assigned a topic?									
31. Does he ask good questions of one who has told something?									
*32. Does he give good suggestions to help others?									
33. Can he give a sentence when asked to?									
*34. Can he help himself by using a self-help guide?									
Written: 1. Can he write a sentence?									
2. Can he write correctly a simple note in form expected at his age level?									
3. Does he use capital letters: a. At the beginning of labels, signs, greetings?									
b. At the beginning of a sentence?									
c. When writing his first name?									
d. When writing I?.............									
*e. When writing the name of a town?									
*f. When writing "Dear" in a letter salutation?									
g. When beginning a title?									
4. Does he use a period after a statement?									
5. Does he use a question mark after a question?									
6. Can he place the items in proper place when filling in a simple form?									

NOTE. The following standardized test is a helpful device not only for determining pupil's ability but also as a means of showing teachers what to include in the language work of the first three grades: Iowa Primary Language Test published by The Bureau of Educational Research and Service, Extension Division, The State University of Iowa.

IN GRADES ABOVE THE PRIMARY

The presentation of the technical aspects of language in *grades above the primary* is limited. Only illustrative patterns using the more important phases of technical language are given. The assumption is that such suggestive illustrations will carry over into all other phases. Perhaps a statement of the *reasons* for acquiring proficiency in the technical aspects of language will be of value at this point. Pupils sometimes ask what benefit grammar is to them. Teachers ask themselves the same question. If a person speaks and writes good English why should he learn the technical, theoretical side of it? A few answers to this question are:

1. Even though a person speaks and writes perfect English, but does not know the basic principles of correct language usage, he will be helpless in respect to these principles when he has to correct an error made by another or when in doubt about a new construction used by himself.

2. In science, mathematics, and other fields, principles rather than individual facts are taught, whenever possible, to save time and to facilitate learning. It would seem that a similar procedure should be followed in language instruction when feasible.

3. A broad concept of language seems impossible without a knowledge of its fundamental principles. Merely to be able to use language is not sufficient. The pupil can command it more completely if he knows something of its foundations.

4. Artistic use of the English language requires an understanding of its principles. The school does not expect a pupil to excel in creating a picture without knowing the principles of perspective and color, or to write a piece of music without being able to use the basic factors involved. It should scarcely expect a pupil to develop beyond the level to which his ordinary experiences would raise him without a command of the foundational tenets of language.

5. We may assume that mastery of the sentence is one essential of training in the English language, or any language, for that matter. To obtain this training, the pupil must have practice in the technical aspects of language.

The following discussion will be concerned with suggestions for presenting some of the *essentials* of the *more technical* side of language including:

1. sentences—combining to make a paragraph
2. the sentence—emphasizing its importance, use, and form
3. the sentence—stressing its main word groups
4. the sentence—stressing types of parts
5. the sentence—emphasizing types of single words
6. the uses of punctuation
7. the uses of capitalization.

It is assumed that the *sentence is* the *basic unit* of language composition and larger or smaller units are composed respectively of sentence multiples or parts.

The *paragraph* is not usually discussed as a part of the beginning of technical language instruction. An important factor in teaching the paragraph is the proposition that a paragraph is about one main idea only. Early in the primary grades pupils may begin to realize this fact. Later they learn that a paragraph may contain other ideas which belong to the main one, and that different sentences of the paragraph may contain these subordinate ideas. Thus paragraph sense grows gradually —beginning with the simple exercises of the reading readiness stage and extending to the multi-sentence paragraph with its main or topic sentence, its supplementary sentences, and possibly its final summary sentence, written by the upper-grade children. If well directed effort is exerted at every step in the child's development, this difficult task may be done satisfactorily.

The *importance* of the sentence as a unit can scarcely be overstressed. It seems to be the only language factor which has remained comparatively unchanged through the ages and we find it useful today. The development of sentence sense in written composition is even more important than that of the paragraph. The written form expands gradually from the pupil's very first dictation of a sentence, directly out of his experience, to the teacher. Of course, the oral-sentence experiences form a background for the written work and assist as the sentence idea develops. Generally a pupil taught to use oral sentences well has less difficulty using written ones. Sentence use, therefore, is first taught when the child starts to school and is kept up until he leaves the elementary grades or until he uses sentences well.

Some *suggestions* for impressing the pupils with the importance of the sentence are: (1) Emphasize that a sentence expresses but one idea, by utilizing the most striking illustrations possible at every opportunity in both oral and written language, as when (a) trying to conduct a recitation without using sentences, (b) asking pupils to communicate with their classmates without using a sentence in some form, such as a statement, question, command, or exclamation, (c) finding what form oral, written, or sign language would take if sentences were not used. (2) Work out factors that make sentences necessary for full expression of ideas, as (a) to express something about an idea, (b) to express many different ideas easily, (c) to record happenings, (d) to express more complicated relationships.

The *uses* of sentences are important. Children should become well acquainted with these uses early in the middle grades, if not before. Pupils use and understand statements in their first days at school. They also ask questions and thus begin to learn that use of the sentence. They employ the command or request and may not recognize this as a different use of the sentence until it is called to their attention. The exclamation is the least familiar but it is also least used and least important of the four uses generally treated technically. Some teachers may prefer to classify the exclamatory sentence as a statement "expressing unusual emotion." If this is done, there will be only three kinds of sentences according to use for elementary pupils to learn.

Plenty of *practice* on the uses of sentences should make the pupil react to them almost automatically. Some of the best exercises are the sentences the pupils write and present to the class for classification. Many teachers find oral exercises helpful because much more practice can be had in a given time. Occasionally, the teacher may test by asking the pupils to write their reactions to oral sentences and then use the results as a check. The pupils may write the number of each sentence and after the number, the kind of sentence it is; for example: "30. Birds fly." "31. Will you come?" Pupil writes: "30. Statement" (or in abbreviation "30. S"), "31. Question" (or in abbreviation "31. Q"). It seems needless to point out that sentences used in practice should be directly connected with the pupil's interests. This will be true if they create the sentences themselves. Teachers frequently make the mistake of using illustrative sentences which are far too difficult. It is better to establish the sentence idea in the pupils' minds by using numerous simple examples. More complicated sentences may be used after the sentence idea has been fixed.

The sentence *form* should not be taken up until the need for it makes it seem desirable. This may occur in the higher-middle or upper grades. Investigation shows that the simple sentence is the one most used by children up to the sixth-grade level, although there is an increasing amount of use of the compound and complex sentences as children progress through the grades. Wherever taught, the learning and practice materials should be kept simple for the pupils until they understand what each form of sentence is, and can distinguish each unfailingly on that level.

The *main parts* of the sentence are usually called the subject and predicate. Children in the early middle grades can easily distinguish these parts as the "idea expressed" and "what is expressed about it," or

perhaps more simply "the thing about which something is said," and "what is said about it." There is nothing mysterious about the parts of a sentence, and pupils should understand that from the first. They know from experience what they are talking about and also what they say about it. Simple illustrations from the schoolroom, playground, the trip to or from school, and other situations directly connected with the pupils' experiences should be used at the beginning of sentence study. A wider range of experiences and sentence forms may be covered in practice and reviews. Some teachers present both the simple subject (word which expresses the main idea) and the complete subject (simple subject and modifiers) at this time. If the examples are kept on a very easy level, the pupils are usually able to acquire a more complete notion of what a subject is. The same is true of the simple predicate and its modifier.

Care should be exercised in presenting the main parts of a sentence in each of its uses and in making preparation for its presentation. For example, in the question type, "Why did the ball bounce?," certain elements, such as word placement, might mislead the pupils and therefore should be studied before this type is introduced. Otherwise the pupils may choose "why" for the subject, especially if a large part of the practice has been on sentences with the subject preceding the predicate. In the study of the question, pupils' attention should be directed toward the thing talked or written about. Is "why" the thing talked about? Usually in a simple sentence such as this, the pupils see at once that "why" is not the thing talked about and frequently are able to select the proper idea. Some teachers secure good results by asking the pupils to put the question into a statement form, as "The ball did bounce. (Why?)" When the query is arranged this way, the pupils see that "why" is attached loosely and that its principal purpose is to put the sentence in question form. The command or request form of sentence frequently causes trouble, especially if the subject is omitted but understood. For example, "Please close the door" might trouble the pupils unless it were explained that in some sentences the subject is not stated but understood. In the sentence above the subject "you" is understood. They should also discover that this is particularly true if the sentence is a command or request. If pupils can be taught to supply the understood subject in their reading and thinking, little difficulty should be experienced. The exclamatory type usually fits into one of the other types of sentence but, in addition, it expresses strong emotion. If this is well understood, little trouble will be experienced with exclamatory expressions. To illustrate: (1) "Whew! Isn't this weather hot?" (2) "Look, a bomb is falling!" (3) "My arm has been broken!" The first sentence expresses emotion in question form plus an exclamatory word. The second one is a statement plus an exclamatory request or command. The third is emotion expressed as a statement.

The study of *word groups* used in sentences may be made as easy or as difficult as desired. Teachers usually help children to find the two main types by using their structural make-up as the basis. If considered from this angle, phrases and clauses are discovered. By reference to the sentence itself, pupils easily find that a phrase, in some respects, is like a subject with no accompanying predicate, whereas a

Simple chalkboard sketches make formal language learning easier.

clause is similar to a simple sentence. After the teacher is sure that all pupils have working concepts of the phrase and clause, she may introduce her pupils to the various kinds and uses of both. It should be understood that this discussion makes no attempt to place the teaching of these concepts at any grade level. That is usually set by the course of study or the textbook used. This would depend upon the detail and difficulty of the subject matter chosen. This learning usually starts with the simple observations that both phrases and clauses are used to tell something about the subject or the predicate, and pupils may learn that they, in some way, change or modify the meaning of the idea they modify. In this way, the concept of modifiers is presented.

This concept should grow out of a wealth of simple yet applicable examples taken directly from the pupils' lives. This means for the most part that illustrative materials must be presented by the teacher to meet the needs of her group and be of the correct difficulty, and of the right amount. For example, phrases may be shown to modify the subject in some such way as this: (1) A boy won the race. (2) A boy from home won the race. (3) A boy from home, having freckles, won the race. Pupils usually see that the boy of the first sentence is just any boy who won the race. But the boy of the second sentence is limited (modified) to the category "boys from home," while the third sentence limits the boy to the more specialized category "boys from home who have freckles." Likewise phrases may be shown to limit or modify the predicate. Clauses (modifiers which have subjects and predicates) may be shown in like manner to limit the subject or the predicate. Examples: (1) The boy (who lived with us) went to school. (2) Jerry spoke (when he was asked).

Finally pupils should see that (1) all *phrases* are weak and cannot "stand alone" that is, make a sentence, and (2) that *clauses* differ somewhat in importance. Some clauses seem to be able to say all that needs to be said and others seem to "hang onto" or depend on something else. Both may be illustrated by one sentence: "The man who came late was elected." The clause (main one) "The man was elected" seems to need nothing more to make it clear, but the other, "who came late," is seen to depend on the subject which is the word "man." Thus by a profusion of varying examples, pupils may be assisted to differentiate clearly between independent and dependent clauses. After the main parts of speech have been learned, it is comparatively simple for the children to discover that phrases and clauses are used as adjectives, adverbs, nouns, and verbs in a great variety of ways.

The same general attack may be extended to learning the types of single words usually known as *parts of speech*. This is the last step in the analysis of the sentence. Perhaps the best approach is from the sentence itself. Attention may be directed to the simple subject "birds" in "The birds fly swiftly," noticing that it is the name of the thing about which something is said. Other sentences may be reviewed to discover that the subject is the name of something, or is a word that is used in the place of a name. With this idea clearly in mind, it may be labeled with the term "noun." Likewise the simple predicate "fly" and similar words in a host of other sentences indicate action, in connection with their subjects. That is, the subject does something which is expressed by the simple predicate. Words which express action also have a name. They are called "verbs." When this type of verb is fixed in mind, the weaker sort may be taken up. They are rather peculiar verbs which do not express direct action but only a half-way kind called "state of being." Such a verb is the word "am." In the sentence "I am here," the verb "am" does not say I am doing anything in any way, I am just being here. Perhaps the children can think of other verbs of this type. Because this family of verbs merely joins ideas it is called "copulative," which means connecting or coupling together. In some such manner as this the idea of what a verb is (already fixed firmly in mind) may be connected with the term "verb." First, the idea should be established, then the name connected with it.

The kinds and forms of *nouns* and *verbs*, if introduced at all in the middle grades, should come slowly, one at a time, introduced in the face of an actual need. For example, some pupil asks why some nouns always begin with a capital letter. The teacher might use this question to introduce the classification of proper nouns. The same thing might be true with other forms and qualities of nouns and verbs, as well as other parts of speech, each in its turn. If pupils do not bring these up, they should be brought in by the teacher. If the teacher desires to follow the textbook order more closely, she at least can introduce the successive items of work by clothing them in the daily language of the school or playground and in an informal manner rather than as merely the next topic in the text. Other types of single words used to express the meaning of the sentence are the *pronoun, adjective, adverb, preposition, conjunction,* and *interjection.*

Some *general suggestions* applicable to the teaching of all types of single words follow. (1) Introduce the type of the single word by using it in simple written and oral sentences with emphasis upon the word being introduced. (2) Call attention to the relation of the idea expressed by the word, to other parts of the sentence. (3) Use a multitude of varied illustrative examples to fix firmly in mind at least the main ideas of the word type being taught. (4) Call on pupils to help find the illustrative examples as soon as they have assimilated the idea. (5) Name the word type just learned. (6) The last step is to test the pupils' ability to recognize the word type as it is actually used in sentences, and their ability to use it themselves in written or spoken composition. In short, the important factor in teaching any one of these word types is the fixing of the concept indelibly in the pupils' minds. Naming and working out a definition help in doing this. Last of all, test the pupils' abilities to use this knowledge by asking them to select the word type from sentences. The danger of presenting the name and definition first lies in the assumption on the part of teachers that if a pupil has memorized the name and definition, he possesses a clear and full concept of what the word type is. Such an assumption may or may not be true. This is evident when pupils glibly recite the definitions but do not know the word types when they meet them in sentences.

More *specific teaching suggestions* for types of single words (using the pronoun as an example) follow. These may, with adaptations, be used as a guide for all.

1. The teacher calls the attention of the class to a word type not previously discussed; some examples: "He went to town," instead of "Father went to town"; "She came early," rather than "Mary came early"; "They crowded the streets," in place of "People crowded the streets"; "It blew a gale," for "The wind blew a gale." Use many examples to indicate the place of the pronoun in the sentence, beginning with the personal use, such as is illustrated above, and then proceed to other uses, such as relative, interrogative, demonstrative, reflexive, indefinite. The various forms of the pronoun should be illustrated in like manner, as, for instance, its form when used as a subject (he), as an object (him), as a possessive (hers). Teaching these uses and forms may and should be spread over several grades. But when first introduced, some such procedure as the above may be followed.

2. As this word type is illustrated by means of sentences, its close relationship to the noun should be noted—that it may be used in the place of a noun in most sentences without changing the meaning greatly.

3. The illustrative sentence materials should show again and again the uses of pronouns in sentences. Pupils should have dozens of opportunities to see, hear, write, and give orally sentences using pronouns of the various types and forms. Perhaps one of the greatest weaknesses of our present language teaching is the dearth of simple illustrative materials from the pupil's environment, used to fix the concepts of

each new factor introduced. Teachers should not depend wholly on textbooks for these but should hand-tailor them to their pupils' requirements.

4. Pupil participation in working with exercises need not be limited to those exercises constructed by others. One of the best evidences of a pupil's mastery is his ability to utilize in actual situations the ideas he has learned. Such uses may consist of writing or giving orally the language aspect involved in exercises or of other more complicated composition forms.

5. With the concepts which go to make up the pronoun idea well in mind, the name and definition of the term may be worked out. This may be done by showing pupils that "pronoun" consists of the two parts, "pro" (meaning "for") and "noun." This gives added meaning to the definition: "A pronoun is a word used in the place of (for) a noun." The suggestion here is that the definition be the outgrowth of the pupil experiences with the idea, not a definition memorized from a book.

6. As a final check on the pupil's knowledge and ability to use pronouns, he should be given the opportunity to recognize and to use them in a wide variety of situations. Furthermore, his more abstract notions of them should be tested. For example, what words are pronouns in the sentence, "The boy who came late lost his hat"? What reasons do you have for your answer? Likewise the adjective, adverb, preposition, conjunction, and interjection (if used) may be taught as each appears in the text or course of study. The particular element which is peculiar to that word type is the element to be emphasized. Adjectives and adverbs modify words with which they are connected. The prepositions and conjunctions each have their own particular connective quality or qualities.

By way of *summary* of this brief discussion of the technical phases of the sentence in its different aspects, a few of the fundamental factors should be repeated. The best way to keep the whole field unified is to base the work on one unit and study this unit in all its relationships. Many teachers feel the sentence is best adapted to this type of attack. Whatever the organization of subject matter, each item, as it is presented, should be illustrated by a wealth of simple examples taken directly from the language of pupils' experience. This means experience of those pupils being taught, not that of any or all pupils. Not only should there be plenty of examples of the kind mentioned, but they should be varied to include all angles of the aspects being studied. Many successful teachers enlist the pupils' efforts in originating and applying various methods of presenting and practicing technical phases of language. Above all, pupils should realize that technical language is a part of their everyday existence; that it is something to be used by them as often as they talk or write; and especially that it is not difficult. Often pupils and teachers too are beaten before they start by the bogey man—"hard grammar."

The *punctuation marks* which most teachers would include in the work of the middle and upper grades are the period, comma, question mark, quotation marks, hyphen, apostrophe, semi-colon, colon, and exclamation point. The course of study, the textbook, or both should indicate the grade placement for the study of these marks. It is sufficient to suggest some underlying *factors of teaching* the various skills connected with the uses of these marks in written language.

First, it is important that the skill be learned in connection with an actual situation growing out of the daily run of pupil activities. For example, the idea that a period comes at the end of every statement may be discovered when the teacher calls attention to it while writing a sentence on the blackboard dictated by her beginning pupils. They may note this fact again when they read sentences from readers, and later when they themselves write sentences. Thereafter they get practice in the use of this skill in the writing of their daily tasks.

The second factor which seems to apply in teaching punctuation skills emerges from the first one. If the pupils use the natural situations to learn and practice the required skills, such situations must be provided. This is the teacher's task and it is not always easy. She should use all the written composition forms possible and teach the necessary skills as she teaches letter or note writing, making records, filling forms, doing creative writing, and other written language forms.

The third factor is that additional practice or drill exercises are needed unless the actual situations provided supply enough practice to establish the skills connected with each punctuation mark. These may be supplied by the teacher as she finds her pupils in need of such practice, or she may supply them from language textbooks or workbooks or other commercial forms. The individual differences of pupils and their variability of performance in learning should be met at least partially by variation of practice work.

The fourth factor in developing pupil skill in the use of punctuation marks is teacher alertness in checking written work. If pupils realize the importance of punctuation in written composition and are convinced that it is best for them to do it properly, the chances of good habits being formed are greater than if the opposite is true. It would seem wise, therefore, for teachers to take time to show how good punctuation does help.

A fifth factor relates directly to the evasive yet fundamental language skill we sometimes call "sentence sense." This of course reaches back to the pupil's early and subsequent training. Often this explains the failure to place the period at the end of a sentence. If such a defect exists the pupil's efforts should be directed toward growth in sentence recognition, starting with its elements—the subject and predicate. Examples in printed form may be used to illustrate the sentence. Oral exercises may be employed to help develop the feeling for and knowledge of it. Actual use of sentences by the pupil, both orally and in writing, would serve as a check. Sentence comprehension helps in training pupils to know the use of all punctuation marks. For example, if a pupil decides the sentence is a question, he knows a question mark should follow; if writing a quotation, he knows that the quotation marks should be used.

Testing in punctuation will be done mostly by teacher-made tests. There seems to be little need for standards of performance since the pupils should be able to use all marks correctly, and a level below this is not satisfactory no matter how it compares with a norm. The form of test used may vary to fit existing needs. Some suggestions follow. (1) Sentences with faulty punctuation may be used, as *John, ran home?* asking the pupil to correct the errors or fill in the omissions. (2) Another form lists the marks for each line (with sometimes an extra one) but does not state where they are to be used, such as *Harry said Hurry Edward* (" " , . ;). (3) A third form puts two or more marks at each location of a punctuation mark, and sometimes where none (*N*) is needed. The pupil selects the mark needed for the given place and puts it in the proper answer space at the right of the sentence, as

1. (N , .) 2. (N " ; , ') 3. (. N " ,)   Answers

Jane came to the door   and called   Dinner   1. ( ) 2. ( ) 3. ( )

Tests such as these can be made easily and duplicated for use in a group
of any size. If teachers keep the data from year to year and use the
same or equivalent tests, approximate levels of pupil achievement for
that school may be acquired. Some standard tests are available.[1]

In general, the methods of teaching and testing suggested for
punctuation may be used in *capitalization*. Since little has been said
about practice materials, perhaps a word as to the different types would
be helpful. First, those which the teacher furnishes may be of several
types: (1) Exercises to fit general class needs, placed on the board.
(2) Those she may duplicate for the class to fit the general situations
which eliminates the writing of the exercises by the pupils. (3) Those
she may duplicate by carbon paper to fit the needs of small groups in
a class. These may differ in content from group to group. (4) Special
remedial exercises for individual pupils. (5) Dictation exercises given
by the teacher. These dictation exercises more nearly simulate the actual
writing situations and hence are probably more valuable. Such exercises may vary from the simplest forms of capitalization or of punctuation to the most difficult and should in all cases be fitted to the needs of
the group or individuals. The second kind of helps is available in commercial form. There is a wide range of workbooks, practice sheets, and
the like which cover all items of capitalization and punctuation. If
funds are available for their purchase, these will save the teacher a good
deal of time. The danger in using these materials lies in the fact that
teachers frequently allow them to dominate the group practice, instead
of using them as tools to develop their pupils by fitting the materials
into their respective needs.

Some teachers use a *check sheet* to keep a record of pupil progress.
This may be in a variety of forms and may be used for either capitalization or punctuation. The one below is only a suggestion.

[1] Test C, Basic Language Skills. *Iowa Every-Pupil Test.* Bureau of Educational Research
    and Service, State University of Iowa.
  Iowa Elementary Language Tests. Bureau of Educational Research and Service, State
    University of Iowa.
  Leonard Diagnostic Test in Punctuation and Capitalization. World Book Co.

Skill	Tom	Mae	Edw.	Etc.
1. Writes own name.....................	X	X	X	
2. First word in a sentence capitalized...	X	X	X	
3. Pronoun "I" capitalized.............	X	X	X	
4. Date written correctly..............	X			
5. City and state written correctly......	X	X	X	
6. Period at end of sentence............	X	X		
7. Question mark after question.........		X		
(and so on to cover all items learned)				

This type of chart may be used in a schoolroom of two or more grades by indicating each pupil's name and his grade level. It may be built up as the various skills are taught and the items may be checked when the teacher is sure the pupil has mastered that skill. Another way of using such a chart is to put on it a list of skills which each pupil of the group should know and in addition all those which are to be taught in that grade. The results of an inventory test at the beginning of the year and of the review tests during the year are checked on the chart and show the skill level at the beginning and at various times throughout the year. The different test checks may be indicated by different colored check marks—the inventory checks may be blue, the first semester red, the second semester yellow. Deficiencies of individual pupils can be made to stand out clearly by such a device. Individual pupil charts of the same form kept by each pupil may be used if the teacher for some reason does not want a large class chart. If the class chart form is used for individual charts, the checks for the various tests may be put in the different columns with dates at the top in place of the pupils' names.

Although the skills in capitalization are quite definite, a large degree of ignorance in their use is found even at the college level. One study [1]

[1] Harap, H. "The Most Common Grammatical Errors." *English Journal*, pp. 440-446, June, 1930.

showed that the types of error were as follows: mistakes in capitalizing proper nouns, titles, direct quotations, first word of a sentence, proper adjectives. Apparently there has not been enough of a follow-through. Possibly our checks have not been sufficiently thorough and our remedial work not carefully and individually done.

In *closing* the discussion on this section it may again be suggested that there is nothing difficult about the basic aspects of technical language unless teachers make it so. If its phases are attacked one at a time and if each is built upon the one before and illustrated by hundreds of simple uses, pupils should find technical language easy and interesting because it is directly connected with the language they use hundreds of times every day. Perhaps teachers work too hard at language teaching. Probably they should tackle the simple elements of the technical side of language through the use of easy examples. If necessary, they should leave the more difficult levels to the high school and college. In the elementary grades teachers should be sure their pupils get a command of the fundamentals and a wholesome attitude toward the technical aspects of language.

CHAPTER 10

SPELLING

A HISTORICAL STUDY of the books and methods used in spelling instruction shows marked changes from colonial times to the present. In the late eighteenth and early nineteenth centuries, spelling was used to introduce children to reading. They learned the alphabet, syllables, and words in order to read religious material. Some early books published were a combination of speller and reader, such as the *New England Primer* and the *American Spelling Book*. At present, spelling takes its place as a partner of writing, serving as a tool for written expression. The spelling books have not reached the degree of attractiveness of some of the reading, arithmetic, and language texts. The subject matter of modern spellers, however, is scientifically compiled and arranged.

Is correct spelling *important*? What spelling ability does the average individual need to fill his place in society effectively? The ability to spell words commonly used in written expression is expected of all people. Misspelling in correspondence may mean loss of business, inability to secure a position or it may even affect the entire course of one's future. Automatic ability in spelling frees the individual from attention to this mechanical phase of writing and enables him to give more consideration to the thought involved. Even the form and style of written composition may improve because of improvement in ability in spelling.

Spelling is a tool used for the *purpose* of meeting actual writing situations effectively. Three important factors in accomplishing this purpose are: (1) that children realize the importance of accurate spelling and that they develop the desire to spell correctly, (2) that they learn to spell selected words which are essential, and (3) that they develop a technique for learning to spell words.

WORD SELECTION AND GRADE PLACEMENT

The scientific studies which determine the *word selection* and the *grade placement* are of two important types: those dealing with the words used in adult writing and those used by children in their written work. The 38th Yearbook [1] gives the following in regard to the selection of words: "Careful selection of the words to be taught in the elementary school involves two major steps. First, the words most important for children to learn to spell must be identified. Second, it must be ascertained which of these words are so simple that they can be learned by the end of the elementary-school period without definite and direct instruction in spelling. Some of these latter words offer considerable spelling difficulty to children at the early grade levels in which the words are needed in writing and should be included to facilitate the writing done in those grades. The emphasis, however, at all grade levels should be upon the words of persistent difficulty." Children learn to spell as part of their normal routine and require no direct teaching of the many simple words they see over and over again in their reading. There is an overlapping of the most important words used in the writing of adults and children. These are the ones to be taught in the elementary grades. They number about 3000.[2] "In any grade any word not included in the basic list should be taught as the need for it arises in connection with other school activities."[3] Some words in such a list may be of a temporary nature and no effort for permanent learning need be made, as in the case of names of pets. Other words pertaining to a certain district in which children live may have continued use and deserve mastery, although they are not in the regular

---

[1] Horn, E. and McKee, P. "The Development of Ability in Spelling." *38th Yearbook of the National Society for the Study of Education*. Part I, pp. 241-242. Public School Publishing Co. 1939.

[2] *Ibid.*, p. 247.

[3] *Ibid.*, p. 251.

current list, such as those pertaining to industries or environment. These special words may become the supplementary list for a class and a record should be kept of them for teaching and review purposes. If this supplementary list makes the load too heavy for the pupils, its words may be substituted for some of those least frequently used in the regular list.

In assigning words from the selected list that are to be learned at the different grade levels, it is well to consider the children's need for knowing the word at that particular period and the difficulty of learning it. The number of words in a weekly unit will vary chiefly according to the grade level. Probably not more than twenty words should be presented in any grade—fewer for the lower grades.

METHODS OF TEACHING

Undoubtedly the *methods* for teaching spelling have been more definitely outlined than for any other subject. Therefore, it would seem that the results obtained in teaching spelling should be better than results in other fields.

Some activities for the purpose of establishing a *spelling readiness*

One way to teach small   Learning through play.
and capital letters.

may profitably precede regular instruction in spelling. A few such suggestions follow: (1) seeing the teacher write labels, sentences, and accounts as the children dictate them, using either manuscript or cursive form, depending upon which form is taught; (2) having attention called to the difference between the capital and small letters in recorded compositions; (3) learning the names of the letters of the alphabet as the opportunities occur for talking about them (this does not imply knowing the letters in alphabetical order); (4) playing with alphabet blocks; (5) calling attention to the likenesses and differences in the appearance of words in reading material; (6) hearing the teacher use the word "spelling" in situations which will make clear that "to spell" means arranging letters in the order in which they come in words; (7) copying their own names, labels, and short messages; (8) helping children feel the need for spelling.

There are *two general plans* of procedure advocated for teaching spelling: the *study-test* and the *test-study*. In the former the children study the words first and are tested after study. It is claimed that in this way they get the correct initial concepts of the words and avoid writing them incorrectly. The second or test-study plan provides that a test be given over the list for the week, and that the studying include only those words which are missed. This saves time and effort since the pupils discover what words they need to study and avoid spending time on those they already know. Perhaps it would be well to use the study-test plan for the younger children since they are more completely guided by the teacher; and the test-study for the older ones after better techniques of independent study have been developed.

If direct spelling instruction is to be given in the *first grade* a good *plan* to follow for pupils' *studying with* the *teacher* is that given by Horn.[1] The words to be taught are put on the board or read from the book. He says: (1) Choose one of the words to be taught. (2) Have the pupils look at the word carefully as you say it. (3) Have them say it after you. Be sure that the word is pronounced correctly. (4) Then write the word on the board. Say each letter as you write it. (5) Have the pupils say each letter after you. (6) Ask them to notice how you make each letter. (7) When you have finished writing the word have the pupils pronounce it again individually or in concert, and (8) again say the letters.

Horn[2] also gives the following steps for first grade pupils to use in *studying independently*. "(1) Look at the first word. Say it softly. Look at each part of the word as you say it again. Now say the letters.

---

[1] Horn, E. "How to Teach and Study Primary Spelling." *The Classroom Teacher*, Vol. 2, p. 552. The Classroom Teacher, Inc. 1927. Adapted.

[2] *Ibid.*, pp. 552-553.

(2) Close your eyes. Say the word softly and try to see it as you say the letters. (3) Open your eyes and look at the word to see if you said the letters right. (4) Look at the word again. Say it. Look at each part carefully as you say it. (5) Close your eyes. Say the word and try again to see it as you say the letters. (6) Open your eyes and look again at the word to see if you said the letters right. (7) Do this enough times to be sure that you can spell the word. (8) Now try to write the word. If you are not sure how to make a letter, ask your teacher to help you."

The following is the *teacher's plan for the week* in the first grade as adapted also from Horn.[1] Monday: Introduce the words to be learned for the entire week. Teach as directed above according to the plan for pupils' studying with the teacher. Tuesday: Help pupils to study the words by themselves, and to write them well. Wednesday: Repeat the work of Monday. Have the children write each word after seeing it written. Thursday: Help pupils to study as on Tuesday. Friday: Ask the pupils to write each word as it is pronounced. Study the papers for the purpose of helping the pupils the next week. This same procedure may be used in the second grade unless the children are especially advanced.

A successful plan for more *advanced levels* using a week-unit originated by Dr. Ernest Horn and Dr. E. J. Ashbaugh and based upon the *test-study* principles is now used generally with some modifications. The following is an adaptation of this plan.

Monday: Present the words for the week. First, pronounce the words and have the pupils look at and pronounce each one. Calling attention to the syllables is often helpful. Second, give the meaning of a word if there is any doubt about the pupils' knowing it. The teacher may use a word in a sentence if she thinks it necessary or she may ask a pupil to do it. Pronounce the words and ask the pupils to write them in a column. The words that each individual misspells are the ones he needs to study. These should be written in another column for study. (See the study sheet plan given below.)

Tuesday: Help each pupil to learn how to study the words he missed on Monday. Use the plan of study given below. Work with them as a group at first and until they have the habit of following the steps presented. Then help them individually as the need suggests.

[1] *Ibid.*, 553-554.

Wednesday: Test again using the list of the week together with the most difficult words from the list of the month before. Pupils who made no errors Monday may be excused from this study period but should write all of the tests since they may spell words correctly on Monday and miss them in the following tests.

Thursday: Help each to study the words he has missed on Wednesday.

Friday: Test again on the words used on Wednesday. The correct spelling of any that are missed should be written in notebooks provided for this purpose. Check the errors. Sometimes children correct each other's lists. If this is done it is well for the teacher to re-check when there is any question of accuracy.

In the *study-test* plan the pupils are taught the words before they are tested on them. The following is a procedure based upon this plan:[1]

First day: New words are presented clearly to the pupils and study assignments are made. Each word should be pronounced clearly by the teacher, written on the blackboard, and attention called to difficulties of spelling. The pupils are asked to close their eyes in order to visualize the words. Different pupils may pronounce them and write them on the board.

Second day: An exploratory test is given by the teacher who pronounces each word, uses it in a sentence, and again pronounces it. When the pupils hear the second pronunciation, they write the word in a column on their papers. The pupils check their lists as the teacher spells the words. The words which each pupil misses should be written in a spelling notebook. Each child thus has his own list for study.

Third day: This day is devoted to the "intensive supervised study of the words missed in the exploratory test." Those missed by most of the group may be studied by the entire class, the other words individually.

Fourth day: The words in the review list (words studied four weeks earlier) are used in a test. More recent words which have caused trouble should be studied and tested, and also words from other sources.

Fifth day: A written test is given on all words that have been studied. Those that each missed should be put in each child's notebook

[1] Ayer, F. C., Oberholtzer, E. E., Woody, C. *Modern Life Speller*, pp. x-xi-xii. World Book Co. 1936. Adapted.

and studied. Each child's progress should be noted on the progress record.

The following may be given to children as a *pattern for learning to spell a word*.[1] (1) Pronounce the word correctly. Look at each syllable carefully as it is pronounced. (2) Close your eyes and think how the word looks as you say it syllable by syllable in a whisper. Look at the word again, thinking of the spelling. (3) Close your eyes and spell it to yourself. Look at the word to see if you spelled it correctly. If you did not, do 1 and 2 again. Repeat until you can spell it to yourself correctly. (4) When you feel that you have learned the word write it without looking at the copy. Then check with the copy. If you have made a mistake, do 1, 2, 3, and 4 again. (5) Repeat this two or more times. If you make a mistake in any of these trials write the word in your notebook and study again later. The above-mentioned plans suggest that learning to spell should include four types of activities; vocal, auditory, visual, and muscular.

Other texts in spelling use a *modification* of this plan. The following is one.[2] (1) Say the word clearly and softly to yourself. (2) Carefully copy the word on your paper. (3) Look at your copy and spell the word twice. (4) Close your eyes or cover the word and make believe you are writing the word twice on paper. (5) Write the word on paper without looking at your book or the copy you made. (6) Check your word. Did you spell it right? (7) If you missed the word, go over the steps again. Then study the next word.

All teachers should try to develop an attitude toward correct spelling which would impel children individually and of their own initiative to work on their spelling deficiencies in their spare time. The following form of *spelling sheet* (8 × 11 inches) may aid in helping children to study independently. These sheets when finished may be kept in notebook form.[3]

[1] Adapted from *18th Yearbook of the National Society for the Study of Education*, p. 72. Public School Publishing Co. 1919. Horn-Ashbaugh. *Progress in Spelling*, p. XV. J. P. Lippincott Co. 1935.

[2] Newlon, J. and Hanna, P. *The Newlon-Hanna Speller*, p. II-1. Houghton Mifflin Co. 1933.

[3] Ritter, E. L. and Wilmarth, Alta L. *Rural School Methods*, p. 8. Charles Scribner's Sons. 1925.

FRONT

1	2 Wednesday	3 Wednesday

Spelling Sheet

Name: Tom Jones   May 10

1 Monday new words	2 Wednesday new words	3 Wednesday review words
1. next	1. next	1. loose
2. their	2. their	2. coff
3. wicht	3. which	3. knew
4. piece	4. piece	4. shure
5. rigt	5. right	5. color
6. etc.	6. etc.	6. etc.
7.		
8.		
9.		
10.		
11.		
12.		
13.		
14.		
15.		
16.		
17.		
18.	Fold	Fold
19.		
20.		

BACK

Spelling Sheet

4 Friday new words	5 Friday review words	6 Study column
1. next	1. loose	Tuesday
2. their	2. cough	1. which
3. which	3. knew	2. right
4. piece	4. shure	3.
5. right	5. color	4.
6. etc.	6. etc.	5.
7.		6. etc.
8.		
9.		Thursday
10.		1. cough
11.		2. sure
12.		3.
13.		
14.		Notebook
15. etc.		1. sure
		2.
	Fold	3.
	Fold	

The following are directions for using this form.[1] "The new words when pronounced on Monday are written in column 1. Words misspelled in column 1 are written correctly in column 6 under 'Tuesday.' On Wednesday the new words (words pronounced on Monday) are written in column 2, and the review list (lesson of one month before) in column 3. Fold column 1 under when column 2 is written; in fact, only the column which is being used should be exposed during any writing. Words misspelled in columns 2 and 3 are correctly written in column 6 under Thursday. Likewise Friday's spellings are written in columns 4 and 5, and the correct spellings of words missed in column 6 under 'Notebook.' If there should be a large number of misspellings, use an additional sheet for column 6."

Although there is evidence that spelling is learned better when words are in column rather than in context form, it is well, nevertheless, to use some short sentences as dictation exercises from time to time

[1] *Ibid.*, p. 8.

since the sentence is the form in which pupils will need to write the words correctly.

Often in a one-room rural school it is advantageous to *combine classes* for spelling. The program which follows shows how this may be done for a fifth and eighth grade.

FIRST WEEK [1]

	Monday	Tuesday	Wednesday	Thursday	Friday
Schedule for 8th Grade	Write new list words	Study new list words	Write new and review words	Study new and review words	Write new and review words
Schedule for 5th Grade	......	Write new list words	Study new list words	Write new and review words	Study new and review words

SECOND WEEK

	Monday	Tuesday	Wednesday	Thursday	Friday
Schedule or 8th Grade	Notebook	Write new list words	Study new list words	Write new and review words	Study new and review words
Schedule for 5th Grade	Write new and review words	Notebook	Write new list words	Study new list words	Write new and review words

THIRD WEEK, ETC.

	Monday	Tuesday	Wednesday	Thursday	Friday
Schedule for 8th Grade	Write new and review words	Notebook	Write new list words	Study new list words	Write new and review words
Schedule for 5th Grade	Study new and review words	Write new and review words	Notebook	Write new list words	Study new list words

There is some evidence to show that learning focused on the spelling of individual words is more effective than fixing attention on learning to spell by *rules*. However, there are certain groups of words to which rules do apply and effect economies of time and effort. Foran[2] gives the following principles regarding the teaching of rules: "(1) Only a

[1] *Ibid.*, p. 9.
[2] Foran, T. G. *The Psychology and Teaching of Spelling*, pp. 144-149. The Catholic Education Press. 1934. Abbreviated.

few rules should be taught. There is no justification for the practice of requiring children to memorize rules which apply to only a small number of words. (2) Some rules should be taught, for children will generalize what they have learned and such generalizations should be directed as far as the spelling of English words permits. (3) Only one rule should be taught at a time. (4) A rule should be taught only when there is need of it. It would be plainly absurd to teach children in the third grade such a complex rule as that regarding the doubling of the final consonant when adding a suffix. (5) The teaching of the rules should be integrated with the arrangement or grouping of the words in the textbook. (6) Rules should be taught inductively rather than deductively. . . . The children should be shown the spelling of several words covered by the rule and their attention directed to but not focused upon the common features of the words. Thus they discover the ways in which the words are alike and state the generalization which they have discovered. (7) There should be ample reviews of the rules both in the grades in which they have been learned and in the following grades. (8) Tests of knowledge of the rule should insist not so much upon logical precision as on comprehension and ability to use the rule."

The following are some common rules which should help: (1) The plural of most English nouns is normally formed by adding *s* or *es*. When the word ends in a sound that does not combine well with the sound of *s*, as that of *j*, *s*, *x*, *ch* or *sh*, *es* is added—as dog, dogs; bee, bees; dress, dresses; church, churches. (2) If a noun ends with *y* preceded by a consonant the *y* is changed to *i* and *es* is added to form the plural, as in baby, babies; city, cities. (3) Some nouns ending in *f* and *fe* have these endings changed to *v* and *es* added to form the plurals, such as shelf, shelves; wife, wives. (4) If a word ends in a silent *e* the *e* is dropped when a syllable beginning with a vowel is added, such as come, coming; name, naming. (5) *Q* is always followed by *u*, as quick, quail. (6) There is only one final *l* in words ending with *ful*, as careful, cupful. Hildreth [1] recommends postponing the introduction of spelling rules until the fourth grade.

There are certain *spelling problems* of which children should be

[1] Hildreth, G. *Learning the Three R's,* Second Ed., p. 538. Educational Publishers, Inc. 1947.

aware. Some of them are: knowing (1) that certain classes of words should begin with capital letters, such as names of places, persons, months, days, and many others; (2) that some words need the apostrophe, such as can't; (3) that some need the hyphen, as self-help; (4) that some nouns have the same form singular and plural, as sheep; (5) that some change one or two vowels to form the plural, as man-men and foot-feet; (6) that the ending with the same pronunciation is sometimes *le* (humble) and sometimes *el* (travel); (7) that some words

Teaching meanings through sketches aids in correct spelling.

with the same pronunciations are spelled differently according to meaning, such as to, too, two. Written exercises based on words selected from one or two of these classes (and including other words) stimulate pupils' interest—such as proper nouns together with some common nouns; names of the months together with names of seasons, etc.

Textbooks commonly plan for *systematic reviews* of the words taught. Reviews are essential for the more difficult words. Some of the points to remember are: (1) One of the best types of review involves the use of words taught in written work of all fields. This, however, is uncontrolled and indefinite; therefore some additional systematic plan should be provided. (2) Writing the review words in the tests twice a week, as suggested in the one week plan, is really a review for maintaining spelling skill. Words not used are likely to be forgotten. (3) Since a pretest is not possible with the supplementary list of words, it is well to keep a list of them and to provide periodic reviews and tests either with the regular reviews or independently. (4) The amount of time given to a spelling lesson is not nearly so important as the plan for conducting the work and the methods of presentation and study employed. The modern spelling texts generally use a week unit of words rather than a one-day unit. (5) Phonics as an aid in spelling should be used judiciously. It may help in the spelling of some words but in others its use may be very misleading—for example, the f sound for *ph* in telephone and similar situations. (6) Reed[1] advises that homonyms be taught separately to avoid confusion, as in the case of bear and bare. (7) Pupils should realize that the dictionary is a source of correct spelling and meanings. They need definite instruction in how to use a dictionary for these purposes as well as for the others. (8) Pupils should realize that good penmanship is essential, since words are often judged incorrect because of poor letter formation.

TESTING AND RECORDING RESULTS

Testing in the field of spelling is more definitely developed and more easily conducted than in most subjects. Testing is desirable as a means of showing children the status of their achievement and as a means of indicating the direction of their efforts.

There are *three types of tests*, (1) those used for the weekly unit of words as a means of determining what words individuals need to study and the progress made during the five days devoted to each unit, (2) those given at longer intervals to determine the skill maintained over the review words, and (3) the standardized tests used for the purpose of comparing individuals and groups with established norms.

There are different procedures for *presenting* spelling *test words*. Foran[2] recommends three methods of administering recall tests: "the list method, the sentence method, and the modified sentence method. The three methods yield approximately the same results but the modified sentence enjoys the advantages of eliminating ambiguities and of economizing time." In the list method the teacher pronounces the words and the children write them. In the sentence method the teacher

[1] Reed, H. R. *Psychology of Elementary School Subjects,* pp. 234-235. Ginn and Co. 1938.
[2] *Op. cit.,* pp. 185-186.

dictates sentences containing the words to be tested and the pupils write each sentence. Only the words of the test are scored. In the modified sentence method the teacher gives the word, repeats it in a sentence, and gives it again, and the children write only the test word. The latter seems to be most helpful because it emphasizes meaning, yet only the pertinent words are written.[1]

The convenience and effectiveness of *graphs* and *charts* as an objective means of showing children their levels of achievement are readily recognized by teachers. Class charts may be posted, but those showing individual attainments had better be kept in each pupil's spelling notebook in order to avoid the making of misleading comparisons of progress by the children. Such personal records can generally be used best to help each pupil to try to surpass his own previous record.

Many of the *modern spellers* offer interesting features in their construction. For example, they give specific directions to teachers as to how to conduct the work. Study helps for pupils are given. Words are presented in meaningful settings, such as a short story or paragraph. They are usually also given in lists. Meanings of words and word analysis are stressed. Different activities which require the use of the words are presented as part of the learning process. Reviews and tests are provided. Notebooks accompany some of the texts or space is provided in the book for writing the words and the tests. These notebooks often contain a form for a graph to show progress.

Let us *summarize* by saying that, with the available helps, the present teaching of spelling should be a challenge to the earnest teacher who desires to develop in children a real interest in this skill subject. Such an interest should lead to a high degree of skill. This will provide the ability to meet effectively situations requiring accurate spelling and will contribute toward successful living.

[1] *Ibid.*, pp. 179 and 186.

CHAPTER 11

HANDWRITING

O NLY in relatively recent times has handwriting become one of the common means by which ideas are expressed. Early man used pictures. For a long period, different types of manuscripts made by the limited groups who knew the techniques of writing were the media of preserving ideas. The different mechanical devices of expression and communication at the present time lessen to some extent the importance of handwriting. These devices, however, are not by any means universally used; indeed in some situations nothing but handwriting suffices. Furthermore, the individuality expressed in handwriting is difficult to duplicate mechanically. Hence writing is used now as a means of expression and probably will so continue for some time to come. It is used also for identification purposes in countless ways. Handwriting and spelling are the tools of language expression. Therefore, there should be close correlation in the teaching of all three. The situations in which these tools are needed have been discussed in the section on written language.

The most important *goal* in teaching handwriting is the ability to express ideas readily and rapidly in symbols easily read by others. This involves legibility of form and speed of movement. Speed of writing and good letter formation are best developed together. One should not be sacrificed to the other. Rhythmic motion in handwriting affects the rate, and grows from harmonizing the necessary movements of fingers, arm, and shoulder. Rhythm should be stressed from the first.

There are certain *factors* to remember when teaching children to write. (1) Learning to write, unless the manuscript form is used, should be delayed. It is a complex process involving the smaller muscles. The younger children find such co-ordination difficult. (2) It should be taught as it is to be used—as a tool for expression. This implies that children should begin by writing whole words, not individual letters. (3) Practice is necessary since writing is a skill. The ability to write is usually attained more easily by some pupils than by others. (4) The prime essential in attaining legibility is a favorable attitude of the pupil; that is, he should have the desire to make his handwriting legible to others.[1]

Techniques of teaching writing are definitely set up in manuals for the different systems of handwriting. Therefore, detailed suggestions are unnecessary here and only some *general phases* are discussed. They are writing readiness, manuscript writing, and cursive writing.

A *writing readiness* period may precede the introduction of any form of writing. The following activities during this preliminary period should help prepare children for it: (1) Drawing is a natural and related activity. Children draw lines with their fingers on frosty window panes, trace pictures with sticks in the sand, and find pleasure in using different mediums of graphic expression. So drawing with chalk on the blackboard and with chalk and crayons on paper gives children an easy, natural means of expressing their ideas before they learn to write. Drawing also develops certain muscular control. (2) Another related activity is the making of rhythmic movements. Making lines to picture ideas, such as curves for swinging ⌣, slanting lines for sliding ╱, and others furnish practice in rhythmic muscular motion. The children's work corresponding to these illustrations and those which follow should all be on a much larger scale than the ones shown here. These exercises are recommended by some authorities to be done according to the rhythm expressed in appropriate rhymes. Freeman [2]

---

[1] Children may be encouraged to use the typewriter where they have the opportunity. Some reasons for its use in school are that children enjoy using the machine and they learn a skill used commonly for expression in the home and business. Freeman claims in his article "An Experiment in the Use of the Typewriter in the Elementary School," *The Elementary School Journal*, Vol. XXXII, No. 10, June, 1932, that children tend to produce more written material when the typewriter is used and that its use does not appreciably lessen quality or rate of handwriting.

[2] Freeman, F. N. "Primary Handwriting." *The Classroom Teacher*, p. 141. The Classroom Teacher, Inc. 1927.

illustrates this by suggesting that a picture of a candle be drawn on the board and the child make curved lines over the top as he says the rhyme about Jack-be-nimble.

Circular movements may likewise be the expression to accompany Pat-a-Cake. (3) Watching the teacher write stories and verse which children dictate is another device. Thus they see the motions involved in writing as well as the finished form and should more clearly realize that writing is a means of expressing and conveying ideas. (4) Making lines and scribbling may appear trivial but are helpful and should be encouraged. In this way, children get practice in holding the writing tools and they gain in muscular control.

There are two forms to consider when introducing children to handwriting: the manuscript or printscript and the traditional cursive. Many instructors prefer using the manuscript for about the first two years then changing to the cursive. Others would teach cursive from the first. Manuscript writing might be taught throughout the grades but the public, as yet, seems not ready to accept it in place of the cursive. Therefore, if children begin by using manuscript, it is probably best that later they learn cursive also.

MANUSCRIPT

Manuscript writing is not new. It is similar to that used in making books by hand before the invention of the printing press. Marjorie Wise of England in 1922-23 introduced manuscript writing at Teachers College, Columbia University. Since then interest has spread throughout the United States. The letters are easily made, consisting of circles, or parts of circles, and straight lines. The following[1] is one of the several good forms used. The arrow indicates the direction and the number the sequence of the stroke.

Some *advantages* of manuscript writing over cursive as given by its advocates are: (1) It is easier because of the simple manner in which the letters are formed and because the letters in the words are unconnected. (2) Early manuscript writing attempts surpass the first cursive

[1] Freeman, F. N. and The Zaner-Bloser Co. *Print to Script, Practice Book I*, pp. 32 and 33. The Zaner-Bloser Co. 1936.

writing of children in legibility. (3) It is more like drawing, to which children are accustomed. (4) Children can express themselves in the manuscript earlier than in the cursive form. (5) It helps in learning to read and to spell. (6) There is less eyestrain and general physical strain involved. (7) It gives children satisfaction because they can obtain results more quickly and easily. (8) It is more attractive for lettering on booklet covers and other such work. (9) It closely re-

abcdefghijklm

nopqrstuvwxyz

sembles the print children meet in reading materials; therefore they are not burdened at first with learning two symbols for each letter. (10) It can be learned without much teacher supervision.

Some of the *disadvantages* given are: (1) It means learning two forms of letters since children also usually learn the cursive. (2) Children sometimes have difficulty when they change to the cursive form. (3) It handicaps children in reading cursive. (4) Children do not write as rapidly as with cursive. (Some claim that manuscript is as rapid. As yet there are insufficient data on this point.) (5) It is not as rhythmic. (6) It lacks individuality.

Some suggestions concerning the *method* of teaching follow:

1. Teachers, themselves, need to be able to use manuscript writing. It is not difficult. With an alphabet as a guide it can be acquired with little practice. Whether or not children use it, teachers will find it effective when making experience reading charts, doing blackboard work, and making cards for different purposes.

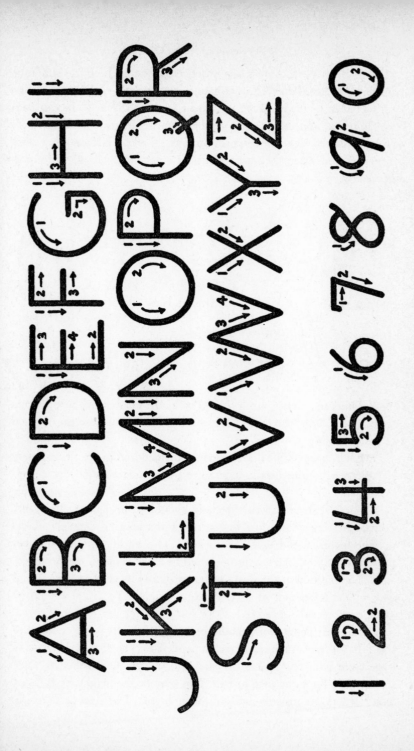

2. It is better to connect the practice in writing with the children's interests, rather than to do it on unrelated forms. A child is always interested in his own name. When he is able to write it, he can label his drawings and other work. Other motives for early work may be copying labels, signs, and words in lists. Later, children copy short sentences and when they have sufficient ability in spelling, write independently.

3. Children's first writing should be at the blackboard, where there is room for large letters and the teacher can easily note the method of work.

4. Later, lines on the blackboard aid the children in acquiring ability to keep the bottom of the letters even and to determine the correct height.

5. For blackboard work the chalk should be held inside the hand, grasped by thumb and first finger, not like a pencil. Only the chalk, not the hand, should touch the board. This encourages larger, freer movements. Children's writing should be about on their eye level.

6. The position at the desks or tables should be comfortable. If the seats or desks are not of proper height, suitable provision should be made to correct the defects.

7. The first paper work should be large, gradually being reduced in size. Paper without lines is recommended for the first work, later a large piece with few spaces may be used. Paper used for later work should have lines one inch apart. This may be the height for capitals. Small letters are usually one-half inch high. The size of letters is

gradually decreased by using paper with narrower spaces. Pencils with large soft leads are best.

8. The paper should be square with the desk. Then the straight down strokes will be perpendicular to the top of the desk.

9. Children need a copy of the alphabet to which they can refer.

10. Most commercial primary writing books use words common to children's vocabulary and can be used as sources of words needed. These are a help to teachers whether or not they are in the children's hands.

11. Two factors that especially contribute to good manuscript writing are: (a) letters rather close together in the words and (b) a space about the width of one of the wider letters between the words.

12. It is well to use some scale for checking children's progress.[1]

13. Cursive writing is often introduced in the latter part of the second grade or first part of the third. By that time children have used manuscript long enough to have acquired fluency in expressing themselves and probably will have matured sufficiently to be able to learn the cursive form easily. Manuscript writing should continue to be used where appropriate, as for labeling, making titles on booklets, and the like.

14. Alertness on the part of teacher may prevent the common tendency of children to bring their eyes too near the paper.

CURSIVE

Most of the suggestions given for teaching manuscript writing apply to the teaching of the *cursive form*. If the latter is to be used exclusively, the writing readiness period should be extended until children have sufficient maturity and muscular control for making the more difficult script forms with their connecting lines.

If manuscript writing has been taught, little difficulty is experienced in the transition from manuscript to cursive. The following suggestions may aid in avoiding trouble or in overcoming it if encountered:

1. Direct the pupils to slant the top of their writing paper about 30° from the top of the desk. The right-hand person slants the top to the

[1] Wahlert, J. and Leutheusser, A. O. *Teachers Manual* to accompany *My First Writing Book* and *My Second Writing Book*. Laurel Book Co. 1935.

left, the left-hand person to the right. This for the most part takes care of the slant in the cursive form.

2. Call the pupils' attention to the fact that the downward strokes for the right-hand person are approximately perpendicular to the top of the desk in cursive writing just as they were in manuscript.

3. Write a familiar word on the board using the cursive form and point out the differences between cursive and manuscript, as slant, connecting lines.

4. Ask pupils to copy the word on paper. Check and aid pupils when necessary.

5. Continue the board and copy exercises with checking until proficiency has been acquired.

Some additional suggestions applicable to *methods* of procedure in teaching cursive writing are as follows: (1) The slant of the writing is determined by the angle at which the paper is placed in relation to the body. (2) Children should continually strive for improving the legibility of their writing. Speed can be emphasized as legibility is being established. (3) The use of the pen is usually recommended for the third grade. There is no reason for barring fountain pens. Children will use them later anyway. (4) Better results are probably attained when children actually copy words than when they trace forms or write in the air. (5) The naturally left-handed pupil should be allowed to use his left hand, especially if the degree of left-handedness is pronounced. His paper should be placed on the desk, slanting from the upper right corner to the lower left corner of the desk. His left hand should be held in the normal writing position, resting on the third and fourth fingers and holding the pen or pencil with the thumb, first, and second fingers.

The *aim* of writing instruction in the *intermediate grades* is improvement of those techniques already acquired to some degree during preceding years. The degree of mastery achieved will be not only the result of practice but also of maturation. Both affect ability in writing. The handwriting done in all fields of work should receive attention, not only those of a definite writing period. After all, the acid test of handwriting teaching is in the manner it functions in daily use. Some teachers, when giving periodic marks, take into consideration random samplings of the handwriting done in all ordinary regular work. For example, samples might be taken from a history examination, the outline of a section on geography, or the notebook work on problem solution in arithmetic and used with the writing period marks to make up the pupil's average semester mark. The same plan may be followed in departmentalized schools with co-operation between the handwriting teacher and those of other subjects. It might well be that a marking procedure of this type would stimulate pupils to greater care and consequent improvement, as it seems to be more accurate than one which takes into account only their writing period work. Some teachers mark their pupils entirely on the daily run of written materials. This plan might function very well in junior or senior high school. It seems that direct instruction should be given in the middle grades, and the results of this should be incorporated in the pupil's final mark. One good way of stimulating pupils to improve their handwriting is to set a definite standard, for example, 60 in quality on the Ayres scale. Pupils should know when they reach this standard and should practice enough to maintain this level of accomplishment. This should include a reasonable rate of writing, possibly 60 to 70 letters per minute.

Freeman [1] gives the following factors involved in good handwriting; speed, uniformity of slant and alignment, quality of the line or stroke, letter formation, and spacing. Perhaps a brief explanation of these factors will suggest to the teacher ways of helping children analyze their handwriting and improve it.

The *rate* at which a pupil writes may be found by asking him to write material that has been memorized (so that time will not be consumed in looking at the copy), counting the number of letters he writes during a designated time, and dividing the total number of letters by the number of minutes he wrote. That is, if he wrote 120 letters in three minutes his rate would be 40 letters per minute.

The *factors constituting legibility* are not so easily checked. (1) In order to determine and compare the uniformity of the slant of the letters, lines may be drawn parallel to the down strokes of some of the letters. This may also be done for the standard scale. If these lines are transferred to a transparent paper and the paper laid over the

---

[1] Much that follows in this section is adapted from Freeman, F. N. *The Teaching of Handwriting*, pp. 118-139. Houghton Mifflin Co. 1914, and *Directions for Using Freeman's Chart for Diagnosing Faults in Handwriting*. Houghton Mifflin Co.

pupil's writing, the comparison is easily made. (2) The uniformity of alignment of the letters is determined by considering the relation of the bottoms and tops of one-space letters to the real or imaginary lines. This may be judged also by using two parallel lines about one-fourth of an inch apart, drawn on a transparent paper and placed over the pupil's writing. The variation from these lines can easily be seen. (3) The strokes are even, smooth, and firm in good writing. Variations in the quality of strokes, Freeman states, are more easily detected by the use of a reading glass in order to magnify the lines. (4) Letter formation is the most important factor in determining legibility. There are many variations from the conventional form and certain individualities in pupils' writing should be accepted. At the same time it should be remembered that "legibility and beauty" are the bases for judging this factor. With these in mind, the teacher should direct children to make comparisons with standard alphabet forms or with well written sentences, in order for pupils to see where improvement is needed. (5) Spacing has to do with the space between letters, words, and lines. The last aspect is controlled for children if they write on ruled paper. The spacing between letters and words may be too wide or the letters and words may be crowded. The following standards are suggested as a bases for comparisons of pupils' work.[1]

Quality	Grades							
	I	II	III	IV	V	VI	VII	VIII
Ayres		38	42	46	50	54	58	62
Speed (in letters per min.)		31	44	55	64	71	76	79

Ability in *self-criticism* in handwriting should be developed in all grades. A good penmanship scale[2] is indispensable in reaching this objective. Perhaps the simpler forms of handwriting scales should be used in the lower grades such as the Ayres "Gettysburg" Scale. If a teacher has no means of securing a handwriting scale, she should arrange three to five handwriting samples in approximate order, from very poor to very good, for her pupils to use in comparing and rating

[1] Ayres, L. P. *Measuring Scale for Handwriting.* Russell Sage Foundation, New York 10, N. Y.
[2] West, P. V. *American Handwriting Scale.* A. N. Palmer Co.
Freeman, F. N. *Chart for Diagnosing Faults in Handwriting.* Houghton Mifflin Co.
New York City Penmanship Scale. The Macmillan Co.

their own specimens. In any case, the teacher should make sure that her pupils develop a sincere attitude of self-criticism. This is a fundamental factor in handwriting improvement. It often produces a desire on the part of the pupil to write better. Without these two basic elements, the best development in handwriting is impossible.

Summarizing the teaching of handwriting, it may be said that: Writing is a tool of expression. It is a complicated process. Children should have some maturity before beginning. Its teaching should be motivated, it should not be a series of mechanical practice periods. The teacher should set good models in her writing. The major objectives are speed and legibility, with formation of letters, slant, alignment, the stroke, and spacing as contributing factors. Each pupil should realize his weaknesses and the teacher and pupil should work together for improvement. Writing scales help children to make their individual analyses.

QUESTIONS—PROBLEMS—REACTIONS
READING

SECTION ONE: *Facts*

1. What are the values of good reading ability?
2. How is reading classified on the basis of purpose? Of form?
3. Name four purposes for reading.
4. What modern conditions affect the amount of reading done?
5. What have been some methods used in teaching reading?
6. What four broad periods in reading instruction are given in this chapter?
7. What are different techniques for recognizing words independently?
8. What movements do the eyes make when reading?
9. What are some reading readiness activities?
10. What are the two phases of the Period of Beginning Reading?
11. What is the main task to be accomplished in the Preprimer Phase?
12. What are four materials and procedures that may be worked out by the teachers and children for this phase?
13. Give some appropriate topics for experience reading charts.
14. State some advantages in using experience charts.
15. What are the purposes of the Primer and First Reader Phases?
16. Name the six steps of procedure for reading a selection as suggested for the Primer Phase.
17. Give the objective for the end of the Period of Expanding Power.
18. What are some purposes for silent reading, re-reading silently, and oral reading?

19. List in one column some specific reading defects. In a parallel column give some remedial devices for these defects.
20. What uses can be made of a school library?
21. Where can materials for a library be obtained?
22. What aims and objectives for reading are set forth for the intermediate and upper grades?
23. In ranking the aims for this period, which one should be given a high place?
24. Which is the more complicated process, oral or silent reading?
25. Outline the values of recreational reading and the cautions that should be considered. Do the same for study reading.
26. What attitudes, habits, and skills in oral reading should a teacher aim to develop?
27. What two approaches for teaching oral reading are suggested?
28. What are some situations for audience reading?
29. What are some values of choral reading?
30. How can silent reading ability be tested?

SECTION TWO: *Problems*

31. "Reading is a complex process." Explain.
32. Compare the importance of oral reading with that of silent reading.
33. What are the relations of oral and silent reading to recreational and study reading?
34. Why is reading instruction important in the teaching of all subjects?
35. Why is attention to word meanings important at all levels?
36. Show the relation of rate of reading to eye movement.
37. Explain the meaning of reading readiness given in the text.
38. Why is it desirable for children to become accustomed to handling books before reading from them?
39. How do silent reading exercises in the Preprimer Phase help develop the understanding of the main purpose of reading?
40. Which of the four activities of the Preprimer Phase help children to acquire vocabulary independently?
41. Why do some teachers urge the reading of several preprimers before a primer, while others suggest the reading of the primer directly following the preprimers of that series?
42. What level of material would you select for the beginning reading of any year? Give reasons for your selection.
43. Why should reading and unit work be correlated?
44. Illustrate each step recommended for presenting a phonetic element to children.
45. Are there dangers in checking free reading too strictly? Reasons for your answer.
46. Explain the meaning of "extending and enriching pupil experience" through reading.
47. Compare ability with the desire to read.
48. What type of reading did you employ when you read this chapter? Give reasons for your answer.

49. Show the relationship of the voice quality to good oral reading.
50. Evaluate the work recommended for the laboratory periods.
51. In comparing the materials listed under "Laboratory Plan" and "Old Plan," which would fit better in the Function of the School outline, Chapter One?
52. Explain the meaning of "audience reading."
53. What evidence have we that study-reading skills can be improved? How can it be done?
54. Evaluate the plan of procedure as outlined for the content subjects.
55. Show the value of testing reading ability.

SECTION THREE: *Personal Reactions*

56. Do you think people tend to read more or less at present than formerly?
57. From your observation, do people do more recreational or study-reading?
58. Which stage of reading do you think the most important? Why?
59. How would you attempt to improve some of the conditions that may create the necessity for remedial work in reading?
60. Which of the factors mentioned in this chapter do you feel are of special importance for determining reading readiness?
61. Do you believe re-reading a selection necessarily helps pupils to understand or remember the subject matter? Why?
62. Would you recommend grouping of primary pupils according to reading ability? Would you recommend the same for middle and upper grades?
63. What procedure do you follow when you meet a new word?
64. Do you think it better for a pupil to read "big little" books than not to read at all? Why?
65. Which pupil do you consider more often neglected in reading instruction, the good or poor reader?
66. Which of the materials and methods suggested for remedial-reading work do you rank as the most important? Why?
67. In your opinion, what should be the order of the aims in teaching literature when arranged according to value in pupil development?
68. Compare the presentation of literature to children by the method of oral reading with that of silent reading. What are the advantages and disadvantages of each?
69. In your judgment, does the text suggest undue precautions in preparing for successful story-telling? Why?
70. Justify teaching literature in a crowded rural school program.
71. If you have not enjoyed poetry, how would you make it attractive to elementary grade pupils?
72. Which in your opinion is the most effective way of presenting the major portion of literature to children—by radio, phonograph, motion picture, teacher presentation, or silent reading? Why?

LANGUAGE

SECTION ONE: *Facts*

73. What is language?
74. Upon what natural tendencies is language development based?
75. What are the main uses for language?
76. What changes in teaching language have occurred?
77. What is the main aim of language instruction?
78. What are the nine general ideas suggested for all phases of language teaching?

ORAL LANGUAGE

79. What different phases of oral language should be stressed in the primary grades?
80. How can teachers help children to increase their speaking vocabularies?
81. About what topics do children talk most readily?
82. How may the assigned language periods be used eeffctively in developing conversation ability?
83. What school situations may necessitate oral composition work?
84. What occasions do children have for selecting names?
85. What are some common situations which involve forms of social courtesy?
86. What essentials should children understand in order to convey messages or give announcements effectively?
87. What are some procedures for pupils to remember: (1) when answering the telephone, (2) when calling someone on it, (3) when answering or calling?
88. What situations do children often pretend in their dramatic play?
89. What factors deserve consideration in arranging for and conducting dramatic play? What values result?
90. What additional dramatic factor is introduced by puppets?
91. How should a pupil prepare for a conversation period?
92. When talking, what mannerisms should be avoided?
93. What principles seem fundamental for teaching story-telling?
94. What abilities are required for public speaking?
95. What factors are involved in answering questions?

WRITTEN LANGUAGE

96. What preliminary work should precede actual written language?
97. What is the most common use of written language?
98. List the steps in grading the difficulties in early letter writing.
99. What occasions are there for keeping accounts?
100. What are the outstanding language benefits to be derived from keeping diaries?
101. Outline the basic factors underlying the teaching of written language. Make at least one sub-heading when suitable material is offered.
102. How may pupils, generally speaking, be tested for achievement in this field?

103. What elements make social letters interesting?
104. What devices should teachers refrain from using in checking children's letters?
105. What additional types of written composition need emphasis in these grades?
106. What basic factors are given concerning reports?

Creative Expression

107. What is meant by creative expression? In what forms is it manifested?
108. What conditions in school are essential for creative expression?
109. What attitudes and reactions on the part of teachers and classmates aid pupils in developing in the creative field?

Formal Aspects

110. For what reasons are the formal aspects of language taught?
111. What twofold problem does a teacher often meet in this field?
112. In the grades above the primary, what unit is used as the basis for presenting the technical forms?
113. What are the common uses of sentences?
114. What is meant by sentence form? When should it be taught?
115. Which sentence forms may make difficult the recognition of parts of speech?
116. What is a practical way to present word groups?
117. What understandings should pupils have about phrases? About clauses?
118. Which should come first, the definition of a word or the development of the concept of what it stands for?
119. What type of illustrations are preferable when emphasizing formal aspects?
120. When may children first make their acquaintance with the period? With other punctuation marks?
121. In what way does "sentence sense" influence the ability to punctuate correctly?
122. How may children be tested for ability in punctuation?
123. When do children usually first meet capitalization?
124. What types of practice material in punctuation are suggested?

SECTION TWO: *Problems*

125. Compare the importance of oral with that of written language.
126. Show the relation of language to the other school subjects.

Oral Language

127. Of what importance is it for teachers to know that children's greatest vocabulary development comes between the ages of one and six.
128. Describe a schoolroom situation which is conducive to growth in conversational ability.

129. Evaluate the use of plans or outlines as aids for children in oral composition work. In giving invitations. In making introductions.
130. Show by illustrations how the teacher can function most effectively in dramatic play work.
131. Explain how language teaching in the grades above the primary differs from that in the lower grades.
132. Show why content is more important than form.
133. Evaluate as a procedure of language instruction the suggestion of visiting a telephone exchange.

WRITTEN LANGUAGE

134. Why should dictated letters precede the actual writing of them by children?
135. Show the value of accounts children may dictate before they are able to write.
136. Summarize the paragraph pertaining to the school newspaper in the primary grades.
137. What forms of written language would you select for beginning work? Give reasons.
138. Compare frequency of use with the importance of written language forms. What implications has this for teaching?
139. Check a social letter by the Score Card for Social Letters.
140. How may pupils be guided in developing ability in making notes or outlining?

CREATIVE EXPRESSION

141. Evaluate the suggestions offered for encouraging and directing attempts at creating.
142. Show how creative writing may function in child development.
143. Discuss the importance of the evaluation of children's efforts in creative work.

FORMAL ASPECTS

144. Discuss the motives and methods of copying. Of dictation.
145. What is the value to pupils of using self-help guides in any language work?
146. Justify teaching the technical aspects of language.
147. Why is the sentence a suitable unit to use in teaching the formal aspects?
148. How may the main parts of a sentence be presented?
149. Illustrate how you would present one part of speech.
150. What is the relation of pupil attitude to the acquisition of skill in punctuation?
151. Why are standards superfluous in testing for punctuation and capitalization?
152. Compare teacher-made practice materials with commercial practice materials.
153. On what phases of capitalization should the most effort be put? Why?

SECTION THREE: *Personal Reactions*

Oral Language

154. Do you see any value, in addition to that given, for children showing objects when giving oral compositions?
155. How important do you consider the knowledge and correct use of the forms of social courtesy?
156. What have you found most commonly lacking in the directions which people have given you?
157. What do you regard as the most important language values derived from dramatic play? Why?
158. On what occasions have you found the ability to tell stories or jokes especially desirable?
159. Which of the fourteen abilities needed in conversation do you think should be given special emphasis?
160. Set up a situation which would involve the conversation needed in a business interview.
161. What is your opinion of the questions people ordinarily ask in conversation?

Written Language

162. What do you think are the reasons why people often dislike to write letters?
163. Do you think children are often given written language work too early? Why is this done?
164. How did you learn to take notes? How important do you consider this skill?

Creative Expression

165. Which of the illustrations of primary children's work do you consider the best attempt at creative expression? Reasons.
166. Do you see reasons for fostering creative expression especially at the present time?
167. Do you think all pupils can achieve creative results if they make the effort?
168. Do you think it of special value that children get a good concept of the sentence in the primary grades?
169. Give your reactions to the use of the score sheet, as suggested for the first two grades.
170. Do you believe that a knowledge of grammar is of outstanding importance in good oral and written expression?
171. Evaluate on the basis of your educational theories, the use of a check sheet for recording results of inventory and periodic review tests.

SPELLING

SECTION ONE: *Facts*

172. What is the main purpose of learning to spell?
173. Give some activities for establishing spelling readiness.
174. What are the two general plans for teaching spelling?
175. Suggest the steps by which pupils may be taught to study independently.
176. How may time be saved in teaching spelling in a rural school?
177. What principles does Foran give in regard to using rules?
178. List the three methods of administering recall tests. Explain each in a sentence.

SECTION TWO: *Problems*

179. Show the relationship of spelling to other subjects.
180. Why are reviews important in learning to spell?
181. Show the value of graphs and charts that indicate the rank of members of the class in spelling.

SECTION THREE: *Personal Reaction*

182. In your estimation, which has the better psychological basis, the test-study or study-test plan?
183. To what extent have you yourself found rules helpful in spelling? Tell which ones, if any.

HANDWRITING

SECTION ONE: *Facts*

184. What, at present, are the two common forms of handwriting?
185. What are the fundamental elements in manuscript writing?
186. What two factors contribute greatly to good manuscript writing?
187. Indicate the writing position recommended for a left-handed pupil.
188. What is the real test of handwriting ability?
189. By what standards can children criticize their own work?

SECTION TWO: *Problems*

190. Show how each activity suggested for writing readiness prepares for actual writing.
191. Evaluate the advantages and disadvantages of manuscript writing and give the bases for this evaluation.
192. Outline the section which gives Freeman's factors involved in handwriting. Make this complete enough to serve as a guide for analyzing a piece of handwriting.

193. What provisions could be made to remedy a situation where seats or desks are not the proper height for writing?
194. What do you consider the best plan for grading pupils' handwriting?

SECTION THREE: *Personal Reactions*

195. Do you think teachers are justified in taking time for "writing readiness" activities? If so, what physiological and psychological reasons would you give?
196. How do you explain the poor handwriting done by adults who have been taught penmanship in school?
197. What is your opinion about the use of the typewriter by elementary school children?

SUGGESTIONS FOR FURTHER READING
READING AND LITERATURE

Arbuthnot, May Hill. *Children and Books.* Scott, Foresman and Co. 1947. This is a fine comprehensive book on all phases of children's literature, splendid as a textbook for a literature class, and for reference on a teacher's desk.

Betts, E. A. *Foundations of Reading Instruction.* American Book Co. 1946. This is a comprehensive well illustrated book "with emphasis on differentiated guidance." It includes good material on reading readiness and beginning reading instruction, a glossary of terms, and list of tests.

Betzner, J. and Moore, A. E. *Everychild and Books.* Bobbs-Merrill Co. 1940. This delightfully written book should prove a real inspiration to those interested in children's voluntary reading.

Bond, G. L. and Bond, E. *Teaching the Child to Read.* The Macmillan Co. 1945. This is an easily read and helpful book on different phases of teaching reading in the elementary grades with strong emphasis on the primary level.

Broom, M. E., Duncan, M. A. A., Emig, D., and Steuber, J. *Effective Reading Instruction.* McGraw-Hill Book Co., Inc. 1942. This is a presentation of teaching reading from various technical aspects. Contains many suggestions for class procedures.

Cole, L. *The Elementary School Subjects.* Rinehart and Co., Inc., New York. 1946. Part I of this book is devoted to technical phases of reading, also vocabulary, study reading, reading readiness, and remedial work. Part II is devoted to handwriting, spelling, and language.

Dolch, E. W. *Problems in Reading.* The Garrard Press, Champaign, Illinois. 1948. This book in remedial reading emphasizes helping the good reader as well as the poor reader to improve. It includes material on phonic teaching. Chapter 8 discusses the relation of phonics to spelling; Chapter 27 tells of the inferences made from studies in this field; and Chapter 28 deals with "The Modern Teaching of Spelling."

Dolch, E. W. *Teaching Primary Reading*. The Garrard Press. 1941. This easily understood book is a good help in teaching reading and phonics. The 220-word sight vocabulary is given and explained.

Fernald, G. M. *Remedial Techniques in Basic School Subjects*. Mc-Graw-Hill Book Co., Inc. 1943. This book explains procedures using kinesthetic techniques in remedial reading.

Forty-eighth Yearbook of the National Society for the Study of Education. Part II. "Reading in the Elementary School." The University of Chicago Press. 1949. This is the newest yearbook dealing with the subject of reading. The leading writers in the field have contributed to it.

Gates, Arthur I. *The Improvement of Reading*. The Macmillan Co. 1937. This book is helpful in diagnostic and remedial teaching of reading. It suggests ways and means of doing both. Contains many tables of data, charts, and illustrations bearing directly on the reading problems; also specific suggestions for the teaching of normal pupils are given.

Gray, W. S., compiled and edited. *Basic Instruction in Reading in Elementary and High Schools*. No. 65. The University of Chicago Press. 1948. This is the 1948 report of the annual reading conference held at the University of Chicago. The theme is "Changing Conceptions of Basic Instruction in Reading." The report deals with the present-day thought concerning many phases, such as grouping pupils, essential equipment, word perception, and many more.

Gray, W. S. *On Their Own in Reading*. Scott, Foresman and Co. 1948. This book deals with word perception. It is helpful on word attack for teachers of both the elementary and the high school.

Harris, A. J. *How to Increase Reading Ability*. Longmans, Green & Co. 1947. Gives attention to reading readiness and a survey of reading instruction in general. The major part of book pertains to diagnostic and remedial instruction. Practical suggestions are a desirable feature.

Harrison, M. Lucile. *Reading Readiness* (Revised Edition). Houghton Mifflin. 1939. This is an aid to kindergarten and first-grade teachers in developing and determining children's readiness to read. Part Two of the revision deals with reading readiness in grades "beyond the preparatory level." This is an extensive bibliography.

Iowa Elementary Teachers Handbook, Vol. XIII "Elementary Literature." Department of Public Instruction, Des Moines, Iowa. 1948. This offers teachers suggestions for good techniques in helping children enjoy literature. It also contains a "Basic List of Books for Recreational Reading for Children from Kindergarten through Junior High School."

Iowa Elementary Teachers Handbook, Vol. II "Reading." Department of Public Instruction, Des Moines, Iowa. 1943. This is a splendid presentation of the practical teaching of reading. The first part deals with methods on different levels; the latter part with material, general in nature, as phonics, seatwork, and study guides.

McKee, P. *The Teaching of Reading in the Elementary School,* Houghton-Mifflin Co. 1948. This is a comprehensive book to help teachers prepare children to read and teach children to read in grades one through sixth.

Seventeenth Yearbook, Department of Elementary School Principals. "Newer Practices in Reading in the Elementary School." Department of Elementary School Principals, National Education Association. 1938. One interested in teaching reading on any level will find helpful information in this yearbook.

Witty, Paul and Kopel, David. *Reading and the Educative Process.* Ginn and Company. 1939. The teaching of reading is viewed from both the theoretical and practical standpoints. It is practical and contains extensive bibliographies on the various phases of reading teaching and learning.

Language—Spelling—Handwriting

Conard, Edith U. *Show Me How to Write* (in manuscript). A. N. Palmer. This is a teacher's guide which gives general facts for understanding the basic principles and clear, detailed methods for teaching manuscript writing. It also sets up standards and gives help for testing and scoring.

Foran, T. G. *The Psychology and Teaching of Spelling.* Catholic Education Press. 1934. This book is based upon exhaustive study of all phases of teaching spelling. It is good for one interested in making a careful study of this subject.

Freeman, Frank N. "An Evaluation of Manuscript Writing." *Elementary School Journal.* February, 1936. pp. 446-455. In pamphlet form, furnished by The Zaner-Bloser Co. This pamphlet furnishes "arguments for and against the teaching of manuscript writing in the elementary grades." Also some facts are given concerning the time for changing from manuscript to cursive form.

Hildreth, Gertrude. *Learning the Three R's,* Second Ed. Educational Publishers, Inc. 1947. This revision has chapters devoted to the importance of language teaching and methods of oral and written instruction. Help is also given for teaching spelling and handwriting.

Horn, Ernest and McKee, Paul. "The Development of Ability in Spelling," *38th Yearbook of the National Society for the Study of Education.* Part I, pp. 241-254. Public School Publishing Co. 1939. One finds material in this book dealing with the selection of words to be taught and the allotment of words to the different grade levels.

McKee, Paul. *Language in the Elementary School, Spelling, Composition, and Writing*. Houghton Mifflin. 1939. Chapters II to V, inclusive, give the historical background of teaching spelling, the summary of investigations for the selection of words, fine suggestions for teaching spelling, and also for testing the results. Chapters VI to IX, inclusive, deal with "The Program in Composition" both oral and written, stressing the common uses of each in daily living. Capitalization, punctuation, and correct usage are also discussed. Chapter X brings to the elementary teacher results of research and practical suggestions concerning when to begin to teach handwriting, practice, standards, (manuscript as well as the cursive form), and use of the typewriter.

Stretch, Lorena B. *The Curriculum and the Child*. Educational Publishers. 1939. Chapter XIII furnishes help to a teacher of handwritng in any grade, since it includes material dealing with handwriting scales, objectives, techniques, beginning work, and general techniques. Chapter XIV consists of a concise presentation of the present-day teaching of spelling. The Test-Study and Study-Test methods are explained. Definite plans of work are outlined. Chapter XV deals with the teaching of language and grammar, showing its inclusive relationship to other subjects. This book also contains material on the teaching of other elementary school subjects.

"Teaching Language in the Elementary School." *The Forty-third Yearbook*. Part II. The Department of Education, The University of Chicago. 1944. This is a comprehensive survey of present-day thinking on teaching language, spelling, handwriting, and allied topics.

PART THREE

Elementary Mathematics

CHAPTER 12

BEGINNING NUMBERS

THE use of number dates back to very early times. Many early civilizations have contributed to modern arithmetic. The Greeks seem to have been mainly responsible for the development of at least two types of arithmetic, the practical and the theoretical. Some of the early arithmetic teaching in our country apparently was of a practical nature as is indicated by the following quotation:[1] "The Dutch West India Company, as the controlling factor in the New Amsterdam Colony, wanted men trained in figuring to act as 'keepers and assistants.' Schools for the teaching of arithmetic were accordingly organized." As time went on, however, purely theoretical arithmetic came to be incorporated in arithmetic textbooks. This was the outgrowth of the belief of educators that beneficial mental training resulted from the use of wholly theoretical number. Although arithmetic was introduced into our country at a comparatively early date, its progress was slow because the early colonial schools emphasized the teaching of reading.

PRESENT-DAY TRENDS

The *present-day trends* show many changes. In the first place, arithmetic is taught chiefly for its values in everyday life situations. This means that many parts of the old curricula have been eliminated. Studies show that "90% of adult figuring is covered by the four funda-

[1] Wilson, G. M., Stone, M. B., Dalrymple, C. O. *Teaching of the New Arithmetic*, p. 3. McGraw-Hill. 1939.

mental processes—addition, subtraction, multiplication, and division. Simple fractions, percentage, and interest if added to the four fundamental processes, will raise the percentage to over 95%. Mastery of these essentials becomes the drill load in arithmetic for the grades. Beyond that, the work is informational-problem work adjusted to child interests." [1] In the second place, some topics are given more emphasis than formerly. An example is the theory of the decimal system, which is related to every process of arithmetic. In the third place, there seems to be a general trend in the direction of the use of life processes and materials in the teaching of arithmetic. No doubt children get better values from their elementary mathematics if they have wide experiences involving different uses of money, if they study buying and selling and realize that certain profits are justified, if they learn of different kinds of taxes, and if they become familiar with other social number practices. Not only should they learn business facts and procedures, but they should form opinions concerning them.

Besides these major tendencies there are other less general ones, such as: (1) more attention to the fact that children have many pre-school number experiences which result in definite number learnings, (2) much more emphasis upon taking time at the start to build number concepts, (3) more lifelike textbook problems, (4) shifting of the difficult combination work of the lower grades to the middle and upper grades, since much useless material has been omitted from the program of these grades, (5) more attention given to the differences in individual ability, especially in drill exercises, (6) more effective books for beginning number work which help to build number vocabulary preceding the more formal work with combinations, (7) more attention given to helping children to discover arithmetical truths for themselves through experiences and activities, (8) more attention given to presenting materials in the order of difficulty.

Along with these changes there have developed different *basic theories* of teaching arithmetic. William A. Brownell[2] gives these three: the drill, incidental, and meaning theories. According to the *drill theory* arithmetic consists of groups of facts and elements of knowledge loosely related. These are mastered by the child through

---

[1] *Ibid.*, p. 7.
[2] Brownell, William A. *10th Yearbook of the National Council of Teachers of Mathematics*, pp. 1-31. Bureau of Publications, Teachers College, Columbia University. 1935.

drill, whether or not he understands or uses them. Excessive flash-card drills and games used chiefly for the purpose of mechanical repetition of answers to combinations are evidences of this theory. The *incidental theory* postpones systematic instruction until the children have been in school two or three years. It allows arithmetic to be brought in only as fitting situations occur. For example, pupils might count the children who are at school, find pages by reading numbers, or do other types of number work when occasions arise. Thus the teaching would be related entirely to experiences involving numbers. The *meaning theory* conceives of arithmetic as a closely knit system of understandable ideas, principles, and processes. Each theory contributes to present-day teaching. The meaning theory has weight if arithmetic is viewed as "a system of quantitative thinking." The incidental theory aids by showing the advantages of postponing the teaching of formal arithmetic and of presenting much of it only when pertinent occasions arise. It cannot, however, be left entirely to chance as to what these occasions are or when they will arise. Practice is necessary to recall facts and processes rapidly and accurately, as is indicated by the drill theory.

Whichever theory predominates, one factor is essential for later intelligent work in the arithmetical processes; the building of clear *number concepts*. Much of the difficulty that children have in the intermediate and upper grades is due to insufficient teaching of basic concepts at the start. Teachers should emphasize three kinds of concepts: (1) those of a broad social nature, such as understanding why the storekeeper should charge more for his oranges than he paid for them, why we pay for the stamps we put on letters, and reasons for other social activities involving number within the children's comprehension at each age; (2) the concepts of the different operations, such as what it means to count, to add, to subtract, and to perform other operations; (3) the concepts of individual numbers, such as the meaning of 6 in its various relationships, for example, 6 representing six objects, 6 in a series, or two groups of objects as $5 + 1$, or $3 + 3$. Generally speaking, the broader the experiences are, the richer the concepts are likely to be. It is especially advantageous to build up these basic concepts in the primary grades.

Reasonable present-day *objectives* in arithmetic teaching for the elementary grades are: to develop the ability to compute with a high degree of accuracy and speed in appropriate situations, to develop the ability to read and interpret a problem in such a way as to analyze the steps necessary for its solution, to develop an understanding of economic situations, which help children to solve social problems, and to develop an enjoyment of arithmetic.

A *good procedure* to follow in teaching arithmetic so as to reach these objectives is: (1) Find out what the children already know. This will indicate what needs to be taught. (2) Grade the difficulties, that is, present the easiest materials first in small amounts. (3) By means of intelligent practice, help children to develop the ability to use this knowledge accurately and rapidly. (4) Finally, test the results of teaching to locate defects which need reteaching or continued practice.

Investigations of *pre-school number experiences* show that children have considerable arithmetical skill and knowledge when they enter school. This depends to a great extent upon the home surroundings, their playmates, mental capacities, and general experiences. The Buckingham-MacLatchy study[1] based upon interviews with 1,356 six-year-old children shows a good deal of number knowledge among them when they enter grade one. In rote counting by ones about 90 per cent of the children succeeded at least as far as 10 and about 60 per cent of them at least as far as 20. In counting objects, 75 per cent counted at least as far as 14.

Smith[2] studied the ways first-grade children use number and reports the following results from her investigation:

Transactions carried on in stores	30%
Games involving counting	18%
Reading Roman numerals on the clock	14%
Reading Arabic numerals in finding pages in books	13%
Dividing food with playmates and pets (fractions)	6%
Depositing money in and withdrawing money from toy banks	5%
Playing store	3%
Other miscellaneous activities (15 activities)	11%

[1] Buckingham, B. R. and MacLatchy, Josephine. "The Number Abilities of Children When They Enter Grade One." *29th Yearbook, National Society for the Study of Education*, p. 508. Public School Publishing Co. Adapted.

[2] Smith, Nila B. "An Investigation of the Uses of Arithmetic in the Out-of-School Life of First-Grade Children." *The Elementary School Journal*, XXIV: pp. 621-626. April, 1924.

William L. Connor,[1] Director of the Bureau of Research of the Cleveland Public Schools, concluded from an investigation of the kindergarten children in Cleveland that children have much more number knowledge than we have recognized and that the tendency has been to retard children in this field by the texts and courses offered.

When to begin to teach arithmetic is a much disputed topic. The results of investigations indicate that many pupils are ready for some kind of arithmetic work when they enter school or at six years of age. The question as to when arithmetic should be taught often simmers down to what arithmetic should be taught, or to what is meant when the word "arithmetic" is used. If we include building number concepts, the chances are that arithmetic is taught in every primary grade room. It certainly would be if a child is taught what he needs when he needs it. At this level he has experiences with "more or less" clay, with "big and little" blocks, he comes to school "once or twice" a day. Thus children learn the arithmetic they need and understand it.

There are many everyday situations in which number appears during the children's early school life. The brief list which follows is suggestive of much *incidental teaching*: (1) knowing there is a time to come to school, (2) putting on a "pair" of rubbers or mittens, (3) sharing and distributing blocks and playthings, (4) realizing differences in distances from their various homes to school, (5) seeing sizes of materials used, (6) bringing money for lunches, (7) counting children needed for games, (8) knowing how old one is. If the teacher realizes the numerous opportunities for using number during a day and has in mind objectives based upon the children's and society's needs, much arithmetic may be taught incidentally and meaningfully. This may be done when occasions arise, whether in a definite number period or not. There are several reasons for promoting incidental teaching of arithmetic from the time a child starts to school. It is a continuation of experiences children have already had. It is necessary if children are to work with the materials they use in the beginning years. It clears up misunderstandings. It offers the chance to establish good number concepts which are essential for effective work later.

[1] Connor, William L. *29th Yearbook, National Society for the Study of Education*, pp. 509-12. Public School Publishing Co. 1930.

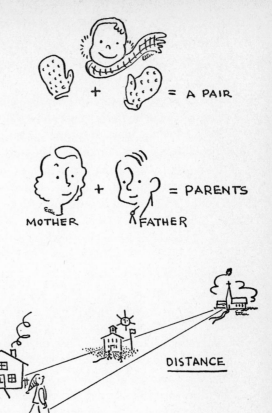

+ = A PAIR

MOTHER + FATHER = PARENTS

Sharing

DISTANCE

Distributing

Common experiences help build number concepts. Why not use them more often?

LUNCH 15¢

NUMBER CONCEPTS

Plenty of time should be devoted to building *basic number concepts*. In this the inexperienced teacher usually needs help. She often attempts formal combination work before the children have concrete bases for understanding the abstract forms. Often this work is presented too soon because she does not know what other material to teach.

Counting is one of the first steps in building these basic concepts, and is very fundamental in later arithmetic work. History contains interesting stories about the ways in which early peoples counted. One story is that of a shepherd who let his sheep out in the morning to graze. In order to know how many left the sheep cote, he laid down a pebble for each sheep that passed him. At night when they returned he checked them in the same manner. That is, he checked by comparison—the number of pebbles and sheep should be the same. Another story is told of a more rapid method in which the shepherd's daughter helped. The shepherd raised a finger for each sheep that passed until he had raised all his fingers. Then the little daughter raised one of hers and the shepherd began over again. At the finish, if the child had four fingers raised and the father two, how many sheep had he turned out? It is surprising to note that the hand probably was the means by which our numerical system based on ten was evolved. The hand was also used to represent numbers in bargaining among early tradesmen who did not speak the same language. In more recent times, Pestalozzi made use of teaching with objects. His theory that a number was a mental image—the result of sense experience—and that in learning number there should be sense experiences of different kinds, has greatly influenced our teaching.

Many children know how to count when they come to school. For some children this counting is rhythmic. They may have learned to count as they might learn the words of a Mother Goose jingle. This is valuable because they have learned the number names in order. Other children can use the number names and actually enumerate the number of objects in a group. The first is *rote* counting, the second *rational* counting. The second is much more important and the child is fortunate who has been taught to count things from the start, not to say the words in parrot fashion. It is well to check each child when he enters school to find what ability he has in these skills. This enables the teacher to know where to begin her teaching. Should there be wide variations of ability in the group, the teacher may arrange activities of a broadening nature for those of greater ability while she directs those with less ability along the lines of beginning counting and other basic concepts.

In rational counting there are *two concepts* to be developed. One is the idea of position in the number series—the *ordinal* concept. To illustrate, a child counts a row of pennies and reaches five. This penny should represent to him the fifth penny. Often very little attention is given to learning the ordinal numbers, that is, first, second, third, and so on. Since they are common in the daily conversation, little practice should be necessary to help children associate these terms with the correct serial positions, such as the first desk in the row, the second drawer from the top, or the third turn to use the swing.

The other concept is that of total number or amount—the *cardinal* concept. For example, a child holds five pennies in his hand and puts them into his pocket one by one as he counts. This moving of the pennies from one group into another is more likely to give him the

Proper use of fingers in counting.

idea of the total amount he possesses. In rational counting, whatever the objective, it is desirable to urge children at first to handle, touch, or point to each object enumerated. If they do not they often count glibly and do not associate the number names with the corresponding objects. Thus, in counting a group of six toy animals, unless each animal counted is touched, the total reached by counting may be different from six. Klapper[1] summarizes rational counting in this man-

[1] Klapper, P. *The Teaching of Arithmetic*, pp. 242-243. D. Appleton-Century Co. 1934.

ner: (1) "The acquisition and control of a series of number names. (2) the recognition of the identity of the individual elements in a group. (3) The making of a one to one correspondence between object and name."

In rational counting the things counted may be *stationary*, such as blocks, buildings, trees; or they may be *consecutive* or moving, such as signals, sounds, or cars on a moving train. Life situations do not call for much consecutive counting, yet there are occasions for it. The techniques of this kind of counting are different and because this is true the concepts of number are broadened by teaching it. There are four apparent phases of this aspect of counting: (1) Visual counting is the counting of visible and moving objects. The skill necessary to count the number of automobiles that pass a corner is different from that of counting them if they are standing in a parking space. (2) Auditory counting is the counting of sounds. Children need this skill in listening to the striking of the clock or the signals given by the ringing of a bell or the blowing of a whistle. (3) Muscular counting is the counting of muscular sensations. A child should be able to carry out directions for taking three steps or for making a certain number of muscular movements for signals. (4) Tactile counting is the counting of sensations of touch. One child counts the taps a playmate makes on his arm. All of these approaches to counting—rote and rational, both the stationary and the four kinds of consecutive counting, visual, auditory, muscular, and tactile—broaden children's basic number concepts.

It is desirable to use many everyday *school situations* in helping children to learn to count. Many such situations become apparent to the alert teacher. A few for rational counting are:

Stationary: Children in different rows, children who are wearing any identical color, buttons on clothing, chairs for the children in a class, materials needed by a group, napkins or papers for lunch, days on the calendar, new books on the reading table, number of stories listed on the chart, children needed for games, or votes for a favorite poem.

Consecutive: Visual—pictures shown in a toy movie, children marching, cars in a train, animals grazing, a flock of chickens, the number of goldfish in a bowl. Auditory—signals, whistles, tones on piano or other musical instruments. Muscular—number of steps to stand from the teeter, number of claps, nods of the head, number of times the ball is bounced or caught. Tactile—sensations made with pencil, eraser, handle of scissors, handkerchief, paper, flower.

Grade the difficulties in presenting the skill of counting when children have little or no ability in it. First, use objects and work with only small groups of pupils at a time. Use 1 to 10 first, then 10 to 20. The use of counting in many different situations and with a variety of materials extends the concepts. Second, when the idea of counting objects is fairly well established, use pictures of objects cut from advertising pages of magazines or found in illustrations of readers. Third, after that use forms of a semi-concrete nature such as circles, lines, or other conventional forms, placed on the blackboard or cards. Finally, present the actual symbols 1, 2, 3, 4, etc. Thus a child is introduced gradually to the symbol that stands for the group with which he has had various experiences. Hence, "5" or any other digit is the sign or symbol that stands for "5" as met in various ways, not just a symbol of which he learns the name. Care should be taken, however, to avoid the extended use of objects in building concepts to keep children from forming habits of thinking objects when they should be seeing abstract number symbols. "Objective exercises should be used to teach the meaning of the first twelve or fifteen numbers. After these have been taught by the use of objects, the ones following should be taught from the serial meaning. Thus, the conception of 34, for example, is different from that of 9, which has a number picture associated with it, as ⦙⦙⦙ or ⠸ ⠒⠒, while 34 has a relational meaning somewhere between 30 and 40 and just between 33 and 35." [1] It is no doubt easier if children learn the order of decades by counting by 10's to one hundred before learning the series in the decade of twenty. Experiences should be given later in counting by 5's, by 2's, both forward and backward.

Recognizing small groups of objects should receive attention. Almost everyone can look at a group of four or five objects and tell at a glance how many are in the group. Some people are more proficient in this respect than others. The order of arrangement facilitates this

[1] Bond, Elias A. *The Professional Treatment of the Subject Matter of Arithmetic,* p. 37. Bureau of Publications, Teachers College, Columbia University. 1934.

ability. For example, :: is probably much more easily recognized as 4 than if the dots were arranged .:· in a hit-and-miss fashion. This skill saves time. Children can develop the ability with little practice. Why should they enumerate each object in a small group, if they can tell the total at a glance? They can recognize two, three, four, and five objects in groups at the primary grade level. It is not feasible to go beyond six. Domino cards are especially helpful as drill material. Different arrangements of the objects in other pattern forms should be used. They should not always see 4 as :: , but as ·:· , and .:. as well. The following patterns are suggested:[1]

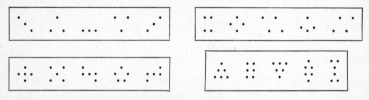

Drills should be given also with irregular patterns. It is best to have them on cards, so they can be flashed quickly with no chance given for the pupils to count the dots. The teacher should be aware of the fact that pupils learn the patterns quickly and may respond to these instead of actually sensing the number of objects.

Closely allied to the idea of estimating the number in a group is that of *comparing* sizes, lengths, and distances. It is fun to use this as a game, guessing the number of objects, sizes, lengths, and then checking to see if correct. This fun continues into adult years in guessing beans in a jar or pennies in a bank.

READING NUMBERS

Practice in *reading numbers* should precede writing numbers. The number names become a part of a child's vocabulary as he hears and uses them in daily activities and in counting. The next logical step is to associate these words with the Arabic symbols 1, 2, 3, etc., in counting. Many pupils may have some pre-school ability in reading numbers. So, again, it is desirable to check individual skills. Reading numbers may be first presented so as to extend concepts further. Utilize

[1] Buswell, G. T., Brownell, W. A., John, L. *Beginners' Course, Teachers' Manual, Daily-Life Arithmetics*, p. 41. Ginn.

cards, such as $\boxed{4}$. One child uses this to tell how many blocks

there are in his pile, setting the card beside them. Another takes $\boxed{3}$

to designate the number of books on the table, and another $\boxed{1}$ to

stand beside the doll. In designating certain materials desired, the teacher says, "We need five pieces of paper," as she writes 5 on the board. This has the additional advantage of permitting children to see how numbers are written as they associate them with the spoken word. Charts which children can make easily help at this stage. Chart I organizes children's previous knowledge with the new symbols. Chart II should be a growing chart, rows being added as the work advances.

Chart I			
⚇ (one figure)	one 1		
⚇⚇ (two figures)	two 2		
etc. to ten			

Chart II

	10	20	30	40	50	60	70	80	90	100
1	11	21	31	41	51	61	71	81	91	
2	12									
3	13									
4	14									
5	15									
6	16									
7	17									
8	18									
9	19									

Another type of card is especially good for this part of the work. The cards may be made by using drawings or pictures of individual objects from magazines mounted on cards with the number and name of objects underneath, while on the reverse side is only the number.[1]

front   back

$\boxed{\begin{array}{c} \text{↑ ↑} \\ \text{2 trees} \end{array}}$ $\boxed{2}$ Cards like these without the digits may be used

in counting. Ability not only to read numbers individually but to know them in order, is essential. At this stage no special emphasis need be placed upon the zero. It may be referred to in connection

[1] Studebaker, J. W., Knight, F. B., Findley, W. C. *Standard Service Teacher's Handbook for Primary Arithmetic*, p. 38. Scott. Foresman & Co. 1929.

with no score made in a game or in record keeping of the number of objects brought for a collection, such as, Kinds of Leaves: John 4, Helen 0, Mary 6, Jack 2.

The number forms "10," "11," "12," need to be connected with the words ten, eleven, twelve, as the symbols 1 to 9 inclusive were. There

Place value in numbers is best understood if pupil-discovered.

seems to be no helpful device to assist children in making this connection. The numbers from 13 (thir-teen) to 19 (nine-teen) are less difficult since second digits give clues of the syllables to be combined with "teen." The reverse order of syllables in saying the teens should cause little difficulty if this decade is presented carefully and slowly enough. This work precedes any number reading in the higher decades, such as 21 or 31, in which the 2 indicating twenty, and the 3 indicating thirty, come first and are read first.

The *concept* of the *teens* consisting of tens and units may be established later by the use of money, such as a dime and different numbers of pennies. For example, when presenting eleven, show the children a dime and one penny; twelve, a dime and two pennies; thirteen, a dime and three pennies. Then say, "Fourteen," and ask them to show what coins are required. Also the old device of using bundles of ten sticks and single sticks is another objective method. When talking of 16, for example, the remark can often be made, "Sixteen is ten and how many more?"

The *decades* beginning with 20 should cause little trouble, since integers are simply substituted for the zeros, and when once started "twenty-one," "twenty-two," and so on, come easily. When reading the three-place numbers, explain that the third digit is hundreds and that 367 is read "three hundred, sixty-seven," which is preferable to "three hundred and sixty-seven." The latter form may cause trouble when decimals are being read. There are occasions for primary grade children to read large numbers, such as automobile license numbers and telephone numbers. These are read as a series of single digits. For example, 1692 is read "one, six, nine, two."

The understanding of the *relationships of numbers* is of special importance in building early number concepts. Attention should be given to: Which is more, 4 or 6? Does 7 come before or after 9? What number is between 4 and 6? and other similar exercises. If a child has many number experiences of this type, his understanding of relationships usually comes as a natural result. To illustrate more concretely: One child brought 4 stones for the museum, another brought 6. Which child brought more? Thus children form concepts of each number's place in the number series. A child may be able to count or read the numbers in the correct order and still not know the relative position of one number to the others of the series without counting. He may count objects from one to ten but not know what number comes before 8 without counting from 1.

WRITING NUMBERS

The daily school procedure presents many opportunities which require children to know how to *write numbers*. It may be in recording a score made in a game, in writing the date on the school calendar, in making price tags for articles in the school store, or in numbering books in the school library. Such situations may be used to stimulate children to write figures clearly. Generally speaking, pupils should have had many occasions to see numbers written before attempting to write numbers themselves. Their first number writing is better controlled at the blackboard. If the class is large the teacher may advantageously divide it into small groups and work with the children individually as much as possible. This is a good sequence to follow. (1) The teacher writes a number as the child watches the direction of the chalk movements. (2) After doing this two or three times, the child tries to write one for himself. (3) Again he watches the teacher's movements and writes one himself. After repeating this two or three times, the chances are that he will have a proper start on the correct form and manner of making the number.

Different devices are suggested for helping children to remember where to begin and in which direction to go in writing the different numbers. In posting a copy for the class, the arrow is as simple a way

1 2 3 4 5 6 7 8 9 10

as any. This should prevent the trouble children often have from beginning 4's and 7's at the bottom instead of the top, making 3's in reversed form, and using other less effective methods when writing the figures. Commence with the number most easily made and teach the writing of only one number at a time. The order of difficulty usually given is: 1, 4, 7, 10, 9, 6, 2, 3, 5, 8. It is essential, at first, that the work be supervised and that more attention be paid to the movement than to the form. Good results come from plenty of practice in an uncrowded space, accompanied by the understanding of the reason why well formed, legible figures are needed. Children should realize that poorly formed figures often cause trouble in later dealings with examples and problems, and that they should write good number forms because of legibility and accuracy, not for the sake of appearance alone. Careless habits may creep in later if good standards are insufficiently stressed.

QUANTITATIVE UNDERSTANDINGS

Measurements affect children's lives from birth. Klapper[1] makes the following classification of measuring units: "The first is the 'undefined unit' which measures by 'more or less,' by 'much or little,' by 'many or few.' The second is the 'defined unit,' the pace, the hand, the step—measures that vary within certain limits but which convey a reasonably satisfactory idea of dimension. This unit pertains to linear measuring more than to other areas, such as money and time. The third is the 'standardized unit,' the recognized unalterable unit like foot, yard, meter, gallon." There are places in elementary school activities for the inclusion of all three. For example, children's ideas of measurement are often undefined. They are familiar with such measurements as big, high, long, heavy, much, and others, which always imply indefiniteness. Such terms should be in the children's number vocabularies. More attention should be given to the "defined unit" than is usually done, since such knowledge is useful on many occasions when measuring tools are unavailable. The "standardized units" will receive greater emphasis in the following paragraphs dealing with different areas of measurement.

Money has *limited meanings* to most six-year-old children. Some children get an allowance at home. They spend it for toys, candy, and other personal items. Some have banks into which go the pennies, nickels, dimes, which come their way. They empty these periodically, count the contents, and deposit their savings in the commercial banks. Some children earn money by going on errands, doing tasks at home and in the neighborhood. Probably more real knowledge concerning the uses and values of money is gained outside school by the majority of children than during school hours. One child of four showed unusual insight into business customs. She often went to the store for her mother and invariably returned with a sack of candy given to her by the storekeeper. Her mother disapproved and admonished her to bring home no more candy unless she paid for it. The next time Mary was

---

[1] *Op. cit.,* p. 231.

sent, she returned with the desired articles and also a sack of candy. To her mother's objection Mary replied, "I did pay for the candy, but I charged the bread."

Primary school children need to know the values and names of the following coins: penny, cent, nickel, dime, quarter, and the fifty-cent piece. Interesting games can be centered around finding all possible equivalents for a dime, a quarter, and fifty cents. Use real money in initial lessons, teaching the names of coins and their relationships. After that substitute toy money for practice purposes.

Time means very little to the five- and six-year-olds. Adults are impressed with this fact again and again as they watch children leisurely

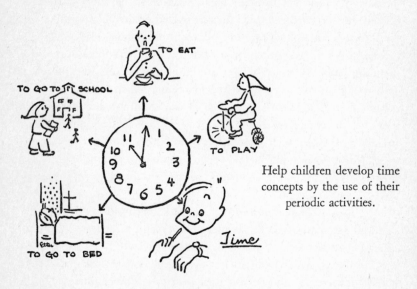

Help children develop time concepts by the use of their periodic activities.

strolling to school, giving their attention to flowers, animals, people, or anything else that attracts them. Beginning primary pupils know that there is a time for arriving at the building and the majority usually come on time. They know also that there are certain times for the routine events of the day; such as getting up, eating meals, going home from school, going to bed, and that the clock is the instrument for telling the time for these events. A year or so later, they begin to read the time on the timepieces and learn to tell the time for their daily procedures. The order of difficulty in learning usually corresponds with the size of the unit; first the hour, then half-hour, quarter-hour, and finally the five-minute and one-minute periods.

They can soon learn to understand today, yesterday, and tomorrow. They talk of days of the week and learn them in proper order. Later, they locate the proper spaces on the calendar, count the number of days in a week, and locate and read the number which stands for each day. One regularly recurring day of importance to a child is his birthday and he soon learns the month in which this day appears. The watchful teacher, with the arithmetic objectives in mind, can find numerous opportunities for frequently bringing number terms and experiences into this area of measurement.

Capacity as a unit of measuring is a part of many childhood experiences both in and out of school. Often mothers send their children

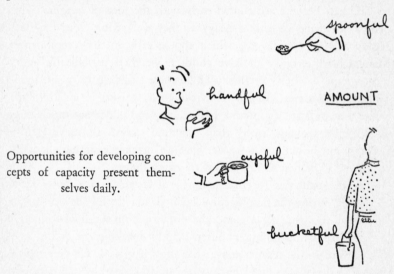

Opportunities for developing concepts of capacity present themselves daily.

to get a quart or pint of milk. Many children in small schools bring milk for their noon lunches in a pint jar. They see their mothers canning fruit in different-size jars. To the rural child the peck and bushel are common units of measure, to the town child, the bushel basket. These same containers are used most commonly in the primary grades for clarifying information which children already have, or for presenting these units of measurement if the out-of-school experiences have not included them. Equivalents and parts are easily presented objectively, such as by using two pints to fill a quart bottle, and two cups to fill the pint bottle. If children are preparing food for a party or other festivity, they find good reasons for measuring with the cup, tablespoon, and teaspoon. This uncovers the need for more practice. By recording the results of experimenting with equivalents, the information is organized and made vitally meaningful. Records such as this might be made:

"We found it took 2 pints of water to fill the quart bottle."
"A pint bottle held 2 cups of water."

This procedure is a desirable one to use with other units of measurement, such as time, money, or length. These facts will be met in table form in future grades.

Children become acquainted early with the idea of *weight*. They delight in lifting objects as heavy as they can swing from the floor. Heavy and light are words which appear early in their vocabularies. Many schools arrange to have children weighed periodically and a record kept of their weights. Thus, these children have first-hand contacts with scales and can soon read their weights in even pounds. Scales that indicate the pound, half-pound, and ounce are much more desirable for playing "store" than imitation scales. By playing store, children can be taught to know what articles are commonly sold by the pound as well as to know how to weigh them.

The opportunities for measurement of *length* and *distance* occur frequently during the first year in school. It may be for the sides of the playhouse, the space for a game, the distance from the floor to hang a picture. At the beginning, children help by marking the end of each foot or yard as the teacher moves the ruler along. Later they master that technique themselves. Each will want to know how tall he is and will use the foot ruler to find out. He may be satisfied, at first, with the fact that he is over two or nearly three feet tall. Later, when the inch is presented, he can be more exact. Some may have a very clear idea of the mile and others of street blocks, because of the distance of their homes from the school. Probably more should be done in teaching how to read the speedometer than has been customary.

Terms denoting groups are more or less commonly used by children of primary age. They often talk about and look at a pair of new shoes or mittens. The store sells oranges for so much a dozen. Santa Claus brought a set of new dishes. The museum has a collection of shells. The story told of twin lambs. The box of crayons has eight pieces of different colors. These are illustrative of the situation which may be found by the teacher and pupils for dealing with measurements of this type in any schoolroom.

Temperature affects the child's daily activities. Whether he is to wear an extra sweater on a winter morning depends upon how cold it is. This is determined by the reading of the thermometer or by the

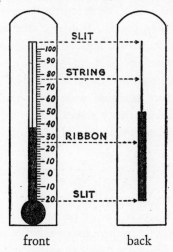

front   back

weather report in the morning radio broadcast. The children are taught to realize the purpose of the thermometer. After they have learned to read numbers, they can find to which number the mercury is nearest even though they cannot make an accurate reading. The thermometer offers occasions for learning terminology and gaining fraction concepts, such as one-half a space. It furnishes a real reason for counting by twos. In reading temperatures children gain an idea of zero, not only from the standpoint of comfort, but as a starting point for counting above and below zero. A good device for practice is a cardboard thermometer about eighteen inches long showing the lines and numbers. The mercury may be imitated with a narrow colored ribbon and an equal length of inconspicuous string. These are fastened together end-to-end so as to form an endless band after having been passed through slits in the top and bottom of the thermometer background. With this arrangement, the colored ribbon can be pulled up to any desired temperature reading and much practice is possible. Later problems in addition and subtraction based upon different thermometer readings may be worked out, such as: Yesterday it was 12° above zero, today it is 4°. How much colder is it today?

Fractions play some part in young children's activities. Miss Polkinghorne[1] found from a study of primary children that everyone understood to some degree selected common fractions, such as one-half, one-third, one-fourth, or three-fourths. Fractions of a unit are more easily grasped than parts of a group. For example, half of an orange is a common experience but half of a dozen cookies is not so common. The equalness of fractional parts seems to be a common hazard. It is not unusual to hear children say, "I have the biggest half." Perhaps, if more attention were given to establishing correct fractional concepts in the primary grades, many of the present common misunderstandings in later grades would not exist.

NUMBER VOCABULARY

Number vocabulary occupies a most important place in efficient problem solving. One day a study-type reading class was attempting to answer the question, "Are there fewer cakes of soap than bottles of milk on the table?" No one was able to answer it correctly. Diagnosis showed that the children did not know the meaning of the word "fewer." Adults tend to assume that word meanings are as clear to children as to themselves, often forgetting that children may not have had an opportunity to hear them or have had no associations that could produce an interpretation. Miss Reid[2] reports a study of the quantitative terms found in a stenographic report of the children's conversations, using first-grade children during their first three months at school. "All" was used 69 times, "little" 49 times, "big" 47, "more" 28, "whole" 27, "long" 24, "bigger" 5, "part" 5, "half" 5, "a lot or lots" 5, "tall" 4, "much" 4, "most" 3, "longer" 3, "less" 3, "biggest" 2, "small" 2, "large"

[1] Polkinghorne, Ada R. "Young Children and Fractions." *Childhood Education,* XI; 354-358. May 1935.

[2] Reid, Florence. "Incidental Number Situations in First Grade." *Journal of Educational Research*, Vol. 30:36-43, September, 1936.

2, "smaller" 2, "higher" 2. The report also shows some use of the cardinal number names "one" to "ten" inclusive, and ordinal names "first" to "fifth" inclusive. Studies of this type make us aware of this particular kind of vocabulary problem and give information as to what can be reasonably expected of children at the time they enter school.

Each area of subject matter has words pertinent only to its own field, and in addition, words common to everyday vocabulary which have new connotations when used in connection with that subject matter. This is true of arithmetic, as in "foot," "pair," "left," "whole," "rest," "yard," "spent," "lost," "found," "gained," and the like. It was many years before one child dissociated a foot, as a unit of measure, from the length of an adult's foot.

Language and reading exercises using these words in the field of arithmetic are of immeasurable value in enriching and clarifying children's number vocabulary. What better composition work can children have than the making of number stories concerning a modern school experience? For example, "We made our library. We needed two orange crates. We spent five of our pennies for them. We spent five more for a brush. We spent ten pennies for paint. We hadn't any money left. The whole school likes our library." The wording of simple problems by children is a way of helping them to think clearly, to select fitting vocabulary, and to express themselves concisely. It is probably best at first to give children plans or guides for creating problems; otherwise the task may be too complicated. In the early stages of combination work, the combinations themselves may be used, as $\frac{2}{4}$.

A child may create a problem similar to: "Two of Harry's kittens were drinking milk, four were playing with a ball. How many kittens did Harry have?" When working with higher decade facts, a plan such as this helps: "A toy bank. Two chances to earn money." A child with a little imagination thus directed makes this problem: "Mother gave Jane a bank for her birthday. The next day Jane earned five cents for dusting and ten cents for raking. How much did Jane put into her bank on that day if she put in all she earned?" Children should have time, when starting to solve textbook problems, for reading the problems and analyzing their meanings before attempting the computation. Later problem solving undoubtedly is aided materially by giving careful attention to number terminology throughout the early elementary grades.

Record keeping aids both children and teachers. It is frequently desirable for each primary child to have a book for recording what number knowledge and skill he has achieved, because the attainments in arithmetic during the early periods vary greatly depending upon the pupil's experiences, abilities, and the kind and amount of guidance the teacher gives. The chart below may serve as one page for his achievements in counting.

How Far I Can Count	to 10	to 20	to 30	to 40	to 50	to 60	to 70	to 80	to 90	to 100
By rote										
Rationally Stationary										
Consecutive Visual										
Auditory										
Muscular										
Tactile										

Other pages in similar form will show a child's ability in reading and writing numbers, what groups he recognizes easily, and other skills important in establishing number concepts.

What is implied by *arithmetic readiness*? Three interpretations follow: (1) It implies that children are ready for formal computation since they have acquired understandings of basic number concepts through experiences in handling materials, by counting, by recognizing groups, by seeing relationships of one number to other numbers, by reading and writing numbers, by measuring, and by using number vocabulary. These varied experiences should build meaningful concepts of numbers, so that when a pupil hears 6, he will not think 6 sheep or 6 books but a generalized 6. Having mastered these concepts, pupils should be ready to carry on computation efficiently in the four fundamentals. The individual child's record sheet should give the teacher a clue to his ability. This interpretation of arithmetic readiness is comparable to interpreting reading readiness as ability to read symbols from books. (2) Brueckner's [1] interpretation is readiness for counting and other initial work. He gives different stages or levels to be considered in organizing arithmetic material. The first one covers the preschool, kindergarten, and usually at least part of first-grade periods. Children have experiences at this time in which "quantitative concepts and a small quantitative vocabulary" are acquired through incidental or guided experiences. These concepts help children to be ready for the more systematic instruction in counting, reading, writing numbers, and other initial phases. Some would, therefore, call this stage the arithmetic readiness period. (3) The third interpretation implies readiness for each phase of arithmetic as it is met in any grade. For example: pupils are ready for multiplication, fractions, decimals, etc., when they have the knowledge and skills necessary to do work in them.

To *summarize* this section it may be said that children come to school having had many number experiences and with a good deal of interest in the "how many" and "how much" of things. The wise teacher utilizes all the opportunities available to establish broad, basic number concepts. She creates opportunities in the arithmetic period and all through the day for counting in different ways; for recognizing groups of objects; for determining relationships; for reading and writing numbers; for gaining concepts of measuring time, money, quantity, weight, and distance; and for developing an understanding and use of a number vocabulary. With this as a background the difficulties of formal arithmetic should be easily and satisfactorily met. It should function effectively in pupil growth and efficiency, serve as a tool to meet number situations, and be a source of real enjoyment.

[1] Brueckner, L. J. "The Development of Ability in Arithmetic." *38th Yearbook of the National Society for the Study of Education.* Part I, p. 280. Public School Publishing Co. 1939.

CHAPTER 13

ARITHMETICAL PROCESSES (I)

COMPUTATION with numbers dates back to very early times. *History* shows that addition and subtraction in ancient Babylon, Egypt, or Rome required little knowledge of our contemporary combinations. Rather it necessitated ability to count the symbols of each denomination and to change the result to the next higher unit. They may have used some form of the *abacus* to parallel computation with numerals and to serve as a mechanical aid. Smith[1] thinks that this device, like many other mechanical devices, had probably been developed over a long period of time. When an early Roman wished to add, it is thought that he drew lines on a board, one to represent units, one to represent tens, and one to represent hundreds. By manipulating pebbles on these lines he could add quite well. The Latin word for "pebble" is "calculus," from which we derive our word "calculate." Sometimes a board with grooves cut into it to hold the "calculi" was used. This device was called an abacus. Later these counters, "calculi," were strung on wires or rods and slid in the grooves. The abacus in different forms was used very generally. A form called "s'choty" by the Russians, "soraban" by the Japanese, and the "suan-pan" by the Chinese, was used in comparatively recent times.

The basic procedure was the same wherever the abacus was used. Suppose a merchant wanted to add 48 and 76. This is what he probably would do: (1) place eight counters on the units or right hand line and

---

[1] Smith, David E. *Number Stories of Long Ago.* Chap. 4. Ginn. 1919.

four counters on the next one to the left, or tens line; (2) place six more on the units, and seven more on the tens line; (3) take ten counters from units, carry one to tens, and leave four on units line; (4) take ten counters from the tens, carry one to hundreds, and leave two on the tens line. So he obtained the sum one hundred twenty-four. Graphically it would appear like this:

(a)   (b)   (c)

It is easy to see how our term "carry" came from the time when one counter was actually carried over to the next space or line or rod.

The exact date of the *invention* of the *zero* is not known. Sanford[1] says it was at least as early as the ninth century A.D., but it may have been as early as the second century B.C. It came from India. It is remarkable that so much was accomplished in mathematics before the zero was invented. Probably one reason was that in those days many of the students were more interested in the theory of number than in computation.

The zero is important in our number system for two reasons: (1) it fills a place or order, and (2) it indicates "no value" in the place or order it occupies. For example, in the number "10," it occupies the units place, putting the "1" in the tens place; and it shows there are no units. In the number "1009," the zeros in the tens and hundreds places put the "1" in the thousands place and the "9" in the units place and indicate that there are no tens or hundreds. The zero is sometimes called a "place-holder," which may not express its full importance.

[1] Sanford, Vera. *A Short History of Mathematics*, p. 93. Houghton Mifflin Co. 1930.

Addition as we know it today has been general only about two centuries—because "there was no cheap paper and that computers had not learned to use the primary combinations."[1]　Addition was common in our elementary school curriculum by 1800.　However, it was taught in a formal manner, stressing memorization of rules and giving practically no attention to the development of concepts.

As time went on, more *phases* of arithmetic were taught and much time in the schools was devoted to their teaching.　Since 1900, many arithmetic operations less commonly used in life have been eliminated from the curriculum.　An illustration of this is the tendency to omit long mechanical practice examples because the school time devoted to arithmetic has been shortened and calculating machines have eliminated the need.

ADDITION

One *definition* for addition is that of finding the total sum of units in two or more like numbers.　If this concept is stressed, there should be less danger of adding units to tens, or tens to hundreds, and the same with higher orders.　This principle, if well established, should carry over into addition of common and decimal fractions.　The technique of adding two or more numbers is a mental process today, and the figures are used as the aids in presenting the situation and in recording results.　The technique of adding two or more numbers has not been changed recently.

Addition is important in our daily lives.　Studies have shown that addition, if mental multiplications are excluded, is used more than any other operation in present-day living.　Many of the problems, however, require adding in very simple forms.　Textbook makers have analyzed the studies concerning its use with the result that newer textbooks show careful planning to prepare children for their present-day needs.　The example below shows the type of difficulty which most life problems do not exceed.　A few more difficult examples and problems than this should be introduced in order to give experience with these types and to show the procedures.

[1] Bond, E. A.　*The Professional Treatment of the Subject Matter of Arithmetic,* p. 44.　Bureau of Publications, Teachers College, Columbia University.　1934.

$3.25
12.60
.78
6.49
.08
3.48
———————

The following *steps* of *development* in teaching addition show a tendency toward greater efficiency. (1) In the early teaching, there was lack of organization. "Authors did not appear to know how many addition facts there are." [1]   (2) By 1880, attention was directed to the forty-five addition combinations. (3) Later, attention was directed to the zero in adding, as an extra hazard. (4) Teaching the addition facts in family arrangement as 1 plus the nine digits, then 2 plus these digits, and so on, was one manner of presentation. (5) At present, the order of difficulty in learning the facts is emphasized. (6) Another recent change has been the postponement of the organized teaching of the 100 addition facts until the second or third year of school attendance.

Students in the arithmetic field advocate a much higher degree of *mastery* than was formerly deemed necessary. A greater degree of achievement is possible because of present theories and practices, such as grading of difficulties, presenting number facts gradually, postponing systematic work in drill, using thoughtful motivation, and making the learning of the number facts a natural outgrowth of learning situations. There are two especially good reasons to strive for this mastery: (1) The value of accuracy in using numbers in all life situations is important. Errors may make a significant difference in all fields of business and living. (2) For a child to know that he knows and can use a group of number facts accurately and effectively gives him assurance which influences his mental and emotional attitudes favorably and has immeasurable effect upon his learning. More will be said later as to the methods for obtaining this mastery. No doubt one of the reasons for children's failing to reach 100 per cent mastery in the addition facts is that they are subjected to formal drill before they have sufficient opportunities to discover and rediscover these facts for themselves. They must have many experiences of putting groups together as they handle materials and play with others. In these ways they gain the concepts of

---

[1] Wilson, G. M. and others. *Teaching the New Arithmetic,* p. 101. McGraw-Hill Book Co., Inc. 1939.

what adding means, as well as learn the individual facts themselves.

What are the 100 addition facts? The 100 addition facts now taught are a development of the original 45 combinations. The 45 combinations include the total number of combinations which are derived by adding any two numbers having one digit each, whose sum does not exceed 18. In the 45 combination organization only one arrangement of addends was taught, such as $2+3=5$, on the assumption that the reverse $3+2=5$ would be learned concomitantly. There is probably some degree of transfer, but teaching the direct forms only is insufficient. Therefore, the more recent theory and textbooks suggest both the direct and reverse forms: $2+3=5$ and $3+2=5$. Since there are 9 doubles, there are only 36 reverse forms, making 81 facts. With the 19 zero facts, the total is 100. The tables below show these organizations.

The 45 direct facts   *The 36 indirect or reverse facts*

```
 1  1  1  1  1  1  1  1  1        2  3  4  5  6  7  8  9
 1  2  3  4  5  6  7  8  9        1  1  1  1  1  1  1  1
 —  —  —  —  —  —  —  —  —        —  —  —  —  —  —  —  —

    2  2  2  2  2  2  2  2           3  4  5  6  7  8  9
    2  3  4  5  6  7  8  9           2  2  2  2  2  2  2
    —  —  —  —  —  —  —  —           —  —  —  —  —  —  —

       3  3  3  3  3  3  3              4  5  6  7  8  9
       3  4  5  6  7  8  9              3  3  3  3  3  3
       —  —  —  —  —  —  —              —  —  —  —  —  —

          4  4  4  4  4  4                 5  6  7  8  9
          4  5  6  7  8  9                 4  4  4  4  4
          —  —  —  —  —  —                 —  —  —  —  —

             5  5  5  5  5                    6  7  8  9
             5  6  7  8  9                    5  5  5  5
             —  —  —  —  —                    —  —  —  —

                6  6  6  6                       7  8  9
                6  7  8  9                       6  6  6
                —  —  —  —                       —  —  —

                   7  7  7                          8  9
                   7  8  9                          7  7
                   —  —  —                          —  —

                      8  8                             9
                      8  9                             8
                      —  —                             —

                         9
                         9
                         —
```

The 10 direct zero facts   *The 9 indirect zero facts*

```
 0  0  0  0  0  0  0  0  0  0      1  2  3  4  5  6  7  8  9
 0  1  2  3  4  5  6  7  8  9      0  0  0  0  0  0  0  0  0
 —  —  —  —  —  —  —  —  —  —      —  —  —  —  —  —  —  —  —
```

Some teachers of arithmetic deem it best to present the 100 addition facts in the *order of difficulty*. Studies were made by Clapp of the errors children made in all grades, by Washburn and Vogel of the errors at the time of learning, and by Knight and Behrens of the difficulty in learning. There is variation in the order of arrangement of these facts by the various investigators. This is not surprising when one considers the difference in the aims of the investigations and the other factors which influence the learning of number facts, such as method of presentation, interest concerning the setting, kind of repetition, and variation in children's abilities. Perhaps the order of teaching is not as important as some of the other factors just mentioned, and has been unduly stressed. It seems to be commonly agreed: (1) that the 45 facts whose sums do not exceed 10 should be taught first; (2) that the 36 facts whose sums come between 10 and 18 inclusive, should be considered the harder ones and be taught later; (3) that both the direct and reverse facts be taught at the same time. Some urge that the corresponding subtraction facts be presented with addition. More will be said about this later.

There is no question that the *zero* is a troublesome element in computation. Some people would teach the simple 19 zero facts interspersed with the other 81. On the other hand, there are probably very few instances when children need to add zero and any number before they meet such facts in column addition. When that need arises, it is probably best to present a group of these facts and develop the principles that (1) zero and any number equal that number, and (2) any number and zero equal that number, (3) zero and zero equal zero. In this way the zero facts can be learned in a very short time. The word "zero" seems to be a more acceptable term than "naught," which is so often confused with "ought."

Developing the concept of adding is important, as well as the learning of each individual fact. Buckingham and MacLatchy in their study of children entering first grade arrived at the following conclusions concerning their abilities in addition. "Very nearly half the children got five combinations right, and only 11 per cent of them failed to get any right. The combinations ranged in difficulty for these children from $5 + 1$, which 71.5 per cent of the children answered correctly, to

4 + 5, which only 22 per cent answered correctly."[1] This would indicate that because of preschool experiences many children have mastered the addition concept when they enter first grade. In their play they have often put two or more groups together and obtained one mass, group, or total. For any who do not appear to have such a concept, counting is of course the basis on which to start.

Presentation of the easy facts may occur in both incidental and organized arithmetic teaching. The need for adding numbers is felt often when a unit of work is being carried on in the primary grades, such as the study of transportation or others suitable for this age. Much of this is presented very incidentally, without drill, and yet real learning takes place. It is desirable for the teacher to keep a record of all such facts that receive some emphasis. Two approaches to the organized procedure of presenting the addition facts will be explained.

One procedure is based on the idea of *putting groups together* and getting the whole. One argument in favor of this plan is that adding really means putting groups together to make the total. It may be introduced by a gradual transition from concrete experiences to the abstract form.

First, the pupil should discover addition facts by the use of situations involving concrete objects. For example, John has two crayons and takes one more. By counting or recognizing the group as a whole he finds he has three crayons. Mary has two balls and gets another from the box. She then has three. This should be continued with other concrete objects, such as pencils, boys, girls, books, and desks.

Second, semi-concrete objects or pictures are used, such as

Third, geometric forms are used to more nearly approach the abstract, such as

[1] Buckingham, B. R. and MacLatchy, J. "The Number Abilities of Children When They Enter Grade One," *29th Yearbook, National Society for the Study of Education*, p. 509. Public School Publishing Co. 1930.

Pupils make up "stories" about groups of objects or forms, such as "One rabbit and two rabbits are three rabbits." The fourth level is the abstract symbol, such as 1 and 2 are 3. Later, the signs are sub-stituted for the words, as + for "and," = for "are," and the form $1+2=3$ is read. Afterwards, the words "plus" and "equals" should be learned. Very soon children may be shown the shorter forms of

addition $\dfrac{\begin{array}{c}1\\2\\\end{array}}{3}$ $\dfrac{\begin{array}{c}2\\1\\\end{array}}{3}$ which they will use commonly. Some pupils may not

need all these levels to understand the final form. The teacher may skip from the concrete objects directly to the abstract forms or may use any steps between. When pupils have the concept of addition well established, the preliminary steps may be discontinued and only the abstract symbols used.

The other plan [1] is based upon the idea of *starting with the whole* and learning the possible groupings of its units. The argument in favor of this plan is that it should avoid a very common tendency of children to count by ones on their fingers, with dots, or in other ways which may continue long after the time of initial presentation. This is especially true if the more formal teaching of arithmetic is introduced too early. The plan of procedure for this approach is as follows: First, pupils experience number situations involving certain addition facts, such as Joe has 3 marbles. They recognize or count the entire group; then are guided to discover that the group can be divided into two parts. Per-haps 1 marble is white and 2 are blue. Helen has 3 balls, 1 is large and 2 are small. This may be continued with other groups of objects. Second, these facts may be shown on the board in sentence form, as for example, 2 marbles and 1 marble are 3 marbles. 1 marble and 2 marbles are 3 marbles. This should be repeated with other objects. Third, these facts may next be shown in this form

2 marbles	1 marble
1 marble	2 marbles
3 marbles	3 marbles

with proper explanation for reading. Illustrations with other widely varied groups should be made, such as trees in the yard, pictures on

[1] This is a modification of the plan given in Studebaker, J. W., Knight, F. B., Findley, W. C., Ruch, B. M. *Understanding Numbers,* pp. 108-111. Scott, Foresman and Co. 1939.

the wall, books on the table. Fourth, help children draw the conclusion that 1 and 2 of all like things are 3 and express in customary form,

as $\dfrac{\begin{matrix}1\\2\end{matrix}}{3}$ $\dfrac{\begin{matrix}2\\1\end{matrix}}{3}$.

When either plan of presentation is used, the following aids for studying and using these facts bring good results with most pupils. (1) Direct children to make individual cards for each fact presented. (2) Show them how to study by looking at the face of the card, closing the eyes and thinking it, recalling twice in the same way.

$$\boxed{\dfrac{\begin{matrix}1\\2\end{matrix}}{3}} \qquad \boxed{\dfrac{\begin{matrix}1\\2\end{matrix}}{}}$$

face　　　　back

(3) Post for reference on the board or chart the facts taught:

$$\dfrac{\begin{matrix}1\\2\end{matrix}}{3} \qquad \dfrac{\begin{matrix}2\\1\end{matrix}}{3}.$$

(4) Find all occasions possible for applying the facts presented. Help children to make their own problems using the facts presented.

It is better to get the idea of addition well established before introducing the idea of subtraction. There is economy, no doubt, in teaching

the whole unit later, as for instance: $\dfrac{\begin{matrix}4\\3\end{matrix}}{7} \quad \dfrac{\begin{matrix}3\\4\end{matrix}}{7} \quad \dfrac{\begin{matrix}7\\-3\end{matrix}}{4} \quad \dfrac{\begin{matrix}7\\-4\end{matrix}}{3}$. For further

suggestions see the discussion on subtraction.

When to teach addition is still uncertain. These are some of the tentative conclusions of the Committee of Seven consisting of some leading educators in Illinois, as given in the 38th Yearbook.[1] They claim that although the addition faces with sums of 10 or less and the easy subtraction facts can be learned by children with the mental age 6-7, evidence seems to indicate that this period and probably the next year should be devoted to number experience of an informal nature without systematic drill. At the mental age of 7-8 the easy additions

[1] Washburne, C. "The Work of the Committee of Seven on Grade-Placement in Arithmetic." *38th Yearbook, National Society for Study of Education.* Part I, pp. 309-310. Public School Publishing Co. 1939.

"are well learned." The harder addition facts and easy subtraction facts can be learned at this stage but these educators question the practice of systematic drill on these facts until the next level. Morton says[1] "there is no good reason why a program of instruction on the easier additions should not begin in the first grade." One commonly used system of textbooks postpones addition and subtraction until the second grade. Another holds that this teaching may be started in the first grade, but leaves the gate open by saying it may be begun in the second half of the first or the first part of the second grade. The practice in many schools is to teach the simpler addition facts in the first grade. It would seem that much depends upon the development of the children, the attitude of patrons and teachers, and the materials at hand.

The harder facts are the sums of two numbers of one figure each whose sums range from 10 to 18 inclusive. These facts should be taught a year later than the easy group. It is unnecessary to use objects in presenting these, since the idea of adding should be established by this time. Cards for study and practice should be made. The goal is a high degree of automatic response, in terms of the sum, to any fact presented.

When children meet $\frac{1}{4}$ the response at once should be only the sum "5," not "1 and 4 are 5."

As soon as children know the easier facts, *column addition* of three digits may be introduced, provided the sum does not exceed 10. Morton[2] gives the following 31 arrangements of three digits each whose sums are 10 or less.

```
1 1 1 1 1 1 1 1 1 1 1 1 1 1 1 1 1 1 1 1 2 2 2 2 2 2 2 2 2 3 3
1 1 1 1 1 1 1 1 2 2 2 2 2 2 3 3 3 3 4 4 2 2 2 2 2 3 3 3 4 3 3
1 2 3 4 5 6 7 8 2 3 4 5 6 7 3 4 5 6 4 5 2 3 4 5 6 3 4 5 4 3 4
— — — — — — — — — — — — — — — — — — — — — — — — — — — — — — —
```

These can be rearranged into a large number of different examples,

taking as an illustration
$\begin{array}{c} 1 \\ 2 \\ 3 \\ \hline \end{array}$
which may be arranged as
$\begin{array}{ccccc} 3 & 2 & 3 & 2 & 1 \\ 2 & 1 & 1 & 3 & 3 \\ 1 & 3 & 2 & 1 & 2 \\ \hline \end{array}$

The new difficulty which children meet in simple column addition is that of adding an unseen number to a seen number. In order to prepare for this, the figures 1 to 9 inclusive may be written in irregular

[1] Morton, R. L. *Teaching Arithmetic in the Elementary School.* Vol. I, p. 77. Silver, Burdett Co. 1937.
[2] *Ibid.*, p. 124.

sequence on the board and the children asked to add 2 to the number to which the teacher points. This should be repeated, adding to those on the board 3, 4, 1, and so on, which are held in mind. Of course the sums must not exceed 10. It is better to teach children to say only the answers, as in

$$2$$
$$1 - 3 \text{ (think this)}$$
$$3$$
$$^- - 6 \text{ (say or write this) rather than 2 and 1}$$

are 3, 3 and 3 are 6. Adding three-digit columns not only introduces a new phase of addition, but also gives drill in facts already presented. Many more three-digit column examples than those given above are possible after all of the 81 simple addition facts have been learned.

Whether to add "up or down" is often asked. Different facts are used in the same example depending upon whether the adding is "up" or "down" the column. Care needs to be taken to be sure that only facts previously presented are met if the adding is done both up and down. After all the facts are learned it seems to make little difference which direction is adopted, except that it is better to decide on one method and use that one exclusively. Adding in the opposite direction will be taught later as a means of checking.

Learning *higher decade facts* in addition aids in column addition. As work advances in column addition, it is necessary for children to learn the related number facts in the higher decades, such as $\begin{matrix} 4 \\ 14 \end{matrix} \quad \begin{matrix} 4 \\ 24 \end{matrix} \quad \begin{matrix} 4 \\ 34 \end{matrix}$ without bridging, and $\begin{matrix} 6 \\ 17 \end{matrix} \quad \begin{matrix} 6 \\ 27 \end{matrix} \quad \begin{matrix} 6 \\ 37 \end{matrix}$ with bridging. This skill is also necessary in multiplication examples which include carrying. Since the basic fact is always in units place, the term "adding by endings" is sometimes used, and since the sums are always above 10, we see the reason for using also the term "higher decade addition." It really extends the knowledge already acquired from learning the basic addition facts. Omitting the zeros, there are 765 facts possible by adding a one-digit to a two-digit number whose sums do not exceed 99. The facts in the higher decades should be taught by grouping rather than as isolated facts.

Pupils can be led to discover the principles underlying the forming of these sums, first *without bridging*, by seeing a series like this on the board

$$
\begin{array}{ccccc}
2 & 2 & 2 & 2 & 2 \\
3 & 13 & 23 & 33 & 43
\end{array} \text{ etc.}
$$

As they give the sum for each combination listed on the blackboard, they should note that the answer in the units place is always like the key fact, also that the answer is in the same decade as the larger number. Starting with this understanding, they can soon work out relationships, or groupings of their own. There is little need to give practice to elementary school pupils on these facts beyond 49 in the work in higher decades. Eventually these should be known as individual facts, that is $\begin{array}{c}4\\22\end{array}$ should be thought of as "26"; not thinking "6," then "2," and "the answer is 26."

When the sum of the units is equal to or exceeds 10, *bridging* is required. That is $\begin{array}{c}5\\16\end{array}$ requires adding into the next decade. Children should know that five and six are 11. But the sum cannot be 11 since 16 is greater than 11, so the answer must be in the next decade and will be 21. The following principles should be developed by the children in their work in higher decade addition: (1) The unit figure in the sum is always like the unit figure in the key fact. (2) If the sum of the units is less than ten, the total sum is in the same decade as the larger addend. (3) If the sum of the units is more than ten, the total sum is in the decade above that of the larger addend. It is desirable to learn both forms, $\begin{array}{c}24\\3\end{array}$ and $\begin{array}{c}3\\24\end{array}$, since whichever way pupils learn to add columns, the reverse order is used for checking.[1]

The *zero in column addition* requires special attention. The most common situation in which children need to add with zero is in keeping score in games. Perhaps John had three chances to throw the bean bag into the circles. His first two throws counted 2 and 4 respectively. He missed the third. In writing his score he records $\begin{array}{c}2\\4\\-\end{array}$, then needs the

[1] Ritter, E. L. and Albert, M. J., *Individual Easy-Step Decade and Combination Cards*. J. S. Latta & Son, Cedar Falls, Iowa. The complete set of cards contains the 390 basic combinations with related upper decade facts in the margins. Answers appear with all facts on one side only.

$$\frac{\overset{2}{4}}{0}$$

symbol for nothing, so he has He realizes that the zero stands for the one he missed, so in adding he must skip that.

Carrying in addition will probably come in the last year of the primary period. Failure to carry correctly is the source of many errors in addition operations. Brueckner[1] lists frequencies of appearance of certain faulty habits in carrying in addition. The table below shows these frequencies translated into per cents.

(1) Per cent of whole number of errors (faulty habits) made in each grade
(2) Per cent total errors in each habit is of total errors (faulty habits) found

	Grades (1)				(2)
Carrying:	III	IV	V	VI	Total
a. Added carried number last..........	21.6%	26.6%	27.6%	27.7%	25.6%
b. Forgot to add carried number........	20.5%	22.5%	21.0%	18.1%	20.8%
c. Added carried number irregularly...	14.4%	17.7%	17.3%	19.1%	16.9%
d. Wrote number to be carried.........	18.8%	14.8%	11.1%	12.8%	14.7%
e. Carried wrong number..............	15.5%	11.2%	16.0%	14.9%	14.4%
f. Carried when nothing to carry......	3.3%	5.3%	5.6%	5.3%	4.8%
g. Wrote carried number in answer....	5.5%	1.2%	1.2%	1.1%	2.5%
h. Added carried number twice........	0.0%	.6%	0.0%	0.0%	.2%
i. Subtracted carried number..........	0.0%	0.0%	0.0%	1.1%	.2%

This table shows that of all the faulty habits found in grade III, 21.6% of them were in "adding the carried number last;" 20.5% were "forgetting to add the carried number;" and 14.4% were "adding the carried number in different places in the column;" and so on. The second, third, and fourth columns are read the same way. The fifth column shows that of all the faulty habits found in all the grades, 25.6% were made in "adding the carried number last"; 20.8% were in "forgetting to add the carried number"; and so on. When the carried number was added last, pupils often forgot it; hence an error. Therefore, the carried number should be added first. This can be accomplished with careful drill following the initial teaching. Writing the number is a "crutch" in remembering and is not generally desirable. Over 20% of the errors in grade III came of forgetting to add the car-

[1] Brueckner, L. J. *Diagnostic and Remedial Teaching in Arithmetic*, p. 120. The John C. Winston Co. 1930.

ried number and there were larger per cents in grades IV and V. The total of 20.8% errors for all grades in omitting to add the carried number indicates that this faulty habit should be guarded against continuously. A careful teacher, by observing closely how children work, can avoid the beginning of many incorrect pupil habits and remedy early any that she finds already acquired.

If the idea of *tens* and *units is rationalized* pupils have a better basis for understanding carrying. Probably the best device is that of using dimes and pennies. Suppose Mary paid 17 cents for a book and 15 cents for paper. How much did Mary pay for both?

17 cents is the same as 1 dime and 7 cents.
15 cents is the same as 1 dime and 5 cents.

| Adding we have | 2 dimes | 12 cents. |
| or | 3 dimes | 2 cents. |

| So Mary paid | | 32 cents. |

Before putting this statement on the board, the teacher should have 3 dimes and 12 pennies on hand and help the children discover this arrangement themselves, putting the dimes on the table and the pennies in the same order as stated above. Since they know that ten cents are equivalent to a dime, this exchange can be made, and they find they have 3 dimes and 2 cents. Other children may work out other problems in the same way. Later, change the word "dimes" to "tens" and "cents" to "units."

17 is 1 ten and 7 units.
15 is 1 ten and 5 units.

| Adding we have | 2 tens | 12 units |
| or | 3 tens | 2 units |

| or | | 32 units.[1] |

[1] Various devices, such as pocket charts, bundles of sticks, or groups of other objects are used especially to aid slower pupils in visualizing and understanding more clearly the relationships of this operation. Perhaps the simplest and most convenient device is one made by each pupil for himself from a sheet of paper 8″ x 11″. He rules this into 2½″ squares, leaving a 1″ top margin with headings as follows:

Hundreds	Tens	Units

He also cuts ¾″ paper squares, clips or staples them into packs of 10, fastens some into packs of 100 with cord or rubber bands, and retains about 20 loose squares. This device may be used to illustrate the processes of carrying or borrowing in the four fundamental arithmetic procedures. It may also be used in the teaching of the place value of numbers.

From that to the accepted procedure should be an easy step, and probably time is saved by having such a preliminary experience. Not much time should be spent on this explanation, since the habit to be established is, "Write the units and carry the tens", and children should not think through this or a similar explanation each time they meet an example requiring carrying. Rather they should acquire this way of thinking:

$$\begin{array}{r} 17 \\ 15 \\ \hline 32 \end{array}$$

think 7 and 5, 12. Write 2, carry 1. One to carry and 1 and 1, 3. Write the 3. Answer, 32. There seems to be a division of opinion as to whether the number carried should be written or not. In a simple example it seems unnecessary, in long ones it may be desirable, since it helps in re-adding individual columns in long examples.

Pupils find column addition easier if the work is presented in *order of difficulty*. If one stands at the foot of a tower and looks at the top, the climb may seem to be long and hard but if the ascent is made step by step, it usually is easily accomplished. The same is often true in learning. If one new difficulty is met at a time in column addition and 100 per cent mastery achieved, the next is learned with much less effort. Therefore, the following sequence is suggested with the idea that as high a degree of mastery in learning as possible is to be attained in each type of example before work with the next level is begun.

Without carrying

I —1—(three addends, easy facts, sums less than 10)
3
2   II —8—(three addends, harder facts, sums 10 to 18)
  1
  3   III —4 5 0—(easy and harder facts with zero)
     0 6 4
     2 0 7   IV —26 41 461—(two-and three-digit numbers)
              32 38 438   bers)

V —24   3 63—(two-digit and one-digit addends, broken columns)
  2 42 21
  63 51   5   VI —40 35—(broken columns and zero)
         4 11
         22   3   VII —321 413—(three-column addition)
         31 40   263 274
                   312   VIII —$1.00 1.25 .85—
                             .25   .23   .12

(dollars and cents)

With carrying

$\boxed{I}$—1—(higher decade without bridging)
 5

 7   $\boxed{II}$—7—(higher decade with bridging)
 <u>6</u>   5

      9   $\boxed{III}$—46   54—(two columns, right-hand column less than 10)
      8   72   95

                $\boxed{IV}$—46   39   46—(two columns, carrying in each,
                      75   94   84   zero as one digit in the sum

$\boxed{V}$—431   394—(three-digit addends, zero in one addend)
 728   203
 <u>225</u>   <u>726</u> $\boxed{VI}$—36—(longer example and gaps)
                 3
          92   $\boxed{VII}$—$1.20—(money)
          46   14.60
          <u>2</u>   .67
                        8.23
                         .90
                       <u>2.48</u>

In column addition, two methods of *checking* are adding again in the same direction and adding in the opposite direction. The latter has the advantage of being a better check as well as giving additional practice because different facts are added. Not only do we want children to add accurately and rapidly, but to form the habit always of checking their work.

The *terminology* which children learn in connection with the addition process includes: *add, addends, sum, equals, answer, total, the whole, amount,* with different meanings for "and," and "are," and the signs $+$, and $=$.

Practice is necessary for mastery in addition. The basic ideas of both the meaning theory and the drill theory go hand in hand in successful teaching. There is need for a great deal of practice in order that skills may be "on tap" for use quickly whenever the situation requires. Just as musicians need to practice scales and exercises in order to perfect their techniques, so pupils need much purposeful repetition of basic number facts. They also need good habits of work, checking, thinking the answers only, neat work, alertness, and other behavior patterns to perfect their work in addition. The wide-awake teacher consciously plans situations which make necessary the repetition of the number facts formerly introduced. If many of the facts are first met in real situations, where they are a natural part of everyday living, they may be learned with less formal practice. Also the fun children have in discovering some of these facts for themselves lends a big impetus toward the mastery of these facts. Some repetition without definite planning will arise in connection with play and units of work. In addition, however, to these and other situations set for repetition, there is a place for definite practice.

The instructor should be keenly aware of what her pupils are practicing in order to know that the correct fact or skill is receiving emphasis. Practice can establish wrong as well as right knowledge or habit. For example, a boy was observed to be adding by looking at the clock. When he added 2 and 3 he found two on the clock, counted three more numbers, and came to five. This was an original but not a good technique for adding. Such situations are excellent arguments for postponing formal arithmetic until the second grade or until basic concepts are well formed. Children then meet the more formal phases with the stronger ability which accompanies greater maturity and consequently have less need to devise roundabout ways of helping themselves.

Pupils should realize that there is need for drill in order that they may participate successfully in daily activities, such as being storekeeper in the school store, keeping the attendance record, and making purchases.

There are two *purposes* for practice in arithmetic, first, to make the responses to basic number facts automatic and, second, to maintain the skill after it has been acquired. The repetitions should be much more frequent during the first week following the presentation of any bit of subject matter. Later repetitions may be spaced at longer intervals. Unless knowledge and skills are used often, they tend to be forgotten.

The following *suggestions* pertain to practice. (1) Accuracy in the use of basic facts is the prime consideration. (2) Speed usually comes as an outgrowth of accuracy and practice. Some pupils grow more rapidly if stimulated a reasonable amount. The rate at which individual children work differs depending upon each one's reaction time and the habits built upon it. (3) Class and individual drills have their place. Individual drills make it possible for each child to work on what he himself needs. The number cards mentioned in other sections are some of the best materials to use for practice. Copying examples from the blackboard for solution is questionable because time is wasted in copying such examples, eyes are often strained, errors are made in copying, and undesirable habits may be formed, such as counting on fingers, with dots, or using some other "crutch." If the teacher wants to give practice in writing the sums, previously prepared lists of examples may be used or a blank sheet of paper may be placed beneath textbook examples and the answers written on this. It is desirable that such lists furnish also written problems which incorporate basic facts on which practice is desired. (4) Mixed drill including different phases of the operation being practiced should be given. For more suggestions on practice see the section on multiplication. (5) One very effective type of drill is the repetition of number facts in verbal problems which may grow out of the pupil's daily living, be found in texts, or be made by the teacher or the children. The last named has the additional value of helping children clarify problem relationships in their own thinking and in developing better habits of problem-solving. (6) Much out-of-school computation is done "in the head"—without pencil and paper. Children should have practice for rapidity in this "mental arithmetic." For example, as a teacher gives rapidly, "5 plus 2, minus 1, add 3," the pupil thinks, "7, 6, 9," and has the answer "9" as the teacher finishes the example. These oral examples may grow more difficult as pupil abilities grow. The original problems in (5) above may also be solved mentally.

There are numerous *workbooks* available. Three types are those which accompany a series of textbooks, those unrelated to any specific text but which cover basic skills, and those which are preparatory for the regular texts in third grade. If carefully utilized, each may be of value in establishing and maintaining skills. Some points for the teacher to keep in mind in using workbooks are: (1) care in teaching pupils how to use them to conserve materials; (2) alertness to the time element in number fact drills, if no provision is made for this in the workbooks themselves; (3) consideration of reading difficulties; (4) the use of supplementary problems if only examples are given; (5) proper fitting of the workbook to the individual needs of the pupils.

Testing and recording bring satisfaction to both teacher and pupil. Such procedures show what degree of mastery has been achieved as work progresses on any level. One of the best ways of testing the degree of mastery of the basic addition facts is with the cards explained in the section on multiplication (p. 326). The record book (p. 288) may be continued as a permanent record. One page may be devoted to the first 15 addition facts as indicated below.

THE ADDITION FACTS THAT I KNOW

	2 2 —	4 4 —	1 5 —	1 2 —	5 1 —	5 5 —	2 1 —	1 8 —	2 3 —	8 1 —	3 2 —	1 1 —	4 1 —	3 3 —	1 4 —
1st test......															
2nd test.....															
3rd test.....															

Other pages may indicate: (1) the second group of 15 easy addition facts, (2) the third group of 15 easy addition facts, (3) the first group of 12 harder addition facts, (4) the second group of 12 harder addition facts, (5) the third group of 12 harder addition facts. There may be also pages showing achievement in (6) different types of column addition, and (7) higher decade facts, based upon material presented in the textbooks used. The real test, it seems, is the effectiveness with which a child uses all of these facts and skills when dealing with problems. To see one's attainments shown on a chart or in any objective manner is one of the best stimuli for greater effort. Individual records are valuable because each can see his own progress, get pleasure in trying to beat his own former record, without being subjected to comparisons with the records of other pupils.

SUBTRACTION

History shows that a few of the methods we know for subtraction date back to very early times. Smith[1] tells us that there has never been one standardized method as there has been for addition. The complementary method was "already regarded as old by 1150 among the Hindus."[2] The simple borrowing plan, Smith[3] says, was mentioned

[1] Smith, D. E. *History of Mathematics,* Vol. II., p. 97. Ginn & Co. 1925.

[2] Ruch, G. M. and Mead, C. D. A Review of Experiments on Subtraction. *29th Yearbook, National Society for Study of Education,* p. 671. Public School Pub. Co. 1930.

[3] *Op. cit.,* pp. 99-101.

in writings as early as 1140. It appeared in books in 1478 and in American books in 1788. The Austrian method was suggested in 1559, but did not receive much attention until the nineteenth century. "It has been called the Austrian method because it was brought to the attention of German writers by Kuckuck (1874) who learned of it through the Austrian arithmetics of Macnick (1848) and Josef Salomon (1849)."

Subtraction may be *defined* differently depending on the point of view. One definition is the process of taking one like number from another. A second definition is of finding the other addend when the sum and one addend are given. This is the reverse of addition. In subtraction the larger number or sum is called the minuend, the smaller number or the given addend is called subtrahend, and the answer or other addend, the difference or remainder.

Subtraction is important in daily living, although we use it less often than multiplication or addition. "Each of the following words suggests subtraction under certain conditions: discount, margin, profit, loss, advance, increase, off, reduce, decline, net, etc."[1] Children frequently meet subtraction situations, as when giving away sticks of candy from the total number purchased, finding out how much older one is than another, and losing part of a set or collection of playthings.

Usually the situations which give rise to different *problems* in subtraction are *classified* in one of these three groups: (1) How many are left—, Jane bought three oranges and gave one away. How many did she have left? (2) How much more—a bicycle costs $15.00. John has $10.00. How much more must he earn? (3) What is the difference— Ted had 15 marbles. Jack has 20. What is the difference between the number of marbles which Jack and Ted have? Children meet all three types in their daily associations. It is better, however, to take one type at a time, when the systematic teaching of subtraction begins, and help children become familiar with one way of thinking in the subtraction process before presenting another. The following order of teaching is suggested: (1) the "how many left" (this type is nearest to the common idea of subtraction), (2) the "how many more," and (3) "what is the difference." Although problems of each type are solved the same way, children need practice in interpreting the wording of the different problems as meaning subtraction.

[1] Bond, E. E. *Professional Treatment of the Subject Matter of Arithmetic*, p. 73. Bureau of Publications, Teachers College, Columbia University. 1934.

What are the 100 subtraction facts?   In the discussion of addition we found how the 100 addition facts were derived. Since the 100 subtraction facts are directly related to the 100 addition facts, their derivation is obvious, as addition

$$\begin{array}{cc} 2 & 3 \\ 3 & 2 \\ \hline 5 & 5 \end{array} \text{, corresponding subtraction } \begin{array}{cc} 5 & 5 \\ -3 & -2 \\ \hline 2 & 3 \end{array}.$$

The chart below gives the 100 subtraction facts arranged in order of size of the three terms—minuend, subtrahend, and difference.

0	1	2	3	4	5	6	7	8	9	
0	0	0	0	0	0	0	0	0	0	
	1	2	3	4	5	6	7	8	9	10
	1	1	1	1	1	1	1	1	1	1
		2	3	4	5	6	7	8	9	10	11
		2	2	2	2	2	2	2	2	2	2
			3	4	5	6	7	8	9	10	11	12
			3	3	3	3	3	3	3	3	3	3
				4	5	6	7	8	9	10	11	12	13
				4	4	4	4	4	4	4	4	4	4
					5	6	7	8	9	10	11	12	13	14
					5	5	5	5	5	5	5	5	5	5
						6	7	8	9	10	11	12	13	14	15
						6	6	6	6	6	6	6	6	6	6
							7	8	9	10	11	12	13	14	15	16
							7	7	7	7	7	7	7	7	7	7
								8	9	10	11	12	13	14	15	16	17
								8	8	8	8	8	8	8	8	8	8
									9	10	11	12	13	14	15	16	17	18
									9	9	9	9	9	9	9	9	9	9

Several methods for presenting subtraction have had their day. Only two need attention at this time. One has the "take away" idea, the other the "additive," which is commonly spoken of as the "Austrian" method. Since some teachers use one and some the other, a brief explanation will be made for each method of presentation. When one method is used for the initial work, it should be continued. It usually confuses children to switch from one to the other.

The *take-away method* may be easier to understand. All pupils have had experiences of sharing and giving away before they start to school. As a follow-up of such experiences, subtraction may be introduced in the following way: (1) Children should meet situations definitely involving subtraction. For example: there were three balls in the schoolroom. Two are taken out at recess. Children easily see that one is left in the schoolroom. Three children are on a committee. One is absent so only two can work. This is repeated with several groups. Here are three children. Teacher asks them to stand in two groups, 2 in one, 1 in the other. The group of 2 goes away. How many are left? This is repeated, only this time 1 goes away and the group of 2 is left. (2) When first showing this with figures, the horizontal form probably will be more easily understood, as 3 children "take away" 2 children leaves 1 child, and 3 children "take away" 1 child leaves 2 children. 3 balls "take away" 2 balls leaves 1 ball, and 3 balls "take away" 1 ball leaves 2 balls. (3) Later the minus sign "—" is substituted for "take away" and equals "=" for "leaves." Finally this common form is used.

$$\frac{\begin{array}{r}3\\-2\end{array}}{1} \quad \frac{\begin{array}{r}3\\-1\end{array}}{2}$$. Pupils should make individual cards, as suggested for addition facts, for practice purposes. The minus sign is desirable, especially when there are mixed drills.

Some *reasons* for using the "take away" or decomposition method, as it is sometimes called, are: (1) The real concept of subtraction can be developed by this method, that is, the process can be more easily understood and illustrated objectively; (2) this method is much more commonly used; (3) Taylor's [1] study showed that 88 per cent of those who were taught by the Austrian method dropped it by the sixth grade.

The *additive method* utilizes knowledge already acquired in addition. This sequence may be followed in introducing it. (1) Problem situations should be used, such as, four children are needed to play a

[1] Taylor, J. S. "Subtraction by the Addition Process." *Elementary School Journal* **XX**. pp. 203-207. November, 1919.

game before school. Two have come. How many more are needed? Thus the children following the same line of thinking as that used in the addition problems may see that they need 2 more, since 2 and 2 are four. (2) There should be a review of necessary addition forms, as

$$\begin{array}{ccc} 1 & 2 & 2 \\ 2 & 1 & 2 \\ \hline 3 & 3 & 4 \end{array}$$. (3) The teacher then may cover one of the addends and

the children supply the number covered. (4) The next step uses this

form, $\begin{array}{cc} 2 & 1 \\ ? & ? \\ \hline 3 & 3 \end{array}$. The children give the missing number. After having

considerable drill with problems of the how-many-more type and on examples with missing numbers, the children should be shown (5) that

$\begin{array}{cc} 2 & 1 \\ ? & ? \\ \hline 3 & 3 \end{array}$ can be written another way $\begin{array}{cc} 3 & 3 \\ -2 & -1 \\ \hline ? & ? \end{array}$ and that it means the

same. That is, 2 and what make 3, 1 and what make 3?

For the additive method these *arguments* are used: (1) the children are not required to learn 100 new facts, (2) the work in addition is strengthened, (3) the work in the higher decades is simplified, (4) it is more effective in balancing accounts. Research seems to show some evidence in favor of the additive method but this evidence is not strong enough to be conclusive. The final answer will await more searching experiments than we have had to date.

The teaching of addition and subtraction may be combined. Some teachers present the 100 addition facts before attempting any subtraction. Others think they save time and energy by teaching the facts

together as a whole unit: that is, $\begin{array}{cccc} 2 & 4 & 6 & 6 \\ 4 & 2 & -2 & -4 \\ \hline \end{array}$. The procedure

more generally followed is: Teach first several easy addition facts,

such as $\begin{array}{ccccc} 1 & 2 & 2 & 3 & 4 \\ 2 & 1 & 3 & 2 & 4 \\ \hline \end{array}$. Then teach several easy corresponding

subtraction facts, such as $\begin{array}{ccccc} 3 & 3 & 5 & 5 & 8 \\ -1 & -2 & -2 & -3 & -4 \\ \hline \end{array}$. After that teach

both addition and subtraction together as a unit, as $\begin{array}{cccc} 2 & 4 & 6 & 6 \\ 4 & 2 & -2 & -4 \\ \hline \end{array}$.

This gives children time to assimilate separately first the idea of addition and later that of subtraction. After the basic understandings are established in each, it may be an economy of time to present them together as a unit. In either event, present the easy facts first.

The *zero* may be taught objectively by using objects and also with problems, as, there are 4 apples in a sack. If none is given away there are still 4, but if all 4 are passed out none remains, or the sack is empty. Several examples like the following may be shown and solved with explanations.

$$\begin{array}{r} 4 \text{ balls} \\ -0 \text{ balls} \\ \hline 4 \text{ balls} \end{array} \qquad \begin{array}{r} 4 \text{ balls} \\ -4 \text{ balls} \\ \hline 0 \text{ balls} \end{array}$$

. From such situations these general principles may be developed: (1) When zero is taken from any number the answer is the number. (2) When any number is taken from itself, the answer is zero. (3) When zero is taken from zero, the answer is zero.

Subtraction examples having *two* or *more digits* in the *subtrahend*, without borrowing or carrying, may be introduced when children have a fairly good knowledge of the easy subtraction facts. They can undertake written work using the facts they know in such problems as "If Jane had 28 stamps and gave Dorothy 14, how many did she have left?" The points to be made especially clear are that the numbers be written correctly, that is, units are to be written under the units and tens under the tens and that the digit at the right in the subtrahend is to be subtracted first. That is, the subtracting proceeds from right to left. Pupils may meet other difficulties even in examples with no borrowing, such as increasing the number of digits in both minuend and subtrahend

three and four: $\begin{array}{r} 28 \\ 14 \\ \hline \end{array}$ $\begin{array}{r} 346 \\ 121 \\ \hline \end{array}$ $\begin{array}{r} 6258 \\ 3147 \\ \hline \end{array}$ bringing in the zero, as for example

$\begin{array}{r} 67 \\ 50 \\ \hline \end{array}$ $\begin{array}{r} 462 \\ 202 \\ \hline \end{array}$, and having extended minuend figures, such as $\begin{array}{r} 167 \\ 24 \\ \hline \end{array}$ $\begin{array}{r} 3492 \\ 141 \\ \hline \end{array}$.

These difficulties should be met one at a time.

The *higher decade* facts used in connection with short division are the only ones of importance. If the short division form is not used, no attention need be given to facts above the 100 simple ones. Should short division be taught, pupils are materially aided by a knowledge of and practice in the 175 different subtraction facts used in that process. Examples of these may be seen from the following:

$$\begin{array}{c}794 \\ \overline{4)3176},\end{array} \begin{array}{c}31 \\ 28 \ (4 \times 7), \\ \overline{}\end{array} \begin{array}{c}37 \\ 36 \ (4 \times 9), \\ \overline{}\end{array} \begin{array}{c}36 \\ 36 \ (4 \times 9). \\ \overline{}\end{array}$$

These and like subtractions are more difficult because they are made while holding in mind the subtrahend, and in some instances part of the minuend. The pupils will probably use the method they have been taught in making these subtractions. If the "take-away" is used they will probably think "31 take away 28" or "28 from 31." If the "additive" method is used they will think "28 and (?) make 31," or "what added to 28 makes 31." Since short division comes after the primary period, it is perhaps better to postpone any work of this type until it is needed.

Usually *carrying* is used with the additive method and *borrowing* with the take-away. The method employed will generally determine how pupils should react when they first meet problems in which some digit in the minuend is less than the corresponding one in the subtrahend. Each type of operation is considered separately, the borrowing type first. As addition with carrying was explained by the use of money on page 303, so this explanation can be reversed for teaching borrowing in subtraction. Suppose this problem is stated. "Harry had 42 cents. He spent 28 cents for a book. How much did he have left?" 42 cents is the same as 4 dimes and 2 cents. 28 cents is the same as 2 dimes and 8 cents. Have the actual money on hand with which the children can work. Help them to see that 10 pennies can be substituted for one of the dimes. By placing the 10 pennies with the 2 pennies, this story is developed

42 cents is the same as	3 dimes and	12 cents.
28 cents is the same as	2 dimes and	8 cents.
Subtracting we have	1 dime	4 cents.
or		14 cents.

Harry has 14 cents left.

If children have been doing subtraction with the additive process, a problem like this may be used to introduce carrying. "Marion wants a doll that costs 35 cents. She has 16 cents. How much more does she

need?" $\begin{array}{c}35 \text{ cents} \\ \underline{16 \text{ cents}} \\ 19 \text{ cents}\end{array}$. In this case, we cannot add anything to 6 to

make 5, so we think of 5 as 15 and know that 6 and 9 are 15. The 9 is written in units place and the one is "carried" to tens, and 1 becomes 2. Then 2 and 1 are 3. One is written in tens place. Therefore Marion needs 19 cents more. The explanation with money in presenting the additive process may be as follows:

35 cents is the same as 3 dimes and 5 cents.
16 cents is the same as 1 dime and 6 cents.

Subtracting we have   1 dime   9 cents.

or   19 cents.

The children are led to think 6 cents and (?) cents make 15 cents (since 5 cents is smaller than 6 cents). Answer 9 cents. Since 1 dime (10 cents) was thought with (added) 5 cents in the minuend, 1 dime must be added to the subtrahend to keep the same relationship between the numbers. 1 dime + 1 dime = 2 dimes. Think 2 dimes + (?) dimes = to 3 dimes. Answer 1 dime. Hence Marion needs 1 dime and 9 cents or 19 cents. In all subtraction work with carrying or borrowing, it is well from the beginning for children to form the habit of thinking, "Is this number (minuend) larger than the other (subtrahend)?" This way of thinking will aid them when they need to borrow or carry, as the case may be.

Consideration of the *order of difficulty* aids as much in teaching subtraction as in teaching addition. The difficulties in examples not requiring borrowing have been previously mentioned. Illustrations for these as well as for those involving borrowing are given here to serve as a background for the teacher's use of textbooks.

Without borrowing or carrying

I —8 5—(easy facts)
    4 3

    II —36 48—(two digits, easy facts)
        24 35

        III —11 17—(harder facts)
              6   8

            IV —48 36—(higher decade used in
                 45 32   short division)

V —427 859—(three digits)
   314 425

    VI —44 446 532 496—(zero difficulties)
        30 302 521 193

        VII —596 986—(fewer digits in sub-
              45   5   trahend than minu-
                         end)

With borrowing or carrying

$\boxed{\text{I}}$ —52   43   62—(one-step borrowing)
     <u>36</u>   <u>28</u>   <u>54</u>

           $\boxed{\text{II}}$ —62   31—(one-step borrowing—one-digit answer)
              <u>54</u>   <u>26</u>

                    $\boxed{\text{III}}$ —461   563—(one-step borrowing—3-digit
                       <u>328</u>   <u>372</u>   numbers)

                              $\boxed{\text{IV}}$ —432   542—(two-step
                                  <u>175</u>   <u>263</u>   borrowing)

$\boxed{\text{V}}$ —963—(zero in answer)
     <u>958</u>

        $\boxed{\text{VI}}$ —614   1463   322—(extended minuend)
            <u>47</u>   <u>638</u>   <u>8</u>

                  $\boxed{\text{VII}}$ —$736—(money)
                     <u>447</u>

                         $\boxed{\text{VIII}}$ —704   670—(zero in
                            <u>126</u>   <u>245</u>   minuend)

Teachers usually find that the most difficult subtraction examples are those having zeros in the minuends. They therefore postpone these until other subtraction zero difficulties have been mastered, and then give special attention to those in the minuend.

The following are some *general items* concerning subtraction. (1) The habit of using "crutches" is a questionable one. They can be of help in some presentations, and their use as long as needed may be justified for the slower children. On the other hand, children are prone to rely on them longer than is necessary when once started. Judging by the appearance of children's work who use "crutches," it would seem that they are more confused than helped. (2) As in addition, children should form the habit of checking all work. In subtracting, this is done by adding the remainder and the subtrahend and checking the sum against the minuend. (3) The discussion concerning practice in the section on addition applies to subtraction. Accurate automatic response to facts is the ultimate goal. Pupils' techniques or methods of work contribute directly to this goal, and therefore should be given close attention during practice. (4) Subtraction has its own terminology. At first children use the form "8 take away 6 is 2." Later they should know that "less" and "subtract" may be used. "Answer" seems to be more commonly used than "remainder" or "difference." They acquire a new meaning for "left." (5) The methods of testing and recording suggested for addition are applicable to subtraction.

The following *suggestions* for *practice* may help to make drill effective and interesting. Two standards by which to judge the value of practice activities are: (1) The majority of the time should be spent on repetition of the number material rather than on the procedures of the activity, such as moving about and handling materials. (2) The majority of the children, not just one or two, should have practice on the arithmetic facts for the major part of the time. Comparatively little repetition is afforded to all of a group when a number card is flashed to only two at a time.

1. *Guessing game.* Teacher: "I am thinking of two numbers that make 14. Can you guess them?" Either written or oral answers may be given. This game stimulates mental alertness and review of number facts on the part of the entire class.

2. *Who Knows?* Children are divided into sides with a captain for each. The teacher has selected from the usual pack of cards the facts on which she wishes the children to practice. She shows a card, calling on the children irregularly, alternating the sides. Hence no pupil knows when his turn is coming and must pay attention. If a child gives the correct answer to the card shown him, the teacher keeps it and shows another card to the next child. If the answer is incorrect or the response too slow, the card is given to the child failing in the response. At the close, the side with the fewer cards wins. Those who have cards study, answer, and return them to the teacher, as they give the correct sums or differences. This game's best features are that emphasis is placed upon the facts that are missed and slower pupils are given more practice.

3. *Matching.* A special pack of cards is prepared for this game. Each child should have at least three cards. A pack of answer cards which contains the answers to all the facts the children have is also necessary. The teacher sets an answer card, such as 12, on the blackboard ledge. The children who have $\frac{6}{6}$ $\frac{8}{4}$ $\frac{7}{5}$ $\frac{9}{3}$ will set these on the ledge. When the last answer card has been shown, all of the cards should have been played. The object of the game is to see who can get rid of his cards first. This game furnishes much repetition for all. Each child reviews all of his cards each time an answer card is shown. Also, each pupil checks every card played against the answer card to catch errors.

SMALL-GROUP AND INDIVIDUAL ACTIVITIES

Small grade groups of pupils usually exist in the one-room rural school and small groups may be formed in the classrooms having a larger number of pupils per grade. Some of the following exercises may be used by individuals or by two pupils working together.

4. *Using individual packs.* Children make their own packs of number cards, taking the numbers from used pages of calendars and pasting them on oak tag or light cardboard, as ☐ 1 ☐ . These may be used in several ways. (a) Children may arrange small objects in groups on the desks, then place the corresponding number card beside each group. (b) Each child, to develop the concept of correct number series, is asked to arrange his individual pack in the same series as that on Number Chart II, page 277. This chart should be used by the child as a guide at first, if he does not know what number to place next. Later he may arrange his cards as he thinks they should be arranged, then check by comparing his arrangement with the chart.

5. *Three the same.* Three or four children may play and three sets of cards are needed; (a) a set with geometric forms or pictures of objects one to nine, inclusive, (b) a set with Arabic numbers 1 to 9, (c) a set with words "one" to "nine." The dealer gives each child six or eight cards depending upon the number playing, and places three cards in the center face up. The first player takes one from the center and lays down one card from his hand, and so on around. As soon as a player has the three like cards—word, number, and objects—he lays them on the table as a book. The object of the game is to make books containing three cards of the same denomination. The first to play all of his cards wins.

6. *Bingo.* The following materials are needed: (1) one master card containing in consecutive order by rows all the numbers which have been presented, (2) a set of the same numbers on small square or round pieces of cardboard, (3) cards for individual players, each containing in irregular order by rows part of the numbers presented, and (4) some kernels of corn. One pupil, the caller, selects a number at random, reads it aloud, and places it on the same number on his master card. Other pupils place a kernel of corn on the number called if it is on their card.

This is repeated until someone completes a row horizontally, vertically, or diagonally. The first to get a complete row covered by placing corn over the numbers read calls "Bingo" and wins.

7. *Tenpins.* These can easily be made by folding heavy paper, 9″ × 12″, horizontally into four sections, overlapping the two end sections (x), and fastening with a pin.

×			×

. The

tenpins may be placed on the floor in triangular form, as

```
× × × ×
 × × ×
  × ×
   ×
```

. On

each of the "tenpins" thus made, write a number from 1-10 inclusive. Each child in turn rolls a rubber ball no larger than a tennis ball, to see how many he can knock down. After his turn, he sets up the tenpins, reading the number on each, the others checking to see if he is correct. Another child counts the number of tenpins knocked over as he reads the number on each. Another child may record on the board the number knocked over. This is also adapted for addition, and may be used for multiplication if all of the tenpins have the same number.

8. *Reading directions.* Reading may be combined with arithmetic, by giving many directions which the child can read and carry out, such as: Draw 5 balls. Make 2 red. Make 3 blue.

Writing Numbers

9. *Circles and numbers.* Sheets of paper divided into sections are provided. In each of these sections are groups of circles with a blank

space below. Children write the correct number in each blank space which corresponds to the group above.

10. *Telephone directories.* Where telephones are common and numbers not too large, children may like to make a directory for those in their room.

11. *Ticktacktoe.*

1	0			2	0	
2	2	0		2	2	0
3		0		0		2.

This is best played on the blackboard. Two children may play together. The object is to get three numbers in correct sequence or three like numbers in a row. Turns are taken and a number or zero is written. The zero is used to block the sequence. Instead of 1, 2, 3, other groups of three may be designated, as 4, 5, 6, or 7, 8, 9.

Number Facts

```
 3        3
 4        4
--       --
 7
face     reverse
```

12. *Number cards.* The usual cards are no doubt the best material available for individual study and small-group activities. Two or three children can play together, one flashing the cards, the others in turn attempting to give correct answers to each card as it is flashed. The cards each child misses should be given him for further study.

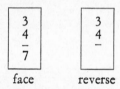

13. *How many.* Individual cards similar to this are given to the children. They are to write on a paper all of the addition or subtraction facts with their answers, that they can make with these numbers within a limited time. These possible facts and answers should be listed on the back of each card, in order that the children may check their own responses. Pupils change cards from day to day.

9	10	7
3	5	8

1
2

face

4
5

face

3

reverse

9

reverse

14. *Find the card.* One large card with answers and a corresponding set of small cards with basic facts are provided for each child. Within a time limit each pupil tries to match each card with the correct answer. In order to check his work, he can turn over the small cards. This may be used for either addition or subtraction.

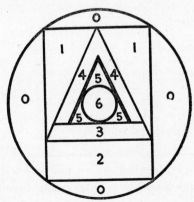

| | 1 | | | 2 |

fold	ㄥ	8	8	ㄥ	ㄥ
	ᘔ	Ɩ	ㄣ	ㄥ	Ɩ
	ㄣ	ㄥ	ㄣ	ϛ	Ɩ
	3	6	2	4	2
	1	2	3	5	2
fold	4	8	5	9	4

15. *Folded paper.* Form 2 is the folded paper that each child receives. On another paper he records the answers within a time limit. By unfolding each edge, he can check his answers.

16. *Throwing the bean bag.* This form may be drawn on the floor or on a paper placed on the floor. Each child has three or four chances to throw, depending upon what length of column work the drill is covering. Another child records the score. The player adds his own score. The others watch to see if the addition is correct. The numbers may be changed to fit the facts being used by the pupils.

MULTIPLICATION

The importance of the concepts of the fundamental processes already discussed holds for multiplication and division. A few well-directed strokes of good teaching can show that multiplication is a shortened form of addition, and division the inverse of multiplication. The *relation* of all of these to counting should be made clear. This in turn may be shown to have grown out of human number needs. The diagram below might help to show these relations:

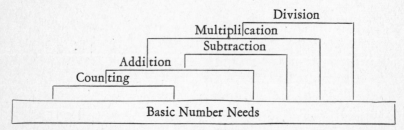

This diagram shows only the relationships of the fundamentals and should not be used as a scale of their importance to us.

History helps us understand that multiplication has been a difficult process for the human race to develop. The Egyptians seem to have multiplied by "duplation" or doubling the multiplicand, as illustrated in the example below:

Our method	Egyptian Method	
124	124 by 1 = 124	— 1— 124
33	124-doubled = 248—(2)	
372	248-doubled = 496—(4)	
372	496-doubled = 992—(8)	
4092	992-doubled = 1984—(16)	
	1984-doubled = 3968	—32—3968
		33—4092

Thus Joseph probably calculated his store of grain during the seven fat years of his rule as prime minister under Pharoah.

Skipping over the centuries we find the "lattice" method which is said to have immediately preceded our own.

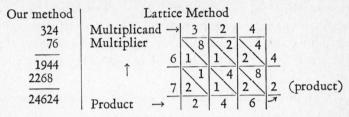

By this method one may multiply either left to right or vice versa and with either figure of the multiplier first. Furthermore, no carrying needs to be done in the multiplying part of the operation, only in the adding. For example in 6×4, the 24 is written out, placing the digits in the proper diagonal space. Likewise the product 12, from 6×2, and the product 18, from 6×3. Begin at the top and right to add the partial products found in the diagonal columns. In the units space is a 4, and $8 + 2 + 2$ in the tens space. This makes 12 tens so one should be carried to the hundreds place when added as $1 + 2 + 4 + 1 + 8 = 16$. The 6 is written in the hundreds place and 1 carried to the next, etc.

It is thought that our $(\times)$ sign of multiplication developed in England about 1600 A.D. from the so-called cross-multiplication, which is manipulated in this way:

Our method	Cross multiplication	
43		
24		
172		
86		
1032		

Solve thus: Think 4×3, 12. Write 2, carry 1. Think 4×4, 16. 2×3, 6, add $16 + 6 + 1$ (to carry), 23. Write 3, carry 2. Think 2×4, $8 + 2$ (to carry), 10. Write 10

If the student is interested in these old methods of multiplying, he will find other very enlightening facts and methods in the histories of mathematics.

The *multiplication concept* is perhaps best developed as a shortened form of addition. Unless the pupils are below normal in number ability, it seems unnecessary to use concrete objects in presenting the multiplication idea. It is easily done, however, should it be advisable. The following suggestions can be readily adapted to the use of concrete materials.

Teachers should start with a problem situation taken from the experience of the pupils: I bought 2 pencils. They cost 5 cents each. How much did the 2 pencils cost? The pupils readily see that 5¢ and 5¢ are 10¢ from their experience with addition. Perhaps several problems using $5 + 5$ should be used to clarify any hazy ideas about relationships in the problem as far as addition is concerned. They also have learned:

$$\begin{array}{r} 5¢ \\ \underline{5¢.} \\ 10¢ \end{array}$$ From this it is comparatively easy for them to discover the two

5's make 10. If the pencils had cost 6¢ each they readily see two 6's make 12, or two 7's make 14, two 4's make 8, etc. By this time pupils will usually run ahead in their thinking and suggest two 9's make 18, two 3's make 6, etc. These at first might be written out in long hand, as in the example above, and placed in order of size. Later these may be reviewed and discussed. During this period the teacher and pupils

might discover a new and shorter way to write these facts, as $\begin{array}{r} 5 \\ \underline{2} \\ 10 \end{array}$ that

is, two 5's make 10. Also

$$\begin{array}{rrrrrrrr} 6 & 4 & 3 & 2 & 7 & 8 & 9 & 1 \\ \underline{2} & \underline{2} & \underline{2} & \underline{2} & \underline{2} & \underline{2} & \underline{2} & \underline{2} \\ 12, & 8, & 6, & 4, & 14, & 16, & 18, & 2. \end{array}$$

Notice that the zero facts are not included. The reasons are that they are difficult for pupils to understand, they are seldom used in actual situations in this isolated form, and in all probability they can be taught later by principle and practiced in the situations where they are actually

used, as in $\begin{array}{r} 60 \\ \underline{4} \end{array}$. Some writers suggest that the 1's be omitted from these

early experiences. It seems, however, that the approach used is just as natural for the 1 as it is for the 5 or any other number.

As the multiplication facts are being learned, they should be used in a wide variety of verbal problems. These for the most part may be oral. Not only may these be presented by the teacher, but they may be thought out and put into good language by the pupils. The following problem types in multiplication will help the teacher to suggest forms to the pupils:

1. Cost of more than one when cost of one is known, e.g., one pencil 5¢, how much for 2 pencils?
2. The amount (spent, earned, saved, etc.) in a long period when the amount for a shorter period is known, e.g., earn $2 per day, how much in a week?
3. The whole number when the number of equal groups and number in each group are given, e.g., two rows, 6 in a row.
4. The number of things or parts in some other quantity, e.g., three feet in 1 yard, how many in 2 yards? Two pints in 1 quart, how many pints in 3 quarts?
5. Distance when time and rate are given, e.g., two blocks in 1 minute, how far in 2 minutes?

If well used, this kind of exercise not only helps to fix the fundamentals, but also gives valuable training in problem relationships which may bear fruit in the solution of problems later. Sets of problems worked out for one related group, such as the 2's, may be readily adapted to other related or unrelated groups of facts.

The *multiplication sign* may be presented by using the following plan after the pupils have mastered the steps suggested above. The $\frac{5}{\underline{2}}$, that is, two 5's are 10, or two 5's $= 10$ may be written this way, 2 times $5 = 10$, or $2 \times 5 = 10$. Great care should be taken to connect the sign $(\times)$ with the word "times," and both of these with the "two 5's $= 10$." Perhaps only a few of these transitional steps need to be used to start the pupils on the way to write all multiplication facts in an orderly fashion, as possibly in a table. Other groups of related or unrelated facts may be written in a similar manner.

If the above-mentioned plan of teaching related groups is followed, the approximate *order of difficulty* is: the 2's first, then the 5's, 4's, 3's, 6's, 7's, 8's, 9's. The 1's of course are included with each related group and a rearrangement of them into a separate table should be easily done and fully understood. The only new combination is $1 \times 1 = 1$. With the exception of the doubles, zeros, and ones, the facts seem to increase in difficulty in proportion to the size of the product. That is $9 \times 7 = 63$ is more difficult, generally speaking, than $2 \times 2 = 4$. The zero facts may be taught later with two or more digit multiplicands. Another gradation of the 100 multiplication facts is by the amount of error pupils make in using them after they have been learned.[1] Still another, possibly the best of all, arranges the facts in order of the difficulty pupils have in learning them.[2] These gradations are called "scientific" because of the methods used in making them. Since there is a wide range of individual differences among pupils in regard to difficulty of multiplication facts, teachers should watch each pupil to catch all troublesome facts at the earliest opportunity.

Suggestions for practice. Regardless of the excellence of the presentation or depth and breadth of concept, the basic facts in multiplication must be mastered if that field of subject matter is to be enjoyed and efficiently used. The sort of mastery necessary is not gained incidentally. It is obtained by plenty of intelligent, well-directed practice, just as skill in any other complicated activity is obtained. Furthermore, there are so many chances for mastery of these basic facts to slip, that a well-organized maintenance program should be followed. (1) Number cards of the usual type,

$$\begin{array}{r} 5 \\ 2 \\ \hline 10 \end{array}$$

and the reverse

$$\begin{array}{r} 5 \\ 2 \\ \hline \end{array}$$

may be made by the pupils at the time the facts are first presented. The face side may be used to aid in the original learning, and the reverse side for later practice. (2) Frequent tests composed of the whole hundred multiplication facts should be used. These should be arranged to put a time limit on each fact. This arrangement will point out the specific facts for each pupil over which he does not have a sufficient degree of mastery. For example, the teacher, after a little practice, can read as a test the facts by rows of ten at a rate sufficiently rhythmical and rapid to prevent counting as the pupils write the products in some pre-arranged order for checking. Or a test of this nature can be made by using large flash cards. The teacher exposes each fact by showing the card to the group for a given amount of time, at regular intervals and at a rate sufficiently fast to prevent counting. The pupils write the answers in a definite order for later checking. Perhaps the best type

[1] Clapp, F. L. *The Number Combinations: Their Relative Difficulty and Frequency of Appearance in Textbooks.* Bulletins Numbers 1 & 2, Bureau of Educational Research, University of Wisconsin.

[2] Norem & Knight. "The Learning of the 100 Multiplication Combinations." *29th Yearbook of National Society for the Study of Education.* Part II, Ch. VII. Public School Publishing Co. 1930.

of number fact test is that given from a phonograph record,[1] because it varies less from the given standard. Such checks will indicate the exact facts inadequately mastered and those on which the pupil might be slipping. These are the ones on which he should practice to raise his degree of mastery. (3) A chart of progress kept by each pupil increases the likelihood of intelligent and earnest co-operation by the pupils. If such a chart could run over a period of six weeks or longer, it would be more valuable than for a shorter time.

If the *basic principles of practice* are followed, greater progress and less difficulty will almost surely result. (1) The pupils should help to determine what facts should be practiced and should share responsibility for mastering them. Many teachers feel they cannot take the time to work this out with their pupils. The fact remains that it usually pays in time, energy, and degree of success to hold the pupils' intelligent co-operation by their participation in planning the practice and determining the outcomes. (2) Pupils should center their efforts on their own specific difficulties instead of wasting them on facts already mastered. To illustrate: If Anna knew the exact multiplication facts which cause her trouble, she could direct her practice more effectively than if she knew only that she needed more practice in multiplication. (3) The conditions under which practice is done often add to its effectiveness. (a) Periods of practice should be comparatively short and frequent. (b) Attention of every pupil should be focused on the practice. (c) Each pupil should work at top speed and accuracy during the practice period. (d) Checks should be rigid, frequent, and self-administered by the pupil immediately after the test, if possible. (e) Practice should be specific yet tied up directly with the larger objectives of arithmetic. For example: Jack reviews and makes $9 \times 6 = 54$ a habit today because it gives him a feeling of mastery now and he knows it often will be of benefit to him in his work later. (f) Practice can be made pleasant but not effortless. The pupil needs to work if he is to develop. Most pupils are willing to do so if there seems to be a good reason for it. (g) Plenty of review and maintenance practice should be provided. Otherwise the pupils may bog down with too much unassimilated fact material. Perhaps a good summary statement might

[1] Ritter, E. L. *Phonograph Record Tests in Arithmetic.* J. S. Latta & Son, Cedar Falls, Iowa.

be: "Keep every pupil busy profitably all of the time in every practice period." Any device or procedure which fails to do this should be challenged.

Some teachers and textbooks recommend that the *multiplication* and related *division* facts be taught together. For example:

$$
\begin{array}{llll}
2 & 3 & & \\
3 & 2 & & \\
\hline
6, & 6, & 2\overline{)6}, & 3\overline{)6}
\end{array}
$$

would make a unit of work and could be taught as a group. This plan requires the reverse be taught with each fact. Usually this causes no trouble. Pupils easily see that three 2's are the same as two 3's. Such a plan could be followed whether the gradation is that of related groups of facts, as the 2's or 3's, or that of a scientifically arranged group as Clapp's or Norem's and Knight's. Usually the pupils are taught at least 15 to 20 easy multiplication facts before the related division facts are introduced. After catching up with the division facts the two operations are taught together. (See division section for introductory suggestions, p. 340.)

Teaching the *higher levels* of multiplication involves several factors. At this point the zero becomes functional. It is probably best introduced by using a familiar verbal problem situation. Example: Harold bought 2 tablets costing 10 cents each. How much did Harold spend for both? The pupils easily arrive at 20¢ by $\begin{array}{r} 10¢ \\ +10¢ \\ \hline 20¢ \end{array}$. By the same process of thinking followed when introducing multiplication facts, the teacher shows that: two 10¢'s = 20¢, or 2 × 10¢ = 20¢, or

$$
\begin{array}{r}
10¢ \\
2 \\
\hline
20¢.
\end{array}
$$

If Harold had bought 3 tablets the example would have been three 10's = 30¢ or

$$
\begin{array}{r}
10¢ \\
3 \\
\hline
30¢.
\end{array}
$$

Use examples until pupils understand the general relation of multiplication to this problem and the use of the zero. Then take up the detailed inspection by suggesting that in each instance

$$\left(\begin{array}{ccc} 10 & 10 & 10 \\ \underline{2} & \underline{3} & \underline{4} \\ 20, & 30, & 40, \text{ etc.} \end{array}\right)$$

when a zero (0) was multiplied by a number the product was always 0, as $2 \times 0 = 0, 2 \times 1 = 2, 3 \times 0 = 0, 3 \times 1 = 3, 4 \times 0 = 0, 4 \times 1 = 4$. Point to the numbers multiplied and usually no trouble is experienced with the 2-digit number in the multiplicand. If necessary use $\frac{100}{\times 2}$ or two 100's and other examples of this type until the rule is worked out, namely: when zero is multiplied by a number the product is zero. The inverse is taught at once by noting that if $2 \times 0 = 0$, then $0 \times 2 = 0$, in the same way that products of 2×3 and 3×2 both are 6. Thus, a second principle in the use of zero is established; namely, that when any number is multiplied by zero the product is zero. Use dozens of examples to illustrate this rule.

Easy examples provide the best way to introduce *two- and three-digit numbers* in the multiplicand, with no carrying and with zeros in the 3-digit examples. These should be very simple at first, and the introduction need not wait until all the multiplication facts are learned. They are good exercises to use in practicing the primary number facts. Examples:

$$\frac{12}{2}, \quad \frac{34}{2}, \quad \frac{11}{3}, \quad \frac{22}{3}, \quad \frac{40}{2}, \quad \frac{202}{3}, \quad \frac{100}{6}, \quad \frac{32}{2}, \quad \frac{93}{3}, \quad \frac{71}{4}, \quad \frac{523}{3}, \text{ etc.}$$

Perhaps pupils should (when it is first met) work out under supervision the difficulty in the double left-hand numbers of the product in such examples as $\frac{63}{2}$. Teachers should be careful, however, to do nothing for the pupils which they can think out and do for themselves.

When *carrying* in multiplication is introduced, extreme care should be observed. Graded materials should be provided to fit the abilities of the pupils and every development of each pupil noted. Start with examples pupils may add easily, as

$$\frac{16}{2}, \quad \frac{15}{2}, \quad \frac{17}{2}, \quad \frac{25}{2}, \quad \frac{24}{3}.$$

First find out that two 16's = 32 by adding. Then suggest that something new is to be learned and immediately teach the mechanics of the process.

After the process is well established, rationalization may be taken up. If the rationalizing is done before the process is well learned, pupils are frequently confused by the explanation and fail to get the process. This is the exact opposite of what an explanation of principles is supposed to do, but because of the lack of pupil ability to see abstract principles or the lack of artistry on the part of the teacher, the rationalizing process may mystify rather than clarify the minds of the pupils. It is safer, therefore, to teach the mechanics of the process first and make sure each pupil can use it even though he does not know why. After the mechanics have been learned, the reasons why the various steps were taken may be thought out. Some pupils may never understand why they carry in multiplication, but can do it just as well as if they did. In using this plan of attack some think, perhaps rightly, that we rob the pupils of a chance to develop by imposing a mechanical procedure upon them without giving them an opportunity to get a meaningful background for it. In one way this is true. But an opportunity may be given to fill in the background if the pupil or teacher or both should feel a need for it after the mechanics have been learned. To those who maintain that the pupils will not learn the operation as well without the background, we reply that if pupils do not have sufficient ability to follow a purely mechanical procedure they probably would not have the ability to understand the background. After all, the order suggested above is the one used very commonly in life. To illustrate: How many of us took a background course in automobile engineering and construction before we started to drive? Most of us know precious little about automobiles after years of operation, yet we use them more or less successfully.

Taking up again the mechanics of carrying, let it be noted that the pupils have found that two 16's are 32 by adding. The new and very interesting process about to be learned is what to do when the first multiplication is 10 or more. For example: in

$$\frac{16}{2,}\ 2 \times 6 = 12.$$

The question arises as to what may be done with the "1" in the 12. Perhaps the easiest and safest method is to write the 12 where it should be, as

$$\begin{array}{r} 16 \\ 2 \\ \hline 12. \end{array}$$

Then, $2 \times 1 = 2$, and the example would be

$$\begin{array}{r} 16 \\ 2 \\ \hline 12 \\ 2 \\ \hline \end{array}$$

putting the "2" one place to the left "under" the "12." Then by adding

$$\begin{array}{r} 16 \\ 2 \\ \hline 12 \\ 2 \\ \hline 32 \end{array}$$

the right product is found, as is proven by addition. Likewise

$$\begin{array}{r} 15 \\ 2 \\ \hline \end{array}$$

would be

15	17	25
2	2	2
10	14	10
2	2	4
30,	34,	50

all of which may be tested out by addition. These may be extended later into

24	12	45
3	6	3
12	12	15
6	6	12
72,	72,	135

and so on to the more difficult examples. After pupils have become accustomed to this form the teacher might ask if they would like to learn a short cut in which they use the head a little more and the pencil less. Then show that in

$$\begin{array}{r} 16 \\ 2 \\ \hline 12 \\ 2 \\ \hline 32 \end{array}$$

one may write only the "2" of the "12" and hold the "1" in mind, as

$$\begin{array}{r} 16 \\ 2 \\ \hline 2 \end{array}$$

Then $2 \times 1 = 2$, $+$"1" in mind makes 3 which is written

$$\begin{array}{r} 16 \\ 2 \\ \hline 32. \end{array}$$

Thus continue with

$$\begin{array}{r} 15 \\ 2 \\ \hline \end{array} \qquad \begin{array}{r} 17 \\ 2 \\ \hline \end{array}$$

and plenty of other examples always keeping the "1 in mind." All of this ought not to be interpreted to mean that the teacher should always "show" the pupils or "explain" to them "how it is done." The teacher who is an artist would maneuver the learning so that her pupils "discover" all or most of these new procedures. For example, when reaching the "short cut" stage, she might remark that it takes a lot of pencil work to do the multiplication examples and suggest that "we" hunt for a shorter way to do it. Or, if the pupils are not able to tackle a problem that difficult, the teacher might ask when she comes to

$$\begin{array}{r} 16 \\ 2 \\ \hline 2. \end{array}$$

"If the '1' is not written, what may be done so as to be sure to have it to add after multiplying 2×1?" The idea behind this procedure is to give pupils every possible chance to think their own way through new situations.

Two or more digits in the multiplier is next met in multiplication. If the form

$$
\begin{array}{r}
16 \\
2 \\
\hline
12 \\
2 \\
\hline
32 \\
\end{array}
$$

had been used to introduce carrying followed by the short cut form the 2-digit multiplier should cause very little trouble. Again the beginnings should be on the easiest levels. For example, the pupils know

$$
\begin{array}{r}
12 \\
2 \\
\hline
24,
\end{array}
\qquad
\begin{array}{r}
13 \\
2 \\
\hline
26,
\end{array}
$$

etc. Suppose

$$
\begin{array}{r}
12 \\
12 \\
\hline
\end{array}
$$

is to be multiplied, how might it be done? Pupils should readily see that multiplying by the "2" is the same as they did previously,

$$
\begin{array}{r}
12 \\
12 \\
\hline
24.
\end{array}
$$

If some pupil does not suggest it, the teacher might "discover" that "we" might multiply by the "1" just as was done with the "2." In multiplying by "2" the first number of the product "4" is put under the multiplier "2." The same thing should be done with the first number of the product when multiplying by the "1." There is a "2" already under the "1" so a new row must be started, as

$$
\begin{array}{r}
12 \\
12 \\
\hline
24 \\
12 \quad .
\end{array}
$$

That is, $1 \times 2 = 2$ and $1 \times 1 = 1$ writing the "12" with the left hand number "2," under the "1" of the multiplier. The partial products already found must be added to get the final product, as

$$
\begin{array}{r}
12 \\
12 \\
\hline
24 \\
12 \\
\hline
144.
\end{array}
$$

Likewise other examples

$$\begin{array}{ccccc} 13 & 22 & 23 & 11 & 30 \\ \underline{12,} & \underline{13,} & \underline{21,} & \underline{27,} & \underline{15,} \end{array}$$

even to

$$\begin{array}{c} 112 \\ \underline{23} \end{array}$$

should be practiced. The difficulty should be increased by easy steps in carrying when using easy 2-digit multipliers, as

$$\begin{array}{ccc} 16 & 18 & 26 \\ \underline{12,} & \underline{12,} & \underline{32.} \end{array}$$

Later, the difficulty may be increased to

$$\begin{array}{ccc} 47 & 68 & 70 \\ \underline{23,} & \underline{34,} & \underline{67,} \end{array}$$

and to larger digits in both multiplier and multiplicand.

In order to prepare in advance for carrying in larger multiplication examples, pupils may be given exercises of a special type. Preceding examples like

$$\begin{array}{c} 68 \\ \underline{47,} \end{array}$$

pupils might practice $7 \times 6 + 5 =$, also $4 \times 6 + 3 =$. These exercises give pupils experience and practice with the exact multiplications and carryings they will have later in the example, without the detracting influences of the work on the example itself. Undoubtedly such exercises help in some cases, but a teacher needs to be very careful in using any type of practice work out of its natural setting. She must be reasonably sure that it carries over to the actual situation. Pupils should know that $7 \times 6 + 5$ will appear in examples and where they will appear. Time and energy are often wasted if these direct connections are not made. This is another use of higher decade addition as presented in the discussion of addition.

Zero situations in the multiplier and in the multiplicand beyond the simple ones already included should perhaps be made items of special attention. To illustrate, sometimes it is necessary to multiply numbers like these:

$$\begin{array}{c} 202 \\ \underline{34} \end{array}$$

(no carrying) or like these:

$$202$$
$$\underline{36}$$

(carrying to the zero). Pupils should think $6 \times 0 + 1 = 1$ (not 7). Possibly the principles covering multiplication of zeros by other numbers or other numbers by zeros should be reviewed before the new work is taken up. This may be continued using examples, as

$$24$$
$$\underline{10}$$

which may be

$$24$$
$$\underline{10}$$
$$00$$
$$\underline{24}$$
$$240$$

or to save the time the pupils usually see that multiplying by 10 is done by multiplying by "1" and annexing a "0," that multiplying by 100 is done by multiplying by "1" and annexing two 0's to the number multiplied. Later they find that to multiply a number by 20, 30, 40, etc., one multiplies by 2, 3, 4, etc., and annexes a "0" to the product. The usual form for this is

$$242$$
$$\underline{20.}$$

Some object to this form because it is hard to explain mathematically. However, it has the advantage of being easily learned. Perhaps the most difficult is

$$232$$
$$\underline{203}$$

which may be taught by using a row of zeros in the partial product, as

$$232$$
$$\underline{203}$$
$$696$$
$$000$$
$$\underline{464}$$
$$47096$$

or perhaps more efficiently by application of the rule: "Place the first right-hand figure of the partial product under its multiplier," as

$$
\begin{array}{r}
232 \\
203 \\
\hline
696 \\
464 \\
\hline
47096.
\end{array}
$$

If the first form is used, the teacher should change to the second form when the placement of the partial products is learned. Zeros in both multiplier and multiplicand are sometimes met and should be at least introduced, as

$$
\begin{array}{ccc}
304 & \text{or } 306 & \text{or } 209 \\
120 & 204 & 300.
\end{array}
$$

If the previous forms have been well learned, the pupils themselves will probably be able to think and work out the procedures used in these examples.

Perhaps the *rationalization* of the multiplication process should be discussed more fully. As stated above, it is suggested by some that in processes with complicated theoretical explanations, the theory should be left until the mechanical skills necessary to perform the operations have been acquired even though some of the learning may be following or imitation to a large degree. In other words, learning the process is the end sought and anything that stands in the way of that should be avoided. The whole process may then be reviewed and better fixed in mind by finding out why certain things were done as they were in that particular process.

Undoubtedly the primary multiplication facts are well understood from their connection with addition. Also their products are all in the units and tens order of the number system. If, however, there should be any chance of the pupils not having learned about the organization of our number system of whole numbers or of having forgotten what they did learn, it should be reviewed. Probably a diagram of the names of the whole number places in our number system would help.

millions	hundred-thousands	ten-thousands	thousands	hundreds	tens	units
1	2	4	6	7	5	4

This should probably be followed with a study of numbers, such as

10 = 0 thousands 0 hundreds 1 ten 0 units
20 = 0 thousands 0 hundreds 2 tens 0 units
35 = 0 thousands 0 hundreds 3 tens 5 units
125 = 0 thousands 1 hundred 2 tens 5 units
253 = 0 thousands 2 hundreds 5 tens 3 units
2284 = 2 thousands 2 hundreds 8 tens 4 units

or another way to look at these numbers is:

$$
\begin{array}{rl}
2284 = & 2000 + 200 + 80 + 4 \\
253 = & 200 + 50 + 3 \\
125 = & 100 + 20 + 5 \\
35 = & 30 + 5 \\
20 = & 20 + 0 \\
10 = & 10 + 0 \\
\hline
2727 = & 2000 + 500 + 210 + 17.
\end{array}
$$

The steps in the multiplication process are taken up in order in the discussion below.

First:

10
2
——
20 Two 10's are 20, or 2×0 units = 0 units.
         2×1 ten   = 2 tens.

The "0" is written in the units place and the 2 in the tens place.

Second:

16
2
——
32 2×6 units = 12 units.

12 units make 1 ten and 2 units. Write the 2 units in the units place and "carry" (in mind) the 1 ten and add it to the product after multiplying the tens column, as 2×1 ten = 2 tens plus 1 ten (carried in the mind) = 3 tens. Write the "3" in the tens column.

Third:

84
4
——
336 4×4 units = 16 units or 1 ten and 6 units left over.

Write the 6 units left over in the units column and carry the 1 ten. 4×8 tens = 32 tens + 1 ten (carried) = 33 tens. But 33 tens are 3 hundreds and 3 tens left over. Write the 3 tens and carry the 3 hundreds to the hundreds order. There are no hundreds to multiply so the 3 hundreds are alone in the hundreds order.

Fourth:

```
        24
        12          24
        ──          12
        48          ──
        40          48
       200          24
       ───          ───
       288   or    288.
```

Begin with the right-hand digit in the multiplier 2 × 4 units are 8 units. Write the 8 units in the proper place. 2 × 2 tens = 4 tens or 40 units. Put the 4 tens in the tens place. This gives the partial product of 48 (40 units + 8 units). 10 × 4 units = 40 units. But 40 units would be exactly 4 tens so we put the 4 tens in the tens column under the other 4 tens. (This could be written as 40 units.) Then 10 × 2 tens = 20 tens, which is the same as 2 hundreds. (This may be written as 200 units.) Write the 2 in the hundreds column. Add to get complete product.

Fifth:

```
       203
        50
       ───
       000
       150
         0
     10000
     ─────
     10150
```

0 × 3 units = 0 units, 0 × 0 tens = 0 tens, 0 × 2 hundreds = 0 hundreds. 50 × 3 units = 150 units. Write the 150 units in its proper place (may be thought of as tens and hundreds). 50 × 0 tens = 0 tens. 50 × 2 hundreds = 100 hundreds (may be thought of as 10,000 units). Teachers use shortened forms of these explanations. But such forms are often not understood thoroughly and time is wasted in teaching them.

Some *checks* more commonly used in multiplication follow. (1) Reverse the multiplier and the multiplicand and multiply, as

```
63      8      16     25
 8     63      25     16
────   ──     ──     ──
504 to 24      80    150
       48      32     25
      ───     ───    ───
      504 or 400 to 400
```

If the multiplicand is concrete (suppose the 16 were $16) this would be considered unmathematical by some. In this case, however, the 16 could be thought of as the "number of dollars" and thus become an abstract number. (2) Divide the product by the multiplier. If pupils have not learned division this cannot be used; moreover, it is a long method of checking. (3) Do the multiplication again in the same form. In this event the same errors may be made. (4) Cast out the nines is sometimes used. Example:

```
67 excess of 9's is   4
×56 excess of 9's is ×2
───                  ───
402                   8 − 8
335
────
3752 excess of 9's is      8
```

Explanation

Add the digits 6 and 7, 13 − 9 = 4.
Add the digits 5 and 6, 11 − 9 = 2.
3 + 7 + 5 + 2 = 17 − 9 = 8. Since the product of the excesses of the multiplier (56) and the multiplicand (67) is 8, the same as the excess of the product (3725), the example is correct. An error of the arrangement of the digits in the product is not discovered by this method. For example: a product of 2573 or 7352 or 5327 or any other number with these digits would prove correct.

Some types of *error in multiplication* made by pupils as found by research are:[1] (1) errors in multiplication facts (these are most frequent); (2) errors in carrying: (a) carrying wrong number, (b) forgetting to carry, (c) adding the number carried; (3) errors in connection with zeros: (a) zero in the multiplier, as

```
346          294
 30   and    102,
───          ───
```

<hr>

[1] See Brueckner, Leo J. *Diagnostic and Remedial Teaching in Arithmetic*, pp. 79-84. John C. Winston Co. 1930. Also, Buswell, G. T., John, Lenore. *Diagnostic Studies in Arithmetic*, pp. 173-180. Univ. of Chicago Press. 1926.

(b) zero in the multiplicand, as

$$\begin{array}{r} 102 \\ \underline{4} \\ \end{array}$$

DIVISION

A bit of *historical perspective* shows some of the difficulties our predecessors had with this operation. The galley method used in an arithmetic of about 1475 A.D. is illustrated in the example below: (1728 ÷ 12)

1st step	2nd step	3rd step
	4	4
5	54	54
1728(1	1728(14	1728(144—quotient
12	12	12
	12	12
		12

In these examples the divisor is rewritten for each figure of the quotient. They show them written in a slightly different form from that in the original—perhaps more easily understood. See if you can think it out. Another method used by the writers of the century between 1500 and 1600 was the Italian method. This is an abbreviated one and uses additive subtraction. Take the same example used above:

$$\begin{array}{r} 144 \\ 12\overline{)1728} \\ 5 \\ 4 \\ 0 \end{array}$$

Explanation: 12 into 17 is 1; 1 × 2 = 2; 2 and "5" = 7; 1 × 1 = 1; 1 and "0" (not written) = 1. 12 into 52 = 4; 4 × 2 = 8; 8 and "4" are 12; carry 1; 4 × 1 = 4; 4 + 1 = 5; 12 into 48 is 4; 4 × 2 = 8; 8 + "0" = 8; 4 × 1 = 4; 4 + "0" (not written) = 4, no remainder.

Whether division is taught concurrently with multiplication or following it, the pupils should be given plenty of opportunity at the beginning to *comprehend* the *meaning* of the operation. That is, understand what is really done in division. There are two aspects of the process of division; one is *partition*. A rather satisfactory way to teach either aspect is to start with actual situations taken from the pupils' experiences. To illustrate partition problems: Here are 6 pennies. I want to divide them equally among Mary, Tom, and Jane. How many should each child receive? Pupils come to the table and actually divide the 6 pennies into 3 groups of 2 pennies each, thus discovering this fact for themselves. Suppose only Mary and Tom were in the class. How could I divide the pennies equally between them? Someone does it and gets 2 groups of 3 pennies each. The same thing is done with groups of pencils, pieces of chalk, apples, etc., until the pupils understand well that a whole group of things may be divided into a number of smaller equal groups. In partition the dividend and quotient are like numbers. The divisor is an abstract number. In the first example, 6 pennies are the dividend, 2 pennies the quotient, and 3 (the number of groups) the divisor.

The second type is that of *measurement*. To illustrate, problem situations like these may be used. Here are 9 pennies. If it takes 3 pennies to buy a pencil, how many pencils can be bought with the 9 pennies? (Pupil shows how this is done using the pennies.) Here is a pile of 12 blocks. Here is a pile of 4 blocks. How many piles of 4 blocks can be made from the 12 blocks? (Pupil does this to illustrate.) Here is a string 6 feet long. Here is another 2 feet long. How many strings 2 feet long can be made from the one 6 feet long? (Pupil actually measures.) This type of illustration should be continued until the pupils clearly see that a group of things may be divided into smaller groups the same size as a given group. In measurement, the dividend and divisor are like numbers. The quotient is an abstract number. In the second problem, 12 blocks is the dividend and 4 blocks the divisor. The quotient is 3 (the number of groups).

Pupils may not catch the difference but teachers should know that in the first type of problem a group of things was separated into equal parts the number of which was given in the problem. In the second type, a small group of the same kind of things as the large group was used as a measure to find how many times the large group would contain the smaller one. The first process is called partition because in it the large group is "parted" (separated) into equal smaller groups. The second process is called measurement because the small group is used as a "measure" to divide the large group into parts the same size as the small group. Calling attention of the pupils to these terms would probably only complicate the process. So it is safer to refrain from mentioning them.

After these basic meanings of division have been firmly planted in the minds of the pupils, they are ready to begin the *computation in division.* (1) This may be made to grow out of the examples used to fix the meanings, as 9 pennies divided among 3 pupils make 3 pennies for each pupil. Or reduced to shorter form: 9 pennies divided by 3 is 3 pennies or 9 pennies divided by 3 = 3 pennies or 9 pennies ÷ 3 = 3 pennies. After generalizing, the pupils see that not only is this true with pennies but everything the teacher may use, always 9 ÷ 3 = 3 or in another form

$$\frac{3}{3)9}$$

Some steps may be skipped with pupils of higher mental age. (2) Many teachers use the multiplication facts as a starting place for teaching the facts of division. In this event, the procedure is something like this: The pupil knows that two 3's make 6, and three 2's make 6. From these facts he knows, or can get the answer to: How many 3's in 6? or, How many 2's in 6? The pupil answering these questions responds: There are two 3's in 6, three 2's in 6. Then: 6 contains how many 3's? 6 contains how many 2's? Then: 6 divided by 3 is 2. 6 divided by 2 is 3. Then: 6 ÷ 3 = 2. 6 ÷ 2 = 3. In another form

$$\frac{2}{3)6} \qquad \frac{3}{2)6} .$$

(3) When teachers desire to use a short cut it may be something of this nature:

(a) 6 = 2 × 3 in multiplication.   (b) 6 = 3 × 2.
    Then, 6 = two 3's.   Then, 6 = three 2's.
    So, 6 divided into 3's makes   So, 6 divided into 2's makes
    2 parts.   3 parts.
    Then, 6 divided by 3 = 2.   Then, 6 divided by 2 = 3.
    Finally, 6 ÷ 3 = 2 and $\frac{2}{3)6}$.   Finally, 6 ÷ 2 = 3 and $\frac{3}{2)6}$.

Gradation of simple facts in division follows closely to that in multiplication. If the division facts are taught with the multiplication facts, they may be taken in the same order as suggested for the latter operation. The same order may be followed if they are taught separately. Difficulties that appear for multiplication will probably be present for division. It usually is most convenient to follow the order of the text used by the pupils. The zero facts should be taught in connection with the decade divisions, such as $2)60$. These will be mentioned later in that connection. The major steps of difficulty for division with *one-digit* divisors are approximately as follows:

1. The 90 primary division facts, such as $6\overline{)24}$
2. Two-three digit dividend—no carrying, such as $2\overline{)84}$, $4\overline{)124}$, or $4\overline{)844}$
3. One-two digit dividend—with remainder, as $2\overline{)9}$, $9\overline{)65}$, $5\overline{)38}$
4. Two-three digit dividend with carrying but no remainder as $2\overline{)52}$, $5\overline{)130}$, $6\overline{)144}$
5. Same as "4" except 4-digit dividend, as $4\overline{)1652}$—one carrying, $3\overline{)6432}$—two carryings, $4\overline{)7316}$—three carryings
6. Examples of any size with or without carrying and with remainder
7. Zero in the quotient
   a. at the end, as $2\overline{)20}$, $5\overline{)450}$, $4\overline{)43}$
   b. within, as $7\overline{)1407}$, $5\overline{)2515}$, $8\overline{)4817}$.

It is possible to make more steps in this gradation, but these seem to be sufficient for a normal group of pupils.

There are two *forms of division examples* in current use, the short and long. In recent times questions have been raised about using the *short division form* when presenting division with one-digit divisors. The short form seems to be more difficult to use on all levels and in the harder examples not any faster than the long form. Some newer textbooks recommend that the long form, as

$$
\begin{array}{r}
15 \\
5\overline{)75} \\
5 \\
\overline{25} \\
25 \\
\overline{}
\end{array}
$$

be used from the very beginning and the short form,

$$
\begin{array}{r}
15 \\
5\overline{)75}
\end{array}
$$

if used at all, be taught later as a short cut. Common sense indicates that the long form is easier for pupils to learn because more of the figures are written out and not so many carried in mind. If the short form were taught well as a short cut, the pupils would probably apply that to the easier division examples having a 1-digit divisor. Since the longer examples in practical life are so few (95.8% have dividends of 3 digits and less, 83% have 2 digits or less [1]) they may be disregarded.

The suggestions made concerning the *rationalization* of the simple and complicated processes of multiplication hold for those in division with a *single digit divisor*. When the theory back of the process can be explained without clouding the actual performance in any way, it may be safely made before the mechanics of the process are learned. If there is any doubt whatever, the explanation should be made after.

If and when explanations are needed they may be made on the several levels of example difficulty. (1) 2)8. This type was rationalized before the learning of the division facts. (2)

$$\frac{21}{2)42}$$

Pupils should see 42 as 4 tens and 2 units. Many texts use money to explain. In this case 42¢ would be 4 dimes and 2 pennies. Then pupils think 4 tens ÷ 2 is 2 tens. 2 units ÷ 2 = 1 unit. The quotient is 2 tens and 1 unit or 21. (3)

$$\frac{212}{3)636}$$

is explained as 6 hundreds ÷ 3 = 2 hundreds. 3 tens ÷ 3 = 1 ten. 6 units ÷ 3 = 2 units. The answer is 2 hundreds 1 ten 2 units, or 212. (4) Carrying is shown thus: in

$$\frac{183}{4)732}$$

7 hundred ÷ 4 = 1 hundred and 3 hundred over. 3 hundred is 30 tens. 30 tens + 3 tens = 33 tens. 33 tens ÷ 4 = 8 tens and 1 ten over. 1 ten = 10 units. 10 units + 2 units = 12 units. 12 units ÷ 4 = 3 units exactly. The quotient is 1 hundred, 8 tens, 3 units, or 183. (5) Explanation of the *long form*, whenever introduced, is somewhat similar. For example:

$$\begin{array}{r} 24 \\ 6)\overline{144} \\ 12 \\ \hline 24 \\ 24 \\ \hline \end{array}$$

[1] Wilson, G. M. *What Arithmetic Shall We Teach?* p. 23. Houghton Mifflin Co. 1926.

14 tens ÷ 6 = 2 tens and 2 tens over. 2 tens = 20 units. 20 units + 4 units = 24 units. 24 units ÷ 6 = 4 units exactly. The quotient is 2 tens and 4 units or 24.

Long division with two or more digit divisors seems to cause much trouble for both teachers and pupils. This discussion outlines the approximate steps in *order of difficulty* and points out some more or less approved methods of teaching.

1. Among the easiest steps of 2-digit divisors are the examples with a divisor ending in 0, not having zeros in the quotient, with or without remainder, as $20\overline{)6420}$, $40\overline{)7468}$, $80\overline{)78496}$, etc.
2. Probably the next easiest step is that of two-digit divisors ending in 1 or 9, with no zeros in the quotient, either with or without remainder, as $21\overline{)441}$, $19\overline{)436}$, $31\overline{)7476}$. In this type the divisors ending in 1 are thought of as one less than the actual divisor; 21 is taken as 20. The ones ending in 9 are thought of as being one more; 19 would be thought of as 20.
3. The next step of difficulty includes 2-digit divisors ending in 2 and 8, no zeros in the quotient, with or without remainder, as $32\overline{)742}$, $48\overline{)6769}$. The divisors are thought of as being two more in case of those ending in 8, and as two less in case of those ending in 2. The trial quotients are in error more often using this procedure with divisors ending in 2 and 8 than with those ending in 1 and 9. This is a contributing factor to the added difficulty pupils have with them.
4. The next group of examples with 2-digit divisors in order of difficulty perhaps would include divisors ending in 3, 4, 5, 6, and 7, again with no zeros in the quotients and with or without remainder.
5. Using 3-digit divisors, no zeros in the quotient—varying from easy examples to more difficult ones.
6. Two and three-digit divisors using zeros in the quotient, with or without remainders. These difficulties are of two main types (a) zeros at the end of quotient and (b) within the quotient. Both cause much difficulty and should be well learned.

Examples (a)   20–   (b)   204–
              $25\overline{)513}$ $42\overline{)8574}$
                 50
                 ――
                 13

The following are *specific helps* for long division. Some teachers suggest that definite steps for solving problems in long division be taught. For example, in

$$\begin{array}{r} 22 \\ 7\overline{)154} \\ 14 \\ \hline 14 \\ 14 \\ \hline \end{array}$$

the steps might be (1) divide, (7 into 15); (2) multiply, $(7 \times 2 = 14)$; (3) subtract, $(15 - 14 = 1)$; (4) inspect, (1 smaller than 7); (5) bring down, (4 from the dividend); then divide, etc., and repeat the procedure. A precise outline of steps of this nature is valuable at the beginning to assist pupils in fixing the order of the steps in their consciousness. Teachers should be careful, however, to keep the attention on the division and not divert it too much to the mechanics of learning the steps. In any case, the steps (if learned) are best assimilated in connection with the actual solution of examples. Some teachers teach successfully without using devices of this nature. They make a direct and immediate attack, using many examples of suitable difficulty to establish the proper procedure, without "crutches" of any kind. If the pupils can learn the steps without special aids, it is useless to teach these aids. If, because of some handicap, pupils seem to be unable to make headway without such props, teachers would undoubtedly be justified in using any such helpful device.

Finding the *correct quotient figure* in each new step causes much of the difficulty in long division. Upton [1] suggests the following rules for two-digit divisors. These do not give a perfect result on every possible long division example, but are much better than the random guessing in which many pupils indulge.

Rule I—Use the first (tens) figure of the divisor as the trial divisor if the second figure of the divisor is less than 6. For example, in $54\overline{)1194}$ the "5" of the divisor would be used, because the "4" (2nd figure) in the divisor is less than "6."

Rule II—Use one more than the first figure of the divisor if the second figure of the divisor is 6 to 9 inclusive. As in $78\overline{)4275}$, the "7" should be increased to an "8" (in thought) for the trial divisor, because the second figure in the divisor is "6" or greater.

Sufficient practice should be provided in finding the correct quo-

[1] Upton, Clifford B. *Teachers Manual for Strayer-Upton Arithmetics for the Lower Grades*, p. 67. American Book Co. Abbreviated.

tient figure through using the above-mentioned rules. One way to get a maximum of practice in a minimum of time is as follows: The teacher is at the blackboard, each pupil is ready with paper and pencil. The teacher places an example (from a list previously prepared) on the board, such as $34\overline{)486}$ and the pupils write how many times 34 is contained in 48. Then the teacher erases the "4" in the dividend and replaces it with a "7" and the pupils write how many times "34" is contained in "78." The teacher changes "3" in the divisor to "1" and asks how many times "14" is contained in "78," and so on. After scores of examples, the teacher checks her pupils' answers from the list previously prepared. If a written record is not desired, oral responses may be made to the different changes as the teacher calls the names of the pupils. If the pupils keep in mind the rules stated above, not only are the rules fixed in mind, but definite practice is received in the actual example situations. Practice in finding the first figure of the quotient usually carries over; hence, large amounts of practice need not be given on the remaining figures of the quotient.

Checking division examples is especially important. Three types of checks follow. (1) Multiplying the quotient by the divisor and adding the remainder is perhaps the best check. (2) Solving the example again and comparing not only the quotients and remainders (if any) but all the operations of the example. (3) Casting out 9's. For example,

6	Excess of 9's in quotient is 6.
$24\overline{)154}$	Excess of 9's in divisor is 6.
144	$6 \times 6 = 36$ (excess of quotient $\times$ excess of divisor).
	Excess of 9's in the remainder is 1.
10	$36 + 1 = 37$ — excess of 9's is 1.

Excess of 9's in dividend is 1, or the same as in $6 \times 6 + 1$. Hence the quotient is correct. There is some possibility of error in the excess of 9's check method. But such a possibility exists in the use of any check. Sometimes a variety of checks sustains the children's interest in the checking process. Furthermore, some pupils may be able to use one check better than another. This might be reason enough for teaching more than one method.

The use of *like* and *unlike* numbers in multiplication and division may disturb teachers. One good way to deal with this situation is to think of any quantity, as for instance: 5 cents, 3 pencils, in the sense of 5 being the "number" of cents and 3 being the "number" of pencils. If this is done the "numbers" may be multiplied regardless of the particular names which happen to be attached to them, and the proper name may be given to the product. This may not be exactly in accordance with the rules governing the use of abstract and concrete numbers, but it does fit in with common sense and common usage. One objective of the rules concerning concrete and abstract numbers is to help the pupils to keep their thinking straight and to be able to identify the answer. This objective is not lost by the above suggestion. If the pupil can interpret the problem, he will have no trouble in knowing what the problem asks and what he should have as his answer. For example, if 1 pencil costs 5 cents, how much will 3 pencils cost? No pupil should fail to see that when he multiplies

> 5—number of cents for 1 pencil
> $\times$3—number of pencils, he gets
> ___
> 15—number of cents for 3 pencils or the cost asked for.

If a pupil is not able to see the relationships involved in the problems, it is probable that the rules on the use of concrete and abstract numbers will help but little. If he does see these relationships clearly, he will know what to do without the rules. Likewise in division, he can divide 15, the number of pennies, by 3, the number of pencils, and get 5, the number of pennies each pencil costs, if he understands fully the conditions of the problem. If the strict mathematical explanation of rules interferes with clear understanding or thinking, the explanation should be postponed until the process or relationship is established, or indefinitely, in some cases.

Brueckner[1] reports the frequency of the most *common faults* in long division of whole numbers as follows:

	Frequency	Per Cent of Whole
1. Errors in division facts....................	191	12.4
2. Errors in subtraction.....................	113	7.3
3. Errors in multiplication...................	105	6.8
4. Remainder larger than divisor............	86	5.6
5. Quotient found by trial multiplication.....	82	5.4
6. Neglecting to use remainder within example	70	4.5
7. All other single faults less than 4.5% of the whole.		

[1] *Op. cit.,* pp. 156-157.   Adapted.

In his discussion Brueckner suggests, "As was found in each of the other processes, the chief faults in division are lack of knowledge of the fundamental facts and counting to get the answer. These difficulties can be remedied by well organized practice. Many errors were made in subtraction, both in carrying in short division and in subtracting in long division examples—much of the deficiency in long division may be due to weakness in the other basic processes involved in the complex long division examples."

An idea of some kinds of *situations* out of which problems in division arise would be helpful to the teacher in making division more meaningful, such as finding (1) amount per acre, when the total yield and number of acres are given, (2) per capita daily cost, when cost per term per pupil, and number of school days are given, (3) average cost of one article, when the cost of many is given, (4) average miles per day, when total mileage and number of days are given, (5) number of miles per gallon, when gallons and total miles are given, (6) daily pay, when monthly salary and days of employment are known, (7) the number of lower units in higher ones, as feet in inches, cubic yards in cubic feet, (8) the number of articles sold, when total receipts and average price per article are given. In making either oral or written problems for the pupils, the teacher should be careful at first to keep these problems simple both in relationships and in the size of numbers.

CHAPTER 14

ARITHMETICAL PROCESSES (II)

COMMON FRACTIONS

HISTORICALLY speaking, the manipulation of quantities less than one seems always to have caused great difficulty. If whole numbers used in multiplication and division were troublesome, fractions were much more so. A mere recital of a few methods of handling such quantities should indicate some perplexities encountered. The Egyptians seemed to have used only unit fractions (except 2/3) to express fractional quantities. For example, 3/4 would be: (1/2 + 1/4), or (1/4 + 1/4 + 1/4); 3/5 might be: (1/2 + 1/10); 5/6 would probably be written: (2/3 + 1/6) or (1/2 + 1/6 + 1/6). The Babylonians are reported to have used the constant denominator of 60 for all their fractions. For example, 1/2 would be 30/60, 2/3 — 40/60, 1/5 — 12/60, etc. The Greeks used denominators limited to powers of 60 for their scientific work, such as astronomy. The Romans used 12 as a base for their fractions. The Hindu and Arabic fractions were written in a form similar to our own without the bar, as 1/2 was 1

$$2, \qquad 3\frac{1}{4} \text{ was } 3$$
$$1$$
$$4$$

The term "vulgar fractions" is found in the early English and early American arithmetics. Later we substituted "common" for "vulgar" and created our present term "common fractions."

What is a fraction? There are at least four conceptions and applications of the fractional idea. (1) Perhaps the most common one is "one or more of the equal parts of a unit."—Jack gave 1/2 of his apple to Harry. How much did Jack have left? (2) A fraction is often "one of the equal parts of several units."—Mary gathered 4 dozen eggs. She sold 1/2 of them. How many dozen eggs did she sell? (3) It can also be thought of as "an indicated division," such as, reduce 8/3 to a mixed number. (4) Finally, a fraction may be thought of as "a ratio," such as,—Seven inches is what part of 21 inches? or 7 is to 21 or 7:21 or 7/21. While the first meaning is the one most commonly used, a knowledge of all is necessary for a full understanding of the fractional concept. Perhaps the idea that a fraction is "one of the equal parts of a unit" should be taught first with thoroughness. The fraction as an "indicated division" would appear in reducing improper fractions to mixed numbers. Number (2) might be introduced at any point after the previous meanings are well fixed. The ratio idea is not widely used and probably will be difficult for the pupils.

Several studies have been made to determine how much *fractions* are *used in life*. A summary table of eight such studies is given by Wilson, Stone, and Dalrymple: [1]

Fraction	Per Cent of Occurrence	
1/2	60.24%	
1/4	13.44%	
3/4	5.26%	All other fractions occurred less than 1 per cent of the total.
1/3	6.44%	
2/3	2.10%	
1/6	2.17%	
1/8	1.30%	
1/12	5.69%	

These studies indicate that a comparatively small number of common fractions are used in life situations. Moreover, the ones used are the simpler ones. If these facts mean anything at all to the teacher, they prove that the simple fractions should be well taught and fully comprehended by the pupils; and that most of the time now being spent on more difficult levels should be devoted to enriching the understanding of the easier fractions.

[1] Wilson, Guy M., Stone, Mildred B., Dalrymple, Charles O. *Teaching the New Arithmetic*, pp. 181-182. McGraw-Hill Publishing Co. 1939.

Methods of teaching depend upon previous learning. The principles of previously learned operations aid in handling of fractions. For example, the rule, "only like numbers can be added" in the addition of whole numbers, applies in the addition of fractions, such as $3/5 + 1/5 = 4/5$.

An *inventory* based on the knowledge of and the ability to use fractions should be made immediately before the formal attack on fractions in the intermediate grades. Such a test should include, among others, items which pupils have not been taught in school. Some pupils may have learned them elsewhere. This check may be written, oral, group, individual, or a combination of all. Whatever its form, it should give a maximum of information concerning each pupil's ability in fractions. Such a test might consist of items of this nature:

1. If anything is divided into 2 equal parts, one part is called _____.
2. One-fourth and one-fourth make _____ fourths, etc.
3. Write one-half, one-fourth, two-thirds, three-fifths, etc.
4. Which is larger, one-half or one-third? Make a drawing to show it.

5. Write what portion of each design is shaded: (a)

_____, (b) _____, (c) _____,

(d) _____, etc.

6. Other checks to find out if pupils know how to reduce, add, subtract, multiply, and divide fractions, or understand such relationships.

The *fraction concept* should be firmly established before taking up the more formal work in reduction and in the four fundamental processes. The amount of time used and the teaching done depends on the needs shown by the inventory tests suggested above. Usually it is necessary to begin the class work with the simplest concrete forms for all pupils. The seatwork (study materials) may be varied in kind and difficulty to fit the individual differences of the pupils. Pupils assimilate ideas more fully if they can see, hear, handle, and work with the materials they are learning. (1) Suppose they are working with the "one-half" idea and the teacher has illustrated this idea with a variety of concrete experiences, such as half of such objects as the ruler, yardstick, quart jar, pint tin cup, window, piece of chalk, etc. Following this, the pupils might illustrate the one-half idea orally by naming other articles, and suggesting the approximate half or actually measuring it before the group. (2) The next step might be that of using drawings: (a) The teacher at the board makes drawings varying widely in shape and size. The pupils assist her by dividing the drawings into halves. (b) The pupils continue this at their desks, making designs of their own and dividing them into halves. (3) Oral work on the one-half idea might follow, through which the pupils name objects or distances divided into halves, such as half of a mile, half of a bushel, half of a day, etc. The teacher might ask what a pupil means when he says "half a day," or "half a bushel." The answer would help to show the pupil's idea of the "one-half notion." (4) Then the notation (writing), first in words (one-half), next in number form (1/2). The teacher should lead by doing this at the board, suggesting how the phrases are read, e.g., 1/2 quart, 1/2 mile, etc. (5) At this stage, the "one-half" might be extended beyond the unit. That is, how many halves are in 2 whole things, in 3, in 10, in 1 1/2, etc. These ideas should be introduced concretely by actual things or drawings. (6) The last step may consist of applying the ideas learned in problem situations. The teacher usually prepares these to suit her pupils. The following will suggest what may be done by using verbal problems (usually oral) to summarize and crystallize the steps thus far presented: (a) Which is longer, 1/2 foot or 1 foot? (b) If you like candy, which would you rather have, 1 pound or 1 1/2 pounds? (c) Tom played 1/2 of a game, James played 2 halves of a game. Which played longer? (d) Show the class 1/2 of anything, 2/2 of anything, 3/2 of anything, etc. (e) Name 1/2 of the pupils in one row or section. (f) Make a problem using 1/2 in it. This type of exercise should give the teacher a better check on the ability of each pupil in her group in the use of this particular fraction, as well as an idea of the general level of his thinking.

The teacher should regard these steps as applicable not only to 1/2 but to any unit fraction (numerator of 1) that she wishes to teach. It is possible that in some groups not all steps need be used, but in others some intermediate ones may be necessary. In any case, she should be sure that the pupils make the fraction idea a part of their thinking. It is impossible to emphasize these first contacts too strongly, provided that they are presented in an interesting manner. Both experience and experiment show that the difficulties pupils have with fractions often spring from faulty concepts. Pupils often do not "see" what method should be followed in the solution of an example or problem. They guess or let previously formed habits carry them along. For instance, a pupil who adds 1/2 and 1/6 and gets 2/8 or 1/4 does not have good basic concepts of 1/2, 1/6, and 1/4.

Terms used in *common fractions* should be learned. Out of the great variety of fractional concepts should come the nature of the fractional form, namely, that a fraction tells two things: (1) the size of the equal parts into which a unit or group of units is divided and (2) the number of these units which is being used. To illustrate: in 1/2, the pupil should be able to see and demonstrate with concrete or semiconcrete materials that the whole thing is divided into 2 parts and that one of them is being used. Much experience of this kind should be given before even these terms are named. When the names are taught, care should be taken to see that pupils attach the correct meanings to them. One device to convey and help fix these ideas is:

$$\frac{2 - \text{how many of the equal parts are being used} \dots\dots \quad \underline{\text{numerator}}}{3 - \text{into how many equal parts the whole thing is divided. denominator}}$$

The teacher may think of other devices to illustrate the ideas. The other terms, such as integer, proper fraction, improper fraction, mixed number, etc., are taught when and where they are encountered. Usually pupils' definitions grow more definite with the expansion of their concepts of fractional quantities. Time spent on verbal definitions is wasted when pupils do not have well-fixed concepts to back them up.

After a few of the *unit fractions* have been taught, a series of drawings might be made showing their relationships, such as:

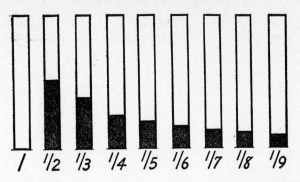

This should help in forming the concepts of the relative size of these unit fractions. The concept may be presented by using circles as well as rectangles. Other concrete or semi-concrete means may be used. Such designs as mentioned in connection with unit fractions offer a convenient way to show the relationship of other fractions, both those which have the same denominator and those which do not. For

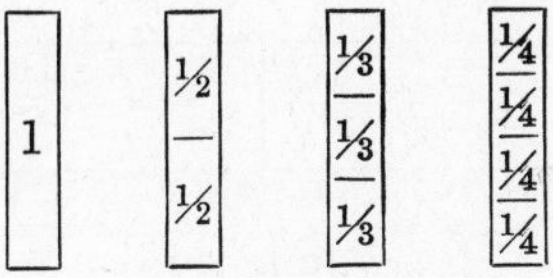

example, it is clear (1) that two 1/2's make 1, or written another way 2/2 = 1; (2) that it takes three 1/3's to make 1, or 3/3 = 1; and 1/3 and 2/3 = 1; (3) that four 1/4's make 1, or 4/4 = 1; three 1/4's and one 1/4 make 1; or 3/4 + 1/4 = 4/4 = 1; and 2/4 + 2/4 = 4/4 or 1. Thus the 1/5's and 1/6's, etc., may be presented and their various relationships (for each denominator) worked out.

Following this, inter-relationships may be shown for 1/2's, 1/3's, 1/4's, 1/6's, and 1/8's. Possibly these should be indicated first in com-

1 whole thing							
½ thing				½ thing			
¼		¼		¼		¼	
⅛	⅛	⅛	⅛	⅛	⅛	⅛	⅛

paratively simple form, as in the "1/2 family." From this it may be clearly seen that one whole thing has two 1/2's, four 1/4's, and eight 1/8's. And that 1/2 has two 1/4's, etc., through all the other relations.

These may be written in figures. $1 = 2/2$ or $4/4$ or $8/8$. $1/2 = 2/4$ or $4/8$. $1/4 = 2/8$. $2/4 = ?$ $3/4 = ?$, etc. Also $2/8 = ?$ $4/8 = ?$ $6/8 = ?$ A chart of this type gives the teacher an excellent base for a multitude of oral examples showing fractional relationships.

Likewise a chart for the "1/3 family" may be used to provide exer-

1 whole thing					
$\frac{1}{3}$		$\frac{1}{3}$		$\frac{1}{3}$	
$\frac{1}{6}$	$\frac{1}{6}$	$\frac{1}{6}$	$\frac{1}{6}$	$\frac{1}{6}$	$\frac{1}{6}$
$\frac{1}{12}$ $\frac{1}{12}$	$\frac{1}{12}$ $\frac{1}{12}$	$\frac{1}{12}$ $\frac{1}{12}$	$\frac{1}{12}$ $\frac{1}{12}$	$\frac{1}{12}$ $\frac{1}{12}$	$\frac{1}{12}$ $\frac{1}{12}$

cises as suggested above for the "1/2 family."

To show the relationships of one family to the other, the teacher probably should prepare a paper chart something like the one that follows, which may be kept for reference.

1 whole thing					
$\frac{1}{2}$			$\frac{1}{2}$		
$\frac{1}{4}$	$\frac{1}{4}$		$\frac{1}{4}$	$\frac{1}{4}$	
$\frac{1}{12}$ $\frac{1}{12}$	$\frac{1}{12}$ $\frac{1}{12}$	$\frac{1}{12}$ $\frac{1}{12}$	$\frac{1}{12}$ $\frac{1}{12}$	$\frac{1}{12}$ $\frac{1}{12}$	$\frac{1}{12}$ $\frac{1}{12}$
$\frac{1}{6}$	$\frac{1}{6}$	$\frac{1}{6}$	$\frac{1}{6}$	$\frac{1}{6}$	$\frac{1}{6}$
$\frac{1}{3}$		$\frac{1}{3}$		$\frac{1}{3}$	
1 whole thing					

Perhaps this would be a good stepping stone to the longer one just below and others even more elaborate.

1 whole thing							
$\frac{1}{2}$ thing				$\frac{1}{2}$ thing			
$\frac{1}{4}$		$\frac{1}{4}$		$\frac{1}{4}$		$\frac{1}{4}$	
$\frac{1}{8}$	$\frac{1}{8}$	$\frac{1}{8}$	$\frac{1}{8}$	$\frac{1}{8}$	$\frac{1}{8}$	$\frac{1}{8}$	$\frac{1}{8}$
$\frac{1}{24}\frac{1}{24}\frac{1}{24}$	$\frac{1}{24}\frac{1}{24}\frac{1}{24}$	$\frac{1}{24}\frac{1}{24}\frac{1}{24}$	$\frac{1}{24}\frac{1}{24}\frac{1}{24}$	$\frac{1}{24}\frac{1}{24}\frac{1}{24}$	$\frac{1}{24}\frac{1}{24}\frac{1}{24}$	$\frac{1}{24}\frac{1}{24}\frac{1}{24}$	$\frac{1}{24}\frac{1}{24}\frac{1}{24}$
$\frac{1}{12}$	$\frac{1}{12}$	$\frac{1}{12}$	$\frac{1}{12}$	$\frac{1}{12}$	$\frac{1}{12}$	$\frac{1}{12}$	$\frac{1}{12}$
$\frac{1}{6}$	$\frac{1}{6}$	$\frac{1}{6}$	$\frac{1}{6}$	$\frac{1}{6}$	$\frac{1}{6}$		
$\frac{1}{3}$ thing		$\frac{1}{3}$ thing		$\frac{1}{3}$ thing			
1 whole thing							

The teacher may find that the step from 1/8 to 1/24 causes trouble. If she anticipates this, she should include only the halves and fourths on one side of the twelfths, the thirds and sixths on the other as shown above. One value of this type of chart is that it helps the pupils to discover and remember the relationships between the fractional values. The wise teacher provides plenty of opportunity to do both, and checks frequently to find what results have been attained.

Usually four kinds of *reduction* (change in form but not in value) are taught in connection with common fractions: (1) to a common denominator, 1/4 and 3/8 to 2/8 and 3/8; (2) to lowest terms, 8/12 to 2/3; (3) to an improper fraction, 2 1/2 to 5/2; (4) to a mixed number, 7/2 to 3 1/2. In teaching these types of reduction, a procedure somewhat similar to the following may be used: (1) Discover the principle which governs the reduction, beginning with the knowledge the child already has. (2) Apply this principle to the fractions needed. (3) Give plenty of practice to fix the principle firmly in mind.

In *reduction* to a *common denominator* a study of the charts given above shows that 1/2 is the same as 2/4, or 1/2 is the same as 4/8, or 1/2 = 3/6, or 1/2 = 6/12. Also that 3/4 = 6/8, 2/3 = 4/6, and so on. From these it is seen that fractions may change in form but not in value. It can also be shown that two or more fractions may be changed to the same denominator without changing the value of either, i.e., 1/2 = 4/8, 3/4 = 6/8. In this way reduction may be taught in using small related denominators. The principle that multiplying both terms of a fraction by the same number does not change the value of the fraction, may be worked out and established at this point. This may be done as follows: Reduce 2/3 and 5/6 to a common denominator. Note the smallest denominator in the group of fractions. Raise this smallest denominator by its multiples until it equals or makes a multiple of the other denominator or denominators. (The largest one may be used in the same way instead of the smallest.) In case of the fractions above, the 3 is the smaller denominator. Two 3's make 6, which is the denominator of the other fraction. Thus 6 contains itself and 3. The example then becomes

$$\frac{2}{3} = \frac{4}{6}$$
$$\frac{5}{6} = \frac{5}{6}.$$

Since there are two 3's in 6, the numerator 2 must be multiplied by the same number. (See the principle above.) Hence, $2 \times 2 = 4$, the numerator of the changed fraction. Changed to the same (common) denominator, 2/3 and 5/6 would be 4/6 and 5/6. The same procedure can be followed with any number of fractions, as 3/4, 2/5, 5/6. Start with 4 (the smallest denominator) and raise it to its various multiples, $4 \times 4 = 16$, $4 \times 5 = 20$. Since 20 contains both 4 and 5 but not 6, our problem is to find a number that contains both 20 and 6. Using 6 times 7, 8, 9, we find no multiple of 20 until $6 \times 10 = 60$. The number 60 contains "4" 15 times, "5" 12 times, and "6" 10 times. So both terms of the fraction

3/4 must be multiplied by 15 = $^{45}/_{60}$, and
2/5 must be multiplied by 12 = $^{24}/_{60}$, and
5/6 must be multiplied by 10 = $^{50}/_{60}$.

Thus any fractions may be reduced to a common denominator. This method reduces them to the "least" common denominator.

Reducing to *lowest terms* is simple after working out the principle, "Both terms of a fraction may be divided by the same number without changing its value." This may be done as follows. From the chart above it is seen that $4/8 = 2/4 = 1/2$. Pupils may discover that both terms of the fraction 4/8 are divided by 2, giving the fraction 2/4. When the same thing is done with 2/4 the result is 1/2. Try out $12/24 = 6/12 = 3/6 = 1/2$ and many other similar fractions. Hence, the statement made above must be true. Then

$$\frac{4 \div 2}{8 \div 2} = \frac{2 \div 2}{4 \div 2} = \frac{1}{2}.$$

Or, using the largest common divsor first, if pupils know what it is,

$$\frac{4 \div 4}{8 \div 4} = \frac{1}{2}.$$

Later, the pupils keep in mind the largest common divisor and see at once, $6/12 = 1/2$ without writing the divisors.

In *reducing* to an *improper fraction*, the pupils should understand that a mixed number is a whole number and a common fraction written together, as: 2 1/2 is 2 and 1/2. In order to reduce this to 1/2's they must know how many 1/2's are in the 2, which are 4. Then add the 1/2 which makes five 1/2's or 5/2. This is usually done in practice by multiplying the whole number by the denominator of the fraction and adding the numerator to this product, then writing this all over the denominator, as

$$2\tfrac{1}{2} \quad \text{or} \quad \frac{2 \times 2 + 1}{2} \quad \text{or} \quad \frac{5}{2}, \ 3\tfrac{4}{5} \quad \text{or} \quad \frac{3 \times 5 + 4}{5} \quad \text{or} \quad \frac{19}{5}.$$

In *reduction* to a *mixed number,* the numerator is divided by the denominator. In reducing 5/2 the following computation is made,

$$\begin{array}{r} 2\frac{1}{2} \\ 2\overline{\smash{)}5} \\ 4 \\ \hline 1 \end{array}, \qquad \frac{19}{5} \quad \text{is} \quad \begin{array}{r} 3\frac{4}{5} \\ 5\overline{\smash{)}19} \\ 15 \\ \hline 4 \end{array}.$$

After the reduction to common denominators is mastered, *addition of common fractions* may be taken up. One principle of addition and subtraction of whole numbers should be employed, namely, "Only like numbers can be added or subtracted." Illustrations:

2 balls	2 apples	2 sixths	
+3 balls	+3 apples	+3 sixths	
5 balls	5 apples	5 sixths	or $\frac{2}{6} + \frac{3}{6} = \frac{5}{6}$.

That is, sixths (parts of a unit) are added in the same way as balls or apples. Attention should be called again to the fact that the numerator tells how many are to be added and the denominator what is being added. In this example it is sixths.

Gradation of examples in adding common fractions is usually made in three steps. (1) The easiest type of examples to add are those with like denominators, such as $3/4 + 1/4$, $2/5 + 3/5 + 1/5$. Pupils can solve examples of this type with little teaching. (2) Addition of fractions with related denominators, such as $1/2 + 1/4$, $3/8 + 3/4$, $2/3 + 1/6$ requires reduction to a related common denominator. If reduction has not been taught, it must be done before starting this level of difficulty. In the easier examples the common denominators may be found by inspection. If enough practice is given in these, the pupils will be more able to make the reduction by computation when the more difficult levels are reached. (3) Fractions with unrelated denominators, such as $1/3 + 1/5$, $2/9 + 1/5$, $2/3 + 2/5$, are the most difficult for pupils to handle because of greater complexities in their reduction to common denominators. These examples, too, should be kept simple at first and the difficulty increased with caution. Competent teachers watch very closely for the tell-tale signs of pupil deficiency as discovered by her numerous and searching checks.

Beginning *addition of mixed numbers* needs special care. As suggested above, pupils should realize that mixed numbers are only whole numbers and fractions written together. They could be added separately just as well and the sums combined, i.e., $2\,1/2 + 1\,3/4$ could be

$2 + 1 + 1/2 + 3/4$, arriving at the same answer. If this is done the pupils will realize more fully the double nature of the operation. In

$$2\tfrac{1}{2}$$
$$+1\tfrac{3}{4}$$

the pupils (1) add the fractions, (2) add the whole numbers, and (3) add these two sums. In this case $1\,1/4$ $(1/2 + 3/4)$ is combined with the whole number 3 $(2 + 1)$ to make a final sum of $4\,1/4$. The form of the computation seems to make little difference if it provides for (1) placing the common denominator in some definite position, (2) placing the numerators of the reduced fractions so as to be easily added, (3) working out the fractional sum so that it is ready to be combined with the whole number sum.

What has been said of addition applies in many instances to *subtraction* of *common fractions*. Practically all the conceptual background laid in addition is usable in subtraction. Moreover, the gradation is the same; namely, (1) like fractions first, (2) fractions with related denominators, (3) fractions with unrelated denominators. The reduction to a common denominator is the same as in addition and the plan of beginning each new step with an abundant amount of easy-level materials should be followed in subtraction. For example, in the first step of like fractions, the beginning examples might be

$$3\tfrac{3}{4} \qquad 6\tfrac{3}{5}$$
$$-2\tfrac{1}{4}, \qquad -2\tfrac{2}{5},$$

that is, like fractions and no borrowing. When borrowing in the fractions is introduced, all other difficulties should be cut to a minimum for it is the most troublesome element in this operation. For example:

$$
\begin{array}{ccc}
(1) & (2) & (3) \\
3\tfrac{1}{4} = & 2\tfrac{1}{4} + \tfrac{1}{4} = & 2\tfrac{5}{4} \\
-1\tfrac{3}{4} = & -1\tfrac{3}{4} \qquad = & -1\tfrac{3}{4}. \\
& & \overline{1\tfrac{1}{2}}
\end{array}
$$

When the minuend is a whole number as:

$$
\begin{array}{rcl}
3 & = & 2\tfrac{4}{4} \\
-1\tfrac{3}{4} & = & -1\tfrac{3}{4}. \\
& & \overline{1\tfrac{1}{4}}
\end{array}
$$

Step (2) in the first example may be omitted after the right habits have been established. Another plan is to reduce the mixed numbers to improper fractions. We find, $13/4 - 7/4 = 6/4 = 1\ 2/4 = 1\ 1/2$. This avoids the borrowing difficulty but adds the reduction to improper fractions. Using improper fractions is necessary only when the subtrahend fraction is larger than the one in the minuend.

An example of fractions with related denominators is:

$$
\begin{array}{rcrcr}
4\tfrac{1}{6} & = & 4\tfrac{1}{6} & = & 3\tfrac{7}{6} \\
-2\tfrac{2}{3} & = & -2\tfrac{4}{6} & = & -2\tfrac{4}{6} \\
\hline
& & & & 1\tfrac{3}{6} = 1\tfrac{1}{2}
\end{array}
$$

Of unrelated denominators:

$$
\begin{array}{rcrcr}
4\tfrac{1}{5} & = & 4\tfrac{4}{20} & = & 3\tfrac{24}{20} \\
-2\tfrac{1}{4} & = & -2\tfrac{5}{20} & = & -2\tfrac{5}{20} \\
\hline
& & & & 1\tfrac{19}{20}
\end{array}
$$

The following *errors in addition and subtraction* of common fractions were found by Morton[1] who gives the following results from his story of errors in addition of fractions:

Types of Errors	Illustration	Per Cent of Error
Wrong operation	$\tfrac{2}{3} + \tfrac{3}{5} = \tfrac{6}{15}$	45.0%
Denominators added	$\tfrac{1}{2} + \tfrac{2}{5} = \tfrac{3}{7}$	30.4%
Error in computation	$\tfrac{3}{4} + \tfrac{2}{5} = \tfrac{16}{20} = \tfrac{4}{5}$	13.6%

No other type of error caused more than 2.3% of the total error.

Brueckner[2] records the results of his study of the errors in subtraction of fractions.

Type of Error	Per Cent of Error
Borrowing	24.3%
Used wrong process	20.3%
Reducing to lowest terms	14.6%
Did not know process	14.6%
Changing to common denominator	8.3%
Computation errors	8.2%
Omitted example	5.6%
Partial operation	4.0%
Copying errors	0.2%

In all probability some of the simple rules covering the *divisibility of numbers* would be useful to pupils in the reduction processes as when used in the addition and subtraction of fractions. Just how

[1] Morton, Robert L. *Teaching Arithmetic in the Elementary School*, Vol. II, p. 218. Silver, Burdett Co. 1939.
[2] *Op. cit.*, pp. 203-206.

many, if any, of these may be used, the teacher must decide. (1) A number may be divided by 2 if the last digit of the number is a zero or is even, as $2\overline{)20}$, $2\overline{)64}$. (2) A number may be divided by 4 if the last two digits used as a number are zeros or are divisible by 4, such as $4\overline{)7500}$, $4\overline{)7332}$. (3) A number may be divided by 8 if the last three digits used as a number are zeros or are divisible by 8, such as $8\overline{)97000}$, $8\overline{)75832}$. (4) A number may be divided by 9 if the sum of its digits is divisible by 9, such as $9\overline{)864}$, $9\overline{)100130202}$. (5) A number may be divided by 5 if it ends in a zero or 5, such as $5\overline{)640}$, $5\overline{)9745}$. (6) A number may be divided by 3 if the sum of its digits is divisible by 3, such as $3\overline{)411}$, $3\overline{)200100}$. (7) A number may be divided by 6 if it ends in a zero or an even number and if the sum of its digits is divisible by 3 (rules 1 & 6), such as $6\overline{)4260}$, $6\overline{)100236}$.

Multiplication of *common fractions* is the simplest operation in fractions and for this reason some think it should be placed first in the teaching of fractions. There seems to be no general tendency to use this order. Work in this operation is usually found to be simple for those pupils who have mastered the difficulties of addition and subtraction of fractions. In finding the rule for multiplication of fractions, the teacher might refer to the charts used in showing the various fractional relationships, or she may construct some charts on the board for the purpose, as in the following:

½				½			
¼		¼		¼		¼	
⅛	⅛	⅛	⅛	⅛	⅛	⅛	⅛

Charts showing thirds, sixths, ninths, and twelfths or fifths, tenths, and twentieths or other related groups may be used in the place of the one suggested above or in addition to it, if the needs of the pupils require. Looking at the chart, the teacher might ask, how much is 1/2 of 1/2?, at the same time writing it on the board. From the chart pupils can see that 1/2 of 1/2 is 1/4. Then 1/2 of 1/4 = 1/8, 1/4 of 1/2 = 1/8, 3/4 of 1/2 = 3/8, etc. Then note again the statement 1/2 of 1/2 = 1/4. What is done with 1 and 1 to make 1? The pupils discover "multiply." What is done to 2 and 2 to make 4? Pupils may say either "add" or "multiply." Take 1/2 of 1/4 = 1/8.

Note that $1 \times 1 = 1$ for the numerator, and $2 \times 4 = 8$ for the denominator. Also, 3/4 of $1/2 = 3/8$, in which $3 \times 1 = 3$ for the numerator and $4 \times 2 = 8$ for the denominator. Use sufficient examples to help pupils find the rule that in finding the fractional part of another fraction, the numerators may be multiplied to make the numerator of the product, and the denominators multiplied to make the denominator. The pupils will also see that "of" means "multiply" or "$\times$" and that $1/2 \times 1/4 = 1/8$ is another way of writing the statement.

Some teachers use a graphic device which pictures the multiplication. Using the $1/2 \times 1/4 = 1/8$, draw a rectangle divided into halves

Then divide the same rectangle into fourths by vertical lines

If now we take 1/2 of one of the fourths, we take the shaded portion of the whole rectangle which is one of the 8 equal parts or 1/8 of it. Likewise 1/2 of $3/4 = 3/8$ or 3/4 of $1/2 = 3/8$ may be shown, as

or 3/8 of the whole. Whatever method of illustration is used, the rule for multiplication of fractions should emerge from it.

Whole numbers and fractions may be taken up next and the above rule applied to them. To make the application easier, the whole numbers may be given their fractional form, i.e., 1/2 of $4/1 = 2$, 3/4 of $8/1 = 6$, $4/1 \times 1/2 = 4/2 = 2$, etc.

Multiplying mixed numbers by fractions, integers, or mixed numbers usually causes more trouble than any other problem type in multiplication of fractions; for example: $1/3 \times 2\ 1/2$, $6 \times 3\ 1/4$, $2\ 1/2 \times 3\ 1/5$. Undoubtedly the least confusing, if not also the most accurate, method is that which changes the mixed numbers to improper fractions and multiplies as the pupils have learned to do previously. The examples above would be solved as follows:

$$(1) \quad 1/3 \times 2\ 1/2 = 1/3 \times 5/2 = 5/6;$$

$$(2) \quad 6 \times 3\ 1/4 = \frac{6}{1} \times \frac{13}{4} = \frac{78}{4} = 19\ 1/2;$$

$$(3) \quad 2\ 1/2 \times 3\ 1/5 = \frac{5}{2} \times \frac{16}{5} = \frac{80}{10} = \frac{8}{1} = 8.$$

The greatest argument against this procedure is the reduction to improper fractions and back again to mixed numbers or fractions, as the case might be. There are chances for pupils to make errors in making these reductions. After cancellation has been learned, it may be used to simplify this method. Another plan of work uses the phases of addition and multiplication of fractions already learned in the straight multiplication fashion as:

(1)	(2)	(3)
$2\frac{1}{2}$	$3\frac{1}{4}$	$3\frac{1}{5}$
$\frac{1}{3}$	6	$2\frac{1}{2}$
$\frac{1}{6}$ ($\frac{1}{3} \times \frac{1}{2}$)	$1\frac{1}{2}$ ($\frac{6}{1} \times \frac{1}{4}$)	$\frac{1}{10}$ ($\frac{1}{2} \times \frac{1}{5}$)
$\frac{2}{3}$ ($\frac{1}{3} \times \frac{2}{1}$)	18 (6×3)	$1\frac{1}{2}$ ($\frac{1}{2} \times \frac{3}{1}$)
$\frac{5}{6}$ (adding)	$19\frac{1}{2}$ (adding)	$\frac{2}{5}$ ($\frac{2}{1} \times \frac{1}{5}$)
		6 (2×3)
		8 (adding)

This plan is somewhat complicated when multiplying mixed numbers by mixed numbers as seen in (3). Frequently pupils leave out one part of the operation. It works very well, however, in examples and problems of the second type which are perhaps more numerous in real life than any other in multiplication of fractions.

Cancellation in multiplication and division of fractions is used to reduce the product to its lowest terms before actually doing the multiplying. This may be done because the processes of multiplication and division can be interchanged without disturbing the outcome. To illustrate, it makes no difference in which order one divides or multiplies in these examples: $3 \times 4 \div 3 = 4$, $1/2 \times 2/3 \div 1/5 = 10/6$ or $1\ 2/3$, or reversing these examples: $3 \div 3 \times 4 = 4$, $1/2 \div 1/5 \times 2/3 = 10/6$ or $1\ 2/3$. In cancellation the dividing is done before the multiplying, thus reducing the labor and chances for error in solving the examples. Pupils usually experience little difficulty in taking this short cut. One source of error which teachers should warn pupils against is the omission of any number when cancelling. A child who writes

$$\frac{\cancel{2}}{\cancel{5}} \times \frac{\cancel{5}}{\cancel{8}}$$
$$4$$

often gets 4 for his answer. If he had written

$$\begin{matrix} 1 & & 1 \\ \frac{\cancel{2}}{\cancel{5}} & \times & \frac{\cancel{5}}{\cancel{8}} \\ 1 & & 4 \end{matrix}$$

he would be more likely to get 1/4. Again, in

$$\frac{\cancel{6}}{\cancel{8}} \times \frac{\cancel{8}}{\cancel{6}}$$

he might get "0." If he wrote

$$\begin{matrix} 1 & & 1 \\ \frac{\cancel{6}}{\cancel{8}} & \times & \frac{\cancel{8}}{\cancel{6}} \\ 1 & & 1 \end{matrix}$$

he probably would get 1/1 or 1 for the answer.

The chief *errors* by pupils in multiplication of common fractions as listed by Brueckner [1] are:

Type of Error	Illustration	Per Cent of Whole
Computation...........	$\frac{5}{6} \times 14 = \frac{58}{6} = 9\frac{2}{3}$	28.7%
Lack of comprehension of process................	$6 \times 2\frac{1}{3} = 6 \times \frac{3}{4} = \frac{18}{4} = 2\frac{4}{4}$	17.3%
Reducing to lowest terms....	$3 \times \frac{4}{16} = \frac{12}{16}$	17.3%
Omitted—no attempt........		11.3%
Reduction improper fractions to mixed numbers........	$4 \times \frac{2}{5} = \frac{8}{5}$	8.8%
Errors in copying..........	$\frac{5}{8} \times 6\frac{4}{5} = \frac{3}{8} \times \frac{\overset{17}{\cancel{34}}}{5} = \frac{51}{20} = 2\frac{11}{20}$	3.5%
Reduction mixed numbers to improper fractions........	$6 \times 2\frac{1}{3} = 6 \times \frac{3}{3} = \frac{18}{3} = 6$	2.8%
Cancellation..............	$3\frac{3}{4} \times 3\frac{1}{3} = \frac{\overset{3}{\cancel{15}}}{4} \times \frac{\overset{2}{\cancel{10}}}{3} = \frac{6}{12} = \frac{1}{2}$	1.6%
Unknown.................	$\frac{1}{4} \times \frac{1}{6} = 46$	8.6%

[1] *Ibid.*, pp. 211-212.

New conditions are met in fractional quantities. When multiplying whole numbers the product is always equal to or greater than either of the terms, as $1 \times 1 = 1$, $6 \times 7 = 42$. In fractions, multiplication produces a product equal to or less than either of the terms such as $1/2 \times 1 = 1/2$, $2/3 \times 1/4 = 1/6$. It is undoubtedly true that this and the reverse in division cause error in computation.

Division of common fractions has one computational factor not found in multiplication of fractions, namely, "inverting the divisor" or multiplying by "the reciprocal," depending on the terminology used. This step in the process seems to cause a large per cent of errors in learning the division of fractions (see table of errors below) and should receive proper attention in teaching. Perhaps the process should be learned before any explanation is made. That is, the pupils should be shown or helped to find out that: $1/2 \div 1/2 = 1/2 \times 2/1 = 2/2 = 1$. This the pupils would know to be correct in whole numbers, since any number divided by itself gives 1. Likewise: $2/3 \div 1/3 = 2/3 \times 3/1 = 6/3 = 2$. They can easily see from a drawing that 2/3 contains two 1/3's. Other simple division examples may be used to establish the form showing the inverted divisor.

After the form has been learned, explanations may be made for inverting the divisor. One simple way is to show that a number may be divided by multiplying it by the reciprocal of its divisor. The idea of the reciprocal of a number is easily understood by illustration, i.e., the reciprocal of 6 is 1/6, of 12 is 1/12, of 1/2 is 2/1, of 3/4 is 4/3, or the reciprocal of any number is 1 divided by that number. Then $6 \div 3 = 2$ is the same as $6/1 \times 1/3 = 2$; $15 \div 5 = 3$ is the same as $15/1 \times 1/5 = 3$; $3/4 \div 1/2$ is the same as $3/4 \times 2/1 = 1\ 1/2$. Dividing in fractions is done by multiplying the dividend by the reciprocal of the divisor, which is the same as inverting the divisor and multiplying the dividend by it.

Errors in division of common fractions as shown by Brueckner[1] appear in table form on the following page.

The pupils using the wrong process (31.1%) multiplied instead of dividing, that is, they did not invert the divisor. This, it seems, could be readily remedied. The various reduction errors (24.7%) could be eliminated with directed practice. The 12.1% who did not com-

[1] *Ibid.*, pp. 213-214.

prehend the example and 6.0% whose solutions were so poor as to be unclassified should certainly challenge our methods of establishing concepts and of teaching procedures. These pupils apparently got little or nothing of value from their experiences with the various processes.

The discussion of *common fractions* may be *summarized* as follows: (1) The socially useful fractions are the ones with small denominators—the 1/2's, 1/3's, and 1/4's plus a few with larger denominators. It would seem reasonable, therefore, that the schools should make sure that children are able to use these simple fractions with a high degree of familiarity and accuracy. (2) Experiment seems to show that little actual computation in fractions is done in real life

Types of Error	Illustration	Per Cent of Error
Wrong process. . . . . (Did not invert the divisor.)	$1\frac{3}{8} \div 1\frac{2}{3} = 1\frac{1}{8} \times \frac{5}{3} = \frac{55}{24} = 2\frac{7}{24}$	31.1%
Computation.	$3\frac{3}{8} \div 1\frac{3}{4} = \frac{27}{8} \times \frac{4}{7} = 2\frac{7}{14} = 1\frac{3}{14}$	13.8%
Did not comprehend processes.	$1\frac{1}{6} \div 3\frac{1}{2} = \frac{5}{6} \times \frac{7}{2} = 3\frac{5}{12} = 2\frac{11}{12}$	12.1%
Reduction—lowest terms	$1\frac{1}{3} \div 3\frac{1}{3} = \frac{4}{3} \times \frac{3}{10} = \frac{4}{10}$	8.9%
Reduction—mixed numbers to improper fractions.	$3\frac{1}{3} \div 1\frac{3}{4} = \frac{\overset{5}{10}}{3} \times \frac{4}{\underset{6}{12}} = \frac{20}{18} = 1\frac{1}{9}$	8.6%
Omitted (no attempt).		8.3%
Reduction—improper fractions to mixed numbers. . .	$3\frac{1}{8} \div 1\frac{1}{4} = \frac{\overset{5}{25}}{\underset{2}{8}} \times \frac{4}{5} = \frac{5}{2}$	7.2%
Errors in copying.	$1\frac{1}{4} \div \frac{1}{8} = \frac{5}{2} \times \frac{3}{1} = \frac{15}{2} = 7\frac{1}{2}$	2.3%
Cancellation.	$\frac{5}{6} \div 4 = \frac{5}{\underset{3}{6}} \times \frac{1}{\underset{2}{4}} = \frac{5}{6}$	1.5%
Unknown.	$1\frac{1}{3} \div 3\frac{1}{3} = \frac{1}{6}$	6.0%

but that use is made of them in thinking in more or less concrete terms. Therefore, the school should present problem situations of a fractional nature to develop pupils in the ability to function in such situations. (3) Emphasizing the practical uses of arithmetic does not mean that all other uses should be disregarded. After all, some persons need more than the bare essentials. (4) The more closely the study of common fractions is connected with the direct experiences of the pupils, the greater the chances are for a maximum development of knowledge in this subject-matter field, as well as in the pupils' more or less general abilities and attitudes.

DECIMAL FRACTIONS

A bit of *historical* background will throw light on this comparatively new process. It would seem natural for the human race to evolve the same kind of number system to deal with quantities less than a unit, as it evolved to deal with those larger than a unit. This was not the case. A system of decimal fractions did not come into existence until about 1585 A.D., long after other systems of handling fractions had been used and forgotten. The decimal point was not used until about 150 years after decimal fractions were invented. In fact, not all civilized countries of the world use it now. People of the United States write 4.62, the English write it 4·62, the French 4,62. Strangest of all, decimal fractions are not used as much as they might be, although they are more convenient to write, easier to interpret, and cause less error in computation than common fractions. Civilization holds to the clumsy common fractions and spends almost endless time and limitless energy in trying to teach and use them. The development of the decimal point shows what a hard time people have in learning and using anything new and different. With the decimal 16.25, the first form seems to have been 16° 2′ 5″. A later form was 1625 (2) (the "(2)" indicating the number of decimal places). Later still, it was 16)25. After that came 16/25. Finally it was 16.25. Sums on checks are still written $16/25 or $16 25/100. Perhaps more progress in the use of the decimal fractions has been made in the last twenty-five years than in the previous fifty years or more. The decimal idea is being adapted to our present awkward units of measure, such as tenths of a foot, hundredths or thousandths of an inch. Automobile tires are 6.50 inches instead of 6½ inches. Athletes run the 100 yards in 10.2 or 10.1 seconds. The scientific world uses the decimal fractions because they are more efficient.

There are two widely used plans of *presenting decimal fractions*. One shows that decimal fractions are a special type of common fractions whose denominators are 10 or multiples of ten. The pupils' knowledge of our monetary system is also utilized. The second plan shows that decimal fractions are the extension of our decimal number system to the right of the decimal point, as the whole numbers extend to the left of it.

Teachers who use the *common fraction approach* generally begin with a discussion about a special kind of fraction which has 10 or some multiple of 10 for its denominator. By enlisting the aid of the pupils, several such fractions are placed on the board, such as 5/10, 2/10, 3/10, 7/10, 12/100, 25/100, 15/100. The teacher suggests a new way to write such fractions, as 5/10 = .5, 3/10 = .3, 25/100 = .25, 15/100 = .15, etc. These new forms have the same name as the old 5-tenths, 3-tenths, 25-hundredths. Enough of these are written in both forms to make sure that the pupils get the connection between the common and decimal fractions. Later the pupils should write them as the teacher dictates. Later still, the class discovers (usually through use of U. S. money) that the first place to the right of the decimal point is tenths, the second place is hundredths. There should be plenty of both reading and writing of decimals at this point. No decimal less than .10 should be used in these beginning efforts. When writing less than .10 is started, the teacher may again use the pupil's knowledge of writing money, as for instance: How is one dollar and six cents written? Pupil suggests $1.06. Then the teacher elicits the facts that $1 is 100 cents and that 6¢ is 6/100 (.06) of a dollar. The suggestion is made that this is the way 6/100 (.06) is written in decimal fractions. The use of dollars and cents also suggests the use of whole numbers with the decimals, and this brings up the point that the word "and" is always used in reading a decimal where the decimal point appears, that is, 2.14 is read, "two and fourteen hundredths." Each step should be accompanied with an abundance of practice. Places to the right should be discussed to the hundred-thousandths, at least, but work need be done only to and including the thousandths.

The *approach* that *extends* our *system* of *notation* of whole numbers would make sure that the pupils understand the orders in any given number. To illustrate: the pupils should know that 3642 contains $3000 + 600 + 40 + 2$, or that the first digit at the right is in units order, the next to the left is tens, etc. In order that pupils become familiar with these, numbers may be read as thousands, hundreds, tens, and units, as 3-thousands, 6-hundreds, 4-tens, 2-units. Perhaps pupils should also write the numbers as suggested in the analysis above. When the pupils have reconditioned their knowledge of whole-number notation, the decimal fractions may be attacked by using some everyday experiences of the pupils, such as the automobile speedometer. Pupils will probably know that the red circle of figures at the right is tenths of a mile. If so, the teacher may show how tenths are written in our system of notation. A speedometer reading may be 2,462.4. Write other numbers until all the tenths appear,— .2, .3, etc. Pupils may think of other ways in which tenths are used —height of pupils in inches and tenths, or weight in pounds and tenths. These should all be written on the board while the pupils watch and read and wait for the teacher to call on them individually. To bring out hundredths, use U. S. money, as $3.25. How many cents in a dollar? What part of a dollar is 25¢ (25/100)? Elicit 25 hundredths or suggest it. Thus, the second place to the right of the point is hundredths. After plenty of practice, the relationships thus far learned may be summarized, as in 1111.11:

$$
\begin{array}{lll}
1 \text{ thousand} & - & 1000. \\
1 \text{ hundred} & - & 100. \\
1 \text{ ten} & - & 10. \\
1 \text{ unit} & - & 1. \\
1 \text{ tenth} & - & .1 \\
1 \text{ hundredth} & - & .01
\end{array}
$$

Some teachers use a table of values to help pupils comprehend the relationship of the decimal fractions, as

$$
\begin{array}{lll}
10 \text{ hundredths} = 1 \text{ tenth} & (& .1 \;) \\
10 \text{ tenths} = 1 \text{ unit} & (& 1. \;) \\
10 \text{ units} = 1 \text{ ten} & (& 10. \;)
\end{array}
$$

They also use the reverse form.

> 1 ten (10.) is the same as 10 units.
> 1 whole (1.) thing is the same as 10 tenths.
> 1 tenth (.1) of a thing is the same as 10 hundredths.

The relationship of the unit to the orders immediately above and below should be very clear to every pupil. This is most important and teachers should be absolutely sure that their pupils realize these fundamental relationships.

The teacher may use the board to check the pupils' degree of comprehension. Write a mixed decimal (whole number with a decimal attached), such as the following: 364.5, 784.46, 8975.426. For each mixed decimal the pupils are asked to name the orders, as the teacher points to them in irregular order. To illustrate, in 364.5 the exercise might be 4 units, 5 tenths, 6 tens, etc. To assure herself that pupils actually comprehend what the various orders stand for, the teacher asks at the beginning: "How many of this order does it take to make one of the next above?"—pointing to the orders in question.

The approximate *steps* of *difficulty* in reading and writing mixed decimals are:

> 1. 14.2, 75.3 also .4, .6, .9, etc.
> 2. 10.15, 31.21 also .42, .71, .45, etc.
> 3. 6.04, 9.02 also .03, .07, etc.
> 4. 14.80, 38.20 also .40, .50, etc.
> 5. 28.674, 18.123 also .742, .975, etc.
> 6. 38.005, 41.08, 6.500 and all other forms.

The first approach has the advantage of using experiences with common fractions which are recent and therefore this approach has greater probability of resting on a satisfactory background for the new operation. The second has the advantage of definiteness and ease of presentation. It also connects at once the system of whole numbers with the system of fractional numbers. The first-mentioned plan must do this sooner or later.

Whether the approach is by the common fraction or the extension of the number system, as before stated, ample *practice* in a variety of ways should be given pupils both in reading and writing all forms of decimals. Pupils should automatically think and write or read hundredths when they hear or see two decimal places, tenths for one place, etc. Not only should the teacher dictate all types of decimals but she should ask the pupils to prepare lists and read them for others of the class to write. The idea is to get as much practice in reading and writing decimals in as many ways as possible in the time available. Brueckner's [1] investigation in 6th, 7th, and 8th grades shows that pupils make an "astonishingly large number" of errors in reading, writing, and converting decimals. He found that approximately 24% of the error came from a lack of "comprehension of the numerical values of decimals." That is, pupils in the upper grades make approximately one error in four when trying to arrange numbers containing decimals in order of size. If the errors arising from a "lack of fundamental knowledge" were combined with those above, we have approximately 36% of the total error made. These data seem to show deficiencies in experience and learning of the basic concepts of decimals. Brueckner [2] also investigated the amount and kind of difficulties experienced by the upper grades in the four operations of decimals which are shown in table form on the next page.

The first horizontal line of this table gives an indication of the relative difficulties encountered in the four operations of decimals.

Type of Error	Per Cent of Error				
	Add.	Subt.	Mult.	Div.	Total
Total error in all operations —6,610 Per cent of total error for each operation..........	8.8%	7.0%	27.4%	56.7%	99.9%
Difficulties basic to each operation.................	27.4%	73.8%	25.5%	16.4%	
Difficulties peculiar to decimal situations...........	61.2%	21.3%	56.9%	69.2%	
Other difficulties...........	11.3%	4.9%	17.4%	14.3%	
Total per cents of specific difficulties...............	99.9%	100.0%	99.8%	99.9%	

[1] *Ibid.*, pp. 229-230.
[2] Ibid., pp. 231-235. Summarized from tables of errors.

Only 8.8% of the total error is made in addition and 7.0% of it in subtraction. There is 56.7% made in division of decimals and 27.4% in multiplication. Following (down) the division column, we find 69.2% of the error made in division is made in situations of a decimal nature. Of this 69.2% of total error, 55% of it pertained to "placing the decimal point" and 13.7% of it was connected with zero difficulties. This seems to show what the task is in division of decimals, namely, placing the decimal point and handling zeros. In multiplication and addition of decimals, a large part of the error made was in connection with purely decimal situations, but in subtraction, the pupils fell down on difficulties of ordinary subtraction examples, such as borrowing, zero difficulties, subtraction fact errors, etc. One should note, however, that comparatively little difficulty of any kind is made in subtraction—only 7% of the whole number of errors in the four operations.

Reduction of decimals should receive due consideration. (1) Changing common fractions to decimals will be discussed under division of decimals because it is best done by using the division operation. (2) Changing decimals to common fractions should cause little trouble if the common fraction approach is used. If it is not, close attention to the reading of decimals should give the cue, as in .5 read "five-tenths" which the pupil knows from his common fraction experience to be 5/10 or in its lowest terms 1/2. Thus a simple decimal, such as .16, is 16/100 = 4/25; .004 is 4/1000 = 1/250, etc. Complex decimals, as .3 1/3 give more difficulty but the same plan is used—

$$\frac{3\frac{1}{3}}{10} = \frac{10\!/\!3}{10\!/\!1}$$

reduced is $10/3 \div 10/1 = 10/3 \times 1/10 = 10/30 = 1/3$. Mixed decimals, such as 4.25, become 4 25/100 or 4 1/4. The whole number remains the same in both forms.

Addition and *subtraction* of decimals present no specific difficulty not found in whole numbers except the placing of the decimal point. This seems to cause slightly more trouble in addition of decimals than in subtraction. In addition usually several numbers are used as addends, while in subtraction only two terms are used. Both operations are made more difficult by examples of irregular form, as in addition

$$.3$$
$$250.007$$
$$6.25 \qquad 756.2$$
$$\underline{1000.105} \text{ or in subtraction } \underline{21.0462}.$$

In adding and subtracting decimals, pupils are confronted realistically with the facts of digit order in the numbers. They find out again that tenths cannot be added to hundredths or subtracted from them. This is perhaps the greatest contribution of these operations to the pupils' basic development.

Multiplication of *decimals* may present the problem of where to place the decimal point in the product. This is complicated when it is necessary to prefix zeros to the product. Of the 56.9% of error due to decimal situations in the table above, 61% was due to misplacement of the decimal point and 11% to its omission. The task in multiplication of decimals is to see that pupils know where to place the decimal point. One pedagogical approach is through common fractions. Starting with this example (integer by decimal) $3 \times .2 = .6$, the pupil knows $3/1 \times 2/10 = 6/10$ or .6. Hence, $3 \times .2 = .6$ is correct. $4/1 \times 6/100 = 24/100 = .24$. Hence, $4 \times .06 = .24$ is correct. The same plan may be used in multiplying a decimal by an integer, as $.14 \times 7 = .98$, or a decimal by a decimal, as $.6 \times .4 = .24$. Thus, by the use of the common fraction form, the rule for pointing off places in multiplication of decimals may be developed, namely, that the number of decimal places in the product is the sum of the decimal places in the multiplier and multiplicand. As in other operations, opportunity for much well-directed and motivated practice should be given in a wide range of examples on easy computation levels. Easy levels allow more practice in varying sorts of examples, make possible more frequent checks, and enable the pupil to place more attention on the specific decimal difficulties, because less attention is required for computation.

The three main types of examples in *division of decimals* are (1) a decimal divided by an integer, as $.6 \div 3 = .2$, (2) an integer by a decimal, as $4 \div .2 = 20$, (3) a decimal by a decimal, as $.6 \div .3 = 2$. An approach to these can be made in the same way as was made for multiplication of decimals.

1. $3\overline{)\,.6} = {}^{6}\!/\!_{10} \div {}^{3}\!/\!_{1} = {}^{6}\!/\!_{10} \times {}^{1}\!/\!_{3} = {}^{6}\!/\!_{30} = .2$, hence $3\overline{)\,.6}^{\,.2}$

2. $.2\overline{)4} = \frac{4}{1} \div \frac{2}{10} = \frac{4}{1} \times 1\frac{0}{2} = \frac{40}{2} = 20$, hence $.2\overset{20}{\overline{)4}}$

3. $.3\overline{).6} = \frac{6}{10} \div \frac{3}{10} = \frac{6}{10} \times 1\frac{0}{3} = \frac{60}{30} = 2$, hence $.3\overset{2}{\overline{).6}}$

Reducing a *common fraction* to a *decimal* is important in percentage work and should be learned as a form of division. In changing 1/2 to a decimal the numerator is divided by the denominator after annexing zeros. As $1/2 = 2\overset{.5}{\overline{)1.0}} = .5$, $3/4 = 4\overset{.75}{\overline{)3.00}} = .75$, etc. Pupils can deduce the rule from illustrations of the type used above.

Suggestions for *locating* the *decimal point* in the quotient are comparatively plentiful. Three are presented below with comments on each. The first one is based on the multiplication idea, namely, quotient $\times$ the divisor $=$ the dividend. Since this is true, the number of decimal places in the quotient plus those in the divisor must equal the number of decimal places in the dividend. This, in practical usage, turns out to be as follows: the number of decimal places in the dividend minus the number of decimal places in the divisor is the number of decimal places in the quotient. In certain types of examples this is rather difficult to apply. In $.2\overset{20.}{\overline{)\ 4.}}$ the pupil cannot apply the rule unless he remembers that if a whole number is divided by a decimal as many zeros must be annexed to the quotient as the divisor has decimal places. Generally speaking, the more regulations the pupils are asked to follow, the greater the chances that one of these regulations will be forgotten or wrongly used.

A second suggestion gives definite directions to the pupil, as follows: If the divisor has any decimal places in it, start at the decimal point of the dividend and count off to the right as many places in the dividend as are in the divisor. Place the decimal point in the quotient directly above this dividing point. Then divide as in whole numbers —annex zeros if needed, as in these examples: $2.43\overset{\bullet}{\overline{)62.43\ 8}}$ or $.462\overline{)825.400}$. If the divisor is a whole number, the decimal point may be placed directly above its location in the dividend without

$$5 \overline{).65}$$ ($.15$ above)

change, as $5\overline{).65}$. This plan involves less learning and computing difficulty than the first one.

A third plan is related to the second one. It asks the pupil to make the divisor a whole number (if it is not one) by multiplying it by 10, 100, 1000, or whatever is necessary. Some teachers place a small (x) after the divisor. Multiply the dividend by the same number, placing the decimal point indicated by a small (x) where it should come after the multiplying. Place the decimal point in the quotient directly above the small (x). Annex zeros if needed. Then divide as in whole

numbers, as $2.32_x\overline{)46.84_x3}$. In actual practice this resolves itself into, "Move the decimal point of the divisor to the right enough places to make it a whole number. Move the decimal point of the dividend the same number of places to the right and indicate it by a small (x). Annex zeros if necessary. Place the decimal point in the quotient directly above the small (x) and divide as in whole numbers." This has the disadvantage of mutilating the original numbers to some extent but is an easily applied procedure that most pupils can learn and use. Some teachers cross out the original point and put it in the new location in both divisor and dividend. This is unnecessary and may be detrimental. This plan is probably as nearly foolproof as any other mentioned.

Checks in multiplication and division of decimals should be encouraged by the teachers. It is easy to make a gross mistake by putting the decimal point in the wrong place, as, for instance, $5.00 can be $500. A large degree of caution should be used from the beginning. Multiplication may be proved by changing the terms of the multiplier and multiplicand and multiplying again. The division may be checked by multiplying the quotient by the divisor and adding the remainder.

Uses of *decimals* later, in the theory and practical applications of percentage, seem to warrant thorough work in at least the few basic principles. Considering also the increasingly greater social usage made of decimals, and the prospects that the future will see a much wider use, it seems that our very best efforts should be put into its teaching. This should include both a knowledge of the principles and the ability to use the various processes in example and problem solution.

PERCENTAGE

Although we now think of percentage as growing out of decimals, it really is the much older process. In fact, the computation of percentage in terms of decimals is comparatively recent. In this problem, taken from an arithmetic written about 1667 by Crocker,[1] no use is made of decimals: "A plummer sold 10 fodder of lead (the fodder containing 19 1/4C) for 204£ 15s. and gained after the rate of 12£ 10s. per 100£. I demand how much it cost him per C." Furthermore, some of the applications of percentage such as interest, are older than the theoretical parts we now use as a background for them. The development of our present per cent sign might be of interest. Smith[2] writes, "In its primitive form the per cent sign (%) is found in the 15th century manuscripts on commercial arithmetic, where it appears, as 'per $\frac{o}{C}$' or 'p $\frac{o}{C}$', a contraction of 'per cento'. As early as the middle of the 17th century it had developed into the form 'per $\overline{o}$', after which the 'per' finally dropped out. The solidus form (%) is modern."

Almost everyone who has expressed an opinion agrees that percentage is not difficult; yet practically every test shows that pupils are woefully ignorant of both the knowledge and use of even the minimum essentials. Whether the opinion is wrong or the teaching bad, we shall not stop to argue. One thing is quite clear. Pupils cannot use percentage in the solution of actual life problems as well as might reasonably be expected. Moreover, they seem to be unacquainted with the reasons for using its various applications. Brueckner[3] found that 405 7A pupils made 73.6% of error on an example, such as "37.5% of 720," 82.2% of error on "120 = ?% of 96," and 96.5% of error on "255 is 125% of ?."

The percentage *concept* seems to be best presented by simple applications of it from pupil experiences. For example: taking half of

[1] Monroe, Walter S. *Development of Arithmetic as a School Subject*, pp. 34-36. Bulletin U. S. Bureau of Education. 1917.
[2] *Op. cit.*, p. 250.
[3] *Op. cit.*, p. 242.

a piece of chalk, or string, ruler, etc., the teacher might ask what fraction of the whole it is in each case. The pupils report this as 1/2. What would 1/2 be if reduced to tenths (decimal)? to hundredths (decimal)? The same procedure may be followed with 1/4 and 1/5. Then the teacher calls attention to the fact that she had stopped with hundredths each time because the class will be working with the hundredths type of decimals for a while. She may explain that just as decimals were a special type of common fractions (denominators of 10 and multiples of 10) so the hundredths type is a special kind of decimal fractions (denominators of 100), as .16, .06, .55, .75, .04½, etc., and further explain that only hundredths are used in this special process called "percentage."

If the teacher could have at hand advertisements of bargain sales which show 1/4 off, or 20% off, she could add to the effectiveness of the introduction. If she does not have such exhibits, the pupils will probably be able to recall some. It may then be shown that 1/4 off means .25 off, or "25 out of every hundred" off, or simply "25 per hundred" off. In percentage this is "per cent"—"per or by the hundred," or in writing, it is "%."

At once it should be made clear that both "%" and "per cent" mean "per (by or for) the hundred"; and if either of them is used, the decimal point to indicate hundredths is left off. To illustrate: .25 would be 25% or 25 per cent, .06 would be 6% or 6 per cent, 1.45 would be 145% or 145 per cent. This idea seems to be difficult for pupils to master and plenty of exercise should be given in changing all sorts of simple decimals to per cents. Some teachers suggest that in reduction from decimals to per cents the decimal point be moved two places to the right. The decimal point is omitted when it comes at the end of a per cent number, i.e., .25 = 25%, .06 = 6%. This also takes care of fractional per cents, as .875 = 87.5%, 6.125 = 612.5%.

In the reverse process—per cents to decimals—the decimal point is moved two places to the left when the per cent sign is removed, as 42% is .42, 325% is 3.25, 12½% is .12½, etc. Pupils should see clearly that if the per cent sign does not say "hundredths," the decimal point must. These two processes could be practiced together.

Another good avenue of *approach* to percentage is through the pupils' knowledge of United States money. This is especially helpful because the bases are the same. The hundredths of a dollar translate readily into per cents.

The *relationships* of *common fractions* to *per cents* are widely and frequently used, so these should be known rather intimately. Not only should pupils know how to change one to the other, but they should have in mind the actual equivalents in the commonly used relationships. For example: $1/2 = 50/100 = .50 = 50\%$, $1/4 = 25/100 = .25 = 25\%$, and so on to include 3/4, 1/5, 2/5, 3/5, 4/5, 1/3, 2/3, 1/6, 5/6, 1/8, 1/10, 1/12, and possibly other of the frequently used common fractions. Pupils should work these out and make a table similar to the one started above. The relations between fractions and per cents will be firmly fixed in mind by this process. Care should be taken to show that the different forms of a given fraction make no difference in per cent; that is: $1/2 = 2/4 = 3/6 = 4/8$, etc. $= .50 = 50\%$. After the pupils know instantly that 2/5 is 40% and 1/8 is $12\frac{1}{2}\%$, the items may be reversed as $12\frac{1}{2}\% = ?$ fraction, $66\,2/3\% = ?$ fraction, etc.

The process of *changing per cents* to common *fractions* should be easy because per cents are known to have 100 as the denominator and can always be written that way. In changing 10% to a fraction one writes 10/100 and reduces to lowest terms to find the fraction 1/10. Thus

$$25\% = {}^{25}\!/_{100} = \tfrac{1}{4},\ 33\tfrac{1}{3}\% = \frac{33\tfrac{1}{3}}{100} = \frac{{}^{100}\!/_{3}}{{}^{100}\!/_{1}} = {}^{100}\!/_{3} \div {}^{100}\!/_{1}$$
$$= {}^{100}\!/_{3} \times {}^{1}\!/_{100} = {}^{100}\!/_{300} = \tfrac{1}{3}.$$

Little time need be spent on actual manipulation. Rather the teacher should be sure to fix the principle that per cents always have 100 as the denominator and may be written that way. Here again United States money may help fix the facts that 50¢ is 1/2 of a dollar (100¢), 10¢ is 1/10 of a dollar (100¢), 25¢ is 1/4 of a dollar (100¢), etc.

The main *problem types* in *percentage* are three in number, as is illustrated below: (1) What is 5% of $300? (Case I) (2) $15 is what per cent of $300? (Case II) (3) $15 is 5% of what number of dollars? (Case III). Teachers seem to be most successful in teaching percentage if, at the beginning, they show the pupils how simple these types of percentage problems are. It is easily demonstrated that there are only three main factors to each problem: the base—the number of which a certain per cent is taken; the rate—which states what per cent is taken of the base; and the percentage—the number obtained after finding the per cent indicated by the rate. Only two of these are given in any problem; and by using them the third one can be found. Sometimes a diagram helps to make these relations clear.

	Base	Rate (%)	Percentage
Case I	Given	Given	?
Case II	Given	?	Given
Case III	?	Given	Given

If the items of the diagram are worked out individually by the class with simple problems, the device will probably be more effective. In any event, everything is done to keep these problems and explanations as simple as possible. It should be noted again and again that two of the factors are given in each problem and one other factor must be found. Also it should be noticed that the different types of problem are made by giving and requiring different factors of the three main types. Attention should be called, before actual problem solution is started, to the fact that percentage problems are just like simple examples in multiplication of decimals with one of the factors or the product left out. Case I is like $.03 \times 8 = ?$, Case II is $? \times 8 = .24$, Case III is $.03 \times ? = .24$. How would the answer be found in Case I? How would it be found in Case II? In Case III? This is the way the answers are found in the three cases of percentage problems. These may be written:

$$
\begin{array}{ccc}
\text{I} & \text{II} & \text{III} \\
8 & 8 & ? \\
\times .03 & \times ? & \times .03 \\
\hline
? & .24 & .24
\end{array}
$$

Attention should be called to the fact that Cases II and III are actually solved by division of decimals even though they are stated in terms of multiplication.

Case I is most commonly used, and fortunately it is the easiest to teach. The word "of" means "multiply" as the pupil already knows and the per cent sign means "hundredths." So the problem stated above for Case I would be $.05 \times \$300 = \$15$. Or using the common fraction form

$$\overset{3}{\$\cancel{300}} \times \frac{5}{\cancel{100}} = \$15.$$

A multitude of problems and examples should be used to establish this concept. Pupils may make lists of this kind of example, using as wide a range of subjects as possible. These practice problems may be oral or they may be written or both. If oral, they should be simple enough to be solved without written computation. The teacher should be careful to get different types of wording and situations into the oral exercises. Dozens, even scores, of problems should be used in the various types of practice. The oral type of practice is not used as much as it might be. It is more rapid, hence it provides more practice in a given time. It seems to make greater use of the child's mental functions. Oral drill has a greater stimulating effect than other types of drill. As the pupils become more proficient in the process, more difficult problems or examples may be used. The teacher should not depend wholly, or even to any great extent, on the text to supply problems or examples for these practices. They can and should be made to fit the needs of the pupils. These problems may include interest, taxes, commission, profit and loss, and in fact any application using Case I.

Case II should be fitted into the pupils' thinking as a part of the general plan of percentage, possibly by using a diagram such as suggested above. The pupils also note what must be found in this type of problem and how that factor is found. Pupils usually have most difficulty in determining which is the base and which the percentage. Sometimes if left to their own devices, pupils form and follow the notion that the larger number is the base. This is true when the percentage is less than 100% of the base, but is not true in any other situation. Usually the best policy is to determine which is base or percentage from the meaning of the problem. Pupils should be taught to discover for themselves, from their interpretation of problems, that one number is a per cent of the other. In the problem "$15 is what per cent of $300?" the words say that $15 is a per cent, or a number of hundredths, of some number and hence is the percentage, and that the other number ($300) must be the base. Even in such a problem as "100 is what per cent of 50?" the wording says that 100 is a per cent, or a number of hundredths, of some number and so would be the percentage; and that the other number (50) of which 100 is a per cent, must be the base. Other problem wordings are more difficult, such as "What per cent is $15 of $300?" If the problem is correctly interpreted, the pupils should know that the percentage divided by the base gives the number of hundredths the percentage is of the base, or the rate in per cent. From the example

$$\overset{.05}{\$300)\overline{\$15.00}}$$ it is clear that .05 or 5% is the factor which the problem requires.

Another type of solution is as follows:

> $300 is 100% of the number.
> $1 is $\frac{1}{300}$ of 100% or $\frac{1}{3}$% of the number.
> $15 is 15 × $\frac{1}{3}$% of the number or 5% of the number.
> Therefore, $15 is 5% of $300 (the number).

Many practical problems may be used to illustrate Case II as was done in Case I. In the problem: Tom (a member of the class) bought a bicycle for $20 and sold it 6 months later for $15, the pupils could easily decide how much money he lost. If they wanted to find what his per cent of loss was, they would need to find what per cent $5 is of $20, the loss and cost respectively. Anna's father bought a house for $5000 and sold it for $6000. Pupils would know at once the gain was $1000. But to find the per cent of gain they must know what per cent $1000 is of $5000. A check for accuracy should be taught with Case II, using the problem type taught in Case I. If in Case II $15 is found to be 5% of $300, the pupils check as follows: .05 (5%) × $300 = $15.00. This proves the solution of Case II is correct.

Case III is used least widely. Its use seems to be greatest in working out prices in the mercantile world, as, for example, in figuring what a thing should sell for to make a certain per cent above the cost price. Moreover, it would seem that most of these problems are too involved and too foreign for sixth-grade pupils. If Case III is taught at all, it should be in simple terms and in connection with its general relationship to the three types of problems in percentage. The example above mentioned would be solved $\frac{\$15.00}{.05} = \$300$. Or analytically it might be

5% of the number is $15.00.

1% of the number is ⅕ of $15 or $3.

100% of the number is 100 × $3 = $300.

Therefore, $300 is the number of which $15 is 5%.

Errors made in percentage examples seem to be largely of the following types:

(1) Per cents less than 1%, such as ½%, .4%

(2) Non-interpretation of equivalent forms, such as 10%, $^{10}\!/_{100}$, .1, .10

(3) Reduction of one-place decimals to per cent form, such as .1 = 10%, .5 = 50%

(4) Reduction of whole numbers to per cents, such as 2 = 200%, 3 = 300%

(5) Reduction of mixed numbers to per cents, such as 1½ = 150%, 2.85 = 285%.

These may not be the specific errors made by any one pupil, but they may be considered the "demons" which cause much of the error in percentage examples and problems.

General suggestions for teaching the uses of percentage are all that space will allow.

It is usually wise to *relate* each type of *percentage* application to the *general theory* problems. For example, interest is a Case I type, as 6% of $100 = $6 interest for one year. Commission of 5% or discount of 10% are problems of the same type. This may serve the double purpose of keeping a lively pupil-interest running throughout, and helping to consolidate the whole percentage field in the pupils' thinking.

Teachers almost always accomplish more in pupil advancement if they make the study in each field of percentage *grow directly out* of *pupil experience*. To illustrate: commission might come from some pupil's experience in selling, or from the experience of some person about whom a pupil knows. Interest, taxes, insurance, investments, banking, and all the rest may be started by the pupils themselves. It is comparatively easy to make the whole study of a field grow out of questions raised by pupils. It is difficult to make specific suggestions to teachers as to how such questions are elicited. What is done depends on the individual school or pupil situation. An observant teacher has practically no difficulty in finding actual pupil or community situations on which to base, or at least to begin, the study of any phase of percentage. More often she has trouble in limiting such situations to proper bounds for study by elementary-grade pupils. Occasionally a question arises in which the pupils of another grade may help. This is particularly true of the one-room school.

A greater degree of success is assured if the *beginning experiences* in any percentage field are of a *simple* nature easily understood by every pupil. Moreover, it seems best that these be kept relatively simple throughout the study. Adjustments must be made for variations of pupil ability. Teachers need to be on guard at this point for problems or experiences introduced by the pupils or coming from the community directly, which are often complex or which have delicate relationships. In the first place, only the simple phases of such a problem should be attacked, and second, common sense and tact should be used in dealing with these phases of it. It is possible that some questions should not be raised at all. For example, a problem on community taxation would not be raised in the schools of a town torn by a six-month old strike or other type of general discord.

Greater interest and benefit would probably come from class *discussion* of the various fields in which percentage is applied, with fewer actual problems of the usual book type. For example, it might be more valuable for pupils to know why there is insurance of various sorts, how it came to be, whether it is good for everyone, than to spend all their time finding what the premiums would be in given situations. This does not mean elimination of all computation. It means giving it a place subordinate to a fundamental conception of the field itself. Usually the computation is easily done if the basic principles are understood.

Concrete materials and *situations* add immeasurably to the possibilities of successful experiences in any field. The same is true in applications of percentage. Wise salesmen have their "materials" with them. Some of them not only have them along, but will "demonstrate" (apply them to a given situation) the value of these materials. Those who sell ideas are a bit handicapped, but even they have with them "materials" (data) to show, and some are willing to "demonstrate" to the pupils in a schoolroom how their ideas work in a real situation. It doesn't take a King Solomon to see that actual blank checks, bank books, deposit slips, bank statements, notes, and other concrete materials (not the ones made by the pupils in the schoolroom) used by a bank, would help pupils to understand banking better. Especially would this be true if they could actually use them in a pupil-made bank in their own room. Add to this a trip to the bank with a look into the vaults, the tellers' cages, the board room, president's office, and the teacher has the setting for realistic pupil experiences and learning in the field of banking. If a whole class cannot go, perhaps a committee can. Or if nobody can go, pictures will help. Books will add their bit, and—well, where is the teacher's initiative?

It is astonishing what a tax receipt will do for the study of taxation, a real life or fire insurance policy for insurance, and a real stock certificate or bond for those fields. If any prospective teacher does not believe this or thinks she cannot obtain such materials, she might be pleasantly surprised upon making the attempt.

Much can be done to make situations "real" in the classroom. Pupils may have a bank in their own room. A stock company may be organized, shares of common and preferred stock sold, or bonds sold later when the company had run into debt or needed a little extra money. It could have salesmen on commission, give discounts on its sale of goods, etc. Such a procedure should be well-planned, however, for time can be wasted easily even if pupils are getting valuable experiences. Furthermore, all such activities should be checked to satisfy the teacher that the pupils are really developing in the direction she intends, and as much as she had planned.

DENOMINATE NUMBERS

Historically, all arithmetic is included in the answers to two questions: How many? which is answered by counting and the processes built upon counting in both abstract and concrete numbers; How much? which is answered by measuring in terms of denominate numbers. Any kind of measuring implies a measuring unit or standard by which to measure, such as a foot, gallon, mile, light year, etc. Apparently it has been difficult for the human race to arrive at exact units of measure. Although our present standard units of measure are quite exact, they are not alike the world over, even among civilized nations.

There are two main systems of measurement: the English, used mainly in Great Britain and United States, and the metric system, used in practically every other nation of the world. The metric system has the advantage of having its units based on 10 and multiples of 10, namely 100 and 1000. Ten of any one unit make one of the next above. The English system of measures in length, weight, volume, and other fields is a conglomeration of almost impossible and unrelated units. For example, there is no unit to relate length and weight directly. The origins of the various units are interesting. A few are given here: inch—Latin: "uncia" = 1/12 or a twelfth part; the yard—English: according to tradition the distance from the nose to the end of the outstretched arm of Henry I of England; the mile—Latin: milla passuum or 1000 paces (running); the bushel—a basket containing the load for a man; the rod—originally the length of stick the ploughman used to prod his oxen (later it was the combined length from heel to toe of 16 men); the meter—one ten millionth of a quarter of a great circle of the earth.

In current *teaching practice,* denominate numbers are taught beginning with the early grades. Some general suggestions will be discussed at this point. (1) The more commonly used sets of measures should be studied in the elementary field. These are generally set out concretely in the textbooks. Only the simpler exercises and problems should be used. (2) Specific application of the various measures, as developed, should be made to the immediate environment. Or, insofar as possible, the different kinds of measures should grow out of the pupils' surroundings. For example: telling time by the clock might begin at school by showing where the clock hands are when school starts or is dismissed for the day. Construction of various types initiates measuring experiences. Later, many types of measurement crowd themselves upon alert pupils and teachers. In fact, almost anything one can think of has measurement connected with it. (3) The units of measure can best be learned in connection with the work done with them, either from concrete experiences or from tables in books, but preferably from the former. For example, a pound, gill, rod, and other unit will be most effectively learned if direct experiences with them are provided. (4) In dealing with areas and volumes, emphasis should be placed on simple and commonly used elements, using practical applications or bringing the problems themselves from the school or community environment.

Reduction (changing of denominate numbers) is essential to learning to manipulate them in the various operations. Only two forms are needed: reduction from larger units to smaller, and from smaller to larger. After tables of the commonly used measures have been obtained experimentally (or otherwise), they may be used to aid in reducing denominate numbers, either simple (as 12 ft.) or compound (as 12 ft. 4 in.), to smaller or larger units. For example the table:

$$12 \quad \text{inches} = 1 \text{ foot}$$
$$3 \quad \text{feet} \quad = 1 \text{ yard}$$
$$5\tfrac{1}{2} \text{ yards} = 1 \text{ rod}$$
$$320 \quad \text{rods} \quad = 1 \text{ mile}$$

may be used to change 10 rd. 4 yd. 2 ft. to feet, as

$$
\begin{array}{lll}
2 \text{ ft.} & & = 2 \text{ ft.} \\
4 \text{ yd.} & 4 \times 3 \text{ ft.} & = 12 \text{ ft.} \\
10 \text{ rd.} & 10 \times 5\tfrac{1}{2} \times 3 \text{ ft.} & = 165 \text{ ft.} \\
\end{array}
$$

$$\text{Total} = 179 \text{ ft.}$$

Or, as in changing to larger units, reduce 179 ft. to larger units of measure.

179 ft. ÷ 16.5 ft. (ft. in 1 rd.) = 10 (number of rd.) and 14 ft. remainder.

14 ft. ÷ 3 ft. (ft. in 1 yd.) = 4 (no. of yd.) and 2 ft. remainder.
Hence, the answer is 10 rd. 4 yd. 2 ft.

Perhaps the only new difficulty in *adding* denominate numbers is the carrying to the larger unit.

$$
\begin{array}{llll}
\text{Add} & 2 \text{ gal.} & 1 \text{ qt.} & 3 \text{ pt.} \\
& 4 & 2 & 1 \\
& 1 & 6 & 3 \\
\hline
& 10 \text{ gal.} & 0 \text{ qt.} & 1 \text{ pt.} \\
\end{array}
$$

Carrying should be shown to be necessary when the sum of the units is equal to, or greater than, the number of units it takes to make one unit of measure of the next larger. In the example above, the 7 pt.— sum of the pints column—reduced to the higher unit make 3 qt. and 1 pt. remaining. Add the 3 qt. to the quarts column and 12 qt. is the sum. But 12 qt. make 3 gal. with 0 qt. remaining. Carry and add 3 gal. to the gallon column and the sum is 10 gal. Since there are no larger units of measure, the example is solved and the sum is 10 gal. 0 qt. 1 pt. If sufficient exercise has been given on reduction of smaller units to larger, little difficulty should be experienced with simple examples in addition of denominate numbers.

Subtraction of denominate numbers presents additional difficulty only when borrowing is necessary. In the following example:

$$8 \text{ yd. } 1 \text{ ft. } 4 \text{ in.}$$
$$-3 \text{ yd. } 2 \text{ ft. } 10 \text{ in.}$$
$$\overline{4 \text{ yd. } 1 \text{ ft. } 6 \text{ in.}}$$

the borrowing is done in terms of a foot to inches and a yard to feet. If reduction from larger to smaller units has been learned, it should be comparatively easy to solve the example given. The borrowed 1 ft. (12 in.) + 4 in. = 16 in. 16 in. − 10 in. = 6 in. The borrowed 1 yd. (3 ft.) + 0 ft. = 3 ft. 3 ft. − 2 ft. = 1 ft. 7 yd. − 3 yd. = 4 yd. Hence the difference is 4 yd. 1 ft. 6 in.

Multiplication and *division* of denominate numbers are used in life situations where doubling or halving (similar operations) of distances, periods of time, recipes, and other denominate quantities are required. The examples below illustrate each of the processes: Triple this time:

$$6 \text{ hr. } 25 \text{ min. } 30 \text{ sec.}$$
$$3$$
$$\overline{19 \text{ hr. } 16 \text{ min. } 30 \text{ sec.}}$$

Explanation: 3 × 30 sec. = 90 sec. = 1 min. 30 sec., 3 × 25 min. = 75 min. + 1 min. (to carry) = 76 min. = 1 hr. 16 min., 3 × 6 hr. = 18 hr. + 1 hr. (to carry) = 19 hr. Product = 19 hr. 16 min. 30 sec. Halve these quantities:

$$2)\overline{5 \text{ gal. } 3 \text{ qt. } 1 \quad \text{pt.}}$$
$$2 \text{ gal. } 3 \text{ qt. } 1\frac{1}{2} \text{ pt.}$$

Explanation: 5 gal. ÷ 2 = 2 gal. and 1 gal. remainder. 1 gal. (rem.) is 4 qt. + 3 qt. = 7 qt. 7 qt. ÷ 2 = 3 qt. and 1 qt. remainder. 1 qt. (rem.) is 2 pt. This added to 1 pt. makes 3 pt. ÷ 2 = 1½ pt. Quotient is 2 gal. 3 qt. 1½ pt.

Instruction pertaining to *graphs* is a phase of arithmetic work, although the facts graphically shown usually come from other fields of subject matter. There are four common types of graph, each with

ILLUSTRATIONS OF SIMPLE GRAPHS SHOWING INFORMATION OF LOCAL INTEREST

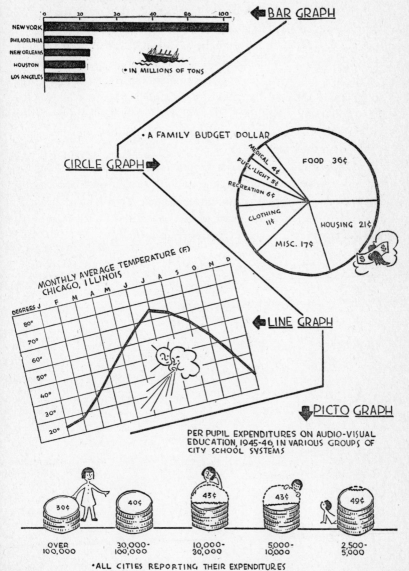

TONNAGE PASSING THROUGH FIVE LEADING PORTS OF THE UNITED STATES IN 1945 •

BAR GRAPH

NEW YORK
PHILADELPHIA
NEW ORLEANS
HOUSTON
LOS ANGELES

• IN MILLIONS OF TONS

• A FAMILY BUDGET DOLLAR

CIRCLE GRAPH

MEDICAL 4¢
FUEL-LIGHT 5¢
RECREATION 6¢
CLOTHING 11¢
MISC. 17¢
FOOD 36¢
HOUSING 21¢

MONTHLY AVERAGE TEMPERATURE (F.)
CHICAGO, ILLINOIS

DEGREES J F M A M J J A S O N D

80°
70°
60°
50°
40°
30°
20°

LINE GRAPH

PICTO GRAPH

PER PUPIL EXPENDITURES ON AUDIO-VISUAL EDUCATION, 1945-46, IN VARIOUS GROUPS OF CITY SCHOOL SYSTEMS

30¢   40¢   43¢   43¢   49¢

OVER 100,000   30,000-100,000   10,000-30,000   5,000-10,000   2,500-5,000

• ALL CITIES REPORTING THEIR EXPENDITURES

a general function: (1) the pictorial, using conventionalized pictures for purposes of comparison; (2) the circle, presenting relationships of parts to the whole and to one another; (3) the bar, showing comparisons of two or more factors; and (4) the line, indicating trends. The main purpose is to teach how to interpret the different types. The secondary emphasis is placed upon how to construct the graphs.

Graph reading is usually taught as situations arise in the fourth grade and continues with more difficult materials in other intermediate and upper grades. One investigation showed that the line graph was the most difficult for pupils to interpret. Many well-planned guiding questions should be used to direct pupils not only in noting what a graph tells but in interpreting the implications and the factors not shown on the graph.

In making graphs the pupils should find or assist in finding the data; decide which type of graph is best for the purpose; use care in making clear and complete headings, explicit legends, and properly related scales; see that one graph does not attempt to tell too much; and make the graphs neat and attractive in form.

CHAPTER 15

PROCESSES APPLIED TO PROBLEM SOLUTION

THE *utilization* of *arithmetic subject matter* in the elementary school is justified in at least two ways. It may be used as a tool to develop pupils mentally and socially; and it puts at their command certain numerical knowledges and skills which are useful now and throughout life. One of the important indications of success in teaching the materials of arithmetic is the level of efficiency at which pupils can use their knowledges and skills in solving numerical problems.

If problem solving is of such significance to the pupils, some questions should be asked concerning it. First, *"What is a problem?"* As the term is ordinarily used in arithmetic, a problem is composed of two parts: a statement usually in numerical terms of a situation partially known, and a question which may be answered using the facts and conditions of the statement. Generally the answer to the question supplies the missing part or parts of the situation. This differentiates a "problem" from an "example" which as a rule consists of computation only and is done according to specific directions, such as "Find the product of—," "Add the following—," "Subtract."

The definition of a problem given above is by no means universally accepted. In the first place, some people would object to its being called a "statement." They would maintain that the problem, if it exists anywhere, is in the mind of the pupil. A "statement" of a problem may or may not produce a problem in the pupil's mind. Even when a pupil's mind is working on the problem, the problem statement may have had but little to do with activating it. Often the possibility of punishment or humiliation or inconvenience is the motive force. Other teachers or leaders in the field of arithmetic would agree that problems occur only in the pupils' minds, but would insist that these problems be evolved by the pupils themselves, under teacher leadership, from their experiences in developing a more or less clearly defined unit of work, which is itself a problem. To illustrate, fifth- or sixth-grade pupils spending a semester on a study of budgeting (personal, family, and community) would bring to light plenty of problems of a numerical nature as well as a host of other types. Moreover, these problems would spring from their own experiences. The newer arithmetic texts utilize pupil experiences as bases for problem situations, as the following show: camp supplies, making a scrapbook, roadside stand, hobby show, a boat trip, visit to the zoo, and building a playhouse. About the only difference between the situations in the textbooks and those of actual pupil experience is that the texts have the data and facts organized while the pupils would need to organize as well as manipulate them in the actual situations.

Perhaps teachers would be interested in the *factors* which seem to be fundamental in the ability to solve problems. (1) Mental power, or what psychologists call intelligence, is one of prime importance. Generally speaking, a pupil with an intelligence quotient of 130 is more likely to be able to solve arithmetic problems from the book or from experience than a pupil with an I.Q. of 80. (2) Skill in the fundamental operations also ranks high in significance in ability levels of problem solving. This is obvious from the fact that these operations are used to solve problems and hence would be certain to condition success in solving them. (3) Skill in reading is closely related to problem solving. Especially is this true of the factor or factors involved in discerning and organizing mentally several relationships stated or implied in printed materials. (4) Attitudes and habits of work are undoubtedly important in the success of solving problems in arithmetic as well as in any other activity. Whether a pupil tries, or whether he cares about what he is doing, must color the result. Attitudes and habits are probably the outcomes of other situations and hence should be sought for earnestly at every step of progress. (5) The pupil's ability to put himself into the problem conditions and think them from "the inside" is probably another way of saying "seeing the problem relationships." If in the problem: "Jack bought a book for $.45, a sweater for $1.15, and a pencil for 5 cents. He gave the clerk two one-dollar bills. How much change should Jack receive?" the pupil could actually think of himself as "Jack," and do all the things mentioned in the problem one at a time and in the order Jack did them, he would have a clear idea of the relationships of the situation, which in turn would insure using the right operations and in all probability lessen the chances of computational error. (6) There are other factors, such as knowledge of arithmetical terms, difficulty of materials, excellence of teaching, and level of performance expected. The teacher should in no way conclude if any or all of these factors are absent that little or nothing can be done to develop deficient pupils. A healthy teacher attitude would find ways and means of using what the pupil has in mental power, reading ability, or skill in fundamentals, to develop him in these same abilities and in his power in arithmetic.

PRACTICAL PHASES

In discussing the more *practical phases* of teaching pupils to attack problems, most teachers admit (to themselves) that they do not know the best method. Perhaps the following steps would be agreed upon by most of them: (1) Sense the situation—which includes reading the problem, noting its vocabulary and relationships if it is a book problem, and getting the idea and information on it from every source possible if a non-book problem. (2) Organize the problem data, noting carefully what the problem asks, everything the problem gives or assumes the pupils to know, and the numbers (if any) connected with each item given in the problem. In case of a non-book problem, organize the facts collected into the various categories required by the problem and check them to be sure all are correctly placed. (3) Decide what the solution will be, determining what steps are necessary and what operation to use in each step. (This would be the same in non-book problems.) (4) Solve the problem, doing the operations decided upon in (3) (same in book and non-book problems). (5) Check the work to prove the answer by asking: Does the answer seem reasonable? Is the answer what the problem asked? Is the computation correct? Steps (3) and (4) are sometimes thought out at the same time. Deciding what operation to use and using it are very closely related, but are separate steps based upon different types of training and habit formation.

METHODS OF TEACHING

Generally speaking, pupils seem to make best progress if some definite plan is taught them for solving verbal problems. If this is started in the early grades, the plan may become habit and little or nothing need be said about it in the intermediate or upper grades. If, however, pupils are in trouble and do not have a definite means of attacking problems, they should be taught one—regardless of grade level. Just what plan is best for any given pupil, no one at this time can be sure. The experimental results seem to point in general to one or two methods; but individual situations may far outweigh these comparatively slight advantages. For example, a teacher's successful experience with a method rated a bit lower experimentally than others, might make it the best method for her. A few of the *methods* of attacking verbal problems are given below.

The *conventional-formula method* has a definite formula which the pupils use in writing out or thinking through each problem situation, as Required, Given, Solution, Proof. This method seems not to rank at the top, according to the experimental data, although perhaps a vast majority of teachers and pupils use it or some adaptation of it.

The *analogies method* utilizes a principle or problem which the pupil already knows to illustrate or teach the new problem type or relationship. Case I in percentage is analogous to multiplying a number by a decimal of hundredths place. This is scarcely a distinct method in itself, but rather a form of association which may be used in any formal method.

The *individual method* refers to the sort of activity a pupil might evolve from his own initiative, the guidance by the teacher, and books. Most individual methods have a core of general procedure such as the steps mentioned above plus the individual techniques built up gradually by the pupil. For example: One pupil solves his problems this way: After reading the problem, he makes a quick computation by setting down figures without names or special order. These are aids to his thinking. If this kind of attack does not produce satisfactory results, he writes out a formal solution including what the problem requires and tells, sets down relationships, and labels each number he uses or derives. If pupils have effective methods of their own, the teacher would probably be wiser to aid them to revise and refine their own rather than attempt to teach them a radically different one. If, however, a pupil seems to have no method of attack, he certainly should be taught one and be required to use it in every problem, even to the extent of writing it out, until his habits of thinking are well rooted in the specific procedure.

Another method named by Hanna,[1] the *dependencies method,* focuses the attention on what is required in the problem. For example: "Harry paid equal fares for himself and three of his friends. He gave the conductor a dollar bill and received 60 cents in change. How much was the carfare for each person?"

The dependencies method would suggest an attack something like this: Since the problem asks what a single fare is, it is evident that a single fare is "dependent" upon the amount spent and upon the number of persons involved. But the amount spent "depends" on the amount given the conductor minus the change received. Finally, a single fare is dependent upon the amount spent related correctly to the number of persons involved. Thus it is seen that one factor is related to or "depends on" another; and this one in turn upon others, until the whole situation is unraveled.

Another plan of attack, called the *graphic method,* emphasizes the use of the diagram in setting out the problem relationships. Using the problem situation stated above, the graphic method would be applied in a manner similar to the following:

$$\text{Cost of 1 fare} \begin{cases} \text{Amount spent} \begin{cases} \text{Amount to conductor—\$1.00} \\ \text{minus} \\ \text{Change received—\$.60} \end{cases} \\ \text{Number of persons 4 or } (1+3) \end{cases}$$

[1] Hanna, Paul R. *Arithmetic Problem Solving,* p. 4. Bureau of Publications, Teachers College, Columbia University. 1929.

This method is said by Clark and Vincent [1] to help the slower pupils more than the brighter ones. It seemed also to give pupils a better opportunity to determine what operation to use.

In *summarizing* the discussion on methods, it should be pointed out that benefit will probably come mostly from the use of a combination of methods or from using one method in one instance, a different one in another; that is, making the method fit the subject matter and the pupils. Although some methods seem to show slightly better results, it is altogether possible that the best one has not yet been found. It may be that a combination of those mentioned above or of others will prove to be more satisfactory. Further, it may be that our idea of teaching problem solving may be radically revised, in which case it is possible that none of the present methods will apply.

A *list* of *difficulties* which pupils experience in *solving problems* may be helpful. Brueckner [2] gives such a list for grades 4, 5, and 6, which was obtained by analyzing 1,014 errors on the Buckingham Scale and the Stanford Reasoning Test, and from which the following table is adapted.

Error	Per Cent of Whole Number of Errors
1. Could not comprehend or analyze problems.......	31.0%
2. Carelessness in reading or work................	19.9%
3. Inability to use fundamentals (simple)...........	16.3%
4. Processes confused............................	15.3%
5. Could not use decimals or common fractions......	7.3%
6. Ignorance of facts or quantitative relations.......	7.1%
7. Lack of interest...............................	3.1%
	100.0%

A glance at the types of errors made by 4th, 5th, and 6th grade pupils is sufficient to indicate the seriousness of the situation. Nearly a third of them made errors because they could not comprehend or could not analyze the problems. Perhaps those who "confused processes" should also be included in this group, because a pupil who does not know enough about a problem to know whether to add, subtract, mul-

---

[1] Clark, John R. and Vincent, E. Leona. "A Comparison of Two Methods of Arithmetic Problem Analysis." *Mathematics Teacher XVIII.* 226-233. April, 1925.

[2] *Op. cit.,* pp. 280-282.

tiply, or divide in it, has not comprehended its relations very well. It should be kept in mind, however, that the pupils were working on problem scales, and at least some of the errors charged to comprehension may have been on problems well above the difficulty level for the grade. The 16.3% of "inability to use simple fundamentals," of course, is scarcely excusable, and the 19.9% of "carelessness of reading and work" is even less so. Such disabilities seem to suggest that our teaching is not what it should be, or else we are trying to use impossible materials.

Several types of *exercises* for *improving ability* in problem solution follow. Teachers ordinarily use them much as a doctor uses medicine. When pupils are healthy and strong in problem-solving ability, no "improving" exercises seem to be needed; but they are quite useful when for some reason, known or unknown, pupils are not what they should be in the above-named ability.

1. Perhaps abilities in the *simple* and *necessary fundamentals* should be checked and all weaknesses overcome. As stated before, pupils will not be able to do both reasoning and computation if they cannot do computation. When such testing is done, it should be of the diagnostic type which shows the actual deficiencies.

2. *Carelessness* in *reading* or *work* is perhaps best met by the type of exercise used in the public schools of Waterloo, Iowa.[1] These exercises are arranged in two sets, "Test" and "Practice." The pupils work out the "Test" exercises on the first level of difficulty and check their answers. If every answer is right, the pupils go on to the second level of difficulty. But if any answer in the "Test" exercises on that level is wrong the pupils must work out all the "Practice" exercises on the first level; that is, they do this extra work as a penalty for carelessness or inaccuracy. The following examples are taken from the first level of the "Test" exercises of decimal fractions; the second from the "Practice Exercises" on the same level.

Test. The distance from City X to City Y is 16.24 kilometers. The distance from City Y continuing west to City Z is 8.87 kilometers. How many kilometers is it from City X to City Z?

a. Do you know what a "kilometer" is?

[1] This was conducted in co-operation with Superintendent Jack M. Logan, principals, and the intermediate grade teachers of the Waterloo Schools.

    b. Must you know what a "kilometer" is to find the answer to
the problem?
    c. What direction is City Z from City X?
    d. What does the problem ask?
    e. What must you do to find what the problem asks?
    f. Will the distance be more or less than 50 kilometers?

Practice. Harley and his brother saved their money for a trip
to the lakes. Harley had $9.10; his brother had $7.20. How many
dollars had both together saved?
    a. What does the problem ask you to find?
    b. Who saved the larger amount of money?
    c. How many persons saved money?
    d. How would you find what the problem asks?
    e. Would it make any difference in the answer if Harley had
saved $7.20 and his brother $9.10? Why?

The plan of penalizing pupils for careless reading or work may be
criticized as being negative motivation. The argument in its favor is
that it seems to work, even with the most shiftless pupils. In fact,
the lazier the pupil the better it appears to function.

3. *Teaching pupils how* to *read problems* is too seldom thought of
by teachers, probably because they assume that a pupil can read a problem if he knows and can say the words and numbers in it. They forget
that reading arithmetic problems is a condensed sort of reading, and
that often much must be read "between the lines." Note some of the
relationships which must be understood before the following problem
can be fully comprehended: "A baby weighed 8½ lbs. at birth. At
the end of six weeks he weighed 12¼ lbs. What was his average gain
per week in ounces?"

    a. Connect "at birth" with the beginning of the period used in
the problem.
    b. Connect "at the end of six weeks" with the end of the period
of the problem.
    c. Note the period is "6 weeks" long.
    d. That 8½ lbs. is weight at "beginning" and 12¼ lbs. weight
at the "end of the period."
    e. Understand that the difference between 12¼ lbs. and 8½ lbs.
is the gain in weight.
    f. Connect this difference with the six-week period.
    g. Connect the idea of average with the same or equal gain each
week.
    h. Know that 1 lb. is the same as 16 oz.

All of this and possibly more, the pupil must know before he can even start to solve the problem intelligently. These ideas come from his reading. Thus, it becomes clear that a little two-line problem has packed in it many relationships which must be read into the problem. This is not done at a speed of 300 words a minute.

4. *Vocabulary* is important in arithmetic. Pupils are more interested if they are familiar with the objects about which they are solving problems, although this is not absolutely necessary. That is, pupils can solve problems about "kilometers," "hectares," or "meters" without knowing what they are, but pupils act toward them much as they do toward beggar lice—pick them off and get rid of them as quickly as possible. The more strictly mathematical vocabulary is needed in the everyday language of the pupils and in their habits of thinking. Sum, product, tenths, improper fraction, base, and so on are needed in mathematical speaking and thinking. The most elusive type of vocabulary is the hidden sort that must be translated from everyday terms to mathematical reactions. In the problem: "Tom had 5 cents in his pocket. He spent 1 cent for an all-day sucker. How many cents did Tom have left?" the pupil must translate "spent" into "subtract" or "take away." It is true this is often done automatically because of well-established habits, but it must be done just the same.

Samples of vocabulary exercises follow:

a. Put (a) after the expression connected with addition.
   Put (f) after the expression connected with common fractions.
   Put (p) after the expression connected with percentage.
   (1) ½ of an apple................................ _____
   (2) 6 is what per cent of 12?...................... _____
   (3) Interest at 6% per year....................... _____

This type of exercise may include any operation in arithmetic and may be made any length. It may also include semi-arithmetical categories, such as things that pertain to a store, a farm, a factory, a home, etc.

b. Fill in the blank with the correct expression.
   (1) ⅜ is called a _____ fraction.
   (2) A pint is _____ of a quart.
   (3) 16 is a _____ denominator of ⅜ and ⁵⁄₁₆.

5. *Problems requiring* only *form* of the *solution* are helpful in focusing the pupils' attention on relationships. Examples:

a. If you know the price of potatoes per pound, how can you find the number of pounds you can get for fifty cents?

b. Given $\begin{cases}\text{average rate per hour} \\ \text{number of hours}\end{cases}$
   Required—total distance traveled.
   (These may be written or given orally to class.)

6. Opportunity for practice in determining the *operation* to be *used* is obtained by using dozens of problem statements, either in written or oral form. If they are given orally by the teacher, they should be numbered and each pupil should write his operation. The answers may be checked later.

   Examples. (Keep the numbers small and relationships simple at first.)

   a. Meat costs 30 cents a pound. What will 5 lbs. cost? *Mult.*

   b. Anna spent 20¢ for pencils. She bought 4. What was the average cost?...................... *Div.*

   c. (In 2-step probs.) John paid 5¢ for a pencil, 10¢ for a tablet. He gave the clerk a quarter. How *Add. and* much change should he receive?.............. *Subt.*

7. *Making drawings* or *illustrations* to help in problem solution is a procedure that often helps when everything else has failed. The problem situation "Jane planted 3 rows of seeds with 4 seeds in each row. How many seeds did she plant?" is made clear by

both as to possible answer and probable operation to use.

8. One device which has not been tried extensively but which seems to work in a reasonable percentage of cases is to engage the pupils in some *concrete mathematical work* that has a definite and immediate purpose. For example: If the class knows the number of square feet of floor to be painted, it can also ascertain how much paint to buy. Again, to settle their argument, Charles and Harry should measure the height of the tall pine. How many gallons does the drinking fountain tank hold? Why not have the class calculate it? etc. One of these problems leads to others—at school, at home, or elsewhere. While this procedure does not assure that many book problems will be solved, it does offer great possibilities for stimulating in the students a vivid interest in number.

9. Although emphasis in elementary arithmetic should be on the concrete and the practical, it is well to bear in mind that subsequent experiences in mathematics will frequently be with abstractions. For that reason, at least the average and brighter pupils should have some experience with problems which do not permit of visualization. It has been shown, for example, that small children find it much easier to obtain the sum of five rabbits and three rabbits than to find the sum of five hours and three hours. For much the same reason, older pupils would have more trouble with problems concerned with kilowatt hours than with similar problems involving speed per hour. Yet it may, at some time, be very important for them to compute problems involving kilowatt hours. It is good policy, therefore, for the teacher to introduce occasional "city" problems for farm children and occasional "farm" problems for city children. But most of their problems should revolve about experiences which are familiar to them all.

QUESTIONS—PROBLEMS—REACTIONS

SECTION ONE: *Facts*

1. What type of arithmetic teaching was needed at an early date in the history of our country?
2. What major and minor changes have occurred in arithmetic teaching because of modern conditions?
3. What are the main objectives in arithmetic teaching at present?
4. What evidence is there that children have considerable arithmetic skill and knowledge when they enter school?
5. List the activities suggested for the purpose of building basic number concepts in the primary grades.
6. What are the meanings of the two main kinds of counting given?
7. How may children be helped to gain the concepts of the numbers between 10 and 20?
8. What sequence of steps is suggested for teaching children to write numbers?
9. What classification of units for measuring should be recognized in the primary grades?
10. In what fields of standardized measurements are teaching suggestions offered?
11. How do children gain their first concepts of time? Of capacity? Of weight? Of temperature?
12. How may language composition work and arithmetic be combined?
13. How was the abacus used by different peoples?
14. Define addition.

15. What present theories and practices make possible a higher degree of mastery of arithmetical processes?
16. What is the relation of the 45 original addition facts to the 100 addition facts?
17. What should be considered in planning the order of presenting the addition facts?
18. What are the harder addition facts?
19. What is the meaning of higher decade facts "without bridging"? "With bridging"?
20. Outline the paragraphs pertaining to practice or drill.
21. In what two ways may subtraction be defined?
22. What is the relationship of the 100 subtraction facts to the 100 addition facts?
23. What is meant by combining the presentation of addition and subtraction? When would it begin?
24. List the items pertaining to the teaching of the zero in both addition and subtraction.
25. What device is suggested for rationalization when carrying in addition, and carrying or borrowing in subtraction?
26. How may the concept of multiplication be developed?
27. What steps may be used in presenting the multiplication sign?
28. Upon what bases may the order of teaching the fundamental multiplication facts be arranged?
29. What are some good basic principles of practice?
30. What is meant by a "unit of work" in teaching multiplication and division?
31. Which should be introduced first: the mechanics or the rationalization of the process?
32. What exercises may be used to prepare pupils for carrying, in multiplication?
33. What are the 5 steps in the rationalization process?
34. What are the two aspects of the division process?
35. What change is recommended by some of the new textbooks in regard to the form of initial division examples?
36. What knowledge is assumed as the basis for rationalization of the division process?
37. What is the chief error made in long division?
38. How may work in division be checked?
39. What were some of the forms in which ancient peoples expressed fractions?
40. Give the four conceptions of the fractional idea and tell when each may be presented.
41. What should be done before starting more formal work with fractions?
42. How should children acquire the terms used in common fractions?
43. What three steps in procedure may help in teaching reduction of fractions?
44. In the addition of fractions, what sequence usually makes the work more effective?

45. What device may help in teaching multiplication of common fractions?
46. What step should receive special attention in division of fractions?
47. What are the two plans for presenting decimal fractions? What is the basis for each?
48. How should a teacher prepare pupils for computing with decimals?
49. What causes pupils to have more trouble with addition rather than with subtraction of decimals?
50. What three plans are suggested for helping to locate the decimal point in the quotient, when dividing with decimals?
51. To what other arithmetical processes is percentage closely related? Which is the oldest?
52. How may the percentage concept be established?
53. Outline briefly the general suggestions for teaching the uses of percentage.
54. What is the main purpose of all arithmetic teaching?
55. What four suggestions are given for teaching denominate numbers?
56. What difficulty presents itself in the subtraction of denominate numbers? When are multiplication and division needed?
57. What is a problem? Give an example.
58. At what level may children acquire a definite plan for problem solution?
59. What explanations are given for the errors made in solving problems, as reported by Brueckner?
60. What can be done to bring about improvement in problem solving?
61. What were the two types of exercises tried in Waterloo, Iowa, to improve problem solution?
62. What special reading ability is required in the reading of problems?

SECTION TWO: *Problems*

63. Explain why theoretical arithmetic was given attention in arithmetic textbooks of former days.
64. Why are the three theories given by Brownell important to teachers?
65. Why is the building of basic number concepts significant?
66. Why should the recognition of small groups of objects be stressed?
67. Explain the relation of reading numbers to the preceding work in building basic concepts. Also to later work in writing numbers.
68. Explain by illustration the meaning of relationship of numbers.
69. Show the importance in computation processes of a good basic understanding of number vocabulary.
70. Compare the interpretations given of arithmetic readiness.
71. Is the use of a number system a modern or an ancient development? Give reasons for answer.
72. Show how the lack of development of basic number concepts may affect the mastery of the addition facts.
73. Compare the two organized procedures for presenting an addition fact.
74. Evaluate the suggestions on when to begin teaching addition.
75. Show the relation of column addition to drill on the basic facts. How does it differ from work on basic facts?

76. Give other illustrations of subtraction problems, designating in which group each would be classified.
77. Compare the two present methods of teaching subtraction.
78. Take four points given as a "good procedure to follow" in the first part of this chapter and illustrate how they apply to the teaching of some phase of addition or subtraction.
79. Explain the diagram which shows the relation of the fundamental arithmetical operations to each other and to basic number needs.
80. Make a verbal problem for each of the "problem types" given for multiplication.
81. Why are the plans for practice and testing, as presented in the multiplication section, valuable?
82. Why is it desirable to use many examples to illustrate the rules about using zero when multiplying?
83. Why is it unnecessary to wait until all the multiplication facts are learned before introducing two- and three-digit numbers in the multiplicand?
84. Explain why teachers are urged to help pupils to "discover," "to think their way through situations," rather than to always "show" them the steps.
85. Write two problems to illustrate each of the two aspects of division.
86. How should a teacher use the idea of gradation of difficulties, as set forth for division, to help her in teaching?
87. Make clear how the steps given as specific helps for long division may be used by the pupils.
88. Construct three problems based on some of the situations suggested for division problems.
89. Which of these groups of fractions should receive the more attention: $\frac{1}{2}$, $\frac{3}{4}$, $\frac{1}{12}$ or $\frac{2}{5}$, $\frac{3}{7}$, $\frac{2}{9}$? Why?
90. Why should the first work in fractions be other than the reduction and addition of fractions?
91. Evaluate the use of drawings and charts for showing relationships of fractions.
92. Why is it so essential that pupils have a clear understanding and adequate skill in the different kinds of reduction of fractions?
93. Why should special attention be given to borrowing in the subtraction of fractions?
94. Explain why cancellation may be used in multiplication and division of fractions.
95. Why would a technician in a chemical laboratory probably use decimal fractions rather than common fractions?
96. What phase of decimal fractions needs special practice, judging from the results of Brueckner's investigation?
97. Why should there be plenty of practice with easy examples in the beginning work in the multiplication of decimals?
98. Justify emphasizing the various ways of writing per cent.
99. How may pupils be led easily to see the relationships of per cents to frequently used common fractions?

100. Show how oral problems may be used in establishing skill, as in the Case I type in percentage.

101. Why is accurate reading needed in the Case II type?

102. Why is skill in reduction of denominate numbers essential?

103. In the first paragraph in the section "Problem Solution," explain the relation of the last sentence to the first. Show its agreement or disagreement with the outline "The Function of the School" in the first chapter of this book.

104. Apply the five general steps for attacking problems to a specific problem.

105. Show how each of the different plans for attacking verbal problems may have its place.

SECTION THREE: *Personal Reactions*

106. Which of the three types of number concepts stated was given the most emphasis in your own training?

107. When in your judgment is a good time to begin the teaching of arithmetic?

108. What values do you see in giving children allowances of money?

109. Which would you consider more useful, a class record or an individual pupil record of attainments in arithmetic techniques?

110. What difficulties have you experienced in arithmetic because of the lack of basic concepts?

111. What arithmetical process do you think should be given the most emphasis? Why?

112. Do you believe enough opportunities for presenting addition facts will occur in incidental teaching?

113. How do you account for the errors made in carrying in addition, as were shown by the table?

114. Which method of subtraction do you use? What advantages do you think it has over the others?

115. Do you consider the results of testing facts and skills of more value to the pupil or to the teacher?

116. What values do you see in presenting the old methods in the fundamental operations?

117. Which of the three methods for checking multiplication do you prefer? Why?

118. Do you see an advantage in basing the introduction of division computation upon the multiplication facts? If so, what is it?

119. What objections, if any, do you find in the suggestion made concerning the use of "like and unlike" numbers?

120. What did you find most difficult in your own work with fractions? How will you capitalize on this in your own teaching?

121. How would you go about avoiding, to a large extent, the errors listed in the table on fractions?

122. Which do you prefer to use in a problem, common or decimal fractions? Why?

123. Do you recommend the use of diagrams as a teaching procedure? Why?
124. Do you think it is easy for pupils to find percentage problems in daily living? Illustrate.
125. Do you know of any attempts to make one system of measuring standards more uniform in the world?
126. Which type of graph, in your judgment, would be easiest for pupils to learn to make?
127. Which of the "factors fundamental in ability to solve problems" do you consider the most fundamental? Why?

SUGGESTIONS FOR FURTHER READING

Brueckner, Leo J. *Adapting Instruction in Arithmetic to Individual Differences.* University of Minnesota Press, 1941. This is a good help to teachers interested in adjusting instruction to meet the needs of pupils of varying abilities. It includes concrete illustrations of procedures.

Brueckner, Leo J. *Diagnostic and Remedial Teaching in Arithmetic.* John C. Winston Company, 1930. This book deals with diagnosing pupils' difficulties in mastering arithmetic and offers remedial exercises for eliminating the difficulties.

Brueckner, L. J. and Grossnickle, F. E. *How to Make Arithmetic Meaningful.* John C. Winston Company, 1947. This is a stimulating discussion of some modern aspects of arithmetic teaching and is valuable to elementary teachers.

Brownell, William A. "Psychological Considerations in the Learning and the Teaching of Arithmetic." *Tenth Yearbook for the National Council of Teachers of Mathematics,* pp. 1-31. Bureau of Publications, Teachers College, Columbia University, New York, 1935. The drill theory, incidental learning theory, and meaning theory pertaining to arithmetic are discussed pro and con.

"This is Arithmetic." *Bulletin of the Association for Childhood Education.* Association for Childhood Education, Washington, D. C., 1945. Many illustrations of arithmetic in primary experiences and activities are given. Dangers to be avoided are pointed out.

Hildreth, Gertrude. *Learning the Three R's.* Educational Publishers, Inc., second edition, 1947. Discusses such topics as teaching arithmetic through the grades, drill, diagnostic and remedial work, and other aspects of arithmetic teaching in the elementary grades.

Morton, Robert L. Volume I, "Primary Grades." *Teaching Arithmetic in the Elementary School.* Silver Burdett, 1937. This comprehensive presentation of what arithmetic to teach, why, and how it should be taught is especially valuable to those teaching in grades below the fourth grade. Volume II covers grades four, five, and six, and Volume III the junior high school period of seventh, eighth, and ninth grades.

Sixteenth Yearbook, The National Council of Teachers of Mathematics. "Arithmetic in General Education." Bureau of Publications, Teachers College, Columbia University, 1941. Leading educators and students in this field have contributed chapters which deal with various phases of arithmetic, such as the social phase, drill, evaluation of learning, and enrichment of the arithmetic course.

Spitzer, Herbert F. *The Teaching of Arithmetic.* Houghton Mifflin Co. 1948. This is a book for teachers which stresses understanding of arithmetic. It helps teachers to provide situations from which children can gain meaningful experiences. Helps are furnished for teaching many phases of arithmetic.

Ulrich, L. E., Sr. *Streamlining Arithmetic.* Lyons and Carnahan. 1943. This is an easily read, practical book of real aid to teachers of arithmetic.

Van Engen, H. No. 1, "Developing the Fraction Concept in the Lower Elementary Grades"; No. 2, "For Developing an Understanding of Place Value"; No. 3, "The Teaching of Fractions in the Upper Elementary Grades." *Bulletins of the Educational Service,* Iowa State Teachers College, Cedar Falls, Iowa, 1946. The suggestions given are very practical, often in dialogue, and are diagrammatically illustrated.

Wheat, H. G. *The Psychology and Teaching of Arithmetic.* D. C. Heath and Co., 1937. By reading this book, a teacher may gain much to help in the formation of a basic philosophy of mathematics. The author seems to believe that with the correct understandings of number and its relationships, a teacher can better instruct children in this field.

Wilson, G. M., Stone, M. B., Dalrymple, C. O. *Teaching the New Arithmetic.* McGraw-Hill, 1939. The general presentation of content and method in arithmetic stresses the teaching of arithmetic for use in the community.

PART FOUR

Social Studies

CHAPTER 16

SOCIAL STUDIES IN THE PRIMARY GRADES

"THE social studies embrace bodies of knowledge and thought pertaining to the relations of human beings—men, women, and children—to one another and to the physical environment in which they live and work. Both terms, knowledge and thought, must be kept in mind if the nature of the social studies is to be grasped."[1] The bodies of subject matter, usually presented in the elementary grades, which pertain to human relationships in the political, economic, and cultural fields are citizenship and civics, safety, health, geography, and history. There are no fixed lines of demarcation between these areas. In reality there is much interrelation. The above definition specifies the consideration of both "knowledge and thought." This is important since writers, in presenting these bodies of subject matter, often include theories and opinions as well as facts. In comparison with the other subjects, history seems to hold a distinctive position, in that it binds all together. It helps us, in the light of past events, to understand the present better and to predict and plan for the outcomes of the future.

PURPOSES

Social studies in the primary grades are usually presented in units centering around themes dealing with history, geography, safety, health, and citizenship. The chief *purposes* are to help children to develop

[1] *14th Yearbook of the Department of Superintendence,* p. 11. Department of Superintendence. 1936.

desirable social attitudes; to gain information and broader understandings; and through all these, to learn to live a richer life in their existing surroundings.

There are certain more *specific factors* involved in the accomplishment of this purpose. (1) Children should develop the ability and desire to participate in meeting the immediate and future problems of community living. They will have an active interest in the broader community affairs of the present and future if they are taught to assume responsibility in the management of their own schoolroom and grounds. (2) Children should begin to feel the interdependence of those engaged in different lines of work. The basis for understanding the interrelationships with those in occupations removed from children's immediate surroundings may be gained by the study of local community workers—the carpenter, mailman, trainman, storekeeper, farmer—with emphasis upon their contributions to the community and to each other. (3) Children should acquire ability to make adjustments to a changing society. They may be guided by comparing processes in order to realize that changes are occurring which vitally affect ways of living. For example, they may compare the pioneer's ways of making cloth with the methods used at the present time. (4) Children should know how to attack problems, to do critical thinking, and to form judgments. Teachers will aid children in forming habits of immeasurable value in meeting life's situations if they guide them to plan effectively the procedures for solving the problems involved in units of work, to carry out their plans successfully, and to pass judgment on the results. (5) This field furnishes opportunities to learn how to do the things usually done outside school. Children are helped to acquire desirable social habits and skills (the acquisition of which is so often left to chance) when they are asked to give a party in school which involves inviting guests and providing for their entertainment. (6) The work in social studies may serve as the motive for work in the tool subjects, and for acquiring knowledge necessary in meeting social situations. It is desirable that children have the ability to read, to spell, and to write, to have mastered some basic number facts, etc., if we expect them to work independently in their investigations of social situations.

The *place* for social studies in the day's program depends upon the circumstances. What is said in the section, "Units of Work," (pp. 25-26) concerning this, applies here. When there is a specific period assigned for unit work and it comes at the beginning of the school day, children will often go to work as soon as they reach the building and will continue through the regular allotted time.

The *length* of time to be devoted to a unit will vary. Some units may have enough different aspects to warrant continuing their study profitably for the entire school year; others for a much shorter time. The children's interest is another criterion by which to determine the length of time to be spent on a unit.

In some one-room rural schools, the *primary grades* are *combined* for the units of work based upon the social studies; or if the whole school is working on the same unit, the primary group works together on one phase of it. In order to avoid repetition of the same units in first, second, and third grades, three different groups of topics from which to select may be listed, and the years in which they are to be used may be indicated.

In order to avoid giving undue emphasis to one field of subject matter, a *schedule* like the following is suggested. Arrange for work in citizenship one day a week throughout the school year. Divide the year into twelve-week periods. In the first or fall period, devote the remaining four days of each week to units in (1) safety and health, (2) science, and (3) history and geography, allowing four consecutive weeks for each of the three. Do the same in the second or winter

period, and also in the third or spring period. Citizenship, if it is interpreted to mean learning how to live together well, is an integral part
of each class period and of all school activities. Special time devoted
to emphasizing certain attitudes in home, school, and community conduct is justified in many instances. This would certainly be true in
teaching respect and care of property, thoughtfulness of others, co-
operation, and many more. Safety and health may come first in the
fall, because it is often necessary to stress safety in coming to and
going from school. Science may be second, because in some localities
seasonal changes are noticeable in autumn. History and geography
may come last in the fall, and first in the winter period, because of
the holidays and their associated activities. Science is suggested for
the second period in the spring because, again, some localities have more
plant and animal forms to observe at that time. There may be chances
for launching safety and health activities just before school closes in
the spring. This will carry over into the vacation period. The following plan of organization for the year includes the above suggestions.

Fall	Winter	Spring
1st 4 weeks—Safety and health	History and geography	History and geography
2nd 4 weeks—Science	Science	Science
3rd 4 weeks—History and geography	Safety and health	Safety and health

An outline of this nature may aid those who desire a balanced program
for opening those fields of subject matter which children study in fuller
detail later. Conditions may make it desirable to modify the plan,
through the occurrence of some event of general interest or a phenome-
non of nature.

SELECTION OF SUBJECT MATTER

The *selection* of the phase of social studies to be considered depends
upon several factors. (1) The unit should be within the range of children's experiences; however, it need not always concern their immediate environment. (2) It should offer chances for a variety of activities, both group and individual. (3) It should lead to other interests,
kindling desires to explore other fields. (4) It should help children to
understand the society in which they live, by presenting some aspects of

living worthy of their expenditure of time and effort. (5) It should offer chances for meeting and solving real problems. (6) It should require the use of other subject matter and tools of learning, and afford chances for growth in them. (7) It should be planned with due consideration (a) of the difficulty of the learning involved and (b) of the abilities of the group participating. Some typical units centered about social studies are based upon the following:

The home	Clothing	Safety and health
Community life	Communication	at home
The farm	Special days	at school
The school	Transportation	on the street or highway
The library	by land	Indian life (Second and
Local industries	by water	Third Grades)
Foods	by air	Pioneer life (Second and
		Third Grades)

An outline of the *procedure in planning* a unit of work is given on page 26 of Units of Work. It includes (1) making the approach, (2) setting up the unit, (3) planning the procedure, (4) determining the activities to be incorporated, (5) arranging the subject matter to be included, (6) summarizing the findings, (7) forecasting the outcomes in terms of anticipated appreciations, knowledges, and skills, and (8) providing the materials and equipment. A wise teacher will make a tentative outline before starting a unit even though she realizes that as the activities progress, many unforeseen conditions will alter the original plan. A more detailed discussion of the different steps of this outline with suggestions for carrying out the procedure follows.

The *approach* may be made by displaying objects and pictures, reading, taking excursions, and utilizing other experiences, such as a report a pupil gives of his ride in an airplane, or the purchase of a new coat. In this way, suggestions for finding out more about travel by plane or about clothing may come from the children, because the teacher has consciously directed their thinking. Children's current interests also may suggest suitable units.

In *setting up* and *planning the unit,* the teacher and pupils decide what is to be investigated. They state the central topic so that everyone will have a clear idea of the goal toward which he is working. Next, it is desirable to plan how to proceed. The teacher's and children's planning continues step by step as work on the unit progresses.

The *activities* to be *incorporated* should be interpreted to include their mental, physical, social, and emotional implications. A unit of work about communication may include the making of a school post office, but the actual building of it is only one phase. The important outcomes are the knowledges, the appreciations, and understandings about communication which become a part of the children as a result of their efforts in the different activities. Some of these activities are carried on individually and some in groups. The scope of possible activities is very broad. (1) Investigative activities have a wide range of usefulness. Even young children soon realize that there are different ways of finding out what they want to know—for example, by reading, by seeing, by studying pictures, and by asking someone. They learn to use the ways which are best adapted to their needs. (2) Constructive activities are usually helpful. Children grow in power by meeting and solving their needs with the use of wood, clay, cloth, paper, and the tools appropriate for the various materials. Materials stimulate thinking and give children a chance to use initiative and to do creative work. (3) Artistic activities may be used far more often and effectively than they are at present. Experiences with stories, poems, music, and pictures help children appreciate the finer and more beautiful phases correlated with the theme.

The *skill and content subject activities* may be utilized. A teacher who plans carefully, arranges opportunities for children to find information in the fields of the social studies other than the one in which they are working. She arranges also for the necessary uses of the tool subjects. Children should be convinced that drill is imperative in order to master certain definite facts and skills which they lack.

The *summarizing activities* of the investigations and experiences of a unit may be effectively organized in different ways, such as a play which the pupils make and perform, a movie which accomplishes the same purpose, or an assembly given for others. An example of an assembly program following the study of milk might consist of reports, songs, and dramatic rhythm, as follows:

Music: Songs.......	*Everybody*	Sending the milk away	*Jack*
Our trip to the farm	*Jane*	Where we get our milk	*Joan*
The dairy barn.....	*George*	Why we drink milk...	*Mary*
The cows..........	*Helen*	Dramatic rhythm.....	*Everybody*

The *outcomes* which may be *expected* are varied. If the units are selected with the above factors in mind, and if the teacher plans to reach specific aims in each unit, the work may result in the following outcomes: (1) facts learned, (2) skills in meeting social situations, (3) abilities to use the steps in the thought process, (4) abilities to use sources of information, and (5) correct attitudes concerning conduct and experiences. In short, these will appear in children's desirable personality growth in direct proportion to the degree of enthusiasm with which they participate in the experiences. In one school conducted on this plan, Jimmie, who rated as rather dull at the beginning of the term, within six weeks was showing initiative, volunteering information in discussion groups, and taking responsibility in various ways. It is desirable to include in the plan a statement of the more specific outcomes anticipated in terms of skills, habits, knowledges, appreciations, and impressions, and to check each child's attainments at the close in the light of these, according to the teacher's judgment and by achievement tests when feasible.

Materials and *equipment* may be got from many sources and the teacher should develop careful preliminary plans for them. Materials are suggested on page 29 of Units of Work.

METHODS OF TEACHING

The *method of conducting* the daily work in carrying out the above program will vary according to the activities used. A period often begins with a discussion by the teacher and pupils, for the purpose of planning the work of the individuals or committees for that day. The plans, references, and names of committee members are usually written on the blackboard. Or the discussion may be for the purpose of evaluating the results of the previous day's investigations, work done with materials, trip, or drill. Following such discussion, children proceed to carry out their plans. Perhaps there is a group which needs the teacher's individual attention while the remainder work independently or as committees on research, construction, or other tasks. This is the opportune time for the teacher to observe, encourage, guide, and direct. It is a good test of her originality, ingenuity, and sympathetic understanding.

The following forms of lesson plans may be suggestive to teachers in making specific lessons for units of work. They illustrate different sections of the unit, such as approach, planning, and activities to be incorporated within the units of work.

INDIAN LIFE

INDIAN FIRE MAKING

Grade 3

Aims

1. To show the difference between primitive ways of living and the present civilized ways
2. To show adaptation of nature to the Indian's needs
3. To use reading as a source of information for social studies material

Materials

1. Pictures of Indians making fire
2. Books
   a. *Indians in Winter Camp*, Deming, p. 72
   b. *How the Indians Lived*, Dearborn, p. 68
   c. Other books

Introduction

1. How do we keep our houses warm?
2. Where do you have fires at home?
3. How do your parents build fires at home?

Development

1. Were there factories to make matches when only Indians lived here?
2. Do you think they had fires?
3. How did they build them?
4. Some Boy Scouts know how.
5. Explain or have read selection concerning primitive methods of fire building
   a. Rubbing dry sticks together
   b. Striking two hard rocks together
   c. Using drills
         Stick drill
         Strap drill
         Bow drill
   d. Using flint and steel
   e. Using tinder

Conclusion: Completion exercise covering information discussed

Follow-up Lesson: Safety lesson—Use of matches

SAFETY

Using Matches

Grade 1 or 2

Aims

1. To help children appreciate the value of matches
2. To help children understand the danger of using matches
3. To help children realize their responsibility in protecting themselves, others, and property

Materials

1. Safety matches
   a. In a box
   b. In a package
2. Common matches
   In a non-inflammable container
3. Pictures

Introduction

1. Showing different forms of matches
2. Discussing who uses matches

Development

1. Discussing how matches help us
   Making list as children enumerate
2. Discussing the dangers associated with matches
   Making list
3. Discussing how to be careful when using matches
   Where to keep them
   How to strike them
   How to throw away the burned match
   Places around room in which matches might be safe—before being lighted and after being used

Summary and Application

1. Developing with the children the following directions for their help
   a. I must not play with matches.
   b. If I see one I should pick it up and put in a safe place.
   c. I should never carry matches in my pockets.
2. Emphasizing which kind of match is safer

Seatwork

Making a clay match container

TRANSPORTATION

Airplanes

Grade 2 or 3

Aims

1. To help children appreciate the importance of air transportation
2. To help children gain a better understanding of air transportation
3. To guide children in research activities

Materials

Lilienthal, Sophie. *Sails, Wheels, and Wings.* Grosset and Dunlap, New York.

Harter, Helen, edited by. *How We Travel.* Follett Publishing Company, 1257 S. Wabash Avenue, Chicago.

Blodgett, C. H., compiled by. *Transport Airplanes.* Charles H. Blodgett, Publishers, St. Paul, Minnesota.

Heiderstadt, Dorothy. *Jimmy Flies.* Frederick A. Stokes Company, New York City.

Introduction (Initiating unit on airplanes)

1. Referring to transportation by land, water, air
2. Asking children about their experiences concerning airplanes, such as riding in them or seeing them

Development (Setting up and planning unit on airplanes)

1. Asking children how much they know about airplanes
2. Starting a vocabulary list of words pertaining to airplane travel
3. Guiding children in formulating questions about what they want to find out about airplanes
    a. By comparing air transportation with that travel with which they have some first-hand contact, such as the railroad
    b. By using pictures
4. Helping children formulate plans for various activities, such as
    a. Reading
        To report
        To discuss
        To make something
        To solve a problem
    b. Experiments
    c. Excursions
    d. Looking and asking at home

Conclusion

Assigning specific duties to the group

COMMUNICATION
THE POST OFFICE
Grades 1 or 2

Aims

1. To help children understand better the function of the mail service
2. To help children appreciate the mail service
3. To help children learn about the use and price of stamps
4. To give opportunities for the use of oral sentences, and those to be recorded

Materials

1. Letters
   a. A friendly letter
   b. A typed business letter
2. Stamps
   a. Envelopes with cancelled stamps on them
   b. New stamps, one-, two-, three-cent, special delivery, airmail

Introduction

Discussion of children's experiences in receiving and sending letters

Development

1. Points for discussion
   a. Why people send letters
   b. Kinds of letters sent
   c. Postage necessary for sending letters by different agencies and different distances
2. Repetition for fixing facts
   a. Answering riddles
   b. Matching cancelled and uncancelled stamps

Conclusion

Summarizing by means of a recorded group composition, using sentences, such as

There are many kinds of stamps.
Some are for mail sent in our country.
Some are for mail sent to other countries.
Some are for airmail.
Some are for special delivery mail.
We put stamps on all mail.

Suggestions for future lessons

1. Discussing the sending of packages by parcel post
2. Understanding the purpose of the cancellation stamp on envelopes
3. Making a post office in school

The three following examples illustrate another simple form which may be used for daily plans.

Grade, Part of Unit, Phase of Work	Teacher's Purpose	Children's Activities	Material
1st Grade	*Unit on Transportation*		
Initiation and development of the unit	To help children realize the different means of transportation To help children organize their information about automobile transportation	Looking at books Telling of trips taken Looking at pictures of automobiles Learning names of different styles of cars	Travel books Picture of coupes, sedans, and trucks
Conversation Oral Composition Vocabulary	To give opportunities for different phases of language expression To set up questions for which children may find answers	Co-operating in setting up the questions	
2nd Grade	*Unit on Light*		
Initiation of the unit Development of the unit Discussion	To help children realize the different ways of lighting To help children appreciate the present ways of lighting To help children use various means of language expression	Looking at a picture book Listing different means of lighting Comparing present and pioneer lighting	Book Candle stick Snuffers Old style lamp
Question making	To set up questions for which children may find the answers	Co-operating in setting up questions	
3rd Grade	*Unit on Christmas*		
Activities that are parts of the unit Discussion Outlining	To help children make comparisons To interest them in nature To help them learn more about Christmas trees	Discussing kinds of trees used for Christmas trees Setting up plans for learning about them Looking at twigs from evergreen trees	Twigs from evergreen trees
Forming questions	To set up questions for which to find answers	Co-operating in setting up the questions	

CHAPTER 17

HISTORY AND CIVICS IN GRADES ABOVE
THE PRIMARY

THE increasing *importance* of studies in social relations is emphasized by almost every recent writer on the school curriculum, and in practically all new courses of study. The same is true with methods of applying the curriculum in the development of potential citizens. Typical of such statements is the one made by a commission[1] to investigate social studies in the schools. "The social sciences, more than any other division of the school curriculum, are concerned immediately with the life, the institutions, the thought, the aspirations, and the far-reaching policies of the nation in its world setting. . . ." "American civilization . . . is passing through one of the great critical ages of history, is modifying its traditional faith in economic individualism and is embarking upon vast experiments in social planning and control which call for large-scale co-operation on the part of the people. It is likewise obvious that in corresponding measure the responsibilities and opportunities of organized education, particularly in the social sciences, are being increased."

History in its larger aspects either furnishes the foundational materials for or is closely related to all social studies, and therefore is of great importance. History, however, as used in the elementary grades, is limited to the facts about people, mostly those of our own country.

---

[1] *Report of the Commission on the Social Studies,* sponsored by the American Historical Association, pp. 1-2. Charles Scribner's Sons. 1934.

Even this small amount if well taught and pleasantly experienced by the pupils is of immeasurable value as a background for living sanely and co-operatively in a democracy such as ours.

OBJECTIVES

Objectives in history or any other social study which may be used in developing pupils are of direct interest to the teacher because they aid her in choosing the most helpful classroom activities and procedures, and in measuring more intelligently the results of her teaching. Such objectives[1] of the social studies curriculum are quoted below.

1. "To give the pupils the truest and most realistic knowledge that is possible of the community, state, and world—the social and physical setting—in which they live." The emphasis in this objective seems to be on "realistic knowledge," that is, of things and conditions as they really are. The emphasis is upon knowledge of a definite sort.

2. "To prepare pupils for promoting a wiser and more effective co-operation among regions, areas, individuals, groups, states, and nations—a co-operation interracial, interreligious, and inter-economic." This aim seems to be focused upon the situation of our increasing dependence upon each other and to suggest that because of this the national and world civilizations must of necessity be changed from their purely individualistic character to a more cooperative and closely knit type.

3. "To develop character by giving pupils a love of truth, an appreciation of the beautiful, a bent toward the good, and a desire and will to use knowledge for beneficent social ends." The evident purpose of this objective is individual character building of the highest kind. It would undoubtedly use all knowledge available from the past and present to develop right attitudes, high ideals, and courageous action.

4. "To train in the intellectual processes indispensable to the functioning of society, such as skill in: (a) locating information, (b) using these sources, (c) exploring and stating both sides of controversial questions, (d) selecting and verifying information, and (e) discussing social problems." Emphasis is placed in this goal on the mental training necessary to function efficiently as a member of a group. It seems, however, to stress the primary importance of evolving useful habits, skills, and attitudes, and to subordinate to it the acquisition of subject matter.

5. "To give pupils knowledge of historical, geographical, social,

---

[1] *Research Bulletin of National Education Association*, pp. 193-4, Vol. XV, No. 5, Nov. 1937. Quoted from the *14th Yearbook, Department of Superintendence*, 1936, pp. 56-59, with slight changes in first four and addition of the fifth.

political, and economic facts which may be of importance to them in later life." This aim seems very frankly to point to the acquisition of facts, information, and knowledge from the past and present for possible use in the future. Some fundamental assumptions of this aim are: (a) That the knowledge useful in the later life of the pupils is now known, (b) that the pupils will still retain this knowledge for when it is needed, (c) that acquiring essential knowledge prepares for citizenship, (d) that by teaching this knowledge the individual interests of the pupils are best served and the fullest possible development is made. These assumptions, as they apply to each objective, are true of all those given above.

It would be well to note at this point that in general, social studies are introduced for the purpose of developing serviceable pupil attitudes, habits, and skills. In other words, the social studies materials

Four aspects of a civic problem.

are used to develop pupils first, and in the developing process the important subject matter is usually learned. Barr,[1] analyzing the classroom activities of good and poor social studies teachers, found that "good" teachers had the following qualifications:

1. Ability to stimulate interest
2. Wealth of commentarial statements
3. Attentive to pupils while reciting
4. An effective organization of subject matter
5. Well developed assignment
6. Good use of illustrative materials
7. Provision for individual differences
8. An effective method of appraising the work of her pupils
9. Freedom from disciplinary difficulties
10. Knowledge of subject matter taught
11. Knowledge of the objectives of education
12. Conversational manner in teaching
13. Frequent use of the experiences of the pupils
14. An appreciative attitude evidenced by the teacher's nods, comments, and smiles
15. Skill in asking questions
16. Definite directions for study
17. Skill in measuring results of teaching
18. Willingness to experiment.

These characteristics were ascertained by careful scientific procedures; and teachers and prospective teachers would do well to study them carefully. Some are comparatively simple and easy to acquire, while others take years of exacting practice.

A short discussion of each of these essentials may make clearer its individual importance.

1. In stimulating interest, good teachers use the direct appeal of the subject matter itself. Often some activity or problem arising from the subject matter is used for this purpose, and quite frequently good teachers will use the interests and experiences of the pupils themselves to add to the interests of the class.

2. The richness of the teacher's comments is illustrated by the following samples. According to your judgment, which type of teacher would make statements such as these? "Don't get too noisy," "I thought so," "Let's try another," "Now, come on," "Say something," "You listen while I tell you." What kind of teacher would make comments of this kind? "Aha, there's a new idea," "Are you satisfied with

[1] Barr, A. S. *Characteristic Differences in the Teaching Performance of Good and Poor Teachers of the Social Studies,* pp. 117-118. Public School Publishing Co. 1929.

that statement?" "Are you with us today, James?" "Fine, Frank thought that one out for himself," "How do you know?" "Let's look it up!" "Probably my question was not a good one," "Who wants to ask James a question?"[1]

3. Teacher's attention to pupils while they are reciting is usually taken for granted. The truth of the matter is, however, that not all of the good teachers are closely attentive, and the poor ones are much less so because they are usually engaged in other more or less irrelevant activities.

4. Organization of subject matter differentiates teachers rather clearly. The good teachers use some sort of topical organization based upon the textbook and such other factors as pupil interests or experiences. The poor teachers follow the textbook directly.

5. Well developed assignments from a mimeographed outline, a topical assignment or a problem project assignment are the kinds of tasks good teachers give their pupils. Poor ones use page to page assignments.

6. Illustrative materials of certain types, such as blackboards, bulletin boards, maps and charts, are used by both good and poor teachers, but pictures, clippings, and pupil-prepared materials are used mostly by good teachers.

7. Provision for individual differences is made by comparatively few of even the good teachers. What is done in this line seems to be in ability grouping and individual instruction to supplement the regular classwork.

8. Effective appraisal of pupil response includes not only that of the teacher but also that of the class. Sometimes this appraisal is accompanied by a question or a discussion from the class or teacher.

9. The good teachers are seldom troubled with disciplinary conditions. Their pupils are busy and interested in doing the things at hand; and hence have no thought or opportunity to create a disturbance.

10. Knowledge of subject matter is a definite factor in successful teaching. Lack of it may cause narrow views or bluffing on the part of the teacher and distrust or horseplay on the part of the pupils.

11. Knowledge of the goals of education both in general and in the specific subject matter field is necessary. Otherwise, a teacher does

[1] *Ibid.*, pp. 40-48.

not know to what end her teaching leads; and cannot know what methods to use to get there.

12. Conversational manner in teaching means a good speaking voice, and one that is well controlled.

13. Frequent use of pupil experience or interests indicates that a teacher is alert to situations as they arise, and that she knows her pupils well enough to make prior preparations for special pupil contributions.

14. An appreciative teacher attitude is indicated by her attention, comments, facial expression, posture, and other factors.

15. Questioning skill is indicated by the type of questions asked as well as the rate at which they are asked. Good teachers ask fewer fact and judgment memory questions, and more questions which involve pupil judging and reasoning than do poor teachers.

16. Definite directions for study include such teacher suggestions as how to read effectively, how to pick out the main thought of a paragraph or section, how to outline, and other basic study skills.

17. Skill in measuring the results of teaching covers the class period as well as term or semester periods with both objective and more or less subjective types of measurement. In short, a good teacher is as skillful in finding out what she has done as she is in doing it.

18. Willingness to experiment indicates that a teacher is sensitive to her problems in two respects: (a) she realizes she has problems, (b) she is trying to find the best way of dealing with them.

METHODS AND AIDS

Methods and aids which teachers of recognized ability use in teaching the social studies were investigated by the Research Division of the N.E.A.[1]

The table below gives the "Per cent of teachers of each school level reporting the use of various instruction technics."

This table is read as follows: 201 teachers or 11.6% of the total teachers included used the textbook type of recitation in some form. In this category were 10.9% of elementary, 7.6% of junior high, and 15.6% of the senior high teachers. The data for the other types of technique may be read in the same way.

[1] "Improving Social Studies." *Research Bulletin of National Education Association*, Vol. XV, No. 5, p. 211. Nov., 1937.

Technic	All Levels		Elem. School Teachers	Jr. High School Teachers	Sr. High School Teachers
	Number Reporting	Per Cent			
1. Textbook recitation.......	201	11.6	10.9	7.6	15.6
2. Socialized recitation.......	585	33.7	30.7	37.0	33.4
3. Individual activities.......	186	10.7	5.9	13.2	12.6
4. Group activities...........	342	19.7	31.8	15.9	12.8
5. Combinations of (1), (2), (3), (4)................	411	23.7	20.5	25.2	25.0
6. Unclassified..............	11	0.6	0.2	1.1	0.6
Total.................	1736	100.0	100.0	100.0	100.0

Perhaps brief explanations of the techniques named in the study would give a better understanding of the table. Teachers using the *textbook* type of *recitation,* (that used by 10.9% of the elementary teachers reporting) generally conduct the recitation with the textbook open. They stress reasons for the facts in the text rather than the facts themselves. Pupils develop power in reasoning and planning by thinking through and finding the reasons for the facts mentioned in the textbook. The work of the study period may grow out of the recitation or, in a more formal procedure, may come from lesson sheets prepared for the purpose. In this event, more of the recitation time would be used in checking the seat work. Some *advantages* of this type of procedure are: (1) Pupils must use the facts of the assignments in lesson preparation and use them again if the check is made in class with each pupil checking his own papers. They learn the facts mostly by using them. (2) The fact-question-and-answer procedure is eliminated because using the open textbook makes asking fact questions senseless. (3) The teacher can more easily detect her weak and strong pupils, and can secure valuable information to help both the weak and the strong to improve. One *disadvantage* teachers sometimes find is the tendency of pupils to neglect the preparation because they can follow the class period discussion from their open books. This, of course, is avoided by an assignment which requires pupils to go beyond the textbook.

The *socialized recitation,* used by 30.7% of the elementary teachers, usually is thought of in terms of class organization. This may range from the extremely formal kind, in which the pupils do all the work of the class according to parliamentary rules, to the very informal sort in which the pupils and teacher talk and work together on the job at hand, using only the common forms of courtesy. The more informal type is frequently found in small class groups. Some *benefits* which may accrue from the socialized class procedure are: (1) Pupils learn to do things together—that is, to divide the task and assign parts to individual pupils or groups. When the tasks are finished they bring them together into a complete whole and finally appraise the outcomes. (2) Pupils learn to take responsibility and to use it properly. (3) Pupils develop qualities of leadership and self-reliance. (4) Pupils tend to do more independent thinking and planning. Some *dangers* connected with its use are: (1) Unless due care is exercised, the whole procedure becomes formalized or stilted. (2) Discipline is often more difficult. (3) Pupils may waste much time in useless discussion if the teacher does not guide them carefully. (4) Constant watch must be kept on individual mastery of the subject matter if that is an objective. (5) The tendency exists for a few of the class to monopolize the recitation.

The *individual* type of *recitation* or class work, used by only 5.9% of the elementary teachers reporting, grew out of the fact that pupils differ in ability to react to the subject matter of instruction. The individual plan makes it possible for a pupil to advance at a rate commensurate with his ability. The assignments are in a very definite form, previously prepared, and when one is completed by a pupil, another may be taken up. Usually about half of a pupil's school time is given to this sort of work, the other half to group work of some kind, such as dramatics, shop, gym, library. The teacher's part in an individualized plan of work is to act as a guide. This may mean: (1) maintaining proper study conditions in the room, (2) rendering assistance of the type needed by any pupil, (3) keeping the pupils happy at their work and making progress. Similar to all other plans the individualized one has some possible *disadvantages*. (1) It tends to degenerate into a mere writing of answers and grading proposition. (2) It is easy for the pupil to do too much copying and writing, and not engage in enough oral activities. (3) Getting the group together for a discussion of points or questions becomes more and more difficult as pupils get farther apart in their assignments. On the other hand there are some *advantages*. (1) No pupil repeats a grade. (2) Each pupil progresses at his own rate. (3) Much pupil time is saved because each pupil is profitably busy all of the time. (4) Usually pupils have a greater amount of time free for other types of work.

Group-activities technique of some kind was used by 31.8% of the elementary teachers reporting. In the more immediate sense, the activity idea is usually connected with class- or group-work projects or units of work selected for special study or development. In general, it is concerned with making more life-like the educational activities of the school. Applied to social studies, this may mean that a class in social problems might actually go into the community, gather data, organize facts, arrive at conclusions, and make recommendations. In elementary grade history, it might mean writing a pageant on community history and staging it for the community; or in civics it might mean resolving the group into the state senate and functioning as a legislative body. In this procedure the nearer the activities approximate the conditions natural in life, the more effective they are likely to be.

Some *difficulties* likely to be experienced in the activity program are as follows: (1) There may be lack of books or materials. (2) Schoolrooms and building are not all planned for work shops. (3) It is hard to find and organize activities for a group of thirty children to participate in all at once. (4) A wide range of activities requires direction in methods and use of materials for which the teacher often is not trained, such as work in iron, wood, chemicals. (5) Teachers and pupils often must be satisfied with mediocre accomplishment because there is not time to perfect all the necessary skills. As a result, pride in workmanship may go undeveloped or even be seriously impaired. (6) Pupils accustomed to learning in connection with bodily action often have trouble in making themselves buckle down to the relatively drab job of drill which may be absolutely necessary to the pupil's development. If a greater opportunity for independence of thought for the aggressive pupils is offered, then a greater chance for domination of the thought and activities of the weak pupil is present also.

Combinations of the four types of class procedure mentioned above were used by 20.5% of the teachers reporting from the elementary field. There is no way of knowing what the combinations were. And so instead of a discussion of possible combinations of these, a few other methods, more or less recognized, are outlined below.

The *problem method* of taking up the social studies, especially history, is very appropriate. For the most part, history consists of the reactions of the human race as a whole or as groups to problem after problem. The steps of procedure in this method, which have been mentioned before, generally are as follows: (1) Get the problem clearly in mind—that is, the actual situation as it existed at the time, not the mere statement of it. (2) Keep the problem in mind by placing it on the board or restating it at opportune times. (3) Read materials which might bear on the problem. Find them by consulting the index. (4) Organize facts and other data into some definite form as:

I. Situations which brought on the problem
      A. . . . .
      B. . . . .

II. Reactions of people to these situations
      A. . . . .
      B. . . . .

III. The outcomes
      A. . . . .
      B. . . . .

(5) Formulate the final solution to the problem. (6) See that the solution agrees with the facts in the outline. Usually in the elementary grades, teacher and class together work out a statement of the problem with possible divisions and sub-topics under each division. The pupils read extensively to supply the necessary information to answer the questions of the problem.

ILLUSTRATIVE MATERIALS

The following example indicates a form of problem frequently used in the upper grades of the elementary school.

How We Made a Better Form of Government Than We Had under the Articles of Confederation

I. Why we needed a better form of government

    A. Main reasons

        1. No one had power to make people obey the nation's laws.

            a. How would this be a reason for needing a better form of government?

            b. Would this be necessary in a new government? Why?

        2. Men in Congress represented states, not numbers of people.

            a. Why might this be unsatisfactory?

            b. What might be done about it?

        3. Nine states had to consent to any national laws that were passed.

            a. How might this cause trouble?

            b. Have you any suggestions?

        4. Amendment to Articles of Confederation needed the consent of all.

            a. Why wouldn't this work?

            b. How would you change it?

        5. No national courts were provided to settle troubles between persons of different states or different states themselves.

            a. Why would such courts be necessary?

        6. Congress could not levy and collect taxes, raise armies, or regulate commerce—just could ask states to act.

            a. Give reasons why this would not work?

    B. Things that made conditions worse

        1. National government had no money.

            a. Why didn't it have money?

        2. Neither interest nor principal had been paid on the Revolutionary War debt.

            a. What reasons were there for this?

        3. Much paper money wasn't worth a "continental."

            a. How did that hinder?

        4. Shay's Rebellion occurred.

            a. What caused it?

        5. Jealousy arose between states.

            a. How could that be?

        6. Tariff troubles developed between states.

            a. How might tariff do this?

II. What we did to make our government better

  A. Alexandria Convention 1785

    1. It considered the use of the Potomac River.
    2. Washington invited commissioners to Mt. Vernon from Virginia and Maryland.
    3. It decided to invite Pennsylvania and Delaware.
    4. Finally Governor of Virginia invited all thirteen states.

  B. Annapolis Convention 1786

    1. Meeting was called by Governor of Virginia.
    2. It met at Annapolis.
    3. Five states were represented.
    4. Four other states appointed delegates.
    5. Little could be done by small group.
    6. Hamilton suggested that a convention be called to plan for all states.
    7. Hamilton's plan received unanimous approval.
    8. Congress passed similar resolution.
    9. Virginia selected delegates first.

  C. The Constitutional Convention at Philadelphia, 1787

    1. Personnel
      a. Fifty-five men
      b. Representatives from all states but one (Rhode Island)
      c. Benjamin Franklin (81 years old), James Madison, Alexander Hamilton, George Washington (presided), John Randolph, Robert Morris, Charles Pinckney
    2. Virginia's large state plan
      a. A national legislature of two houses
      b. A legislature elected by people instead of by states as in Articles of Confederation
      c. Favored by large states
    3. New Jersey's small state plan
      a. Congress to be one house
      b. Members to be elected by state legislatures
      c. Each state to have equal representation
    4. Compromises of the constitution
      a. Connecticut's compromise on representation
        (1) Tie between large and small states
        (2) Question of power necessary to run government divided between states and national government
        (3) Compromise on two houses: Senate, elected by state legislatures; House of Representatives, elected by people in proportion to wealth or population

  b. Three-fifths compromise on taxation
    (1) It made population basis of representation rather than wealth.
    (2) South wanted slaves counted in representation.
    (3) North wanted them counted in determining proportion of federal taxes levied.
    (4) Madison's compromise proposed three-fifths of slaves be counted in apportioning both representatives and taxes, or five slaves count the same as three white persons.
  c. Slave trade or commerce compromise
    (1) Most states were in favor of Congress regulating commerce to some extent.
    (2) South Carolina and Georgia wanted slave trade.
    (3) Most states were opposed to slave trade.
    (4) New England states insisted Congress be given full power.
    (5) Compromise elements were:
      (a) Slave trade to continue for twenty years
      (b) Congress to pass navigation laws and regulate commerce
      (c) No taxes to be levied on exports from any state
 5. The main principles of the constitution
  a. Was the supreme law of land.
  b. Made a government with power to do things.
  c. Saved the rights of the states both large and small.
  d. Kept road open for change and growth.
  e. Formed government of three divisions:
    (1) Executive
    (2) Legislative
    (3) Judicial.

D. Ratification by the states 1788–1790
 1. Nine states were required to start government.
 2. There was much opposition.
 3. Pennsylvania voted first of the large states.
 4. Massachusetts and Virginia ratified by small majorities.
 5. New York had hardest fight.
 6. July 1788, eleven states had ratified.

E. First election—Washington elected President
 1. Congress met first.
 2. Electoral vote counted by Congress showed Washington unanimously elected President; John Adams, Vice-President.
 3. Last of branches to be organized was Supreme Court.

F. Bill of Rights—Amendments
    1. Insisted on by Massachusetts, South Carolina, Virginia.
    2. Guaranteed rights of personal liberty, e.g., freedom of speech, protection against search, trial by jury, etc.

III. Results
  A. Constitution ratified
    1. Eventually by thirteen states
    2. Hard fights in some states

  B. Change from Confederation to Federal Government
    1. Old Congress called new Congress together.
    2. New Congress met March 4, 1789.
    3. It had no quorum until April.
    4. Electoral ballots were opened and President and Vice-President selected.
    5. President appointed Supreme Court Justices—John Jay as Chief Justice.

  C. States gave up some powers to make a central or national government, as
    1. To declare war
    2. To collect taxes
    3. To borrow money
    4. To make laws necessary to carry out provisions of the Constitution.

A *special type* of problem method has functioned successfully in the upper grades of one-room rural schools. It fits well into a situation in which the teacher has a minimum amount of time for class instruction and the pupils a large amount for independent work. It seems to work also under more favorable conditions.

The pupils have in hand an outline of each problem under three general headings:

    I. Conditions out of which the problem developed
    II. Attempts at solution
    III. Results

1. Each problem is introduced in a class period by the teacher. She makes clear its setting in relation to the previous problem, indicates what new factors are involved, and helps the pupils actually to realize the problem which the people of that time had.

2. The core of pupil development comes from carrying one step farther each minor topic (a, b, c, etc.) of the problem outline. Pupils read the references on the section in several histories before actually

filling in the additional topics in rough form. The minor topics in parentheses [(1), (2), (3), etc.] are supplied by pupils from the references they have read. It seems best to have these separate, in short concise form, rather than in a more elaborate paragraph. The emphasis should be on getting the right bits of information in the right place rather than on stressing the form used. The information the pupils gather should be in their own words—not sentences copied from books. The illustration below shows the plan of work.

Problem VI[1]

How to Gain and Hold the Great Valleys of the St. Lawrence and the Mississippi (The Intercolonial Wars)

I. Conditions out of which the problem developed
    A. The growth of New France in America 1608–1689
        1. Explorers
            a. Verrazano—Atlantic coast 1524
                (1) He was an Italian.
                (2) France hired him to find the Indies by sailing west.
                (3) He explored parts of the coast of North America.
                (4) His statue is in Battery Park, New York City.
                (5) He discovered New York Bay.
            b. Cartier—
                (1) The same procedure as for Verrazano
            c. Champlain—
                (1) The same procedure as for Verrazano
    B. The contrast between French and English colonial strength and colonial policies
        1. (The same procedure as for A above)
    C. The same procedure as for A and B

II. Attempts at solution—Wars
    A. Early intercolonial wars
    B. The same procedure as in Section I

III. Results
    A. Treaty of Paris 1763—as it affected America
    B. The same procedure as in Section I

[1] Moeller, H. C., Ringstrom, N. H. *Pupils Guide Book in the Study of History Through the Problem Method*, pp. 11-12. Follett Publishing Co. 1931. Adapted.

3. A class meeting (recitation) may also be called as needed to meet a general difficulty or to discuss a section of the problem completed. Such a meeting is necessary at the end of the reference work on each problem. The purpose is to check facts and to think the relationships of the various major and minor topics through to the main problem. For example, in Problem VI above, the teacher would check first to find if the information which the pupils had secured on Verrazano was correct. Then she might ask, "What did Verrazano have to do with the growth of New France in America during 1608–1689?" Or, "How did Verrazano affect the conditions from which the problem developed?" Or, "How were the intercolonial wars attempts to gain and hold the Mississippi and St. Lawrence river valleys?" In this way, all parts of the problem are related to other parts, as well as the present problem to the ones preceding.

4. Following the final class review period or periods, each pupil takes an objective test over the facts of the problem; and in addition, writes a short essay on some aspect of it. Finally, he places the finished problem outline and filled in test blanks in a permanent notebook for further reference.

5. This final form of each problem is marked by the teacher as it appears in the notebook. The semester mark is usually made up of the average marks on the work in the notebook, objective tests over each problem, and the final test if one is given. These are usually weighted so that at least half the semester mark is based upon the notebook average, one-fourth on the problem tests, and one-fourth on the final semester test. Thus, if a pupil received an average of A (4 points) on his notebook, a C (2 points) on his problem tests, and a D (1 point) on the semester test he would receive

Mark–Points——Weight——Weighted Value
A or 4 × 2 fourths =   8
C or 2 × 1 fourth =   2
D or 1 × 1 fourth =   1
―――――――
4 fourths = $\overline{)11}$

Average weighted mark is 2.75 or nearly B (3 points).

Some *values* of this procedure are: (1) Pupils read widely in many texts as they search for the information needed. (2) Pupils learn a

438 SOCIAL STUDIES

method of attacking subject matter. This method is useful to them now and later, with little adaptation. (3) Pupils are compelled to organize facts, to make decisions, and to arrive at conclusions. (4) Pupils are taught the form of logical outline on an easy level. They use the main topics of the outline as a framework for the items they add. (5) Pupils have a definite task and a definite method of attack. (6) Pupils are encouraged to work independently and in accordance with their respective abilities. (7) Pupils are required to exercise judgment and to think. (8) Pupils of the upper grades learn to use the method readily.

Some *dangers* in using this procedure are: (1) Pupils may receive only fact-finding training in filling in the items under the respective topics. (2) Pupils may flounder about in the readings, dealing with a problem. (3) Pupils may see no existing relationships between the various divisions of the problem and the problem solution. (4) Pupils may get the impression that history is divided into the sections exemplified by the problems he studied. (5) Pupils may not develop a chronological sense.

The *project method* is closely related to the problem method and is probably an outgrowth of it. The problem method is usually thought of as using only the mental processes in working out the solution, whereas the project method encourages in addition the use of concrete materials and physical activity in carrying out a given project. It is comparatively comprehensive, is participated in by a number of pupils, and may involve several different subject-matter fields. The idea is to keep the pupil learning history (or some other social study) while he engages in constructive activities related to his history subject matter and at the same time he works toward a definite goal known to him.

This type of procedure requires careful attention to details of administration both before and during the progress of the project, otherwise much time and energy may be wasted. A few examples of projects through the grades may be helpful in clarifying the project idea further. Pupils in the primary grades may construct a playhouse when developing the idea of shelter, or weave cloth when talking about clothing. The intermediate grades might construct a model village when evolving the notion of community life, each taking a part of the life of the village to add to the completed project. The same may be done for a farm community. A pageant of pioneer life may be written and staged by the upper grades, or a trial by jury carried through. There are marvelous possibilities in such procedures which should challenge a teacher to reach her top level of accomplishment.

Perhaps statements of *criteria for evaluating* projects would be helpful to teachers inexperienced in the use of this procedure. The statements below outline some of the more important factors. (1) The pupils should participate in the selection and development of the project. (2) The project, to be most effective, should grow directly from the work of the class and be undertaken to serve a purpose known to each one of the group. (3) The work of the project should be done in a natural way. This is conditioned by the nature of the project and by the place where it is done. (4) Each project should furnish a wide enough variety of activities to provide fully for individual differences of the group. (5) Projects should increase in difficulty and vary in kind sufficiently to keep pace with individual and collective growth. (6) Each project should stimulate investigations into other fields of subject matter. It should lead pupils into a wide variety of experiences, both in the mental and physical activities. (7) Each project should be intensely interesting, contain developmental values for pupils now and later, help pupils form desirable study and work habits, and contribute to wholesome attitudes toward history.

The *unit method* is probably more valuable as a teaching aid in the upper grades than in the intermediate grades. By it, history as a development of the human race or of a people may be more easily shown. A whole section of materials which might cover a semester, year, or even two years is divided into rather large units, which include significant movements or developmental stages of history. The work for each unit is generally put in outline form which contains, besides the questions and outlines, some references for each major topic. These may be suggested by the pupils, reorganized and mimeographed for them. In addition to the outline, a pupil's guide or work sheet is used. This contains problem statements or questions and various types of exercises designed to aid the pupil in working most effectively toward the main objective of the unit. The teacher's task in this procedure is easily surmised from the suggestions above. (1) She should plan the units and, obviously, know what the goal in each one is. (2) She should make the outlines and guide sheets for each unit. (3) She must be able to start and guide each pupil through the work on the unit. (4) She must check carefully on the work done by individual pupils.

An illustrative unit [1] from early history follows. This subject matter is usually covered in the sixth grade as old world background, or as an introduction to American history. The unit is quoted in some detail because teachers frequently encounter difficulty in teaching this and later periods of history to sixth-grade pupils in the most effective manner.

I. *Unit:* The First Civilized Nations

          Egypt   Phoenicia

          Babylonia   Palestine (Hebrews)

II. *Objectives*

   A. *Controlling theme:* Each of the ancient settled peoples made valuable contributions to civilization.

   B. *Generalization:* The development of the earliest civilizations depended upon favorable geographical conditions.

   C. *Desirable outcomes*

      1. Understandings

         a. The geographical environment greatly influences the civilization developed in a region.

           (1) A fertile valley yearly inundated, such as the Nile or Tigris-Euphrates, favored the development of an early civilization.

           (2) A country little protected against invaders would have many wars, e.g., Mesopotamia or Palestine.

           (3) The people of a narrow country bordering the sea would naturally become great seamen and probably great traders.

           (4) The materials at hand determine the type of structures built. Thus Egypt built with stone, and Mesopotamia with sun-dried brick.

         b. The beliefs of a people determine the customs of a people to a great extent.

[1] This unit is used with permission of Miss Mary C. Anderson, Supervising Critic in the Campus Elementary School of the Iowa State Teachers College, Cedar Falls, Iowa.

(1) The Egyptians, believing in a life after death, embalmed their dead and carefully buried them.

(2) The Babylonians, having no belief in a life after death, got what pleasure they could in the present life and gave little attention to the care of their dead.

(3) The Hebrew belief in one God, a kind father of his people, helped them to remain apart from other peoples and helped them to endure great hardships and suffering.

c. Each nation was influenced by the civilization of the other nations, and each succeeding nation built upon the contributions of the preceding ones.

2. Appreciations

a. To gain an appreciation for the great accomplishments of these first peoples in the long climb toward civilization

b. To have an appreciation of our debt to these early peoples

3. Attitudes

a. To have an open, unbiased mind toward these early peoples

b. To have the desire to find the cause for certain developments or changes

c. To have the desire to share information with each other in class discussion

d. To have the desire to use illustrative material— pictures and articles that may be collected, models or drawings that may be made

4. Habits

a. To form the habit of noting carefully the accuracy with which a date is given   (Is the event given as probably happening in a given century, or about this time, or given exactly as 606 B.C.?)

b. To form the habit of consulting various references and, as far as possible, finding reasons for differences in statements

c. To form the habit of noting the chronological order of events and noting those events that happened contemporaneously

d. To form the habit of locating on a map all the places considered

5. Skills
   a. To have the ability to use reference material effectively
   b. To have the ability to sort out important facts bearing on a topic and to take notes intelligently
   c. To have the ability to make note of a reference correctly
   d. To have the ability to add new words to one's vocabulary and to use them in discussion (Also an attitude)

III. *Terminology*

A. Egypt

Places	People	Terms
Nile	Khufu or Cheops	pharaoh
Mediterranean Sea	Menes	Rosetta Stone
Sinai	Thutmose III	obelisk
Khartoum	Tutenkhamon	shadoof
Thebes	Champollion	inscriptions
Giza	Ramses II	mummy
Karnak	Ra	embalming
Memphis	Osiris	pyramids
Red Sea	Isis	sarcophagus
		papyrus
		hieroglyphics

B. Mesopotamia

Places	People	Terms
Tigris	Semites	cuneiform
Euphrates	Hammurabi	stylus
Babylon	Nebuchadnezzar	ramp
Nineveh	Ashurbanipal	
Persia	Sennacherib	
Chaldea	Cyrus	
Assyria		

C. Phoenicia

Places	People	Terms
Pillars of Hercules	Hiram	bireme
Tyre	Dido	trireme
Sidon	Pygmalion	murex
Byblos	Jezebel	caravan
Lebanon	Ahab	colony
Carthage	Baal	
Marseille		
Cadiz		

D. Palestine

Places	People	Terms
Jerusalem	Abraham	patriarch
Samaria	Jacob	sacrifice
Israel	Joseph	tribute
Judah	Moses	prophet
	David	
	Solomon	
	Goliath	
	Jehovah	

IV. *Outline of the unit*

A. Egypt

1. The Nile valley favored an early civilization.

    a. It was a fertile valley yearly enriched by the over-flow of the Nile.

    b. It was well protected from neighboring people.

    c. It had sufficient water for irrigating crops.

    d. It had a favorable climate.

    e. It had metals to use—gold and copper.

2. The Egyptians had a government and made laws which made it possible for many people to live together.

    a. They had a head or chief called a pharaoh to rule over all.

    b. They placed people into different groups or classes according to the work they did, as pharaohs or rulers, priests and nobles, city workers in metals and pottery, scribes, traders, farmers, slaves.

3. The Egyptians have left many evidences of their early civilization.

    a. They had a system of writing called hieroglyphics which was composed of pictures or signs representing words, syllables, and sounds, about 600 signs in all.

    b. They left their records carved in stone on the walls of tombs and temples, on columns and obelisks; and in writing on rolls of papyrus.

    c. They were great builders as is evidenced by their temples, pyramids, and statues which are still standing.

    d. Much has been learned from the tombs of the Egyptians. Because they believed in a future life they took great care to preserve their dead and became the most successful embalmers the world has known.

4. The yearly overflow of the Nile made it necessary for the Egyptians to learn how to do a number of things.

   a. They needed to re-survey the fields each year. They learned how to run a line at right angles to another—the "rope stretchers."

   b. They could find the area of surfaces, even of a circle.

   c. They divided time into a year of twelve months, that they might predict the time of the overflow of the Nile.

   d. They could add, subtract, multiply, and divide numbers.

5. Egypt has had a varied history.

   a. At one time its power extended into Asia as far as Palestine and Syria.

   b. Later it was overpowered in turn by Persia, Greece, Rome, the Arabs, Turks, and finally England.

   c. Today it is independent.

   d. The dynastic history of Egypt extended form about 3500 B.C. to 332 B.C.

B. Mesopotamia

1. Mesopotamia means "the land between two rivers."

2. Mesopotamia may be compared to Egypt in a number of ways:

   a. Like Egypt, it was in a fertile valley which was yearly inundated by the Tigris-Euphrates Rivers.

   b. Unlike Egypt, it was poorly protected against invaders and its history was one of constant warfare.

   c. Since there was little stone, the buildings were made of sun-dried brick. Consequently, little remains of the buildings of this valley and less is known of these people than of the Egyptians.

3. Many different people conquered Mesopotamia. Each brought some new ideas, but each adopted the civilization of the conquered peoples so that Mesopotamia was truly a melting pot of these early civilizations.

   a. The earliest known inhabitants of Mesopotamia were the Sumerians.

      (1) They farmed with plows and oxen.

      (2) They dammed the water and irrigated their fields.

(3) They built houses of brick and wrote on brick or tile tablets.

(4) They built temple towers from which they worshipped.

(5) They had kings ruling small city-kingdoms.

b. About 2800 B.C., Semitic tribes from the desert conquered the Sumerians. Babylon, one of the city-kingdoms, became so powerful that the name Babylonia was given to the whole country.

(1) A number of the city-kingdoms were united under the rule of Hammurabi about 2100 B.C.

(2) He collected and arranged the old laws and customs. This was probably the first Code.

(3) Since the Babylonians were good business men, they invented many devices for carrying on trade.

(a) They used silver and copper bars for money.

(b) They invented a system of weights and measures.

(c) They kept records and accounts.

(d) They organized banks.

c. The Assyrians, a warlike people living in the mountains north of Babylon, gained control of the Fertile Crescent and completely destroyed Babylon under the leadership of Sennacherib, about 800 B.C.

(1) The Assyrians were successful conquerors.

(a) They used horses and chariots.

(b) They used iron weapons.

(c) They used battering rams.

(2) The Assyrians made few contributions to civilization.

(a) They carved beautiful animals in bas-relief in their stone walls.

(b) They introduced new and more terrible devices for fighting.

d. The Chaldeans conquered the Assyrians about 600 B.C. and completely destroyed their capital, Nineveh.

(1) Nebuchadnezzar was the best known Chaldean king.

(a) He rebuilt Babylon and made it the most beautiful city.

(b) He built the Hanging Gardens to please his queen whose home had been in the mountains.

(c) He conquered the nearby city-kingdoms and united them.

(d) He conquered Jerusalem and carried the Jews to Babylon as captives.

(2) In 539 B.C., the Persians under the rule of Cyrus gained control of Babylon and the Fertile Crescent. Babylon was never able to rise again to power.

4. The peoples living in Mesopotamia contributed many ideas.

a. They built temple towers of six or seven stories and used the ramp.

b. They wrote on clay tablets with a stylus and introduced a form of writing called cuneiform.

c. They were expert in carving animals in bas-relief.

d. They divided time into weeks of seven days each.

e. They used the sun dial and water clock for telling the hour of the day.

f. They introduced better business methods.

g. They introduced a method of counting by 60's.

h. They worshipped many gods, their chief god being Marduk.

i. They believed in no life after death.

C. Phoenicia

1. The Phoenicians were Semitic people who had wandered there from the desert.

2. Phoenicia was on the main highway between Egypt and Babylonia.

a. The Phoenicians could learn the ways of both the Egyptians and the Babylonians.

b. It was easy for them to trade with both countries.

c. It made their country a common battleground.

3. The Pheonicians became great seamen.

a. Since their long, narrow country could not furnish a good living, it was natural that they should turn to the sea.

b. The cedar trees of Lebanon furnished timber for ships.

c. The calm Mediterranean with its many islands invited them to venture farther away from shore.

      d. Fishing trained the people for a life on the sea.

      e. The desire to exchange their surplus dye, glass, and cedar for food, copper, tin, etc., encouraged them to trade with distant lands.

4. The Phoenicians became the great carriers of goods for the rest of the world at that time.

      a. They improved and enlarged their boats, making biremes and triremes.

      b. They learned how to get their bearings from the North Star.

      c. They made a chart of the sea.

      d. They established colonies all around the Mediterranean to carry on business with the natives: Carthage, Cadiz, Marseille.

      e. They kept a record of all business transactions.

5. Although the Phoenicians had few new ideas, they made important contributions to civilization.

      a. They borrowed ideas from other countries, became skillful in improving them, and passed them on to the people with whom they came in contact.

      b. They adopted an alphabet of 22 symbols, each representing a single sound, which was carried in turn to the Greeks, Romans, and the people of western Europe.

      c. They did not build up an empire, but carried civilization to other people.

D. Palestine

1. The early Hebrews were wandering Semites on the Arabian Desert, and were governed by patriarchs.

2. For some reason, probably a great drought or famine, the Hebrews drifted into Egypt.

      a. Through the influence of Joseph, they were treated kindly for a long time.

      b. Ramses II believed they were becoming too powerful and had them treated as slaves.

      c. After much suffering, Moses was called by God to lead his people out of Egypt into Canaan, now called Palestine.

3. The Hebrews became a settled people in Palestine after conquering many enemy tribes.

      a. They changed their habits of living and now chose a king for their head.

      b. While Solomon was king, much was done to build up Jerusalem.

　　　　　　　　(1) He carried on considerable trade with dis-
　　　　　　　　　　tant countries.
　　　　　　　　(2) He built a magnificent temple in honor of
　　　　　　　　　　Jehovah.
　　　　　　　　(3) The building of the temple necessitated the
　　　　　　　　　　levying of heavy taxes.
　　　　　c. The heavy taxes levied by Solomon caused discon-
　　　　　　　tent and finally divided the Hebrews into two
　　　　　　　sections: Israel with its capital at Samaria and
　　　　　　　Judah with its capital at Jerusalem.
　　　　　d. The Northern Kingdom was invaded by Sennach-
　　　　　　　erib and his army in 722 B.C., Samaria was
　　　　　　　destroyed and the Hebrews scattered.
　　　　　e. In 586 B.C. Nebuchadnezzar destroyed Jerusalem
　　　　　　　and carried the best citizens to Babylon as
　　　　　　　slaves.
　　　　　f. These Hebrews were permitted to return to Jeru-
　　　　　　　salem when Cyrus of Persia conquered Babylo-
　　　　　　　nia.
　　　4. The Hebrews made two valuable contributions to the
　　　　　world.
　　　　　a. They gave to the world the idea of one God, a
　　　　　　　kind father of all.
　　　　　b. They gave to the world the Bible, a story of their
　　　　　　　history, traditions, laws, sufferings, and tri-
　　　　　　　umphs.

V. *Approach*

　　Make a careful transition from prehistoric times to the study
　　of these ancient civilizations.
　　Call attention to the slow and gradual development of these
　　early civilizations. The dynastic history of Egypt, for ex-
　　ample, extended over a longer period of time than that which
　　has existed since the birth of Christ.
　　Note that while these peoples were developing a civilization,
　　other peoples were still living in the Stone Age.
　　Call attention to the fact that several nations were developing
　　at the same time around the eastern end of the Mediterranean.
　　This introduction should lead to such questions as:
　　　Why did these regions develop an earlier civilization?
　　　What opportunities did they have to borrow ideas from each
　　　other?
　　　What contributions did each make to later civilizations?

VI. *Assimilative material*

　　A. Activity
　　　1. Class
　　　　a. Reading of references

         b. Taking notes on topics in study guide
         c. Locating places on the map
         d. Sharing information with each other in discussion period
         e. Looking at pictures of the art and architecture of these early nations

    2. Group and individual
         a. Preparing a report to give to the class
         b. Preparing illustrative material to show to the class
         c. Preparing a dramatization to give to the class
         d. Drawing picture maps of these early civilizations

    3. Culminating or unifying
         a. Giving summary talks on the contributions made by each of these early civilizations
         b. Making comparisons of these early civilizations
         c. Preparing an exhibition of the drawings and articles made by the children
         d. Preparing a time line showing the relative time of events in these several civilizations
         e. Giving dramatizations and reading stories that may have been written by some of the children
         f. Making a chart in art class comparing the civilizations studied

B. Materials
    1. Outline map showing the regions of early civilizations
    2. Time line on which events can be placed as studied
    3. Pictures of building and statues
    4. References for pupils

        a. Egypt
             Erleigh, *In the Beginning*, pp. 41–49.
             Freeland-Adams, *America's World Backgrounds*, pp. 111–131.
             Hartman, *The World We Live In*, pp. 81–94.
             Hawley, *Adventures in Old World History*, pp. 15–28.
             Hillyer, *A Child's History of the World*, pp. 24–41.
             Kelty, *How Our Civilization Began*, pp. 51–71.
             Knowlton-Gerson, *Our Beginnings in the Past*, pp. 120–133.
             Lansing, *Man's Long Climb*, pp. 49–70.
             Rogers-Adams-Brown, *Story of Nations*, pp. 29–58.
             Vollintine, *The American People and Their Old World History*, pp. 26–36.

Wells, *How the Present Came from the Past*, pp. 1-41.

b. Mesopotamia

Erleigh, *In the Beginning*, pp. 37-43.

Freeland-Adams, *America's World Backgrounds*, pp. 151-155.

Greenan-Cottrell, *From Then Until Now*, pp. 47-71.

Hillyer, *A Child's History of the World*, pp. 42-48.

Kelty, *How Our Civilization Began*, pp. 74-93.

Knowlton-Gerson, *Our Beginnings in the Past*, pp. 26-28; 135-144.

Kummer, *The First Days of Knowledge*, pp. 126-279.

Rogers-Adams-Brown, *Story of Nations*, pp. 63-79.

Southworth, *America's Old World Background*, pp. 125-139.

Van Loon, *Ancient Man*, pp. 65-87.

Vollintine, *The American People and Their Old World Ancestors*, pp. 40-51.

Wells, *How the Present Came from the Past*, pp. 44-117.

c. Phoenicia

Carus, *Metten of Tyre* (Story).

Freeland-Adams, *America's World Backgrounds*, pp. 155-158.

Hartman, *The World We Live In*, pp. 94-95; 120-124.

Hawley, *Adventures in Old World History*, pp. 62-68.

Hillyer, *A Child's History of the World*, pp. 74-78.

Kelty, *How Our Civilization Began*, pp. 94-103.

Knowlton-Gerson, *Our Beginnings in the Past*, pp. 158-165.

Lansing, *Man's Long Climb*, pp. 145-149.

Rogers-Adams-Brown, *Story of Nations*, pp. 93-99.

Southworth, *America's Old World Background*, pp. 156-164.

Vollintine, *The American People and Their Old World Ancestors*, pp. 52-66.

Wells, *How the Present Came from the Past*, pp. 161-189.

Wilson-Wilson-Erb, *Where Our Ways of Living Come From*, pp. 421-427.

Van Loon, *Ancient Man*, pp. 105-115.

   d. Hebrew People

      Baker-Thorndike, *Everyday Classics*, Book VI,
       pp. 97–115; 122–126.
      Free-Treadwell, *Reading and Literature*, Book VI,
       108–159.
      Hawley, *Adventures in Old World History*, pp.
       68–72.
      Kelty, *How Our Civilization Began*, pp. 104–110.
      Knowlton-Gerson, *Our Beginnings in the Past*,
       pp. 145–157.
      Rogers-Adams-Brown, *Story of Nations*, pp.
       83–93.
      Wells, *How Our Present Came from the Past*, pp.
       142–160.

  5. General references for the teacher

    a. Breasted, James Henry, *Ancient Times*.
    b. Hayes, C. J. H. and Moon, P. T., *Ancient and
     Medieval History*.

C. Study guide for the pupils (Note—only one copy has been
  included as a sample. Plenty of space for writing in data
  should be left on sheets actually used by the pupils.)

  Unit: The First Civilized Nations Name _____
  Topic: The Ancient Hebrews Date _____

  Unit questions:

    1. How were these ancient Hebrews different from the
      other people you have studied?
    2. What contributions did they make to the world?

  References:

    1. Baker-Thorndike, *Everyday Classics*, Book VI, pp.
      97–115; 122–126.
    2. Free-Treadwell, *Reading and Literature*, Book VI, pp.
      108–159.
    3. Hawley, *Adventures in Old World History*, pp. 68–72.
    4. Kelty, *How Our Civilization Began*, pp. 104–110.
    5. Knowlton-Gerson, *Our Beginnings in the Past*, pp.
      145–157.
    6. Rogers-Adams-Brown, *Story of Nations*, pp. 83–93.
    7. Wells, *How Our Present Came from the Past*, pp. 142–
      160.

  Study helps:

    I. Read one of the references and check the topics
      on which it gives some information.
      A. Life of the early Hebrews while they were
        shepherds in the desert

B. Life of the Hebrews in Egypt
C. Life of the Hebrews in Palestine
D. Life of the Hebrews in captivity
Reference used: _____

II. From this reference and others you may read, list ways in which these people were different from the others you have studied.

III. Locate the following places and be ready to tell of some connection each had with Hebrew history.

1. Sinai
2. Jerusalem
3. Samaria
4. Dead Sea
5. Galilee
6. River Jordan
7. Land of Goshen
8. Canaan
9. Palestine
10. Israel
11. Judah

IV. Be ready to tell how the following people were connected with Hebrew history.

1. Abraham
2. Joseph
3. Moses
4. Saul
5. David
6. Solomon
7. Goliath
8. Philistines

V. For many years the Hebrews were governed by patriarchs. Be ready to explain what this means.

VI. Find some reasons for the many wars of the Hebrew people.

VII. The Hebrew people were finally conquered by the stronger nations east of them.
A. Be ready to tell of the conflict between the Assyrians and the Hebrews.
B. Be ready to tell of the conflict between the Chaldeans and the Hebrews.

VIII. What valuable contributions did the Hebrews make to the world?

Interesting things to do:

1. On an outline map, trace the journeys of the Hebrew people.
2. Prepare a play giving the story of some Hebrew character.
3. Mold in clay a model of Solomon's temple.
4. Draw a series of pictures showing the principal events in the life of the Hebrews.
5. Learn some of the Psalms. The following are very beautiful:

First
Twenty-third
One hundred third
One hundred twenty-first

D. Tentative time schedule—Entire Unit: 6 weeks

> *INTRODUCTION OF THE UNIT*—transition from pre-
> history to history   1 day

> *Egypt*   7 days
>> Introduction of the country and setting up of problem
>> General survey of the guide sheet—1 day
>> Reading of references—   2 days
>> Taking an inventory of what has been accomplished.
>> Individuals report accomplishments and difficulties and
>>> suggest references especially good for certain topics.
>> Remaining time spent in further study   1 day
>> Discussion of topics—   2 days
>> Reports, summaries, sharing of results of individual and
>>> group activities—   1 day

> *Babylonia*   7 days
>> Introduction—   1 day
>>> Note the geography of the region.
>>> Prepare a skeleton time line showing time when the
>>> various peoples controlled Mesopotamia.
>>> Note points in the study guide.
>> Study, reading of references—   2 days
>> Inventory of work accomplished, remotivation of some
>>> parts.
>> Remaining time spent in study—   1 day
>> Discussion—   2 days
>> Giving summaries and sharing results of individual and
>>> group activities—   1 day

> *Phoenicia*   5 days
>> Introduction of country and setting up of
>>> problem—   1 day
>> Reading references—   2 days
>> Discussion—   2 days

> *Palestine*   4 days
>> Introduction and setting up of problems—1 day
>>> How were these people different from the
>>> others studied?
>>> Why did they have so many wars?
>>> What contributions did they make?
>> Study—   2 days
>> Discussion—   1 day

> *Summary*   5 days
>> Comparing the civilizations of the four nations and
>>> the contributions of each, noting as far as possible
>>> reasons for differences between them
>> Listing informational facts to be remembered
>> Listing words added to the vocabulary during the study

Planning a wall hanging to be made in the art class depicting these early civilizations

Taking a test

Looking over results of test, clarifying mistaken notions and re-learning some forgotten points

VII. *Evaluation*

    A. Objective evaluation test

        Test: The First Civilized Nations

Name: _____ Possible score _____

                                           Median score _____

                                           My score _____

In the first column below is a list of terms and in the second column a description or explanation for each of those terms. Match the term in the first column with the explanation in the second column by placing the number of the term in the blank.

1. sarcophagus   ____ a. method of writing used by the Egyptians
2. pyramid   ____ b. writing cut in stone
3. trireme   ____ c. a boat with two banks of oars
4. tribute   ____ d. the embalmed body of an Egyptian
5. inscription   ____ e. a coffin
6. papyrus   ____ f. a reed-like plant which the Egyptians used to make paper
7. obelisk   ____ g. tomb of an Egyptian king
8. hieroglyphics ____ h. a one decked vessel
9. galley   ____ i. a boat with three banks of oars
10. bireme   ____ j. a tall four-sided pillar
11. mummy   ____ k. a device for raising water
12. cuneiform   ____ l. method of writing used by the Babylonians
                     ____ m. payment made by one country to another for protection

In the same way match the people in the first column with the description in the second column.

13. Cheops or Khufu ____ a. Egyptian sun god
14. Osiris   ____ b. the Hebrews' God
15. Cyrus   ____ c. rebuilt the city of Babylon
16. Nebuchadnezzar ____ d. builder of the largest pyramid
17. Dido   ____ e. god of the Phoenicians
18. Marduk   ____ f. god of the Babylonians
19. Ra   ____ g. Egyptian god of the underworld
20. Baal   ____ h. a Persian king
21. Jehovah   ____ i. collected and wrote the laws of Babylon
22. Hammurabi   ____ j. founder of Carthage
23. Ashurbanipal   ____ k. Assyrian king who carried the Israelites into captivity
24. Hiram   ____ l. king of Phoenicia
                     ____ m. founder of an early library

Do the same for the following exercise.

25. Babylon	____ a.	Strait of Gibraltar
26. Rosetta	____ b.	port famous for its glass products
27. Sinai	____ c.	island in the Mediterranean
28. Nineveh	____ d.	great trade center of Mesopotamia
29. Lebanon	____ e.	name of one of the mouths of the Nile
30. Sidon	____ f.	the first great city
31. Jerusalem	____ g.	peninsula where much copper was found
32. Carthage	____ h.	the principal city in Assyria
33. Tyre	____ i.	the most important colony of Phoenicia
34. Samaria	____ j.	capital of the kingdom of Israel
35. Pillars of Hercules	____ k.	mountains in Phoenicia
36. Memphis	____ l.	port famous for its dyes
37. Sicily	____ m.	an important river
	____ n.	city in which the Hebrew temple was built

Fill the blanks with a word or words that will complete the sentence correctly.

The land of early Egypt was owned by the (38) _____.
Egypt was called the (39) _____.
The Egyptian scribes wrote on (40) _____ and (41) _____.
Mesopotamia means (42) _____.
Most of the Egyptian writing was about (43) _____.
Most of the Babylonian writing was about (44) _____.
The Babylonians made their buildings of (45) _____.
Both the (46) _____ and the (47) _____ told the story of a great flood.
The Phoenician alphabet had no (48) _____.
(49) _____ constructed the Hebrew temple in (50) _____.
The Old Testament is a history of the (51) _____.

Put a + (plus) before those facts which help to explain the statement above it. The Nile valley was a good place for an early civilization to develop.

52. It was yearly enriched by the overflow of the Nile.
53. It rarely rained there.
54. It had plenty of stone.
55. It had plenty of water for its fields.
56. It was well protected against invaders.

Man has learned much about the early Egyptians.

57. They painted pictures of their history on the walls of the pyramids.
58. Their writing was easily read.
59. They left inscriptions on stone.
60. They buried many articles of the home in the tombs.
61. They constructed their buildings of stone which are still standing.

The Assyrians were able to conquer the Babylonians.

62. They were better civilized.
63. They used horses and chariots.
64. They used weapons made of iron.
65. They came from an older country.

Below are some ideas and contributions of the following people: Egyptians, Babylonians, Assyrians, Phoenicians, and Hebrews. Place the correct name in each blank.

66. _____ carried civilization to other countries.
67. _____ were the first to use columns in their buildings.
68. _____ believed in no life after death.
69. _____ thought their ruler was a god.
70. _____ were the first to use the arch in building.
71. _____ believed there was one God over all nations.
72. _____ divided the year into twelve months.
73. _____ introduced new and terrible ways of fighting.
74. _____ divided time into weeks of seven days each.
75. _____ carved figures of animals with remarkable ability.
76. _____ gave the world the alphabet.
77. _____ taught men how to live together in large groups.
78. _____ were first ruled by small city-kingdoms.
79. _____ believed that all children should be taught to read.
80. _____ gave the first written laws.
81. _____ gave the Bible.
82. _____ carried goods for other countries.

The following people ruled Mesopotamia at some time: Babylonians, Assyrians, Persians, Sumerians, Chaldeans.

Arrange them in the correct order.

83. _____
84. Babylonians
85. _____
86. _____
87. Persians

Place an *S* on the line before the name, if those people were Semites.

88. ____ Assyrians
89. ____ Babylonians
90. ____ Phoenicians
91. ____ Egyptians
92. ____ Hebrews

Write your answer in complete sentences.

93-4. Why do we know less of the civilization in Mesopotamia than in Egypt?
95-6. Give one advantage and one disadvantage that came to Phoenicia and Palestine because of their location.
97-9. Why did the Phoenicians become great seamen? Give three good reasons.

B. Subjective evaluation—(criteria for)

Criteria for judging the unit

1. Have the pupils had an interest in the unit which has been maintained throughout the study?

2. Has there been evidence of a growing interest in historical material?
3. Do the pupils have a knowledge of the more important events?
4. Do the pupils bring in illustrative material?
5. Are the pupils adding new terms to their vocabulary?
6. Are the pupils careful to get accurate information?
7. Do the pupils attempt to trace the relationship between events?
8. Do the pupils have an appreciation for the contributions of these early civilizations?
9. Do the pupils make worthwhile contributions in the class discussion?
10. Do all pupils take part in the class discussion?
11. Do the pupils select and organize material for reports?
12. Do the pupils use reference material effectively?
13. Do pupils use all available helps: maps, time chart, dictionary, encyclopedia, etc.?
14. Do the pupils take good, brief notes?
15. To what degree have the pupils attained the outcomes outlined for this unit?

C. Evaluation of unit as planned (criticism to be noted *after* the teaching of the unit)

Perhaps the reader wonders why so many *methods* of teaching social studies have been suggested and no "best one" selected. The plain truth of the matter is that there is no "best one" for all situations. In fact, excellent teaching is done by each of the methods outlined. Some teachers use adaptations of them and others use parts of several methods. Generally, a teacher finds the method or combination of methods she can best use by trying out the various procedures. A good teacher is always experimenting and improving.

Much has been said and written about a *social studies laboratory*—a room or rooms where all the social studies materials are assembled. In it would be found books, maps, pictures, newspapers, magazines, still and motion picture projectors, tables, filing cases, blackboards, globes, cupboards, bulletin boards, and similar equipment. In short, it should be a place where a social studies class may lose itself in its work on any problem. The extra expense would undoubtedly be justified by the fine results of teaching and pupil development. There usually is a room devoted to social studies and there seem to be good reasons why it should be equipped as well as are the rooms housing the home economics center, manual training shop, or science laboratories. Sound

SOCIAL STUDIES LABORATORY

motion pictures are beginning to play a large part in the teaching of social studies in the rapidly increasing number of schools where sound projectors are found. Pupils learn more subject matter and remember it longer when motion pictures are used.[1] Motion pictures also affect favorably class participation in history reading under classroom conditions. This was found to be true when only one-sixth of the instruction was visual and the remainder of it oral. If it is not possible for a single small-school social studies laboratory to possess such a projector, possibly the schools of a whole county might purchase one in partnership. Laboratory work would undoubtedly take the classes into the community for first-hand studies of social, economic, religious, industrial, or other problems. These studies, of course, must always be prosecuted with common sense and with regard for the welfare of all concerned. In any event, a room with specially adapted equipment would undoubtedly add to the effectiveness of social studies teaching. Much equipment is possible even in a one-room rural school.

MEASUREMENT OF RESULTS OF TEACHING

The *measurement* of the results of teaching history is governed by the same general principles as measurement in other fields. This was discussed in a previous section. Specific applications are different for each subject-matter field. Measuring the results of teaching history means that the teacher must: (1) find whether the aims of the course have been attained; (2) ascertain if pupils have grown in ability in

[1] Knowlton, D. C. *Motion Pictures in History Teaching*, pp. 90-93. Yale University Press. 1929.

using history materials as a means (a) to detect and differentiate between cause and effect, (b) to see relations between events or developments, (c) to judge reliability of statements, (d) to select a few main items from many, (e) to organize materials into a given form; (3) test the pupil's knowledge of history facts; (4) find how pupils retain facts.

An example of a test which measures something more than knowledge of subject matter follows. This form may be used to test progress in the special problem type of study in upper grade history as mentioned above. A test of this nature was made by the teachers of the rural schools of one county[1] each semester, to cover the problems taught during that period.

HISTORY—GRADE 8—FIRST SEMESTER

Pupil's Name_____   Score—Total Number Right ____

Directions to the Teacher.   Read the instructions aloud to the pupils. Start on Part I with the textbook, Guide Book,[2] and some writing paper on the desk.   Allow exactly 3 *minutes*[3] for Part I.   Then all stop work.   Read the instructions for Part II and start pupils together on it.   Allow exactly 5 minutes.   All stop.   Read instructions and allow these amounts of time for the various parts of the test: Part III—3 minutes, Part IV—6 minutes, Part V—10 minutes, Part VI—8 minutes, Part VII—8 minutes, Part VIII—5 minutes, Part IX—5 minutes.

PART I.   Use your textbooks to find the following.   Write the answer on the line after each item.   Your score will depend upon accuracy and speed.

  A. On what page is found the discussion of the Missouri Compromise?..   ____

  B. Find the page of the map that shows what parts of America were claimed by England, by France, and by Spain..   ____

  C. (Continue with 6 or 8 items.)

PART II.   Locate the following facts by giving the number of the page and position on the page as: near top, middle, bottom.   Write the answer on the line after each item.   Your grade will depend upon accuracy and speed.

[1] Osceola County, Iowa.   Mrs. Gladys W. Bradley, County Superintendent.

[2] Moeller, H. C., Ringstrom, N. H.   *Pupils Guide Book in the Study of History Through the Problem Method.*   Follett Publishing Co.   1931.

[3] The time is fixed arbitrarily so that no pupil can complete all the items correctly in the time allowed.

    A. Find the year in which slaves were first brought to
        Virginia.................................... _____
    B. Find what the Freedman's Bureau was.............. _____
    C. Skim the section beginning at the bottom of page ___ and write
        the answers to these questions:
          1. (Put question here.)
          2.   (?)
          3. (Continue with 8 to 10 items.)

PART III.   Read each topic below and underline the two expressions
which would most likely tell something about the topic if looked
up in the index.

    A. The Explorations of England in America

        1. England, 2. Columbus, 3. Explorations, 4. Ships,
        5. Travel

    B. (Continue with 5 to 8 items.)

PART IV.   Fill in this outline.   Use text, pp. ___ to ___.

ACQUISITION OF OREGON

I. Location of Oregon country (a sentence)

II. Claims to the Oregon country   III. Settlement of the Oregon
                                          country

    A. _____   A. By the English
        1. _____   1. _____
        2. _____   2. _____
    B. _____   B. By the Americans
        1. _____   1. _____
        2. _____   2. _____
    C. _____   IV. Acquisition of the Oregon
        1. _____   country by the United
        2. _____   States
                                        A. _____
                                        B. _____

PART V.   Turn to Problem 21 in the Guide Book.

    A. Fill in the minor topics indicated by the lines.
        "I. Conditions out of which the problem developed
           B. Great Westward migrations
              1. Economic pressure in New England

                  a. _____
                  b. _____

             2. Desire to be independent land owners

                  a. _____
                  b. _____"

B. Answer these questions on separate paper.

    1. Explain the meaning of Problem 21 in your own words.

    2. Why was it necessary to think about internal trade?

    3. (Continue with 6–8 general items on this or other problems.)

PART VI. Turn to Problem 24 and write the answers to these questions on separate paper.

A. What does the problem ask you to find out?

B. Why did such a problem arise? (See Section I of Problem 24.)

C. (Continue with 6 or 8 items on the problem.)

PART VII. Write correctly in a sentence, on a separate paper, each of these words or groups of words to show that you know what it means. Be sure to number exactly as in this part.

    (1) crusade, (2) found a colony, (3) circumnavigate, (4) (Continue with 30 words or phrases.)

PART VIII. Write on separate paper, in your own words, the central thought in each of these paragraphs. Number the items as in the test.

A. Page ___, paragraph beginning, "Besides the planter . . . "

B. Page ___, paragraph beginning, "And it was not only . . . "

C.   (Continue with 6 to 8 items.)

PART IX. Do not use your textbook for this part of the test.

A. Answer by "yes" or "no," or complete the statement by filling in the blanks correctly.

    1. The slave trade was prohibited in the District of Columbia.. _____

    2. John Brown's raid was a good thing for the slaves.. _____

    3. (Continue with 8–10 items.)

    4. The Missouri Compromise dealt with the _____ question.

    5. (Continue for 20 blanks.)

B. Select the statement that best completes the sentence.

    1. The South was sorry to have Lincoln elected President because:

        a. He was a republican.

        b. They were afraid there would be war because he was opposed to slavery.

        c. He was a college graduate.

        (Also statements d. and e.)

    2. (Continue with 8 to 10 items.)

Thus tests of skills, knowledge, and judgment can be made objective to a large degree and fit the form and substance of the subject matter taught. Where a large number of teachers are involved in each grade, as in the one-room rural schools of a whole county, all may use the same test with a saving of time and a gain in usefulness of results. Good tests and test data over a given area should be saved; and after the less valuable items have been changed, they may be used again later in a similar situation. This gives eventually not only better tests but also tentative standards for that area. The teacher, however, in checking her pupils, frequently uses other factors which as yet cannot be accurately measured. For example, she considers a pupil's attitude, dependability, willingness to experiment, and accuracy of work, even though she may not record definite marks for them.

CHAPTER 18

GEOGRAPHY IN GRADES ABOVE THE PRIMARY

CONCEPTS AND OBJECTIVES

THE *concept* of *geography* has changed during the twentieth century from factual study about the earth's surface to a study of the relations of man to his environment. Geographical education was concerned forty years ago mainly with teaching the location of cities, rivers, countries, mountain ranges, and other types of facts. Today it is still interested in these things but in addition it asks: Why were they so located? Why did they grow in wealth and influence? What, if anything, in the environment caused men to live and work there? Such questions point to the inter-working of man and environment. The more recent geography is of this nature. These radical changes in basic aims have worked many important changes in methods of teaching, which will be discussed later in this section.

This idea of geography makes it fundamental. It is intimately related to man; to what he eats and wears, how he lives, and what he does. Perhaps the importance of geography might be shown by listing its various well developed and functioning phases. Home geography means man's relations to environment in the community. Industrial geography refers to the part production of great industries play in the life of man. Commercial geography has special reference to business, banks, and other related organizations. Physical geography deals more especially with the natural forces which play around and upon man. Political geography has to do with divisions of the earth arranged by man. Other sub-divisions of this immense field of subject matter could be named but these show its limitless extent. For use in the elementary grades, however, the field is limited to a selected mixture from many if not all of the above-mentioned fields. Even though the selections from the various fields are made with care, geography can easily develop into a very complicated subject. And unless the subject matter is kept very close to the pupils' experiences from the beginning, it can easily become just something to be memorized; and not something to be lived and assimilated.

These intimate relationships of geography are shown also in its connections with other subjects of the curriculum. Geography and history are so closely interwoven that one cannot be taught without the other. All types of production, geographic as well as others, are tied up with arithmetic. Nature study is a step-sister, health or hygiene is a first cousin, and government, the arts, and language have lesser but fairly close ties.

What *objectives* should be attained through developing pupils by using geography? The following may be listed as important:[1] (1) to train the processes of the intellect to function accurately when grappling with any problem connected with man's relationship to his environment; (2) to help pupils understand better the conditions of all peoples of the earth and to develop a spirit of co-operation with each and every one; (3) to develop the highest type of integrity and respect for all that is good, pure, and beneficial to mankind, accompanied by the courage to defend it; (4) to help pupils to secure knowledge of the actual physical conditions of the world in which they live, that is, to learn the world as it really is—not as they or the textbook writers might wish or guess it to be; (5) to teach the geographical facts needed to think intelligently in geographical terms, either by having the facts in mind or a knowledge of where they may be secured; (6) to imprint indelibly on each pupil's mind the advantages of thorough thinking before forming judgments or making decisions about man's relation to his surroundings.

The emphasis is on pupil development, using geography materials to produce it. Teachers should realize that in all probability, the most

[1] "Improving the Social Studies Instruction." *Research Bulletin of the N.E.A.* Vol. XV, No. 5, pp. 193-194. November, 1937. Adapted.

valuable service geography can render will be to help boys and girls to understand their foreign neighbors better and to think a bit more clearly on some of their home geographic problems. These materials should also help pupils realize more fully our great dependence on nature and on ourselves, that nature can be our mutual friend or common enemy, and that friendly co-operation gets mankind farther in the long run than individual or national selfishness.

METHODS OF TEACHING

The *methods* of *teaching* suited to the newer idea of geography are freer and give greater opportunities to teachers to develop latent pupil powers. The statements of a yearbook on geography [1] supply helpful suggestions. The best method of teaching geography, or any social studies subject, seems to include three constituents: "purposing, thinking and activity learning." These should probably not be regarded as three separate parts of a method for they really are different phases of an activity. Any intelligently selected activity, whether it is learning or creating, must have a purpose. This would be preceded by a background of information and experience gained from conversation, books, motion or still pictures, or from a trip from which questions, problems, and ideas would spring. It must be accompanied by thinking, using the background of information to define the purpose and aligning it with other facts in approaching the solution. If anything is done about it, additional learning by physical or other types of activity would follow. A learning activity in this procedure has a definite place in the learning act—it helps in thinking. Or as Reeder puts it, "Activity is a method of thinking." Activity is a positive force valuable in its own right—not something dragged in to bolster a sagging section of the main procedure. Hence, an activity in teaching geography would be valuable only insofar as it aids in "a program of worthwhile learnings." Otherwise it "is likely to be a vapid, unorganized series of doings, resulting in little worthwhile learning and in dissatisfaction and poor study and poor character habits on the part of the children."

The method best suited to utilize the foregoing factors, according to

[1] Reeder, Edwin H. "Method in Geography." *32nd Yearbook of the National Society for the Study of Education.* Chapter XX, pp. 315-331. Public School Publishing Co. 1933. Adapted.

Reeder, is the *problem method*, because these factors are "the backbone of the so-called 'problem method in geography'." It consists of locating a problem by the pupils, generally as a result of stimulation by a wealth of interesting materials or experiences. These usually are presented, or at least organized, by the teacher. After a problem has been found and defined in terms understood by the group, they are ready to work on it (do the thinking); searching books and materials widely to secure the best information available. Activities are a natural part of the procedure. It may be mental activity, such as reading references, summarizing, picking out main ideas, organizing an outline. If the activity is of the construction type, things may need to be made, such as maps, charts, pictures, arranging an exhibit. In any case, the "activity" grows out of the problem or problems being solved. It helps to solve the problem. It is not the whole thing itself, not the end to be attained; only a means through which to reach it.

One other value of activity learning suggested by Reeder is that it necessitates a large mass of details. Children get their broad concepts from the innumerable details they acquire in support of that concept. Children's books bear out the truth of this statement. For example, abstractions or geographical personalities, like "people of the hot, dry

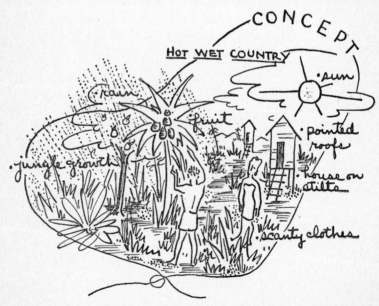

regions," or "people of the hot, wet regions," would need hundreds of details to make the mental picture. The brighter and more interesting the details, the more colorful the picture they evoke, and the more lasting its impression on the pupils' minds.

Some *erroneous conceptions* of the use of the problem method are listed by Reeder: (1) The worth of a problem is not determined by its scope—that is, the amount of materials or territory it covers. Evaluation should be made on the degree of activity it evokes in terms of purposing, thinking, and actual worth-while learning activities. (2) The problem method of study is not in opposition to good journey or to topical geography. The smaller parts of a journey may be organized into the finest type of challenging problem or question. (3) The selection of a problem is not the first step in the study of a new unit or topic. The background comes first if the pupils aid in selecting problems. This background may be the problem just solved; but it must be present in the pupils' minds to enable them to deal intelligently with the new subject matter.

The *project method* is discussed elsewhere (see pp. 438-439). It is used frequently in geography teaching; hence its special application to this field of subject matter might be reviewed with profit.

Some *types* of projects are outlined by Kilpatrick,[1] for example, (1) construction projects—such as making a model farm, making a Swiss mountain scene, making a Dutch landscape; (2) enjoyment projects—such as taking a trip and reporting on it, constructing a model airplane and flying it, reading a book; (3) problem projects—such as gathering information on vocations for use in class and library, making a population survey of the neighborhood for school use, serving a dinner to one hundred persons to build up an expense fund; (4) learning projects—such as reading for information to use on a journey, learning how to operate a tractor, learning how to keep books for a certain company.

Teachers who have had no experience with work in projects would do well to start with rather simple ones and plan them carefully from beginning to end before carrying them out in class. Plans and supervision a bit too strict in these first efforts are more commendable than

[1] Kilpatrick, W. H. "Introductory Statement: Definition of Terms." *Teachers College Record* 22:449. Adapted.

lax control and guidance which might decrease the values or endanger the success of the projects.

Other types of procedure are used by successful geography teachers. One commonly employed is *trips* or *journeys*, either imaginary or real. Even when the journeys are wholly in the imagination, they may be very stimulating and carried out in a good class atmosphere. These are prepared for in the same way real journeys are. Reports of progress along the way may be made in class and a final one should be drawn up after the journey is over. A special program may be conducted to celebrate the safe return. This type of procedure can be made fascinating even though imaginary, if pupils can be induced to report details, such as experience with the rancher's dog when they ran out of gas in the middle of the night, or what happened when they camped in the wildest part of the national forest preserve. The incidents, of course, must be plausible as indicated by the references read and the trip taken. Real trips need planning by teacher and pupils and should have very definite purposes.

Pupils develop effectively when they put themselves into the situations they study.

A PLAY-

Another procedure closely related to the journey idea is that of *dramatization*. This requires definite details and careful organization of the details gleaned from the reading of the class. In turn, these are put into form for dramatizing. Such a project would correlate with both written and oral English and with art, if it were produced in public. The reading might take the pupils into history, science, and other fields. This type of procedure, if staged for other persons, passes on educational benefits to those who see and hear it. For example, in a presentation of the Constitutional Convention, the audience would have a very real portrayal of the scene as well as information about what was said and insight into the characteristics of its members.

Some teachers have used *stories* to focus attention on a given country or region. Pearl Buck's story *The Good Earth* might help a class understand China. Travel stories, either as a whole or in part, serve to clarify geographic concepts and to stimulate learning. Especially is this true if the stories contain interesting detail and are well written.

Geography lends itself quite readily to almost every variety of *socialized class work* whether it be individual questions or work by committees making an attack as a class group upon a selected unit of work. This will hold regardless of the class organization. One member of the group may be the leader directing operations; there may be committee groups each with its leader; or the teacher may at times assume charge to keep activities at top efficiency.

Activities of a *laboratory* type may be carried out in the geography study, such as experiments with apparatus to show moon phases, seasons, causes of tides, rain, dew; or activities, such as making surface maps, various types of shelter, clothing, and tools. It would be best for the geography teacher to utilize different procedures. Undoubtedly, this would add variety and give opportunity to use the method best suited to the subject matter taught.

ILLUSTRATIVE MATERIALS

Common use is made of the *unit-problem* combination in geography as well as in other subject-matter fields. The unit [1] outlined below illustrates that type of organization for the eighth-grade level. This attack may be used in smaller units than the one outlined in some detail here. In that case, the organization would have the same form but the length of time required would be shorter.

I. The Unit: A study of certain phases of the economic, social, and cultural importance of New York City today with historical backgrounds

[1] Organized and used by Mr. David B. Hawk, student teacher under the direction of Miss Ernestine Smith, Supervising Critic in Social Studies, Campus High School, Iowa State Teachers College, Cedar Falls, Iowa.

II. Objectives:
  A. Understandings
    1. Realization of the importance of New York City in modern civilization
       a. America's chief port of entry and departure
       b. Railway and distribution center
       c. Manufacturing center
       d. Financial center
       e. Cultural center
    2. The importance of historical and geographic factors in the development of a great city

  B. Appreciations
    1. Realization of the part New York City plays in our daily life through the radio and newspapers
    2. Realization of the worth of individual contributions by various members of the class who are able to supply special information

  C. Attitudes
    1. Broadening of horizons through the realization that a city hundreds of miles away is important to our daily lives
    2. Creation of attitudes of co-operation and mutual respect through practice in discussion and individual research and reports

  D. Skills
    1. Collecting material from pictures, maps, magazine articles, books, encyclopedias, etc., on a given topic
    2. Integrating the known with the unknown material
    3. Making maps and reading maps
    4. Giving oral reports

III. Vocabulary:

mainland	free port	cantilever bridge
strait	mercantile district	subway
sound	residential district	elevated
harbor	financial center	tubes
tides	suburb	ferries
channel	borough	roof garden
bar	plaza	express highway
shore currents	Palisades	aqueduct
sediment	zoo	housing program
shallows	menagerie	folk festival
draft	botanical garden	immigrant
hinterland	suspension	museum
docks	span	opera
		terminal

IV. Outline of Unit:

   A. New York and vicinity—Principal land and water masses
1. Principal land masses
   a. Long Island
   b. New York mainland
   c. New Jersey
   d. Staten Island
   e. Manhattan Island
2. Smaller islands
   a. Ellis Island
   b. Bedloe Island
   c. Others (Governors Island, etc.)
3. Hudson River
4. Bays
   a. Upper New York Bay
   b. Lower New York Bay
5. Straits
   a. The Narrows
   b. East River
   c. Harlem River
6. Larger bodies of water
   a. Long Island Sound
   b. Atlantic Ocean
7. Bridges and tunnels
   a. Brooklyn Bridge
   b. Triboro Bridge
   c. George Washington Bridge
   d. Holland Tunnel
   e. Lincoln Tunnel

   B. New York Harbor
1. Present mouth of the Hudson at the Battery is 18 miles from the entrance to New York harbor.
2. Divided into Lower Bay and Upper Bay, the harbor is like a giant hour-glass.
3. Through its neck, the Narrows, the sand and refuse-laden tides ebb and flow.
4. The entrance to Lower Bay is the 5-mile stretch of ocean northeastward from Sandy Hook, N. J., to Rockaway Point, Queens.
5. Ambrose Channel, 7 miles long, 2000 ft. wide, and dredged to a depth of 40 feet, is the chief of three channels crossing Sandy Hook bar and allowing ships into Lower Bay.
6. The harbor occupies a northwest angle toward which southwesterly winds sweep from a great distance,

and in the gateway the wind-driven shore currents meet and deposit some of their materials. The Hudson, too, carries down sediment. This bar grows, hooking away from the wind. The bar can obstruct but never close the channel, for the rush of the ebb tide sweeps clean.

7. The Narrows connecting Lower Bay with Upper Bay is a strait about a mile wide between Staten Island and Long Island.

8. As one enters the Lower Bay, Coney Island stands to the right.

9. Farther off is the Rockaway Peninsula, shielding Jamaica Bay from the ocean.

10. As one continues northward through the main or Anchorage Channel of the Upper Bay, Brooklyn lies to the east and Jersey City to the west, while straight ahead the towers of Manhattan thrust at the sky.

11. Main Channel is a half mile wide and 40 to 90 ft. deep.

12. There are two other channels into Upper Bay; one to the east, Buttermilk Channel leading to the East River and separated from the Main Channel by a broad shoal and Governors Island; the second to the west, Kill van Kull, now dredged to 30 ft. and giving access to Newark Bay.

13. The most extensive shallows in the Upper Bay are in the western part. Almost in mid-channel lies Liberty or Bedloe Island. Nearby Ellis Island is really three islands joined by causeways and has been built up from 3 to 27 acres.

14. The rise and fall of the tide in the harbor averages only about 4 feet, thus permitting the pier system. Ships of every size may enter and leave at any time.

15. The total water frontage of New York City is 578.4 miles.

16. From the Battery to about 14th Street, where Manhattan loses its triangular shape, the Hudson is officially the North River.

17. The Harlem River cuts off Manhattan Island to the north and connects the East River with the Hudson.

18. As the East River extends to the east, it widens out into Long Island Sound.[1]

C. Important points to be known about New York City
    1. Phenomenal growth of New York City (Graph)—Three historical movements aided greatly in causing the great increase in population.

[1] Federal Writers Project. *New York Panorama*. Random House. 1939. Adapted.

    a. The Erie Canal—1825

    b. Building of the great railroads—1840 to 1870

    c. Steam-driven ocean ships—1880 on

2. Capital of the United States

    a. Washington, first President of he new government was inaugurated here April 30, 1789.

    b. Place was Federal Hall (now the Subtreasury Building) in Wall Street.

3. The Hudson River

    a. There is enough current and flow of the tide to sweep the sediment out of the channel.

    b. On the east bank of the river opposite upper Manhattan are the high cliffs known as the Palisades.

4. Manhattan Island

    a. Area is about 22 squares miles, about $13\frac{1}{2}$ miles long, maximum width two and one-fourth miles.

    b. Contains great commercial, financial, and mercantile institutions and famous museums, libraries, cathedrals, and railway stations.

5. Staten Island or Richmond

    a. Mainly a residential district with increasing number of industries.

    b. Contains the new "free port," 18 acres of land, 60 acres of adjacent water, 4 piers and a new 7-story building.

    c. The Staten Island ferries are famous.

6. Brooklyn

    a. Mainly a residential district with a considerable number of industries.

    b. Prospect Park is noted for its natural beauty.

    c. The Navy maintains a ship repairing and training yard here.

7. The Bronx

    a. The Bronx Zoo is the world's largest.

    b. The New York Botanical Garden is here.

    c. The Bronx is the home of the Yankee Stadium.

8. Broadway

    a. Begins at the Battery and runs diagonally across Manhattan, crosses the Harlem River, and runs north through the Bronx to the city limits.

    b. Is lined with shops, hotels, hurches, and residences.

9. Wall Street
   a. Historical reason or the name
   b. Important as the great financial center

10. Important bridges
    a. Brooklyn Bridge is oldest.
    b. Williamsburg Bridge connects Manhattan and Brooklyn.
    c. Queensboro Bridge is a cantilever bridge.
    d. Hellgate Bridge is a large span bridge and maintains rail communication with New England.
    e. George Washington bridge newly built, has the second longest span of any bridge.
    f. Triboro Bridge is made up of 4 bridges over water and 12 over land.

11. Statue of Liberty
    a. Statue is of "Liberty Enlightening the World" by Bartholdi and stands on Bedloe Island.
    b. It is 151 ft. high and stands on a pedestal 155 ft. high.
    c. It was finished in 1883 and unveiled in 1886.

12. Radio City
    a. Is on Manhattan around 5th Ave. and 50th St.
    b. Is the greatest building unit of modern times (11 buildings).
    c. Buildings house radio, theatre, and business office units with roof gardens on top.
    d. Rockefeller Plaza is a street and parkway in the center of the unit.
    e. The highest building is the 850 ft. RCA Building.
    f. One of the buildings houses the famous Museum of Science and Industry.

13. Grand Central Station
    a. Covers an area of 70 acres.
    b. Handles annually about 85,000,000 passengers.

14. Central Park
    a. Embraces 800 acres in the heart of Manhattan.
    b. Contains many fine works of sculpture.
    c. Has a menagerie.

15. City Transportation Systems
    a. Subway and elevated are necessary to take care of the traffic in Manhattan, Brooklyn, and Queens.
    b. Brooklyn still uses cable cars, but trolley cars have vanished from Manhattan and the Bronx.
    c. Many express highways are necessary.

      d. Many ferries are necessary for people, autos, and railway cars in addition to the bridges and tunnels.

      e. Subway cars use tubes under the rivers.

16. Times Square

      a. Is the busiest part of New York day and night.

      b. Is the biggest amusement center in the world. (Broadway and 42nd Street)

      c. Crowds gather here on New Year's Eve and on election nights.

17. Holland and Lincoln Tunnels

      a. Holland Tunnel was first to be built, extends from Canal St. to Jersey City, N. J.

      b. Lincoln Tunnel was patterned after the Holland Tunnel. Goes from West 39th Street to Weehawken, N. J. Has wider roadway, glass tiled walls and ceiling.

18. Tenement district

      a. There are nine city blocks each housing more than 3000.

      b. In 5 years $46,000,000 has been spent on public housing.

19. Harlem

      a. Harlem is located on Manhattan Island north of Central Park.

      b. It has a solid negro population.

      c. Less than one-fifth of the city's negro population was born there.

20. Foreign speaking districts

      a. Among the important foreign groups in New York are Greek, Arabian, Syrian, Turkish, Czechoslovak, Chinese, Spanish, English, Irish, Swedish, Finnish, Danish, French, German, Hungarian, Italian, Japanese, Jewish, Swiss, Rumanian, Polish, and Russian.

      b. There is a Folk Festival Council which arranges and announces folk festivals.

21. Metropolitan Museum of Art

      a. Is the largest storehouse of fine arts in the country.

      b. Contains ancient sculptures and other works of art and paintings by the world's greatest painters.

22. Metropolitan Opera Company

      a. The world's greatest singing stars perform here.

        b. Offers the most refined and expensive type of
entertainment patronized by every class of
people.

  23. City water supply

        a. Comes mainly from the Catskill Mountains where
two large creeks have been impounded for
water.

        b. The Catskill aqueduct through the 18-mile Shon-
daken tunnel brings the water to New York
City.

  24. World's Fair

        a. Commemorated the 150th anniversary of the
establishment of our government.

        b. Purpose was to mirror our modern industrial civili-
zation.

  25. City Hall Park

        a. The old City Hall is a good example of nine-
teenth century architecture.

        b. Here Lafayette was feted when he returned to
America after the Revolution.

  26. Ellis Island

        a. Here immigrants are landed for inspection by
health officials before they are permitted to
come into the country.

        b. Ellis Island is really three islands joined by cause-
ways. It has been built up from the floor of
the bay from 3 acres to 27 acres.

  27. Coney Island

        a. Is a sort of sand bar now connected with Brook-
lyn.

        b. Contains a bathing beach and an amusement park.

  28. Jersey City

        a. This city is really a suburb of New York City
except that it is across the state line.

D. A problem to solve: In 1790 New York City was one of the
smaller cities of the United States; why has it
grown so tremendously since then, and especially why has it far surpassed in size cities like
Boston and Philadelphia which were at first
larger?

  1. Large harbor, 578-mile shoreline, deep

  2. Protection from wind, waves; favorable tides

  3. Atlantic location, nearest Europe

  4. Increase in trans-oceanic travel through use of the
steamship

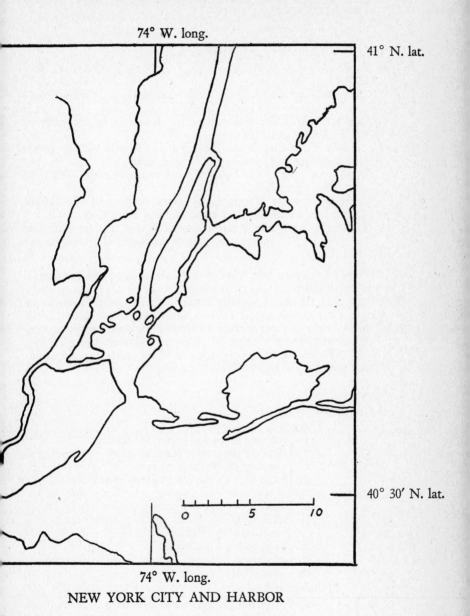

74° W. long.

41° N. lat.

40° 30' N. lat.

0   5   10

74° W. long.

NEW YORK CITY AND HARBOR

     5. Entrance to the Hudson-Mohawk gateway to the West
       a. Trails
       b. Canals
       c. Railroads
     6. Growth of industrialism and trade

V. Approach

We have studied all the important regions of the United States. Now we will study America's largest city. I wonder if you can think of any reason why we should leave the study of New York City until the last?

1. New York City is the focal point of almost all the goods entering and leaving the United States.
2. More industries and kinds of work center in New York than any other place.
3. Some or most of practically every product of the United States sooner or later come to New York City.
4. New York is the greatest American city, and as such sets the lead in radio, newspapers, fashions, and many other things.

One of the very best ways to learn about any place is through studying pictures. That is one of the ways we are going to study about New York. I wonder if each one of you would like to bring some pictures that explain something about New York. (Don't bring just *any* picture of New York you happen to see. Look around for a number of pictures, and then bring for the bulletin board one or two which you think really explain something about the city.)

VI. Assimilative Materials

  A. Activities
    1. Class
       a. Studying maps for important features
       b. Locating important features on an outline map
       c. Listening to oral reports
       d. Discussing things of interest about New York City
       e. Looking at lantern pictures of New York City
       f. Answering test questions from references to the outline map mentioned above
       g. Discussing the problem which was given
       h. Discussing items of current interest about New York City
    2. Individual
       a. Collecting pictures for the bulletin board and for the lantern lesson
       b. Solving a problem

        c. Looking up and giving a report on a special topic about New York City

        d. Making a graph on population growth

B. Materials

   1. Texts

        a. Rugg, H. O. *An Introduction to American Civilization* (maps and graphs only)

        b. Smith, J. Russell, *Men and Resources*, pp. 51–59

   2. Illustrated reference books and magazines on points of interest about New York City

        a. Sun Dial Press, *Going to the Fair*

        b. Bercovici, *Around the World in New York*

        c. Federal Writers' Project, *New York Panorama*

        d. Journal of Geography, Vol. 38, No. 9 (Dec. 1939), p. 355, *Types of River Crossings*

        e. *Fortune Magazine*, Vol. 20, No. 1 (July 1939)

        f. *The World Almanac*, 1939

   3. Maps

   4. Newspaper articles and pictures

C. Study guides and exercises

   1. Points to be located on outline map (principal land and water masses, "A" in Outline)

   2. Map questions for use with outline map prepared by the pupil

        a. What two boroughs are on Long Island?

        b. What two boroughs are separate islands themselves?

        c. What one borough is on the mainland of North America?

        d. What is the name of the bridge that connects Manhattan Island with New Jersey?

        e. What is the name of the strait of water between Brooklyn and Richmond?

        f. What famous street runs the length of Manhattan Island?

        g. A famous bridge connects the Bronx with two other boroughs. What is its name?

        h. What is the largest borough?

        i. Where are most of the skyscrapers?

        j. What is the most famous bridge connecting Manhattan and Brooklyn?

        k. To get to Manhattan, you must go either under or over one of three rivers. What are the three?

   3. Solving the problem

      (Problem and solution in "D" in Outline)

VII. Evaluation
    A. Pupil evaluation
        1. The pupils said they enjoyed studying the unit particularly:
           a. the discussion of common experiences in which knowledge of New York had a part,
           b. the visual education activities.
        2. In a concluding discussion the pupils signified:
           a. they felt they knew more about New York City than they had before,
           b. they would be able in the future to interpret references to New York more meaningfully,
           c. they appreciated better the importance of New York City in our daily lives.

    B. Teacher evaluation
        1. Work of children
           a. Discussion abilities were improved through the inclusion of interesting and meaningful material and the pupils took part enthusiastically.
           b. The ability to find and report on information was fostered, including skill in the use of reference books.
           c. Considerable progress was made in knowledge of maps and use of maps, an outcome which seemed quite important.
           d. Pupils manifested ability in solving the problem.
           e. Interest was stimulated in getting information from the various sources (radios, newspapers, pictures, etc.).
        2. The unit as planned provides for:
           a. Better understanding of the environment,
           b. Appreciation of values coming to us from other localities and other peoples,
           c. Appreciation of the interrelation of human life,
           d. Practice in the skills of
              (1) Making and using maps,
              (2) Using newspapers and the radio,
              (3) Finding information for reference,
              (4) Making oral reports.

In *developing good habits* of *study*, teachers in smaller schools, as in one-room rural schools, face certain problems which apply especially to them; one of which is the problem of time. Good study habits seem to develop best when the teacher and the class work together as for example, in the class instruction period. These periods are usually

Trip to Brazil
1. Where is Brazil?
2. What climate?
3. Why warm....?
4. What exports.....?

Teacher-pupil organized units stimulate
growth in healthy study habits.

short in the smaller schools, which frequently use a somewhat formal or fixed recitation program. Regardless of what our ideas of a formal recitation program are, thousands of schools use it in some form, and probably will continue to do so for years to come. Even when it is exchanged for something better, teachers will still be confronted with the necessity of providing more or less specific practice on fundamental skills in study. Consequently, teachers in these smaller schools need procedures through which they can develop desirable study habits by using portions of the subject matter the pupils are mastering. In this way they teach pupils how to study geography, for example, by using geography subject matter. In general, this procedure approximates the open-book method of study although it differs in some important respects. The materials illustrated below were worked out by a county group of one-room rural school teachers to meet the needs of their beginning fourth grade, with a 20-minute class instruction period twice a week—Monday and Wednesday. The pupils had no previous experience with geography textbooks. The "units" were arbitrarily arranged into convenient sections with work for a week period. This is frankly a textbook arrangement by which pupils use the geography text partly to learn to work and at the same time to get command of geography materials. The outline [1] of the "units" for the entire year should be in each teacher's hands. Only portions of the different sections are given.

4th Grade Geography—Unit Five[2] (Pages 8-10 and Review)

Our Neighbors Near and Far[3]

I. Class instruction period—*Monday* (20 minutes)
    A. Reading directions (or teacher's use)
        1. Vocabulary study (words and phrases pupils might not be able to use in the reading)
        2. Study-type reading exercises (on new materials)
            "Open your book to page 8. Close it on your finger. When I say 'Go,' open your book and find as quickly as you can the word or phrase which tells the answer to the exercise. When you know the answer, close your book on your finger again." (The teacher may read an item (as below) orally before she starts the pupils to work, or it may be read aloud by a pupil after which all start to work. The aim is to see who can find the correct answer first. Answers may be given orally and checked immediately or written and checked later. The idea is to stimulate each pupil to do his best in rate of work and in comprehension. The exercises may be of any desired type. Fact items are usually difficult enough for early intermediate grades using new materials. Exercises covering longer sections of subject matter may be used for a class of better or more advanced pupils.)
            a. Find the name that tells what we use to see our world all at one time.

---

[1] Such outlines may be constructed by combining the efforts of teachers. Each teacher works out a "unit" from sample "units" which are provided. These are combined and in this way a county group of one-room rural teachers may make an outline for a whole year in a very short time.

[2] Outline as used in the rural schools of Crawford County, Iowa. F. N. Olry, County Superintendent.

[3] Carpenter, Frances. *Our Neighbors Near and Far.* American Book Co. 1933.

      b. Find the sentence that tells where we would have to live if we came to explore our earth.

      c. How much more water than land is there on the earth?

      d. What direction are we looking on the earth when we look toward the North Pole?

      e. What do the winding black lines show on a geography map?

      f. (Etc. to utilize the class instruction time)

B. Assignment for seatwork to follow the Monday class instruction period (30 minutes)

    Directions. "Write the answers to the questions and do the things suggested. Begin with the First Section and take the items in order. Then take the second section, and so on. You should do as much of this work alone as you can." (The teacher should see that each pupil does more and more of his work independent of teacher and other pupils. A time limit is likely to induce greater application and concentration of effort.)

  1. First section (facts to find)

      a. What color is water on the globe?

      b. How many great land masses are there?

      c. Name some ways maps may be printed.

      d. (Etc. to cover main facts of unit)

  2. Second section (problems to solve)

      a. Why do we picture our world in two parts? (See top of page 8.)

      b. Why not take globes on a journey instead of maps?

      c. Do you think it would be a good thing to make a museum for geography? Why?

      d. (Etc. to cover the main problem situations of the unit)

  3. Third section (things to do)

      a. Work out the "Globe Exerise" on page 9. Be sure to get each exercise correct.

      b. Bring at least one kind of map to school.

      c. Find the Big Dipper tonight and make a drawing showing the Earth, North Star, and Big Dipper.

      d. (Etc. to keep all pupils profitably busy)

II. Class instruction period—*Wednesday* (20 minutes)

A. Check the seatwork of Monday. (15 minutes) (Time divisions are only suggestive.)

  1. Facts—teacher reads answers and pupils check own papers (2 minutes)

  2. Problems—pupils discuss and react to these (10 minutes)

  3. Things to do—if there is time, if not teacher scores (3 minutes)

B. Continue work on Unit 5 (5 minutes).

(Teacher and class work together on these exercises. Pupils of all abilities should be encouraged to read as rapidly and as well as they can in these directed reading exercises. Pupils complete all unfinished exercises at their seats in the study period.)

1. Exercises (over same subject matter as Monday)
    a. Find the section that tells what we use as a model of the world.
    b. Find the paragraph that begins "The point at the top of the globe," etc. Write two words that tell the main thought of this paragraph.
    c. Find the heading "Map Symbols." Read the second paragraph. Which sentence in the paragraph tells best what the whole paragraph is about?
    d. (Etc. to cover any points which may have been omitted)

2. Review of Units One to Five—pages 1–10
    a. Find the page that shows a picture of a Bedouin home.
    b. Why does the earth seem flat? How could you prove it?
    c. Which section tells how to find directions by the sun?
    d. What is one important thing we must know before we start on a journey?
    e. What paragraph tells you how to make a compass chart?
    f. (Etc. to cover the main points of the units)

III. Class instruction period for *Monday* of the next week
    A. Check seat work of previous Wednesday. (5–10 minutes)
    B. Class reading on new material—page 11 and following— of the textbook (5–10 minutes)
    C. Seatwork assignment
        1. Facts
        2. Problems
        3. Things to do

IV. Class instruction period—*Wednesday*
    Same procedure as previous week

Teachers who have but one grade or subject probably will not need such "cut and dried" plans as outlined above. But the teacher who has six or eight grades working in a more or less formalized program can use all the plans she may get with benefit. Such outlines are not followed slavishly by any teacher, but the ideas and background are used, as well as sections and specific items which fit into the class needs.

Some teachers entrust the abilities to *interpret* and *use maps, pictures, graphs,* and *other tools* of *geography* to incidental teaching. Research shows that such important factors cannot with prudence be left to chance learning or teaching. It has also been demonstrated that intensive training even for a short period greatly improves skill in the use of the tools of geography. Mary Thorp [1] used five tests, one each on: globe study, map reading, climatic elements, index and appendix, and graph reading. These tests were given without previous pupil training (except one group) to 556 pupils of grades IV to VIII inclusive of large city, small city, village, and rural-consolidated school systems. The one group of sixth-grade pupils was given intensive training for a six-week period. The table below shows selected items typical of the results of this experiment in per cents of pupils responding correctly.

Comparison of Untrained and Trained Pupils from Certain Grades in Ability to Use Geographic Tools	Untrained	Trained
	IV VIII	VI Exper.
A. Globe Study: 1. General knowledge of globe factors........	71 91	96
2. Latitude as a means of globe location......	0 41	79
B. Map Reading: 1. Understanding and use of legend..........	16 58	92
2. Ability to find required map and to use legend with accuracy..................	0 62	71
C. Climatic Elements: 1. Knowledge of wind belt.............	0 19	67
2. Understanding of rain-bearing winds..	0 4	38
3. Ability to interpret isothermal readings	0 29	79
D. Index and Appendix: 1. Use made of the key and index......	9 65	92
2. Ability to locate an exact bit of information a.	0 53	75
b.	0 42	75
3. Power to interpret pictures........	34 58	88
E. Graph Reading: 1. Ability to read a picture graph..........	27 74	96
2. Ability to construct a graph from data..	13 87	96
3. Ability to read a bar graph.............	6 74	88
4. Ability to tabulate reading from a line graph.............................	9 79	92

The foregoing data leave little room for doubt that the use of geographic tools should be given special attention, and that direct

[1] Thorp, Mary T. "Studies of the Ability of Pupils in Grades Four to Eight to Use Geographic Tools." *32nd Yearbook, National Society for Study of Education.* pp. 494-506. Public School Publishing Co. 1933.

benefits come if proper training is given. The experiment does not seem to indicate just when this training should be given. It probably would be when each tool is taken up for study, with frequent use made of it in later work until the use becomes habit. Teachers often do not appreciate the variety and difficulty of skills required to use these tools intelligently. In map reading, for example, some of the skills are: symbols for natural features, scale of miles, meridians and parallels, political units, crop regions, climate belts, surface features, such as mountains, rivers, elevation, and slopes. To read a globe, all of these must be known plus information about the earth's rotation, inclination, relation to sun, moon, etc. Reading pictures and graphs is almost as complex, depending on the detail of interpretation required.

Different kinds of *maps* are put to various uses in the average geography class. Outline maps are almost a necessity in the study of facts of location, both in original learning and in reviews or tests of such facts. Relief or surface maps are a distinct aid in understanding the influences of topography. The ordinary wall map is used for locational facts, political divisions, routes of transportation, and other man-made factors. The blackboard maps are used by both teacher and pupils for illustrative purposes. Maps of this type are usually drawn on black rubber cloth and mounted on a spring roller. Materials can be erased from them; hence they can be used indefinitely. If any time at all is put on making formal maps, it probably will be best utilized at the end of a unit of work to summarize the materials covered. Putting a large amount of time on such activities is of doubtful value.

MEASUREMENT OF RESULTS OF TEACHING

Measuring the results of teaching in geography is related closely to doing the same thing in history or any other content subject. The more formal testing is done mostly by two types of tests. (1) Standard tests are a general type. Such tests in geography and other similar subjects are often invalid because they do not cover exactly what has been taught, or the skills which have been developed in a particular classroom. A standard test is helpful when a given field has been completed and the teacher wishes to measure her pupils' development against the standards for that grade. (2) Tests improvised by the teacher are usually in objective or semi-objective form, and are made to include the important items of the subject matter covered. Teachers also set up tests to cover reading or study skills, using the content subject materials studied. The teacher will probably find most value in the tests she herself makes, both of a diagnostic and survey nature. She can use the different types of maps, charts, tables of data, and the like to make interesting and revealing tests. Many present-day teachers are discarding the purely memory tests for the more flexible ones which use textbooks, wall maps, and other helps in the examinations. By its nature, geography is well suited to this type of examination. Instead of facts only, such a test can check ability to solve problems and show the results with a high degree of objectivity. If a teacher wishes to check growth in ability to study geography as well as ability to recall it, a test using the materials covered during the last semester or other period of time may be constructed. The test below is one used for fourth-grade geography by one group of one-room rural teachers. It applies equally well in any classroom organization.

Fourth Grade Study-type Reading Test [1]

Total Test Score_____

Pupil_____ Township_____ Dist. _____ Date_____
Age_____Birthday_____

TEST I (VOCABULARY) 10 POINTS   Score ____

Directions: Look at the first item in Column A. Find in Column B the expression with which the first item of Column A is connected and write a "1" on the dotted line in front of that expression in Column B. The first item is marked correctly. Now look at the second item in Column A. Find the expression in Column B that goes with it and put a "2" in front of it. Then look at the third item of Column A and put a "3" in front of the right expression of Column B and so forth until all the items of Column A are used. Do not use your book.

Column A	*Column B*
1. peninsula	____ A line which runs east and west around the middle of the globe
2. strait	__1__ A body of land almost surrounded by water
3. equator	
4. sand dunes	____ A narrow strip of water connecting two larger bodies
5. isthmus	
6. nomads	____ People that wander from place to

[1] Over subject matter in Atwood-Thomas. *Home Life in Far-Away Lands.* Ginn & Co. 1929.

7. (Continue to 10 points.)   place during the year

_____ Hills of sand

_____ A narrow strip of land connecting two larger bodies of water

_____ (Continue to 12 items—two not applicable.)

TEST II (USE OF INDEX) 8 POINTS   Score _____

Directions: Using your geography, find the answer to each of the following questions and write it on the line at the right. Your score will be the number of answers you have right in three minutes. Work as rapidly and accurately as you can. Do not begin the next test until told to do so.

1. On what page would you look to find out something about Genoa?.................................... _____

2. On what pages is there a map of the United States?.... _____

3. On what page is there a discussion of "lines of latitude"? _____

4. On what pages does the geography tell about the "Big Dipper"?... _____

5. (Continue to 8 points.)

TEST III (SKIMMING) 10 POINTS   Score _____

Directions: Using your geography, find the answers to the following questions and write them on the line at the right. Your score will be the number of answers you can get right in four minutes. Work as rapidly and accurately as you can. Put a number and check in the right column to answer the question. T means "near the top of the page"; M means "near the middle of the page"; B means "near the bottom of the page." Do not begin the next test until told to do so.

Page	T	M	B

1. On what page and part of the page does your book tell for whom the men send when they find a herd of wild reindeer?........

2. On what page and part of the page is Fig. 113?.............. ....

3. On what page and part of the page does your book say that Bergen is "one of the great fishing and fish exporting ports of the world"?..............................

4. (Continue to 5 items.)

TEST IV (RATE AND COMPREHENSION)   Score _____

Words per minute

Directions: In a moment you will be asked to turn to a page in your geography and find the section headed "The Uses of the Walrus." This section has six paragraphs and is continued on the next page. When your teacher says "Go," read these six paragraphs *once* as rapidly and as well as you can.   When you finish raise your hand so your teacher can take the exact time it took you to read the section.   As soon as this is done, turn this page around and answer the questions about the paragraphs you have just read.   Turn to page 44 in your geography.   Find the section headed "The Uses of the Walrus" and at once close your book on your finger and be ready.

Score ———

Questions: (To be answered briefly by the pupils after reading the section of geography *once*)   10 points

1. Who will help Nandla's father bring home the walrus if he kills one? ———
2. What is the name of the thick layer of fat on the walrus just beneath the skin? ———
3. Do Eskimos eat blubber? ———
4. What keeps the meat from spoiling when it is stored away? ———
5. What is made from the walrus hide? ———
6. (Continue to 10 items.)

Test V (Sentence Meaning) 8 Points   Score ———

Directions: Turn to page 49 in your geography.   Find the paragraph headed "Winter Clothes," and number the sentences 1, 2, 3, at the beginning of each one.   There are 3 sentences.   Using your book, answer very briefly the following questions about the sentences:

1. When do the Eskimos put on their winter clothes?.... ————
2. Do men and women dress much alike?............... ————
3. How do the Eskimos dress for the coldest weather?... ————
4. How is the fur of the inside coat worn?............. ————
5. (Continue to 8 points.)

Test VI (Central Thought) 6 Points   Score ———

Directions: Open your geography to page 63.   Find the section headed "How the day is spent in camp."   Number the paragraphs 1, 2, 3, etc., in the margin.   You should have 6 paragraphs (some on page 64).   The expressions below are the main thoughts of the paragraphs with two extra which are not main thoughts of any of the paragraphs.   The main thoughts are not in the same order as the paragraphs.   They are mixed up.   You should read each main thought, then find the paragraph to which it belongs and write the number of the paragraph in front of the main thought.   Remember there are two main thoughts which will have no number.

Main Thoughts: (Put the number of the paragraph on the line.)
———— How Bedouins get their cloth for tent coverings, blankets, and clothes
———— Other reasons why Hirfa's people wear more clothes than Bombo's
———— When the Bedouins retire at night
———— What the men and children do in the morning
———— (Continue to 8 items, two of which are not central thoughts.)

SOCIAL STUDIES

Test VII (Organization) 16 Points   Score _____

Directions: This test includes pages 54–70. It is an outline partially filled in and you are to use your geography to fill in correctly the parts of the outline that are left out. You will not need to fill in any parts except where blanks are left for you.

I. Nomads of the Desert
    A. The Arabs and their home-land
        1. Hirfa's people
        2. The land of the Arabs
        3. _____
        4. _____
    B. A trip across the desert
        1. The Bedouin Arabs
        2. _____
        3. _____
        4. The ship of the desert
        5. _____
        6. _____

C. _____
    1. We reach the Bedouin Camp
D. _____
    1. _____
    2. The need of water
    3. _____
E. A day in the Bedouin Camp
    1. _____
    2. _____
    3. _____
    4. How the day is spent in camp
    5. _____
F. _____
G. _____

Key for 4th Grade Test

Test I
3
1
2
6
4
5

Test II
1. 141
2. 156–157
3. 155
4. 6, 7

Test III

Page	T	M	B
1. 47	X		
2. 83			X
3. 80		X	

Test IV
1. other hunters
2. blubber
3. yes
4. freezing
5. straps and harness

Test V
1. when cold weather comes
2. yes
3. wear two coats
4. against the Eskimo's skin

Test VI
4
6
–
1

Test VII
I.
  A.
    1.
    2.
    3. Our voyage to Arabia
    4. An Arabian seaport
  B.
    1.
    2. The camel caravan
    3. The hot, dusty desert
    4.
    5. The midday rest
    6. Night in the desert
  C. A Bedouin welcome
    1.

D. Why Bedouins are nomads
    1. The search for grass
    2.
    3. How the Bedouins get water
E.
    1. Breakfast with Hirfa's family
    2. Tending the sheep and goats
    3. The tent and its furnishings
    4.
    5. Evening in the camp
F. Traveling with the Bedouins
G. A visit to an oasis town

Sometimes teachers ask pupils to write a story in their own words about a given country, city, or region in a given time, say 45 minutes, and in a limited number of words—perhaps 250-500, according to the grade being tested. Teachers allow or do not allow the use of texts, depending upon the purpose of the test. A skeleton outline should accompany the story. One possible reason why pupils dislike tests is the sameness of them. Teachers would do well to vary them not only for the purpose of pupil interest but for variety in skills and knowledges tested. They need not hesitate to experiment.[1]

[1] The following tests in the social studies are listed for teachers' information and to help them in developing tests of their own in these fields:

Civics: Brown-Woody. Civics Test obtained from World Book Co.; Hill-Wilson Civic Action Test obtained from Public School Publishing Co.

Geography: New Stanford Geography Test, Forms V and W obtained from World Book Co.; Wiedefeld-Walther Geography Test obtained from The Bureau of Educational Research and Service, Extension Division, The State University of Iowa.

History: Analytical Scales of Attainment in American History obtained from Educational Test Bureau; Denny-Nelson American History Test obtained from World Book Co.; Gregory American History Tests (Revised) obtained from The Bureau of Educational Research and Service, Extension Division, The State University of Iowa.

CHAPTER 19

HEALTH EDUCATION

"HOW are you?" "I am fine. How are you?" How often one hears this when friends meet. It may have become a trite salutation. However, the concern about good health and the importance that we all place on it are the reasons for such greetings. It is one of the most valuable assets an individual can have and will bring better chances of happiness and the likelihood of a greater degree of success in personal growth.

Life expectancy has increased in our nation because health conditions have improved. This is shown by these data from the American Public Health Association: [1]

1789 in New England	28 years
1885 in Massachusetts	40 years (approximately)
1901 for the United States	49 years
1935 for United States	over 61 years

This increase was brought about principally by the saving of infants' lives and by the decrease in the number of deaths from communicable diseases and, according to Turner's data, the life expectancy during these periods had increased little for those of 35 and over. Further increases have been made, however, since 1935. In 1942, life expectancy was 63.65 years for men and 68.61 for women in the United States.[2]

---

[1] Turner, C. E. *Principles of Health Education*, pp. 23-24. D. C. Heath & Co. 1939.

[2] Kieran, John, editor. *Information Please Almanac, 1947*, p. 198, Doubleday & Co., Inc. and Garden City Publishing Co., Inc.

There are *two aspects* of healthful living: first, that which pertains to the individual and his personal welfare—physical, mental, emotional; secondly, that which affects the interactions of the individual with the people in his own environment—at home, in school, in his immediate community, his state, the nation, and the world in general. For example, Tom's eating affects his own health. What he eats may depend upon the production and availability of food in his immediate locality and upon essential foods which are produced, processed, and brought to him from distant areas. Mary contracts a disease. She suffers. Her family and friends are concerned and often inconvenienced. This illness may have been caused by lack of local sanitation or by bacteria originating far from her immediate environment.

Since health is so vital to good living, effective health learning and good health practices should have a prominent place in all elementary school programs. In this chapter we will deal primarily with health teaching in the schools, at the same time recognizing the importance and close correlation of health instruction and practices of other agencies in a community.

HISTORICAL BACKGROUNDS

A bit of *historical* background may be helpful.[1] Health education among adults was attempted in Europe as early as the middle of the eighteenth century. About 1760, because general living conditions were poor, some physicians, among them Simon A. Tissot, wrote books to inform adults of better health practices. These men believed that if such information were available, people would use this knowledge and change their health practices. Tissot wrote for the people of Switzerland, but the book was translated into German, Dutch, French, and English. He claimed that the dissemination of such information had caused the elimination in almanacs of "astrological injunctions," which tended to keep up "ignorance, credulity, superstition, and falsest prejudices on the interesting articles of health, disease, and of remedies."[2] He wrote some sane advice—good even today.

[1] Hussey, Marguerite M. *Teaching for Health,* pp. 1-18. Prentice-Hall, Inc. 1939. Adapted.

[2] Tissot, Simon A. *Advice to the People in General with Regard to Their Health.* Dedicated, Lausanne, Dec. 3, 1782. Translated from the French edition. Philadelphia. Printed for John Sparhawk, 1771, pp. iv and 307.

This type of health teaching persisted for a hundred years. In 1869, Dr. W. W. Hall wrote "To prevent the young from getting sick, to enable all to grow old gracefully, with a heart full of the milk of human kindness, a genial smile and a pleasant word for everybody, and to go down to the grave 'like as a shock of corn fully ripe in his season'. . . ."[1] This advice to adults, however, did not improve the general health. Twenty-seven years before Hall's writing, Horace Mann, believing in a positive approach as contrasted with the negative approach of his predecessors, advised the teaching of physiology and anatomy in the public schools. He believed that if pupils learned of the wonders of the human body, interest in good health would be aroused.

Later ideas which contributed to the general picture were that (1) things which harmed the body should be avoided, (2) physical examinations are essential, (3) activities for grown-ups and children should be directed toward the improvement of health. Results, however, were meager. The church believed that things of the flesh were not especially important. Some teachers felt that the teaching of physiology and anatomy held no interest for children and even embarrassed them. There were no texts available for different levels of ability.

In 1885, because of the influence of the Women's Christian Temperance Union, Pennsylvania and Massachusetts passed laws which required the teaching of temperance in schools so that knowledge of the effects of alcohol on the human body would be spread.

In the early part of the twentieth century, through the influence of John Dewey and others, the theory of health education based on the belief that "knowledge of facts" would influence conduct changed, and it was held that "learning by doing" and "the doctrine of interest" were the important factors. In 1922 workers in this field promulgated the plan of helping children form good health habits by actually doing and repeating the activities. Also it was believed that if an interest in good health were developed, good health practices would follow. Later, investigations showed that health practices which were directed against pain and discomfort and toward the satisfaction of feeling well "were not sufficiently continuous or powerful to motivate conduct."[2]

[1] Hall, W. W. *The Guide Book to Health, Peace and Competence*, p. 752. D. E. Fisk & Co., Springfield, Mass. 1869.

[2] Hussey, Marguerite M. *Teaching for Health*, p. 3, Prentice-Hall, Inc. 1939.

It was shown, however, that the "primary interests in life were those related to doing things, to success in these undertakings and to personal characteristics which promote success and self-esteem, as strength, beauty and the like."[1]

Thus we might summarize by saying that there have been three outstanding steps in the development of health instruction:

1. The study of anatomy and physiology based on the idea that knowledge thus gained would result in better ways of living.

2. The practice in health habits based on the belief that these habits, if they were once formed, would continue.

3. The development of interest in, and correct attitudes toward good health, leading to practices which result in living with satisfaction.

PRESENT TRENDS

Present-day trends in health teaching (no. 3 above) show marked changes from the theories and practices of the earlier days. It is no longer considered an accepted procedure in the elementary school to memorize the names of the bones in the cranium. Health facts are no longer presented in fairy-tale guise and taught in fanciful form.

Some of the more recent trends are shown in the following statements:

1. Knowledge is not enough. Reading about health is not enough. Children should learn to plan the correct health activities and should be taught how to check themselves on good practices and beneficial habits.

2. Habit formation is not sufficient to meet all emergencies. In meeting new health situations children need to be guided to use reasoning based on knowledge and experiences.

3. Recognition is given not only to the physical development but to the mental, emotional, and social aspects as well. It is the whole individual that is to be considered.

4. Prevention, not cure or correction, is the slogan.

5. Educators recommend that activities be used to fit the needs of each child—more strenuous and varied activities for children who need such types, less vigorous and simpler activities for others.

[1] *Loc. cit.*

6. The pressure of modern life is such that children will need to be equipped to meet situations which did not concern former generations, for example: how to dress for comfort both indoors and out, in cold areas where rooms have summer temperatures; how to utilize electricity for proper lighting and cooking; and how to use such sources as the radio for weather information.

7. Because of present-day transportation and communication facilities, children should realize that health has become not only an individual concern but also a national and international one.

8. Nowadays, the term "health" implies "state of health" (strength, resistance, vigor)—not just freedom from disease.

9. Although there is continual emphasis on sanitation and immunization (group hygiene), more attention is being given to the teaching and practice of individual hygiene.

CORRELATION WITH OTHER ACTIVITIES

The question usually arises in planning a curriculum as to *when* certain subjects shall be taught. Health education should be thought of not as a subject but as a way of living and as such is a part of all the school's activities, including class periods, play periods, lunch time, and rest periods.

In order that health instruction be given its share of attention it is usually wise when arranging a program to see that special time is allotted, at least beginning with the third grade, to the teaching of the essential phases of health education. This allotment of a definite time to health education does in no way imply that health teaching should be slighted in other general activities of the day and week, such as washing hands, adjusting shades, and conducting lunch periods.

Health teaching often occurs in a science lesson when, for example, children learn about the effect of sunlight; or in an arithmetic class, when they compute time allotments for daily activities; or in geography lessons, when they investigate the source of necessary foods. The following outline gives good suggestions for correlations:[1]

[1] "Health in Schools." *20th Yearbook of the American Association of School Administrators,* pp. 67-68. American Association of School Administrators, 1201 16th St. N. W., Washington, D. C. 1942.

Social Studies

1. Study of food supply, housing, clothing, community services, recreation, transportation, inventions, and disease problems of people of this and other countries.
2. The local community, its health services and problems.
3. Health conditions of past generations and cultures.

Science

1. How animals and plants grow, develop, and reproduce, and the factors which favorably and unfavorably influence these life functions.
2. Microscopic life and the role of disease-producing organisms—nature, spread, and control.
3. Appreciation of and love for the out-of-doors.

Language Arts

1. Health experiences and problems for written or oral discussion.
2. Child-planned dramatizations.
3. Health articles for the school newspaper.
4. Stories and poems which favorably influence attitudes concerning many aspects of living.

Art

1. Posters, borders, murals, illustration of individual health records.

Physical Education

1. Emphasis on big-muscle activities in directed and undirected play.
2. Adaptation of activities to individual health conditions.
3. Safety in physical activities.
4. Mental and emotional values in participation in wholesome activities.
5. Posture and feet conditions.

In a one-teacher school, it may be desirable to combine for some occasions the classes for pupils below fourth grade into one group, those on the fourth, fifth, and sixth grade levels into another, and those in seventh and eighth grades into a third. In schools having one grade to a room, a general scheme for the system should be worked out so that there are new approaches and advanced materials although repetition on the succeeding levels is unavoidable. For example, nutrition may be presented on different levels, but in its different phases and with different approaches.

This is an aspect of the school program which extends into the home and community. Although proper instruction may be given in school, the actual practice is carried out in such of the pupil's home activities as sleeping, eating, and dressing. In terms of a pupil's community responsibility, observing a quarantine sign is as much a part of the teaching of health as is reading about it or discussing its community values. Moreover, it is a good illustration of conduct as a technique of learning.

It is not the function of this chapter to select the subject matter used in the field of health instruction. Since methods are conditioned by what is taught, however, the following is given as the basis for a health curriculum.[1]

"Knowledge of the developmental and behavior needs of all children indicates that health teaching in the elementary school will center around the formation and extension of desirable practices, attitudes and understandings associated with (a) nutrition and growth, (b) relaxation, rest and sleep, (c) activity, (d) fresh air and sunshine, (e) elimination, (f) cleanliness and care of teeth, body, and clothing, (g) importance and means of securing dental and medical attention, (h) control of infection, (i) care of eyes and ears, (j) posture, (k) safety, and (l) emotional and social adjustment. In the upper grades of the elementary school there is, in addition, need to widen the horizons of the pupils to introduce them to health problems of the home, school and community."

FACTORS AND METHODS OF INSTRUCTION

Certain outstanding *factors* affect materially the results of health instruction.

1. There are *two aspects* of *health instruction* in the schools. One is mainly administrative and has a vital part in children's proper development. It deals mainly with the school environment and the physical set-up. The other is guidance and development of children along the lines of happy, efficient living. It has to do with procedures and the activities in which the pupils more directly participate.

2. Health instruction should *begin where children are*, recognize their needs, and guide their activities to lead them from one step to the next. The work of the Alfred P. Sloan Foundation with under-

[1] *Ibid.,* p. 61.

privileged children is a good illustration of efforts to improve family living as to food, clothing, and shelter, beginning with conditions as they exist. Children from more fortunate homes could profitably start their efforts on a higher level than underprivileged children could.

3. It is essential that the whole school system have the *same philosophy of health education*. If there are differences in the underlying principles, conflicts may arise in procedures, such as self-directed versus definitely dictated activities, or strict isolation of those with contagious illnesses versus lax observance of such rules.

4. *Temporary* and *unrelated incentives* are *poor stimuli* for conduct. It is often better to let the reward or punishment of the action come as the natural outgrowth of the activity. The individual is the one who suffers, for eating green apples may result in pain in the stomach, and dirty hands deny one the privilege of handling new books. In contrast to these are the stars on charts, the airplane race, and other artificial incentives. There is much enjoyment in the satisfaction one feels in sensing growth and progress.

5. Sometimes *too much attention called to an undesirable practice* only causes the child to want to continue instead of discontinue it. He is made more conscious of it; he is getting recognition because of it. Therefore, why not do the same thing again?

6. It is surprising how some *superstitious beliefs* continue to influence conduct. Learning and applying sound health facts should help develop scientific attitudes and aid in dispelling such a silly practice as wearing charms to ward off disease.

7. It is possible to make *children too health conscious*. This may result in over-sensitivity to certain unavoidable conditions, in an unhappy attitude, and in such a waste of time as the continual washing of hands to avoid germs.

8. *Fatigue* is a condition to be avoided by both pupils and teachers. One cannot act normally when he is very weary. For instance, if it has been an unusually busy day and the teacher and children have been under nervous strain, it may be better to use the last period for a quiet story hour than to push the program through according to schedule.

9. It is better to *stress* the *positive* and *constructive* than to emphasize the negative with fear and unpleasant aspects of situations. Thus,

it is better to point out that wearing rubbers will enable us to continue in school rather than to stress that if we do not wear rubbers we shall probably have severe colds and shall need to remain at home.

10. It is perhaps most important of all to help children *realize* that achievement in physical and mental activities requires certain *fundamentals of health*.

If a teacher has in mind that the *aim* is promoting health rather than teaching health, she will undoubtedly attempt the following:

(1) to give attention to her own health,

(2) to arrange or strive for healthful surroundings,

(3) to find unhealthful conditions and try to correct them,

(4) to guide the children toward self-direction,

(5) to utilize interesting techniques and materials for health instruction,

(6) to work with the homes, as far as she can tactfully do so, in promoting right practices,

(7) to work with the children for better health conditions in the community.

The alert teacher will incorporate a large variety of *methods* in her plans for reaching these aims. These will be discussed in the order above and techniques suggested for attaining them.

1. Someone has suggested that health instead of disease should be contagious. Surely it is one of the *teacher's responsibilities to have good health herself*, to know how to care for it and to be an example of one who uses good health practices daily. A well person, a person who has sufficient sleep, an attractive and neat person, without question exerts an influence in the schoolroom which cannot be measured. Exuberant spirits and happiness usually radiate to those whom she meets, and a better atmosphere of learning permeates the situation. This implies that she will budget her time, providing time for rest, outdoor exercise, relaxation, reading for pleasure and enlightenment, and cultivating friendships in the community.

2. Children have a right to a *clean, attractive, hygienic school home*. The following chart will help the teacher and children check their environment.[1]

---

[1] Iowa Elementary Teachers' Handbook, Volume VII. *A Plan of Health Education,* pp. 20-28. Department of Public Instruction, State of Iowa, 1946. Adapted.

I. Seating

  A. Are we seated comfortably; that is—

    ____1. Does the height of the seat make it possible for our feet to rest heavily upon the floor, knees at right angles, no pressure under the thighs along the front edge of the chair?

    ____2. Are the chair and desk close enough together so that leaning forward is not necessary while writing, and yet there is enough space to enter and leave easily?

    ____3. Is the height of the desk such that the forearm may rest on it while writing without raising the shoulder too high?

  B. How can we help solve our seating problems so that we meet the above standards?

II. Lighting the classroom

  A. Is our schoolroom well lighted; that is—

    ____1. Do we have double shades mounted, adjustable at both top and bottom of the window? If the ordinary single type of shade is still in use, are they rolled entirely to the top of the window when the sun is not on that side so that the light will carry to the far side of the room?

    ____2. If there are windows on both sides of the room, are the shades pulled to cover the windows on the right side and adjusted for proper lighting on the left side according to Item 1?

    ____3. Are our shades translucent with buff or tan color and wide enough to exclude sun streaks? Are sunstreaks excluded between the rollers of double shades?

    ____4. Are our windows kept clean?

    ____5. Do we have a minimum of 15-foot-candles of light, artificial or daylight, on all working surfaces?

    ____6. Are all our desks placed so that the light comes from the left, or left and rear, causing no objectionable shadows?

    ____7. Are walls light buff or ivory and the ceiling white or light?

    ____8. Is there an absence of direct or reflected glare on working surfaces from sunlight or from artificial light? (Working surfaces include desks, tables, blackboards, and materials.)

    ____9. Are there no sun streaks and no bright reflecting objects?

    ____10. Are we seated during study and recitation so that no one will be forced to look directly into the light? This means:

      a. If children are seated in a semicircle for recitation, the open side should face toward the dark corner

of the room and the semicircle should be small
enough so that no child faces the light.
b. If tables are used, children should sit on one side
only with light coming over the left shoulder.
c. Teacher should not stand at the windows at any
time, especially when conducting recitations.

_____11. Do we keep flowers and plants on a shelf or table below
the window sill, and are sash curtains and decorations
off the window so that we will get all the light
possible?

_____12. Are those of us with defective vision sitting near the
front of the room and in the best light?

_____13. Are those of us who are left-handed seated so that we
need not write in a shadow?

B. How can we help to solve the lighting problem in our room
and share in the duties concerned with them?

III. Temperature and ventilation
A. Do the temperature and ventilation of our classroom make us
comfortable and wide awake so that we can do our best
work; that is—

_____1. Is the temperature 68 to 72° F. with no drafts?

_____2. Are thermometers kept at desk height both near the
the source of heat and at the desk farthest from it?

_____3. Is provision made for intake of fresh air and outflow
of foul air?

_____4. Is the stove (if one is used) adequately jacketed?

_____5. Is some provision made to keep the air moist in winter?

_____6. Do we open windows when we play hard in the school
room?

B. How can we help to solve the heating and ventilation problems and share in the duties concerned with them?

IV. Housekeeping
A. Is our room kept clean and orderly; that is—

_____1. Do we use some means of avoiding dust when sweeping
and dusting?

_____2. Are the seats movable so that the floors may be easily
cleaned daily?

_____3. Do we keep all materials neatly put away except those
we are using?

_____4. Does each of us clean up his materials immediately
after construction work or after lunch?

_____5. Do we have receptacles of sufficient size for refuse?

_____6. Do we clean blackboards thoroughly at least once a
week and wipe them with a damp cloth daily?

_____7. Do we keep erasers and chalk trays clean and dust-free?

_____8. Do we have mats for cleaning our shoes, and do we all use them before entering the schoolroom?

_____9. Do we burn all garbage from our lunches in the winter and bury it or carry it home in fall and spring?

_____10. Do we have definite places, preferably enclosed, for wraps, dinner pails, drinking cups, cooking utensils, books, instructional materials, etc.?

_____11. Do we have screens on doors and windows and do we use spray to keep flies out of our school?

_____12. Do we plan ways of making the room attractive in appearance?

B. How can we share with the teacher in the cleaning program and how can we help solve the cleaning problems? Can we encourage cleanliness and tidiness through teacher-pupil-parent cooperative planning so that the necessary facilities mentioned above are provided?

V. Toilet facilities

Note: Rating items similar to those above may be worked out by teacher and pupils for these facilities and for those which follow:

VI. Water supply

VII. Lunch period activities

VIII. School grounds

3. How can *unhealthful conditions* be discovered and remedied? One of the first things that should occur when children enter the room

Running water and liquid soap without modern conveniences

in the morning is that each take an inventory of himself in order to check the cleanliness of his hands, face, and nails, and his general appearance. Many times children are in proper condition when leaving home, but play on the school grounds may wreak havoc with the neatly combed hair and clean hands. How can standards be provided by which children can judge their personal appearance? A teacher-pupil evaluation guide may be the most effective means. This can be developed in the same manner as other study guides. After a hand-washing experience, the children may exhibit their hands and discuss the success of the use of soap and water, nail file or other instruments used by the different children. In this way those who have not been thorough enough may see the difference in results and set up a criterion by which to evaluate in the future. Those with really clean hands could describe the procedure they used, and this would suggest items for an evaluation chart. Some hands may be stained or chapped, but this should be taken into consideration and help could be suggested. Questions such as the following may be developed in the chart:

Did I use soap and water (warm, if possible)?

Did I wash long enough to remove all dirt?

Did I dry my hands well?

Did I thoroughly clean my nails immediately after washing?

Similar charts may be developed as needed for other health habits. Pictures showing other children carrying on health practices may be used effectively, especially if they also depict the results. Water, soap, and individual or paper towels should be accessible. A mirror, hung low for primary children, permits children to make their own inventory on personal appearance.

It is well for a teacher to take a quick survey to see that nothing unusual is apparent. In one room a child was carrying his arm straight at his side and investigation raised the question of a broken bone. He was taken home and to the doctor for further investigation.

Fortunate is the school with a nurse available, who will check for physical handicaps and recommend corrective procedures. Otherwise, this responsibility rests with the teacher, who often does not have the training for such diagnosis but nevertheless should do what she can. Most of us do recognize symptoms of a cold and can take the steps necessary for isolation. It is certainly important that parents and children realize the necessity of remaining at home until danger of spreading the cold to others is passed. The welfare of the entire room is thus considered. Symptoms of other common contagious diseases should be familiar to teachers (charts may be obtained for this purpose), and children should be excluded when such symptoms are observed until medical advice is obtainable. There may be parents who do not understand the importance of inspections and examinations for defects, the value of tests for certain diseases, and the security obtained from vaccination and immunization. In such cases parent education may break down the barrier. Such an effort should usually be made by the teacher.

Every child has the right to be as healthy as he can be. Science offers many avenues now toward rectifying poor vision, defective speech, impaired hearing, and other defects. These aids surely should be made available whenever possible.

What can the instructor do to instill the desire in children to become self-directing in the use of good health practices?

One good technique for all teaching is using praise when it is deserved. "Your hands are indeed clean this morning, and I did not remind you." "John, how well you combed your hair after looking in the mirror."

Self-help guides, such as the chart given on pages 40 and 211, put responsibility on the pupils. Privileges permitted as rewards for good health habits also stimulate self-direction. "Your position when standing is good. Therefore, would you like to show these pictures to the class?" Sometimes the situation in the act itself will be the incentive to repeat and carry on the practice, or it may necessitate denial or inhibition on the children's part. To illustrate, every child likes to wade in puddles. However, if he is not properly dressed for this sport and the temperature is near freezing, he may need to direct himself to other kinds of fun.

5. The *materials and techniques* which a teacher selects to use in her health instruction program should be determined mainly by the type of children under her care—that is, by their health attitudes, personalities, and home backgrounds. Also, she learns much concerning her pupils' health practices by watching their daily activities, how they sit and stand, how they play, the manner of holding books, their practices of cleanliness, their general appearances, the kind of lunch they bring, and the state of the clothing they wear. She is fortunate if she has access to the results of standard tests or physical examinations.

Some schools provide all necessary equipment without request. Others will secure this if the teacher knows what is needed for the work at hand and makes the request for such items as an electric plate for preparing hot lunches; pictures, slides, and films for illustrating care of teeth and other features; canvas cots for rest periods; and proper window shades.

Pure memorization has little part in this field. The technical aspects of physiology and anatomy have a small place, if any, in the elementary school. However, basic principles and necessary facts should be part of pupils' equipment if they are to have bases for forming judgments when opportunities arise and for developing necessary skills. For example, if a boy knows a little of the structure of the human body, he may see more readily the advantage of good posture over slouching. The knowledge of the value of milk in one's diet, as learned through experiments and pictures, may result in a better balanced noon meal.

In determining which *techniques* are the most effective, it is well for the teacher to ask, "What activities can I use most effectively with children to promote good health practices and to stimulate interest in healthful living?" Some of the effective techniques which she may employ are: (a) discussion, (b) investigation, (c) experimentation, (d) use of visual materials, (e) excursions, (f) demonstrations, (g) organization of units, (h) dramatization, (i) exhibits, or (j) a combination of two or more of these.

It is assumed that all of these procedures will naturally lead into positive action and will develop favorable attitudes. Even though each technique is here discussed separately, the most effective teaching usually results from a combination of them.

Discussion can be utilized on any level. The opportunity may arise from the launching of a dental program in the schools. The group discussion, depending upon the age level, may be on the effects of good health on teeth, the need for proper care of teeth, what care teeth should have, or the importance of an examination by a dentist and of following his recommendations. Children may relate their experiences, assignments may be made to health texts, and the discussion may be continued in later class periods.

Investigation appeals to most pupils because it utilizes a rather fundamental tendency. For example, the teacher and pupils of a one-teacher school are dealing with the problem of flies in the schoolroom.

They investigate breeding places and find out how to combat flies there. They discuss means of obtaining the necessary materials for protecting the schoolroom. This investigation involves various lines of approach and the reaching of decisions based upon information obtained.

Experimentation usually implies the handling of objects—one of the most effective techniques for learning. Probably one of the best ways of showing the effect of proper diet is the common experiment of feeding two animals—white rats or young chickens—giving one the proper diet and the other a diet lacking in one or more of the most important ingredients. The result will be self-evident.

Since *visual teaching* is discussed more in detail in another chapter, it is given only brief consideration here. How can visual teaching improve posture? Pictures of good and poor postures, demonstrations by pupils, anatomy charts to show the effects of postures on bodily structure, graphs to show improvements—all are ways of developing the desire to practice correct standing, walking, and sitting.

The *excursion* is also discussed elsewhere in this book (see pp. 554-556). Some health objectives of excursions may be: to learn, by a visit to a bakery, how breads and pastries are made hygienically; to see, by a trip to a grocery store, how food is protected; to discover, by going to the water plant, how water is made safe for consumption; to find out, by a trip to the dairy, how milk is pasteurized and kept sanitary; or to observe, by a trip to the creamery, how butter is made under healthful conditions.

Demonstration is another phase of visual teaching. It is probably not as practical in this field as in some others, and when used it should be simple, exact, and conducted so that all can see. It is always safer to have a tryout, whether the teacher or the pupil is to demonstrate, in order to be certain that the demonstrator has all the steps well in mind and in the proper order. An example of demonstration is: how to wash hands with running water and liquid soap—one child dispenses the soap and another pours the water, keeping the towels and other necessary utensils handy. The demonstrators should know the directions and advantages of this routine so as to present it concisely and with dispatch. Manicuring nails and brushing teeth may be other health chores to demonstrate.

Unit procedure would in varying instances utilize a few, many, or maybe all of the techniques listed above. The steps in carrying on a unit are given in Chapter Two and illustrated in Chapters Seventeen, Eighteen, and Twenty-one. The approach in this field may be by means of children's questions, such as "Why should our drinking water be tested?" "Why is milk better for us than coffee?" or other situations that children can help solve. An honest piece of work, truly important to a school, would undoubtedly have more educative value than one selected without direct relation to pupil experiences.

Taking care of a pet is a project of practical interest and value to primary children, and around it a unit of work could be organized. The children will thus have occasion to learn of proper foods for animals and of the necessity for sanitation and cleanliness. They will also realize the pet's dependence for comfort and growth upon the care they give it. The children should get information through their own investigation and observation and from the reading material available on this topic at the primary level.

Dramatization of daily experiences is a part of children's spontaneous play. An original play organized and produced by a group of any age or all ages may easily grow out of discussions and experiences centered around the idea of a playmate with a broken leg and the attentions he receives, or a family carrying on home duties when the mother is ill. Thus this technique may help to impress ideas of health and be a fine means of culminating a unit. It gives a good chance to develop powers of organization and of creative expression. Such an activity is a desirable part of a program for parents or other groups.

Utilizing the *exhibit* is the final technique to be discussed. It is a good way to present the principles of healthful living objectively and in well-organized form. One exhibit which may be developed in the school is the showing of the proper types of clothing to wear in different seasons or climatic conditions. It may be a community affair, such as the health exhibit at the county fair, or the Cleveland Health Museum. Teachers use the exhibit to fit the current health instruction in (1) the discussion of the different articles of the exhibit, (2) the comparisons which may be made of these articles, (3) the learning of the steps of a process, (4) observations followed by further investigation, (5) the organization as a culminating feature of a unit.

Some good suggestions for organization are given by Homer N. Calver, who was Director of the Health Exhibits, New York World's Fair, 1939.[1]

1. The exhibit should tell a simple story—drive home a few salient facts. Avoid cluttering up the exhibit with insignificant details.
2. Make the exhibit with the audience who is to see it in mind. See that it is interesting and easily comprehensible to that particular audience.
3. Set down specifically the purpose of the exhibit.
4. With the purpose clearly in mind select the facts for presentation.
5. Design, color, and movement or a sense of movement are elements in an effective exhibit. They should all serve the main purpose of the exhibit. Color can be used to produce contrast, harmony, emphasis, feeling, and a sense of motion.
6. In the lighting of the exhibit, glare from shiny surfaces, shadows, and confusing reflections should be avoided. Emphasis on a particular point may be obtained with a spotlight.
7. The text of exhibits should be reduced to a minimum. Short words and short lines are usually easy to comprehend. The letters should be large enough to be easily read at the distance at which the exhibit is to be viewed. Lower-case letters used with the necessary capitals are more legible than all capital letters.

Most good teaching is a *combination of techniques*, as is illustrated when a cleanup campaign is under way. Much discussion would be necessary, committees might take excursions and investigate, experiments might prove which tools were best to use, charts and pictures would aid in setting aims and recording conditions both before and after the campaign, and these in turn would make a most effective type of exhibit.

(6) *Cooperation with the home* in developing better health practices is of high importance, yet it must be handled most tactfully if it is to be effective. Probably the best ways of ensuring mutual understandings are through the teacher's visits to the homes, parents' visits to the school, the sending of charts and other materials to the homes, and meetings of parent-teacher organizations.

[1] Calver, Homer N. *The Exhibit Medium,* pp. 341-346. American Journal of Public Health, XXIX. April, 1939.

What are some of the phases upon which parents and teachers can direct cooperative action?

a. Entrance age is one phase. Many children begin the more formal work of the first grade too young. Experimental evidence seems to indicate that pupils entering at six years of age progress more naturally and develop with a greater feeling of security and chance of success than if they start at five years of age. Five-year-olds should have a year of kindergarten with no formal work or very little formal work in reading.

b. Rest and sleep are essential. Anything that deprives children of sufficient sleep and rest interferes with effective school living. The following standards indicate in general the amount of sleep necessary for the given grade levels: "Kindergarten through third grade—11½ to 12 hours; fourth through sixth grade—11 to 11½ hours; seventh through ninth grade—10 to 11 hours."[1] Rugs or mats often provided by the homes are essential in beginning grades for relaxation periods during the school day.

c. The school lunch needs atention. Close cooperation between school and home on noon lunches for children who are in school the full day more nearly assures them of a good diet. This may be done in different ways. If the lunch is brought from home each morning, suggestions may be made to parents as to what to prepare. This may be done by discussions at parent-teacher meetings, by sending to the homes pamphlets on good school lunches, and by making use of the children's interests stimulated by class study of nutrition. In some instances this cooperative planning in rural areas has resulted in the lunch's being brought for all by different mothers on designated days. Often a hot dish is prepared at school to supplement lunches the children bring. Many schools take advantage of the lunch program as set up by the federal government.

The proper eating habits emphasized in school, may be carried over into homes where such practices are lacking.

d. Corrective measures should be considered. These may include calling parents' attention to teeth, eyes, ears, speech, and other sources of difficulties. One state conducted county-wide dental programs in

[1] Iowa Elementary Teachers Handbook, Volume VII. *A Plan of Health Education,* p. 44. Department of Public Instruction, State of Iowa. 1946.

which the dentists cooperated in examining and doing the necessary dental work. This is school, home, and community cooperation.

e. Immunization may need to be emphasized. Most parents now know the value of vaccination and other antitoxin programs to individuals and communities. If there is any question, however, time is often well spent in developing a fuller understanding preliminary to such a campaign.

f. Personal cleanliness may carry over to the homes. If a desire to be clean can be developed among children it may be sufficient to help overcome indifference in the home toward such matters, since cleanliness and neatness may become contagious.

g. General activities, such as play, deserve recognition. How much time does the child have to play when at home? Is he encouraged to set up a daily program which will provide a definite time for play? Can he meet his own problems and is he encouraged to work out their solutions? It is well for parents and teachers to discuss these and other questions together so that the efforts of one will enhance the work of the other for the good of the children.

7. *Health* is a community concern. In towns, much space is provided for business people to park cars near their places of business when perhaps more exercise from walking would be of benefit to them. Is there equal thought given to providing play space for children, so essential in any town? This could be a worthwhile community project in which the children would participate by helping clear the space of unnecessary objects, planning and helping to lay out game spaces, and being responsible for some of the upkeep.

It seems wasteful for play equipment to lie idle in a country school during the summer months. With careful planning, arrangements may be made for responsible pupils to take bats and balls and other durable articles to their homes. The neighborhood could then have access to them during the vacation period.

MENTAL HYGIENE

Mental hygiene is a commonly used term in professional books on education. One definition is: "Mental hygiene in education accepts the responsibility of helping the child at every stage of his development to work out a sane, wholesome, and humanly valuable adjustment to the persistent tasks of life in terms of his capacities and unique temperament and personality."[1]   Guidance of a child's emotional health and general personality development means a great deal to his continued happiness and efficiency.   Such training usually produces a person who in adulthood contributes positively toward a stable, effective, and democratic society.   The development of mental health is, therefore, an obligation.

The teacher's personality and emotional responses to her situation, some claim, are more important than her knowledge of subject matter and her skill in teaching.   She needs to know children and the importance of children's emotional reactions.   She should realize the influence of an attractive appearance and pleasant voice and the value to children of smiles of encouragement.   Nagging, ridicule, sarcasm, and domination certainly have no place in the elementary school.   A successful teacher makes a continuous study of each child and frequently asks herself, "Now why did he do *that* in *that* way?"   Furthermore, a teacher is responsible for having a cheerful, attractive, livable schoolroom with an atmosphere in which children can be happy, feel secure, and practice democratic living.   They should have confidence in their teacher.   They should know that she respects them as individuals and that she is vitally interested in the welfare of each one.

A few *more specific suggestions* may aid the teacher who is looking for assistance in dealing with emotional problems.

1. The work of the school should be planned so that each pupil has tasks suited to his ability, tasks at which he can attain a degree of success and its attendant feeling of security and satisfaction.   Such tasks should also be challenging, so that each pupil needs to make efforts to accomplish according to his ability.   Continual failure is most discouraging; too easy work creates habits of idleness and dawdling. This brings up a problem which often puts teachers in a quandary— the inability of a child to do the work expected in his grade.   It is undoubtedly true that a child will have less frustration if the situation is discussed with the parents and arrangements are made so that he can

[1] "Mental Health in the Classroom."   *13th Yearbook, Directors of Supervision and Directors of Instruction,* p. 24.   Department of Supervisors and Directors of Instruction, N.E.A., Washington.   1940.

work on his own level of achievement. When these preliminary arrangements have been made, the whole matter should be talked over with the pupil and a plan worked out for his adjustment to the other children of his group. Remaining in a room a second year or doing different work may be difficult at first, but in the long run the pupil usually finds greater satisfaction than in continually sensing failure.

Teachers and parents often do the children's jobs for them. Instead they should insist that children accept and carry responsibility according to their respective capacities and take the consequences that follow. Rewards which are the natural outgrowth of success in the project, such as the child's becoming the pitcher on the ball team through diligent practice, are usually the best. Justifiable praise is also an effective reward.

2. It is a good idea for children to have contacts with those of different ages, abilities, and home backgrounds. They soon learn that others do not like those who sulk, pout, lose their tempers quickly, and try to dominate. To be able to work successfully with others is a big asset. Children should be encouraged to cooperate in planning for the school program, for daily work, and for larger units. It helps them to feel they are an integral part of this phase of living.

3. Play is a natural function in the early years of children's lives. Big-muscle activity in children's play helps them develop in all aspects. Properly directed play will enable children to meet the many challenges which confront them throughout the range of their development. The growth and maturity of personality are directly influenced by the nature of the play situations in which children have their earliest social experiences. Teachers and parents may profit by the study and the interpretation of children's play. These are vital aids in the understanding of the children themselves. What they play with, where they play, and with whom they play are all matters of high importance.

4. Intellectually retarded children need affection and understanding. They need also be specially planned for and helped if they are to grow into happy, healthy citizens who will be useful in their communities. Our schools are woefully lacking when they expect such children to conform to a program planned for children who are developing normally. Certainly the school can provide such materials

as wood, clay, and paints with which these pupils can work and profit by a reasonable degree of success.

5. Sometimes pupils with unstable nervous systems are overtaxed by too many extra-curricular activities and social functions. It is they who profit especially by avoiding fatigue, by getting more sleep, and by eating wholesome food.

6. Threatening, arguing, and coaxing should be avoided. If a punishment is promised, it should be given promptly. Usually children with good home training are not problems in school. An aggressive pupil may cause the teacher more concern, but usually his case is not as serious and does not need the teacher's guidance as much as the retiring, shy, or passive child who withdraws from the others.

7. Reports in the form of letters telling of children's reactions, traits, and development are considered better than achievements and characteristics graded by numbers or letters. Personal reports will aid parents toward a better understanding of their children's general growth. A large enrollment may, however, make such a plan unfeasible.

In general, the teacher should try to provide an environment in which each child may develop daily in the ability to derive satisfaction from living.

Undoubtedly *sex instruction* can be given most naturally and effectively in the home, since it is a continuous program beginning before school age and since much of the basic information is acquired incidentally. These conditions necessitate close cooperation between home and school if the school attempts to aid in this field of instruction and if the best results are to be achieved.

In general, the home seems to have done none too well in carrying this responsibility, and some parents as well as educators think the schools should gradually take on this added field of teaching, as it is related to health instruction. Regardless of the school's formal policy, however, each teacher meets many problems either directly or indirectly related to sex. To help avoid such problems if possible, or to meet them successfully if they cannot be avoided, is the purpose of these suggestions.

1. Adult attitudes toward sex usually affect the attitudes of children toward it. A wholesome attitude on the part of the teacher

usually engenders a similar one in the pupils or helps in a desirable change from unwholesome attitudes.

2. Honesty and correctness in response to the children's frank questions help build the confidence of children in their parents and teachers and add immeasurably to the chances of successful instruction.

3. Even in the elementary grades the various fields of science may be used to teach the basic facts of reproduction. Rural children have direct experiences with many such phenomena in both the animal and plant worlds. Urban children may obtain knowledge from experiences with pets at home or in school.

4. The most successful teaching seems to be accomplished by the use of the scientific method, with all basic facts in the open and no deep, dark secrets under cover. To small children especially, this is the most natural approach.

5. Both motion and still pictures may be substituted for direct experiences or used for additional instruction to supplement these experiences.

The results of a health education program are difficult to *evaluate*. Changes for the better should be evident in community, school, and individual living. Ruth Strang says:[1] "Although values vary with the situation and with the individual, they usually include a feeling of well-being, physical fitness for the tasks of life, and consideration for the health of others. These ends are the complex resultant of heredity, environmental conditions conducive to healthful growth, healthful ways of behaving in everyday situations, wise choices based on knowledge of health facts, and attitudes which avoid the extremes of anxiety about health and indifference or antagonism to healthful living."

EVALUATION

Certain *procedures* help the teacher evaluate the general health of her pupils.

1. Daily *observation* of children can be used not only to note cleanliness and evidence of illness, but also to find whether they are taking responsibility in carrying on good health practices, such as adjusting

[1] Strang, Ruth. "What are Some Criteria for Evaluating Healthful Living." *Healthful Living for Children*, p. 26. Bulletin, Association for Childhood Education, 1944.

shades to prevent glare on their desks, keeping objects off the floor, and having satisfactory lunches. The teacher may also observe their general participation in the school's activities and their attitudes toward their own activities and those of others. These and other items furnish data for determining the degree of healthful living.

2. Since much of the health program is carried on at home, *reports from parents* contribute desirable information concerning rest, sleep, play, and eating. Such reports of twenty-four-hour activities for a period of a week at a time are more enlightening than reports for a single day and probably give a more accurate picture than a questionnaire which covers general points.

3. *Paper-and-pencil tests* and check forms made out by children show what a child knows and thinks about healthful living and help in diagnosing incorrect practices which the child may not know are harmful. However, the mere fact that one *knows* he should wash his hands before eating or *says* he prefers to play outside instead of indoors does not mean that he will do those things. Sufficient motives may be lacking. Whether the test is objective or a blank to be filled in, the statements may suggest the best procedure to the pupils and influence them to choose the best response rather than the habitual one.

Teacher-pupil interview

The record of an informal discussion pays dividends in better health practices.

4. *Teacher-pupil interviews* should be conducted casually after the teacher is certain that she has the confidence of the pupil. Many facts related to a child's health will come to light in conversing with him about his interests and activities. The idea of the teacher's wanting to help should be paramount, not the thought of her passing judgment, criticizing, or ridiculing. If the latter should show itself, chil-

dren are apt to try to make a good impression and not tell of undesirable practices. Matters that worry children may be brought out. The teacher should try to put herself in the child's place and offer suggestions of an encouraging nature. It is probably better to omit most suggestions at the time of the interview but to use this information as a basis for guidance through stories, moving pictures, or group discussions. Although it takes the most time, conducting interviews is probably the best method of making evaluations.

5. *Anecdotes* about children's episodes which have significance from the health standpoint may be written on cards and filed with the children's records. These add valuable information to the cumulative records.

6. Older children may be interested in *keeping diaries* or *records* of what they do daily. They should be encouraged to think in general of what happened during the day, not to write specifically from the health angle. Such factors as play interests, rest periods, and eating habits, which pertain to healthful living can thus be learned.

7. *Medical examinations* give more accurate information from a scientific aspect. The parents and children may go to the doctor, or some arrangements may be set up whereby children are checked at school. In this case it is better to have the parent present, and it is very helpful to have the assistance of a nurse. The doctor will be aided also if the teacher has assembled all information concerning each child's background. Of course, if a defect is found, corrective measures should follow.

8. *Weight* and *height* records may vary with the season and the individual. If there is no gain in a three-month period, the child should see a physician. Height measurement should be taken twice a year.

9. The *scholastic record* of a pupil, including his cumulative scholarship record, mental test results, number of absences, and other factors are also items for a teacher to consider in making her analysis of a child's health status.

When these items of information pertaining to the child's health knowledge, habits, and attitudes are combined, a picture may evolve (although not necessarily complete) of how he is developing his general pattern to live healthfully.

CHAPTER 20

SAFETY EDUCATION

I N THIS age of speed and mechanical devices the hazards to *safe living* have increased. The Report on Health Education gives these data.[1] "Accidents are the leading cause of death in the United States for young people between the ages of three and twenty-two. . . . Up to five years of age the chief cause of fatalities is burns; beyond that age it is the automobile."

The fact that the accident rate has decreased immediately after safety education has been stressed indicates the value of such a program. Hussey says,[2] "It has been established that the number of accidents is not in ratio to the traffic density and dangerous crossings but rather in ratio to the education of children in observing traffic signals and crossing streets at the proper places. Some dangerous thoroughfares have been found singularly free from accidents where the children were taught proper safety practices."

Society establishes schools and requires children to attend. Therefore, it is society's obligation to provide safe conditions enroute to and from school as well as at the school itself. This implies regulation of traffic and conditions in and about the building. Equipment should be continuously checked. It also implies the best kind of safety education of children—that which helps them build the proper attitudes

---

[1] "Health Education," pp. 89, 91. *Report of the Joint Committee on Health Problems in Education of National Education Association and the American Medical Association.* N.E.A., Washington, D. C., 1941.
[2] *Op. cit.,* pp. 125-126.

and acquire the necessary skills to insure their own safety and that of others.

Most accidents are preventable, and many causes of accidents can be eliminated. Hence, one of the main objectives is to direct pupils into practices which result in knowledge and skills to do dangerous things, if necessary, with poise and success. Such teaching should be conducted, insofar as possible, in actual situations with sufficient repetition so that the desirable attitudes and practices will be instilled in the children and will function independently when the real need develops. This, however, is not enough. Children should also think of what they can do to prevent accidents by being courteous (courtesy plays a big part in safety), by being able to think clearly, and by seeing the foolishness of taking unnecessary chances. They should also be taught to consider the protection of property which might be destroyed through carelessness.

OBJECTIVES

If rather definite *objectives* are then set up, the following should be considered:[1]

"Children should learn to avoid unnecessary and undesirable dangers.
Children should learn to face courageously and intelligently dangers that are either unavoidable or necessary. Life to be interesting and challenging must be adventurous, and adventure involves some degree of uncertainty and danger.
Children should learn what society is doing to make life safe so that they in turn can cooperate effectively in such activities.
Children should learn to help one another avoid dangers. This is especially important in the upper grades and in the secondary schools."

No safety program can be carried on efficiently without the *cooperation* of *parents* and *public officials*, such as policemen, councilmen, inspectors, firemen, legislators, and others. A word of precaution from parents as children start to school that they walk on the left side of road or highway may be the reminder needed to fix this habit. In addition there are the innumerable opportunities in and about the home to carry on a safety campaign.

[1] "Health Education," p. 143. *Report of the Joint Committee on Health Problems in Education of National Educational Association and American Medical Association.* N.E.A., Washington, D. C. 1941.

Friendly relations with public
officials aids cooperation and
avoids a feeling of fear
or hostility.

A visit to schoolrooms by a fireman or a policeman who will answer
questions or give explanations not only helps the safety program but
develops the proper attitude toward these officers. A highway patrol-
man may with profit stop at a rural school when passing.

CORRELATION WITH OTHER ACTIVITIES

If schools are to help children to live fully, there is no question
that safety should be *part* of the *daily program*. Perhaps no definite
period is used, but it should be part of a day's procedure, just as other
phases of health instruction are.

It is said to be dangerous not to have suitable play equipment at
school. If this is not available, some children who are not capable of
meeting the social situation created by the lack of play equipment may
stand around idle, annoy one another, find undesirable pursuits, and
miss the physical development that balls, swings, and organized play
bring.

The *assignment of topics* to different age levels may be based upon
a course of study or on a good series of textbooks. Much needs to be
taught as occasions arise. A school should be provided with first aid
equipment, and the teacher should know how to use it. The use of
this in caring for cuts, scratches, burns, and other injuries is a lesson
in itself to the injured and to the playmates observing.

The opportunities for practicing safety are far flung: in the home,
at school, on the highways and streets, at play, and when camping.
Some of the most common causes of accidents which might be pre-
vented are automobiles, water, fire, poisons, firearms, explosives, trains,
live electric wires, and sharp pointed objects.

TECHNIQUES AND EVALUATION

How can the attitude of respect for safe practices and the many habits and skills be developed most effectively in school? Certainly much depends upon the locality and the children. Different procedures are required for different circumstances. Some *techniques*, however, are quite constant.

1. Often it is well to make analyses of accidents, to locate the danger points, and to discuss and plan preventive measures. An item from a paper posted on the bulletin board could start the discussion. The following chart given by Strang and Smiley[1] offers a good plan for analysis:

What was happening	*Where*	*When*	*The accident*	*How it could have been prevented.*

2. One child follows another down the slide too quickly and both receive hard bumps. This incident leads to discussion, and a chart is

worked out stating rules for safe sliding. This is posted for future reference.

3. Safety on the highway or streets, including use of bicycles and riding ponies, is discussed, and safe practices are shown by dramatization with imaginary streets marked on the schoolroom floor. However, it should be later practiced in the real situation with a limited number of pupils taken at a time.

4. Washing hands before eating and after going to the toilet becomes a habit in time if practiced daily.

[1] Strang, R. M. and Smiley, D. F. *The Role of the Teacher in Health Education*, p. 192. The Macmillan Co. 1941. Used with permission of the publishers.

5. When there is to be climbing on apparatus, using and putting away tools, carrying pointed and sharp objects, and carrying on other activities, it may be desirable for the teacher, or for a child who knows how, to demonstrate the correct way so that accidents may be avoided.

6. Seeing movies or pictures that show what is to be done in case of a fire will no doubt make a strong impression on children.

7. Serving as a monitor to see that the floor and playground are free of obstacles which may cause falls should develop in the child a good attitude of responsibility toward the safety of others.

8. Reading about poisonous plants and studying their pictures will show children the need of avoiding such plants when hiking and camping. An American Red Cross[1] book of instructions should furnish older children with good first aid advice.

9. Good themes for experience charts are "How to Play with Scooters" and "What to Do at the Zoo."

10. Two items a small child should know as memory facts in case of emergency are his name and his address.

11. Testing hot objects quickly with the finger will show little children the technique and importance of avoiding burns when picking up hot objects.

12. An excursion is planned and taken for the specific purpose of checking children's habits concerning their behavior in traffic, keeping away from machinery, or in handling unfamiliar plants.

13. During Fire Prevention Week children may make surveys for the purpose of detecting fire hazards in their homes or surroundings.

14. A committee of older children may find it worth while to have an interview with a fireman in order to plan for fire drill at school.

15. Situations should be presented to children with responsibility and *positive* guidance, such as calling to a child coasting, "Hold on tightly," not, "Don't fall"; or to one who has a pretty vase for his flowers, "Set it down when you put the water in," not, "Don't drop it." Children blossom under the glow of having confidence placed in their abilities.

16. The teacher's own regard for safety practices is shown in her daily conduct and her unmistakable attitude toward carelessness. She

[1] *First Aid Text Book,* revised edition. P. Blakeston's Son & Co., Philadelphia. 1937.

will thus indicate that carelessness is foolishness and at the same time set good examples for the children to emulate.

Some of the best ways of *checking* results of safety education are:

1. To observe children's actions in all situations involving safety.

2. To ask children to list both safe and unsafe places in which to play and have them give reasons in both cases.

3. To test with objective examinations children's knowledge of good practices.

4. To test their attitudes by showing appropriate pictures and observing and listening to their actions.

A good safety education program should teach children to observe safety rules to protect themselves and others, not because of fear of accident but in order to be ready to do the adventurous things skillfully and without mishap.

QUESTIONS—PROBLEMS—REACTIONS

SECTION ONE: *Facts*

SOCIAL STUDIES IN THE PRIMARY GRADES

1. What bodies of subject matter are usually included in the field of social studies?
2. What is the purpose of work in the social studies?
3. Outline briefly the section dealing with "specific factors in accomplishing this purpose" in teaching the social studies.
4. What should a teacher consider when selecting a social studies unit?
5. What methods may be used in conducting the daily work in a unit?
6. What are the steps in the outline of the procedure in planning a unit?

SECTION TWO: *Problems*

7. Show how the social studies materials considered in school may be closely related to daily living.
8. How is history related to other fields of subject matter?
9. Why will the method of "setting up and planning the unit" vary with schools?
10. What is the greatest value of unit teaching in teaching the skill subjects?

SECTION THREE: *Personal Reactions*

11. What advantages or disadvantages do you see in the schedule for a year's work, as outlined for a rural school?
12. How important do you consider the making of lesson plans?

HISTORY AND CIVICS

SECTION ONE: *Facts*

13. What is the value of good teaching of history in the elementary grades?

14. What activities may a good teacher employ to reach the objectives in social studies teaching?
15. List the methods and aids investigated by the Research Division of the N. E. A., noting the advantages and disadvantages (when given) of each.
16. What are some group activities that might be used?
17. What are the steps in the problem method?
18. To what other method is the project method related? What does it encourage?
19. What is the unit method? What steps are given?
20. What should tests in history attempt to do?
21. What factors need consideration when making history tests?

SECTION TWO: *Problems*

22. How do current world affairs affect the teaching of social studies?
23. Outline the objectives for the social studies curriculum.
24. Compare the benefits and dangers inherent in the socialized recitation.
25. Show in what type of school the individual type of recitation might serve to good advantage.
26. Why is the problem method especially appropriate for teaching the social studies?

SECTION THREE: *Personal Reactions*

27. What difference do you see between a textbook assignment and open textbook recitation?
28. Do you consider the special type of problem method, as explained heretofore, difficult to teach?
29. Which method—problem, project, or unit—would you like to use in this field? Why?

GEOGRAPHY

SECTION ONE: *Facts*

30. What are the different phases of geography?
31. In what ways can the study of geography help growth in desirable ways of living?
32. What are the teaching corollaries to the idea that a satisfactory method is one of teaching the "whole child"?
33. List the types of methods suggested for geography teaching.
34. What specific teachers might need a definite plan, such as explained in this section?
35. What evidence is there that it pays to have training in the use of the tools of geography?
36. List the different kinds of maps, with statements explaining their uses.
37. What types of tests may be used in this field? Which are probably the most valuable?
38. What do the sample tests show how to check?

SECTION TWO: *Problems*

39. Give reasons for the change in geography study in the last twenty-five years.
40. How is geography related to the other subject-matter fields?
41. Select one type of project and show its relationship to some phase of geography.
42. Show how the samples, from the outline of "units" made by a rural group of teachers, could be used "to learn to work" and "to get command" of geography material at the same time.

SECTION THREE: *Personal Reactions*

44. Which in your estimation would develop individual initiative more, taking an imaginary trip or dramatization? Why?
45. How could more pupils be helped to enjoy the study of geography?

HEALTH

SECTION ONE: *Facts*

46. Of what importance is good health?
47. What has been the trend in life expectancy in the last 150 years?
48. Summarize the development of health education, beginning with the eighteenth century.
49. If classes in a rural school are combined, how can repetition in succeeding years be avoided?
50. About what subject areas in school is the formation of desirable practices, attitudes, and understandings usually associated?
51. What is the teacher's responsibility in regard to her own health?
52. How can a teacher check for signs of physical handicaps or symptoms of disease?
53. What techniques are effective in conducting health education?
54. What suggestions are given pertaining to sex instruction?

SECTION TWO: *Problems*

56. Compare the influence of the home with that of the school in bringing about the desired results in healthful living.
57. Illustrate how giving too much attention to an undesirable practice may cause a child to want to continue rather than to discontinue the practice.
58. Explain the difference between promoting and teaching health.
59. Give three good reasons for using the chart to check the school environment.
60. Plan a teacher-pupil evaluation or chart for another health activity.
61. Select three of the techniques listed, and show how each may be used satisfactorily in some phases of health education.
62. In the light of the definition given for mental hygiene, explain how one may apply this instruction to some individual child.
63. Of the nine procedures suggested for evaluating the general health of

children, which would you consider most appropriate for the primary levels?

SECTION THREE: *Personal Reactions*

64. How can you personally protect the health of your associates?
65. Do you think we should give stars as rewards for observing daily good health practices? Explain.
66. Give an illustration from your experience when deserved praise has served as an incentive for desirable conduct.
67. What do you think we can do specifically to promote better mental hygiene in our public schools?

SAFETY

SECTION ONE: *Facts*

68. Give two reasons why the teaching of safety practices is of especial importance at the present time.
69. Where in the day's program should safety be taught?

SECTION TWO: *Problems*

70. Which of the techniques stated for teaching safety would be best for use in a one-room rural school? Why?

SECTION THREE: *Personal Reactions*

71. What is your opinion of the second objective as stated for safety education, namely, that "Children should learn to face courageously and intelligently dangers that are either unavoidable or necessary"?
72. What other means of checking the results of safety education would you add to the four already mentioned?

SUGGESTIONS FOR FURTHER READING

"Materials of Instruction." *Eighth Yearbook of the Department of Supervisors and Directors of Instruction of the National Educational Association.* Bureau of Publications, Teachers College, Columbia University, New York, 1935. This study tells of books and other sources of information to aid in acquiring "knowledge and understandings" as well as of those materials to be used as means of expression. It should be especially useful in conducting work on the unit plan.

"The Social Studies Curriculum." *Fourteenth Yearbook of the Department of Superintendence.* The Department of Superintendence, 1201 16th St., N. W., Washington, D. C., 1936. This yearbook sets forth the result of studies concerning the teaching of social studies and "suggests the contribution that education may be expected to make to American democracy" (p. 5). The content of courses, grade placement of material, and procedures are discussed.

Horn, Ernest. *Methods of Instruction in the Social Studies.* Scribners, 1937. This is a thought-provoking discussion of fundamental factors underlying the teaching of social studies based upon scientific data, containing definite suggestions for applying them in the classroom.

Hussey, Marguerite M. *Teaching for Health*. Prentice-Hall, Inc., 1939. This book gives the history of the steps in promoting health through education. It applies the educational philosophy of John Dewey to presenting the idea of helping the individual to know the necessary pertinent facts, to use good health practices, and to acquire an interest in and proper attitude toward health.

"A Plan of Health Education for the Rural and Elementary Schools of Iowa." *Iowa Elementary Teachers' Handbook, Vol. VII*. State of Iowa, 1946. This is a course of study prepared by a committee for the elementary grades. It includes many charts to be used by the teacher, parents, children, and others for checking health and safety practices.

Lacey, J. M. *Teaching the Social Studies*. Burgess Publishing Co., 1941. This contains good material for aid in conducting unit work in all of its phases.

Nineteen-Fifty Yearbook, Association for Supervision and Curriculum Development. "Fostering Mental Health in Our Schools." This book deals primarily with the techniques for diagnosing the well-being and furthering the mental health of "normal" children. It has practical down-to-earth suggestions, very usable by teachers in their regular classroom situations.

"Health Education." *Report of National Education Association and the American Medical Association*, N.E.A., Washington, D. C., 1941. This report has sections dealing with the various problems of health in many aspects.

Nineteenth Yearbook of the National Council for the Social Studies. "Geographic Approaches to Social Education." Washington 6, D. C., 1948. This is a splendid book for teachers on any elementary level to read. Not only is there a part on general goals and philosophy but discussions of objectives, materials, and instruction on the elementary level.

Salt, E. B., Fox, G. I., Douthett, E. M., Stevens, B. K. *Teaching Physical Education in the Elementary School*. A. S. Barnes and Co., New York, 1942. This book presents the present-day philosophy of physical education. It also gives directions for many activities.

"The Study and Teaching of American History." *Seventeenth Yearbook of the National Council for the Social Studies*. Washington, D. C., 1946. This gives the "newer interpretations and emphases in American history" and presents methods as well as materials for teaching. It discusses the place of reading in learning history.

"Democratic Human Relations." *Sixteenth Yearbook of the National Council for the Social Studies*. National Council for the Social Studies, 1201 16th St., N. W., Washington 6, D. C., 1945. This is a discussion devoted primarily to helps for promoting better human relationships.

"Social Studies," *Iowa Elementary Teachers Handbook*. Vol. VI. Department of Public Instruction, Des Moines, Iowa, 1944. This is a good guide for teaching social studies for the third through the eighth grades. It shows how to correlate the teaching of history and geography. Most of the work is presented in definite sample units.

Storm, Grace E. *The Social Studies in the Primary Grades*. Lyons and Carnahan, 1931. This is a helpful book for those interested in presenting social studies in the kindergarten and primary grades. It gives suggestions for working out units, information on the various fields, illustrative lessons, and other practical help.

Strang, R. M. and Smiley, D. F. *The Role of the Teacher in Health Education*. The Macmillan Co., 1941. This is a usable book to give teachers a general picture as well as specific suggestions for a health program on different levels. Has good sections on safety, sex, and mental hygiene.

Thirty-second Yearbook, The National Society for the Study of Education. "The Teaching of Geography." Public School Publishing Co., Bloomington, Illinois, 1933. This is a general survey which discusses objectives and methods of presentations on different levels as well as measurements of students' progress.

Turner, C. E. *Principles of Health Education*. D. C. Heath & Co., 1939. Some history of the health education movement and a good outline of the phases of health are given. The book brings in also the coordination of other community agencies and is helpful to a school planning a health education program.

"The Social Studies in the Elementary School." *Twelfth Yearbook, National Council for the Social Studies*. Washington, D. C., 1941.
Part One: The Child, the School, and Society.
Part Two: Curriculum Development in the Social Studies.
Part Three: Unitary Samples of Social Learning.
Part Four: Evaluation in Social Studies.

Wesley, E. B. and Adams, M. A. *Teaching Social Studies in the Elementary Schools*. D. C. Heath and Co., 1946. A helpful book in this field, it deals with organization of the social studies curriculum, shows its place in child development, sets up objectives, and gives suggestions for procedures.

Wild, Monica R. and White, Doris E. *Physical Education for Elementary Grades*. A bulletin of the Iowa State Teachers College, Cedar Falls, Iowa. Revised 1950. This volume contains the latest theories and practices in teaching physical education to elementary-school children, with implications for higher grades. It has a very complete collection of folk songs (with music), games (with directions for playing), as well as excellent suggestions for teaching modern games, exercises, etc., both individual and group for indoors and outside. These are all arranged by approximate grade level for most effective use.

PART FIVE

Science

CHAPTER 21

BACKGROUND AND OBJECTIVES

IMPORTANCE OF SCIENCE IN PRESENT-DAY LIVING

THERE can be no question in the mind of any reasonable person as to the *importance* of *science* in the world of today. Science helps us to produce our food, clothing, shelter, recreational facilities, and all types of communication. A knowledge of science helps us to have better health and longer lives and changes basically our social, economic, and political relations. In fact, it is difficult to find any phase of life which is not affected to some degree by science. Furthermore, a thoughtful look to the future indicates that in all probability the extent of this influence will increase and spread to areas as yet practically untouched.

In view of the almost universal application of the principles of science to our everyday living and the place science has occupied in the development of our civilization, it would seem that, in spite of recent advances, it has an inadequate place in our elementary school curricula. Perhaps we are even more negligent in the preparation we give our elementary teachers, especially those with two years of training or less. If there can be but one course in science for prospective teachers, it would seem reasonable that it should be concerned with the materials and methods of teaching which these elementary teachers will be likely to use with their pupils. A traditional first course in physics, biology, or chemistry is too remotely related to the schoolroom needs of the teachers. If, in addition, the college science teachers could use methods in their classes which their students with slight adaptation could use effectively with their elementary pupils, a giant stride would be made toward more efficient elementary science teaching. Until such conditions are more nearly met, many prospective teachers and some experienced elementary teachers hesitate to attempt science teaching because of their lack of training and knowledge. Although these factors are highly essential to the most successful teaching and should be obtained before science teaching is attempted, much may be done, even with the lack of proper training and sufficient knowledge at the start, if the teacher uses common sense and is willing to spend a little extra time learning, as she teaches, what she should have obtained in training.

At this point a bit of *historical background* may be helpful in clarifying present-day status of science teaching in elementary schools. By 1850, public elementary schools were taking root in our country, and Pestalozzi's concepts that a child should be an active participant in the learning process and that his individuality should be emphasized were slowly but surely leavening our methods of teaching children. Teachers and pupils used more often the concrete materials of the environment in addition to books. For example, instead of *reading* about a rose, pupils would bring a specimen into the classroom for first-hand study. These "object lessons" were direct and made use of the senses of sight, touch, smell, and encouraged realistic pupil reactions to the "objects" in the form of discussion, opinion, and stimulation of further activity. Such learning activities seemed to be much more effective than the commonly used formal method of study from textbooks with memory as the chief agent of learning.

OBJECT TEACHING

This technique, "object teaching," which aroused formidable criticism in the 1870's, had two rather serious weaknesses—the "object lessons" were too often disconnected, and frequently they were unrelated to the pupil's environment. Therefore, the tasks of those interested in the teaching of elementary science of that day seemed to be (1) to unify or organize the science materials and (2) to connect them directly with the pupil's environment. It took about twenty years to get this done (1870-1890). The transition was made more difficult by (1) the oncoming industrial revolution, which clearly indicated that science should be "practical" as well as "cultural" and (2) the rather radical changes in thinking about the nature of the learning process, which insisted strongly on the individuality of the child and emphasized the importance of insight and the values of reflective thinking even with primary children.

NATURE STUDY

Around 1890, educators began to introduce the study of nature into the schools. They continued to emphasize the use of the senses; much of the study came directly from pupil's environment; and the materials could be organized without undue difficulty. Out of this background grew the *nature-study* movement, much as we have it today.[1] From the beginning, the lack of trained teachers often blocked more notable advances in science teaching. To help remove this difficulty, numerous nature-study manuals were prepared to assist teachers and pupils in content materials and in methods of teaching and study. Work done at Cornell University under the leadership of Professors L. H. Bailey, Anna B. Comstock, and later by Dr. E. Lawrence Palmer and his talented wife Katherine V. Palmer have set, and are setting, high standards for this new field of science study. The "Nature Study Leaflets" from that institution continue to furnish teachers effective help in top-rank science teaching.

The nature-study movement, as well as its antecedent, "object teaching," started and developed in the elementary schools through the help of teacher training institutions of the day. The main purposes of each movement were (1) to bring the pupils into direct contact with the physical aspects of their environment, and (2) to use these experiences effectively in the mental, social, physical, and spiritual development of the children. Although they may be stated differently, these aims are basic in the science teaching of today. One thing, however, that nature study seemingly did not do was to organ-

[1] Underhill, Orra E. *The Origins and Development of Elementary-School Science.* Scott, Foresman and Co., Chicago. 1941.

ize sufficiently well the children's experiences so as to realize rather definite outcomes in scientific knowledge, habits of thought, and attitudes.

ORGANIZED SCIENCE

To complete the study of present-day science in the elementary school, another line of development must be mentioned—namely, that of so-called *organized science teaching*, which came from the colleges to the senior high schools in the form of more or less formal science reading, discussion, and experiment. Later, a simplification of the materials used in the high school appeared in "general science" courses in the junior high school. These frequently stressed practical applications of science and illustrative demonstrations by the instructors. Some of this science content has in turn sifted down to the intermediate grades and to some extent into the primary grades. The content in the newer series of elementary grade science texts comes from many science fields and seems to be selected on the basis of usefulness to the child. It is written and illustrated in terms easily understood by him. For example, one series[1] lists as content materials for Grade I the following: The Seasons; Animals, Plants; Things That Are Not Alive; Weather; The Magnet; What Makes Things Go; An Easy Way; Water; Homes. Undoubtedly this wide spread of science content even in the first grade is due in a large degree to the amazing scientific development of the last twenty-five years. Daily we use the principles and facts of science in integrated forms whether it be meteorology ("seasons," "weather"), biology ("plants," and "animals"), geology ("things that are not alive"), physics ("magnets," "an easy way"), or some of the other first-grade science materials. Moreover, we try to help these young pupils (and those on all other grade levels) to develop scientific attitudes and learn to use scientific method, and above all to recognize the great truths of science.

Thus we find *present-day elementary science* is truly the child of its forebears. It is not the exact reproduction of any one of them but has some characteristics of all. One can find some prototypes of the old science stories and poems for children. We still use the method

[1] Craig, et. al. *Our World of Science.* Ginn and Company, Boston. 1946.

of object teaching; and most certainly we consider the child as the center of attention in developing both content and method. We now have an enlarged environment that takes in the whole scope of science. We are careful to organize materials and to employ only such methods as will most surely develop a scientific attitude and, from their very first school experiences, attempt to make the scientific method perfectly natural to the children.

A discussion of the *objectives* of today's science teaching should assist the prospective teacher and even the experienced teacher to use science materials more proficiently. Teachers should have good reasons "why" they use any subject in guiding the development of their pupils. This is especially true of science. The ultimate goals of science teaching should be crystal clear and should light every step of progress toward their realization.

Science teachers may state their general aims differently, but usually they include the following: (1) to help pupils acquire the essential scientific knowledge and skills which will help them meet the problems of life successfully; (2) to light up fields of science which are new and useful to the pupils and to secure, if possible, the pupils' permanent interest in them; (3) to develop in the pupils a scientific attitude toward natural phenomena and to help them acquire a systematic method of procedure in dealing with them; (4) to introduce the pupils, as they develop, to constantly broader scientific experiences, concepts, and principles; (5) to establish in the pupils' thinking the intimate and increasingly significant relations between science and the social studies.

SCIENTIFIC CONCEPTS AND HABITS OF THOUGHT

Each of these basic purposes of science teaching seems to be of such importance as to warrant a brief amplification.

1. The acquisition of scientific knowledge and skills is a necessity in this rapidly accelerating machine age. Take, for example, the matter of safety. Most certainly, the school should supply the truths about safety as well as equip pupils with skills and influence their attitudes in the right direction in this field. Health knowledge and habits are perhaps even more vital to the individual, family, and community. Pupils readily understand that each one must know these

and other scientific facts and attitudes before he will know how to be the best possible citizen of his home, school, or community. Teachers will realize that this means instruction that somehow will *function* in the place where it is needed. They know that such learning may or may not be connected with books. Pupils who walk on the highway facing the on-coming traffic, or sneeze into their handkerchiefs display evidences of good science teaching whatever its source.

2. Opening new fields of interest to pupils is often thought of (whether correctly or not) as a main purpose of science teaching. This aim is weighed with high potential for both teacher and pupils. Science as viewed from this objective is the teacher's opportunity to start her pupils on a self-developing, self-interesting, and self-continuing journey. It is the pupils' chance to observe a never-ending panorama of delightful surprise. A pupil who starts into the field of science with proper guidance should never lack in scope or intensity of interests. Lively interests almost assure optimum learnings, favorable attitudes, and deep satisfactions. To illustrate, a 4-H Club boy undertakes the project of raising baby beef. The housing, feeding, record keeping, rate of development, and other items keep an unending stream of interests passing in almost constant review. This boy is sure to learn valuable facts, acquire useful skills, and comprehend more clearly the underlying relationships growing out of his scientific experiment. If successful, he will have the satisfaction that comes with carrying an experiment through to a triumphant end. He may even win honors because of the excellence of his work. Some teachers are quite sure that this type of experience, involving a new field of science, is most fruitful in terms of pupil development and that it may enrich the pupil's life beyond our power to measure. Apparently the type of learning exeprience in science, especially in a new science field, helps to determine not only the amount of pupil growth but also the kind of procedure to be used.

3. The acquisition of a scientific attitude and the ability to use scientific method are usually considered parts of high school or college level development. Certainly these are both in evidence on the higher levels but their elements may be, and frequently are, acquired before or during the years of the elementary school. It is these beginnings with which we are concerned during the early years—not the refined

thinking and methods of the trained specialist. For example, a six-year-old asked his grandfather what made thunder. The grandfather said it was caused by potatoes rolling down the porch roof and was surprised to find that his grandson accepted the explanation. There may be satisfactory reasons why this boy did not sense the incongruities of the situation but, in general, if the science experiences had been effective and the elements of the scientific attitude had begun to take hold, even six-year-olds would ask such questions as these: Where did the potatoes go? How big were they? Why don't we eat them? Do they fall on all the roofs in town? Why do they fall just after lightning? In other words, very early in their lives, children may be encouraged and directed in forming habits of asking about strange experiences and in trying to align their observations with what they already know to be true. With this attitude may be developed a mistrust of all situations that do not seem to square up with the truth as already known. These are the basic elements from which scientific attitudes and methods are formed. In adult life we call it "making up one's mind," "looking at a question from all sides," or "getting all the evidence" before saying or doing something.

The field of science is especially useful for aiding elementary children in forming sound habits of thinking and in meeting problem situations. With proper guidance they may be helped to understand that there is a reason for everything; that things do not "just happen"; that there is a cause-and-effect relationship in all of life's events. This type of teaching and learning may carry over into other fields, such as the social studies, and encourage the scientific spirit and procedures to function there also. If children were taught respect for scientific principles from their first days of school, much would be done to combat the various forms of superstition, such as belief in luck and charms. Games and devices of chance would be understood for what they really are. We would not have in our land three million[1] people who believe in astrology (founded on the assumption that the planets revolve around the earth) and who have their horoscopes plotted to see whether the signs are right to marry, to invest money, to take a trip, to die, or to make any important decision.

4. It is important that pupils learn the facts of science and become

[1] *Life.* Vol. 21. No. 27. December 30, 1946, p. 45.

able to transform them into habits of living; that they be guided into new and interesting fields of scientific endeavor; and that as these things are being done they develop an impartial attitude toward facts, together with a sound procedure of dealing with them. All these aims will be achieved more readily if pupil experiences are directed toward the underlying scientific principles and the pupils realize that their environment has in it forces which operate always in the same way. If, in addition, they understand that knowing how these forces always work enables people to use them, they have further incentive to study science.

The next problem teachers face is the presentation of these scientific concepts in such form and manner that pupils of the various ability levels will understand and be able to use them. The newer curriculum materials and textbooks with their manuals for teachers give direct aid in the organization of materials and methods of teaching on the various levels. Prospective teachers should be warned, however, that the assimilation of scientific concepts is a matter of mental growth, not a matter of memory. A pupil may recite glibly a statement of scientific principle but fail miserably when asked to illustrate from his own environment or to tell in his own words what it means. Pupils establish a scientific concept by many and varied experiences. As the pupils mature they are able to interpret their experiences on higher and higher levels. The teachers' task is to keep the difficulty level high enough to challenge the ability of every pupil as his mental power develops.

5. The excellent opportunities for developing pupils which science offers the elementary teacher are not enough. There must be added the numerous implications which science focusses directly on the general welfare of all human beings. For example, science has released atomic energy. We can use it to raise our plane of living or to destroy ourselves. The necessity of fixing indelibly in pupils' minds the close relationship between science and social well-being is obvious. It is evident that we must make sure of certain controls which will keep science a servant of mankind and not allow it to become our master. In science teaching as well as in the teaching of the social studies, teachers should make clear that the power which science gives *must be used for the good of all*, not for the benefit of a few, and that it must never be used to harm anyone. Ownership of a bicycle does not give

one the right to run over those who walk; the person who drives an automobile does not possess the right to crowd the bicycle rider off the street. Science creates machines to help people live better and more happily. Unfortunately it also creates machines which may be used to spread distress and destruction. Relationships such as these with all their human implications *may* (perhaps the word is *must*) be taught effectively in the elementary school. Moreover, this teaching should be started with the earliest science experiences.

Perhaps this discussion of the long-view aims may be *summarized* by stating that elementary science teachers should be concerned with using the materials of science to guide their pupils in the acquisition of important scientific facts and skills and orderly habits of thinking. This learning should be so directed as to develop a favorable attitude toward both the scientific method and the conclusions reached by means of it. Finally, extreme care should be exercised in aiding children to assimilate the great truths of science and to assure ourselves that neither now nor in the future will science be anything but the servant of mankind.

To reach the goals of science teaching, one must utilize (1) the proper *materials* of science as determined by curricula, textbooks, and the pupils' environment and experiences, and (2) the proper *methods* of teaching as determined by experimentation in handling group or individual problems.

Since a statement of the materials of science is usually available to the teacher in the curricula, textbooks, and pamphlets adopted by her school, and since this chapter is devoted principally to the methods of science teaching, only illustrative examples of science subject matter are included. The following quotation from a recent work reveals the broad concepts of science which present-day educators think should be attempted. One writer has called them the "abiding massive facts of life." They are "the modern scientific ideas of space, time, change, adaptation, interrelationships, variety, and man's attempt to control his environment."[1] It is quite obvious that this concept of science grants it an almost all-inclusive domain. It permits the greatest freedom in selecting science materials to fit the needs of life and to adjust to the

[1] Craig, G. S. *Science for the Elementary-School Teacher*, p. 8. Ginn and Co., Boston. 1940.

spread of pupil ability on various levels, from the first to the last of the elementary grades. There is also the utmost freedom of adjustment to such conditions as time of year and school equipment.

Perhaps a word of explanation would help the teacher to envision the broad expanse of the field encompassed by these ideas. Space exists between electrons as well as between stars. Time covers the millions of years already past as well as the untold aeons of the future. Change is all about us and affects everything, even our so-called "truths" of science. Perhaps the only unchanging fact in the world is that all natural things change. The concept of adaptation may contain the explanation for the existence of all forms of life, at least on this earth. Without the power to adapt to our environment or change our environment to meet our needs, we would have ceased to exist long ago or perhaps would never have begun to exist. Possibly all life depends on a host of relations of two or more natural forces or factors. These reactions are sometimes gathered under the general term *inter-relationships*. For example, the earth is being acted upon by natural forces, such as heat and cold; life on the earth is affected in many ways by the movements of the ocean of air which surrounds it; sunlight is necessary for life. Variety or difference is present in all life as we know it. For example, no leaf on the big elm tree is exactly like any other; your nose is not exactly like any other person's, for even identical twins have many rather basic differences. In man's attempts to control his environment he has made use of the forces of nature. As a result he has evolved what we know as scientific concepts, principles, methods of study, and attitudes toward life around him.

CHAPTER 22

ILLUSTRATIVE MATERIALS

PRIMARY MATERIALS

THE preceding chapter may seem to have little to do with the kind of science materials a teacher can use for her first grade tomorrow. The irrelevance, however, is apparent rather than real. Space may be the distance from home to school, or the length of the schoolroom, or the difference between Jane's height and Tom's. Time may be indicated by the number of candles on Harry's birthday cake, or the number of days in a week, or the length of the school year, or by the position of the clock's hands when we go to lunch. Change may be observed in differences in the weather, variation in the color of leaves, growth of plants, or changes in the height of pupils. Thus, we could go on through the list, always using materials to illustrate and teach the various concepts that fit most nearly the ability levels of the pupils. Furthermore, two or more of these phenomena may with advantage be taught together. Time and distance are illustrated by Mary's trip between home and school; time and change by noting that a large lump of coal burns longer than a small one. Illustrating two or more general concepts at once may create a more natural learning situation than would exist if each one were taught in isolation. Moreover, important interrelationships may thus be brought together in the experiences of the pupils. The more recent science curricula, textbooks, and teachers' manuals, with their numerous aids and suggestions, save time and aid the teacher in her original planning and organization.

Some science activities[1] suitable for younger children are listed below, together with suggestions as to when they may be used advantageously. Teachers should expect to find such materials in their curriculum or texts or in both.

A. Activities continuing throughout the year

KEEPING PETS: Rabbits, turtles, guinea pigs, insects, salamanders, canaries, white mice, hen and chickens. Making animal cages, feeding the animals, watching them, listening to them, observing their habits, learning care in handling them, collecting them from the country, buying them from the pet shop.

KEEPING AN AQUARIUM: Washing sand and pebbles, helping to arrange plants, helping to carry water, feeding fish (only three times per week), watching fish, observing habits, watching development of tadpoles.

MAKING A MUSEUM: For exhibits of rocks, shells, nuts, insects, nests, plants, quills, bark, bones, cotton, wool, fungus growth, gourds.

B. Seasonal activities

FALL—*Leaves:* Collecting and sorting as to size, shape, etc.; making leaf prints or blue prints; mounting; scuffing, jumping, raking, piling; putting over bulbs for winter protection; using for decoration of room; pressing and pasting in leaf books.

WINTER—*Feeding winter birds:* Making feeding tray, watching habits of different birds which come to feeding station, making birds' Christmas tree, making bird houses for spring, finding out what birds come to feeding tray, finding out what to feed them, planting trees and shrubs which will furnish food and shelter for them.

Snow and ice: Watching snow as it falls, modeling snow man, catching snowflakes on coat sleeve to see form of snowflakes, bringing in ice to watch it melt, playing with sleds, putting dishes of water out to freeze and noticing that ice takes more room than water, melting ice and noticing that it takes heat to melt ice.

SPRING: *Birds:* Watching for robin, bluebird, other birds; keeping record of date when first robin is seen, first bluebird, etc.; putting out short pieces of string or worsted for birds to use in building nests.

Experiments with plants: Planting lima beans or scarlet runner beans and from time to time pulling up one plant to see how it grows; watching sprouted potatoes growing in dark and in light; planting potato cutting with an eye and watching it

[1] Bulletin: Science Committee. Suggested List of Science Activities for Young Children. *Science and the Young Child*, pp. 22-24. Association for Childhood Education. Adapted.

grow; bringing twigs into room in the early spring and watching them develop; having a bean race, each child having a bean; growing sweet potatoes and carrots in water.

C. Activities connected with physical science

PLAYING WITH MAGNETS: Noticing what things magnets will and will not attract, fishing with magnets from boat—catching paper fish with nail put through them to be attracted by magnet.

CHEMISTRY: Dissolving things in water—salt, ink; watching salt and crystals form as water is evaporated from salt water.

MECHANICS: Balancing see-saw, playing with blocks, learning balance relations of one block with another, hammering nail to make it go straight, experiments with steam, observing machines in construction—steam shovels, cranes.

WATER: Playing with water, finding out what will float and what will sink, catching steam on glass when water is boiled, observing differences between dew and rain, watching rain wash houses and make rivers in gutter, boiling water and watching it disappear from pan, putting water on floor in sun and shade to see which dries faster.

The materials[1] of the next section serve several purposes. (1) They illustrate science materials arranged in the form of a unit. (2) They may be used on all grade levels, such as those found in a one-room rural school, provided pupils participate in ways best suited to their respective abilities. (3) They show how a wide variety of activities may be taught through the use of one science unit. (4) They point out how various fields of subject matter and skills may be co-ordinated to achieve certain ends through science teaching. (5) They bring the school and community into direct, cooperative efforts of lasting value to the community and to the school. The same procedures may be followed and similar results may be achieved in other subject matter fields, as suggested elsewhere in this book.

CONSERVATION OF WILD LIFE
(Appropriate for Autumn and Winter)

I. *The Introduction*. Conservation of wild life is a present-day problem. Children can study the problems and participate in their solution through first-hand experiences. They can see results of their efforts and these results may add to their present and future welfare.

---

[1] Martin, C. F. and Shepherd, L. A. *Conservation and the School.* Klipto Loose Leaf Co. 1941. Adapted.

II. *The Approach.* Interest may be initiated in the following ways: seeing flocks of birds migrating, finding birds' old nests, seeing squirrels carrying or hiding nuts, seeing other wild life, hearing or reading stories and poems pertaining to this topic.

III. *Setting up and planning the unit.*
A. Realization of the problems of animals' winter living (1) among migrating and non-migrating birds, (2) among animals that hibernate, store food, or those who do neither
B. Plans for the protection and care of wild animals, game birds, and song birds, by (1) taking a census, (2) constructing feeders for song birds and wild animals and game birds, (3) studying the environment for wild life habitats and natural supply of food, (4) selecting a location for a station for shelter and feeding, (5) ascertaining sources of food supply, (6) planting for cover and natural food supply, (7) releasing foundation stock, such as coveys of quail, (8) keeping records of activities, such as number of stations maintained, number of wild life fed, amount of food consumed, kind of plantings made (trees, cover), plantings of foundation stock (kind, place of release)

IV. *Activities incorporated.*

A. Activities for creating and constructing; such as building the shelters and feeders, making pictures, creating stories and verse, and carrying on dramatic play
B. Activities for developing attitudes of service, as (1) inspecting shelters and feeders regularly, (2) reporting on observations at feeding stations, (3) keeping predators from stations, (4) providing food when needed, (5) assisting with the planting of cover and feed lots, (6) caring for new plantings
C. Activities for investigating, such as (1) observing the environment in relation to wild life habitats, types of protection, the presence of natural food supply, tracks in the snow (from these they may draw conclusions), (2) taking excursions to find location for the shelter, (3) asking people in the community for information pertaining to the census and about soliciting food, (4) looking at pictures used for reference material, (5) listening over the radio to conservation or related programs, and for information about weather forecasts, (6) reading
D. Activities for appreciating, as (1) learning of birds' ways of living, (2) seeing their beauty, (3) hearing their calls and songs, (4) listening to and reading nature stories and poems, (5) listening to music and singing, (6) enjoying pictures

E. Activities for developing abilities in the skill subjects

1. Arithmetic: (a) with the primary group, building number concepts through counting the kinds of song birds on the feeder, recognizing the number of impressions made in individual tracks in the snow, and making comparisons of size; (b) with the upper grades, measuring, making graphs showing comparisons in size of flocks migrating, solving problems in buying seeds and trees, and many more

2. Reading and literature: (a) for the lower grades, "reading" pictures, making and reading experience charts, reading labels, signs, captions, bulletin board material, science material in books; (b) for the upper grades, reports of committees' reading of science books, reference books, reading for developing study skills or simply reading for pleasure

3. Language: giving committee reports, planning for the activities, making riddles (descriptions of animals), giving directions for mixing the food, acquiring new words, making compositions about the experiences at the stations, writing letters asking for information about wild life, filling in report forms, and others

4. Spelling: special words pertaining to conservation not included in the regular spelling lists (cover, conservation)

5. Writing: picture making by the younger children, manuscript form for making signs and labels, cursive for the older ones when filling in forms, and lettering for signs

F. Activities correlating with content subjects

1. History: learning of the events making conservation necessary and how it was practiced at different periods

2. Geography: acquiring the understanding of the value of plantings for cover for soil conservation and the dependence of wild life on environment, for food and protection

3. Citizenship and civics: children actually co-operating with other agencies, such as Izaak Walton League and conservation officers to improve their community

4. Elementary Science: learning of the food value of certain grains, of the habits of wild life, of the effect of seasons on animal life, and many more

5. Agriculture: learning the benefit to crops of insect-destroying birds, and the value of cover to encourage their presence

G. Activities for summarizing: (1) writing reports, (2) making booklets with pictures (snapshots and drawings) organized around the unit, (3) giving assembly programs or meetings to which the parents are invited to hear about the pupils' activities concerned with the unit, (4) making and showing movies telling of the activities

V. *Outcomes which may be expected*. These are varied and extensive. The following suggest the possibilities of more: (1) Children derive pleasure from these experiences with wild life. (2) Children may become more interested in living in rural districts. (3) The activities offer opportunities for co-operative endeavor. (4) Children have the satisfaction of actually aiding in community betterment. (5) They develop desirable personality traits of kindness and protection. (6) They gain in knowledge and learning skills through interesting experiences.

VI. *Materials and equipment*. The important material is the wild life of the community. In addition there should be science books, reference books, government and state bulletins, pictures, carpenter tools, lumber for constructing forms, grains, other food supplies, etc.

The unit quoted below, entitled "Making and Using Weather Forecasts,"[1] illustrates the type of science materials which may be used perhaps most successfully in the middle- and upper-grade range. The reading, experimentation, observation, and conclusions are of a more technical nature and in general require more mature abilities. This type of problem, if once started, may well be continued for an indefinite period during the year; or, if discontinued, it may be taken up later in the study of certain interesting weather phenomena appearing only at that period of the year.

MAKING AND USING WEATHER FORECASTS

Weather it always with us. We talk about it a great deal but can do practically nothing to change it. Hence, all man has been able to do about weather is to try to forecast it and make suitable preparation for it. Scientific study has improved forecasting in accuracy and lengthened the period of the forecast. Many people rely on these forecasts a great deal.

[1] "Science and Nature Study," pp. 40-43. *Iowa Elementary Teachers Handbook*, Volume V. Department of Public Instruction, Des Moines, Iowa. 1943. Adapted.

I. Studying the work of the Weather Bureau

    A. List the ways in which the farmer may be benefited by weather forecasts.

    B. State ways in which members of the farmer's family benefit by weather forecasts.

    C. Make lists of other occupations and people in various parts of the United States that profit by weather forecasts.

    D. Find information by visiting a weather station, or by reading a text or a reference book, about the following topics:

      1. Information needed by meteorologists for forecasting the weather.

      2. Manner of getting this information.

      3. Time of getting this information.

      4. Instruments needed for getting the necessary information.

      5. Number of weather stations in your state.

      6. Number of weather stations in the United States.

      7. Location of nearest weather station.

      8. Location of main Weather Bureau of the United States.

      9. Date on which the first Weather Bureau was established in the United States.

      10. Amount of salaries and other expenses annually.

      11. Manner in which Weather Bureau is financed.

      12. Per cent of accuracy of weather forecasts.

      13. Reasons for inaccuracies of weather forecasts.

    E. Form you opinion, after careful consideration, of the advisability of continuing or discontinuing the U.S. Weather Bureau, and state your conclusions.

II. Studying weather forecasts

    A. Study a newspaper's weather map daily for two weeks.

      1. See what weather conditions are shown.

      2. Watch to see whether predictions are accurate in your locality.

      3. Find out whether the forecasts were accurate in localities near you.

      4. Find a reason for forecasts' accuracy in some localities and not in others.

    B. Send for a few of the daily weather maps from the U.S. Weather Bureau at Washington, D. C. (Current maps are not always available.)

    C. Study a U.S. weather map.

      1. Observe the symbols for snow, rain, hail, sleet, clear condition, cloudy condition, partly cloudy, and wind.

2. Find the places having the same temperature in the Mississippi Valley.

3. Find the places east and west of your state having the same barometric pressure.

4. Notice the general directions of the winds in the United States.

5. Observe the weather conditions of your state and of Alaska. Is Alaska on the U.S. weather map?

6. Find a low-pressure area.

7. See whether a "high" follows this "low."

III. Reading about low air pressure

A. List the ways in which cyclones, tornadoes, thunderstorms, and hurricanes differ.

B. List the ways in which cyclones, tornadoes, thunderstorms, and hurricanes are alike.

IV. Making your own weather forecast

A. Record daily on a chart at 8:00 A.M. the following information:

1. Temperature.
2. Kinds of clouds.
3. Direction of cloud movement.
4. Movement of clouds—slow or fast.
5. Sunshine, cloudy, partly cloudy.
6. Direction of wind.
7. Velocity of wind.
8. Relatively humidity (if hygrometer is available).
9. Air pressure (if barometer is available).
10. Precipitation.

B. Observe the clouds.

1. Learn to recognize the cumulus, nimbus, stratus, and cirrus clouds, finding facts concerning their color, shape, height, and composition.
2. Record and learn the weather indicated by each kind of cloud.

C. Make observations about the wind.

1. Observe the wind's direction. Note that:
   a. A wind blowing from the south to southeast and a steadily falling barometer indicate a storm from the west or northwest.
   b. A wind blowing from the east to northeast and a steadily falling barometer indicate a rain from the south or southwest.
   c. A wind blowing from the west to northwest and a rising barometer indicate cool, fair weather.
2. Observe the velocity of winds.

  a. A breeze barely moves the leaves of trees and has a velocity of 1 to 5 miles per hour.

  b. A fresh wind moves small branches of trees and has a velocity of 5 to 15 miles per hour.

  c. A brisk to strong wind sways large branches of trees and has a velocity of 15 to 25 miles per hour.

  d. A high wind sways the trees and has a velocity of 25 to 35 miles per hour.

  e. A gale breaks branches of trees and has a velocity of 35 to 75 miles per hour.

  f. A hurricane destroys houses and uproots trees and has a velocity of 75 to 100 miles per hour.

  g. A tornado tears down buildings and pulls up trees and may have a velocity of 200 to 300 miles per hour.

 D. Read the thermometer.

  1. Note that a rising thermometer is favorable for rain.

  2. Refer to a text or reference book for information about the relation between humidity, temperature, air pressure, and winds.

V. Forming conclusions

 Do not become discouraged if your first attempts at forecasting are unsuccessful. Remember that forecasts made by experienced weather men are sometimes wrong.

VI. Evaluating weather signs and superstitions

 A. After observing, reading, and reasoning, decide which of these proverbs are based on reliable weather signs and which are based on superstition. Give reasons for your decision.

  1. A ring around the moon indicates a storm.

  2. A dog eating grass is a sign of rain.

  3. Rain before seven, clear before eleven.

  4. Rainbows in the morning, sailors take warning.

  6. Clear sunset, fair day tomorrow.

  6. Thick fur on animals in the fall indicates a very cold winter.

 B. Add to this list some other weather signs and superstitions you know.

 C. Decide as to their reliability.

VII. Finding other interesting customs and myths

 A. Find in a reference book some interesting ways by which people have tried to control the weather.

 B. Read the myths containing explanations given by people in early times for the causes of:

  1. Seasons.

2. Thunder.
3. Lightning.
4. Drought.
5. Rain.

VIII. Correlations

Agriculture, geography, health, history, language, literature, reading, spelling

IX. Grade range: 5–8

X. References[1]

[1] Pupil references include four series of science texts: *Compton's Pictured Encyclopedia, A Basic Science Education Series,* and the *World Book Encyclopedia.* Among the teacher references included are *Handbook of Nature Study* by Anna B. Comstock, several sets of Science Readers, and suggestions for leaflets from various sources. (The Handbook from which this unit is taken has a very usable reference list keyed to the various science units.)

CHAPTER 23

METHODS AND MEASUREMENTS

METHODS

THE next problem to consider is: *How* may science materials be used in the development of elementary school children? Any worthwhile answer to this question must indicate (1) what "development of children" means, (2) what types of classroom procedures, teaching aids and techniques are usually effective in this developing process, and (3) in what ways these methods of instruction may be applied in the field of science.

First, what is meant by *development of children*? Some teachers are satisfied if children memorize and are able to give back to them the main facts of the subject matter studied. Other teachers insist that efficient habits of study, abilities to use effectively the facts of subject matter in solving problems or in answering questions, and other useful habits be included. Still other teachers would extend the word "development" to the growth and establishment of favorable pupil attitudes toward the subject-matter field being studied and to an abiding faith in the principles established in the field covered. Certainly the finest type of growth would encompass all of the levels mentioned— conditioned of course, by the pupils' capacities to grow in these respects.

Second, what *instructional aids* and *techniques* are usually helpful in encouraging pupil growth on the different levels of development?

1. Those procedures which give pupils a clear insight into the values *to them* of the subject-matter field being studied. For example, the introduction of each new section in science might indicate the new ideas, interesting experiments, or field trips which may come up during the study and might show how these are of importance to the pupils.

2. Those procedures which exhibit most realistically the facts, relationships, and principles of the materials being studied. To illustrate: an excursion to see gullies caused by erosion; demonstration of a bottle broken by the expansion of water frozen into ice.

3. Those procedures which tend to enlist pupil thought and powers of imagination (wisely guided) in organizing the materials with which they themselves later will work and in discovering the most effective means of doing this work. For instance, the next job is to find out how weather may be forecast for 48 or more hours. Before any reading is done, pupils in class may discuss or suggest what they would like to know about this problem and what the most effective procedures would be in getting answers to the questions which might arise.

4. Those procedures which by their nature serve as measures of pupil development through the daily classroom activities. For example, the kinds of questions a pupil asks are usually indicative of his present stage of development, or the difficulty level on which he can answer questions might be a better measure of his growth to date. Is he limited in answering to the level of fact questions, or can he put two or more facts together and answer a problem question? Or do his answers show not only a knowledge of facts and the ability to use them in meeting definite situations but also effective habits of thinking and reasoning or even favorable attitudes toward the field studied? Thus the technique of questioning may indicate to the teacher the stage of pupil development. Other techniques besides questioning may do the same thing. These will be discussed later in this chapter.

Third, in what ways may these and other *principles of method be applied* in the teaching of science?

1. Assuming that a *favorable pupil attitude* toward a field of study, together with good reasons for studying it are advantageous in stimulating pupil growth, what techniques may be used to obtain these in the field of science?

a. Since pupils, especially those of lower grades, are naturally curious, the wise teacher uses a part of her classroom space to stimulate this natural bent in the direction of science. She may use collections of different sorts varying with the class work. The line of interest may be guided by the happenings in the fish bowl, in the herbarium, on the weather chart, or in the pen for pets. Every teacher can acquire an interesting classroom environment. Furthermore, every teacher can have at least an occasional school visitor to make additions to the current studies or to introduce new ones.

b. In addition to developing a stimulating classroom atmosphere the teacher may generate further interest by connecting the new science learning with the everyday experiences of her pupils in their community environment. This connection can be made through the organization of class work outlines, by discussions in class, and by excursions to various points of scientific interest in the community. All this tends to make science more real and to help pupils to realize more fully that both they and their communities are a part of the scientific world their textbooks mention.

c. This last suggestion is related directly to the activities by which each new science idea is introduced. The teacher may make this new experience a most intriguing one or just another chapter from the science book. Successful teachers use many and varied ways of making the approach inviting. One may describe an experience that opens the gate to a whole series of revealing experiences. Another may do it with just the right kind of picture. Perhaps the surest way to do it is to present the new experience by means of actual materials, by a demonstration, or by an experiment. In any case the approach gives a clear indication of thrilling experiences ahead.

Summarizing, if a favorable pupil attitude toward science is an asset to good teaching, teachers may secure it by enriching the classroom environment in the direction of science, by relating the new science facts and principles to the pupil's own experiences and community environment, and by taking great care in introducing each new science experience.

2. Again assuming that procedures are most desirable which *reveal most realistically* to the pupils the facts, relationships, and principles of science, the following suggestions would seem to be pertinent:

a. Perhaps the most useful technique in a realistic study of science is that of *observation*. Abilities acquired by observing intelligently the phenomena of the environment may equip pupils for a life filled with pleasures impossible without such abilities. There can be but little doubt of the possibilities for growth of a child whose eyes see, whose ears hear, and whose mind asks questions of every new experience, especially when it is connected with his natural environment. In teaching children to observe carefully and intelligently, science has a supreme opportunity to help develop lifelong habits of every-increasing value. Elementary school pupils (adults as well) differ greatly in ability to observe. Some seem to look almost without seeing, others apparently focus on objects without seeing much else, and a few seem to be able almost instinctively to see all these and also to distinguish significant relationships. Teachers use several types of aids in and out of the classroom to develop these varying powers of observation. Among them are bulletin boards, pictures, a science corner containing constantly changing science materials. Occasionally a written or oral check is made on the extent and nature of pupil observation of these. Ordinarily nothing beyond this check made with an eye to guidance is needed. However, should some pupils be unable to observe what a picture, herbarium, or fish bowl tells, the teacher may help them to improve their powers of observation by one or more of the following:

(1) Use very simple materials, such as a picture with a title, a drawing with a plain purpose, a weed seed with obvious means of dispersal.

(2) Note that with children observations are more useful if the observer sees the main factor as well as important details or facts in what is observed, such as title of the picture, words in the cartoon.

(3) Note that with children the "main factor" is often determined by the purpose of the observation, such as looking for kinds of trees or birds.

(4) If the main purpose is not predetermined, it is often well for the pupil to connect the observation with something already in his experience, or to try to see why the thing is or behaves that way, or whether it is likely to change, etc.

(5) Perhaps most important of all—pupils should be given much *practice in observing* such things as kinds of plants or animals.

(6) This practice should begin with simple situations and be ex-

tended to all levels of observation (to the extent of the pupils' abilities) from simple objects to complicated relationships.

b. The *excursion* is closely related to observation and tends to present first-hand experiences to the pupils. Moreover, its use as an educational practice is apparently on the increase. One writer observes: "The school journey has developed to a greater extent in the last five years than in the previous twenty. . . . Now educators feel that students need to be aware of what is going on in their community, in the world, and that there is a need for greater understanding not only of the world within reach but the world at large."[1]

Possibly more concrete evidence of the increase in interest in this technique is found in a comprehensive bibliography of articles and books dealing with the school excursion.[2] This compilation lists some 480 references dealing with the excursion in teaching. It probably is more important to note that over 380 were published between 1930 and 1938.

How can teachers make the most effective use of this technique in teaching science?

(1) Be reasonably sure that a trip is the best way to solve the science problem at hand. That is, an elaborate procedure should not be used if a less complicated one will serve the purpose as well or better.

(2) Plan every detail very carefully. This is a joint responsibility of the teacher and pupils. In this type of procedure it is possible to integrate social studies and science. Pupils may learn basic democratic group cooperation at the same time that they learn principles of science. Opportunities should be given the pupils whenever possible to participate in group planning. The following outline suggests step by step what good plans include. It is adapted from "An Excursion to Study Breeding Habits of Mosquitoes and Methods of Control."[3]

(a) Some suggested aims:
  To discover some of the ways in which mosquitoes breed.
  To realize the importance of co-operation in solving community problems.

[1] Hersey, P. R. "The School Journey," p. 332. Educational Screen, Vol. 19. October, 1940.

[2] *Field Studies in Schools and Colleges,* Bureau of Field Studies, New Jersey State Teachers College, Montclair, New Jersey. 1938.

[3] Pitluga, George E. *Science Excursions into the Community*, pp. 48-55. Bureau of Publications, Teachers College, Columbia University, New York. 1943.

To develop some understanding of methods that may be used to combat mosquitoes.

(b) Contributing facts and generalizations:
Some animals take very little care of their young.
Animals which have three body parts and six legs are called insects.
Insects lay eggs.
Diseases are spread by man and other animals.
Man has learned to prevent and check many diseases.

(c) Possible approaches:
Mosquito bites.
Sample of pond water with wrigglers.
Book or newspaper stories.

(d) Introduction to material involved:
Kinds of mosquitoes involved.
Sources of information.
Life history of mosquitoes.
How to control mosquitoes.
What children can do.

(e) Teachers bibliography:
Books on insect control.
Books on insect life.

(f) Preparation for the excursion:
Location of breeding places.
Care of trespass.
A cup lashed to a long wood handle to dip for specimens in suspected spots.
Places to find pupae or larvae.
Children visit several different breeding places rather than spend the whole time at one.

(g) Suggestions for the excursions:
Equipment—several cups attached to poles; glass jars with punctured lids.
Teacher preparation—cannot be prepared for all questions; should know most or refer to later study.
Teacher use of pupil questions to introduce meaningful relationships.
Individual trips—children make and bring reports after the first one.
A map of the neighborhood—equipped with colored pins for actual and suspected breeding places.

(h) Follow-up activities:
Projects
Find effect of oils and larvicides on wrigglers and pupae.
Discover how goldfish get on with wrigglers and pupae.
Make drawings showing life cycle.
Take photographs showing breeding places.

Write a story for a newspaper concerning mosquitoes.
Breed mosquitoes from eggs to adults.
Other excursions
Visit to Board of Health office.
Excursion to see area drained.
(i) Children's bibliography:
Elementary science books.
Primer of sanitation.

Certain elements may accrue from the excursion technique. Curtis[1] found that the excursion procedure "contributed to the *understanding* when used as a summary technique" in teaching conservation. He recommends "that the excursion be used as a major instrument of instruction in cases where illustration of subject matter is readily accessible in the community, and especially in cases where the concrete experiences of the pupils have been limited."

The *exploratory* or discovery element is present in every worthwhile excursion. The thrill of making a discovery is a highly motivating factor in any type of learning, especially in science. One science student proudly tells of his discovery of sand dunes quite near a university but overlooked until then by the university's nationally recognized geology department. Teachers often need to take care that this element does not overshadow the goals originally set up.

The *social* element may and usually does afford excellent opportunities for integration of group behavior with the purposes of science. Should pupils help set up the excursion, help control it while enroute, and help organize the follow-up activities? Is each member responsible for the good name of the whole group while at or away from school? With proper precaution and careful organization beforehand discipline, one of the most potent foes of the excursion, can be turned into a valuable channel of social training.

c. The *experiment* is another procedure used in science teaching to demonstrate in a realistic way many, if not all, scientific facts, relationships, and principles. Types of experiments vary with the subject matter, equipment, level of pupil ability, and purposes for which the experiments are being used. In the elementary grades pupils do experimenting mostly to prove or disprove certain ideas they may have and to solve problems for which they are seeking solutions. In these

[1] Curtis, Dwight K. "The Contribution of the Excursion to Understanding," *Journal of Educational Research*, pp. 201-212. November, 1944.

conditions children may repeat experiments again and again. Usually this procedure is most effective if both pupils and teacher work together in performing the experiments. More rarely the teacher may serve as demonstrator.

More specific suggestions for using this technique in the elementary grades are: (1) Keep the experiments simple. (2) Be sure the pupils focus attention on the principle which is being illustrated or proved, not merely on the experiment which is performed. (3) Illustrate the principle by different experiments, if possible calling attention to the principle in each instance. (4) Keep pupil attention through an experiment made by teacher or a pupil by (a) a discussion of the possibilities before the experiment is started, (b) questions and discussion by pupils and teacher at each step, and (c) discussion and reasons why the experiment came out as it did. (5) Be ready for a repetition, possibly in a simpler form, if some pupils did not catch the point or principle of the experiment. (6) Quick-learning pupils, rather than the teacher, should make explanations to slower pupils.

One rather good indication of success in the use of this procedure is the amount of carry-over to individual experimentation outside of class, either at home or at school. In some instances this "outside research" ranges widely, even beyond the ken of the teacher. For example, in one midwestern rural school two boys, one seventh grader and one eighth grader, having learned the Morse Code, made and used a telegraph outfit. Later they besieged every visitor for aid in constructing a telephone set, their current interest.

In summarizing the procedures used to present the materials of science in a striking and concrete manner (realistically), one can readily see that observation heads the list in importance. In fact this technique so pervades all the others that there is some doubt as to whether it should be singled out as a separate one. Certainly the excursion is helpful in numerous ways and offers almost unlimited opportunity for pupil growth, not only in science but in the art of living and working together. Finally, the experiment, with all its possibilities of use both in school by groups or individuals and outside of school either with or without the direction of the teacher, offers entrancing new fields for the development of elementary school boys and girls.

3. If we assume that it is a good thing for both teaching methods and teaching results for the pupils to have a part in setting up the science problems or units as well as in working them out later, what are some helpful suggestions for doing this successfully? There seem to be three types of techniques which may be helpful:

a. Those which are connected with teaching pupils how to help in the organization of their science materials.
b. Those which are related more or less closely with working out the problems or units originated in the first step.
c. Those which may be used for putting into good form the solutions to problems, answers to questions, charts, completed units, tables, and other outcomes of the second step.

The first type of technique, mentioned in "a" above, is connected with teaching pupils how to help in organizing their own materials of study.

(1) Start with problems in a field familiar to the pupils. For example, work out plans to discover what happens in a cocoon; or plan to show that air has weight; or plan to observe how a seed germinates.

(2) Start on a comparatively easy level early in the year.

(3) Encourage all pupils to contribute ideas and suggestions. Undoubtedly most of the best ones will come from a few pupils. Pupils can learn to do thinking and imagining of this type if they have the proper training.

(4) Stimulate pupil reaction by helping the pupils to put themselves more nearly into the environment of the problem being attacked. For instance, before *we* can find out what happens inside a cocoon, what must *we* do? After *we* get one, what should *we* do with it? Why? Do *you* think *we* can find out at once what *we* wish to know? Why? If not now, when? Why should or shouldn't *we* cut it open now to see what is inside? Is there any way to know now what may happen later? Interested pupils raise questions of this nature. If these pupil reactions are placed on the board and later organized by class and teacher into a plan of attack with definite portions for given pupils or committees of pupils to work out, the class will have had a part in originating, organizing, and assigning its own work in science. Furthermore, pupils will have had practice in one of the most stimulating types of discussion—creating something new and interesting. They

will have had challenge after challenge to use their best efforts in thinking out ways and means to meet definite situations in an environment somewhat familiar to them. They will have been encouraged to do this thinking on their own with an almost immediate check on the effectiveness of it. Finally, they will have helped put their thinking, stated mostly in the form of questions or statements, into a more nearly *organized whole* which they as a group or as individuals will be ready to attack.

The second type of technique, mentioned in "b" above, has to do with finding the facts, solving the problems, and answering the questions raised in the period of organization. The over-all consideration here is the ability to use the various skills in study. Some of these are: (1) locating materials in a book or elsewhere, (2) finding the correct answer to a question or problem and proving it is the right one, (3) knowing when a problem is solved, (4) being able to comprehend materials essential to the work at hand, (5) reading and working with reasonable speed, accuracy, and continuity to accomplish desired results, (6) finding the proper concrete materials if needed; carrying out an experiment if necessary; in short, meeting all conditions of work out of class. Wise science teachers do not assume that their pupils already know how to study. They check to find out and act on the results of the check.

The third type of technique, mentioned in "c" above, is the outgrowth of the first two and is connected with the arrangement of the results of study in a usable form. This assumes that some sort of written record as well as a mental record should be made and that this is a part of the procedure in which pupils help set up and work out their study activities in science. Undoubtedly every teacher realizes the advantages of summaries of results at opportune times to pupils working in science. Perhaps most teachers agree that it adds to the effectiveness of teaching if pupils put these summaries into written form—in notebooks, workbooks, or record books. If this is done, the following suggestions may be of use to the teacher:

(1) Pupils should have in mind and be able to give orally the main items or factors of the unit or problem being summarized.

(2) Pupils can usually summarize more effectively if they have in mind such important factors as: (a) statement of the problem or

unit title, (b) facts, information, materials necessary, (c) solution, answers to questions, data in the unit, (d) proof of correctness of solution, answers.

(3) If the teacher desires a written record, it usually pays to show pupils how best to make and keep it. This may be done by having a model for children to see, by providing pupils with full directions in written form, or by class discussion, with teacher and pupils co-operating in determining form, contents, size, etc. The last suggestion is best, of course, since pupils are drawn into the decisions and the reasons for written records are more likely to be brought out and understood. Written records include all types of drawings, pictures, tables, and other descriptive or numerical data related to the materials being studied.

By way of summary, the hope is again expressed that teachers will see the value of pupil participation in initiating problems and organizing the science materials they study as well as in working them out; that they will see this in terms of the mental and social growth of their pupils; and that they will further refine these types of procedure.

(4) The final type of procedure is, by virtue of its form and use, an integrated part of the activities of each day's work—those procedures which tend frequently to *check pupil abilities* and thus to serve as a constant measure of pupil growth.

These techniques are used in both class and study periods. Among those more commonly found in the class period are:

a. Teacher questions (usually oral) used to check pupil knowledge of science facts, such as, "What are two distinguishing characteristics of insects?"

b. An oral statement of a condition or situation to check on pupil ability to use the facts of science, such as, "Observe these mounted specimens and find out how many and which ones are insects."

c. The use of science problems which may require knowledge of, and ability to use, science facts as well as the mental power to apply scientific principles, such as: "Prove to the group that the earth moves."

While the variations of difficulty represented by these questions are not objective measures of ability, they are used daily by science teachers to approximate the level of development of their pupils. As mentioned above, this measuring is usually done as an integral part of the class work, with the teacher making mental or written notes of level of pupil response. Such measurements often result in a more accurate and valuable estimate of a pupil's present status or of his growth than do the results of a formal test.

Among the techniques used in the study period which may aid in measuring the growth of pupils is a well-arranged pupil study-guide for attacking science units or other materials. Teachers accomplish this by arranging the study materials in approximate scale form with the simplest materials at the beginning and the most difficult at the end. The level to which a pupil can climb day after day in his study is a rough estimate of his power or growth. This type of assignment technique has other values besides that of indicating the approximate growth levels of the pupils. It can be made to take care of a wide range of ability. It may serve as a stimulus to better work. It undoubtedly gives pupils of lower levels of ability a better chance than they would otherwise have.

To summarize, this section points out that the daily teaching techniques which tend to measure pupil growth are important and can probably be used to excellent advantage in many ways not now being exploited. They are worthy of the attention of the best teachers and deserve further experimentation and refinement.

Teachers and pupils need *periodic tests* of the results of teaching and learning in addition to those used as an integral part of the daily work. Standard tests are available commercially.[1] These may be used for purposes of comparison with general standards and, if the pupils' papers are studied carefully, some insight into specific difficulties as well as points of development of individual pupils may be discovered.

Usually a teacher cannot depend solely on commercial tests. She undoubtedly will need to make her own measuring instruments to fit

[1] The following test batteries have science tests of some type in them:

Analytical Scales of Attainment, Dvorak, A. and Van Wagenen, M. J. Educational Test Bureau, Minneapolis, Minnesota. 1932.

Unit Scales of Attainment, Brannon, M. E. et al. Educational Test Bureau, Minneapolis, Minnesota. 1932.

The New Stanford Achievement Test, Kelly, T. L. et al. World Book Company, Yonkers-on-Hudson, New York. 1940.

The Modern School Achievement Tests, Gates, A. I. et al. Bureau of Publications, Teachers College, Columbia University, New York City. 1931.

Public School Achievement Tests, Orleans, J. S. Public School Publishing Company, Bloomington, Illinois. 1931.

the various levels of her pupils' abilities, the specific subject matter taught, and her own methods of teaching. If she also has reliable tests of her pupils' capacities, such as mental ability, it is always interesting and sometimes helpful to compare the growth in science as measured by various achievement tests with the pupils' basic capabilities as measured by the mental tests or other tests of pupil capacity.

Whether tests are teacher-made or not, each pupil, as well as the teacher, should become fully aware of his growth or lack of growth in science. Perhaps one of the most delicate tasks connected with measuring pupil growth is that of using the test results to help pupils realize what their difficulties or successes mean and to help them improve their techniques of work.

MEASUREMENT

Evaluation of the results of teaching by the science teacher means far more than determining a test score or a class mark. It includes the interpretation of these and other evidences of pupil change as related to individual capacity, background, and other important factors. A final step in this evaluation seeks to help the pupil apply the findings to improve his own work in science.

1. *The measurement of science knowledge.* Although growth in science may not be measured wholly on the basis of knowledge of facts, meanings of terms, and statements of principles, very little real growth can be made without them. Hence, they should be found in a measuring instrument of ability or growth in this field.

Illustrative types of science tests follow:

a. *True-False*
   Directions: If the statement is true put an *x* on the *T*, if false put an *x* on the *F*.
   (1) The school drinking water should always be healthful   T   F
   (2) Our moon is larger than our sun . . . . T   F

b. *Multiple Choice*
   Directions: Check the phrase which makes the statement complete and true.
   (1) An insect always has
        (   ) (a) eight legs and two wings.
        (   ) (b) four body parts and eight legs.
        (   ) (c) six legs and two wings.

( ) (d) a poisonous sting and dark color.
( ) (e) three body parts and six legs.
(2) A calorie is a
( ) (a) unit of heat.
( ) (b) cross section of a plant.
( ) (c) unit of energy.
( ) (d) part of a flower.
( ) (e) measure of electricity.

c. *Completion*
Directions: Write *one* word in each blank that makes the sentence true.
(1) _____ in the air is necessary for human life.
(2) The force that draws objects toward the center of the earth is called _____.
(3) _____ is distance north or south from the equator.

d. *Filling in an outline*
Directions: Supply the proper subtopics under each heading in the spaces indicated.
(1) Four gases found in the atmosphere
(a) _____
(b) _____
(c) _____
(d) _____
(2) Illustrations of the kinds of simple levers
Directions: Use as many boxes as necessary to show the use of all simple levers.

(a) [ ] (b) [ ]

(c) [ ] (d) [ ]

(e) [ ] (f) [ ]

Teachers may find other test types in texts on educational tests and measurements or statistics. The purpose for which a test is used may largely determine which type will be most effective as a measuring instrument.

2. *Measurement of ability to solve science problems.* Knowledge of the facts of science is necessary to pupil growth, but the proper develop-

ment of power to use these facts in meeting problem situations in the field of science is perhaps even more essential to the fullest and healthiest type of pupil development. Suggestive types of written tests to measure ability to meet science problem situations follow:

a. How would you find the answer to this question if the needed materials were available?

   Problem

   What part of a gallon of water would a gallon of light snow make?

   Solution

   Step 1_____
              (write fn)
   Step 2_____
              (write in)
   Step 3_____
              (write in)

b. The noon shadow on the fourth grade's window shadow stick is exactly the same length today as it was last September 21.

   (1) What date is today?_____
   (2) Is the shadow growing longer, shorter, or remaining the same length?_____
   (3) Reason for your answer to No. 2_____
   (4) When will the shadow be longest or shortest if it is changing?
       _____
   (5) Reason for answer to No. 4_____

c. Connect with wavy lines for wires the two cells of the battery and the buzzer so the buzzer will buzz.

   (1) Step 1 _____
                      (write in)

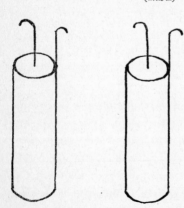
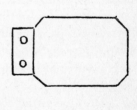

(2) Reason for step 1 _____

_____

(3) Step 2 _____
_(write in)

(4) Reason for step 2 _____

_____

(5) Step 3 _____
_(write in)

(6) Reason for step 3 _____

_____

d. Jack's bicycle has three sizes of sprocket gears on the rear wheel, a large, a middle-sized, and a small one.   Jack can shift from one to the other as needed.   What gear would he likely use when—

(1) Riding up a long hill?_____

(2) Reason for answer to No. 1_____

_____

(3) Riding on level ground or slight down grade?_____

(4) Reason for answer to No. 3_____

_____

(5) Taking a long ride over easy up and down grades?_____

(6) Reason for answer to No. 5_____

_____

3. *Measurement of changes in attitude toward and appreciations of the field of science.*

a. Important factors in changing attitudes and building appreciations are mentioned because they may aid teachers in measuring these significant but highly elusive attributes.

(1) The teacher's own attitude toward science as well as the strength and quality of her personality are perhaps of prime importance.

(2) The pupil's background of experience and present environment also rank high in determining his attitudes and appreciations.

(3) The quality of teaching as adjusted to individual needs, utilizing pupil environment, and stimulating to pupil thinking is a major factor.

(4) The kind of teaching is closely related to the success of the pupil's activities in the science field and in all probability is the influence which finally decides what his attitude will be.

b. Some types of checks found helpful by teachers are listed below. Perhaps no single check is always best; rather one should use a combination of several of the most effective ones. There seem to be no objective means of measuring all these changes, important as they are.

(1) Oral and written reactions by pupils to direct or indirect questions concerning their own attitudes and appreciations of science.

(2) Teacher observations, recorded as they are made, are valuable if kept over a sufficient length of time.

(3) Class marks and test scores in all other phases of science work may give a hint as to the pupil's attitude toward the subject.

(4) Individual conferences between teacher and pupil are frequently illuminating. They often reveal the pupil's attitude toward science and indicate how it may affect his future.

(5) One other indication of a pupil's attitude toward and his appreciation of science is his tendency to use his knowledge and abilities in science when working in other fields of study.

(6) Some teachers keep their class records in chart form. Others have a file for brief notes or data for the whole class. Others have blank leaves in their class record books for such information. In whatever form the records are kept, they should be readily available when needed.

QUESTIONS—PROBLEMS—PERSONAL REACTIONS

SECTION ONE: *Facts*

1. What were "object lessons"?
2. About what year did nature study appear in the elementary school curriculum? Who have been directly connected with movement? How?
3. State briefly the objectives of today's science teaching.
4. What two factors in teaching should be considered in reaching the goals of science education?
5. What are the "abiding massive facts of life"?
6. State three good science activities for primary grades for each season of the school year.
7. How is the unit on "Conservation of Wildlife" connected with the social studies, arithmetic, language, and science?
8. What does "development of children" mean?
9. Name two techniques which are likely to show "realistically" the facts relationships, and principles of science.
10. What are some elements of training that may accrue from the use of the excursion in teaching science?
11. What three types of technique are closely connected with getting pupils to aid in setting up and working out science problems?
12. How may pupil growth in science be checked daily?
13. Give two good reasons for using periodic tests in science teaching in addition to the daily class work checks.

14. What levels of growth in science may be checked by elementary teachers?

SECTION TWO: *Problems*

15. Should two-year elementary trained teachers be given more practical courses in college science? Why?
16. How would the "oncoming industrial revolution" indicate that science should be practical?
17. Show how "meteorology" can be taught to first-grade pupils.
18. Why should the ultimate goals of science teaching be "crystal clear" in the minds of science teachers?
19. Are the people who believe in astrology just "a little bit off"? Why?
20. Write out five lasting benefits a pupil may derive from the unit "Making and Using Weather Forecasts."
21. Give two good reasons why pupils should help organize the materials they are to study. Be able to defend these reasons.
22. Why should pupils be convinced that the materials of science are important? Is this true for all subject matter fields?
23. Should pupils be taught how to study science more effectively? Why?
24. Is the average elementary teacher able to test her pupils on the different levels suggested? Give reasons for your answer.

SECTION THREE: *Personal Reactions*

25. Do you agree that the training of elementary teachers is inadequate? Give reasons for your answer.
26. Does the idea that science should be used to develop children square with your thinking? If not, how does it differ?
27. Do you really think that six-year-olds can be taught to think scientifically, as was suggested by the "potato" story? Why?
28. Some science teachers disagree with the statement of the text that it is the business of science to teach people how to live together and to teach that the power science gives be used for the "good of all." What is your reaction?
29. In your opinion, is the "development of children" as important as the the text indicates? Why?
30. Arrange the four types of instructional techniques in order of importance as you view them.
31. Are notebooks in elementary grade science worth the time and effort it takes to make them? Be sure your answer is not prejudiced by your own past experiences.
32. You are an elementary teacher who must teach science. You feel you are not able to make tests to check fully the results of your teaching. What should you do?
33. Have your ideas of science teaching with regard to the part of the pupils in their own growth, the place of the subject matter of science, the role of the teacher, the uses of books, and the place of the community in this whole picture changed since you started work on this chapter?

SUGGESTIONS FOR FURTHER READING

Craig, Gerald S. *Science for the Elementary-School Teacher.* Ginn and Co., Boston, 1940. This is a book of basic information for teachers of elementary science from the viewpoints of philosophical background and everyday teaching methods. In addition, the teachers with inadequate science training will find welcome assistance in the science materials— reading and pictures, drawings, etc.

Noll, Victor H. *The Teaching of Science in Elementary and Secondary Schools.* Longmans, Green and Company, New York, 1939. This is a clear statement of the principal aims of science teaching. The author gives a clean-cut statement of what he thinks the "scientific attitude" is and suggests several types of relatively objective measurements of this factor. One chapter is devoted to practical suggestions on methods.

Pitluga, George E. *Science Excursions into the Community.* (A Handbook for teachers of grades Four through Eight.) Bureau of Publications, Teachers College, Columbia University, New York, 1943. A very helpful manual of suggestions for the classroom, this contains definite information not only on the use of the excursion as a teaching device but includes detailed directions for carrying them out in several widely different fields.

"Science Education in American Schools," Sections I and II. *Forty-sixth Yearbook of the National Society for the Study of Education, Part I,* University of Chicago Press, Chicago, 1947. This book contains excellent suggestions and helps for science teachers including general and specific problems in science teaching, objectives, in science instruction, and some 70 pages of practical directions in teaching science in the elementary grades. It also has a section on science teaching in high school.

"The Measure of Understanding in Science," Chapter VI. *Forty-fifth Yearbook of the National Society for the Study of Education, Part I,* University of Chicago Press, Chicago, 1946. This chapter assumes that "science understandings," are "objectives" in science teaching. It contains many illustrative types of tests which may be used to measure various kinds of science understandings which the average classroom teacher can construct.

Teaching films and filmstrips for science in elementary grades and guides for teachers in using them may be secured from:
     Encyclopedia Britannica Films Inc., Chicago, Illinois
     Young America Films, Inc., 18 E. 41st Street, New York 17, N. Y.
     Popular Science Publishing Co., Inc., (Audio-Visual Division) 350 4th Ave., New York 10, N. Y.

PART SIX

Development Through The Arts

CHAPTER 24

GROWTH THROUGH MUSICAL EXPERIENCE*

T HERE are *two definite courses* of procedure to choose between in the teaching of music in graded schools. One is the traditional course, in which the dominating aim is to teach the children to read music independently at sight. The attempt to develop this technical skill places the emphasis on an analytical study of musical detail and involves extensive drill in note-by-note reading. This approach to music, which closely parallels the alphabetic method once used in the teaching of reading, of necessity leaves limited opportunity for music itself, as an art, to figure in the program.

The other procedure is to base the program on a rich and varied musical experience for *all* of the children, and to allow them to grow naturally in musical skill and understanding through their own participation in re-creating a wide repertoire of songs accurately and beautifully. This basic singing experience, which is the heart of an effective modern music program, is also its most significant contribution to the child's musical development and appreciation. For if music is to succeed in the schools, the first essential is that it be made from the beginning an enjoyable and rewarding experience for the entire group. To acquaint the children with the wealth of song literature that is their heritage from the past by re-creating it on a high musical level is the first and the all-important goal.

* Written by the late Professor C. A. Fullerton, Iowa State Teachers College, Cedar Falls, Iowa. Revised by Margaret Fullerton, and based upon material in *Together We Sing,* by Charles A. Fullerton and Irving Wolfe (Head, Division of Music, George Peabody College for Teachers, Nashville, Tenn.). Follett Publishing Co., 1950.

HISTORY AND OBJECTIVES

How can this basic experience be successfully realized in the schools today during the precious minutes allotted to music? A brief *history* is necessary at this point to show what was done to find the answer to the problem for the rural teacher—an answer that serves equally well for the village or town teacher. In 1922 some one-room rural schools were selected for demonstration purposes, and one of the authors was asked to help in working out a course in music for them. It was evident from the start that the *note-by-note* reading of music in the rural schools could not be carried on successfully by the rural teachers themselves. By that time, the phonograph had been so improved that it could really convey the charm of a song to the listener. Quite naturally the thought occurred that the phonograph could furnish the solution of the rural school music problem. Within a few months a phonograph company had a record made of several simple, attractive children's songs, and the plan was tried. The first lesson was a pronounced success from the standpoint of the interest of the children; and their accurate and beautiful singing seemed to transform the school. The plan went from school to school, from county to county, and from state to state. In the years that it has been in use, there has not been one failure when it has been given a fair chance. Here was a situation in which not only were the ears automatically involved in every music lesson but a means was in operation by which the children always could hear the song sung accurately. At the same time, the progress of each pupil could be checked by tests with the phonograph.

PHONOGRAPH USE AND CHOIR PLAN

These phonograph tests dealt with what might be considered minimum essentials, and the expectancy was that everyone should pass them successfully. This developed in the children the confidence that usually goes with success in what is attempted. The daily participation of children in re-creating songs with the recording artists gradually developed in them good singing habits. As time went on, the pupils who always heard songs sung correctly and sang them correctly themselves attracted the attention of the public by their beautiful singing. The children who learned to sing a selected list of songs exactly with the

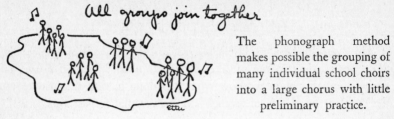

All groups join together

The phonograph method makes possible the grouping of many individual school choirs into a large chorus with little preliminary practice.

phonograph were called the school choir, hence the name *Choir Plan*. These choirs were quite generally assembled into county choruses and sometimes into state choruses. Where the course of procedure which had been developed was strictly adhered to, the singing of the groups was uniformly excellent. When 4000 children from rural schools sang at a state fair after only one short rehearsal, music critics in the audience reported that they sang in correct pitch with perfect diction, true rhythm, precise phrasing, and with splendid tone quality.

The choice of song material is, of course, basic to the success of any music program. Unless songs of the finest musical quality, inherently interesting and appealing to children in both words and melody, are used, no worthwhile musical education can take place. Especial care has been given to this in the development of the Choir Plan. By means of the recordings, a wide repertoire of songs of child life, folk songs of many nationalities, songs related to the story of America's growth, seasonal songs, songs that have lived through the ages are brought directly into the schoolroom to become a permanent part of the children's musical experience.

THE CHOIR PLAN IN DETAIL

The following are the *steps* of procedure *in learning a song* by the choir plan.

First: The class listens to an easy song rendered a few times by the phonograph.

Second: The class joins with the record in some very easy parts of the song—the parts marked "Sing" in the musical score. (See "An Easy Song," page 575.)

Third: After the class sings the easy parts correctly, it exchanges parts with the machine and sings the more difficult ones—the parts marked "Listen."

Fourth: The class sings the entire stanza softly with the machine.

Fifth: The class sings the stanza softly without the machine.

Except for frequent trials, only those who can sing accurately sing with the recording. The best plan to transform non-singers into singers is to have them listen to accurate singing most of the time without attempting to sing.

Parallel to the simple, interesting singing program, the phonograph is also used in vitalizing and establishing *rhythmic movements*. Wide experience has shown that the series suggested below, which

begins with simple arm movements and ends with marching, is of surprising value in unifying a school in preparation for singing, as well as preparation for the mastery of rhythm.

1. Slide hands upward alternately, palms touching.
2. Clap hands, touch shoulders.
3. Clap loudly, softly.
4. Imitate marching with hands. (With elbows at side, and palms parallel, move forearms up and down alternately in the manner of a toy soldier.)
5. Add marking time with the feet to marching with hands.
6. Mark time with feet.

Use "Sailor Lads,"[1] (three stanzas) to test these movements.

The equipment needed to teach by the Choir Plan is a phonograph that by actual count makes 78 revolutions per minute, a supply of

[1] Fullerton, C. A. and Wolfe, Irving. *Together We Sing.* Follett Publishing Co. 1950.

records, and enough copies of the song so that all above the second grade can see the words and music while learning it from the phonograph. The importance of the quality of the equipment used cannot be overemphasized. With the tremendous increase in the use of audiovisual materials, a phonograph has become standard equipment in the modern schoolroom. A good machine can be obtained at a reasonable price and with proper care can render long and invaluable service to the school. In the Choir Plan, careful adjustments of the speed of the machine to insure proper pitch, the choice of the best type of needle for fine tone reproduction, and special care in handling and storing records are matters of first importance.

By making every music lesson so interesting and so easy that practically all pupils can succeed, one not only demonstrates democracy in music education, but gradually transforms an unmusical school into a musical school. From the standpoint of democracy the beautiful singing of simple songs by nearly the entire school furnishes a much better environment for the talented pupils than the school in which the few especially gifted in music do all the singing.

In all of this program there is nothing peculiar to rural children, for music is music, and children are children, whether in cities, villages, or rural districts. To understand precisely how the Choir Plan is *introduced* and *conducted*, imagine a one-room rural school or a graded school where the conditions are decidedly unfavorable for carrying on the music program, where the children have had practically no musical training, and are well below the average in musical aptitude.

To start the Choir Plan in a rural or graded school, it is well to begin with rhythmic movements in order to unify the group and to insure unanimous participation from the first. "The Music Box" is well adapted to this introductory activity. After playing this song once or twice, have the entire group make the following movements to the rhythm of the record: slide hands upward alternately, hands touching as they pass each other. Pupils should stand erect, using sprightly movements. This process should be made contagious by the vigorous leadership of the teacher. The second rhythmic movement, clapping hands lightly and touching shoulders, may also be introduced. From day to day these two movements may be used until the class can keep

The Music-Box

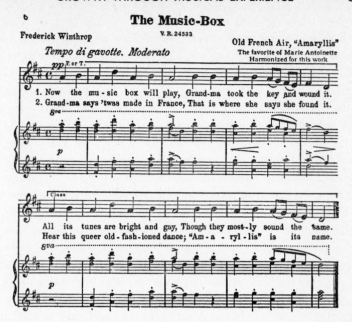

time exactly with the instrument. The additional movements should be introduced gradually as the children become ready for them. Much of this first practice in rhythm may be done without the instrument, but it should always be used for testing.

"An Easy Song," included on a record with thirteen other primary songs, is a good choice for an introductory song in *starting the choir plan*. Have the children listen to the record several times with copies of the song in hand. Then have the class sing lightly (so each can hear the phonograph) the second "cuckoo"—the part marked "Sing" —the teacher joining with them. In this first lesson divide the class

An Easy Song

into two sections: those who can sing the second "cuckoo" with the machine and those who cannot. Have those who cannot sing with the instrument listen without singing. A child is not getting an opportunity to learn to sing correctly when his ears are filled with his own discordant tones. His chances to learn to sing perfectly are much better when he is listening most of the time to the others who sing accurately than when singing inaccurately himself. Ask the singers to do the parts marked "Sing" several times. Give the entire class one or two more chances, and then have the singing group exchange parts with the machine, singing the phrases marked "Listen." When the singing group can sing these more difficult parts with the phonograph with accuracy and assurance, have them sing the entire stanza, the others listening. After singing the first stanza several times, have the entire class try singing with the phonograph again. Next, have the singers, including the teacher, sing both stanzas by themselves once more. Give especial attention to the rhythm, prolonging the long notes and observing the rests. The next and final step is singing the song without the machine. A little more volume may be used here, but the same fine tone quality must be preserved.

To *summarize*, the first steps in simple rhythm have now been sketched out and the class has learned to sing one easy song. In some schools such songs as "The Farmer in the Dell" or "The Muffin Man," both of which are on the same record, will probably be easier for the children to learn because some of them may have heard them sung. It is important that the easiest songs be learned first, not only at the beginning but throughout the year. From now on it is not necessary to ask the children to listen. They cannot proceed in singing alternate parts with the instrument without listening. This is one of the reasons why learning songs with the phonograph produces such fine results.

It is a unique feature of the Choir Plan of teaching music that *direct testing* is not merely desirable, it is absolutely necessary. The children do not realize they are being tested. They are merely experiencing an interesting way of studying music. Those who have succeeded in all tests thus far, have passed. Those who have not succeeded are failing. The process [1] is extremely simple but very exacting. The spark plugs in an automobile are no more essential to its successful operation than

---

[1] The process is outlined in *Together We Sing*.

are these individual tests to the success of a music class. Every pupil either gets what is undertaken here or he misses it. There is no middle ground. The constant goal is one-hundred per cent choir membership.

Nearly all so-called "monotones," or perhaps better named "off-tune" singers, have a tendency to sing too low. Experience has shown that a very small percentage of them are incapable of learning to sing. Their need is for specific help in finding themselves musically. The plan is to start at their low pitch. A successful device is to have the entire group sing the first stanza of "The Farmer in the Dell" in the key of C several times and in a spirited manner. Next, sing it in the key of E♭, with everybody singing. Then sing it in the key of F and, finally, in the key of G. Other simple songs may be used. Some children will do best in one key and some in another. Teachers get much better results in this undertaking by having the entire school join in the singing than by individual work. The results of using such methods have been beyond expectation. Matching tunes with the class or the phonograph is a much more interesting musical experience than matching tones individually with a piano or even a teacher's voice, and self-confidence is more quickly and easily developed.

Getting all the pupils, or nearly all, to sing one simple song accurately with the phonograph is the most important initial achievement. It is suggested that the teachers, with "encouragement" as their watchword, set out to reveal to the boys and girls their capacity for musical growth. When music itself is brought directly to these children and their growth is constantly measured by a high standard (the phonograph record) both in singing and rhythmic activities, talent has adequate opportunity to reveal itself.

The *objective for the year* in the *rural schools* is to learn a selected list of songs—some very easy ones for the junior choir, and a well-balanced group for the regular choir. The regular choir lists recommended for use contain some very easy songs, school songs suitable for upper grades; standard songs, such as are used for mass singing by adults; and two-part songs. The entire school learns the junior songs early in the year, but they are generally sung in public only by the junior choirs. An eight-year cycle of recorded songs, without repetition, has been planned so that fresh material will be available for each year's work and a county or state can follow a uniform program. With this plan, groups of children in different communities can be assembled for choral singing.

Below is given the first-year list in the eight-year cycle. There are fifteen new songs each year without repetition, all of them on phonograph records.

First Year[1]

	Victor Record
Junior List	
Mary Had a Little Lamb	24533
Hobby Horse	24533
Easy Song	24533
Music Box	24533
Farmer in the Dell	24533
Regular List	
Sailor Lads	24533
Going to Market	24533
Keys of Heaven	24538
Glendy Burk	24538
Follow On (two parts)	24535
London Bridge (two parts)	24535
Marianina	24538
Over the Summer Sea	24538
Long, Long Ago (alto optional)	24536
Santa Lucia (alto optional)	24536

Choir membership charts are available for recording the progress made by each individual. In this way a superintendent or supervisor can see at a glance what pupils are eligible to sing in the choir. Two-part songs can be sung by the choir with accuracy and confidence by having the alto recorded separately and learned by the entire group before they sing the soprano. In some records the alto is not sung separately, but is made so prominent in the recording that classes can generally learn to sing it separately. In passing the tests for choir membership, singing either part accurately is sufficient. Singing by four's or by two's is good preparation for passing individual tests.

Although singing and rhythmical activities are the outstanding phases of music for rural schools as well as for graded schools, it is important that the essentials of *theory* be mastered. A firm foundation

[1] The songs in this list can be found in *Together We Sing*.

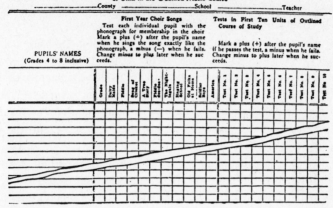

is provided for this by the extensive singing and rhythmic program. By following the music in the book while hearing it sung by the recording artist and by using their own voices, children develop an awareness of phrasing, rhythmic pattern, note values, melody line, etc. This is audio-visual learning in action. By learning as an added stanza, the syllables to a number of songs in various keys, children begin to

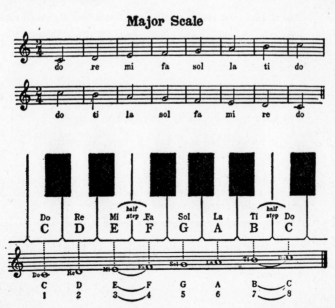

understand key signatures and tonal relationships. The program of rhythmic activities serves the same purpose. By clapping the rhythm to a variety of songs, the children experience the underlying pulse and the grouping of pulses that furnish the key to the rhythmic pattern. Further experience in moving with the music by stepping the note values of the songs (described in detail later in this chapter) gives them a first-hand understanding of this phase of music structure. To the rhythm of the phonograph, the various musical characters are made at the blackboard—notes, rests, sharps and flats, clef signs, and the staff itself.

The keyboard of the piano is used as a basis for the study of theory. The staff, the keyboard, and the syllables are combined in such a way as to be understood by all. The same simple thoroughgoing procedure is used here as in the rhythm and singing. The nine-step method, which for over thirty years has vitalized the study of elementary theory by keeping it related *to the song*, is a series of nine objective tests that begins with the singing of a simple song and ends with the recording of it on the blackboard in any required key. Success in the nine-step method is positive evidence of real growth.

An illustration of the nine-step method using "The Fiddle" follows:

First.....Sing it as a rote song, with clear tones and light movement.

Second...Sing it by syllable, committing the syllables to memory as follows: mi mi sol sol, fa mi re, do re, mi do, mi mi sol sol, fa mi re, do, do.

Third....Have pupils write initial letters for syllables on entire song on board or writing tablets.
m m s s, f m r, d r, m d, m m s s, f m r, d, d

Fourth...Sing it by syllable and clap rhythm, accenting first beat in each measure and touching others lightly.

Fifth....Now have the pupils sing the song by syllable, following letters, and place a dot over each strongly accented note, while teacher claps rhythm. Thus:
ṁ m s s, f́ m r, d́ r, ṁ d, ṁ m s s, f́ m r, d́, d́.

Sixth....Let all sing again and have pupils place a vertical bar before each accented note, extending the bar through the staff above or below.
ṁ m s s, | f́ m r, | d́ r, | ṁ d, | ṁ m s s, | f́ m r, | d́, | d́.

Seventh..Now clap the rhythm again, observe carefully what notes receive more than one beat and place a dash for each beat below the letters. Thus:

m m s s, | f m r, | d r, | m d, | m m s s, | f m r, | d, | d.

In seventh step where two notes occur to a beat, make a long dash under the two notes, and a short dash below the one-beat notes.

Eighth...Next write the corresponding notes beneath the syllables, or above. Thus:

Phonograph may be used with steps 1, 2, 3, 5, 6, 7.

Special devices for *rhythmical development* for vocal and instrumental classes in rural and graded schools are suggested for those passing the tests in the six basic rhythmic movements.

There is no rhythmic device that is more successful in giving the children the feeling and flow of the melody and an understanding of the meaning of the notes as symbols than that of stepping the note values to a song. This is a simplification of Dalcroze Eurhythmics.

As an introduction, it is well to have the class experiment in stepping the notes to a song such as "Music Box." They will soon decide to walk for the quarter notes and to run short steps for the eighth notes. For the half notes there will be an extra count. As they step for the first count, then bend the knee for the second, it is helpful to have them clap their hands lightly on the second count:

"Walk, walk, walk, walk, walk, walk, step, bend,
Walk, walk, walk, walk, run, run, run, run, walk, walk.
Walk, walk, walk, walk, walk, walk, step, bend,
Walk, walk, walk, walk, run, run, run, run, step, bend."

The whole note will offer them a challenge in devising movements for the four counts. For the sake of uniformity, have them step with the left foot for count one, extend the right foot forward for count two, extend the right foot to the side for count three, and extend the right foot to the rear for count four, touching the floor with the toe of the foot for each count. "Song of the Cricket" and "Sky Music" are songs well adapted to this activity.

For stepping a combination of the dotted quarter and eighth note, the best introduction is to have the group step this series of notes first: quarter-eighth-eighth-quarter-quarter; *i.e.*, walk-run-run-walk-walk— several times. To achieve the dotted quarter-eighth-quarter-quarter combination, progress from walk-run-run-walk-walk to walk-change-step-walk-walk, which substitutes a "catch-step" or two-step for the regular run-run that preceded it. "All Through the Night" and "America the Beautiful" are especially good for stepping these note values.

For stepping a dotted eighth and sixteenth note combination, a small skip step can be used. "Battle Hymn of the Republic" illustrates this rhythmic pattern well.

A good device for helping the children to observe the rests in a song and sustain its rhythmic flow is to have them clap lightly for each rest. This is an aid in such songs as "The Linden Tree," "An Easy Song," and others where the observation of the rest may present a rhythmic difficulty.

In addition to the stepping of note values, there are many other rhythmic responses that may be used in helping the children to feel and express the movement of the music. For example, the following procedure is successfully used with "An Easy Song":

1. After learning to sing this song accurately from the phonograph and printed music, the class claps "loud-soft" for each measure, singing the entire stanza with the machine.
2. Class recites the words in strict time, saying "Hm, Hm," for the first rest, a single "Hm" for the second rest, and the same in the second line.
3. Class sings the song with the machine, this time including the "Hm's."
4. Class stands and marks time in place, beginning with the left foot.
5. Class marches about the room, singing the song precisely as it is, maintaining silence for the rests.

"Dancing Song" may be used for the same purpose.

1. Class listens to the first phrase (four measures), claps loud-soft-soft for the second phrase, listens to the third phrase, and claps for the fourth.
2. Class claps loud-soft-soft for the first and the third phrases and listens for the second and the fourth phrases.

The possibilities for rhythmic activity are unlimited, for the sense of rhythm is as natural in the child as his ability to sing. The development of this innate rhythmic sense is a vital part of the music program, and the creative teacher, with the interested co-operation of her class, will find a variety of ways of expressing it. It is essential, however, always to keep in mind that the purpose is to establish firmly the rhythmic feel of the *music itself*. Each simple movement, as soon as it has been mastered, should be experienced *in time with the movement of the music*, preferably a song that is familiar.

A further contribution to increased musical skill and enjoyment for the children is the playing of simple accompaniments to some of the easier songs. A number of accompaniments have been written with the child player in mind, as well as chording accompaniments in various keys.

The whole program is further enriched by experience in listening to recordings of fine music. With the major role that the radio is playing in the daily lives of all Americans, the schools have an important responsibility in helping the boys and girls to become discriminating, intelligent listeners. Although their own experiences as musical performers furnish the true basis for this, listening to recordings of the music of the great composers is an important part of their musical education. The compositions suggested for use with the Choir Plan have been selected for their musical worth and their appeal to children. The acquisition of a record library and some useful music reference books is a worthwhile and rewarding investment.

The Choir Plan may be used in *graded schools without music supervision*. The following brief outline suggests how. For each of the eight grades there are two choir lists of ten songs each, 160 songs in all. For *four-room schools* the course of study is built on four levels, with two lists of songs equally difficult for each grade. With two grades in a room, the lower grade work will be taken the first year, the upper grade work the next, then the lower grade work again. The boys and girls who learn to sing all of these songs accurately, as they pass through They will have received excellent training in the only kind of sight singing that over ninety-five per cent of the singers use, and they will the grades, will have little trouble in learning to sing the 161st song.

have acquired this skill by the gradual, enjoyable processes of growth in musical experience.

Introducing the Choir Plan in *three-room* schools, where there are three grades in some of the rooms, involves no new problems except those of adjusting the course of study and the choir songs to the schools. In general, with three grades in a room, begin with the material for the lowest grade, selecting the easiest songs first. At the worst, the problems here are not so difficult as in the one-room school where it is necessary to treat the entire group as a unit. Passing the tests of the six basic rhythmic movements standardized by the song "The Quaker's Wife," and passing the singing tests of even ten selected songs, gives positive evidence that these children are getting superior training in music.

Many *two-room* schools prefer to begin with the rural list selected for the year, the lower grades taking the junior songs and the upper grades taking both. Additional songs, if needed, may be taken from the graded school lists. Solving the problem of how to teach music in the one-room rural schools has solved it for the two-room schools.

The Choir Plan can be used in *graded schools with music supervision*. Regardless of whether the attempt is made to teach children to sing by reading music note by note, or to teach them by the Choir Plan, the measure of success will be determined by the quality of their singing.

For standardization tests in singing, the minimum requirement should be the first list of choir songs for each of the eight grades; for testing rhythm, the minimum requirement should be the six basic movements for the first six grades.[1] In testing the singing with the phonograph, use groups of four at first. Eight pupils standing in a row can take the rhythm tests at the same time. Two songs well adapted for use with the six preliminary rhythm tests are "Sailor Lads" and "Quaker's Wife."

If the course of procedure suggested previously is adhered to in teaching the songs, a new music world may be opened up to the children. When they join with recording artists in re-creating songs, they become interested, sensitive listeners. The musical atmosphere created in this way establishes a friendly relationship between the children

[1] *Ibid.*

and music. In this type of music lesson the children's enjoyment increases their skill; and skill, in turn, increases enjoyment.

Schools that are using the *note-by-note reading* program with any series of music books will find that some features of the Choir Plan will help decidedly in their undertaking. The rhythmic activities represent the best methods known for developing a sense of rhythm. In the absence of a phonograph and the records, they can be used in giving children much valuable training, and with the phonograph and the records they can bring the rhythmical development of every pupil to an effective level.

This will increase very decidedly the ability of the children in reading music. The Choir Plan for teaching the rote songs can be used without a phonograph if the teacher and some of the better singers take the phonograph part, and the remainder of the pupils take the class part. The practice of committing to memory syllables of numerous easy songs, and also clapping the rhythm to them furnishes valuable preparation for independent reading of music. In fact, it is doubtful if anyone is expert in reading music by syllable who cannot sing the syllables to familiar songs without seeing the music. Using Choir Plan materials as supplementary merely to passing the tests on ten songs and passing the tests in the six basic rhythmic movements, will establish a standard of singing with all the pupils that will be far above what is ordinarily achieved in the average school.

As school music begins its second century in the United States, it seems reasonable that a thorough investigation be made concerning the best use of the precious school time allowed for this subject. The scientific method which has contributed so much to agriculture by improving crops and stock, and has raised the level of efficiency so much in the industrial world, should be drafted into serving the interests of children's education. No one will deny that the children are worth the effort, and this research work should not be left entirely to the trained experts in psychological laboratories. Music supervisors and grade teachers are in a position to render valuable service. One strong point in favor of their active participation is that when teachers make an important discovery they are likely to do something about it, whereas much of the research work done in colleges and universities is hidden away in the archives.

Learning to sing by singing seems to be a sensible procedure. For more than a quarter of a century, the phonograph method for teaching music in the schools has been accumulating evidence on what happens when music itself comes into direct contact with school children. Little effort has been made to teach the children to read music note by note. They have learned to sing by singing just as they learn to play ball by playing ball, to run by running, to jump by jumping. In all of these activities they increase their ability through experience. The growth is gradual and natural. In every music lesson with the phonograph, they receive training in all these elements needed in good singing—tone quality, rhythm, diction, intonation, attack and release, phrasing, pronunciation, and interpretation. While this course of procedure has been carried on wholly from the children's standpoint, a constant effort has been made to check every feature of the program with the writings of contemporary psychologists. In fact, a book written by one of the leading modern psychologists [1] who is particularly interested in music education reads like a laboratory report of what had been going on with the Choir Plan for fifteen years.

The progress children make in musical skill by using the Choir Plan depends in part on the fact that they are not asked to develop any artificial skills. They gain in rhythmic control and singing ability by re-creating good songs and engaging in interesting rhythmic activities. Every class under proper conditions may become a choir. Pupils exhibit decided growth in ability to learn new songs readily and in the mastery of rhythm. Theory becomes easy for them because it is vitally associated with the songs and rhythm. Furthermore, their preparation for the study of vocal and instrumental music is much increased.

This emphasis on music as an art in the schools is doing a great deal to restore the interest of the public in children's singing. It is a sad commentary on music education in the schools that so little attention has been given in the past decade to the singing of grade children. It is probably true that children in the grades, given the same time and attention, can sing as artistically as the *a cappella* choirs in high school. This is particularly true in schools where careful listening attitudes and the accompanying beautiful tone qualities are developed in the children. From the standpoint of the patron who is both tax-

[1] Mursell, James L. *The Psychology of Music.* W. W. Norton & Co. 1937.

payer and parent, it should be remembered that three-fourths of the children will get, while in the grades, all the training in music that the public schools give them; and that the high school groups in the contests represent a very small proportion of the entire school population. Music is robbed of much of its charm when it is used merely for winning in a contest. When music functions normally, it develops a feeling of good will and friendliness among people. A music festival in which the masses of the school population sing beautifully and where the audience joins with them occasionally in this uplifting experience, is a fine picture in democracy.

A well conducted *rhythm orchestra* or *band* is good fun for a school. Better results may be obtained if such an organization is delayed until the six basic rhythmic movements are mastered and at least ten songs

Rhythm Band

Only three of the several "instruments" commonly used.

are sung accurately. Unless the singing is well established, a rhythm orchestra may be a liability as far as rhythm is concerned. Using a song such as "Dancing Song"[1] for rhythm training will help in securing light, accurate rhythm. Safe directions for organizing a rhythm orchestra should be followed.[2] It is a tragedy for any school to develop a rhythm orchestra as a substitute for teaching children to sing.

[1] Victor Record 19891.
[2] Fullerton, C. A. and Wolfe, Irving. *Together We Sing*. Follett Publishing Co. 1950.

CREATIVE MUSIC

Something may be done along the line of *creative music* in the schools. In the natural sequence of children's development in music, most teachers would agree the first objective, apart from those rhythmical activities consisting of physical movements, is to have the children acquire a singing experience corresponding to the talking experience which they have upon entering school. As most children enter school without much singing experience, the singing program should be extensive. If the school music is to harmonize with the best educational ideals, these songs should come to the children as complete songs and be sung so beautifully that they will create a musical atmosphere in the schoolroom. One of the most urgent needs in school music is for teachers to realize how charmingly children sing when given a fair chance. The practice of teaching children songs with a piano will probably need to be abandoned before the real beauty of children's singing can be realized. All that the piano can bring the children is the pitch and duration of the tones; the song itself, with all its musical flavor, cannot be presented to the children in this way. Another serious handicap is the approach to music which builds up little tunes out of intervals and measures, with one-beat notes and two-beat notes. The five-year-old child who enters school with a vocabulary of 1000 or more words has not confined himself to one and two syllable words.

Children's singing should rise above all this. Songs and rhythm, and rhythm and songs, should be the body of the program until all, or nearly all, of the boys and girls are steeped in songs of good musical quality. Assuming that there are some future composers in every music class, this rich experience in singing songs of good quality is the ideal background for their future work as composers. The advantage is that while the school is giving them this preparation for composing, it is also giving all of the taxpayers' children the best possible musical experience. The Choir Plan, therefore, furnishes healthy conditions for creating music by building a background of fine songs, by developing a keen sense of rhythm and accurate pitch, and by helping pupils to learn a minimum of theory.

The first efforts in the creative field will undoubtedly be elementary and very simple. The teacher and class may work together to write a tune to fit a verse some member of the class had written, much as they might work together to draw or paint a picture illustrating an oral or written description. The following song[1] was created in just this way.

HALLOWE'EN

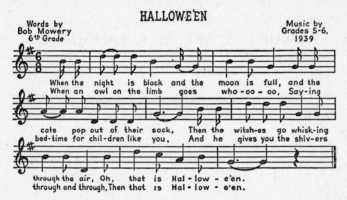

Words by
Bob Mowery
6ᵗʰ Grade

Music by
Grades 5-6,
1939

When the night is black and the moon is full, and the
When an owl on the limb goes who - oo - oo, Say-ing

cats pop out of their sack, Then the witch-es go whisk-ing
bed-time for chil-dren like you, And he gives you the shiv-ers

through the air, Oh, that is Hal - low - e'en.
through and through, Then that is Hal - low - e'en.

Words are never adequate to express the *nature* and the *mission* of *musical culture*; music is its own best spokesman. Fortunately visual beauty is showered upon us in abundance by nature. Nature has not been so lavish with the beauty that comes to us through our ears. Birds charm the world with their singing; waterfalls, running brooks, dashing waves, rustling leaves, contribute their share of the pleasing sounds that we hear; but most auditory beauty is man-made. Man's success in this field is one of his outstanding achievements.

Music is eloquent in expressing love, patriotism, nostalgia, or adoration for the Deity. Good music, sung spontaneously and beautifully creates an atmosphere of kinship and pleasure.

[1] Public Schools of Ambia, Indiana.   Rose Margaret Leak, music instructor.

CHAPTER 25

ACQUIRING ART AS A LANGUAGE*

PHILOSOPHICAL BACKGROUND

T HE *experience of creating* is not only the highest pleasure possible to man but it is also the most productive of individual growth. To understand the difference between a creative and a noncreative experience, observe a seventh-grade boy who builds model airplanes "for fun," and attends arithmetic class "because he has to." This boy probably attains more real growth with his hobby than with his arithmetic, not only in skills and information acquired, but also in the integration of his personality. The intensive focusing of all the faculties upon a creative undertaking seems to pull a person together. Growth and creation are essential to happiness. Why else should spring be so universally hailed as the happiest time of year? Things are developing most rapidly; nature is in her most creative mood. Why is childhood remembered by adults as the most pleasant time of life? Because the experiences of growing, learning, and creating have, for too many adults, slowed down or stopped. The human organism is dynamic. It must grow in order to remain healthy, happy, and alive. To grow, it must engage in creative endeavors which demand the expansion of its powers.

It is an essential responsibility of the teacher to see that *conditions* permitting wholesome creative experience are maintained for the child; and the purpose of this section is to suggest what these conditions may be.

* Written by Professor John W. Horns, Supervisor, Contra Costa County, Calif.

It is necessary to inquire briefly into the qualities of a genuine creative act which will bring to the child the pleasure and growth desired. It should be emphasized that the experience and its consequences to the child are what concern us. The finished work is merely a valuable indication of what has happened to the child.

Creative experience is not confined to the realm of what is known as art. The creation that counts is never limited to the external object. A painting is truly art only if it represents an *extension of understanding* and real growth within the personality of the individual. Travel may be considered creative experience, if the traveler absorbs his new experiences and really grows in his conception of the world. That is why some people enjoy traveling more than others. Reading also becomes a pleasure and an art to the degree that it promotes inner development.

What is desired for the child is adventure—the leading on from something new to something new again with an ever keener feeling of anticipation and ever more alert senses to find the yet unknown. Art means the spirit in which an act is performed. Painting pictures may or may not be art just as teaching school may or may not be art. Whether an act is to be thought of as art depends upon whether the person carries it out in a spirit of voluntary, open-eyed eagerness or whether he proceeds under coercion—the blind slave of some external force.

It is ultimately desirable that this positive spirit of art be carried into all the activities of the child. The special problem, however, is to see that the spirit is developed and preserved in the field commonly called art. Existing here in maximum purity and intensity, the spirit should thrive as does wild life in a reservation, so that it can continue to furnish new vigor to other areas of the child's experience.

There are *two phases* necessary for any truly creative undertaking. The creator *conceives* a worthy purpose and *invents* the means by which to accomplish it. An artist may observe a certain aspect of beauty in a particular landscape. He then invents the means with which to transmit his concept of beauty. Another artist may conceive possibilities of greater comfort in the design of a chair, and then proceed to invent a more comfortable chair with his knowledge of needs and materials. These two phases, conception and invention, always over-lap because the finest conceptions of purpose always grow with the process of experimentation and invention. Conceptions and purposes, furthermore, can never be adequately expressed in words. It is apt to be embarrassing to a child for the teacher to demand a preliminary explanation of what he is about to do. He should be allowed time for experimentation.

Those who take sides on the matter of *realistic or abstract* art may be judging with too narrow a view. One child may be just as in-tensely interested in portraying the beauty he has discovered existing in the flight of an airplane as another is in inventing new color com-binations. Some people have rejected modern abstract painting when extended contemplation would convince them that this field of inven-tion is as sound as that of music which also uses abstract elements.

A notion prevails that the aim of the artist is to make something beautiful in terms of *rules or principles*. No rule or principle has any validity aside from the *idea*. Many forgeries in the name of art have done nothing more than fulfil conventional schemes for picture mak-ing. A painting or a statue or even a design must say something which comes from the very heart of the creator. The final test of true art is sincerity.

Art is of the greatest importance as a *means of communication*. An artist paints a picture because he has discovered some new, interesting truth about which he wishes to tell others. A poem or a song may serve his needs, but the nameless quality which he finds of interest may call for a painting or a carving. Because the success of democracy depends upon the interplay of free minds, we cannot afford to neglect art, which provides the finest opportunity for freedom of expression.

The greatest barrier to the general acquisition of art as a language is the erroneous idea that only the few are talented. The following quotation from L. Maholy-Nagy is presented on this point. "Our profoundest belief is that everyone is talented; that every healthy person has, deep in him, a capacity for developing his creative nature. Every-one is naturally equipped to receive and assimilate sensory experiences. Everyone is sensitive to musical tones, to colors, to touch and to space. That is to say, everyone is able to participate in the whole of sensory experience, which is the basis of every expression. This means that any healthy man can become a musician, a painter, a sculptor, just as when he speaks he is a speaker. Thus he can give non-verbal expression to his reactions as well, expressing himself in any material." [1]

How is art to be acquired as a language? Truly miraculous is the process by which a child learns to talk. He first plays with sounds, and then by trial and error and by subtle imitation, he gradually "catches on" to the language. He learns, too, by using it to make himself understood even before he knows any grammar. As a child learns to speak by playing with his voice, he must learn to paint by playing with this new material of expression. Art, in a sense, is always play. Even the most profound art may be shown to have been produced in a spirit of play and experimentation. Play does not mean endless dabbling. It is likely to become more purposeful than any exercise the teacher can assign.

Punishment and coercion are destructive to the development of creative expression. It is inconceivable that a child could be coerced into learning to talk by threats of physical punishments, and it should be just as clear that a child cannot be forced into expressing his ideas in paint or clay. Artificial rewards are scarcely more advisable. Most schools have discarded the use of physical punishment and the offering of prizes; but many still persist in the use of marks, failures, and promotions which often provide such severe coercion that the child's impulses are irrevocably stifled.

This does not mean that *criticism* of the child's work by the teacher is to be eliminated. The teacher serves two purposes as a critic. She should be a fair sample of humanity upon which the child can test the effectiveness of attempts at expression. On the other hand, she should be able to sense the child's purpose and provide guidance in the use of materials, so that more adequate expression may be possible. The satisfaction that comes to a child when his idea is genuinely appreciated may be all that is needed to lead him on to greater achievements. Courage is the foundation of art and this can generally be developed better by giving major attention to what is right. What is wrong should be dealt with as incidentally as possible.

[1] Maholy-Nagy, L. "Fundamentals of Design: Bauhaus Education," p. 23. *Art Education Today*. Teachers College, Columbia University. 1939.

ENVIRONMENT AND MATERIALS

A child must have an *environment* conducive to "playing his way" into art. He needs (1) time to experiment and to play with materials, (2) a place to work in which he may move about freely and not be too worried about spoiling the furniture or the floor, (3) materials which are plentiful and suited to his present manipulative abilities, (4) a teacher who is an artist—because art can only be caught, it cannot be taught. The teacher should serve as a "source of contagion."

When one considers the importance to the child of real creative expression, it seems only fair to allow it an *impressive place in the school day*. Perhaps many can recall anticipating Friday afternoon with great pleasure. After recess came art, such as it was. This treat served as the needed stimulant to pull the fagged pupils and teacher through the final forty-five minutes of the week's ordeal. The tendency persists to give the time of the child's greatest efficiency to the so-called solid subjects and salvage the ragged margins of time for art. Regular daily or bi-weekly periods should be provided in which the child is free to try his hand at art. Naturally the younger child has the shorter attention span, and art periods will increase in length from perhaps twenty minutes in the first grade to at least an hour in the seventh and eighth grades.

The potentiality of creative activities in *stimulating interest* and *motivating learning* has led to the extended use of many art materials in units and projects, whose primary purpose is the acquisition of knowledge concerning history, geography, or some other field. Such uses of art materials and techniques are of great value and the teacher should be resourceful in promoting them. To assume, however, that these group projects had provided sufficiently for the needs of the individual child to develop his own creative language would be wrong.

All through his school life, the child needs some *time to himself* during which he can put his dreams into concrete form for others to see. It may be possible to give more time and also improve the use of this time for individual expression if the children are allowed to work in any of several materials including words, music, dancing, paint, and clay. One task of the teacher, then, is to see that each child tries each of the available means of expression. A sort of law of interest cycles will usually provide the child with a transition from one material to another.

A good plan is to provide a certain section of the room, or a special art room with materials and equipment and to permit the children to spend *extra time* there. An opportunity to do a bit of painting before school may be a real incentive to promptness. It is good to keep the child feeling that his time with his art materials is a time when he may, not must, do things.

The *room arrangement* should permit and encourage natural moving about to permit the children to observe the experiments of others and to procure materials for themselves. Movable tables are preferred to fixed desks. The teacher and the pupils should experiment with frequent rearrangements of this equipment to meet the special needs of the group. Many schoolrooms are small, but some *free floor space* should be arranged for easels. Many undertakings call for a generous floor area to work on. Wall space for murals should also be available. Often halls may be utilized.

Each room ought to have running water and a large sink, but substitute arrangements can be made by using pails and pans. Closets and shelved cabinets of easy access to children are a necessity for stocks of materials and storage places for children's work in progress. A teacher with ingenuity and interest can plan shelves, cabinets, easels (see page 609), etc., which can be built at small cost by a carpenter. The children and the teacher may build their own equipment and gain worth-while experience. The problem is to provide a room which may be kept in reasonable order by the children and still permit them to use things.

The *selection and handling of materials* is one of the teacher's chief problems. The expense of art materials often causes administrators to deprive the child of this important experience. Therefore, some materials with their sources and methods of preparation are suggested below. It is a real part of the teacher's responsibility to continue the search for new materials. This is a task with which the children may help, with accompanying educational benefits. Suggestions for the use of these materials will also be given. The teacher should try out the ideas suggested; partly to verify and understand the methods of work, but mostly because one must be an active, producing artist in order to teach art. Methods and processes suited to the school's particular needs will develop for the teacher who works with her pupils in a creative manner. Methods of work should not become so routinized that no new ones are permitted to develop.

A *new material, process,* or *technique* should be presented to a child at the moment he finds a need for it. This, however, would be completely possible only with small classes. Formally directed art lessons may be deadly, and should be presented only when necessary for the sake of efficiency and economy of time. Most dictated lessons are the result of rationalization on the part of the teacher who might often find a much more individualized procedure possible even with large classes. The typical formal art lesson persists largely because of habit and custom. It is foreign to the fundamental nature of art, which is based upon unique, individual, voluntary expression. To dictate the construction of a poster and call it art may serve as a sort of inoculation against further art expression.

The *teacher* should be a *real artist,* not necessarily one who paints pictures, but an artist in the sense that she has real live interests of a creative nature. She can understand the conditions necessary to the development of such interests in children only if she expresses her own ideas in some material and does it for fun. More will be accomplished toward real growth if the teacher takes part in the experiments of the children as a learner herself. Nothing is more fatal to art than having a dictator or a "master" in charge. She should of course be an intelligent participator and may be expected to contribute special resources for the solution of such problems as arise. She should enjoy teaching as a continuous adventure.

It is argued by some that the art lesson ought to teach first of all the ability to follow directions. There are plenty of tasks in which the child will be eager to follow directions if he can see that it will help him achieve his purpose. The chief need of the artist is to direct his own undertakings, the success of which will call for the occasional following of directions from a book or other source. In such a situation, the teacher may be called upon to help.

To illustrate the manner in which a teacher may present a *new material,* consider this possible procedure for the introduction of clay modeling. A first-grade class has observed the teacher working with clay. She has displayed several simple clay objects that she has made.

In response to a request on the part of the class to be allowed to use clay, a half hour is taken to present this new material. The children are allowed to "play" with it. The teacher and children may talk about clay as they work. Where does it come from? What is it used for? What can we make of it? Only a few precautions should be suggested, such as keeping it on the boards and cleaning up the desks at the close of the period. But how are the inexperienced children to do anything without being shown? Children often show greater ingenuity than expected. There is almost sure to be a number of real artists in any group—some who will succeed in carrying through an idea the very first time. It is the task of the teacher to extend the enthusiasm of the pupils who have caught on to those who have not. It is much better if the teacher herself is a source of inspiration. Success with clay as with any other material, depends upon the child catching on to what can be done.

Many of the children will "waste" time and have nothing to show for the first period except a much squeezed lump of clay; but the *period of manipulation,* longer for some children, is not really wasted time. This method of presenting a new material will bring less of finished work at the beginning, but will just as surely yield much richer ultimate results in real creative expression. Those children who proceed with sufficient courage need no suggestions—only help with technical problems when they arise. Others who fail to generate an idea from manipulation of the material may need the teacher to help call to mind some experience or interest of the child which may start an idea. Enough help must be given to forestall discouragement but not enough to cripple resourcefulness.

The small child generally will draw, paint, and model vividly from *his own observation and experience*. The very boldness and disregard of unimportant detail gives his work a unique power. As the child grows older, however, a natural avenue for progress is to make his work more expressive of what he sees as the real nature of things —more representational. Teachers commonly observe that older children become dissatisfied with their drawing and seem to demand better "technique." It is at this period, usually during the upper four grades and high school, that the most serious error in art teaching is made: that of diverting the attention of the child from his natural purpose of expressing ideas to irrelevant drills and assigned problems in techniques. Children so treated either lose interest or become hacks, proficient only at meaningless exercises.

The *chief resource* in this vital period is *life itself*. If a child cannot draw well enough to serve his needs for expression, he should be encouraged to go back to the subject which interests him and study it further. The best means for observing the essential character of a street car, for example, is to look at one and make a sketch of it. Sketching from reality will serve to improve drawing skills without imposing mechanical schemes and systems. It will teach the child to observe and will also provide an abundance of subjects for painting.

SUBJECT MATTER

Subjects for sketching may at first be hard to find, but ideas will multiply as time goes on. The artist needs a subject which will serve as a symbol through which he can express his ideas and feelings. Such a subject must first of all be one with which the artist has considerable acquaintance and also one with which others have had enough experience to enable it to carry a meaning. The subject most commonly used is the human figure. Certainly, human beings offer the artist an endlessly fascinating field for study. People who are doing things make good subjects: workmen, farmers, players in a game, spectators, circus performers, picnickers, street car passengers, shoppers, and members of the family in their characteristic occupations. No doubt the very best works of real art by school children are caricatures of teachers, the best of which surely have been promptly destroyed.

Among other subjects of sufficiently general appeal, the following may be listed: pets, farm animals (boys sometimes become intensely interested in horses, which seem to be a symbol of life, and power), buildings, trees, landscapes, airplanes, trains, ships, automobiles, and machines. While children often learn to draw these from pictures, it is well to encourage sketching of the actual subject, wherever possible.

Drawing and painting from memory are to be encouraged, provided that the subject has made a strong enough impression upon the child. The memory serves as a sort of a filter through which the main idea may pass, but which strains out superfluous details. Of course even in a sketch from life, the child should be encouraged to select and emphasize the important things.

Technique and procedure in sketching should be left almost wholly to the child. Many beautiful drawings are made with a direct, hard line, while some children may prefer to use some system of blocking in the sketch to get proportion, action, and composition established before final lines and "shading" are put in. Habits which result in ineffective drawing will become apparent as the drawing is viewed with those of the other children. The teacher should not force the acceptance of any narrow standard—for example, that all drawings be large, or heavy, or be made with a certain type of line. The only point at which a child needs advice is where his methods of drawing have not been suited to his idea. The child should be encouraged to experiment with techniques, some of which may be suggested by the teacher. The teacher should grant the legitimacy of an unlimited variety of objectives, and so should also grant the child's right to use an unlimited variety of techniques, so long as the means adopted serves the individual best in achieving his objective.

Older pupils should be encouraged to keep *sketch books* and to make sketches of interesting subjects every day. A simple ten-cent loose-leaf notebook with unruled paper will do. Soft, kindergarten pencils are good, though sketching with a variety of materials, such as pen, brush, and crayon, should be encouraged. One effective scheme for stimulating sketching is to keep a bulletin board on which children are encouraged to post their daily sketches. The teacher may comment upon these from day to day and select some of the more interesting ones for a more permanent display.

The problem of *learning to understand* as well as to speak the language of art must be considered. As in language, the development of expressive ability is largely based on understanding, and familiarity with the expression of others. What has passed for the study of art appreciation, however, has been largely destructive to the development of real understanding on the part of the children. Sentimental and hackneyed observations concerning a few old favorite paintings kill genuine interest and real understanding of art. To get the artist's message, the observer must have a sufficiently similar background of experience to permit the subject to serve as the medium for the idea. For that reason, the very best place to begin art appreciation study is with the work of the other children in the class. The range may then be extended to the expressions of adult artists in the community, provided of course, that their work is authentic expression based on their own real experience.

As early as possible the teacher should make a thorough survey of *all the resources of the community* which may be used to promote a finer appreciation of art. The specific values and means of access to these should be investigated. Some may be visited by the class as a whole, while individuals with special interests may study others. Many local enterprises will be pleased to co-operate in other ways, such as lending exhibition material or furnishing special demonstrations.

While there may be few recognized and well-established artists in the community, it is certain that there are a number who are, notwithstanding their lack of recognition, real artists. The most genuine achievements in the teaching of art appreciation may be to help the children to appreciate beauty in the work of local craftsmen. A carpenter, cabinet maker, or other craftsman may be found who will be glad to have the class visit his shop. To observe the work of artists of any kind may furnish the germ of enthusiasm which is the basis of both true appreciation and creative initiative. Machine shops and manufacturing plants of all kinds are worth investigating.

Local stores will usually co-operate in the study of the aesthetic qualities in manufactured articles. Pupils should be encouraged to take an increasing part in the selection of their own clothes. They should also be encouraged to take an intelligent interest in the decoration and furnishing of their homes. Study of community problems can provide valuable experience. The improvement of housing and the general appearance of the community may seem a long way from the level of school-age ability, but some study will show the teacher that there are practical undertakings well-suited to her children. Improving the appearance of the schoolroom, building, and school grounds may be a good place to start.

Fine art expression of the past and present has recently been made more available through increased distribution of low-cost books and prints. The school should own enough of this material so that the children can use it freely. Some color reproductions may be framed; however, they should not be hung in any one place too long. Other prints may simply be placed in folders and put on a browsing table. Many magazines contain good reproductions, and old copies of the magazines may be secured for clippings. Children can help build up a library of these reproductions.

Appreciation of any work of art will of course be aided by a *greater knowledge* of the *conditions* under which it was made. The teacher may promote this growth of appreciation by suggested readings and by class discussion. Study of the art of any people will both enhance and be enhanced by a more general study of that people. Thus a study of the social system of the Egyptians may be fruitfully combined with a study of their art. The art of a people furnishes the chief resource for understanding that people.

The *pictures for selected study* should be well within the comprehension of the children. However, the subjects need not be sentimental or trivial. Even young children ought to have access to genuinely fine art; they are often more capable than older people of appreciating real esthetic values. The use of pictures for stimulation of oral and written expression is no doubt valuable, but good photographs would often serve better for such purposes. To assume that one can tell in words what a fine painting means is misleading and likely to leave the child with a notion that the story is all that matters.

Because of the varied interests and backgrounds of teachers and children, specific recommendations of pictures to be studied in each grade will not be offered here. The teacher should see that the children always have access to a rich variety of material from which something will occasionally emerge for special consideration. Sometimes this will happen because of interest in a certain technique that a child needs to use, sometimes because of a child's interest in the subject matter treated in a painting. The work of contemporary and recent painters is likely to be more interesting and helpful to children than the work of earlier periods.

TECHNIQUES FOR TEACHING

A *rigid course of study* is not advisable in art because it is never possible to anticipate precisely what interests, needs, or facilities may develop. Some guiding advice is nevertheless needed to aid the inexperienced teacher in estimating the difficulty of certain undertakings, as well as in their evaluation in terms of the needs of a child at each age level. For this purpose the following chart has been made. The teacher and children ought to make their own plan of work in the light of their needs and interests. This chart is offered only as one source of information necessary for organizing such a plan.

	Grades									
	K	1	2	3	4	5	6	7	8	9
Tempera Paint (page 607)										
At easel with large bristle brush.......	x	x	x	x	x	x	x	x	x	x
With small soft brush.................					x	x	x	x	x	x
With brush outline-chalk coloring......					x	x	x	x	x	x
With crayon outline-tempera wash coloring............................					x	x	x	x	x	x
With "dry brush" for texture and shading..............................							x	x	x	x
On clay objects.......................	x	x	x	x						
Transparent water color (page 608)										
Using large bristle or soft brush........			x	x	x	x	x	x	x	x
Using small soft brush.................							x	x	x	x
Finger Paint (page 611)										
Free expression on 12 × 18 paper.......	x	x	x	x	x	x	x	x	x	x
Using notched cardboard or other devices for all-over pattern effects.......							x	x	x	x
Oil Paint (page 612)										
On canvas and board..................								x	x	x
Enameling and protective painting on clay and wood objects..............			x	x	x	x	x	x	x	x
Wax Crayon (page 613)										
Large kindergarten crayons on 18 × 24 manila paper.......................	x	x	x	x	x	x	x	x	x	x
Paper off crayon, using side for graded tone drawing.......................						x	x	x	x	x
Crayon outline with chalk, tempera or water color..........................					x	x	x	x	x	x
Crayon on unbleached muslin or other cloth for wall hangings..............						x	x	x	x	x
Chalk (page 614)										
Chalk drawing with fixative...........	x	x	x	x	x	x	x	x	x	x
Modified by using crayon or brush line and rubbing in chalk. (Use rough surface paper such as manila or bogus.)..					x	x	x	x	x	x

					Grades					
	K	1	2	3	4	5	6	7	8	9
Pencil (page 614)										
Drawing with large kindergarten pencil	x	x	x	x	x	x	x	x	x	x
Contour drawing.....................								x	x	x
Ink (page 614)										
Use of lettering pens and India ink......								x	x	x
Cartooning...........................								x	x	x
Brush drawing with ink..............						x	x	x	x	x
Charcoal (page 615)										
General use..........................	x	x	x	x	x	x	x	x	x	x
Drawing from posed figure............						x	x	x	x	x
Paper (page 615)										
Making soft cover, simply tied, or sewed books.............................	x	x	x	x	x	x	x			
Making stiff covered books with loose leaf, tied fillers.....................					x	x	x	x	x	x
Making stiff covered books with sewed fillers..............................								x	x	x
Making cloth-covered portfolios and books..............................								x	x	x
Making masks........................	x	x	x	x	x	x	x	x	x	x
Making posters.......................				x	x	x	x	x	x	x
Making May baskets..................	x	x	x	x						
Making Christmas decorations.........	x	x	x	x	x	x	x	x	x	x
Cloth (page 613)										
Making crayon wall hangings..........						x	x	x	x	x
Printed designs on cloth (linoleum).....						x	x	x	x	x
Making book covers..................								x	x	x
Weaving large rag rugs on frame loom (separate pieces).....................	x	x	x	x	x					
Weaving on cord and cigar box looms...				x	x	x	x			
Weaving with carpet warp and yarn or with coarse thread on commercial loom				x	x	x	x	x	x	x
Sewing doll dresses....................	x	x	x	x	x					
Sewing aprons........................	x	x	x	x	x	x	x	x	x	x

	Grades									
	K	1	2	3	4	5	6	7	8	9
Metal (page 617)										
Making soft wire and sheet metal figures, animals, and inventions............						x	x	x	x	x
Using soft sheet metal for tooling and tapping............................						x	x	x	x	x
Pounding pewter and copper bowls, etc.								x	x	x
Leather (page 617)										
Tooling, sewing, and dyeing leather objects................................								x	x	x
Clay (page 617)										
Free expression (figures, animals, beads, pottery, plaques, abstractions, etc.)...	x	x	x	x	x	x	x	x	x	x
Firing and glazing clay objects.........					x	x	x	x	x	x
Casting from clay with molding plaster							x	x	x	x
Making puppet heads—paper and paste shell over clay......................							x	x	x	x
Making masks—paper and paste shell over clay............................							x	x	x	x
Soap										
Carving................................							x	x	x	x
Wood (page 620)										
Carving (figures, animals, abstractions, totem poles).....................							x	x	x	x
Making furniture (see library unit) using boxes and orange crates..............	x	x	x	x	x	x	x			
Making better furniture...............							x	x	x	x
Making kites.........................					x	x	x	x	x	x
Making airplanes......................	x	x	x	x	x	x	x	x	x	x
Building cars, trains, etc...............	x	x	x	x	x					
Using coping saw and jig saw.........					x	x	x	x	x	x

	Grades									
	K	1	2	3	4	5	6	7	8	9
Puppets and Masks (page 621)										
Making stick puppets with cardboard figures or paper bag heads...........	x	x	x	x	x					
Making hand puppets—paper and paste heads.............................				x	x	x	x	x	x	x
Making string puppets—simple bodies of paper and cloth....................						x	x	x	x	x
Using head of paper shell over molded clay with wooden, hinged body......								x	x	x
Sawdust and paste heads..............				x	x	x	x	x	x	x
Masks of paper bags and cut paper......	x	x	x	x	x	x	x			
Masks of paper and paste over clay.....						x	x	x	x	x
Printing (page 623)										
Stick printing........................	x	x	x	x						
Printing with potatoes or other vegetables..............................			x	x	x	x	x	x	x	x
Linoleum block printing on paper and cloth..............................						x	x	x	x	x
Lettering and poster design (page 624)										
Making informal posters with crayon and chalk.........................	x	x	x	x	x	x				
Using India ink and lettering pens......								x	x	x
Using tempera paint..................						x	x	x	x	x
Using cut paper......................				x	x	x	x	x	x	x

A general discussion of *color* will apply to several of the materials mentioned. Successful use of color in any form for design or pictorial expression depends upon an understanding of the three factors in color variation: hue, value, and intensity. A child may develop a workable understanding of color without knowing the terminology or schematic arrangements used here, but the teacher will be better prepared to advise if she will make a study of them.

All colors that exist have a place in a three-dimensional arrangement known as the color tree. (See page 610.) Two-dimensional charts can never present a complete representation of color relationships, and so it is advisable for the teacher to construct a simple color tree on this plan. The Munsell tree has about 10,000 colors. For school use, 100 colors would be sufficient to serve to demonstrate the idea.

Hue is the factor first distinguished by children. Red, yellow, blue, and possibly green are the hues first recognized. The color wheel is simply the color spectrum tied into a circle. Study of the rainbow or the spectrum band, made by a prism in sunlight, will reveal the natural source of this arrangement of hues: red, orange, yellow, green, blue, and violet. (Indigo is often inserted between blue and violet). It is possible to divide the wheel into 100 hues which will still be quite distinguishable.

Hues may be classified generally as warm or cool. A warm red would be toward orange, and a cool red toward violet; a warm green toward yellow, and a cool green toward blue. Brilliant and exciting color schemes often result from playing complementary (opposite) hues against each other. Close harmonies and quieter schemes may be obtained by using single or neighboring hues.

The term *value* is generally used to mean the light and dark quality of color. It can be measured by the common photo-electric light meter, and refers to the amount of light the surface of the color reflects. Value is the most important factor and the most commonly misused. The importance of sufficient value contrast in a picture is illustrated by the trick of showing a pure white piece of paper and explaining that it is a picture of a polar bear on a snowdrift. Colors will show up against each other only if they possess sufficient value contrast. Strongest accents may be achieved where desired by relatively sharp value contrasts. The value pattern may be studied by squinting at the painting. If the edges of the adjoining areas merge into one another, little value contrast is indicated; if the line remains sharp, the value contrast is greater. Active, dramatic effects generally call for sharp value differences, whereas, quiet effects may require a more subtle relationship of values.

The remaining factor, *intensity,* is the one which may offer the greatest scope for study and refinement. In general, large areas call for soft or neutral colors. These can be mixed from the bright colors by the addition of black, white, or both; or by the addition of some of the opposite hue (for example, red to green). Bright colors are commonly reserved for small areas to furnish accent and climax to the general scheme.

Tempera paint [1] is one of the most useful materials. It is easier to handle than transparent water color and less expensive than oil. Being opaque, tempera color can be better observed in mixing than can transparent water color. In painting with tempera one need not be so afraid of making a mistake because it can be painted over after it is dry. The great variety of ways in which it can be used is suggested in the chart. Tempera can be made. [2] The children might well join in the experiment, to the advantage of all. The old masters of necessity prepared their own paints and many of the best modern painters have resumed the practice, feeling that it not only gives them finer materials but enables them better to understand their craft. The exact proportions must be determined according to the nature of the particular materials; but an experiment in making tempera, or any other art material for that matter, should prove an exciting and instructive experience. Because of the danger that some of the pigments may be poisonous, it is not recommended that small children make or use home-made paints.

The painting easel [3] has come to be almost a symbol for the kindergarten. It should be available to children of all grades. At least eight colors should be provided with possibly more in the higher grades. The eight colors are indicated in the chart. [4]

In the kindergarten, first, and second grades a brush should be provided for each color. In the higher grades one brush will do, with a can of water for washing and a soft cloth for wiping the brush between dips. A half sheet of newspaper makes an ideal palette on

[1] *Tempera paint,* as commonly offered on the market for school use, is also known as show card color, poster color, or opaque water color. High grade tempera generally runs about $2 per quart retail, although very good paint is now offered by most companies at about half this price. Powdered temperas are common, but one needs to test them to see that they contain sufficient glue or other binder. Glue or paste can be added to prevent their rubbing off. Generally, too, they do no keep long after mixing with water.

[2] A satisfactory tempera can be made by combining the following ingredients: one part dry pigment (secured at local hardware or paint store), one part white clay or barite (modeling clay may be put through a fine screen or "settled out"), a little glue or even flour paste, a little glycerine to retard drying and prevent brittleness, and some disinfectant to preserve the glue. Sodium benzoate will serve as a preservative.

[3] See page 609.

[4] See page 610.

which the child may mix any colors he wishes. Of course some paint is "wasted" when the paper palette is discarded at the close of the work period, but the tendency is not to mix so much of one color as when using dishes to mix in. Doll muffin tins are good when larger quantities of each color are needed for designs or murals. Heavy cream manila paper is better for the more careful work of older children, although newsprint is still good for quick experiments. For a large group, where easels are not available, 18″ × 24″ "quarterboard" boards may be used as desks. Movable desks may be arranged so that four children may use one set of paints, each child standing as he works. (See page 609.)

Since *experimentation* is the very essence of art, the teacher should encourage the invention of new colors and combinations, new brush strokes, textures, and effects of all kinds. Here are a few of the things that children will discover, possibly after some suggestion from the teacher: (1) using tempera as a transparent wash, (2) painting one color into another while it is wet, (3) painting lines or dots over a piece of work when dry, (4) using a nearly dry brush to get textures or soft lines, (5) shading one color into another by rubbing the brush back and forth between them, (6) obtaining a graded tone by filling the brush with water and the tip with color, and then using the brush flatwise (beautiful tree trunks may be made in this way). The possibilities of invention with these materials are unlimited. The best technique is that which is invented or adapted to serve a particular need, so that an open mind should be maintained toward methods of applying the paint. Anything that works is right.

Transparent water color has long been a standard item in school use. It is more difficult to handle than tempera, but it has unique possibilities which should be opened up, particularly to the upper-grade children. Painting a water color is like singing a song. One needs a sureness of touch and a boldness of treatment which can be left to carry its message without too much retouching. The attainment of this typically broad watercolor effect will be helped by the use of a large brush and large paper (cream manila is good). Experimentation will soon show a student many tricks in handling water color, for example: to get a hard edge, use dry paper; to get a soft line, work on wet paper; to get a swift gradation of color, fill the brush with water

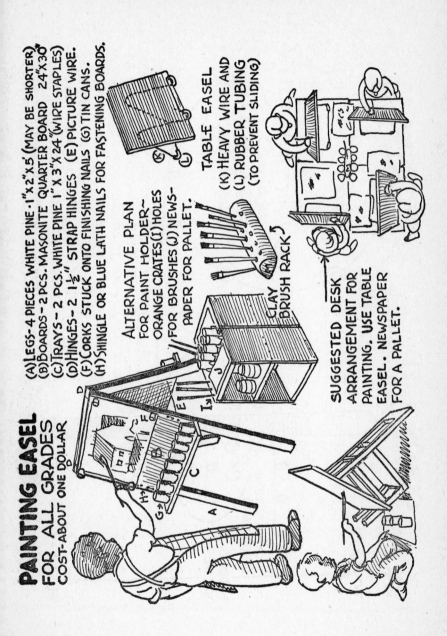

PAINTING EASEL
FOR ALL GRADES
COST-ABOUT ONE DOLLAR

(A) LEGS—4 PIECES WHITE PINE · 1"x 2"x 5' (MAY BE SHORTER)
(B) BOARDS—2 PCS. MASONITE QUARTER BOARD 24"x 30"
(C) TRAYS—2 PCS. WHITE PINE 1" X 3"x 24" (WIRE STAPLES)
(D) HINGES—2 1½" STRAP HINGES (E) PICTURE WIRE.
(F) CORKS STUCK ONTO FINISHING NAILS (G) TIN CANS.
(H) SHINGLE OR BLUE LATH NAILS FOR FASTENING BOARDS.

TABLE EASEL
(K) HEAVY WIRE AND
(L) RUBBER TUBING
(TO PREVENT SLIDING)

ALTERNATIVE PLAN
FOR PAINT HOLDER—
ORANGE CRATES (I) HOLES
FOR BRUSHES (J) NEWS-
PAPER FOR PALLET.

CLAY
BRUSH RACK

SUGGESTED DESK
ARRANGEMENT FOR
PAINTING. USE TABLE
EASEL. NEWSPAPER
FOR A PALLET.

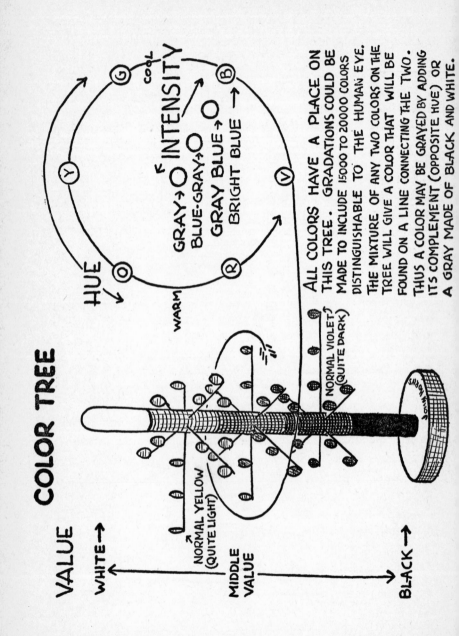

COLOR TREE

VALUE

HUE

INTENSITY

GRAY→○
BLUE-GRAY→○
GRAY BLUE→○
BRIGHT BLUE

COOL

WARM

ALL COLORS HAVE A PLACE ON THIS TREE. GRADATIONS COULD BE MADE TO INCLUDE 15000 TO 20000 COLORS DISTINGUISHABLE TO THE HUMAN EYE. THE MIXTURE OF ANY TWO COLORS ON THE TREE WILL GIVE A COLOR THAT WILL BE FOUND ON A LINE CONNECTING THE TWO. THUS A COLOR MAY BE GRAYED BY ADDING ITS COMPLEMENT (OPPOSITE HUE) OR A GRAY MADE OF BLACK AND WHITE.

NORMAL VIOLET (QUITE DARK)

NORMAL YELLOW (QUITE LIGHT)

MIDDLE VALUE

WHITE→

BLACK→

and the tip with color, then use the side of the brush; to lay on an even wash, keep the board at a uniform tilt and work back and forth at a uniform speed, moving a small flood of water down over the area while it deposits its color.   Other less common devices of painters include: pressing with a blotter or sponge to give texture, and scratching through the paint with a razor blade for details.

Finger paint [1] offers a great range of possibilities.   There are no limits either way—the youngest and the most inept child can do something with finger paint that will be interesting to him.   The fact that no experience with ordinary tools of drawing is needed puts such a child on a more equal footing with the others.   The equality thus gained may help to bolster the child's courage and put him on the road to real voluntary expression.   On the other hand, there are no limits to the inventions possible with finger paint in the hands of an older or more experienced person.   It is a particularly apt material for invention because of the speed with which new experiments can be made.

The *paper* to be used in finger painting must have a glazed surface which will resist water for some time. Good quality notebook paper will work, but it usually comes in too small sheets.   (12″ × 18″ or 18″ × 24″ are preferred sizes.)   Glazed shelf paper is good but somewhat expensive.   Certain highly glazed magazine stocks work very well and are available in large sizes.   Most paper-supply houses can supply satisfactory paper if specifications are given.

A *water pan* as long as the width of the paper is needed.   The sink may be stopped up to serve this purpose.   The paper is first dipped into the water by submerging one edge, held taut, and the whole sheet is pulled through under the water. After draining off excess water for a few seconds, the paper is spread out smoothly on the desk top. The more highly glazed side of the paper is the one on which to paint. A teaspoonful of each color is then placed in front of the child's paper where he may dip into it at will. Finished paintings

---

[1] Good finger paint may be made as follows: (1) Mix ½ cup laundry starch with ½ cup cold water. (2) Pour one quart of boiling water over this, stirring briskly. This should produce a thick starch. (3) Add ½ cup tempera paint. Beat it in thoroughly. Two tablespoons of sodium-benzoate will help preserve the paint. Blue works the best if you are using only one color. However, to get the most out of the experience a child should have access to three colors (red, yellow, and blue). The paint may be made in tin cans and a wooden paddle put into each for dishing up.

should be laid out on newspapers to dry. Surplus paint may be taken up at the close of the work period by means of a flexible spatula or palette knife. This paint will not injure well-waxed desks which have a painted or varnished surface. Children can easily clean the desks if cloths or sponges wrung out of clear water are provided.

Some *demonstration* on the part of the teacher is desirable in introducing finger paint. However, the possibilities of experimentation and invention which are so typical of this medium should not be hampered by directions. A liberal period of manipulation must be allowed. Progress may be assured by intelligent criticism on the part of the teacher. One valuable feature of finger painting is that many successive trials may be made quickly on a single sheet of paper, and the chance of getting something good without direction is multiplied (granting that the teacher is at hand to help the child recognize a good thing when it occurs).

Experiments in pattern and abstract design are the best subjects for finger painting. Only a few pictorial subjects, such as plants, fish, under-sea life, and birds, seem suited to it. Drawing objects in outline with the fingers is not the best use of the material, as that may be done better with crayon or paint. A leaf or a wave can be created in finger paint with one deft move and can be made to exist in three dimensions with a force that is possible with finger paint only.

Oil paint is generally regarded as suited only to the advanced student or professional painter, because of the supposed difficulty of handling and the cost. Of course this medium has been a favorite with painters for centuries, because it is relatively permanent. Oil paint is really the easiest of all paints to handle. It is similar to tempera in that it is opaque, but it is superior in that the colors do not change perceptibly in drying. Oil also dries much more slowly and so permits greater blending and manipulation. Since great permanence is not generally desired, oil paints for school use can be bought quite cheaply. Ordinary decorators' colors are available at 10¢ a tube. Canned paint sold for buildings will serve to give the older children experience in handling this material.[1]

The chief *advantages* of oil paint will be obtained only if it is used

[1] Dry color may be ground with linseed oil and, when necessary, made opaque with the addition of a little white clay.

on a properly sealed surface. Canvas is the traditional material, but many painters now are using "masonite" or "pressed wood" boards, sealed the same as canvas.[1]

A *pallet* for mixing colors can be made by carefully sealing and sandpapering a piece of wall board. A flexible pallet knife or spatula is needed for mixing colors. A jar of turpentine, a paint rag, and bristle brushes (the kindergarten type is good) complete the necessary equipment.

Preliminary drawings for oil paintings are generally laid in with charcoal or pencil. If this is done lightly and surplus charcoal is blown off, it will not be necessary to spray the drawing with fixative before painting. Many painters prefer to draw directly with a brush, using paint thinned greatly with turpentine. As the paint is applied, it may be thinned or used thick. Experimentation again is desirable.

Wax crayons are so commonly used as to be known by many children simply as "colors." The large, soft kindergarten crayons (8 color box) are the best for all grades. To gain experience with a great variety of colors, a child can do better by mixing tempera paint.

There are *endless ways of using* wax crayons, including that of the old standard "filling-in" technique. One method is to apply a light color underneath and a dark one on top, then scratching lines through the top layer. Crayons without paper wrappings will be found most useful. They may be bought that way if specified, or the paper may be removed. This permits the use of the side of the crayon. Very effective, quick gradations of color can be made thus, by bearing down harder on one end than the other and drawing broadside. Crayon line drawings with water color, tempera paint, or chalk, for filling in color, will be found effective. Manila and bogus papers have a surface on which crayons work very well.

Crayon designs on unbleached muslin or other *cloth* have been popular lately. The colors become fairly permanent when pressed in with a hot iron (between papers). Wall hangings and draperies may be so decorated. Boxes and other wooden objects may be decorated with crayon and made permanent by shellacking.

---

[1] Canvas or wall board must be first sized with a glue solution and, when dry, painted with white lead and linseed oil. Any good white oil paint will do. In the case of wall board, the surface should be slightly sanded after two coats of paint. A cheap prepared canvas called "wall-tex" is now sold in wallpaper stores at about 4¢ per square foot. Good, prepared canvas sells for 50¢ and up, per square yard.

Chalk [1] is a soft, sensitive material to use. Its chief drawbacks are untidiness in use and tendency to brush off when finished. It has some disadvantage for very small children, but with the use of fixative [2] chalk is very valuable for most grades. Chalk can also be rubbed into the surface of the paper to prevent dusting off and to get certain effects. Felt pads for this purpose are sold in some newly promoted sets of materials. Chalk may be rubbed through a stencil with cotton or soft cloth.

Since children use *pencils* so much in all kinds of school work, it is not necessary to encourage their use for art expression. Large, soft, kindergarten pencils are recommended for all age levels. These will yield good, bold lines and minimize the possibility of drawing too small. In the higher grades, however, where daily sketches are desired, the child should be encouraged to use whatever pencil he has at hand. He should understand that even a humble lead pencil can produce drawings of real merit. Short pencils generally do better work than long ones.

Pen and ink is a favorite medium with many artists, partly because of the ease with which strong effects may be obtained and partly because ink drawings are the easiest to reproduce in papers and magazines. Older children will like the lettering pens too—both for lettering, as suggested in the manuals issued by the makers of the pens, and for creating designs. Use a soft brush to fill in solid areas.

The "funnies" are so universally devoured by children that they may offer an approach to art for children who otherwise would not be interested. Many boys who feel that art is feminine are excited at the idea of cartooning. Caricature forms a sound basis for art expression. A study of the pen techniques used by favorite comic artists may promote experimentation by the pupils. The teacher may lead children to observe that the most effective comic drawings are also the simplest. She should place a premium on originality and invention. Pen and ink artists generally "block in" their drawings in pencil before starting with ink.

[1] Colored chalk can be made by mixing dry color with plaster of paris or molding plaster. A greater proportion of dry color makes a softer chalk. This should be mixed dry and then with water, after which it may be poured into molds made by forcing a stick into wet clay.

[2] Fixative can be made by mixing white shellac and alcohol. Pour off the clear liquid from the top and apply it with a small fly spray.

Charcoal has the special advantage of being versatile in the hands of a person of any age. Heavy darks or delicate grays may be attained at will. Big sticks of soft charcoal should be used. Many artists use a chamois to rub off light lines and to modify tones. Kneaded erasers are used to "lift" out lights from dark areas. The fixative suggested for chalk (page 614) is especially suited to charcoal. Manila paper is good, although real charcoal paper is not expensive. Charcoal is ideal for blocking in water color, oil, or tempera paintings.

Several *kinds of paper* should be available for use with all media so that the child can try out different textures, colors, and sizes. (1) A liberal supply of newsprint in large sizes (24″ × 36″) is a necessity. This can be bought from the local printer. (2) Cream manila in 18″ × 24″ size has many uses. It is inexpensive and has a fine surface for paints, crayon, or chalk. (3) Wrapping papers are good for murals and large construction work. (4) Interesting results can be had by painting on colored construction paper with tempera paint. Poster paper is lighter in weight and cheaper. It is good for cutting and pasting. Gray or cream bogus, American white, manila tag, and chipboard are also very useful.

In *book construction* (see chart of materials) the children should be given access to a variety of kinds and colors of paper as well as cord for tying and sewing. Colored construction paper is good for covers, and newsprint or wrapping paper for filling. If the teacher will take time to experiment with variations on simple methods of book construction, she will soon have a series of suggestions to stimulate the children's experiments. Neatness will be facilitated if plenty of clean newspapers are used and a clean damp cloth kept handy. It is better to apply paste with the fingers because then it can be thoroughly worked into the surface of the paper.

The making of *May baskets* affords a better activity if the methods suggested by the teacher are not so "tricky" as to require precise following of directions; although some trick ways of folding and cutting paper may be stimulating to the child's imagination. Baskets based on a simple box-construction are practical because many variations and inventions are open to the child after he has mastered a simple principle of construction.

SIMPLE BOOK CONSTRUCTION

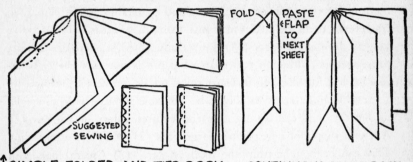

FOLD

PASTE FLAP TO NEXT SHEET

SUGGESTED SEWING

SIMPLE FOLDED AND TIED BOOK CONSTRUCTION PAPER COVER

CONTINUOUS SCRAP BOOK

HINGE COVER BOOK MADE WITH CHIPBOARD (OR OTHER CARDBOARD), GUMMED PAPER TAPE, CONSTRUCTION PAPER, AND FILLER

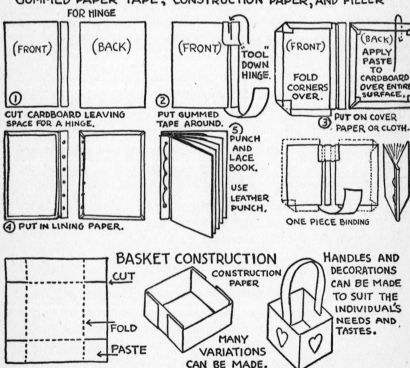

FOR HINGE

(FRONT)   (BACK)

① CUT CARDBOARD LEAVING SPACE FOR A HINGE.

(FRONT)   "TOOL" DOWN HINGE.

② PUT GUMMED TAPE AROUND.

(FRONT) FOLD CORNERS OVER.

(BACK) APPLY PASTE TO CARDBOARD OVER ENTIRE SURFACE.

③ PUT ON COVER PAPER OR CLOTH.

④ PUT IN LINING PAPER.

⑤ PUNCH AND LACE BOOK.

USE LEATHER PUNCH.

ONE PIECE BINDING

BASKET CONSTRUCTION

CUT

FOLD

PASTE

CONSTRUCTION PAPER

MANY VARIATIONS CAN BE MADE.

HANDLES AND DECORATIONS CAN BE MADE TO SUIT THE INDIVIDUAL'S NEEDS AND TASTES.

Christmas decorations offer one of the best opportunities for invention. By encouraging originality, it is possible to avoid too much repetition of outworn forms.

Weaving can be done with very simple means and offers no end of opportunity for invention. A cigar box or a piece of cardboard with notches cut in either side makes the simplest loom. A long, smooth stick with a hole in one end will serve as a shuttle. Driving a row of nails into each end of a board also makes a good loom, particularly for mats and rugs. Weaving a mat from local reeds, straw, and grasses can be very interesting. For small children, single strips should be used for cross weaving. Simple looms used by the Indians should be studied. Small looms can be bought for as little as $2 and are excellent for the higher grades.

Embroidery with colored yarns on coarse materials will help a child to appreciate textiles, as well as being a good medium for expression. Children should create their own designs and use easy stitching.

Discussions of *metal* work will not be undertaken here apart from saying that soft sheet metals and various sizes of wire are very useful materials to have on hand for general experimental and inventive purposes.

Leather may be sewed and tooled to good advantage with very few special tools. Most tools may be made from nails. Nut picks and nail files may be used. The leather must be dampened and placed on a block or glass to be tooled. Calf skin is generally the best.

Clay is a most useful material and is furnished in such abundance by nature that it ought to be always on hand for pupils of all ages. Children enjoy clay because it can be so easily manipulated and invites so many fascinating experiments. Young children gain a great deal in dexterity simply through playing with it. Very soon they begin to express real ideas; and before leaving elementary school, many children can become practiced sculptors and potters.

Clay may be kept in *good condition* more easily if a large quantity is prepared at once.[1] Inexpensive clay may be secured from a brick

---

[1] A twenty gallon garbage can will hold two hundred pounds of clay. Using a pound coffee can or similar measure, alternate four measures of clay powder with one of water until the can is nearly full. Better save a little dry clay to add later if the mixture is too wet. After standing a few days, the clay will be uniformly moist and ready to use. Very little mixing is necessary.

factory or tile works. Such clay is commonly stocked in lumber yards under the name of mortar-mix and sells for about 60¢ per 50-pound bag. Before buying a large quantity of this, however, the teacher should try the clay out, because it is not always of uniform quality.

Within walking distance of many schools will be found *clay deposits* suitable for school use. To prospect for such clay, test it, prepare it, and put it to use can furnish a valuable experience. Few opportunities remain to use nature's resources directly, and this experience may furnish the child with a clearer conception of the relationship of human culture to the natural world.

Clay may be used to good advantage through the whole of a child's school life *without firing facilities*. Clay pieces may simply be dried and painted with tempera or quick-drying enamel. Clay may be easily mended with a solution of sodium silicate, commonly known as water glass. This may also be used to cement cardboard bases onto clay objects. For firing, however, a clay slip (see below) should be used for mending.

Firing clay objects is such an interesting process, however, that every school ought to provide the facilities for it. Satisfactory electric kilns may now be had for $100 or less. They are simple to operate and very usable. A variety of schemes may be devised for outdoor firing. A kiln to be fired with wood or coal may be built for from eight to ten dollars. Pieces may be fired simply by placing them in an 8″ drain tile and blocking the ends with stones. This should be blocked up a few inches on stones, and then a good-size wood fire should be built under, around, and over the whole thing. The fire must be kept going briskly for four or five hours, after which it may be allowed to die out, and the following day the clay objects may be removed. Firing has also been done satisfactorily by placing a dry clay object in a coffee can and packing sand around it, after which the whole thing is put into a coal furnace with a hot fire. Turning this occasionally, through a period of four or five hours, will produce uniform firing.

If the clays mentioned above are to be fired, they should be treated to remove stones and pieces of shale. Forty mesh brass screen (strainer cloth) can be secured at the hardware store and stretched on a frame. Clay mixed quite thin (in the potter's language called "slip") may be put through this screen easily. To dry sufficiently for use, permit clay to settle, pour off the water, and let stand until sufficiently dry. Clay may be dried out more quickly by putting it on a plaster slab which will absorb the surplus water. Stones and impurities may be made to settle to the bottom by mixing the clay thin with water and allowing it to stand, a process that may be found just as effective as using the screen.

Clay objects larger than 1½″ in diameter should be *hollowed out* to prevent breakage in firing. Clay should be thoroughly kneaded before work begins. Breakage will be minimized also by slow heating and slow cooling. Clay must be thoroughly dry before firing.

Objects may be *decorated* by painting over dry clay with a thin slip of a different kind of clay which will give a contrast in color when fired. Pottery is generally finished by a process called "glazing." This is done after the first (biscuit) firing, by coating the piece with a mixture of clay and metal oxides which will melt and give a surface of glass, the color of which is determined by the metal used. Glazing requires special study, but it is fascinating and within the abilities of older children if a kiln is available.

Tools for clay modeling can be made of maple, white pine, or other wood, with a pocket knife. Boxwood is used for most commercial tools. Meat skewers, tongue depressors, and such things make very good tools. These should be waxed or coated with vaseline. Children should be encouraged to work large enough so that most of the work can be done with their hands. It is true of clay as well as all other materials that anything that works is right. Objects may either be modeled in one piece or made by adding pieces, provided the clay is not too dry and each new piece is well attached to the rest of the object.

A *small board* should be provided for each child to model on. Pressed composition board with an oil binder is good because it will not warp. The clay object may be left on the board and covered with a damp cloth and oil cloth, or it may be put into a moisture-proof cabinet to keep moist for continued work on successive days. Coffee cans, gallon lard pails, or other metal containers furnish good storage places for clay pieces.

Of all the methods commonly used for *pottery making,* the ball method is easiest for children. A *ball* of clay is placed upon the board and as the ball is turned, the thumbs are forced slowly down into the top to form a bowl or vase as desired. The *slab* method may be used for either cylindrical or rectangular forms. Bottoms and sides are cut from a slab of clay and "welded" together by rubbing and using some water. The *coil* method is a favorite with some Indian tribes. It consists of making a disk of clay for the base and building the walls with rings of clay. Each round of clay must be welded to the preceding one by rubbing it with water. The *potter's wheel* is, of course, the most useful device for making pottery. Simple wheels may be devised, and electric wheels are available at low cost.

Wood has been such a standard material for building and construction that most children will be fairly familiar with its possibilities. Throughout all the grades an assortment of wood should be kept on hand. Orange crates and other packing boxes are useful sources of wood, although the school should buy some standard material, such as 1″ by 2″ white pine strips for large constructions, and quarter-inch basswood for coping saw work. Mattress boxes furnish a good supply of heavy cardboard with which to build large things.

Tools for wood work should include, for the lower grades, about twelve 10 oz. claw hammers, cross-cut saws, coping saws, several small planes, a wood file, screw driver, pliers, and several braces with a variety of wood bits. The assortment of nails should include roofing, lath, shingle, and 4, 6, and 8 penny common. Coping saw work should not be encouraged among the very young children because of the detail and difficulties involved. Older children should have access to some machines, such as the jig saw and the lathe, which are both quite safe to use.[1] *Wood carving* can be done in the upper grades. Wood chisels and mallets should be furnished for this purpose. Substantial benches and vises are suggested for all grades.

Making a xylophone can be a thrilling experience. Strips of wood 1″ × 2″ can be cut to various lengths so as to produce a perfect scale. The pitch is raised by shortening the piece and lowered by sawing into the back of it. This makes an excellent motivation for studying different kinds of wood because each has a different sound. Maple

---

[1] A magnetic jig saw which needs no motor is now available for $5 to $10. It is absolutely safe and will cut all kinds of wall board easily.

and cedar work nicely, but others may be found to work better. These pieces may be tacked to a "V" of clothesline rope and played flat on a desk top. Supports should be one-fifth of the distance from the end. The hammers may be made of halves of spools or large wooden beads stuck onto pieces of reed or dowelling.

Masks and puppets (page 623) offer the child valuable opportunities for dramatization and also encourage invention with a variety of materials. A professional method of making masks is to model a face of clay. This is covered with waxed paper and then with three or four layers of two-inch wide newspaper strips dipped into flour paste. A last layer of paper toweling gives a good outside surface. Then when dry the clay is removed and the mask painted with tempera or enamel. Puppet heads can be made in a similar manner, but of course the shell must be cut in two to remove the clay. It can easily be spliced with paper and paste. Simple masks can be made with paper sacks and cut paper. Imagination and fantasy should be given full sway so that new color arrangements and designs will result.

Puppets are dolls with remote control. From the simplest stick puppet made with a paper doll tacked to a stick to the most intricate string puppet, there is enough range for invention to suit any age level. Puppetry, incidentally, makes an ideal hobby for a teacher. The objective here again ought to be invention, and the most we can do is to suggest things for the children to try.

A simple method for hand puppets is to fill a small paper sack with crushed newspaper and tie it over the end of a stick. Next, the features may be modeled over this with crushed paper, held in place with strips of pasted newspaper. When this is dry, it can be painted with tempera or enamel. The hole left when the stick is removed is for the finger. If this head is to be used for a string puppet, the body may be made of rolls of newspaper and gummed tape fastened together with stout cord.

Other materials used for puppet heads are sawdust and paste, carved wood, plastic wood, and stuffed cloth. Whatever the method chosen, it ought to be simple enough so that the child can have time to experiment with the action of the puppet, and so that he may evolve new ideas with each new generation of his puppets. The stick puppets may consist of figures cut from cardboard and fastened to

MASKS AND PUPPETS

CUT-PAPER MASK ON PAPER BAG

PROFESSIONAL METHOD

CARBON PAPER DUPLICATION →

A   B

(A) MODEL FACE OF CLAY.

(B) COVER WITH WAXED PAPER.

(C) COVER WITH THREE LAYERS OF NEWSPAPER HEAVILY PASTED ON BOTH SIDES AND APPLIED IN SMALL PIECES.

(D) APPLY ONE LAYER OF PAPER TOWELING.

(E) WHEN SHELL IS DRY REMOVE CLAY AND PAINT MASK.

VARIOUS MATERIALS MAY BE GLUED ON FOR DECORATION SUCH AS COTTON AND YARN.

THE SIMPLEST PUPPET IS A PAPER DOLL TACKED TO A STICK. →

HEADS FOR STICK, HAND, AND STRING PUPPETS CAN BE MADE IN THESE WAYS. NEW METHODS CAN BE DEVISED.

SMALL PAPER BAG FILLED WITH NEWSPAPER →

GUMMED TAPE OR CORD AT NECK

FEATURES BUILT BY MODELING WITH DRY CRUSHED PAPER HELD IN PLACE BY PASTED STRIPS

PAINTED WHEN DRY

FOR HAND PUPPET MAKE TUBES TO FIT FINGERS.

YARN OR COTTON FOR HAIR

PUT STRING PUPPET TOGETHER THIS WAY.

USE ROLLS OF PAPER FOR ARMS, LEGS, AND BODY.

FASTEN WITH STRONG CORD.

DRESS OR PAINT ATTACH STRINGS.

PULL CURTAINS

TRANSPARENT BACK CURTAIN

WALL BOARD OR MATRESS CARTONS ON 1"x2" WOOD FRAME

HINGES

ON TABLE OPERATORS STAND ON TABLE

HEAD MODELED OF SAWDUST AND PASTE

STAGE FOR HAND PUPPETS AND REVERSED FOR STRING PUPPETS

A STRING PUPPET SHOULD BE VERY FLEXIBLE.

sticks. They are the easiest for children to make and manipulate. The finger puppets are more difficult to handle. In using these, the hand is hidden by the figure's costume and controls the action. The forefinger is inserted into the hollow head which may be made of clay or sawdust, according to the formula given below.[1] The thumb forms one arm and the second finger the other. By such arrangement the head can nod, the arms make gestures, and the conversation be made much more expressive. The use of string puppets is more suitable for those beyond the primary years.

The stage for puppetry is as open to invention as the puppets. Fist and stick puppets may be induced to perform by simply thrusting them up over the edge of a table. Turning one table upside down on top of another and hanging a curtain across the legs, may work. A very good folding stage may be built using strips of wood, mattress cartons, and hinges. For string puppets, the manipulators may stand on a table behind the stage.

Printing is so important in modern life, and children enjoy it so much, that more opportunity should be made for experimentation in various phases of the craft. It combines opportunity for the invention of technical processes with the expression of ideas, so that there are endless possibilities. The simplest material with which to print is the potato. Cut it evenly across with a sharp knife and rub the surface smooth and dry on a piece of newspaper. Then cut a simple shape on the surface. Printing may be done on paper or cloth with either tempera paint or quick-drying enamel. The paint may be applied to the surface of the potato with a brush, or by stamping it into a pallet of paint spread out on a newspaper.

[1] *Directions for Making a Finger Puppet Head.* Make some flour paste, using one part flour to four parts water. Mix the flour with a little water until it is smooth. Add slowly the remainder of the water. Stir and boil until it is clear. It should be fairly stiff when cold. Mix powdered alum with the paste in the proportion of one heaped teaspoonful of powdered alum to one pint of paste. Mix sawdust with the paste to make a mixture that is about the consistency of biscuit dough. The paste holds the sawdust together and the alum hardens it. A hollow cylinder into which the forefinger slips is the foundation on which to model the head. Make this of light-weight cardboard, the width depending on the height of the head. Tie with string and cover by pasting on strips of cloth which extend below the head and cardboard. The dress is to be sewed to these ends of cloth. Cover the foundation with the sawdust material to make a core, and let it dry in some warm place for twenty-four hours. Then finish modeling the head, using more sawdust material on the core.

Adapted from Fickler, B. A. *A Handbook of Fist Puppets,* pp. 41-45. Frederick A. Stokes Company. 1935.

Linoleum printing may be done easily with the help of such inexpensive tools as a soft rubber ink roller and a glass pallet which are good for applying the paint to the block. Standing on the block or pounding it with a mallet should give enough pressure for printing on either paper or cloth. Printer's ink is the best, but oil paint will work, particularly if a little varnish is added. Quick-drying enamel works well if it is thick enough. The addition of a little acetic acid will aid in making colors fast when printing on cloth.

The invention of *other printing processes* can be very stimulating, particularly to the older children. For example, shapes might be cut from inner-tube rubber and cemented to blocks of wood. These could be used just as other rubber stamps are used. "Dry paint" etching on celluloid has been used to good advantage with older children. The process consists simply of scratching lines in a celluloid sheet and rubbing printer's ink into the scratches, after which the whole thing is pressed against a dampened paper so that the ink is transferred.

Lettering and poster design have been commonly overrated as projects for teaching. Mechanical, hackneyed posters on meaningless subjects have too often been used simply as busy work. Cutting small letters of paper is too tedious for small children. When there is a real need, poster-making can be a meaningful and worthwhile activity in the primary grades, but it should be undertaken with easily manipulated materials, such as crayons or chalk. Cut paper can be very useful for giving the strong, simple effects needed in posters. Some of the most effective posters are bold and informal. Lettering can be casual if it is legible. The originality and effectiveness with which an idea is presented is more important than conventional skills of lettering.

The mastery of two or three simple, basic alphabets is of more use than an attempt to execute a variety of "fancy" styles. Legibility is the first requisite. Fine design and spacing are worth more than "fancy" lettering. This does not mean that originality is to be limited. The same amount of originality might better be given to the fine balancing of a letter than to decorating it.

The most useful alphabets are the upper and lower case modern Gothic and script. Gothic lettering is distinguished from Roman by the uniform width of its elements and by the absence of serifs. Script is, of course, more related to the written letter. Any letter that is slanted

LETTERING

Mastery of these simple styles will provide a basis for good lettering. Variations can be devised if they are consistent and if attention is given to spacing.

ABCDEFGHIJKLMNOPQRSTUV
WXYZ 123456789 AMNWYE

abcdefghijklmnopqrstuvwxyz

In using a pen the strokes should generally be made down and to the right. (( )) O O

VARIATIONS: CONDENSED TO FIT A SPACE   EXTENDED HORIZONTALLY

HIGH CROSS BARS-LOW BARS-BOWLEG STYLE

ITALICS MEANS SLANTED. Script is like writing.

○ SERIFS AND VARIED THICKNESS ○

ARE TAKEN FROM THE ROMAN. GOTHIC
DOES AWAY WITH BOTH FEATURES. MODERN
LETTERING FAVORS THE SIMPLER GOTHIC. RRRI

SPACING

RELATIVE WIDTHS
OF LETTERS SHOULD
REMAIN THE SAME
IN ALL LETTERING.

IF CENTERING IS
DESIRED!— FIND
CENTER OF SPACE
AND COUNT THE
LETTERS.

ABOUT EQUAL AREA BETWEEN LETTERS.
DISTANCES MUST THEREFORE VARY DUE
TO OPEN SPACE CONTRIBUTED BY SOME.

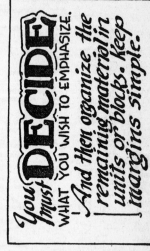

You must **DECIDE**
WHAT YOU WISH TO EMPHASIZE.
And then organize the
remaining material in
units or blocks. Keep
margins simple.

IN PREPARING A

LAYOUT

Make several small
trial sketches. then
block in the poster
lightly in pencil.

is said to be in italics. Modified German black letter and old English are fairly simple to master, but they are neither so legible nor so rapidly printed as the others. Basic alphabets are shown on page 625.

Spacing of letters and words is more important than good letter forms. Each word should stand as a unit. Letters within the word should be evenly and compactly spaced. The average space of one letter should be left between words. There is no mechanical rule that will guarantee good spacing, but the area between letters should be uniform. Since some letters are "open," (A, V) and contribute some area to the space between, less distance is needed than with other letters (H, B). A well-lettered word should present a uniform tone.

A collection of lettering samples clipped from magazines and newspapers furnishes good material for the study of letter styles and layouts. Such letters should not be imitated, however, unless the child can devise a simple, direct way of making the letters with the instruments at his disposal. Outlining and filling in letters is tedious and misleading.

What can be accomplished by good art teaching is suggested by the two true stories which follow. These stories are printed here just as they were told by the art teacher.

"John Anderson, an eighth-grade Negro boy of 16, was a serious discipline problem. His apparent hatred of school and society was somewhat explained by the fact that his teeth were in very bad condition due to chronic undernourishment. During his first few months in my art class he did nothing beyond making occasional attempts to annoy some of the other children. He met my repeated suggestions by not too polite refusals. I had almost given up trying to interest him in undertaking any art projects.

"When we tried finger painting, John was somewhat interested, but for a while he continued to sulk at his desk. When he volunteered to pick up a paper and started for the sink, I held my breath. I was sure that the distance to the sink and back was too far for John's good intentions. It was! Half-way there, he paused before an industrious little Italian and smacked his paper down upon a completed finger painting. There was a splitting yell and a gleeful laugh, then silence. I was busy elsewhere. Then the two boys came running, each carrying a very interesting painting such as I had never seen.

"My praise of John Anderson's wonderful discovery was given substance by the acclamation of the class, many of whom immediately tried the idea. John was ahead of them, though. He made one after another until he had perfected a really new technique. He asked to come in and do extra work and made several paintings which he sold for $1 each, after I had helped him to mount them.

"We got along all right after that. John tried other things too and became more agreeable. Those who observed the case agreed that his awakened interest in finger painting had considerable influence on his attitude toward life."

"The principal had the appearance of grasping at the last straw when he handed William Ball over to me, the new art teacher. William had been expelled several times during the previous year for insubordination, but had always been reinstated because of his amiable disposition. His chief infraction was drawing funny pictures in defiance of teachers' commands to stop. Additional charges were that he made queer noises (squeaks and squawks and hoots and howls) and that·he laughed at the teachers.

"He was assigned to my special care because the principal had learned that I liked to draw funny pictures too. Bill was told that he could come to the art room and work whenever he could get excused from any class, which proved to be quite often.

"Provided with pen and ink and an inexhaustible supply of suitable paper, Bill required scarcely any attention from me—that is, if I didn't happen to be annoyed by the continual din of unearthly vocal experiments. I wasn't bothered. I was only curious. It soon became apparent that the sound effects were meant to go with the pictures. (Walt Disney does it.) His drawings were good and surely justified his alleged neglect of some other more common means of expression. He drew a fire scene in which insects of undoubted rarity were madly administering all kinds of fire-fighting techniques. Another large 22″ × 28″ drawing portrayed a hundred or more figures engaged in a mountaineer moonshine feud.

"During the first three months of school, Bill reeled off an amazing succession of these elaborate creations; and at the same time, I began to hear reports of his improved behavior in other classes. He finished the year without a single expulsion and three years later graduated from high school near the top of his class.

"Bill's mother would give testimony that this opportunity for a legitimate exercise of his terrific creative energy saved him from failure. So far as the other teachers in the school were concerned, Bill's success proved to be the greatest support to a method of teaching which had previously been regarded with suspicion."

QUESTIONS—PROBLEMS—REACTIONS

GROWTH THROUGH MUSICAL EXPERIENCE

SECTION ONE: *Facts*

1. What are two types of procedure for teaching vocal music in the grade school?
2. What uses of the phonograph for teaching vocal music are set forth in this chapter?
3. What are the five important steps in learning to sing a song?
4. What equipment is needed to teach music by the Choir Plan?
5. Explain how so-called "monotones" may be helped.
6. What is meant by the "Junior List" and the "Regular List"?
7. What is the purpose of the short course in conducting?
8. For what are the choir membership charts to be used?
9. What are the steps in teaching theory according to the nine-step method?
10. What different types of rhythmic exercises are suggested?
11. What features of the Choir Plan can be adapted to a note-by-note program?
12. In what elements involved in good singing do children receive training from lessons with the Choir Plan?
13. Why is theory usually easy for those using this plan?
14. How does the piano help in teaching children to sing?
15. In what way does the Choir Plan prepare for children's creativeness in the field of music?

SECTION TWO: *Problems*

16. Why does the Choir Plan lend itself easily to singing in large groups?
17. How important a place do the rhythmic exercises hold in obtaining good results? Explain.
18. Why is it important that children alternate singing with, and listening to, the phonograph?
19. Indicate the outstanding differences in using the Choir Plan in the rural and in the graded schools.
20. How is the plan adapted to four-, three-, and two-room schools without music supervision?

21. Why are the advantages set forth for learning to sing by the Choir Plan of special significance?
22. Show the results of the neglect of teaching singing in the elementary grades in the past.
23. What dangers are involved in conducting a rhythm band? Give reasons.
24. Illustrate how some occasion in school might serve as an incentive for composing.
25. How does music function in helping us to work and live better?

SECTION THREE: *Personal Reactions*

26. Would you maintain that a person who has had no musical training could teach children to sing effectively by using the Choir Plan?
27. If you have had a chance to hear some of the songs on the lists, how would you describe them?
28. From your observation and experience, which procedure do you think children would enjoy more, learning by the Choir Plan or the note-by-note reading program?
29. What do you imagine would be the results of conducting an investigation of children's ability to read music independently by sight? Do you think the names of the notes when you sing?
30. Do you think the arguments given for the need of more teaching of singing in the elementary grades are justified? Why?

ACQUIRING ART AS A LANGUAGE

SECTION ONE: *Facts*

1. What does creative activity do for man?
2. With what two phases of a creative act should the teacher be concerned?
3. What two phases are necessary to any creative undertaking?
4. What is the final test of true art?
5. What comprises the background of small children's expression?
6. What resources are aids to expression?
7. How can the teacher best serve as a critic?
8. Discuss the four factors desirable in an environment conducive to art expression.
9. What is the importance of the period of manipulation, as with clay?
10. What technique and procedure for sketching are suggested?
11. At what point does a child need advice in his drawing?
12. What artists, in the broader interpretation, are found in almost every community?
13. What is the purpose of the chart showing some art materials and their uses?
14. What are the meanings of hue, value, and intensity of color?
15. Give three reasons for using tempera paint.
16. List the materials desirable for use when working at the easel.
17. What are some of the ways of using transparent water color?
18. Give the procedures for finger painting.

19. What are some of the advantages of oil paint?
20. What can be done to prevent chalk from rubbing off the paper?
21. What materials are suggested for use in book construction?
22. Why do children like clay?
23. How may clay pieces be decorated?
24. What materials and tools should be provided for wood work?
25. What are the different types of puppets?
26. What is the most important feature of lettering?

SECTION TWO: *Problems*

27. Why is creating pleasurable and conducive to individual growth?
28. Show by an illustration how art is a means of communication.
29. How can most of us be artists according to this broad interpretation of art?
30. Compare the effect of play with that of punishment and coercion upon creative expression.
31. What does the expression, "The teacher should be a real artist" mean?
32. Why can art appreciation be best begun by looking at the work of other children?
33. Show why the study of the arts of a people aids toward understanding those people.
34. How may pictures best be used in teaching appreciation of art values?
35. List the materials on the chart that you have not used and should like to try first. Give reasons.
36. Show how experimentation is possible with tempera paint.
37. Which of the reasons given for using finger paint shows that it would be especially well adapted for the child with little initiative?
38. Why are crayons more useful with the wrappings removed?
39. How may weaving be simplified for young children? Give illustrations.
40. Give the reasons for using clay in school. Be able to interpret two of these reasons.
41. Indicate with what language activity the use of puppets correlates best. Give reasons.
42. Show how the printing process may be adapted to different levels of ability.
43. Name some of the present weaknesses in poster-making. Be able to state why they are weaknesses.
44. What factors make lettering legible? Show why they do.

SECTION THREE: *Personal Reactions*

45. What place do you see for rules or principles in furthering creative expression?
46. Using the illustration for presenting clay as a guide, choose another material and tell how you would introduce it.
47. Of what value to you are the suggestions for appreciation given in this chapter?
48. Give an illustration of some outstanding use of one of the three factors in color variation, which has come to your attention lately.

49. Since the forms of expression by means of finger painting are limited, should one stress its use?
50. Do you think that we do enough to encourage children to express humor in their pictures? How can the idea be promoted?
51. Which of the methods of making pottery do you consider the simplest?
52. Why should puppets be popular with all ages?
53. How do you explain the change in the behavior of John and Bill in the two stories?

SUGGESTIONS FOR FURTHER READING

GROWTH THROUGH MUSICAL EXPERIENCE

For the Teacher:

Mursell, James. *Music in American Schools.* Silver Burdett, 1943. A review of music education in America, with ways and means for making it a powerful cultural force in the lives of the people today.

Mursell, James and Glenn, Mabelle. *The Psychology of School Music Teaching.* Silver Burdett, 1938. A noted psychologist and progressive music educator discusses the psychological bases of music education, stressing the importance of continuing group participation if musical results and democratic goals are to be achieved.

For the School Music Library:

Burch, Gladys. *Modern Composers for Boys and Girls.* A. S. Barnes, 1941. A companion volume to "Famous Composers," containing twenty biographies, from Moussorgsky to Gershwin. These are useful reference books for both teachers and children.

Burch, Gladys and Wolcott, John. *A Child's Book of Famous Composers.* A. S. Barnes, 1939. Biographies of twenty outstanding composers, arranged chronologically, with portraits. Written for the younger child.

Kinscella, Hazel G. *Music and Romance.* RCA Victor Co., 1941. Gives useful background information for a varied listening program, covering a wide variety of song, opera, and instrumental material.

Lacey, Marion. *Picture Book of Musical Instruments.* Lothrop, Lee & Shepard, 1942. Drawings of the instruments, with some historical information on each. Designed for use in Grades 5 to 8.

ACQUIRING ART AS A LANGUAGE

Art Education Today, by Fine Arts Staff, Teachers College, Columbia University. Contributions by leading art educators on a variety of subjects including philosophies of art, education, and reports of specific achievements.

Dewey, John. *Art as Experience.* Milton Balch, 1934. A definition of the quality which characterizes an experience as art. A thorough study of this book should furnish a sound philosophy for teaching art.

Haggerty, Melvin E. *Art a Way of Life.* University of Minnesota Press, 1934. A statement of the larger motives which art and art education are adopting.

Moholy-Nagy, L. *The New Vision: Fundamentals of Design, Painting, Sculpture, Architecture.* W. W. Norton, 1938. This states a genuinely creative method of teaching, emphasizing the use of modern machines.

The Visual Arts in General Education. Appleton-Century, 1940. It is the report of the Committee on the Function of Art in General Education for the Commission on Secondary School Curriculum of the Progressive Education Association. This report states the position of this association.

Tolstoi, Leo. *What is Art?* Oxford University Press, 1930. This is one of the finest essays on art and should provide any reader with a sounder basis of art criticism.

INDEX

Abacus, 290
Addition
  carrying in, 302
  of columns
    of easy facts, 299
    taught in order of difficulty, 304
  of common fractions, 359
  concept of, 295
  definition of, 292
  development of teaching of, 292
  of decimals, 373
  of denominate numbers, 387
  importance of, 292
  of mixed numbers, 359
  practice in, 305
  and subtraction, combined in teaching, 312
  up or down, 300
Addition facts, 294
Additive method of teaching subtraction, 311
Alphabetic method of teaching reading, 65
Alphabets, types of, 624
Analogies method of solving arithmetic problems, 394
Arithmetic
  basic theories of teaching, 267
  early teaching of in America, 266
  errors in solving problems in, 396
  in everyday life situations, 266
  incidental teaching of, 270
  lifelike processes and materials in teaching, 266
  methods of solving problems in, 394
  objectives in teaching, 268

Arithmetic—(*Continued*)
  present trends in teaching, 266
  when to begin to teach, 270
Arithmetic readiness, 288
Art
  alphabets for lettering in, 625
  book construction in, 616
  Christmas decorations in, 617
  clay in, 618
  color in, 605
  color tree in, 610
  community resources and appreciation of, 600
  correlation of with other subjects, 594
  course-of-study chart for, 604
  creative experiences in, 591
  criticism in, 593
  drawing from memory in, 598
  easels in, 607, 609
  embroidery in, 617
  environment for, 594
  experimentation with paints in, 608
  finger painting in, 611
  hue in, 606
  intensity in, 606
  leather in, 617
  linoleum printing in, 624
  manipulation in, period of, 597
  masks in, 622
  materials and recipes in, 614
  May baskets in, 616
  meaning of, 591
  as means of communication, 592
  metals in, 617
  need for of each child, 594
  oil paint in, 612
  painting from memory in, 598
  philosophical background for, 590